Collins

second edition

# SOCIOLOGY A2 FOR OCR

Stephen Moore Dave Aiken Steve Chapman Peter Langley

# INTRODUCTION

## Features of the textbook

The book is divided into chapters that match the OCR A2 topics. Each chapter contains a number of features designed to help you with learning, revision and exam-preparation.

### Getting you thinking

The opening activity draws on your existing knowledge and experiences to lead in to some of the main issues of the topic. The questions are usually open and, although suitable for individual work, may be more effectively used in discussion in pairs or small groups, where experiences and ideas can be shared.

**Getting you thinking**

1 Look at the two photos on the right. Which of the two areas do you think has the higher rate of crime? What reasons can you give for your answer?
2 What different sorts of crimes might take place in the city during the day and during the night? What reasons can you give for your answer?
3 When you are walking home in the evening, do you feel more concerned than during the day? Are there any precautions you take if you are walking alone at night? What are they?
4 If you see a group of young males standing ahead of you on the street, do you alter your behaviour or route in any way? Give reasons for your answer.

### OCR specification table

At the start of each chapter, a clearly laid out table shows how the topics in that chapter cover the OCR A2 specification.

| OCR specification | | | Coverage |
|---|---|---|---|
| Patterns and trends of inequality and difference related to: | • social class<br>• gender | • ethnicity<br>• age | Social class inequalities covered in Topic 3, gender inequalities in Topic 5, ethnic inequalities in Topic 6 and age inequalities in Topic 7. |
| Theoretical explanations of the patterns and trends: | • functionalist<br>• Marxist<br>• Neo-Marxist | • feminist<br>• Weberian<br>• postmodern views | Explanations of social class inequality covered in Topic 2, gender inequalities in Topic 5, ethnic inequalities in Topic 6 and age inequalities in Topic 7. |
| Sociological explanations of the changing class structure | | | Covered in Topic 4 with definitions and measurements in Topic 1. |
| Explanations for inequality through the intersection of: | • class<br>• gender | • ethnicity<br>• age | Covered in Topics 2, 5, 6 and 7. |

### Key terms

These are simple definitions of important terms and concepts used in each topic, linked to the context in which the word or phrase occurs. Most key terms are sociological, but some of the more difficult but essential vocabulary is also included. Each key term is printed in **bold type** the first time it appears in the main text.

**Key terms**

**Compensatory education** making more resources available to schools in poorer areas in order to compensate (make up) for deprivation.

**Cultural deprivation** 'cultural deprivation' theory suggests that some pupils' backgrounds are in some way deficient or inferior.

**Deterministic** in this context, making it appear inevitable that people will react in a particular way.

**Differential educational achievement** the extent to which educational achievement differs between social groups.

**Educational Maintenance Allowance (EMA)** a means-tested sum of up to £30 per week given to post-16 students to support them in meeting the daily costs of coming to school.

**Material deprivation** lack of money leading to disadvantages such as an unhealthy diet and unsatisfactory housing.

**Self-fulfilling prophecy** a prediction that causes the outcome it predicts.

**Underclass** term used by the New Right to describe group below the working class with unstable domestic lives, reliance on benefits and fatalistic values.

### Activities

At the end of each topic, there are two types of activity that will help you take your learning further:

- *Research ideas* – Suggestions for small-scale research which could be used for class or homework activities.
- *Web tasks* – Activities using the internet to develop your understanding and analysis skills.

**Activities**

**Research idea**

1 Interview a range of your teachers. Ask them to explain the values which they consider are encouraged by the following aspects of school organization and routine: assemblies, sports days, school uniform, registration, house competitions, school rules, prefects, detention.

Evaluate the extent to which their responses subscribe to functionalist, Marxist, interactionist, social democratic or New Right views of education.

2 Organize a small research project to discover what people consider to be the primary purpose of education. Compare class, gender and age patterns in terms of the extent to which the wider social purposes are recognized. Which groups see school as most beneficial to individuals – for example, as helping someone to get a better job?

**Web.tasks**

Search for government educational policy documents and statements at www.education.gov.uk. What are the government's stated aims? How do these aims relate to the sociological views you have been introduced to in this chapter?

## Focus on research activities

A recent piece of interesting and relevant research is summarized, followed by questions that encourage you to evaluate the methods used as well as the conclusions drawn.

### Focus on research

**Ameli *et al.* (2007)**
The ideology of demonization

Ameli *et al.* (2007) analysed the mainstream news programmes of *BBC News*, *Newsnight*, *ITV News* and *Channel 4 News* before and after the events of 7 July 2005. They particularly examined the language used by journalists to discuss that event. They found that 'asylum-seekers' and 'immigration' were frequently focused on, despite the fact that the suspected bombers were British born and raised. The researchers argue that this had the effect of reinforcing the view that all Muslims are of the same mind and that they should be suspected of being 'others', i.e. not integrated into British society. Moreover, the media also focused on the issues of 'loyalty' and 'belonging' and it was generally accepted that, despite a British upbringing, Muslim youth had the potential to develop extremist views and be led away from 'normality'. They had now become 'the enemy within'. In fact, this media portrayal strongly implied that *any* Muslim, especially any young male, had the potential to become an extremist. Ameli and colleagues conclude that despite the good intentions of these news networks, issues regarding Islam were discussed within a very narrow ideological framework.

Adapted from Ameli, S., Marandi, S., Ahmed, S., Kara, S. and Merali, A. (2007) *The British Media and Muslim Representation: The Ideology of Demonisation*, London: Islamic Human Rights Commission

**What evidence does the passage contain to support the researchers' conclusion that 'issues regarding Islam were discussed within a very narrow ideological framework'?**

## Check your understanding

These comprise a set of basic comprehension questions – all answers can be found in the preceding text.

### Check your understanding

1. Explain the difference between equality of outcome and equality of opportunity.
2. According to functionalists, what are the main functions of schools?
3. For functionalists, what is the role of education in creating a meritocracy?
4. What does Althusser consider to be the main purpose of education, and how is it achieved?
5. Why do you think the theory of Bowles and Gintis is sometimes called 'correspondence' theory? Give examples.
6. Why, according to Bowles and Gintis, do White, middle-class pupils do better in education?
7. How does Willis's work appear to support the views of Bowles and Gintis?
8. In what ways might it be claimed that Bowles and Gintis' theory has relevance today?
9. What is the key difference between interactionist approaches and those of Marxism and functionalism?
10. Contrast the approach taken to education by social democratic and New Right thinkers.

**An eye on the exam** Ethnicity and stratification

Describe only – no need for evaluation

Prejudice and discrimination expressed through media representations, policing, housing allocation, employer attitudes, employment, unemployment and pay, racial name-calling and attacks etc.

**(a)** Outline the evidence that racism exists in modern British society. (20 marks)

Statistical trends and patterns, research findings and contemporary examples from any module studied and/or your wider sociological knowledge

Describe the main explanations for ethnic inequality using appropriate theories, concepts and writers

These should focus particularly on employment, unemployment and pay although references to education, housing etc. would be relevant too

**(b)** Outline and assess sociological explanations for ethnic inequalities in modern Britain. (40 marks)

Compare the strengths and weaknesses of different explanations before reaching a balanced conclusion

Focus on comparing the main ethnic minority groups in the UK - Asians such as Pakistanis, Indians and Bangladeshis, and African-Caribbeans - with the White majority

**Grade booster** Getting top marks in question (b)

Outline some of the ethnic inequalities that exist in the modern UK today including access to skilled jobs, pay, unemployment as well as poverty, housing and education. You need to consider a range of different sociological explanations in your answer including functionalism, Weberianism, Marxism and postmodernism. In discussing explanations, make use of relevant concepts, such as assimilation, reserve army of labour, primary and secondary labour markets, underclass, and racialized class fractions. You can develop evaluation by considering evidence for and against different views, using one theory to argue against another and by considering how different ethnic minority groups compare against one another in the labour market.

## An eye on the exam

OCR-style exam questions with some helpful hints and Grade Booster advice to help you get top marks. Use these to assess your progress, as well as to provide regular exam practice.

## Exam practice

At the end of each chapter is a complete exam-style question of the type you will find in the relevant OCR A2 exam paper. A candidate's answer is provided, together with comments and a mark. The comments point out where the answer scores good marks and where it fails to score.

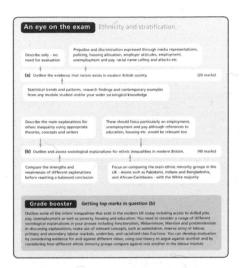

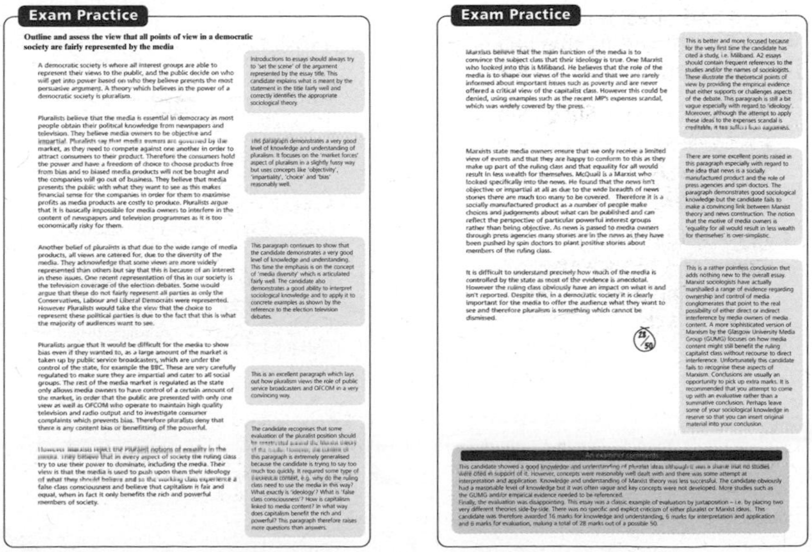

**Exam Practice**

**Outline and assess the view that all points of view in a democratic society are fairly represented by the media**

**Exam Practice**

# CONTENTS

# Sociology A2 for OCR

# Sociological theories

# TOPIC 1

# Consensus, culture and identity

## Getting you thinking

**1 Look at the photograph above. Do you feel we are all puppets of society? Explain your answer.**

**Use your knowledge from your AS-level studies to match each of the sentences below with the sociological theories they are most closely associated with. Explain your decisions.**

1. **Society is like a human body – every part of it helps to keep society going.**
2. **The ruling class benefits in every way from the operation of society while the workers get far less than they deserve.**
3. **Britain is a patriarchal society. Men generally have more power and prestige than women across a range of social institutions.**
4. **People do not feel that they are the puppets of society, rather that they have an active role in creating society.**
5. **Society has experienced such major upheavals from the late 20th century onwards that the old ways of explaining it just won't work any more. We are entering a new sort of society.**

**If you are not sure, the possible answers are given on the right (upside down). The actual answers to the questions are provided at the end of the topic.**

Possible answers: functionalism – feminism – Marxism – social action theory or interactionism – postmodernism

During your AS-level Sociology studies, you will almost certainly have met most of the main sociological theories. The exercise above will have reminded you of some of these. In this chapter, we will be drawing these ideas together and exploring them further.

This topic explores what are known as modernist theories. '**Modernism**' or 'modernity' refers to a period of history in 19th- and 20th-century Western societies that was characterized by major technological, social and political advances. It was within this period and driven by these ideas of rational, progressive thought that sociology was born. The main modernist approaches are Marxism, functionalism and **social action theory** (**interactionism**), and these have dominated sociology for much of the subject's existence.

Modernist theories are divided into two main perspectives – **structural approaches** and social action approaches:

- *Structural approaches* attempt to provide a complete theory of society. They begin their analyses from the 'top', by looking first at society as a whole and then working down to the individual parts, and finally to individuals. There are two main structural theories: Marxism or conflict theory (and its development, neo-Marxism), and functionalism or consensus theory (and its development, neo-functionalism). These theories may start from the same position, but they come to very different conclusions.
- *Social action theories* do not seek to provide complete explanations for society; instead they start by looking at how society is 'built up' from people interacting with each other. Quite how far 'up' they arrive is a matter of debate – though one version of social action theory, known as **labelling** theory, does seek to explain the construction of social rules.

# Functionalism

Functionalism is closely associated with the work of Talcott Parsons. His work dominated US sociology and vied with Marxist-based approaches in Europe from the 1940s until the 1970s. Today, it still provides us with a useful and relatively simple framework for approaching the study of society.

Parsons' aim was to provide a theoretical framework that combined the ideas of Weber, who stressed the importance of understanding people's actions, and those of Durkheim, who emphasized the necessity of focusing on the structures of societies and how they function.

Parsons' starting point, taken from Durkheim, was the organic analogy – that is, he imagined society as similar to a living being that adapts to its environments and is made up of component parts, each performing some action that helps the living being to continue to exist. In the case of human beings, for example, our organs provide functions to keep us alive – for example, the heart pumps blood. It exists for that purpose and we would not have it if there was no need to pump blood. Other creatures have developed alternative methods of survival – for instance, reptiles do not have hearts as they do not pump blood around the body. Similarly, institutions exist, or don't, because of their functions for the maintenance of society.

Just as our bodies need to resolve certain basic needs in order to survive, so do societies. Parsons (1951) suggests that there are four needs (or **functional prerequisites**) that all societies have to satisfy:

1. *Adaptation* (the economic function) – Every society has to provide an adequate standard of life for the survival of its members. Human societies vary from hunters and gatherers to complex industrial societies.
2. *Goal attainment* (the political function) – Societies must develop ways of making decisions. Human societies vary from dictatorships to democracies.
3. *Integration* (social harmony) – Each institution in society develops in response to particular functions. There is no guarantee that the different institutions will not develop elements that may conflict. For example, in **capitalism** the economic inequalities may lead to possible resentment between groups. Specialist institutions therefore develop that seek to limit the potential conflict. These could include religion, notions of charity and voluntary organizations.
4. *Latency* (individual beliefs and values) – The previous three functional prerequisites all deal with the structure of society. This final prerequisite deals instead with individuals and how they cope. Parsons divides latency into two areas:
   - *Pattern maintenance*: this refers to the problems faced by people when conflicting demands are made of them, such as being a member of a minority religious group and a member of a largely Christian-based society. In contemporary sociological terms, we would call this the issue of identity.
   - *Tension management*: if a society is going to continue to exist, then it needs to motivate people to continue to belong to society and not to leave or oppose it.

## Pattern variables

For a society to exist, it must fulfil the functional prerequisites listed above. However, 'society' is a concept that does not exist in itself, but is rather a term for a collection of people. When Parsons says that a 'society' must resolve certain problems, what he actually means is that *people* must act in certain ways that enable society to fulfil its needs and ensure its continuation. This is the role of culture, which emphasizes that members of society ought to act in particular ways and, in doing so, ensure that the functional prerequisites are met.

Parsons claims that in all societies there are five possible cultural choices of action. The different answers the cultures provide lead to different forms of social behaviour and thus different ways of responding to the functional prerequisites. It is within these five sets of options that all cultural differences in human societies can be found.

Parsons calls these cultural choices of action **pattern variables**. They are:

- *Affectivity or affective neutrality* – Societies can be characterized either by close interpersonal relationships between people, or by relationships where the majority of interactions are value free. For example, a small rural society may well be based upon personal knowledge of others, whilst in a large, urban society people hardly know each other.
- *Specificity or diffuseness* – The relationships people have can be based on only one link or on many. We may know others simply as a teacher or a colleague, whereas in simpler societies, they may be cousin, healer, ceremonial leader and so on.
- *Universalism or particularism* – In contemporary societies, we believe that rules should apply equally to

# Focus on research

## Pete Saunders (1996)
### Do the best reach the top?

Functionalist theory suggests that society is formed as it is because that is functionally the best way of maintaining its existence. This includes inequalities in class and status. Many critics argue it is not true that the most gifted achieve the top positions, but that success has more to do with inheritance and parental support. Saunders wished to demonstrate that in fact the best do achieve. He used evidence from the *National Child Development Study*, a longitudinal study of 17 000 children born in 1958 to assess their chances of social mobility. In 1991, he had access to information from the study on 6800 individuals in full-time employment, and concluded that occupational status was closely related to ability and effort. His results, therefore, support the functionalist argument.

Saunders, P. (1996) *Unequal but Fair? A study of class barriers in Britain*, London: IEA

**In what ways do Saunders' results 'support the functionalist argument'?**

everyone (even if they don't), yet in many societies rules are not regarded as necessarily being applicable to all. Royalty, ethnic groups, religious leaders may all be able to behave differently.

- *Quality or performance* – This is linked to the previous pattern variable. Should people be treated according to their abilities or by their social position at birth?
- *Self-orientation or collectivity orientation* – Do societies stress the importance of individual lives and happiness or that of the group?

The answers that the culture of a society provides for these five pattern variables determines the way that people behave, which Parsons describes as social roles.

## Criticisms within the functionalist approach

Robert Merton (1957) belonged to the same functionalist approach as Parsons. However, Merton was critical of some of Parsons' arguments and proposed two amendments to functionalist theory:

1. Parsons assumed if an institution was functional for one part of society, then it was functional for all parts. But Merton points out that this ignored the fact that some institutions can be both **dysfunctional** (or harmful) for society, and functional. In particular, he cites the example of religion, which can both bring people together and drive them apart.
2. Merton suggests that Parsons failed to realize the distinction between manifest (or intended) functions and latent (or unintended) consequences of these actions. Merton says that this makes any analysis of society much more complex than Parsons' simple model.

## Criticisms outside the functionalist approach

Sharrock *et al.* (2003) argue that there are several main criticisms of functionalism:

- Functionalism overemphasizes the level of agreement or consensus in society. Apart from the simplest of societies, people have different values and attitudes within the same society.
- Parsons suggests that society is rather like an organism, yet this is not true. Organisms actually exist as biological entities, have a natural form and a natural life cycle. Society, on the other hand, is a concept, consisting of the activities of possibly millions of people. There is no natural cycle or natural form.
- Functionalists have real problems explaining social change. If, as Parsons claims, institutions exist to fulfil social needs, then once these needs are fulfilled, there is no reason to change them. Unless, therefore, there are some external changes which impact on the four functional prerequisites, societies should never change in form.
- Parsons seems to ignore differences in power. Yet differences in power can have strong impacts upon the form that society takes and whose interests it reflects.
- Finally, as interactionists point out, human beings in the Parsonian model of society seem rather like puppets having their strings pulled by all-powerful societies via pattern variables. Interactionists, postmodernists and late-modernists all combine to argue that people are much more 'reflexive', making choices and constructing their lives.

## Neo-functionalism

Other writers following in the functionalist tradition include Mouzelis (1995) and Alexander (1985). Both these writers argue strongly for the overall systemic approach provided by Parsons. They dispute criticisms of Parsons that suggest he is not interested in how people act, and argue that with some modification Parsonian theory can allow for people to be 'reflexive', making decisions for themselves. These modifications to the theory also help explain social change.

# Marxism

The second major sociological perspective that, like functionalism, aims to create a total theory of society by linking individual motivations and wider structural context is the tradition that has developed from Marxism. Marxism derives from the 19th-century writings of Karl Marx (1867/1973), who sought to create a scientific explanation of societies. His starting point was that the economic system of any society largely determined the social structure. The owners of the economic structure are able to control that society and construct values and social relationships that reflect their own interests. Other groups in society, being less powerful, generally accept these values and social relationships, even though they are not in their interests.

Marx began by suggesting that all history can be divided into five periods or epochs, which are distinguished by ever more complex economic arrangements. The history of all societies begins with what he entitled 'primitive **communism**' – simple societies, such as hunters and gatherers, where there is no concept of private property and everything is shared. From that point it passes through the ancient societies, such as those of Asia and Rome, through feudalism until it reaches the crucial stage of capitalism. According to Marx, capitalism would inevitably give way to the final stage of history, that of communism.

## The Marxist model

Marx developed a theoretical model to describe the development of societies through these epochs. In each of the five epochs there is a particular economic structure (the economic base or **means of production**), which, except in primitive communism, is always controlled by a ruling class. This ruling class then constructs a whole set of social relationships (the **relations of production**) that benefit them and allow them to exploit all others who do not share in the ownership of the means of production. According to Marxist economic theory, the means of production are always advancing, becoming more complex and capable of producing greater wealth – nothing can stop this onward march of technology. However, the values that the ruling group create to benefit themselves tend to move much more slowly. Within each epoch, at the beginning, the values of the ruling class help technology move forward, but over time, because the values do not move as fast, they begin to get in the way of the move forward of technology – in fact, they actually impede it. At this point, a new, challenging group arises with values and ideas that would help the means of production advance, and, after a degree of conflict, they gain control of society and begin to construct their own relations of production. A new epoch has started and the process begins again.

### *Applying the model to capitalism*

Marx believed that contemporary society has reached the stage of capitalism. The majority of his work was about the state of capitalist society and the factors that would, in his opinion, lead on to a communist society.

Within capitalism, there is a ruling class, or 'bourgeoisie', that owns the industry and commerce. All other people who work for a wage, no matter how prestigious or well paid, are members of the working class or proletariat. The bourgeoisie construct relations of production to their own benefit, including concepts of private property, wage labour and the justification of wide inequalities of wealth. The majority of the population accept the inequalities of the system because of the way that dominant institutions, such as religion and education, justify the prevailing economic and social situation. Marx describes this majority as suffering from '**false consciousness**'. However, there is always a degree of conflict between some groups in society who are aware of their exploitation, and the bourgeoisie – Marx saw these people as being 'class conscious'.
**Class consciousness** manifests itself in terms of strikes and political protest, all examples of **class conflict**.

Over time, capitalism will enter a period of crisis, caused by ever-increasing competition amongst industries, leading to fewer and fewer large employers – who are able to lower the wages on offer to such an extent that the majority of the population live in poverty. At such a point, with a tiny minority of very rich capitalists and a huge majority of relatively poor people, radical social change is inevitable. This change will usher in the final epoch of communism.

## Criticisms of Marx

Marx's work has probably been subjected to more critical discussion and straight criticism that any other sociological theory. This is mainly because it is as much a political programme as a sociological theory. However, specific sociological criticisms of Marx's work include the following:

- The description of capitalism and its inevitable move towards a crisis has simply not occurred. Indeed, capitalism has grown stronger and, through globalization, has spread across the world.
- The polarization of people into a tiny rich minority and an extremely poor majority has also not occurred. There is huge inequality, but at the same time there has been a massive growth in the middle classes in society – the very group that Marx predicted would disappear.
- Capitalism changed significantly after Marx's death with the introduction of a wide range of health, pension, housing and welfare benefits, all of which were missing from Marx's analysis.

## Neo-Marxism

The basic model of Marxist theory has provided the platform for an entire tradition of writing in sociology. His ideas have been taken up and developed by a wide range of sociologists, keen to show that the model, suitably amended, is still accurate. Neo-Marxists seek to overcome the criticisms listed above.

The extent of writings within the Marxist tradition is too great to cover in any detail, but three versions of neo-Marxism provide us with a fairly representative sample of developments.

### *The Frankfurt School*

The Frankfurt School is associated with the works of three major neo-Marxists: Marcuse, Adorno and Horkheimer, all of whom were originally at Frankfurt University. In separate books, Marcuse (1964/1991), Adorno (1991) and Horkheimer (1974) criticized Marx for being an **economic determinist** – that is for believing society is mainly determined by the economic system. They argued that people's ideas and motivations are far more important than Marx ever acknowledged. Their critique contained three important elements:

1. *Instrumental reason* – According to Adorno, Marx failed to explore people's motivations for accepting capitalism and the consumer goods it offers. Adorno suggests that it was wrong of Marx to dismiss this as simply 'false consciousness'. People work hard to have a career and earn money, but quite why this is their aim is never explored. Thinking in capitalism is therefore rational, in terms of achieving goals, as long as the actual reasons for having those goals are not thought about rationally.
2. *Mass culture* – Marcuse argued that Marx had ignored the importance of the media in his analysis. Marcuse suggested that the media play a key part in helping to control the population by teaching people to accept their lot and to concentrate on trivial entertainment.
3. *The oppression of personality* – The third element of their critique of Marx focused on the ways that individuals' personality and desires are controlled and directed to the benefit of capitalism. Before capitalism, there was no concept of 'the work ethic'; people did the work that was required and then stopped. Capitalism, and particularly industrial production, needed people who accepted going to work for the majority of their lives and having little leisure. In the early stages of capitalism, therefore, pleasure and desire as concepts were heavily disapproved of – hence the puritan values of Victorian England. But in later capitalism, when it was possible to make money out of desires (and in particular sex), they were emphasized. Sex is now used, for example, to sell a wide range of products. According to the Frankfurt School, therefore, even our wants and desires are manipulated by capitalism in its own interests.



### *Althusser and the concept of relative autonomy*

One of the most sociologically influential neo-Marxist approaches was provided by Althusser (1969), who argued that Marx had overemphasized how much the economic system drove society. Althusser suggested that capitalist society was made up of three interlocking elements:

1. the economic system – producing all material goods
2. the political system – organizing society
3. the ideological system – providing all ideas and beliefs.

According to Althusser, the economic system has ultimate control, but the political and ideological have significant degrees of independence or autonomy. In reality, this means that politics and culture develop and change in response to many different forces, not just economic ones. Althusser used the term **relative autonomy** to describe this degree of freedom of politics and values. This may not at first seem very important, but what it suggests is that society is much more complex and apparently contradictory than in traditional Marxist analysis. So, the march towards a communist state is not clear, but confusing and erratic.

Althusser also used this argument in his analysis of politics and the state. For Marx, the role of politics was simply to represent the interests of the ruling class, but for Althusser, the state was composed of two elements:

1. **repressive state apparatuses** – organizations such as the police and the army
2. **ideological state apparatuses** – the more subtle organizations including education, the media and religious organizations.

Both sets of apparatuses ultimately work for the benefit of capitalism, but there is a huge variation in the way they perform this task, with some contradictions between them.

Althusser's work provided a huge leap forward in neo-Marxist thinking, as it moved away from a naive form of Marxism (rather similar to functionalism), which simply said that everything that existed did so to perform a task for capitalism. Instead, while recognizing this ultimate purpose, Althusser highlighted the massive contradictions and differences between the various institutions of society.

### *Harvey: a late-modernist approach to Marxism*

Some of the most recent and interesting sociological theorizing within neo-Marxism comes from the work of Harvey (1990). Harvey is extremely unusual for a neo-Marxist in that he develops Marxism within a postmodernist framework. As we see in the next topic, postmodernism is a movement that sees a fragmentation of society and a move towards image and superficiality in culture. Harvey argues that this move to postmodernity is the result of economic changes in the 1970s, which led away from manufacturing to commerce, media and retail as the main employers. Coupled with the development of globalization, these changes have presented massive challenges to capitalism.

According to Harvey, capitalism has, however, been clever in its responses to these economic changes, developing new sources of profit through the creation of whole new areas of commerce – what he calls **flexible accumulation** – in particular, through the manipulation of identity, with developments in fashion, travel and new forms of music. Globalization, too, has been utilized to produce cheap goods, which are given added value by being marketed in the more affluent nations.

At the same time, Harvey points out that there have been many real changes that have affected capitalism quite drastically. For example:

- National governments are less powerful than ever before in modernity, and so change now lies at the global, rather than national, level.
- Real political discourse within the traditional frameworks of government and political parties has been replaced by image politics, where what *appears* to happen is more important than what *actually* happens.
- Social class as the dominant form of division between members of societies has been partly replaced by a range of divisions linked to gender, ethnicity, religion and even alternative political movements, such as the green movement.

# Social action theories

According to social action theories, the way to understand society is not to start analysis at the top (analysing the structure of society, as Marxism and functionalism do), but to begin from the 'bottom' – analysing the way people interact with each other. Social action theorists do not set out to construct a grand theory along the lines of Marxism or functionalism, but are much more content to sketch out the rules of social interaction. These approaches (which are sometimes referred to as 'phenomenological approaches') explore the day-to-day, routine actions that most people perform. Interactionists (social action theorists/ phenomenologists) set out to see how individuals actually *create* society through these routine actions.

## Symbolic interactionism

**Symbolic interactionism** – the full name for interactionism – derives from the writings of Mead (1934) and then Blumer (1962) at the University of Chicago. Both Marxism and functionalism seemed to suggest that people were like puppets controlled by the 'relations of production' or the 'pattern variables'. Instead, symbolic interactionism sees people as actively working at relationships, creating and responding to symbols and ideas. It is this dynamic that forms the basis of interactionists' studies.

The theory of symbolic interactionism has three core ideas: the symbol, the self, the interaction.

1. *The symbol* – The world around us consists of millions of unique objects and people. Life would be impossible if we treated every separate thing as unique. Instead, we group things together into categories which we then classify. Usually, we then give each group a name (which is a symbol). Examples of symbols include 'trees', 'women', 'gay men', 'terrorists'. You will immediately see that the symbol may evoke some feelings in us; they are not necessarily neutral terms. So, the world is composed of many symbols, all of which have some meaning for us and suggest a possible response or possible course of action. But the course of action that we feel is appropriate may not be shared by everybody.
2. *The self* – In order for people to respond to and act upon the meanings that symbols have for them, they have to know who they are within this world of symbols and meaning. I cannot decide how I ought to behave until I know who I am and therefore what is appropriate for me to do in certain circumstances. Crucially, this involves us being able to see ourselves through the eyes of others. Blumer suggests that we develop this notion of the self in childhood and, in particular, in games playing. When engaging in a game with others, we learn various social roles and

**Figure 1.1** The difference between structural theories and social action theory

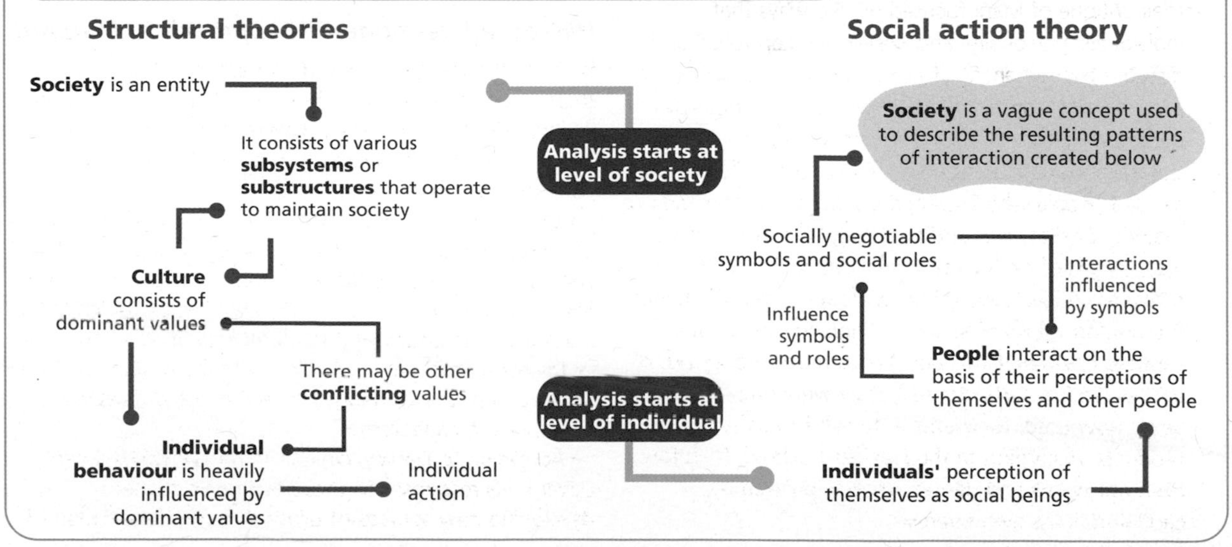

also learn how these interact with the roles of others. This brings us to the third element of interactionism, the importance of the interaction itself.

3 *The interaction* – For sociology, the most important element of symbolic interactionism is actually the point at which the symbol and the self come together with others in an interaction. Each person in society must learn (again through games) to take the viewpoint of other people into account whenever they set out on any course of action. Only by having an idea of what the other person is thinking about the situation is it possible to interact with them. This is an extremely complex business – it involves reading the meaning of the situation correctly from the viewpoint of the other (What sort of person are they? How do they see me? What do they expect me to do?) and then responding in terms of how you see your own personality (Who am I? How do I want to behave?). There is clearly great scope for confusion, error and misunderstanding, so all people in an interaction must actively engage in constructing the situation, reading the rules and symbols correctly.

## Goffman and the dramaturgical approach

Erving Goffman (1968) was heavily influenced by symbolic interactionism in his studies of people's interaction in a number of settings. Goffman's work, which has been called the **dramaturgical** approach, is based on similar ideas to symbolic interactionism in that he explores how people perceive themselves and then set out to present an image of themselves to others. Goffman suggests that people work out strategies in dealing with others and are constantly altering and manipulating these strategies. The basis of his ideas is that social interaction can best be understood as a form of loosely scripted play in which people ('actors') interpret their roles.

## Evaluation of symbolic interactionism

Interactionism provides a rich insight into how people interact in small-scale situations. However, as a theory it is rather limited in scope and is as much psychological as sociological. Its main weakness lies in its failure to explore the wider social factors that create the context in which symbol, self and interaction all exist and the social implications of this. This means that it has no explanation of where the symbolic meanings originate from. It also completely fails to explore power differences between groups and individuals, and why these might occur.

Some of these criticisms were answered by Becker (1963) and other writers within the labelling perspective. Labelling theory is explored in Chapter 2, so we will deal with it only very briefly here. An offshoot of symbolic interactionism, labelling theory focuses on explaining why some people are 'labelled' as deviant and how this impacts on both their treatment by others and their perception of themselves. Becker specifically introduces the notion of power into his version of symbolic interactionism and demonstrates how more powerful groups are able to brand certain activities or individuals as deviant, with consequences that are likely to benefit themselves and harm those labelled deviant. One particular study which combines ideas about power and labelling is his analysis of the imposition and repeal of the laws on prohibition (making alcohol manufacture and sales illegal) in the USA in the early 20th century. He showed how powerful groups came together, based on a mixture of genuine zeal and self-interest, to introduce the prohibition laws, and he explores the consequences for society. It is, therefore, possible to apply symbolic interactionism to broader social situations and also to include power in the analysis.

# Conclusion

In this topic, we have explored a variety of modernist theories, which provide two approaches to understanding society. The first is the structural approach utilized by Marxism and functionalism. This approach starts from the 'top' and works downwards and claims to provide a total theory of society. The second approach starts its analysis from the bottom and works upwards. This is the social action approach utilized by symbolic interactionism. Both approaches have strengths and weaknesses, leading to sociologists taking sides in a debate that lasted more than 20 years. However, changes in society during the 1980s led many sociologists to be dissatisfied with both approaches. We move on to see the results of this dissatisfaction in the next topic.

## Answers to 'Getting you thinking'

1 Functionalism
2 Marxism
3 Feminism
4 Social action theory or interactionism
5 Postmodernism

# Key terms

**Capitalism** term used originally by Marx to describe industrial society based on private ownership of property and businesses.

**Class conflict** in Marxist analysis, the inevitable conflict arising between social classes based on their differing economic interests.

**Class consciousness** in Marxist analysis, the awareness of belonging to a social class.

**Communism** term used originally by Marx to describe societies where ownership of land, businesses and so on is shared and not privately owned.

**Dramaturgical** refers to Goffman's version of interactionism, in which he sees people rather like actors in a play, with some of the script written and some ad-libbed.

**Dysfunctional** in functionalist theory, activities or institutions which do not appear to benefit society.

**Economic determinism** belief that the form of society is mainly determined by the economic system.

**False consciousness** in Marxist analysis, the lack of awareness of being exploited.

**Flexible accumulation** a term used by the neo-Marxist writer Harvey to explain how capitalism has continued to find new ways of profiting from people.

**Functional prerequisites** in functionalist theory, societal needs.

**Ideological state apparatuses** a term used by the neo-Marxist writer Althusser for those institutions which he claims exist to control the population through manipulating values, such as the media.

**Interactionism** shorthand term for symbolic interactionism.

**Labelling** a theory developed from symbolic interactionism which was adapted for use in studies of deviance.

**Means of production** in Marxist analysis, the economic structure of a society.

**Modernism (modernity)** a period in history characterized by the belief that rational thought can be used to understand and explain the world.

**Pattern variables** in functionalist theory, cultural choices as 'suggested' by the society.

**Relations of production** in Marxist analysis, the social relationships in a society.

**Relative autonomy** a term used by the neo-Marxist writer Althusser to suggest that society is not determined as much as Marx suggested by the economic base.

**Repressive state apparatuses** a term used by the neo-Marxist writer Althusser for those institutions which he claims exist to control the population through aggressive means, such as the police.

**Social action theory** another name for symbolic interactionism; social action theories focus on how society is built up from people interacting with each other.

**Structural approaches** these attempt to analyse society by looking it as a whole and then working down to its constituent parts and then to individuals.

**Symbolic interactionism** a theory associated with G.H. Mead that argues that people constantly work via symbols (language, writing, and so on) to construct society through the process of social interaction.

# Check your understanding

1. **Explain what is meant by 'modernism' or 'modernity'.**
2. **What is the 'organic analogy'?**
3. **In your own words identify and briefly explain 'functional prerequisites'.**
4. **Identify and explain two criticisms of functionalism.**
5. **For Marx, what are the 'means of production' and how do they relate to the 'relations of production'?**
6. **What is meant by neo-Marxism? Give one example of a neo-Marxist approach.**
7. **What does Harvey mean by 'flexible accumulation'?**
8. **In your own words, explain the key difference between social action theories and structural theories.**
9. **Why are the concepts of the 'symbol', 'self' and 'interaction' important to interactionists?**
10. **Explain any one criticism of interactionism.**

# Activities

## Research idea

Conduct a small study of your own in which you explore the nature of symbolic interaction in the classroom. How do people respond to symbols? Do they respond differently?

## Web.task

Use the links provided on the website for Pip Jones' book 'Introducing Social Theory' to add to your notes and depth of knowledge.

Go to: **www.polity.co.uk/jones/web.htm**

# TOPIC 2

# Feminist, late-modern and postmodern sociological theories

## Getting you thinking

### She's gotta have it

*By Polly Vernon*

Kate Rainbow, the 31 year old owner of a communications company, says ... 'It's only now becoming obvious, but the market in accessorizing is huge – Swarovski crystal covers for Blackberries, laptop bags, phone fascias and phone charms. The potential to customize phones and gadgets will grow immensely. People, women in particular, want to make their gadgets individual in some way. Lee agrees: 'Increasingly the lines between jewellery or accessory and gadget are being blurred. You can literally wear your phone or your digital camera around your neck on necklaces designed for that purpose.'

Source: *The Independent Technology Magazine*, Issue 1, 31 July 2005

### iPhone gets faster and sexier – but will UK pay more?

*By Martin Hickman, Consumer Affairs Correspondent*

APPLE is to sell a new version of its iPhone with faster internet connection speeds and new applications for about £100, slashing the price of the gadget by more than a third.

The device will use Wi-Fi, 3G and Edge networks, automatically switching between them to ensure the fastest download speeds.

Apple said: "The new iPhone 3G also makes it easier to multi-task with simultaneous voice and data communications, so with iPhone 3G you can browse the web, get map directions, or check your email while you are on a call."

Mr Jobs said there would be software upgrades for the phone, on sale in the UK through an exclusive tie-up with the mobile company 02.

"The thing for Apple is to be able to leverage the iPhone for further innovation, or they run the risk of being the next [Motorola] RAZR, which was iconic in its own way, but for which innovation did not come fast enough," said Shiv Bakhshi, director of mobility research for the market research firm IDC.

Source: *The Independent*, 10 June 2008

**1 What do you think the text and photo tell us about:**

**(a) the changing pace of technology**

**(b) the relationship between fashion and technology?**

**2 Do you think that males and females have different attitudes to modern technology (phones, computers, etc.)? Does this have any impact on what they buy?**

**3 Can you suggest ways in which the following have brought about social changes:**

**(a) mobile phones (b) the internet?**

**4 In what ways do you think the developments reflected in the material above affect society? Explain your answer.**

Topic 1 explored the emergence of sociology during the period of modernity and how the subject was shaped by the dominant ways of thinking of that time. Reflecting the natural sciences, sociology searched for a theoretical perspective that could explain how society was structured, how it functioned and how it changed over time. The theoretical approaches of Marxism and functionalism both claimed to do this, but by the 1970s, sociologists began to accept the fact that these major theoretical approaches simply failed to provide an adequate explanation for the existence of society. It was during this period that social action perspectives became popular, but for most sociologists these had limited value as they never claimed to provide the overarching theoretical frameworks that functionalism and Marxism had claimed. By the 1980s (and ten years earlier for feminists), sociologists were aware, through their studies of culture, gender, social class and the economy, that enormous changes were taking place. The traditional 'modern' social characteristics of strong social classes, clear gender roles and party-based politics, all linked to an economic system based on industrial production, were no longer an accurate reflection of British society (and most other Western societies). Sociological theory was simply unable to explain these changes. It was in this vacuum that a new breed of theorizing emerged.

One group of writers believed that modernity had moved towards what is now commonly known as '**late modernity**' (or '**high modernity**' according to Giddens (1984)). A separate, much more radical group of theorists argued that society really had totally changed and had moved into a **postmodern** era – hence the term 'postmodernists'.

A third group of sociologists are feminists, who provide the bridge in sociological theorizing from structural and interactionist theories through to postmodern approaches.

# Feminism

Gender roles and the issue of patriarchy are explored in a number of units in this book. Feminism as a social and political movement has been concerned to expose the inequalities that exist in the treatment of women in society. However, linked to this movement has been a development in theoretical approaches to explain the situation of women in society.

In many ways, feminism could be seen to be the battering ram that smashed down the closed doors of sociological thinking. Feminism initially emerged from a Marxist theoretical framework, but many feminist writers soon found this approach too constricting and moved beyond this towards more radical theories. Eventually, feminism began to question some of the very basic concepts upon which sociology was built – in fact, the very notion of male and female came under attack.

For a detailed analysis and evaluation of the various types of feminism, see Chapter 6, Topic 5.

# Late modernity and postmodernity

## The distinction between late-modern and postmodern theory

Most students of sociology are understandably confused over the distinction sociologists make between late modernity (or 'high modernity') and postmodernity.

Perhaps the simplest way of dividing the two is that late modernity sees society as having changed and developed new aspects. The task of the late-modernist theory is to adapt more traditional theories of sociology.

Postmodern theorists argue that the whole 'sociological project' was part of a period of history – modernity – in which a particular way of viewing society developed that was closely related to a set of economic and social circumstances. We have now moved into a new set of economic and social circumstances based largely on communication and image, and therefore traditional sociological models have no value at all.

## Late or high modernity

In the previous topic on modernism, we saw that the major split between theoretical approaches concerned which 'end' of human society sociologists emphasized. On one side of the argument were 'structural' theorists, such as Marx and Parsons, who, no matter what their differences, stressed that the only way to understand human behaviour was to locate it firmly within a dominant, controlling, structural framework. Their theories suggested that people were manipulated by their cultures.

On the other side, however, writers from the social action tradition, such as the interactionists, argued equally passionately that the only way to see society was as an abstract concept consisting of the interaction of individuals and groups. People were actively engaged in defining the world around them and then responding to these definitions.

By the 1980s, most sociologists began to tire of this argument and looked for ways out of it – there had to be a way to combine the two perspectives.

## Giddens' structuration theory

The best-known and currently highly influential attempt to resolve the argument can be found in the work of Giddens (1984). Giddens calls his theory **structuration theory**, which, as you can tell from the name, combines the concepts of structure and action.

> *«The difference between society and nature is that nature is not man-made, but society is. While not made by any single person, society is created and recreated afresh, by participants in every encounter. It is indeed only made possible because every member of society is a practical social theorist who draws upon their knowledge and resources, normally in an unforced and routine way.»* (Giddens 1993)

### *Structure in Giddens' writings*

The starting point for Giddens is that there is such a thing as structure, but only as a way to describe patterns of behaviour of people in society. Structure has no existence beyond this. He therefore rejects the traditional modernist notion of something 'out there' that determines how we behave.

> *«Society only has form, and that form only has effects on people, in so far as structure is produced and reproduced in what people do.»* (Giddens and Pierson 1998)

The simple way that Giddens himself explains this is by using the example of a language. We all use a series of words and grammatical rules to communicate. We may not know all the words and we may not be aware of what the rules actually are – we just use them. The language therefore exists, but it only does so because we make it exist through our use of it. Giddens calls this 'structure'.

Bearing this in mind, structure consists of two key elements: *rules* and *resources*. Both of these combine to influence how we act:

- Rules are procedures we generally follow in everyday life. They can be formal or informal depending upon the situation and their perceived seriousness. Rules are not fixed and may be changed over time. (Again, think of his analogy with language.)
- People have differing resources – by which he is referring to access to different levels of power. These resources consist of material resources (such as wealth and income), symbolic resources (such as personal or job-related prestige), biological resources (such as physical attractiveness) and cognitive resources (such as intelligence or skills).

The structure of society, then, consists of people following rules, but different people have different resources to deploy in order to use or amend these rules.

### *Agency and the duality of structure*

If structure is actually only people (or '**agents**' as Giddens calls them) behaving in certain ways, then why is it important? Because, Giddens argues, people draw from society the shared stock of knowledge that they use to guide their actions (that is, 'the rules' above). People therefore make society, but in doing so give themselves the rules and structure to guide them in their actions. This intimate two-way relationship is described by Giddens as the '**duality of structure**'.

### *Ontological security*

Ontology refers to the issues to do with the reality of the world. According to Giddens, humans have a need for a sense of security, provided by rules and resources. As he puts it, people wish to believe that the 'natural and social worlds are as they appear to be'. He describes this situation as '**ontological security**'.

The desire for security and the existence of shared understanding helps people engage in regular patterns of social life. This regularity then helps society to remain stable.

### *Reflexivity and transformative capacity*

In seeking ontological security, people are clearly seeking stability. However, we know that people also seek to bring about social change. You may also recall from your study of functionalism (see Topic 1) that there was a real problem with the theory in explaining social change. Giddens says that this change takes place because people are constantly monitoring their situation and their place in society, and assessing whether they match their idea of self-personality – this process is known as 'reflexive monitoring'. If people are unhappy or have an ideal of what they want, then they will actively seek change. Unlike the Marxist or functionalist view, people are not puppets controlled by others. By engaging in **reflexivity**, people have a '**transformative capacity**' to change society.

As a way of illustrating his theory, Giddens points to Willis' *Learning to Labour* (Willis 1977) as an example of structuration, where the young lads' choices of action and the wider structure of society interact to provide an outcome that reflects both. Willis studied a group of 12 working-class boys for 18 months at the end of their schooldays, and then briefly into their first employment. The 'lads' showed little interest in studying, as they knew that their future lay elsewhere in unskilled physical labour. At school, they passed their time by 'having a laff' in lessons and making fun of teachers and the harder-working pupils ('ear 'oles'). Their choice of behaviour in school guaranteed their school failure, thus ensuring that the future that they knew would come about for them actually did come about. When they later entered these unskilled jobs, the skills of 'having a laff' and passing time enabled them to cope with the work. To summarize, the boys made choices based on their awareness of the wider society and their place in it. It is possible that they could have made other choices, but did not do so. The interaction of their choices and the 'reality' of society resulted in the outcome they predicted.

### *Criticisms of Giddens*

Although Giddens' work is very influential and has attracted much attention, Cuff *et al.* (1990) question how original his ideas actually are. They suggest that these are really just a collection of ideas drawn from a variety of sources. Much of Giddens' work, they suggest, goes little further than the work of some of the founders of sociology. Many would argue that Giddens is merely updating Weber. Despite Giddens claiming the originality of ideas such as 'transformative capacity', sociologists such as Craib (1992) suggest that similar ideas can also be found in Marx, who once wrote that 'men make their own history albeit not in circumstances of their own choosing' or even in Parsons' concept of pattern variables. Cuff and colleagues also suggest that Giddens' theory has rarely been successfully applied, least of all by Giddens himself. Giddens has used the example of Willis' work, yet Willis himself was working from a Marxist perspective. Chapter 3 Topic 1 contains more on Willis.

## Beck and the sociology of risk

Another sociologist pushing forward the boundaries of sociology within the 'late modernity' framework is the German sociologist Ulrich Beck. Beck (1992) argues that a central concern for all societies today is that of risk, and this concept has permeated the everyday life of all of us. There are three elements to Beck's thesis: **risk society**, **reflexive modernization** and **individualization**.

### *Risk society*

According to Beck, modernity introduced a range of 'risks' that no other historical period has ever had to face. Note that Beck uses the term 'risk' in a very specific way. Throughout history, societies have had to face a wide range of 'hazards', including famine, plague and natural disasters. However, these were always seen as beyond the control of people, being caused by such things as God or nature. Yet the risks faced by modern societies were considered to be solvable by human beings. The belief was that industrialization, public services, private insurance and a range of other supports would minimize the possibility of risk. Indeed, the very project of sociology began with a desire to control society and minimize social problems.

However, in late modernity (which Beck calls 'advanced or reflective modernization'), the risks are seen as spiralling away from human control. No longer can risks be adequately addressed to the same standards as they were in modernity. Problems such as global warming and nuclear disaster are potentially too complex for societies to deal with.

### *Reflexive modernization*

Late modernity, in which people are reflexive (as outlined in the work of Giddens), leads to their questioning how these risks became uncontrollable – that is, they begin to question the political and technological assumptions of modernity. People begin to be aware of risk and how they as individuals are in danger. They also seek ways of minimizing risk in all spheres of their lives. Risk and risk avoidance become central to the culture of society. This helps explain the growth in control of young children by parents trying to minimize any possible risk to them from cars, paedophiles and the material they watch on television. At the level of politics, there is a huge demand for governments to seek to identify and control every possible risk.

Beck argues that although it is the global political and technological 'system' itself that is the cause of the risk, there has been little attempt to confront the problems at this level; rather, risk avoidance operates at the personal and lower political levels.

### *Individualization*

Beck links the move towards individualization with the move away from 'tradition' as an organizing principle of society. In modern societies, most aspects of people's lives were taken for granted. Social position, family membership and gender roles, for example, were all regarded as 'given'. In late modernity, however, there has been the move towards individualization, whereby all of these are now more open to decision-making. So, the background is of risk and risk awareness, and the foreground is of people making individual choices regarding identity and lifestyle as they plan their lives.

### *Criticisms of Beck*

Beck has been criticized by a number of writers. Turner (1994) argues that Beck's distinction between 'hazard' and 'risk' is dubious. People have always faced 'risk' and have always sought to minimize this in whatever ways were available at the time, such as religion or some other means that we might now consider of little value. Nevertheless, there was an awareness that something could be done to combat the 'hazard'.

A second criticism derives from Beck's argument that the response to risk was largely individual. Yet a range of political movements have been formed to combat global warming, eradicate poverty in Africa and stop the spread of HIV/AIDS. These are all political movements which are international in scope and which indicate that people do believe that it is possible to control the risks that Beck identifies. In July 2005, a G8 summit took place at which the richest countries in the world committed themselves to seek to resolve poverty in Africa and global warming. A series of rock concerts was also put on across the world to draw attention to the need for the G8 leaders to tackle these issues. However, in defence of Beck, his writings have been so influential that one could equally reply that it is his work that has led people to believe it is possible to challenge global threats.

Elliot (2002) argues that Beck's work fails to recognize differences in power. Beck has suggested that the risk is spread across all groups in society and that differences in power are relatively unimportant. Elliot disputes this, suggesting instead that rich and powerful groups are able to limit risk and to have greater influence on the context in which the risk occurs.

# Postmodernism

Postmodernist approaches to sociology emerged in the 1980s, providing a powerful challenge to traditional 'modernist' theories that sought to create an all-encompassing theory to explain society.

Two key postmodernist writers are Baudrillard (1980, 1994) and Lyotard (1984). Although Baudrillard had originally been a Marxist academic and his early works supported a neo-Marxist perspective, he later attacked the 'grand theories' such as Marxism and functionalism. Lyotard and Baudrillard dismissed these as merely **meta-narratives**, or elaborate stories, that effectively gave comfort to people by helping them believe there was some rational, existing basis to society. According to the postmodernists, sociological theory, like science and most other academic subjects, was simply a set of stories or narratives belonging to a specific period in history – the period of modernity, whose roots lie in the 18th-century historical movement known as the Enlightenment. This was the term used by those at the time for an academic movement which applied rational thought to solving scientific, economic, political and social questions. It is difficult for us today to accept that it was really not until then that academics began to believe that the natural and social worlds were governed by forces or laws that could be uncovered through scientific endeavour. The more the laws of economics and science could be uncovered, it was argued, the greater would be the progress in ridding the world of hunger, disease, war and all other problems.

The Enlightenment gave birth, in turn, to modernity, the period of 19th- and 20th-century history characterized by significant technological, social and political advances in Western societies. It was within this period that sociology was born. All of the founders of sociology were very strongly influenced by the idea that societies were progressing from traditional or premodern societies through to modern ones based on science, technology and the industrial process. This belief in scientific and social progress based on the application of rational thought was taken for granted until the 1970s when the postmodernist movement began to emerge.

At their simplest, postmodern theories argue that there cannot be any overarching theoretical explanation of society. This is because society exists only as a reassuring 'narrative'. In order to understand society as it is today, we need to have a deep awareness of the role of the media in creating an image of society that we seek to live out.

## Lyotard

Lyotard argues that economic expansion and growth, and the scientific knowledge upon which they are based, have no aim but to continue expanding. This expansion is outside the control of human beings as it is too complex and simply beyond our scope. In order to make sense of this, to give ourselves a sense of control over it and to justify the ever-expanding economic system, grand narratives have been developed. These are political and social theories and explanations that try to make sense of society, which in reality is out of control. Marxism and functionalism and all other sociological theories fall into this category. The role of sociology, therefore, has been to justify and explain, while the reality of life for most people has simply not accorded with the sociological explanations. Lyotard sees contemporary society not as described in sociological theories, but as one that consists of isolated individuals linked by few social bonds.

## Baudrillard

Baudrillard is also a critic of contemporary society. Like Lyotard, he sees people as isolated and dehumanized. Lyotard was particularly interested in the notion of knowledge as serving to justify the narratives of postmodern society. He argued that knowledge was a commodity that was bought and sold, and this buying was usually undertaken by big business and government. The result was that what people know about the world (knowledge) was that filtered through business and government. Baudrillard was also interested in the way that knowledge and understanding of the world are created, but his main emphasis was on the media.

### *The death of the social*

Baudrillard notes that, in contemporary societies, the mass of the population expresses a lack of interest in social solidarity and in politics. The hallmark of this postmodern society is the consumption of superficial culture, driven by marketing and advertising. People live isolated lives sharing common consumption of the media, through which they experience the world. According to Baudrillard this can best be described as the 'death of the social'.

### *Media and the experience of the world*

The media play a central role in the death of the social. Baudrillard argues that people now have limited direct experience of the world and so rely on the media for the vast majority of their knowledge. As well as gaining their ideas of the world from the media, the bulk of the population are also influenced in how they behave by the same media. Rather than the media reflecting how people behave, Baudrillard argues that people increasingly reflect the media images of how people behave. Of course, at some point, the two move so close together that the media do start once again to mirror actual behaviour, as actual behaviour 'catches up' with the media images.

### *Sign-objects and the consumer society*

In the 21st century, a significant proportion of Western societies are affluent. Members of those societies are able to consume a large number of commodities and enjoy a range of leisure activities. However, Baudrillard argues that this consumption moves people ever further away from social relationships and ever closer to relationships with their consumer lifestyles. Yet the importance of objects in our lives has little to do with their use to us, but much more to do with what meaning they have for us. We purchase items not just because they are functionally useful, but because they signify that we are successful or fashionable. Consumer goods and leisure activities are, in Baudrillard's terms, '**sign-objects**', as we are consuming the image they provide rather than the article or service itself.

### *Hyperreality and the simulacrum*

Baudrillard argues that, in modern society, it is generally believed that real things or concepts exist and then are given names or 'signs'. Signs, therefore, reflect reality. In postmodern society, however, signs exist that have no reality but themselves. The media have constructed a world that exists simply because it exists – for example, take the term 'celebrity'. A celebrity is someone who is defined as a celebrity, they do not have to have done anything or have any particular talent. It is not clear how one becomes a celebrity nor how one stays a celebrity. Being a celebrity occurs as long as one is regarded as a celebrity. Where a sign exists without any underlying reality, Baudrillard terms it a '**simulacrum**'. He believes that the society in which we live is now increasingly based upon simulacra. The fact that so much of our lives are based upon signs that have no basis or reality has led

## Key terms

**Agents** Giddens' term for people.

**Duality of structure** the notion that people both make society and are strongly influenced by it.

**High modernity** Giddens' term for late modernity.

**Hyperreality** the idea that we live in a world that is increasingly perceived and experienced via the media.

**Individualization** a decline in accepting socially approved roles and an increasing stress on personal choices.

**Late modernity** a term to describe contemporary society, in which the traditional social groupings, economic organization and culture have all changed so profoundly that traditional sociological explanations no longer hold true.

**Meta-narratives** a postmodernist term used to refer to the structural theories of Marxism and functionalism.

**Ontological security** the idea that people want to believe there is some reality beyond them in society, giving them the psychological confidence to engage in interaction.

**Postmodern** a different perspective on contemporary society that rejects modernism and its attempts to explain the world through overarching theories. Instead, it suggests that there is no single, shared reality and focuses attention on the significance of the media in helping to construct numerous realities.

**Reflexive modernization** the idea that risk avoidance becomes a major factor in social organization.

**Reflexivity** Giddens' term for the ability to perceive yourself as others see you and to create your own identity.

**Risk society** Beck suggests that contemporary societies are best characterized as ones where people are aware that they face complex risks that are not open to individual control.

**Sign-objects** Baudrillard's term for the notion that we buy items to express ourselves, not for their function.

**Simulacrum** (plural 'simulacra') media images that have no basis in reality, but which people increasingly model their behaviour upon.

**Structuration theory** the term used for Giddens' theory, which seeks to combine both structural and social action theories.

**Transformative capacity** the ability of people to change society.

Baudrillard to suggest that we now live in a world of '**hyperreality**' – a world of image.

## Criticisms of postmodernism

Postmodernism has been very influential in sociology and can probably claim to have generated the huge growth in the academic subject of media studies. However, its success has been more in pointing to the failure of grand theories rather than in putting anything positive in its place. Of course, postmodernists in reply would argue that that is precisely their point! Baudrillard or Lyotard, though they reject any idea of value-free sociology, do appear to be more critics of society than sociological theorists. Their work is shot through with value-judgements about what is real and what is worthwhile – so their dismissal of contemporary media-based society is less a sociological statement than a political one.

Postmodernists have also been criticized for their failure to accept that not everything is hyperreal. People do live in reality, and some people have much greater access to goods and services than others.

## Check your understanding

1. **Identify three of the social changes that led some sociologists to believe that traditional sociological theory was out of date.**
2. **Identify the key difference between late-modern and postmodern theory.**
3. **How does Giddens use the example of language to explain the idea of structure?**
4. **What does Giddens mean by 'duality of structure'?**
5. **What piece of research does Giddens use as an example of structuration theory?**
6. **How has Giddens' work been criticized?**
7. **What is a 'risk society'?**
8. **How do postmodernists criticize sociological theory?**
9. **What does Baudrillard mean by the 'death of the social'?**
10. **Identify two criticisms of postmodernism.**

## Activities

### Research idea

Ask a sample of young people the extent to which they anticipate being able to control their future. Focus on factors such as choice of partner, higher education, job, friends and family relationships. Use the results to assess the extent of individualization.

### Web.task

The site **www.theory.org.uk.** is run by the media sociologist David Gauntlett. Go to the page **www.theory.org.uk/giddens.htm** Make your own notes on at least one aspect of Giddens' thinking as described here.

Then head for **www.theorycards.org.uk/main.htm** Choose three of the theorists mentioned in this topic along with any others you have come across in your Sociology course. Print them out and turn them into playing cards.

An amusing area of his site is the set of 'Lego theorists', including the 'Anthony Giddens in his study' set (shown here), which shows the sociologist 'composing new works, reading books and discussing ideas in his office at the London School of Economics'. See: **www.theory.org.uk/lego.htm**

# TOPIC 1

# The definition and measurement of crime and deviance

## Getting you thinking

**Item A** Trends in crime 1981–2008/9

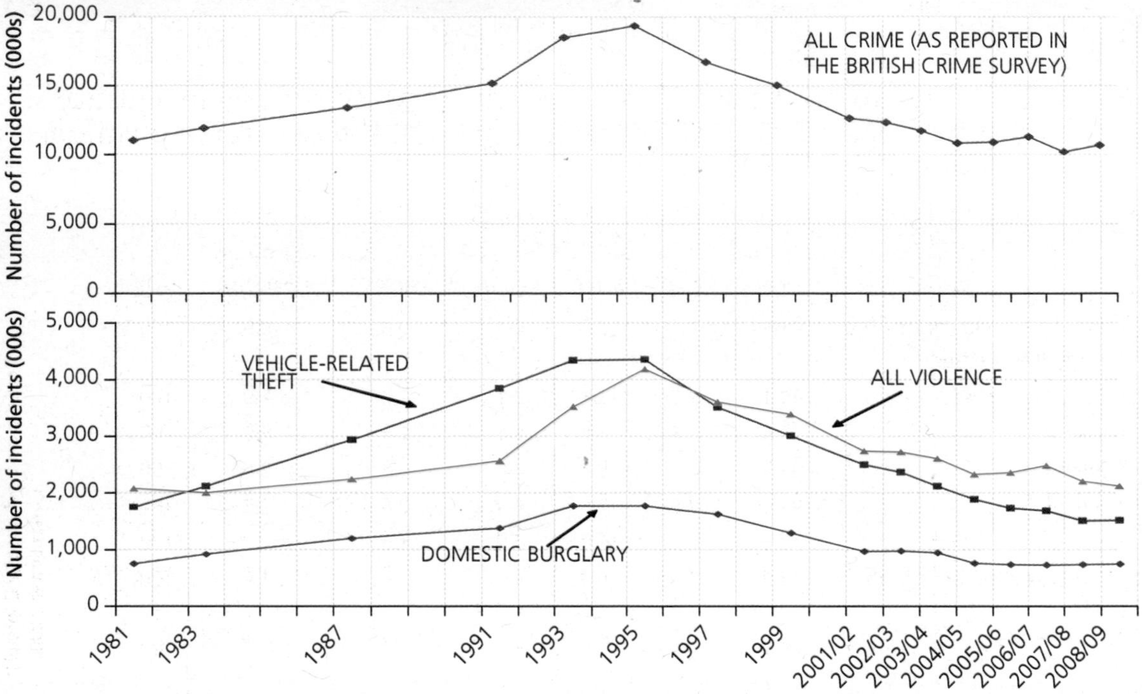


British Crime Survey 2008/9

**Item B** Offenders as a percentage of the population by age, 2006, England and Wales

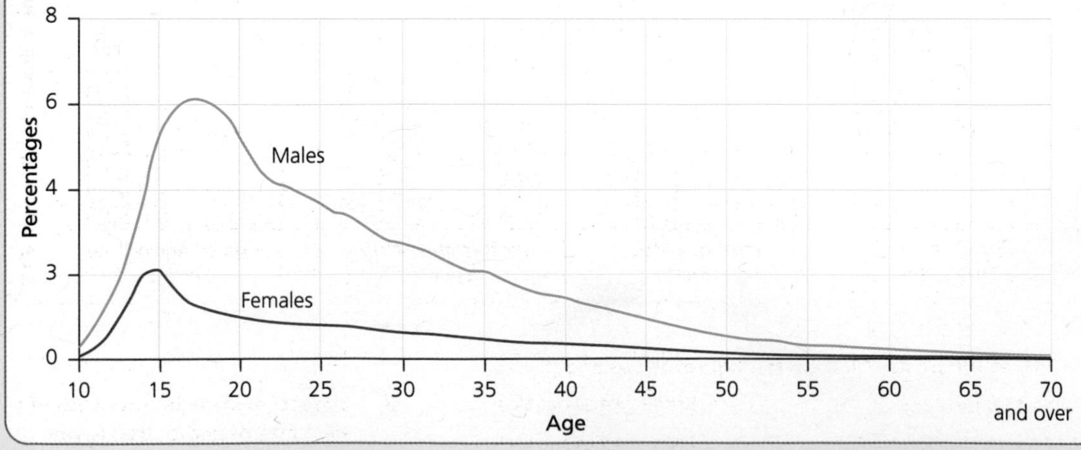


British Crime Survey, 2007/08

continued on the next page

## Getting you thinking continued

### Item C Serious or persistent youth offending, by social class

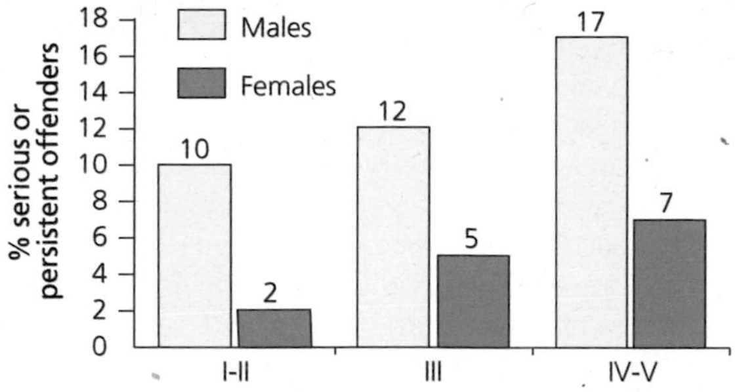


Note: 1. The Registrar General's social classification is used to measure social class. The individual's social class is derived from their father's occupation (or their mothers, if father's is unknown or not applicable).
I – professional, II – managerial or technical, III – skilled manual and non-manual work, IV – partly skilled, V – unskilled.

Youth crime: findings from the 1998/99 Youth Lifestyles Survey, a self-report study

### Item D Percentage of ethnic groups at different stages of the criminal justice process compared to the ethnic breakdown of the general population, England and Wales 2007/08

| | Ethnicity | | | | | | |
|---|---|---|---|---|---|---|---|
| | White | Mixed | Black | Asian | Chinese or Other | Not stated/ Unknown | Total |
| General population (aged 10 & over) @ 2001 Census | 91.3 | 1.3 | 2.2 | 4.4 | 0.9 | 0.0 | 100 |
| Stops and searches | 68.1 | 2.5 | 13.1 | 8.1 | 1.2 | 7.0 | 100 |
| Arrests | 79.3 | 2.8 | 7.4 | 5.1 | 1.4 | 4.0 | 100 |
| Cautions | 82.5 | | 6.5 | 4.6 | 1.4 | 5.0 | 100 |
| Youth offences | 84.8 | 3.5 | 5.8 | 3.0 | 0.4 | 2.5 | 100 |
| Tried at Crown Court | 73.5 | | 14.0 | 8.0 | 4.4 | * | 100 |
| Court ordered supervision by probation service | 83.6 | 2.5 | 6.3 | 4.6 | 1.2 | 1.8 | 100 |
| Prison receptions | 79.1 | 2.9 | 10.6 | 5.9 | 1.2 | 0.2 | 100 |

Statistics on Race and the Criminal Justice System, 2007

### Item D Recorded crime rates per 10,000 population by area type

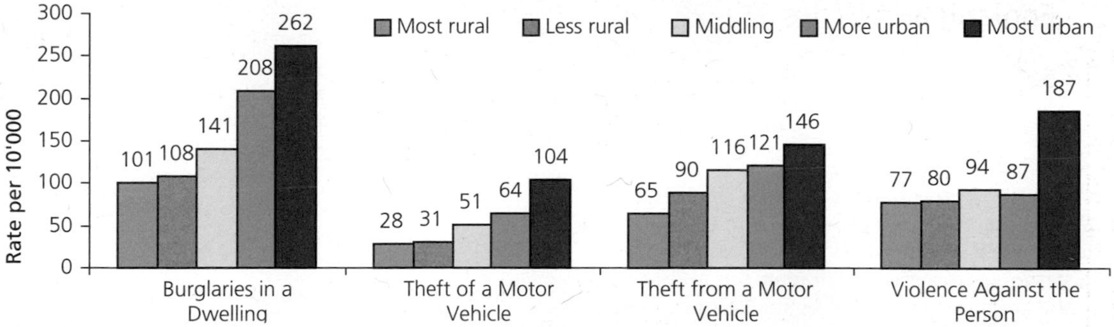


Rural crime in England and Wales, 2001/2

Look carefully at the Items. What do the figures tell us about:

1 **Crime rates over time?**
2 **Crime and age?**
3 **Crime and gender?**
4 **Crime and social class?**
5 **Crime and ethnicity?**
6 **Crime and type of area?**
7 **Suggest explanations for each of the patterns and/or trends you have identified in questions 1–6.**

Hopefully you will have seen from the statistics above that there are quite strong connections between crime rates and various social factors such as gender, age, ethnicity and social class. When it comes to explaining these patterns and trends you might have come up with two types of view. The first accepts the statistics as accurate and looks for differences in the culture, values and social position of particular groups to explain why they might be more or less likely to engage in criminal activities. The second explanation questions the statistics themselves. Are they accurate or do they tell us more about the reporting of crime by the public and stereotyping and labelling by the criminal justice system than about the 'real' crime rates? Much of this chapter will be concerned with exploring these issues in more depth.

But before we start on this exploration it is important to work out exactly what we mean by the terms 'crime' and 'deviance' and to investigate how crime statistics are actually collected. These two issues provide the central themes of this first topic.

Sociologists have suggested two, distinct definitions of deviance: the normative definition and the relativistic.

## The normative definition of deviance

The normative definition is perhaps the common-sense one, a version of which most people suggest when they are questioned as to the meaning of deviance. A typical example of a normative definition of deviance would be that it 'refers to actions which differ from the accepted standards of a society' or more sociologically, 'it consists of the violation of social norms'.

The normative definition provides a simple and clear image of a society in which there are shared values and ways of behaving (norms) and the deviant is a person who breaks these shared values. Finding out what the shared values are is relatively easy, as these can be found by various surveys (a good example is The British Attitudes Survey, published annually).

Underpinning this definition of deviance is the belief that society is essentially **consensual** – that is, the vast majority of people share similar values. Indeed, it was this approach that was used by Durkheim in his explanation of deviance and its relationship to crime. Durkheim suggests that every society shares a set of core values, which he called the '**collective conscience**'. The more behaviour differed from these core values, the more likely it was to be viewed as deviant.

This normative definition of deviance has a number of consequences for the study of offending. Perhaps most important is that, if there are core values that most people subscribe to, then the main aim of the sociology of crime and deviance is to explain why some people act in a deviant manner. Therefore, sociologists who accept the normative definition of deviance will often set out to discover what differences there are between people who deviate (including criminals) and people who behave conventionally. Much research goes into exploring how such things as family differences, social-class differences or the influence of the peer group make some people into deviants.

# Focus on research

### Definitions of crime and deviance

The American sociologist Marshall B. Clinard (1974) suggested that the term 'deviance' should be reserved for behaviour that is so disapproved of that the community finds it impossible to tolerate. Not all sociologists would accept this definition, but it does describe the area usually covered by studies of deviance. In terms of Clinard's definition, crime and delinquency are the most obvious forms of deviance. 'Crime' refers to those activities that break the law of the land and are subject to official punishment; **'delinquency'** refers to acts that are criminal, or are considered antisocial, which are committed by young people. Social scientists who study crime are often referred to as **criminologists**.

However, many deviant acts that are disapproved of are not defined as criminal. For example, alcoholism and attempted suicide are not illegal in Britain today. Some criminal acts are not even typically seen as deviant. Sometimes, outdated laws are left on the statute books even though people have long since stopped enforcing them. For example, under British law it is technically illegal to make or eat mince pies on Christmas Day and to shout 'taxi' to hail a cab.

Deviance is also **relative**: there is no absolute way of defining a deviant act. Deviance can only be defined in relation to a particular standard, and no standards are fixed or absolute. As such, what is regarded as deviant varies from time to time and place to place. An act considered deviant today may be defined as normal in the future. An act defined as deviant in one society may be seen as perfectly normal in another. Put another way, deviance is socially constructed.

Adapted from Haralambos, M. and Holborn, M. (2004) *Sociology: Themes and Perspectives*, London: Collins Education

**Give an example of each of the following:**

**A** an act generally disapproved of, but not criminal

**B** a criminal act often not seen as deviant

**C** an act likely to be considered deviant in one culture, but not in another

**D** an act that used to be seen as deviant but is not today.

## The relativistic approach

The normative definition of deviance starts from the basis that there is a common set of shared values. The relativistic approach argues, instead, that the basis of society is a diversity of values, not a consensus. Societies are just too complex for there to be a clear set of shared values. Sociologists from this perspective point to the conflicts of interest and diversity of beliefs and values that characterize modern societies. The relativistic approach to deviance therefore suggests that there are different sets of competing values that coexist and that are constantly in a state of change, jockeying for positions as the more 'socially valued' values of society. So, the values of society are to be understood less in terms of a consensus of fundamental beliefs and values, and much more as the outcome of some form of dynamic process through which some values become adopted by society at the cost of other values.

There are two main approaches to how this dynamic process works:

1. *the interactionist or labelling approach* – according to which the values that emerge as most highly rated are the result of complex interactions between different groups and individuals in society
2. *the conflict approach* – most commonly associated with Marxists, which argues that the values of society are dominated by, and reflect, the interests of the ruling class, and beneath that the dynamics of the dialectic.

The implications of a relativistic approach, as opposed to a normative approach to understanding deviance, are very important indeed for the study of crime and deviance. Before, we saw that the key question for the normative approach was, 'What is the difference between deviants and conforming people, which makes the deviants act the way they do?'. However, the relativistic approach argues that dominant values are just the outcome of a struggle to get one group's values accepted rather than another's. In this case, studying the personal or social characteristics of deviants is not that important; what is far more important is to ask the question, 'Why do some groups' values become the socially accepted ones at the expense of other groups' values?'.

So, the normative definition suggests that the focus of study is to explain the causes of deviant behaviour and the focus of the relativistic definition is to uncover the processes whereby one set of values dominate.

# The measurement of crime and deviance

In order to understand why people commit crime, we need first to find out who commits crime and what sorts of crimes are committed. Sociologists use three different ways to build up this picture of crime. Each method provides us with particular information, but also has a number of weaknesses that need to be identified if our picture is to be accurate. The three methods of collecting information are: police-recorded statistics, victim surveys and self-report studies.

# Police-recorded statistics

Police-recorded statistics are drawn from the records kept by the police and other official agencies, and are published every six months by the **Home Office**.

The **official statistics** are particularly useful in that they have been collected since 1857 and so provide us with an excellent historical overview of changing trends over time. They also give us a completely accurate view of the way that the criminal justice system processes offenders through arrests, trials, punishments, and so on.

## Police-recorded statistics as social constructions

Police-recorded statistics are **social constructions** – they cannot be taken simply at their face value because they only show crimes that are reported to and recorded by the police. When we dig a little deeper, a lot of hidden issues are uncovered.

**Figure 2.1** Comparing a victim survey (BCS) and crimes recorded to the police

Kershaw, C., Nicholas, S. and Walker, A. (2008) *Crime in England and Wales 2008*, Home Office RDS/Ministry of Justice

**Compare these two pie charts which show the differences in the image of 'crime rates' between the two methods of collecting information.**

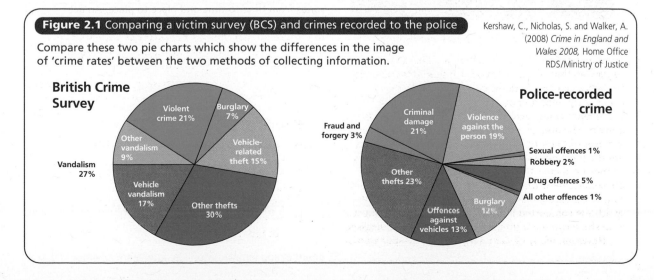

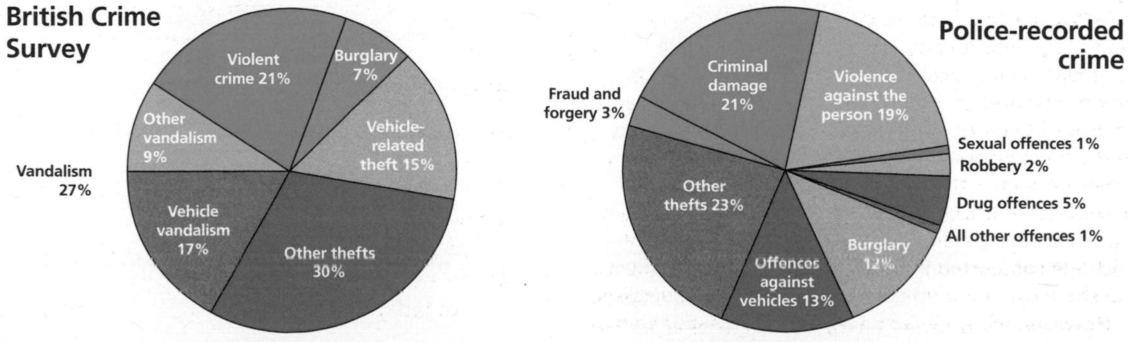

### *Reporting crime*

Police-recorded statistics are based on the information that the criminal justice agencies collect. But crimes cannot be recorded by them if they are not reported in the first place, and the simple fact is that a high proportion of 'crimes' are not reported to the police at all. According to the **British Crime Survey** (Home Office 1998), we know that individuals are less likely to report a 'crime' to the police if they regard it as:

- too trivial to bother the police with
- a private matter between friends and family – in this case they will seek redress directly (get revenge themselves) – or one where they wish no harm to come to the offender
- too embarrassing (e.g. male rape).

Other reasons for non-reporting of crimes are that:

- the victim may not be in a position to give information (e.g. a child suffering abuse)
- they may fear reprisals.

On the other hand, people are more likely to report a crime if:

- they see some benefit to themselves (e.g. an insurance claim)
- they have faith in the police ability to achieve a positive result.

### *Recording of crimes*

When people do actively report an offence to the police, you would think that these statistics at least would enter the official reports. Yet in any one year, approximately 57 per cent of all crimes reported to the police fail to appear in the official statistics. Figure 2.1 above shows the proportion of the crimes committed that are reported to the police and the proportion recorded by the police.

### *The role of the police*

Clearly, the police are filtering the information supplied to them by the public, according to factors that are important to them. These factors have been identified as follows:

- *Seriousness* – They may regard the offence as too trivial or simply not a criminal matter.
- *Social status* – More worryingly, they may view the social status of the person reporting the matter as not high enough to regard the issue as worth pursuing.
- *Classifying* – When a person makes a complaint, police crimes officers must decide what category of offence it is. How they classify the offence will determine its seriousness. So, the police officer's opinion determines the category and seriousness of crime (from assault, to aggravated assault for example).
- *Discretion* – Only about 10 per cent of offences are actually uncovered by the police. However, the chances of being arrested for an offence increase markedly depending upon the 'demeanour' of the person being challenged by a police officer (that is, their appearance, attitude and manner). Anderson *et al.* (1994) show that youths who cooperate and are polite to police officers are less likely to be arrested than those regarded as disrespectful.

## **Focus** on **research**

### The British Crime Survey

The British Crime Survey (BCS) was first introduced in 1982, heavily influenced by a similar type of survey which had been undertaken in the USA since 1972 (funded by the US Department of Justice). Originally, the UK studies were every two years, but since 2000, they have been carried out every year. The sample size is enormous, with almost 40 000 people being interviewed. The idea behind the study is that by asking people directly what crimes have been committed against them, the problems of crime reporting and police recording are avoided. Supporters of the survey suggest that it is more 'valid' than the police statistics.

The sampling technique is based on (a) all households in England and Wales and then (b) anyone over 16 living in these households. The households are selected using the Postcode Address File, developed by the Post Office to recognize all households in Britain. Interviews last 50 minutes and each person is asked if they have been the victim of a list of selected crimes. There is then a smaller 'sweep' (a subsample), who are asked to answer questions on selected (sometimes sensitive) issues directly into a laptop computer.

Is the BCS more accurate than the police-recorded statistics? The answer provided by Maguire (2002) is that the BCS is neither better nor worse, but simply provides an alternative, overall picture of crime which helps fill in some gaps in the police-recorded statistics.

1. **What steps does the BCS take to maximize the representativeness of the survey?**
2. **Can you identify any groups who may still be left out of the survey?**
3. **Why do you think respondents in the smaller subsample are asked to input their answers directly into a laptop computer?**

- *Promotion* – Police officers, like everyone else, have concerns about career and promotion. This involves trying to impress senior officers. However, at work they also need to get on with other colleagues, who do not like officers who are too keen (as this makes more work for everyone). Arrests reflect a balance between comradeship and a desire for promotion (Collison 1995).

### *The role of the courts*

Official statistics of crimes committed and punished also reflect the decisions and sentences of the courts. However, these statistics, too, are a reflection of social processes.

British courts work on the assumption that many people will plead guilty – and about 75 per cent of all those charged actually do so. This is often the result of an informal and largely unspoken agreement whereby the

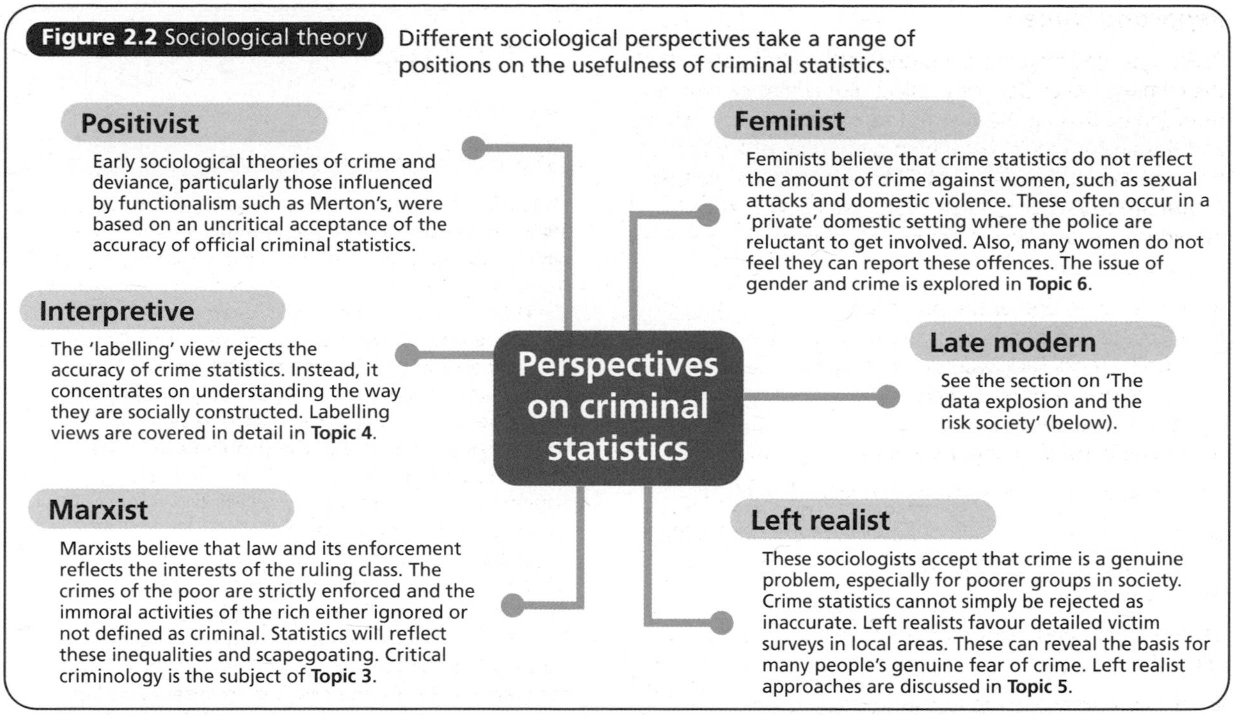

Positivist
Early sociological theories of crime and deviance, particularly those influenced by functionalism such as Merton's, were based on an uncritical acceptance of the accuracy of official criminal statistics.
Interpretive
The 'labelling' view rejects the accuracy of crime statistics. Instead, it concentrates on understanding the way they are socially constructed. Labelling views are covered in detail in Topic 4.
Marxist
Marxists believe that law and its enforcement reflects the interests of the ruling class. The crimes of the poor are strictly enforced and the immoral activities of the rich either ignored or not defined as criminal. Statistics will reflect these inequalities and scapegoating. Critical criminology is the subject of Topic 3.
Perspectives on criminal statistics
Feminist
Feminists believe that crime statistics do not reflect the amount of crime against women, such as sexual attacks and domestic violence. These often occur in a 'private' domestic setting where the police are reluctant to get involved. Also, many women do not feel they can report these offences. The issue of gender and crime is explored in Topic 6.
Late modern
See the section on 'The data explosion and the risk society' (below).
Left realist
These sociologists accept that crime is a genuine problem, especially for poorer groups in society. Crime statistics cannot simply be rejected as inaccurate. Left realists favour detailed victim surveys in local areas. These can reveal the basis for many people's genuine fear of crime. Left realist approaches are discussed in Topic 5.

**Figure 2.2** Sociological theory Different sociological perspectives take a range of positions on the usefulness of criminal statistics.

defence will try to get the charges with the lightest possible punishment put forward by the prosecution. (In the USA, this bargaining is far more open than in Britain, and is known as **plea-bargaining**.) The result is an overwhelming majority of pleas of guilty, yet these pleas are for less serious crimes than might 'really' have been committed. The statistics will reflect this downgrading of seriousness.

### *The role of the government*

What is considered to be a crime changes over time, as a result of governments changing the law in response to cultural changes and the influence of powerful groups. Any exploration of crime over a period is therefore fraught with difficulty, because any rise or fall in the levels of crime may reflect changes in the law as much as actual changes in crime. A good example of this is the way that attitudes to cannabis use have shifted – while there has been an increase in the numbers of people possessing and using cannabis (both of which are a crime), the number of arrests for its possession has actually declined, as the police respond to public opinion. The police statistics might make it look as if cannabis use is actually declining, when it is not.

## Victim surveys

A second way of estimating the extent and patterns of crime is by using **victimization** (or **victim**) **surveys**. In these, a sample of the population, either locally or nationally, is asked which offences have been committed against them over a certain period of time.

### *Strengths of victim surveys*

This approach overcomes the fact that a significant proportion of offences are never recorded by the police. It also gives an excellent picture of the extent and patterns of victimization – something completely missing from official accounts. The best known victimization study is the British Crime Survey which is now collected every year and has been in operation since 1982 (see 'Focus on research', on p22).

### *Weaknesses of victim surveys*

- The problem of basing statistics on victims' memories is that recollections are often faulty or biased.
- The categorization of the crimes that has been committed against them is left to the person filling in the questionnaire – this leads to considerable inaccuracy in the categories.
- Victim surveys also omit a range of crimes, such as fraud and corporate crime, and any crime where the victim is unaware of or unable to report a crime.
- Despite victim surveys being anonymous, people appear to underreport sexual offences.
- The BCS itself suffers from the problem of not collecting information from those under 16, although this is not necessarily a problem of victim surveys as such. The British Youth Lifestyles Survey (2000), for example, was carried out specifically to obtain detailed information on crimes against younger people.

### *Local victim surveys*

The BCS is a typical cross-sectional survey, and as such may contain some errors – certainly, it does not provide detailed information about particular places. This has led to a number of detailed studies of crime, focusing on particular areas. These provide specific information about local problems.

The most famous of these surveys were the **Islington Crime Surveys** (Harper *et al.* 1986 and Jones *et al.* 1995). These showed that the BCS underreported the higher levels of victimization of minority ethnic groups and domestic violence and were influential in the development of left realism (see Topic 5).

### *The media and sensitization*

Victim surveys are dependent upon people being aware that they are victims. This may seem obvious, but in fact this depends very much on the 'victim' perceiving what happens to them as being a crime. The media play a key role in this as they provide illustrations of 'crimes' and generally heighten sensitivity towards certain forms of behaviour. This is known as **sensitizing** the public towards (certain types of) activity that can be seen as a crime worth reporting. A positive example of this has been the change in portrayal of domestic violence from a family matter to being a criminal activity. See Topic 8 for a more detailed discussion of the media and crime.

## Self-report studies

The third method for collecting data is that of **self-report studies**. These are surveys in which a selected group or cross-section of the population are asked what offences they have committed. Self-report studies are extremely useful as they reveal much about the kind of offenders who are not caught or processed by the police. In particular, it is possible to find out about the ages, gender, social class and even location of 'hidden offenders'. It is also the most useful way to find out about victimless crimes, such as illegal drug use.

### *Weaknesses of self-report studies*

- The problem of validity – The biggest problem is that respondents may lie or exaggerate, and even if they do not deliberately seek to mislead, they may simply be mistaken.
- The problem of representativeness – Because it is easy to study them, most self-report surveys are on young people and students. There are no such surveys on professional criminals or drug traffickers, for example!
- The problem of relevance – Because of the problem of representativeness, the majority of the crimes uncovered tend to be trivial.

Nevertheless, the only information that we have available of who offends, other than from the official statistics of people who have been arrested, comes from self-report studies, and they have been very widely used to explore such issues as crime and drug use. Figure 2.3 summarizes the processes and problems involved in different methods of finding out about patterns of crime.

## The data explosion and the risk society

Maguire (2002) has pointed out that since the 1970s there has been a huge increase in the number of statistics gathered on crime and 'antisocial behaviour'. Before then, the main source of information was the government publication *Criminal Statistics*, which relied solely upon criminal justice agencies for the figures. Since the 1970s, information has come to be gathered on wider aspects of crime:

- *Unreported and unrecorded offences* – Information is collected through the BCS.
- *Specialist subcategories of crime* – There are now literally hundreds of crime categories that official statistics record.

**Figure 2.3** Patterns of crime: accurate or social construction?

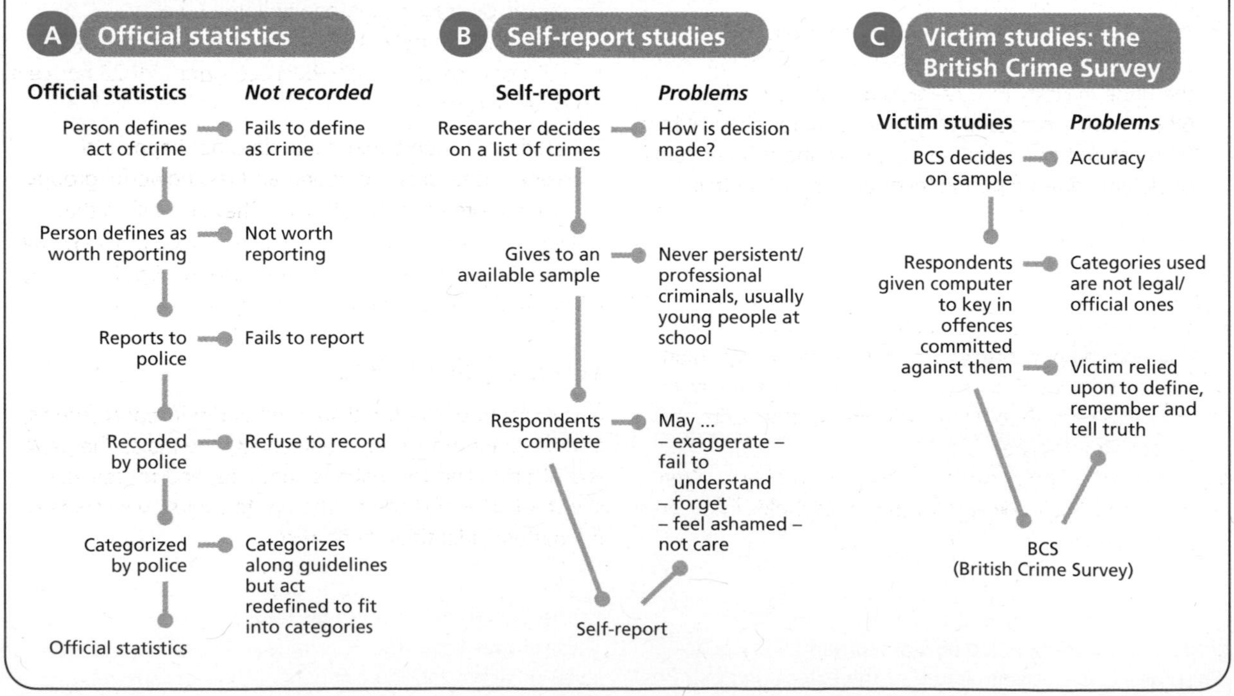

- *Hidden crime* – Information on sexual offences, domestic violence, white-collar crime and, most recently, corporate crime has started to be gathered.
- *Victim perspectives* – Possibly the most recent innovation has been the collection of information from the victims of crime.

Garland (2001) suggests that it is not just an expansion of knowledge for its own sake that has driven the explosion of statistical information. He suggests, instead, that the answer can be found within the concerns of late modernity. During modernity, governments took upon themselves the task of controlling crime and punishing criminals. According to Garland, most people believed that the government had crime control in hand. Garland suggests that in late modernity, there is a much greater sense of uncertainty and risk, and governments are no longer believed to catch and punish all criminals. Instead, the government engages in **risk management** – it gathers statistics on crime so that it can better assess and manage this risk. Garland has also introduced the notion of '**responsibilization**' – part of risk management is to push responsibility for avoiding becoming victims of crime back onto individuals. The statistics are part of this process of informing individuals how best to avoid becoming victims of crime.

# Patterns of offending

Using the three methods of gathering information, sociologists have managed to construct an interesting picture of offending and victimization patterns.

## Types of offences

- *Property crime* – According to the British Crime Survey, 54 per cent of crime in 2008/9 was accounted for by some form of property theft, with burglary and vehicle theft forming the bulk of these.
- *Violent crime* – All forms of violence account for approximately 20 per cent of BCS-reported crime, but the huge majority of these acts of violence – about 68 per cent – consisted only of very minor physical hurt (at most slight bruising). In fact, only about 5 per cent of violent crimes reported involved more than trivial injury.

## Types of victims

- *Victims of violence* – Young males, in particular the unemployed and low-waged, have a particularly high chance of being victims (see Fig. 2.4). Interestingly, in about 88 per cent of cases of violence, the victim and perpetrator know each other.
- *Victims of property crime* – Victims of property crime are most likely to be low-income households living in poorer areas.

**Figure 2.4** Risks of being a victim of crime

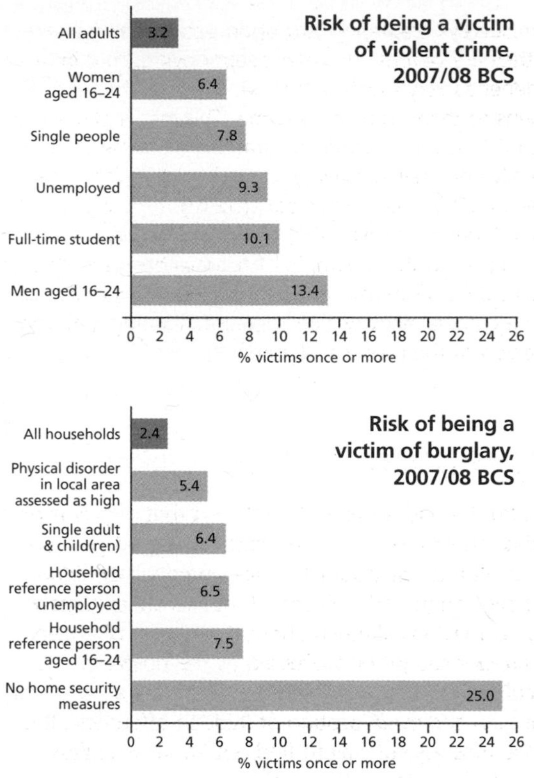


- *Repeat victimization* – Victim surveys demonstrate not only that some people are more likely than others to be victims in the first place, but that a proportion of the victims are likely to be targeted more than once (**repeat victimization**) – see Fig. 2.4. Of all households burgled, 20 per cent experienced repeat burglaries, and one tiny group has a disproportionately high chance of being victimized: 0.4 per cent of householders accounted for 22 per cent of all burglaries.

The statistics suggest that crime does not happen to everyone – it targets the poorer and less powerful groups in society more than the affluent. They also tell us that violent crime tends to happen between people who know each other, even live together. More detail about victimization can be found in Topic 5.

## Types of offenders

According to both official statistics and self-report studies, offenders are most likely to be young and male. The peak age of offending for males is about 18, and for females about 14. The next topics attempt to explain why some of the patterns identified here exist.

# Key terms

**British Crime Survey** annual victimization survey carried out by the Home Office.

**Collective conscience** a term used by Durkheim to describe the core, shared values of society.

**Consensual** where the vast majority of people share similar values

**Crime** activities that break the law of the land and are subject to official punishment

**Criminologists** social scientists who study crime.

**Critical criminology** work of criminologists influenced by Marxist thinking.

**Delinquency** criminal or antisocial acts committed by young people.

**Deviance** behaviour that is different from the normal expectations of a society and is viewed as 'wrong' or bad'.

**Home Office** government department responsible for criminal justice matters.

**Islington Crime Surveys** famous local victimization studies focusing on one area of North London.

**Official statistics** statistics released by government agencies.

**Plea-bargaining** where there is an informal (sometimes unspoken) agreement that if an accused person pleads guilty to a lesser crime than that of which he or she is accused, they will receive a lighter sentence.

**Relativity** In this context, the idea that values vary from society to society and between groups in a society so it is impossible to define clearly what counts as deviance.

**Repeat victimization** where people are victims of the same crime more than once.

**Responsibilization** Garland suggests this is the shift towards blaming people for becoming victims of crime, by suggesting they have not taken adequate precautions.

**Risk management** the process whereby governments stop trying to prevent all crime and instead see it as their job to limit the risk of crime for the population.

**Self-report studies** where people are asked to note down the crimes they have committed over a particular period.

**Sensitizing** refers to the extent of disorder or minor criminal activity that people will accept.

**Social construction** created by society, so subject to cultural variation and change.

**Victimization (or victim) surveys** where people are asked what crimes have happened to them over a particular period.



# Check your understanding

1. **Identify and briefly explain the two views on defining 'deviance' supported by sociologists.**
2. **Explain why official statistics give a completely accurate picture of the workings of the criminal justice system.**
3. **Explain why official statistics do not give an accurate picture of the number and types of crimes committed.**
4. **Why might official statistics give a more accurate picture of the amount of car theft than the amount of domestic violence?**
5. **How might a person's 'demeanour' affect their likelihood of arrest?**
6. **Explain why so many people plead guilty in court.**
7. **Do reductions in arrests for possession of cannabis reflect a decrease in the use of the drug? Explain your answer.**
8. **Suggest three crimes that you think people might be willing to admit to being victims of when questioned in a victimization study.**
9. **Why might some people exaggerate the amount of crime that they have committed in a self-report study?**
10. **Suggest two reasons why young males might make up the majority of victims of violence.**
11. **Explain why repeat victimization may occur.**

# Activities

## Research ideas

Carry out interviews with a small sample of people of different ages and genders to discover the factors that influence public reporting of crime. Does it depend on seriousness, whether the crime has a victim or other factors? Does likelihood of reporting correlate with variables such as age or gender?

## Web.tasks

Go to the government's statistics site at **www.statistics.gov.uk**. Select 'Crime and justice' and explore the latest trends and patterns in criminal statistics.

## An eye on the exam The definition and measurement of crime and deviance

A detailed description of the usefulness of official statistics of crime is required, using sociological concepts, theories and studies

Weigh up the strengths and weaknesses of official statistics of crime in some detail, then present alternative methods of finding out about crime before reaching a balanced conclusion

**Outline and assess the usefulness of official statistics of crime to sociologists. (50 marks)**

Why do sociologists need an accurate picture of the amount and types of crime?

This refers to data collected by the police and the state

### Grade booster Getting top marks in this question

A clear explanation of the various types of official statistics would be helpful and the essay would also benefit from an early link to the positivist view of official statistics with examples of some explanations based on the accuracy of official statistics, for example those within the functionalist tradition. The left realist view that official crime statistics should not be dismissed out of hand should also feature here (although it could also be usefully included as part of a balanced conclusion).

A range of views can be introduced that are critical of the accuracy and, therefore, usefulness of official criminal statistics. These are likely to include the interactionist view of crime statistics as a social construction and the more structural criticisms of Marxism and feminism.

# TOPIC 2

# Functionalist and subcultural explanations

## Getting you thinking

### Youngsters 'turning to gangs instead of parents'

Gangs are the new families for many youngsters. One in three teenagers do not consider their parents to be role models, according to a survey.

The Prince's Trust youth charity found that young people were turning instead to gangs and 'youth communities' for support: 58 per cent of young people claimed that finding a sense of identity is a key reason for joining a gang; 22 per cent said young people were looking for role models in gangs, with 55 per cent citing friends and peers as role models.

Martina Milburn, chief executive of The Prince's Trust, said: 'All the threads that hold a community together – a common identity, role models, a sense of safety – were given by young people as motivations to join gangs. Our research suggests that young people are creating their own "youth communities" and gangs in search of the influences that could once have been found in traditional communities.'

It found that young people with a problem were twice as likely to turn to a friend for advice as to a parent.

Last month, South Wales Chief Constable Barbara Wilding warned that gangs based on drugs and violence had replaced traditional families for many youths.

'In areas of extreme deprivation there are almost feral groups of very angry young people. Many have experienced family breakdown, and in place of parental and family role models the gang culture is now established.

'Tribal loyalty has replaced family loyalty, and gang culture based on violence and drugs is a way of life.'

www.dailymail.co.uk/news/article-1042760/Youngsters-turning-gangs-instead-parents.html

1. **Who do you turn to for advice over difficult or embarrassing issues, your parents or friends?**
2. **Do you 'hang around' most evenings with your friends?**
3. **Are there any 'gangs' in your area?**
4. **Define what you mean by a 'gang'.**

You may well feel that your friends exert a considerable influence on your life. Sometimes, groups of friends develop norms and values that are unconventional and may encourage deviant acts. **Subcultural theories** share the common belief that people who commit crime usually share different values from the mass of law-abiding members of society. However, crime-committing people do not live in complete opposition to mainstream values, rather they have 'amended' certain values so that this justifies criminal behaviour – hence the term '**subculture**'. (The relationship between offending and subculture is illustrated in Fig. 2.5.) The concept of subculture has been used by sociologists representing various perspectives, including functionalism (Cloward and Ohlin and A. Cohen), interactionism (Young) and Marxism (Hall).

**Strain** is a term that is used to refer to explanations of criminal behaviour that argue that crime is the result of certain groups of people being placed in a position where they are unable, for whatever reason, to conform to the values and beliefs of society. Strain theory is associated with functionalism because it tends to start from the view that there are shared values in a society. However, the origins of the functionalist approach to deviance go back to the work of Durkheim.

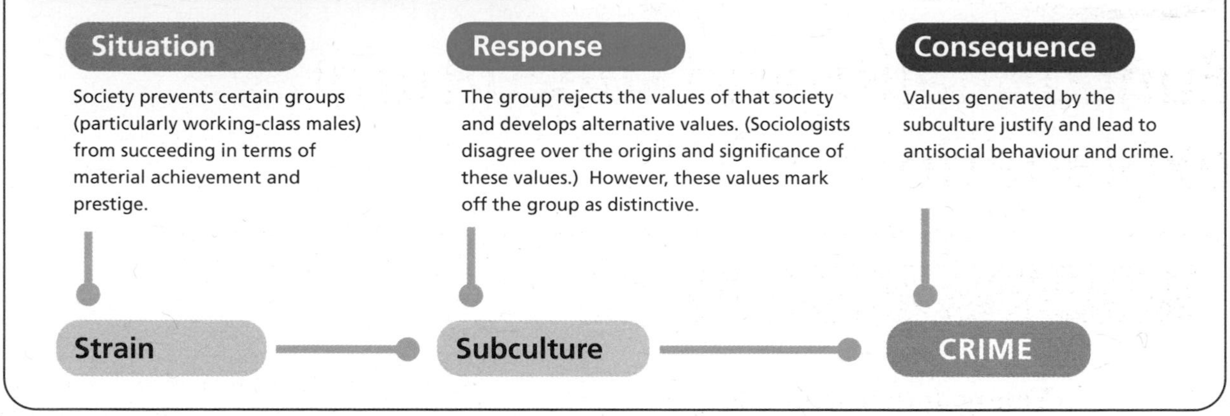

Situation
Society prevents certain groups (particularly working-class males) from succeeding in terms of material achievement and prestige.
Response
The group rejects the values of that society and develops alternative values. (Sociologists disagree over the origins and significance of these values.) However, these values mark off the group as distinctive.
Consequence
Values generated by the subculture justify and lead to antisocial behaviour and crime.
Strain
Subculture
CRIME

**Figure 2.5** Subcultural formation and effects

# Durkheim and the functions of deviance

The first, and still one of the most valuable, sociological explorations of the relationship between deviance and crime was provided by Durkheim, who identified two different sides of crime and deviance for the functioning of society:

- a *positive* side that helped society change and remain dynamic
- a *negative* side that saw too much crime leading to social disruption.

## Positive aspects of crime: social cohesion

According to Durkheim (1895), crime – or at least a certain, limited amount of crime – was necessary for any society. He argued that the basis of society was a set of shared values that guide our actions, which he called the collective conscience. The collective conscience provides a framework with boundaries, which distinguishes between actions that are acceptable and those that are not. The problem for any society is that these boundaries are unclear, and also that they change over time. It is in clarifying the boundaries and the changes that a limited amount of crime has its place. Specifically, Durkheim discussed three elements of this positive aspect:

1. *Reaffirming the boundaries* – Every time a person breaks a law and is taken to court, the resulting court ceremony and the publicity in the newspapers, publicly reaffirms the existing values. This is particularly clear in societies where public punishments take place – for example, where a murderer is taken out to be executed in public or an adulterer is stoned to death.
2. *Changing values* – Every so often when a person is taken to court and charged with a crime, a degree of sympathy occurs for the person prosecuted. The resulting public outcry signals a change in values and, in time, this can lead to a change in law in order to reflect changing values. An example of this is the change in attitude towards cannabis use.
3. *Social cohesion* – Durkheim points out that when particularly horrific crimes have been committed, the entire community draws together in shared outrage, and the sense of belonging to a community is thereby strengthened. This was noticeable, for example, in the UK following the July 2005 London Underground bombings.

## The negative aspects of crime: anomie

While a certain, limited amount of crime may perform positive functions for society, according to Durkheim, too much crime has negative consequences. Perhaps his most famous concept was that of '**anomie**', which has been widely used and adapted in sociology. According to Durkheim, society is based on people sharing common values (the collective conscience), which form the basis for actions. However, in periods of great social change or stress, the collective conscience may be weakened. In this situation, people may be freed from the social control imposed by the collective conscience and may start to look after their own selfish interests rather than adhering to social values. Durkheim called this situation anomie. Where a collapse of the collective conscience has occurred and anomie exists, crime rates rocket. Only by reimposing collective values can the situation be brought back under control.

Durkheim's concept of anomie was later developed and adapted by Merton, who suggested Durkheim's original idea was too vague.

# Strain theory

In the 1930s, Robert Merton (1938), took the functionalist view a stage further by arguing that crime and deviance were evidence of a poor fit (or a strain) between the socially accepted goals of society and the socially approved means of obtaining those desired goals. The resulting strain led to deviance.

Merton argued that all societies set their members certain goals and, at the same time, provide socially approved ways of achieving these goals. For example, a well-paid job might be a shared goal in modern Britain and educational qualifications the socially accepted means of achieving that goal. Merton was aware that not everyone shared the same goals; he pointed out that, in a stratified society, the goals were linked to a person's position in the social structure. Those lower down had restricted goals. The system worked well as long as there was a reasonable chance that a majority of people were able to achieve their goals. However, if the majority of the population were unable to achieve the socially set goals, then they became disenchanted with society and sought out alternative (often deviant) ways of behaving. Merton used Durkheim's term anomie, to describe this situation.

The following five different forms of behaviour could then be understood as a strain between goals and means:

1. *Conformity* – The individual continues to adhere to both goals and means, despite the limited likelihood of success.
2. *Innovation* – The person accepts the goals of society but uses different ways to achieve those goals; criminal behaviour is included in this response.
3. *Ritualism* – The means are used by the individual, but sight of the actual goal is lost, e.g. the bureaucrat or the police officer blindly enforcing the letter of the law without looking at the nature of justice.
4. *Retreatism* – The individual rejects both goals and means. The person dependent upon drugs or alcohol is included in this form of behaviour.
5. *Rebellion* – Both the socially sanctioned goals and means are rejected and different ones substituted. This is the political activist or the religious fundamentalist.

### Evaluation of Merton

Merton has been criticized by Valier (2001), amongst others, for his stress on the existence of common goals in society. Valier argues that there are, in fact, a variety of goals that people strive to attain at any one time. Taylor, Walton and Young (1973) accuse Merton of ignoring the crimes of the powerful while exaggerating the significance of working-class crime.

Reiner (1984) defends Merton against these attacks. He believes that Merton was well aware of the issues that he is criticized for ignoring. For example, Merton did explain middle-class crime by pointing out that there was no limit to success so the wealthy may still be greedy for more.

There can be little doubt of the influence of Merton's view that a key cause of crime in modern societies is the mismatch between people's aspirations for material success and their ability to achieve that success. This idea reappears throughout this chapter, in the work of subcultural theorists, (see below), left realists (see Topic 5) and Marxists (see Topic 3) for example.

## Illegitimate opportunity structure

The idea of strain between goals and means had a very significant impact on the writings of Cloward and Ohlin (1960), who owed much to the ideas of Merton.

They argued that Merton had failed to appreciate that there was a parallel opportunity structure to the legal one, called the **illegitimate opportunity structure**. By this they meant that for some subcultures in society, a regular illegal career was available, with recognized illegal means of obtaining society's goals. A good example of this is given in Dick Hobbs' book *Bad Business* (1998). Hobbs interviewed successful professional criminals and demonstrated how it is possible to have a career in crime, given the right connections and 'qualities'.

According to Cloward and Ohlin, the illegal opportunity structure had three possible adaptations or subcultures:

1. *Criminal* – There is a thriving local criminal subculture, with successful role models. Young offenders can 'work their way up the ladder' in the criminal hierarchy.
2. *Conflict* – There is no local criminal subculture to provide a career opportunity. Groups brought up in this sort of environment are likely to turn to violence, usually against other similar groups. Cloward and Ohlin give the example of violent **gang** 'warfare'.
3. *Retreatist* – This tends to be a more individual response and occurs where the individual has no opportunity or ability to engage in either of the other two subcultures. The result is a retreat into alcohol or drugs.

### Evaluation of Cloward and Ohlin

This explanation is useful and, as Hobbs' work shows, for some people there really is a criminal opportunity structure. But the approach shares some of the weaknesses of Merton's original theory:

- It is difficult to accept that such a neat distinction into three clear categories occurs in real life.
- There is no discussion whatsoever about female deviancy.

## Status frustration

Writing in the mid 1950s, Albert Cohen (1955) drew upon both Merton's ideas of strain and also on the **ethnographic** ideas of the Chicago school of sociology. Cohen was particularly interested in the fact that much offending behaviour was not economically motivated, but simply done for the thrill of the act. (This is as true today as it was in the 1950s, for vandalism typically accounts for about 18 per cent of current crime recorded by the British Crime Survey.)

According to Cohen, 'lower-class' boys strove to emulate middle-class values and aspirations, but lacked the means to attain success. This led to **status frustration** – that is, a sense of personal failure and inadequacy. The result was that they rejected those very values and patterns of 'acceptable' behaviour that they could not be successful within. He suggests that school is the key area for the playing out of this drama. Lower-class children are much more likely to fail and so feel humiliated. In an attempt to gain status, they 'invert' traditional middle-class values by behaving badly and engaging in a variety of antisocial behaviours.

### Evaluation of Albert Cohen

- There is no discussion of females. His research is solely about males.
- The young 'delinquents' need to be brilliant sociologists to work out what are middle-class values and then invert them!

**Figure 2.6** Matza: techniques of neutralization

**Denial of responsibility** – The offender denies that it was their fault: 'it wasn't me, it was the alcohol/drugs'.
**Denial of victim** – The offender claims that in this particular case the victim was in the wrong – for example in a rape case where the woman was dressed in a way that 'led him on'.
**Denial of injury** – The offender claims that the victim was not really hurt or harmed by the crime. Often used to justify theft from a company as opposed to stealing from individuals.
**Condemnation of condemners** – The offender feels a sense of unfairness of being picked on for something others have done and not been punished for.
**Appeal to higher loyalties** – The offender claims that the rule or law had to be ignored because more important issues were at stake. The offender was, for example, 'standing up for his family/community/race'.

- Cohen fails to prove that school really is the key place where success and failure are demonstrated.

## Focal concerns

In the late 1950s, Walter Miller developed a rather different approach to explaining the values of crime when he suggested that deviancy was linked to the culture of lower-class males. Miller (1962) suggested that working-class males have six '**focal concerns**' that are likely to lead to delinquency:

1. *Smartness* – A person should both look good and also be witty with a 'sharp repartee'.
2. *Trouble* – 'I don't go looking for trouble, but ...'.
3. *Excitement* – It is important to search out thrills (see Katz, Topic 6).
4. *Toughness* – Being physically stronger than others is good. It is also important to be able to demonstrate this.
5. *Autonomy* – It is important not to be pushed around by others.
6. *Fate* – Individuals have little chance to overcome the wider fate that awaits them.

According to Miller, then, young lower-class males are pushed towards crime by the implicit values of their subculture.

### Evaluation of Miller

Miller provides little evidence to show that these are specifically lower-class values. Indeed, as Box (1981) pointed out, they could equally apply to males right across the class structure.

## Applying subcultural theory: the British experience

The studies we have looked at so far have mainly been American ones. However, subcultural studies were being undertaken in Britain too – though with a variety of results. Howard Parker (1974) successfully applied Miller's focal concerns in his study of working-class 'lads' in inner-city Liverpool, although he could probably have applied these equally successfully to rugby-playing students at Liverpool University.

On the other hand, studies by David Downes (1966) of young working-class males in London could find no evidence of distinctive values. Instead, Downes suggested that young working-class males were 'dissociated' from mainstream values, by which he meant that they were concerned more about leisure than their long-term future or employment, and were more likely to engage in petty crime. So, in the UK, evidence of distinctive subcultures has been fairly difficult to obtain.

## Subterranean values

One consistent criticism of subcultural theories was that there was little evidence to demonstrate a distinct set of antisocial values. Even if there were subcultures, were they a response to middle-class values or to a distinctive set of working-class values?

Matza put these criticisms together to make a strong attack upon subcultural theory (Matza and Sykes 1961). Matza argued that there were no distinctive subcultural values, rather that all groups in society used a shared set of **subterranean values**. The key thing was that, most of the time, most people control these deviant desires. They only rarely emerge – for example, at the annual office party, or the holiday in Agia Napa. But when they do emerge, we use **techniques of neutralization** to provide justification for our deviant actions (see Fig. 2.6). The difference between a persistent offender and a law-abiding citizen is simply how often and in what circumstances the subterranean values emerge and are then justified by the techniques of neutralization.

Matza's critique of subculture is quite devastating. He is saying that all of us share deviant, 'subcultural values', and that it is not true that there are distinctive groups with their own values, different from the rest of us.

# Subculture: the paradox of inclusion

In his book *On the Edge*, Carl Nightingale (1993) studied young Black youth in an inner-city area of Philadelphia. For Nightingale, subculture emerges from a desire to be part of, rather than to reject, mainstream US society that has rejected and marginalized them. Nightingale notes the way that Black children avidly consume US culture by watching television with its emphasis on consumerism and the success of violence – yet at the same time they are excluded economically, racially and politically from participating in that mainstream US culture. The response is to overcompensate by identifying themselves with the wider culture by acquiring articles with high-status trade names or logos. Once again, drawing upon Merton's ideas, the subculture reflects the belief that it is not so much how these high-status goods are obtained, rather the fact of possessing them. In the USA, these are often obtained through violence, expressed in violent gangs and high crime rates.

Similarly, Philip Bourgois' study of El Barrio (2002) looks at the lives of drug dealers and criminals in this deprived area of New York and finds that they, too, believe in the 'American Dream' of financial success. The values of their 'subculture' are really little different from mainstream values, the only difference being that they deal drugs in order to get the money to pursue an all-American lifestyle.

So, both Nightingale's and Bourgois' versions of subculture take us back to the strain theory of Merton, and Cloward and Ohlin, emphasizing that the desire to be included leads, paradoxically, to the actions that ensure that they are excluded from society.

# Contemporary alternatives to subculture

## Postmodernism

Most of the approaches we have looked at here, as well as the Marxist subcultural approaches described in Topic 3, seek to explain deviant behaviour by looking for some rational reason why the subculture might have developed. Recent postmodern approaches reject this explanation for behaviour. Katz (1988), for example, argues that crime is seductive – young males get drawn into it, not because of any process of rejection but because it is thrilling. In a similar manner, Lyng (1990) argues that young males like taking risks and engaging in '**edgework**' as he puts it. By edgework, he means going right to the edge of acceptable behaviour and flirting with danger.

## Neo-Tribes

Maffesoli (1996) introduced a postmodernist innovation in understanding subcultures, with his argument for the existence of neo-tribes. Maffesoli was unhappy with the idea that the idea of subculture had been transformed from a concept based on values more into one of a group sharing a set of values. He suggested that it was much better to think of subcultures in terms of 'fluidity, occasional gatherings and dispersal'. Neo-tribes then referred more to states of mind and lifestyles that were very flexible, open and changing. Deviant values are less important than a stress on consumption, suitably fashionable behaviour and individual identity that can change rapidly.

Goths: subculture or neo-tribe?

## Masculinity

Subcultural theory is overwhelmingly male subcultural theory. The assumptions underlying the vast bulk of the writings we have looked at within this tradition have been discussing masculine behaviour. However, as Collison (1996) points out, they may well have missed the significance of this. In order to explain male offending behaviour, it is important to explain the nature of being male in our society and the links masculinity itself has to crime. The work of Connell (1995) is particularly interesting here, in that he sees the existence of a hegemonic masculinity which males both conspire with and aspire to. The emphasis of this hegemonic masculinity is very similar in values to Miller's early work on 'lower-class values'. However, Winlow (2004) argues that the values are best seen within the context of a changing economic social structure. Winlow suggests that the traditional (working-class) male values fitted physical work undertaken by men in industrial settings. These have now gone and the values are inappropriate for contemporary employment. He suggests, too, that the problem may be even greater for those young men excluded completely from employment.

## Gangs and subcultures

Despite the widespread media coverage of youth gangs, which give the impression of widespread gang membership, only about 6 to 9 per cent of young people claim to belong or to have ever belonged to a 'gang', and just 2 per cent claim to carry or ever carry a knife, according to research by YouGov (2008).

Indeed researchers suggest that the idea of a gang is defined differently by different young people. This has led Marshall *et al.* (2005) to suggest that there are three distinct categories of youth groupings, which vary in the degree of seriousness of offending behaviour, but which are often mixed together under the term 'gang':

1. *Peer groups or 'crews'* – These are unorganized groups of young people who tend to hang around together in a particular place. Any offending behaviour is incidental and does not reflect any great estrangement from society.
2. *Gangs* – Youth gangs in Britain tend to have similar characteristics to peer groups or crews, but instead have a focus on offending and violence. These are the sorts of youth gangs that the majority of the theoretical models of subculture in this topic were intended to explain.
3. *Organized criminal groups* – These are the most serious types of groups, who are heavily involved in serious crime. The age of the members varies and there is a clear hierarchy. For the gang members, the illegal activities comprise their occupation. These are the sorts of gangs to which Cloward and Ohlin's analysis can most easily be applied.

## Focus on research

### Smith and Bradshaw (2005)
### Gang membership and teenage offending

Smith and Bradshaw undertook a longitudinal research study to explore gang membership and youth offending. The project used a wide range of research methods including self-report questionnaires with young people conducted in annual sweeps to identify any changes and patterns. This was followed by semistructured interviews, for depth of detail, with a subsample of the young people. At the same time, a sample of teachers and parents completed questionnaires. The researchers also examined the records of social work reports and children's hearings (a type of youth court).

A variety of schools were used as the basis for the research, which included 23 state secondary schools, eight independent schools and nine special schools. However, there is a problem with these as a sampling frame, as the research only reached young people in education.

In terms of findings, Smith and Bradshaw concluded that rates of gang membership fell with age, with 20 per cent of respondents reporting that they were members of a 'gang' at age 13, falling to 5 per cent at age 17, suggesting that young people mature out of gang membership.

They found that rates of membership were higher in more deprived neighbourhoods, among respondents from manual households and among one-parent families. They also found that there was a 'close association' between gang membership and offending, and also drug use.

Smith, D.J. and Bradshaw, J. (2005) *Gang Membership and Teenage Offending*, Edinburgh: Edinburgh University, Centre for Law and Society

1. **Why is a longitudinal study useful in explaining why people join (and leave) gangs?**
2. **What problems can you see in using self-report studies about gang membership, offending and drug use?**
3. **What advantages do semistructured interviews have compared to structured ones?**
4. **What relationships did the researchers find between gang membership and social background?**

## Key terms

**Anomie** term, first used by Durkheim, to describe a breakdown of social expectations and behaviour. Later used by Merton to explain reactions to situations where socially approved goals were impossible for the majority of the population to reach by legitimate means.

**Edgework** derives from Lyng. Refers to activities of young males which provide them with thrills derived from the real possibility of physical or emotional harm (e.g. stealing and racing cars; drug abuse).

**Ethnographic** form of observational research in which researcher lives amongst, and describes activities of, particular group being studied.

**Focal concerns** term used by Miller to describe key values.

**Gang** term applied to a wide variety of youth groups, but should only be used for organized groups that regularly engage in offending.

**Illegitimate opportunity structure** an alternative, illegal way of life that certain groups in society have access to.

**Status frustration** according to Cohen, this occurs when young men feel that they are looked down upon by society.

**Strain** term used by Merton and other functionalists to describe a lack of balance and adjustment in society.

**Subculture** a distinctive set of values that provides an alternative to those of the mainstream culture.

**Subcultural theories** explanations of crime and deviance focusing on the idea that those who deviate hold different values to the majority.

**Subterranean values** a set of deviant values that exist alongside the socially approved values, but are usually kept hidden or under control. They may emerge in certain social situations, such as at parties or after drinking alcohol.

**Techniques of neutralization** justifications for our deviant actions.

## Check your understanding

1 How, according to Durkheim can deviance be functional for society?

2 How does Merton use the idea of anomie to explain deviance?

3 How, according to A. Cohen, does failure at school lead to the formation of subcultures?

4 How does the idea of 'techniques of neutralization' undermine some subcultural arguments?

5 What do we mean by the 'paradox of inclusion'?

6 Why is the idea of 'masculinity' relevant to understanding criminal behaviour?

# Activities

## Research idea

Check the graffiti in your area – are there any tags of particular groups which appear regularly? What does this suggest?

## Web.task

**www.law.ed.ac.uk/cls/esytc/**
This is the website of an extensive research project about young people in Edinburgh. If you work in groups, you can divide the study into themes; each group can work on a theme and then present a poster summarizing the main points of your theme to the rest of the class. For example, you could use the themes: context to the research; methodology; gang membership; offending; drug use, and so on.

## An eye on the exam Functionalist and subcultural explanations

A detailed description of subcultural theories is required, using sociological concepts, theories and studies.

Weigh up the strengths and weaknesses of subcultural theories in some detail, then present alternative perspectives before reaching a balanced conclusion.

**Outline and assess subcultural theories of crime and deviance. (50 marks)**

The concept of subculture has been used by a range of sociologists representing several perspectives

### Grade booster Getting top marks in this question

The introduction should discuss the concept of subculture and show awareness that the concept has been used by sociologists representing a variety of theoretical approaches.

Move on to a discussion of some of the theories that have emphasized the idea of subculture. These will include those within the functionalist tradition such as A. Cohen, Miller and Coward and Ohlin and the more recent work of Nightingale and Bourgois. It is also worth looking through Topic 3 for examples of Marxist subcultural approaches (e.g. Hall) and Topic 5, which includes a discussion of the concept of subculture in relation to left realism.

These theories vary widely so it would be helpful to assess them against each other as the essay progresses. Most sociologists accept the importance of subcultures in explaining crime and deviance but they use the concept in slightly different ways.

# TOPIC 3

# Marxism and the New Criminology

## Getting you thinking

Today, more than 350 million children, aged from 5 to 17, are at work. They can be differentiated on the basis of their age, the effect that working has on their basic rights and, in particular, the extent to which their work causes them harm.

More than 140 million of the total are old enough to be working under international standards. Nevertheless, getting on for half of these – 60 million – suffer harm because they are involved in the abuse of the 'worst forms' of child labour, from which they should be protected. The remaining 80 million have reasonable jobs, either in industrialized or developing countries.

Out of approximately 211 million working children under 15, more than half (over 120 million) are involved in the 'worst forms'. So, together with older adolescents, almost 180 million young people below 18 are involved in the 'worst forms', approximately 1 in every 12 children in the world today. The vast majority of these, more than 170 million, are engaged in work that is hazardous, posing a health risk and, in some cases, even threatening their lives.

www.unicef.org.uk/publications/pdf/ECECHILD2_A4.pdf

**Look at the photos of the children working. Although it would be illegal in the UK for them to work like this, it is legal in their countries. The girls making the fluffy toys work up to 12 hours each day in a factory in south-east Asia and earn a pittance. The boy works in a battery recycling factory in Bangladesh, spending the day breaking up batteries to get reuseable parts and metal out of them.**

1. **Do you think it is wrong? Do you think it should be made illegal (as it is in the UK) or do you think that each country should be left to sort out its own laws?**
2. **Suggest why an act should be made illegal.**
3. **Using your own ideas, can you find any examples of activities that you think ought to be crimes, but are not? Can you suggest why they are not crimes?**

*<<I wake up at the first cockcrow, I clean the house and the kitchen, I collect kindling, which we sell in bundles at the market and we survive thanks to the money it brings in. I do the cooking and washing. I go to the market, I chop wood. My aunt's children go to school and I stay home to do everything. I only eat once a day … If I happen not to sell enough oranges they tell me I am cursed and 'good for nothing'. And if I'm ever unlucky enough to lose any, I have to pay them back out of the little money that my parents give me whenever they stop by to visit. I want to go back to my parents … I often have headaches. At night I tremble, I'm so tired.>>*

Matou, a 12-year-old in Guinea, working for a woman 85 kilometres away from her home. When Matou's parents learnt about her suffering, they urged her employer to send her to school. Her employer promised she would, but nothing has come of it.

Recorded for UNICEF, 2003

The activity on the previous page should have alerted you to the possibility that laws, and the way they are applied, may favour certain groups – in most cases, the rich and powerful. This is the starting point for Marxist and neo-Marxist approaches.

# The traditional Marxist approach

Karl Marx himself wrote very little about crime, but a Marxist theory of crime was first developed by Bonger as early as 1916 and then developed by writers such as Chambliss (1975). The overall background to this approach was based on the Marxist analysis of society, which argues that society is best understood by examining the process whereby the majority of the population are exploited by the owners and controllers of commerce and industry. Marxists argue that this simple, fundamental fact of exploitation provides the key to unlock the explanations for the workings of society.

The key elements of the Marxist or critical criminological approach include:

- the basis of criminal law
- the dominant **hegemony** of the ruling class
- law enforcement
- individual motivation
- crime and control.

## The basis of the criminal law

The starting point for Marxist analysis is that all laws are essentially for the benefit of the ruling class, and that criminal law reflects their interests. For example, concern with the laws of property ownership largely benefit those with significant amounts of property. For those who are poor, there is little to steal. Personal violence is dangerous, and the ruling class wish to control the right to use violence in society through their agents – the police and the army. Criminal law therefore operates to protect the rich and powerful.

## Law creation and the dominant hegemony

In capitalist societies, the ruling class impose their values – that is, values that are beneficial to themselves – upon the mass of the population. They do this through a number of agencies, such as the education system, religion and the mass media. (This concept of ruling-class values being imposed upon the population is commonly known as 'hegemony'.)

This dominant set of values forms the framework on which laws are based in a democracy. However, we have just seen that, according to Marxists, the set of values is actually 'forced' on the people. Thus, what they believe they are agreeing to as a result of their own beliefs is, in reality, in the interests of the ruling class.

## Law enforcement

Despite the fact that the law-making process reflects the interests of the ruling class, many of these laws could provide benefits for the majority of the population if they were applied fairly. However, even the interpretation and enforcement of the law is biased in favour of the ruling class, so that the police and the judicial system will arrest and punish the working class, but tend not to enforce the law against the ruling class.

## Individual motivation

Marxist theory also provides an explanation for the individual motivation underlying crime. Bonger (1916), the very first Marxist writer on crime, pointed this out. He argued that capitalism is based upon competition, selfishness and greed, and this formed people's attitudes to life. Therefore, crime was a perfectly normal outcome of these values, which stressed looking after oneself at the expense of others. However, Bonger also said that in many cases, poor people were driven to crime by their desperate conditions

## Crime and control

For Marxists, the ruling class in capitalism constantly seeks to divert the attention of the vast majority of the population away from an understanding of the true causes of their situation, and to impose their values through the mass media, religious organizations and the education system. These institutions provide alternative accounts of reality justifying the capitalist system as the natural and best economic system. Crime plays a significant part in supporting the ideology of capitalism, as it diverts attention away from the exploitative nature of capitalism and focuses attention instead on the evil and frightening nature of certain criminal groups in society, from whom we are only protected by the police. This justifies heavy policing of working-class areas, 'stop and searches' of young people, and the arrests of any sections of the population who oppose capitalism.

## An example of the traditional Marxist approach

William Chambliss' study of British vagrancy laws provides an illustration of the ways in which laws may be directly related to the interests of the ruling class. The first English vagrancy laws appeared in 1349, one year after the outbreak of the Black Death plague that was to kill more than one-third of the country's entire population. One result of the catastrophe was to decimate the labour force, so that those who were left could ask for high wages – and many people did this, moving from village to village in search of high pay. To combat this, the vagrancy laws were introduced, requiring every able-bodied man on the road to accept work at a low, fixed wage. The law was strictly enforced and did produce a supply of low-paid labour to help the workforce shortage. For almost 200 years the laws remained unchanged, but in 1530, changes were introduced which altered the emphasis of the laws to protect the concerns of an increasingly powerful merchant class from the many highway robbers who were preying on the traffic of goods along major highways. The vagrancy laws were amended so that they could be used to punish anyone on the road without a job, who was presumed to be a highwayman.

In both cases, the law was introduced and imposed in such a way as to benefit the ruling class – whilst apparently being concerned with stopping vagrants from travelling around England.

### Criticisms of the traditional Marxist approach

1. The victims of crime are simply ignored in this analysis. The harm done by offenders is not taken into account. This is particularly important, as the victims are usually drawn from the less well-off sections of the population.
2. The explanation for law creation and enforcement tends to be one dimensional, in that all laws are seen as the outcome of the interests of the ruling class – no allowance is made for the complexity of influences on law-making behaviour.

## The New Criminology

Partly as a result of these criticisms of what was a fairly crude Marxist explanation of crime, and partly as a result of the influence of interactionism (see Topic 4), Taylor, Walton and Young attempted to produce a fully social theory of deviance in *The New Criminology* (1973). This became an extremely influential book – possibly because it was a fairly successful fusing of Marxism and interactionism, the two most prominent theories of that time.

The new criminologists argued that in order to understand why a particular crime took place, it was no use just looking at the individual's motivation (e.g. alcohol or jealousy) and obvious influences (e.g. family background), which is what traditional positivist sociology might do. A Marxist perspective must be taken, looking at the wider capitalist society that is helping generate the circumstances of the crime and police response to it. It is also important to use interactionist ideas to see how the behaviour of victim, offender, media and criminal justice system all interact to influence how the situation develops.

### Ideology and the New Criminology

A further element of the New Criminology was that, apart from the actual analysis that is suggested, it also argued that any sociology of crime and deviance had to be critical of the established capitalist order. This meant that instead of accepting the capitalist definition of crime and seeking to explain this, its role ought to be to uncover and explain the crimes of the rich. There was no attempt to be unbiased; rather, the approach looked critically at the role of the police, the media and the criminal justice system in general – pointing out how they serve the needs of the ruling class.

Part of this critical approach to crime and criminal justice was to look in a fresh way at the ordinary criminal, who should best be seen as someone who is angry at capitalism and mistakenly expresses this anger through crime, rather than politics.

A good example of critical criminology is the work of Stuart Hall *et al.* (1978) in *Policing the Crisis: The State and Law and Order.* In the 1970s, London witnessed a growth in 'muggings' – assault and robbery of people in the streets. The media focused on this crime and a wave of publicity forced the problem to the top of the political and policing agenda. Although Hall did not exactly follow the model put forward in *The New Criminology*, the general critical criminological framework was used – see Table 2.1.

### Criticisms of the New Criminology

Traditional Marxists such as Hirst (1975) argued that the New Criminology strayed too far from the Marxist tradition. Others, such as Rock (1988), who were concerned directly in combating crime, argued that it gave far too romantic a view of criminals (in later

**Table 2.1** The New Criminology

| What a fully social theory of deviance must cover, according to Taylor *et al.* (1973) | Application of these ideas in Hall *et al.* (1978) |
|---|---|
| The wider origins of the deviant act | The 1970s was a period of considerable social crisis in Britain, the result of an international downturn in capitalist economies. |
| The immediate origins of the deviant act | This turmoil was shown in a number of inner-city riots, conflict in Northern Ireland and a high level of strikes. The government was searching for a group that could be **scapegoated**, to draw attention onto them and away from the crisis. |
| The actual act | Mugging – which according to the police was more likely to be carried out by those from African-Caribbean backgrounds. |
| The immediate origins of social reaction | Media outrage at the extent of muggings, linked to racism amongst the Metropolitan Police. |
| The wider origins of social reaction | The need to find scapegoats and the ease with which young men from African-Caribbean backgrounds could be blamed. |
| The outcome of social reaction on the deviants' further action | A sense of injustice amongst ethnic minorities and a loss of confidence by ethnic-minority communities in the criminal justice system. |
| The nature of the deviant process as a whole | The real causes of crime were not addressed and were effectively hidden by the criminal justice system. |

writings, Young echoed this criticism and suggested it was one of the reasons for his development of left realism – see Topic 5). Feminist criminologists, such as Pat Carlen (1988), pointed out that there was absolutely no specific discussion of the power of patriarchy in the analysis, which simply continued the omission of women from criminological discussion.

Methodologically, it has always been extremely difficult to apply this perspective, as it is so complicated. In fact, no sociologist has actually managed to use this approach and so it remains more as an interesting model than an approach that guides research – as we saw earlier, the nearest attempt was made by Hall.

**Figure 2.7** A subcultural analysis of skinheads

Skinheads: a 'magical' attempt to rediscover the working-class community

*'Skinheads' football violence reflected a concern with their territory – linked to the redevelopment of traditional working-class communities in London in the '60s.'*

*'Skinheads' clothes were closely linked to the style of a traditional manual worker.'*

Based on Cohen, P. (1972) *Knuckle Sandwich: Growing up in the working-class city*, Harmondsworth: Penguin

# Marxist subcultural theory

A second strand of thought that developed from Marxism, was a specific explanation for the existence of subcultures amongst the working class. According to The Centre for Contemporary Cultural Studies (a group of writers at Birmingham University), capitalism maintains control over the majority of the population in two ways:

- ideological dominance through the media
- economic pressures – people want to keep their jobs and pay their mortgages.

Only those groups on the margins of society are not 'locked in' by ideology and finance, and thus are able to provide some form of resistance to capitalism. The single largest group offering this resistance is working-class youth.

According to Brake (1980), amongst others, this resistance is expressed through working-class youth subcultures. The clothes they wear and the language they use show their disdain of capitalism and their awareness of their position in it. Brake argues that this resistance, however, is best seen as '**magical**'. By magical, he means that it is a form of illusion that appears to solve their problems, but in reality does no such thing. According to him, each generation of working-class youth face similar problems (dead-end jobs, unemployment, and so on), but in different circumstances – that is, society changes constantly so that every generation experiences a very different world, with the one constant being that the majority will be exploited by the ruling class.

Each generation expresses its resistance through different choice of clothes, argot (slang and patterns of speech), music, and so on. But each will eventually be trapped like their parents before them.

## Criticism of the Marxist subcultural approach

### *Methodological Problems*

Stan Cohen (1980) pointed out that these writers were simply biased in their analysis. They wanted to prove that working-class youth cultures were an attack on capitalism, and therefore made sure that they fixed the evidence to find this. He pointed out, for example, that there were many different ways to interpret the subcultural style of the groups, and that the interpretation that the Marxist writers had imposed was just one of many possibilities. The researchers using this method knew what they wanted (signs of subcultural resistance) when they started looking at youth culture, and so they extracted what they needed to prove their theory and ignored what did not fit it.

### *Theoretical problems*

Blackman (1995) points out that the emphasis on the working-class basis of subcultural resistance ignores the huge variation of subcultures based on variations in sexual identity, locality, age, 'intellectual capacity' and a range of other social factors. Thornton (1995) argues that there is simply no 'real' social-class basis to youth subcultures at all; these are, in fact, creations of the media.

# Occupational and corporate crime

The study of **occupational crime** and **corporate crime** developed from the original work of Sutherland in the 1940s. Sutherland used the term '**white-collar**' **crime** to refer to crime committed by people who worked in offices. However, Sutherland's work overlaps with the interests of Marxist writers who were interested in the 'crimes of the powerful'. Both approaches share the concern that traditional research into crime centres on such things as robbery and burglary, and in doing so focuses on working-class offenders. People committing offences such as fraud, who tend to be at the other end of the class structure, are generally ignored.

Although there has been general agreement with Sutherland's argument that crime committed by the powerful needed studying, there remains considerable debate between sociologists about exactly what should be studied under this term. Sutherland (1940) originally defined white-collar crime as 'crime committed by a person of respectability and high social status in the course of his occupation'.

The definition is unfortunately very vague and includes within it two, quite different activities: on the one hand, it means crimes against the organization for which the person works, and on the other, crimes for the benefit of the organization for which the person works or which they own.

### Occcupational and corporate offending: the problem of law

There is one more problem in the debate about what occupational/corporate crime actually is. Very often, when sociologists talk about white-collar or corporate crime, they may actually not be discussing actions that are illegal – that is, if the company or person is 'caught', no one is likely to go in front of a judge and face the possible personal risk of going to jail. Instead, the crime studied may actually be the breaking of supervisory codes (as in financial services) or technical standards (chemical content of consumer goods), or may refer to a whole range of actions that are, it could be argued, harmful and may even lead to death, but are not strictly speaking illegal – low safety standards at work, but that meet minimum legal criteria, for example. In fact, as Nelken (2002) points out, the debate about corporate crime is as much about corporate practices and sociologists' biases about what is morally wrong, as it is about breaking the law.

Some writers, such as Pearce and Tombs (1998), argue that corporate crime ought to extend to the manufacture of cigarettes and alcohol – both of which are linked to illness and death. Others point out that transnational companies that manufacture in poorer nations, where safety standards are negligible, are engaging in human-rights violations and are therefore committing crime – even if they are acting in a perfectly legal way according to the laws of the country where they are manufacturing.

So, much of the debate about occupational or corporate 'crime' goes beyond the limits of the law and looks at actions that have harmful consequences – and, in doing so, takes us beyond the limits of conventional criminology, opening up debates about what the sociology of crime and deviance ought to study.

### The distinctions between occupational and corporate crime

This has led to two confusing and overlapping traditions:

- Studies of *occupational crime* – How and why people steal from companies and the public in activities associated with their jobs; for example, the employee who claims false expenses from the company or who overcharges customers and keeps the additional amount.
- The study of *corporate crime* – Much more important as a field of study in sociology, this is crime by corporations or businesses that has a serious physical or economic impact on employees, consumers or the general public. Corporate crime is motivated by the desire to increase profits.

## Occupational crime

### The impact of occupational crime

Theft by employees is a major source of crime in Britain – though whether the action of depriving an employer of goods, services or money is actually defined as theft is a real issue. Ditton (1977) and Mars (1982) have both studied theft by employees and found that in the range of industries they studied – from workers in the tourist industry to bakery delivery drivers – minor theft was regarded as a legitimate part of the job and redefined into a 'perk' or a 'fiddle'. Indeed, according to Mars, fiddling was part of the rewards of the job. For their part, according to Clarke (1990), management generally turned a blind eye to fiddles, accepting them as part of the total remuneration of the job and taking these into account in determining wage structures.

Levi (2007) estimates that direct losses from fraud in Britain total £12.98 billion. Fraudulent health and unemployment benefit claims total about £3 billion and frauds within the NHS are estimated at a possible £6 billion.

Practices of occupational crime extend into the professions too. Functionalist writings on the reason for the existence of the professions (Parsons 1964) stress that the key difference between professionals and most other workers is the degree of trust placed in them by their clients/patients. According to Nelken (2002), however, there is a considerable body of evidence pointing to fraudulent claims made by doctors and dentists against insurance companies in the USA and, to a smaller extent, against the NHS in Britain.

Barclay and Tavares (1999) found that theft by shop staff amounts to £350 million each year, which is about 25 per cent of all retail losses.

In an earlier study by Levy (1987), he found that 75 per cent of all frauds on financial institutions such as banks and building societies were by their own employees. Of 56 companies he surveyed, over 40 per cent had experienced fraud of over £50 000 by employees that year. However, employers were very reluctant to prosecute as they feared that by doing so, they could attract negative publicity.

## Corporate crime

### The impact of corporate crime

Many sociological approaches – particularly that of left realists – have pointed out the enormous costs of conventional crime to society, as well as the damage it does to the quality of people's lives. Those interested in studying corporate crime argue, however, that the costs of conventional crime are dwarfed by those of corporate crime. There are no clear calculations of the costs of corporate crime in Britain, but one contemporary study in the USA suggests that the annual cost to American society is in the region of $400 billion. This compares to an annual cost of $13 billion for all forms of other crime combined.

The 'costs' of corporate crime are not just economic, however. Tombs and Whyte (2007) point out that in the UK, Great Western Trains were fined £1.5 million for their role in a train crash in London in 1999, when seven people were killed and 150 injured. In 2006, Balfour Beatty were fined £10 million for four deaths and 150 injuries caused by their failure to maintain the railway lines adequately.

We pointed out earlier the way that corporate 'crime' can transgress the boundaries of crime through acts that may not actually be illegal, but are regarded by sociologists as morally reprehensible and often a violation of certain human rights. Mokhiber (1988) points out that, in the USA, 800 people die each day from smoking related diseases; 8000 a day die from asbestos-related cancers and 85 000 cotton textile workers suffer breathing problems from dust related to their jobs.

## Corporate crime: an invisible issue

Corporate crime is clearly a major problem for society and actually costs economies more than conventional crimes. What is particularly interesting is just how little attention is paid to it and how sanctions against those engaged in this form of crime are relatively minor.

The invisibility has been explained in several ways:

- *Differences in power* – Marxist-influenced writers, such as Pearce (1976), argue that the laws governing corporate crime, as well as the enforcement of these laws, reflect the inequalities in power of a capitalist society. The owners of the corporations are members of the ruling class, and they ensure that the law and its enforcement reflect their interests. However, it is not just Marxist writers who stress differences in power; most other sociologists exploring this area, such as Braithwaite (2000) and Tombs (2002), also suggest that the way the laws are defined and enforced are a reflection of the economic and political influence of large corporations. They can be distinguished from Marxist writers in that they do not see a coherent ruling class that manipulates power to its own ends.
- *Media representations of crime* – Tombs and Whyte (2003) have pointed out that corporate crimes are rarely considered newsworthy, partly because the crimes are often too complex to summarize in an article, or are too dull or have no clear victims. Often, when such crime is reported, media coverage is less about it being a crime than a 'scandal' or 'abuse' or even an 'accident'.
- *The policing of corporate crime* – According to Braithwaite (2000), business and finance tend to be controlled through 'regulation' rather than policing, and a different set of terms are used in the policing of corporations: agencies are developed by government to 'oversee' the activities of companies. A good example of this is the financial sector in Britain, which is meant to be controlled by the Financial Services Authority and the Bank of England. However, these agencies rarely call in the police if they find violations of procedure (the term 'lawbreaking' is rarely used); companies are advised or educated. They are generally negotiated with and, at the most extreme, they receive sanctions, which usually take the form of a company fine.
- *Lack of research* – As Tombs (2007) points out, each year the British government spends considerable effort in finding out how many 'crimes' are committed through the British Crime Survey (see Topic 1), yet nothing similar is attempted to find out the extend of corporate crime. (However, Hopkins (2002) has noted that, in recent years, the government has become very active funding research into crimes *against* businesses.) Even academic research into this area is relatively limited, with sociologists having limited access to large corporations and little expertise in business methods.

## State–corporate crime

There is a close relationship between large corporations and governments. At its simplest, governments rely upon large corporations for tax revenues and to provide employment. Corporations rely upon governments for a sympathetic and organized environment in which they can engage in their activities. They are therefore mutually dependent.

It has been suggested that this can lead to a situation in which 'serious harms' can result from the interaction between them. An example of this is Kramer's (2006) research into the circumstances surrounding the US space shuttle *Challenger*, which exploded soon after take off in 1986, killing all its crew. Kramer argues that the explosion was actually a result of political decisions by NASA to maintain the space exploration programme but with large budgetary cuts. This resulted in one large corporation being pressured to provide components for the Space Shuttle that were known to be potentially dangerous. The corporation agreed to continue providing the parts, as they were influenced by the high level of profits and the need to fulfil contractual obligations. The executives of the corporation did this even though, Kramer argues, they knew what the possible consequences of component failure might be.

Before the launch of the space shuttle, both NASA (the government space agency) and the company MTI knew the potential dangers. However, the explosion was described at the time as an 'accident'.

# Globalization and crime

Giddens (1964) defines **globalization** as 'the intensification of worldwide social relations which link distant localities in such a way that local happenings are shaped by events occurring many miles away and vice versa'. By this, Giddens means that modern forms of communication have made distance and national borders far less important than barriers between social groups. What happens in one society can quickly impact on other societies – anywhere in the world.

The importance of globalization on crime cannot be overestimated. According to the United Nations Development Programme (1999), the result of globalization has been a massive growth in the following forms of crime:

- dealing in illicit drugs
- illegal trafficking in weapons
- iillegal trafficking in human beings
- corruption
- violent crimes, including terrorism
- war crimes.

The importance of this can be seen by the fact that the total value of transnational organized crime is estimated by the United Nations to be approximately £1 trillion per year.

Ian Taylor is interested in how the broader effects of globalization have impacted upon crime. Taylor (1999) suggests that the impact of globalization on economies provides fertile soil for the growth of transnational crime. Taylor's analysis is extensive and complex, but two examples from his work illustrate the very diverse ways that globalization can generate new forms of crime:

1. The ability to move finance around the world with limited controls enables a whole range of financial crimes, from tax evasion and insider trading to the laundering of profits from illegal activities such as drugs production and distribution.
2. Cheap international transport and effective communication systems have allowed companies to shift production to countries where production costs are lowest. This generally involves moving from high-tax countries, such as those of Western Europe, with decent welfare provision and health and safety laws, to low-tax countries with no welfare provision or employment laws – typically in South East Asia. The resulting decline in employment and income levels in Western European countries has led to increased levels of crime and social disorder.

Ruggiero (1996) points to a further consequence of this shift in production. He argues that the decline in employment encourages the growth of small firms in Western Europe that avoid labour laws and operate outside the formal economy. Furthermore, these countries will employ the cheapest labour they can find, often focusing their recruitment on illegal immigrants.

However, the impact of globalization can also be felt in the way that even normal transnational companies can engage in practices that are either illegal or morally discreditable. According to Michalowski and Kramer (1987), modern transnational corporations can practise a policy of **law evasion**, for example setting up factories in countries that do not have pollution controls or adequate safety legislation, rather than producing in countries with stricter standards. They may sell goods to poorer countries when the goods have been declared unsafe in the more affluent countries (a fairly common procedure with pharmaceuticals). Box (1983) has claimed that multinationals dump products, plants and practices illegal in industrialized countries onto undeveloped or underdeveloped countries. They are able to do this because the poorer countries do not have the resources to control the large companies and also because officials are likely to accept bribes.

*Pearce and Tombs (1998) argue that the manufacture of cigarettes should be regarded as a corporate crime. What do you think?*

## Organized crime

Globalization has also brought about the growth of transnational organized crime. The same ease of communication that has enabled legal industries to develop production and distribution around the world has also allowed the growth of organized crime groupings. Organized crime is involved in a number of activities including:

- *The drugs trade* – According to the United Nations Office on Drugs and Crime (UNODC 2005), the value of the illegal drugs trade is $13bn at production level, $94bn at wholesale level and $332bn based upon retail prices.
- *Human trafficking* – According to Raymond (2002), this is worth about $5 to $7 billion, with 4 million persons moved from one country to another and within countries. This includes about 500 000 a year to Western Europe alone, for use in the sex industry.

Both these are closely linked to money laundering. According to the International Monetary Fund, it is estimated to involve between $800 billion to $1.5 billion dollars per year.

# An overview of Marxist approaches

Marxist criminology has provided a very powerful counterbalance to explanations of crime and deviance that focus on the individual, their family or the community in which they live. Marxist criminology has forced sociologists to explore the wider social, economic and political factors which shape society. Perhaps most of all, they point out that crimes can only happen when people break the law, but that the law itself reflects differences in power between groups. Powerful groups, they claim, can ensure that the law, and the enforcement of the law, reflects their interests.

However, Marxism as a significant theoretical perspective in sociology has been on the wane for a number of years. The questions it raises remain as important, but the answers provided by critical criminologists have been less influential in the subject.

# Focus on research

## Tombs and Whyte (2003)

### State and corporate crime

Jean Charles de Menezes: a victim of state crime?

Tombs and Whyte set out to explore why so little attention has been paid by British criminologists to state and corporate crime. They pointed out that out of 298 articles published in the *British Journal of Criminology* over a ten-year period, only one article discussed crimes of the state and six discussed corporate crime. Tombs and Whyte suggest that there are three reasons for this silence on the matter:

1. Research in Britain is increasingly 'policy oriented', with the government, local authorities and other state agencies asking for very specific pieces of research on particular policies. In effect, these agencies set the research agenda and they are simply not interested in paying for sociologists to criticize them. This has had the effect of limiting research into wider, more critical areas.
2. Even if research is done, it is difficult to get the conclusions widely distributed. For example, the government often makes researchers sign agreements that they can only publish their research if they are given permission from the government.
3. It is extremely difficult to gain access to the more powerful groups in society. They have the power to deny access to information and to refuse to be interviewed. This leaves the sociologists who research these areas struggling to obtain evidence. Without evidence, criticisms of the role of the state can easily be refuted.

One final point that Tombs and Whyte make is that sociologists in non-democratic countries may well face threats if they seek to research areas which might threaten the interests of the powerful.

Tombs, S. and Whyte, D. (2003) *Unmasking the Crimes of the Powerful: Scrutinizing States and Corporations*, New York: Peter Lang

**1** **In your own words, explain why sociologists rarely publish articles on the crimes of the state and of the powerful.**

**2** **Do critical criminologists believe that a 'value-free' sociology is possible? Explain your answer.**

**3** **What methods could sociologists use to uncover the 'crimes of the powerful'?**



# Check your understanding

**1** **How does the ruling class impose its values on others?**

**2** **According to Marxists, how neutral is the law?**

**3** **What is Bonger's explanation of individual motivation for crime?**

**4** **How does Chambliss' research on vagrancy support a Marxist view of crime?**

**5** **In what ways does the New Criminology utilize both Marxism and interactionism?**

**6** **Why is it convenient for capitalism to find scapegoats?**

**7** **How do Marxists explain the development of working-class subcultures?**

**8** **How do working-class subcultures resist capitalism?**

**9** **In what way is their resistance 'magical'?**

**10** **How have different Marxist approaches to crime and deviance been criticized?**

**11** **Explain the difference between corporate and occupational crime.**

**12** **Which costs society more, white-collar crime or 'conventional' crime? Illustrate your answer with figures.**

**13** **What do we mean by state–corporate crime?**

**14** **What do we mean by the term 'globalization', and give one example of how this relates to crime?**

**15** **Why are Marxists particularly interested in studying corporate crime?**

# Key terms

**Corporate crime** crimes committed by companies against employees or the public.

**Crimes of the state** actions performed, or permitted to be performed, by the government that harm groups within society and breach their human rights.

**Entrepreneuriality** qualities of people with original ideas for making money.

**Globalization** better methods of communication allow goods, knowledge and services to cross distances and national borders easily.

**Hegemony** the ideas and values of the ruling class that dominate thinking in society.

**Law evasion** acting in such a way as to break the spirit of laws while technically conforming to them.

**Left realist** a development from Marxist criminology which argues that it is better to work within capitalism to improve people's lives, than to attempt wholesale social change.

**'Magical'** illusory; in this context, something that appears to solve problems, but in reality does not.

**Occupational crime** crimes committed against a company by an employee.

**Scapegoats** groups in society (usually relatively powerless) who are blamed by the powerful for the problems of society, thus drawing attention away from the real causes of crime.

**Transnational crime** crime that is organized and committed across national boundaries.

**White-collar crime** a term originally used by Sutherland for both occupational and corporate crime.

# Activities

## Research idea

Get hold of a copy of *Private Eye* magazine and read its investigations on corruption in commerce and of the way that the presentation of news is influenced by the media:

**www.private-eye.co.uk**

## Web.tasks

Look up the website **www.socialistparty.org.uk**

1. To what extent do you think the Marxist analysis contained in it accurately explains today's social problems.
2. Corporate Watch is a website packed with examples of corporate irresponsibility: **www.corporatewatch.org**
   Prepare a report on one or two examples.

## An eye on the exam Marxism and the New Criminology

A detailed description of Marxist perspectives is required, using sociological concepts, theories and studies.

Weigh up the strengths and weaknesses of Marxist perspectives in some detail, then present alternative perspectives before reaching a balanced conclusion.

**Outline and assess Marxist perspectives on crime and deviance. (50 marks)**

You will need to include both traditional Marxist and neo-Marxist perspectives

### Grade booster Getting top marks in this question

It is worth using the introduction to provide a brief explanation of the key ideas of Marxism and their application to deviance. The main body of the essay needs to describe traditional Marxist approaches such as the work of Bonger and Chambliss. Perhaps limitations of the traditional approach could lead into the neo-Marxist approach of the New Criminology, which attempted to reconcile Marxist positions with labelling theory – the work of Hall is important here. Examples of Marxist subcultural theory and the insights Marxists have provided into corporate crime could also be introduced.

Left realists (see Topic 5), among others, have criticized Marxist approaches for assuming that all laws favour the ruling class, ignoring the effects of crime on victims and having something of a romanticized approach to crime and criminals. Feminists have also pointed out that many Marxists ignore the gendered dimensions of crime.

# TOPIC 4

# Interactionist approaches

## Getting you thinking

**The New Labour government 1997–2010 introduced a range of laws concerning 'antisocial behaviour'. The official definition of antisocial behaviour is 'behaviour which causes or is likely to cause harassment, alarm or distress'. This has caused considerable problems for the police, as one person's sense of harassment, alarm or distress may well be different from another's.**

### Crackdown on young drinkers

UNDERAGE drinkers are being targeted in a police crackdown. Officers have stepped up evening patrols in the trouble hotspots of Littleport to make sure youngsters behave themselves. Letters have been written to parents of children caught drinking alcohol.

Police have also broken up gangs of up to 10 teenagers in recent weeks after complaints from residents who felt intimidated by them.

Pc Dave Bishop, community beat manager for Littleport, said: "We have ongoing action plans for underage drink and noise complaints, particularly in the old medical centre area.

"I was out recently with my sergeant and moved on a group of 10 youths. There were small groups gathered over the Christmas period, but I wouldn't call them 'gangs'.

"We have increased patrols in the evenings as there are isolated groups around the place. However, if they are hanging around the play area, I don't think that's a problem, provided they are behaving themselves."

The increased police presence follows a raft of complaints to police about antisocial behaviour in Littleport in the past few months.

"Elderly people are terrified of leaving their homes after dark because of these gangs and if you see a police car after dark it's a rarity.

"I've seen gangs of 15–20 youths hanging around, so it's no wonder people feel so threatened. Many of them are very abusive, but they know they will get away with it."

*Cambridge Evening News*, 15 January 2008

1. **Do you think that young people hanging around are engaging in antisocial behaviour?**
2. **The article above states that people are 'terrified' of the 'gangs'. Do you think this is a reasonable reaction? Explain your answer.**
3. **What behaviour do you consider is antisocial – give one example that annoys you and you would like to see the police 'crack down' on?**
4. **Do you think the official definition of antisocial behaviour means that young people are more likely to be labelled as troublemakers and picked on by the police?**



## Understanding deviance: reaction not cause

Most approaches to understanding crime and deviance (with the exception of Marxist approaches) accept that there is a difference between those who offend and those who do not. On the basis of this assumption, they then search for the key factors that lead the person to offend.

However, since the early 1950s, one group of sociologists influenced by **symbolic interactionism** have questioned this approach, arguing that it is mistaken in its fundamental assumption that lawbreakers are somehow different from the law-abiding. **Labelling theory**, derived from symbolic interactionism, suggests, instead, that most people commit deviant and criminal acts, but only some people are caught and stigmatized for it. So, if most people commit deviant acts of some kind, it is pointless trying to search for the differences between deviants and non-deviants – instead the stress should be upon understanding the reaction to and definition of deviance rather than on the causes of the initial act. As Howard Becker (1963) puts it:

> << *Deviancy is not a quality of the act a person commits but rather a consequence of the application by others of rules and sanctions to an 'offender'. Deviant behaviour is behaviour that people so label.* >>

This is a radically different way of exploring crime; in fact, it extends beyond crime and helps us to understand any deviant or **stigmatized** behaviour. Labelling theory has gradually been adopted and incorporated into many other sociological approaches – for example, Taylor, Walton and Young (1973) have used it in their updating of Marxist criminology, while postmodernist approaches also owe much to it.

The best-known exponent of 'labelling theory' is Howard Becker. In *The Outsiders*, Becker gives a very clear and simple illustration of the labelling argument, drawing upon an anthropological study by Malinowski (1948/1982) of a traditional culture on a Pacific Island.

Malinowski describes how a youth killed himself because he had been publicly accused of **incest**. When Malinowski had first inquired about the case, the islanders expressed their horror and disgust. But, on further investigation, it turned out that incest was not uncommon on the island, nor was it really frowned upon provided those involved were discreet. However, if an incestuous affair became too obvious and public, the islanders reacted with abuse, the offenders were ostracized and often driven to suicide.

Becker, therefore, argues the following:

1. Just because someone breaks a rule, it does not necessarily follow that others will define it as deviant.
2. Someone has to enforce the rules or, at least, draw attention to them – these people usually have a vested interest in the issue. (In the example of the incestuous islanders, the rule was enforced by the rejected ex-lover of the girl involved in incest.)
3. If the person is successfully labelled, then consequences follow. (Once publicly labelled as deviant, the offender in Malinowski's example was faced with limited choices, one of which was suicide.)

## Sociological theory

### Symbolic interactionism

Labelling theory and symbolic interactionism provide similar analyses of individual behaviour. Symbolic interactionism argues that the social world consists of 'symbols' that have a culturally defined meaning to people and suggest appropriate ways of acting. These symbols are not fixed and may change over time. Every time two or more people interact with each other, they amend their behaviour on the basis of how they interpret the behaviour of the other people. A second element of symbolic interactionism is the way that people develop images of themselves and how they should 'present' themselves to other people, which is known as the 'self'.

The ideas of labelling theory are very similar, with some changes in language, so instead of symbol, the word 'label' is used. Instead of using the term 'the self', the term 'master status' is used.

There is one great difference between symbolic interactionism and the form of labelling developed by such writers as Becker: symbolic interactionism is not interested in power differences, whereas labelling theory focuses on the way that differences in power can lead to some people imposing labels on others (and the consequences of this).

# Responding to and enforcing rules

Most sociological theories take for granted that once a person has committed a deviant or criminal act, then the response will be uniform. This is not true. People respond differently to deviance or rule-breaking. In the early 1960s, when gay people were more likely to be stigmatized than now, John Kitsuse (1962) interviewed 75 heterosexual students to elicit their responses to (presumed) sexual advances from people of the same sex. What he found was a very wide range of responses from complete tolerance to bizarre and extreme hatred. One told how he had 'known' that a man he was talking to in a bar was homosexual because he had wanted to talk about psychology! The point of Kitsuse's work is that there was no agreed definition of what constituted a homosexual 'advance' – it was open to negotiation.

In Britain today, British Crime Survey statistics show that young Black males are more likely to be stopped for questioning and searching than any other group. This is a result of the police officers' belief that this particular social group is more likely to offend than any other; for this reason, they are the subjects of 'routine suspicion'.

## Criticism

Akers (1967) criticized labelling theorists for presenting deviants as perfectly normal people who are no different from anyone else until someone comes along and slaps a label on them. Akers argues that there must be some reason why the label is applied to certain groups/individuals and not to others. As long as labelling fails to explain this, then it is an incomplete theory.

## The consequences of rule enforcement

As we have just seen, being labelled as a deviant and having laws enforced against you is the result of a number of different factors. However, once labelled as a deviant, various consequences occur for the individual.

The clearest example of this is provided by Edwin Lemert, who distinguished between '**primary**' and '**secondary**' **deviance** (Lemert 1972). Primary deviance is rule-breaking, which is of little importance in itself, while secondary deviance is the consequence of the responses of others, which is significant. To illustrate this, Lemert studied the coastal **Inuits** of Canada, who had a long-rooted problem of chronic stuttering or stammering. Lemert suggested that the problem was 'caused' by the great importance attached to ceremonial speech-making. Failure to speak well was a great humiliation. Children with the slightest speech difficulty were so conscious of their parents' desire to have well-speaking children that they became overanxious about their own abilities. It was this very anxiety, according to Lemert, that led to chronic stuttering. In this example, chronic stuttering (secondary deviance) is a response to parents' reaction to initial minor speech defects (primary deviance).

The person labelled as 'deviant' will eventually come to see themselves as being bad (or mad). Becker used the term '**master status**' to describe this process. He points out that once a label has successfully been applied to a person, then all other qualities become unimportant – they are responded to solely in terms of this master status.

## Rejecting labels: negotiability

The process of being labelled is, however, open to 'negotiation', in that some groups or individuals are able to reject the label. An example of this is Reiss' (1961) study of young male prostitutes. Although they had sex with other men, they regarded what they did as work and maintained an image of themselves as being 'straight'.

## Deviant career

These ideas of master status and negotiability led Becker to devise the idea of a '**deviant career**'. By this, he meant all the processes that are involved in a label being applied (or not) and then the person taking on (or not) the self-image of the deviant.

# Creating rules

Once labelling theorists began the process of looking at how social life was open to negotiation and that rule enforcement was no different from other social activities, then attention shifted to the creation of rules and laws. Why were they made? Traditionally, sociologists had taken either a Marxist perspective (that they were made in the interests of the ruling class) or a functionalist/pluralist perspective (which argued that laws in a democracy reflected the views of the majority of the population). Becker (1963) doubted both these accounts and argued instead that:

> << *Rules are the products of someone's initiative and we can think of the people who exhibit such enterprises as* '**moral entrepreneurs**'. >>

So, labelling theorists argue that laws are a reflection of the activities of people (moral entrepreneurs) who actively seek to create and enforce laws. The reasons for this are either that the new laws benefit the activists directly, or these activists believe that the laws are truly to the benefit of society.

Becker's most famous example is his study of the outlawing of cannabis use in the USA in 1937. Cannabis had been widely used in the southern states of the USA. Its outlawing was the result of a successful campaign waged by the Federal Bureau of Narcotics which, after the repeal of the prohibition laws (that had banned alcohol), saw cannabis as a growing menace in society. Through a press campaign and lobbying of senior politicians, the Bureau was successful in outlawing the growing and use of the drug. However, Becker points out that the campaign was only successful because it 'plugged in' to values commonly held in the USA which included:

**Figure 2.8** The process of labelling

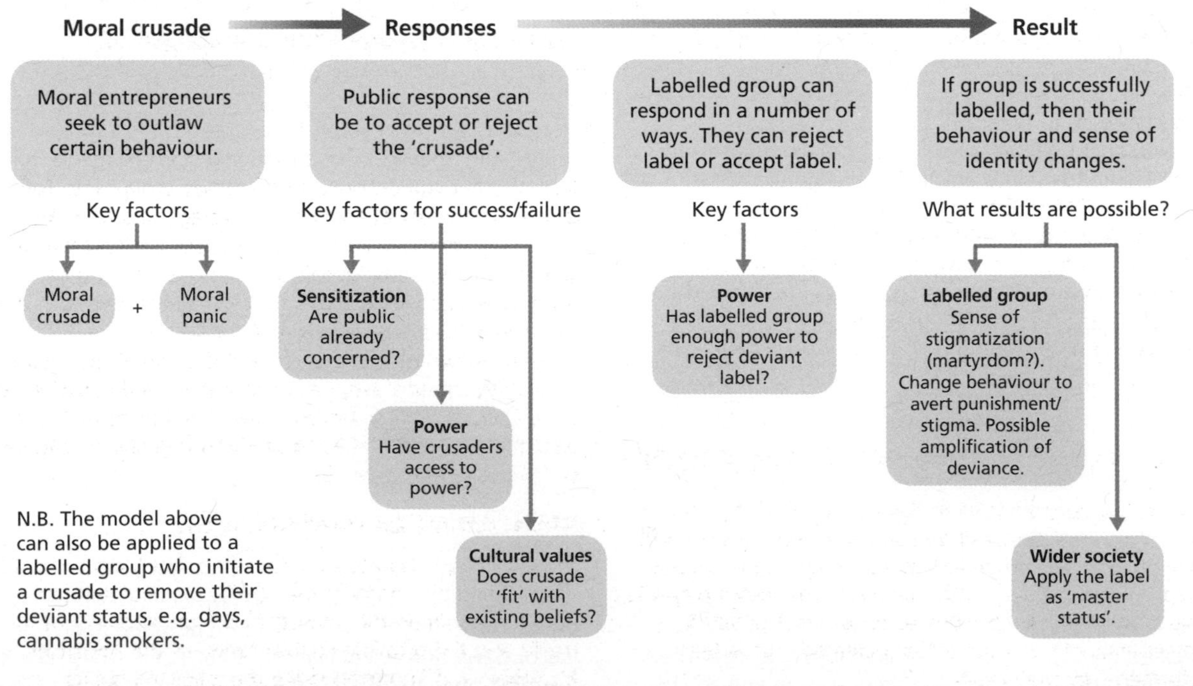

1 the belief that people ought to be in control of their actions and decisions
2 that pleasure for its own sake was wrong
3 that drugs were seen as addictive and, as such, 'enslaved' people.

The term Becker used to describe the campaign was '**moral crusade**', and it is this terminology (along with the concept of moral entrepreneurs) that sociologists use to describe movements to pass laws (see Fig. 2.8).

### Criticisms

The idea that there are those who seek to pass laws or to impose rules upon others has been accepted by most sociologists. However, Marxist writers, in particular, have pointed out that there is a wider framework within which this is placed. Are all laws just the product of a particular group of moral entrepreneurs? If so, then what are the conditions under which some groups succeed and others fail? Labelling theory does not really answer this issue very well; in fact, labelling theory does not have a coherent theory of power, as it argues that more powerful groups are able to impose their 'definition of the situation' on others, yet does not explain why some groups have more power than others and are more able to get laws passed and enforced that are beneficial to them. In defence of labelling theory, Becker (1970) does suggest in a famous article ('Whose side are we on?') that there are differences in power and that it is the role of the sociologist to side with the underdog. However, no overall theory of differences in power is given.

## Labelling and values

We have just mentioned a famous article by Becker, in which he argues that labelling theory has a clear value position – that is, it speaks up for the powerless and the underdog. Labelling theorists claim to provide a voice for those who are labelled as deviant and 'outsiders'.

However, Liazos (1972) criticizes labelling theorists for simply exploring marginally deviant activities as, by doing so, they are reinforcing the idea of pimps, prostitutes and mentally ill people as being deviant. Even by claiming to speak for the underdog, labelling theorists hardly present any challenge to the status quo.

Gouldner (1968) also criticizes labelling theorists for their failure to provide any real challenge to the status quo. He argued that all they did in their studies was to criticize doctors, psychiatrists and police officers for their role in labelling – and they failed ever to look beyond this at more powerful groups who benefit from this focus on marginal groups. Gouldner is putting forward a Marxist argument, by claiming that labelling theorists draw attention away from the 'real crime'.

## Crime, labelling and the media

Labelling theory alerts us to the way in which the whole area of crime depends upon social constructions of reality – law creation, law enforcement and the identities of rule breakers are all thrown into question. The media play a key role in all three of these processes, as most people's perceptions of crime are actually created – or at least informed – by the media.

Labelling theory has contributed two particularly important concepts to our understanding of the relationship between the media and crime: deviancy amplification and **moral panics**.

### Deviancy amplification

The term '**deviancy amplification**' was coined by the British sociologist Leslie Wilkins to show how the response to deviance, by agencies such as police and media, can actually generate an increase in deviance. According to Wilkins (1964), when acts are defined as deviant, the deviants become stigmatized and cut off from mainstream society. They become aware that they are regarded as deviants and, as a result of this awareness, they begin to develop their own subculture. This leads to more intense pressure on them and further isolation, which further confirms and strengthens them in their deviance.

Jock Young (1971) used this concept in his study of drug use in North London. He showed that increased police activity led to drug use being 'driven underground'. This had the effect of isolating users into a drug subculture, with 'a distinctive style of dress, lack of workaday sense of time, money, rationality and rewards', thus making re-entry to regular employment increasingly difficult – which, of course, made it difficult for them to afford the drugs. The scarcity of drugs drove the price up and this drew in professional criminals who regarded it as worthwhile entering the illicit drug business; criminal rings developed and the competition between them led to violence. It also led to the use of dangerous substitutes and adulterants in drugs by suppliers, interested only in maximizing profits, thus creating a situation where users no longer knew the strength of drugs and were consequently more likely to overdose. The process described here caused wide public concern which spurred the police to intensify their clampdown even further, which only served to accelerate the spiral of this 'amplification' process.

### Moral panics

The idea of moral panics both overlaps with and complements the concept of deviancy amplification. The term was first used in Britain by Stan Cohen in a classic study (1972) of two youth subcultures of the 1960s – 'mods' and 'rockers'. Cohen showed how the media, for lack of other stories, built up these two groups into **folk devils**. The effect of the media coverage was to make the young people categorize themselves as either mods or rockers. This actually helped to create the violence that took place between them, which also confirmed them as troublemakers in the eyes of the public.

The concept of moral panic and the role of the media in helping to create them, has been widely used in sociology since Cohen's original British work – though perhaps the best adaptation of this is the study by Hall and colleagues of 'mugging' (see Topic 3).

#### *Moral panics: an outdated idea?*

McRobbie and Thornton (1995) argue that 'moral panics', as described by Cohen in the 1960s, are outdated and have to be seen in the context of the development of the media and the growing sophistication of the audiences. McRobbie and Thornton make the following points:

- *Frequency* – There has been an increasing number of 'moral panics' – they are no longer rare or particularly noteworthy.
- *Context* – Whereas moral panics would scapegoat a group and create 'folk devils' in the 1960s, today there is no single, unambiguous response to a panic as there are many different viewpoints and values in society.
- *Reflexivity* – As moral panics as a concept are so well known, many groups try to create them for their own benefit. However, the same knowledge means that the media know this and do not necessarily wish uncritically to start a moral panic over an issue.
- *Difficulty* – Moral panics are much more unlikely to start in society because it is far less clear today what is unambiguously 'bad'. Society is too fragmented and culturally pluralistic.
- *Rebound* – People are more wary about starting moral panics as there is the possibility of it rebounding on them. Politicians who start a campaign about family values or drugs have to be very careful about their own backgrounds.

Labelling has been very important in helping to understand the role of the media. However, if what McRobbie and Thornton say is true, then by their very success, sociological concepts such as moral panic have gradually filtered into the wider society, so that journalists and politicians are now aware of them and use them in their decisions about what actions to take.

**Figure 2.9** Crime and the media

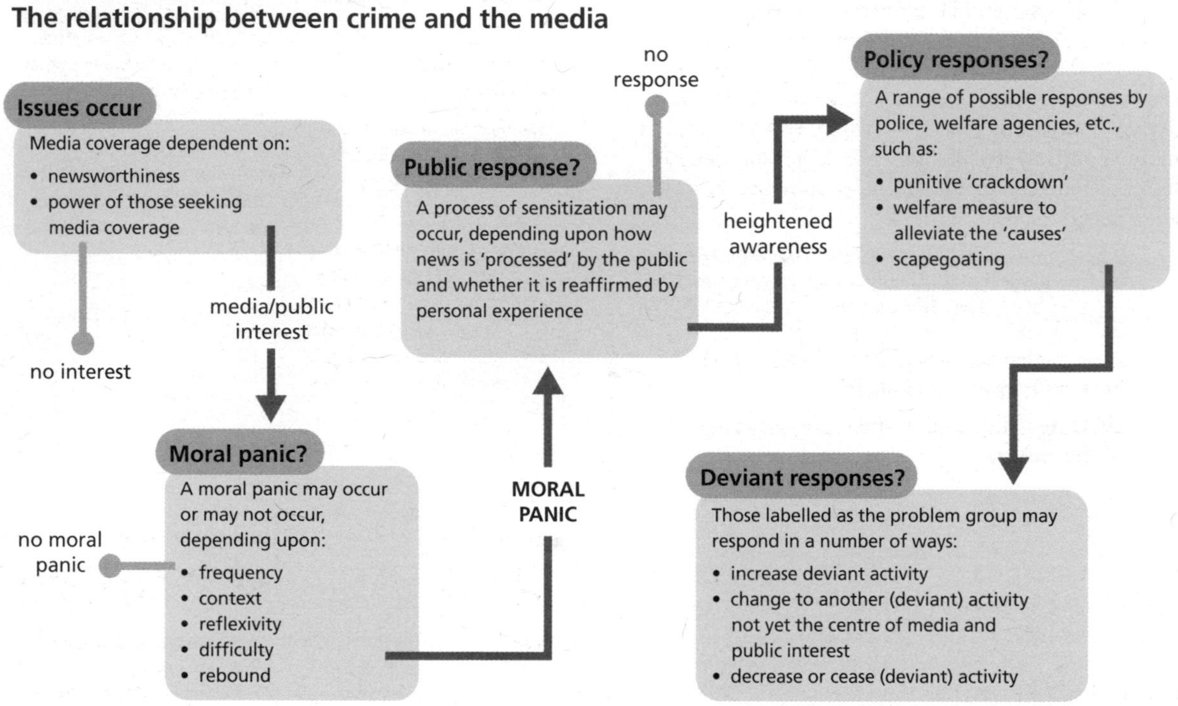


The relationship between crime and the media is complex and may result in a number of different outcomes.

# Focus on research

## Heckert and Best (1997)

### The stigmatization of red hair

Heckert and Best conducted a study into the impact of having ginger hair. For some years there has been a negative image promoted about ginger-haired people and the researchers argued that people with ginger hair are negatively labelled and are treated as deviants. They interviewed 20 ginger-haired people in all, nine males and eleven females, using open questions. They found that ginger-haired people were viewed as having all or some of the following characteristics – hot tempered, clownish, weird, wild (women) or wimpy (men). They were typically treated more negatively in childhood and as a result had low levels of self-esteem. Interestingly, both researchers were ginger-haired!

Heckert, D.N. and Best, A. (1997) 'Ugly Duckling to Swan: Labeling Theory and the Stigmatization of Red Hair', *Symbolic Interaction*, 20(4), pp. 365–84

**1 How might the researchers' own ginger hair have influenced respondents?**

**2 Evaluate the reliability and representativeness of this research.**

# Key terms

**Deviancy amplification** when the action of the rule enforcers or media in response to deviance brings about an increase in the deviance.

**Deviant career** the various stages that a person passes through on their way to being seen as, and seeing themselves as, deviant.

**Folk devils** groups associated with moral panics who are seen as troublemakers by the media.

**Incest** sex between close members of a family (other than man and wife).

**Inuits** previously known as 'eskimos'.

**Labelling theorists** a theory developed from **symbolic interactionism**, adapted for use in studies of deviance

**Master status** when people are looked at by others solely on the basis of one type of act (good or bad) which they have committed; all other aspects of that person are ignored.

**Moral crusade** the process of creating or enforcing a rule.

**Moral entrepreneur** person or group which tries to create or enforce a rule.

**Moral panic** outrage stirred up by the media about a particular group or issue.

**Primary deviance** the act of breaking a rule.

**Secondary deviance** the response to rule breaking, which usually has greater social consequences than initial rule-breaking.

**Stigmatized** labelled in a negative way.

**Symbolic interactionism** a theory derived from social psychology which argues that people exist in a social world based on symbols that people interpret and respond to. **Labelling theorists** tend to substitute the term 'label' for 'symbol'.

# Activities

## Research idea

Conduct a survey to discover young people's perceptions of the elderly. Do their views represent particular labels and stereotypes?

Then interview a small number of elderly people. Are they aware of stereotypes and labels? How do they feel about these labels? Do they affect them?

Be sensitive in your interviewing technique, following the usual ethical guidelines.

## Web.task

Search the worldwide web for newspaper and other information about any moral panic of your choice (e.g. concern over film violence, drugs such as mephodrone, underage sex). To what extent can you identify the key features of a moral panic, such as media exaggeration, the creation of 'folk devils', the activities of moral entrepreneurs, and so on?

# Check your understanding

1. **Instead of looking at the cause of crime, what does labelling theory focus on?**
2. **What theoretical approach does labelling theory derive from? How?**
3. **Explain and give one example of what labelling theorists mean when they say that the response to lawbreaking is variable.**
4. **Explain the importance of the term 'master status' in understanding deviance.**
5. **In what way does the labelling approach to the introduction of laws differ from the Marxist approach?**
6. **How has labelling theory been criticized?**
7. **Explain the importance of the idea of 'deviancy amplification'.**
8. **What criticisms have been made of the term 'moral panic'?**

## An eye on the exam Interactionist approaches

A detailed description of interactionist theories is required, using sociological concepts, theories and studies.

Weigh up the strengths and weaknesses of interactionist theories in some detail, then present alternative perspectives before reaching a balanced conclusion.

**Outline and assess interactionist explanations of deviance.** **(50 marks)**

These centre around labelling theory

### Grade booster Getting top marks in this question

The introduction needs to demonstrate an understanding of the key points of interactionism and apply these to the study of crime and deviance – the concept of labelling is likely to appear here. The work of Becker is the classic account of labelling and key interactionist concepts such as primary and secondary deviance, deviant career, deviancy amplification and moral panic should also feature (there is a further account of moral panics in Topic 8).

Labelling theory has been criticized as incomplete for failing to explain primary deviance and Marxists in particular are not happy with the way it ignores wider power relations in society. However, there is no doubt that interactionism has had a major impact on the sociology of crime and deviance and its influence can be seen in approaches such as the New Criminology and left realism.

# TOPIC 5

# Realism, victimization and locality

## Getting you thinking

1. **Look at the two photos on the right. Which of the two areas do you think has the higher rate of crime? What reasons can you give for your answer?**
2. **What different sorts of crimes might take place in the city during the day and during the night? What reasons can you give for your answer?**
3. **When you are walking home in the evening, do you feel more concerned than during the day? Are there any precautions you take if you are walking alone at night? What are they?**
4. **If you see a group of young males standing ahead of you on the street, do you alter your behaviour or route in any way? Give reasons for your answer.**

The last few topics have dealt with theoretical perspectives on crime and deviance but have these perspectives presented realistic, practical suggestions for what to do about crime? And have they noticed that fear of crime and becoming a victim of crime can be very damaging to individuals and to communities?

This topic looks at perspectives that have become known as realist approaches because they try to take a more practical view of crime and deviance, offering suggestions for what might be done to reduce crime and to make communities feel safer.

In Topic 1, we looked at criminal statistics. We learned that the victims of crime are, perhaps surprisingly, more likely to be poor and the disadvantaged than the rich. Furthermore, the majority of crime occurs in inner-city areas and in large social-housing developments where there is real concern over the amount of crime - a concern which sociologists had previously simply missed. It was within this context of uncovering the true extent, victims and location of crime that two very different approaches developed:

- **Right realism** – deriving from the **right-wing** theories of James Q. Wilson and emphasizing '**zero tolerance**'.
- **Left realism** – deriving from the writings of Lea, Young and Matthews who emphasize the importance of tackling deprivation and of getting policing to respond to the needs of the local population.

Before discussing right realism it is worth examining New Right approaches to crime in general.

## The New Right and crime

Many New Right thinkers believe that the relationship between the family and social control is the key to understanding the causes of crime. For example, Dennis and Erdos (1993) argue that the correlation between crime and certain family characteristics is a reflection of a much wider change in society. In particular, the traditional three-generation family structure had provided stability and a place in which moral values and a sense of community belonging had been passed on. However, since the 1960s, a series of changes in the family, in particular the decline in the role and presence of fathers, has weakened the external patterns of social control based on families and communities (where community members felt able to restrain extreme behaviour or young offenders) and also undermined the internalized forms of social control that had traditionally occurred through family socialization. However, Scraton (2002) rejects Dennis's argument. He accuses Dennis of mixing up a moral argument, reflecting his own views, with a sociological one supported by evidence.

The close relationship between family, community and offending was taken up by the American writer Charles

Murray (1990). He argued that over the previous 30 years, there had been an increase in what he termed 'the **underclass**'. By this, Murray refers to a clearly distinguishable group of young people who:

- have no desire for formal paid employment, preferring to live off benefits and the illegal economy
- have a range of short-term sexual liaisons
- routinely have children born outside serious relationships, so that fathers do not regard their offspring as their responsibility.

The children of these people are brought up with little or no concern for the values of the society in general. The result is that there is now a generation of young people who do not share the values of the wider society and who are much more likely to commit crime. Poorer communities are being destroyed by the underclass, who are driving out the law-abiding majority, and thus the members of the underclass are becoming ever more isolated and confirmed in their behaviour. Dennis and Murray's writings link very closely with the work of the right realists, foremost among whom is James Q. Wilson.

# Right realism

Right realism originated in the USA with the writings of James Q. Wilson. In 'Broken Windows' (Wilson and Kelling 1982), Wilson argued that crime flourishes in situations where social control breaks down. According to his analysis, in any community, a proportion of the population are likely to engage in 'incivilities', which might consist of such things as dropping litter, vandalism or rowdy behaviour. In most communities, this behaviour is prevented from going further by the comments and actions of other members of the local community. Effectively, the amount and extent of incivilities are held in check by the response of others. However, if the incivilities go unchecked, then the entire social order of the area breaks down and gradually there is a move to more frequent and more serious crime. The parallel which Wilson drew was with abandoned buildings; he asks whether anyone had ever seen just one window broken? The answer was, of course, that once one window was broken, then they all were.

Once crime is allowed to happen, it flourishes. Wilson was strongly influenced by the work of the American theorist Amitai Etzioni, and his theory of communitarianism (1993) – which stresses the fact that only local communities by their own efforts and local face-to-face relationships can solve social problems.

The conclusion that Wilson drew was that the police should have a crucial role to play in restoring the balance of incivilities and helping to recreate community. He argued that most police officers engage in law enforcement – that is ensuring that the law is not broken and apprehending offenders if they have committed an offence. He argued that this did relatively little to reconstruct communities and prevent crime (after all only about 3 per cent of offences result in successful prosecutions). Police should instead be concentrating on order maintenance. By this he means using the law to ensure that the smaller incivilities – groups of rowdy youths, noisy parties, public drug use – are all crushed. According to him, this would help to create a different view of what was acceptable behaviour, and would make public areas feel safe again for the majority of people.

## Evaluation of right realism

After a version of his ideas was adopted in New York, under the slogan 'zero tolerance', and there appeared to be a decline in crime, the term was adopted throughout America and to some extent in the UK as a description of a much harsher form of street policing. Platt and Takagi (1977) criticize this approach for concentrating exclusively on working – class crimes and ignoring the crimes of the powerful. Furthermore, it ignores ideas of justice and law enforcement and advocates instead the maintenance of social order – even if it is at the expense of justice.

# Left realism

Left realism developed primarily as a response to the increasing influence of right realism over the policymakers in Britain and America. In the USA, the main writer has been Elliot Currie, while in Britain left realism is associated with Jock Young, John Lea and Roger Matthews.

Young was one of the founders of 'the New Criminology' (see Topic 3) that introduced elements of interactionist theory into Marxism in order to provide a 'complete' theory of crime. However, Young became increasingly disenchanted with the Marxist approach that stressed that criminals should be seen as the victims of the capitalist system and that sociological analyses of crime should stress the criminality of the rich and powerful. This disillusionment was fuelled by a series of local victimization surveys, e.g. in Islington and Merseyside, which showed that the real victims of crime were the poor and powerless, and that these people viewed street crime and burglary as one of the main social problems they faced.

Young (1986) argued that it was the role of criminology to provide relevant and credible solutions for policymakers to limit the harm that crime was doing to the lives of the poorer sections of the community. This approach led to a bitter debate in sociology, with many influential left-wing criminologists attacking Young for selling out. (The implication of Young's new argument is that the role of sociologists is to help the government to combat crime. For Marxists, crime exists because of capitalism, and the government represents capitalism.) Young responded by labelling Marxist criminology as 'left idealism', meaning that it was great in theory, but had no practical solutions.

The left realist explanation of crime has three elements: relative deprivation, marginalization and subculture.

### *Relative deprivation*

The concept of **relative deprivation** derives from the writings of Runciman (1966), who argued that political revolutions only occurred when the poor became aware of the sheer scale of the differences between themselves and the rich. Without this knowledge, they generally accepted their poverty and powerlessness. It is not, therefore, poverty that leads to revolution, but awareness of their relative poverty.

Applying this concept to crime, Lea and Young (1984) pointed out that poverty or unemployment do not directly cause crime, as despite the high unemployment experienced in the economic depression in Britain from the late 1920s to the 1930s, crime rates were considerably lower than they were in the boom years of the 1980s. According to Lea and Young, the expectations of 1930s youth were much lower than those of contemporary young people, who feel resentful at what they could actually earn compared with their aspirations.

### *Marginalization*

**Marginalization** refers to the situation where certain groups in the population are more likely than others to suffer economic, social, and political deprivation. The first two of these elements of deprivation are fairly well known – young people living in inner cities and social-housing estates are likely to suffer from higher levels of deprivation than those from more affluent areas. The third element – political marginalization – refers to the fact that there is no way for them to influence decision-makers, and thus they feel powerless.

### *Subculture*

This draws partially upon the Marxist subcultural approach (see Topic 3), but more heavily from the ideas of Robert Merton (see Topic 2). Subcultures develop amongst groups who suffer relative deprivation and marginalization. Specific sets of values, forms of dress and modes of behaviour develop that reflect the problems that their members face. However, whereas the Marxist subculture writers seek to explain the styles of dress, and forms of language and behaviour as forms of 'resistance' to capitalism, Lea and Young do not see a direct, 'decodable' link.

For Lea and Young (1984), one crucial element of subcultures is that they are still located in the values of the wider society. Subcultures develop precisely because their members subscribe to the dominant values of society, but are blocked off (because of marginalization) from success. The outcome of subculture, marginalization and relative deprivation is street crime and burglary, committed largely by young males.

## Evaluation of left realism

Marxist or 'critical criminologists' writers have attacked realism for ignoring the 'real' causes of crime that lie in the wider capitalist system and of ignoring the crimes of more powerful groups in society by simply concentrating on street crime. Feminist and Postmodernist criminologists, such as Pat Carlen (1992) and Henry and Milovanovich (1996) have argued that left realist criminology accepts the establishment's view of what crime is and so concentrates its attention on issues to do with street crime and burglary. They argue, instead, that one role of criminology ought to be exploring the way that society harms less powerful groups.

Realist approaches to crime have actually been put into practice, in a modified form, by New Labour governments between 1997 and 2010. More detail can be found in Topic 9.

# Victimization

During the 1980s criminologists became aware that much of their work focused on the causes of crime and the motivation of those who break the law – but it paid little attention to the victim. Work needed to be done to find out about the risks and experiences of victimization for different groups and areas.

## Victim surveys

Victim surveys are discussed in some detail in Topic 1. The best known victim survey is the annual British Crime Survey. But there have also been a range of local victim surveys which were very influential for left realists as they showed that risk of victimization was greatest in poor areas and that official statistics – and the British Crime Survey – were under-representing the higher levels of victimization of minority ethnic groups and domestic violence.

## Risk of victimization

Young males, who form the majority of the unemployed and low-waged, have a particularly high chance of becoming a victim of crime. In most cases, victim and attacker know each other. Victims of property crimes such as burglary are most likely to be low-income households in deprived areas.

According to the British Crime Survey (see Figure 2.10), people from minority ethnic backgrounds are at greater risk of being a victim of crime than the White population. However, this can largely be explained by the fact that the age profile of ethnic minorities in Britain has a much higher proportion of younger people. Younger people (from any ethnic background) are more likely to be victims of crime than any other age group. However, there are some differences in the types of crime that ethnic minorities experience – particularly 'mugging' and other forms of street crime.

The statistics suggest that crime does not happen to everyone – it targets the poorer and less powerful groups in society more than the affluent. They also tell us that violent crime tends to happen between people who know each other, even live together.

## Fear of crime

Fear of crime is not necessarily linked to the real risks of victimization. As we will see in Topic 8, perceptions of crime are often influenced by sensational and selective media coverage of deviance, rather than the results of, say, the British Crime Survey.

### *Ethnicity*

People from minority ethnic backgrounds are more likely to be worried that they will be victims of most forms of crime compared to the majority White population. As we saw above, they are at greater risk of victimization because of their presence in high risk groups such as younger people.

**Figure 2.10** Adults most at risk of violence, 2008/09 BCS

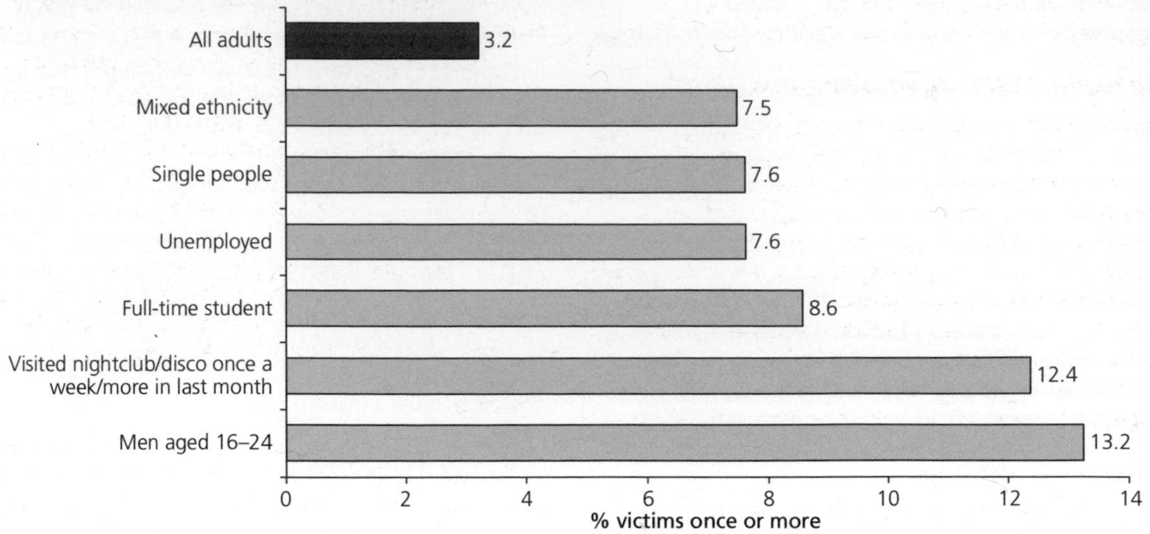


### *Age*

Both males and females under the age of 25 report the highest levels of worry for nearly all crimes, in particular sexual assault. This worry about crime is lower among men and women aged 60 and over, reflecting the higher chances of people in younger age groups becoming victims. However, the number of sexual offences against women by strangers is very small.

### *Gender*

Women are about three times more likely than men to be worried about physical attack yet men are slightly more likely than women to be a victim of violent crime.

## Feminism and victimization

Feminist approaches to crime are discussed in detail in Topic 6. In terms of victimization, feminists have been influential in bringing attention to issues such as sexual and domestic violence – crimes which are very hard to obtain accurate data about. Recent feminists such as Smart (1990) have attempted to push the boundaries of criminology beyond understanding law breaking to take into account a range of activities that harm women (see Getting you thinking in Topic 6 for some examples).

## Marxism, corporate crime and victimization

Marxist perspectives and corporate crime are discussed in detail in Topic 3. Marxists, like recent feminists, want to move beyond the boundaries of conventional criminology as they see the law and criminal justice system as serving the interests of the ruling class rather than protecting the public. Marxists have been influential in spelling out the costs of corporate crime for its victims – who are often all of us. It has been suggested that the annual cost of corporate crime in America is $400 billion compared to a cost of $13 billion for all other crime put together. The 'costs' of corporate crime are not just economic however, Tombs and White (2007) point out that in the UK, Great Western trains were fined £1.5 million for their role in a train crash in London in 1999, when seven people were killed and 150 injured. In 2006, Balfour Beatty was fined £10 million for four deaths and 150 injuries caused by their failure to maintain the railway lines adequately.

We pointed out earlier the way that corporate 'crime' can transgress the boundaries of crime through acts that may not actually be illegal, but are regarded by sociologists as morally reprehensible and often a violation of certain human rights. Mokhiber (1988) points out that, in the USA, 800 people die each day from smoking related diseases; 8000 a day die from asbestos-related cancers and 85 000 cotton textile workers suffer breathing problems from dust related to their jobs.

# Locality and crime

Both right and left realists have attempted to explain why crime occurs in some places more than others, particularly poorer urban areas. We now move on to look at the issue of geographical location and crime in more detail.

## Chicago sociology

### *The pattern*

In the late-19th and early-20th centuries, one of the fastest growing cities in the USA was Chicago. The city also possessed one of the new university departments of sociology, and two of its researchers, Shaw and McKay (1931) began plotting the location of the addresses of those who committed crimes in the city. The results showed that, if they divided the city into **concentric zones**, each of the five zones they identified had different levels of offenders, with zone two (which was nearest the city centre) showing the highest rates.

This was interesting in itself, but they also found that because of rapid social change, the population living in zone two was changing regularly, so that although the various zones maintained their different levels of offenders over time, they were different offenders. This meant that there was something about the zones, rather than individuals who lived there, that was linked to crime rates.

### *The explanation: social disorganization*

Shaw and McKay suggested that as each successive wave of immigrants arrived in the city, they were moved into the cheapest and least desirable zones – that is, the **zone of transition**. Over time, some were successful and they moved out to the more affluent suburbs, while the less successful remained. The places of those who had moved on were taken by newer immigrants, and so the process started again. This pattern of high population turnover created a state of **social disorganization**, where the informal mechanisms of social control that normally hold people back from criminal behaviour were weak or absent.

### *Cultural transmission*

In their later writings, Shaw and McKay (1942) altered the meaning of 'social disorganization' to refer to a distinct set of values that provided an alternative to those of the mainstream society. This amended approach came to be known as **cultural transmission** theory. They argued that amongst some groups in the most socially disorganized and poorest zones of the city, crime became culturally acceptable, and was passed on from one generation to the next as part of the normal socialization pattern. Successful criminals provide role models for the next generation by demonstrating both the normality of criminal behaviour and that a criminal career was possible.

## Differential association

One criticism of Shaw and McKay and other members of the Chicago School of Criminology was that their theories were too vague and difficult to prove.

In response, Sutherland and Cressey (1966) introduced the concept of **differential association**. This states that someone is likely to become criminal 'if they receive an excess of definitions favourable to violation of law over definitions unfavourable to violation of law'. This simply means that if people interact with others who support lawbreaking, then they are likely to do so themselves.

Further tightening his approach in order to avoid criticisms of vagueness, Sutherland suggested that these definitions vary in frequency, duration, priority, and intensity:

- *frequency* – the number of times the definitions occur
- *duration* – over what length of time
- *priority* – e.g. at what stage in life (childhood socialization is more important than other periods)
- *intensity* – the status of the person making the definition (e.g. family member rather than a stranger).

## Housing policies

Most British research failed to reproduce the clear pattern of concentric circles that the Chicago School had identified. Crime rates certainly varied by areas, but in more complex patterns.

One early study by Morris in 1957 found no evidence that people in areas of high delinquency held a coherent set of values that was any different from that of mainstream society. Morris suggested that a key factor in the concentration of delinquents in certain areas was linked to the local council's housing policies. For example, in his study of Croydon, the local council's policy of housing problem-families together meant that these areas became, almost by definition, high-crime areas.

The impact of local-authority housing decisions was clarified much later by the work of Baldwin and Bottoms (1976), who compared two similar local-authority housing estates, separated by a dual carriageway. One of the estates 'Gardenia' had a 300 per cent higher number of offenders and a 350 per cent higher level of crimes than the other 'Stonewall'. The difference according to him was the result of a process that he named '**tipping**'.

### *Tipping*

Most estates consist of a mixture of people from different backgrounds and with different forms of behaviour. Informal social control imposed by the majority of residents limits the offending behaviour of the antisocial minority. However, if for whatever reason (such as local-authority housing policies), the antisocial minority grow in number, their behaviour drives away some of the law-abiding families. Those who wish to enter the estate tend to be relatives of the antisocial families and this leads to a speed up in the law-abiding residents leaving. The estate has 'tipped' and becomes increasingly regarded as a problem estate. Those who are able to flee, do so. In Baldwin and Bottom's analysis, Gardenia had tipped, whilst Stonewall had not.

### *Disorder*

W.G. Skogan (1990) in the USA has fleshed out this idea of tipping. He suggests that social control breaks down when, for example, there is a combination of physical deterioration in local buildings and parks, and an increase in social disorder in the form of public alcohol and drug use. This leads to a situation of disorder, which has three consequences:

1. It undermines the mechanisms of informal social control and leads people to withdraw, thus undermining the bonds between people.
2. It generates worries about neighbourhood safety, so that people avoid going out at night, thus making it easier for street crime to be committed.
3. It causes law-abiding people who can afford it to move out of the area, and leads to a decrease in property values and the growth of housing to let.

## Social capital

Social disorganization explains crime and deviance by a lack of common, shared values, although there is relatively little evidence to support this. However, more recently, there has been a shift back to understanding the role of values. Putnam (2000) argues that there has been a decline in the extent to which people are linked into family and friendship networks. The result is that individuals feel more alone and less confident about engaging in community activity. According to Putnam, this results in a weak community unable to impose social control on those who engage in offending.

## Focus on research

### Bernasco and Nieuwbeerta (2005)

### How burglars choose their targets

Bernasco and Nieuwbeerta conducted a detailed study of burglary patterns in The Hague, in the Netherlands. They obtained information on 548 residential burglaries and from 290 (arrested) burglars across the city over a period of one year. They concluded that there were some very clear patterns of burglary. The affluence of the neighbourhood was not very important; instead, homes were more likely to be broken into if they were relatively near to where the offender lived and if there was perceived to be limited 'guardianship', meaning people keeping an eye on the property. Other factors were the high rate of burglary in areas of the city where there were mixed ethnic groups and a high proportion of single-parent families. Bernasco and Nieuwbeerta did not find any evidence for concentric zones where crimes were more likely.

Bernasco, W. and Nieuwbeerta, P. (2005) 'How do residential burglars select target areas?', *British Journal of Criminology*, 45(3)

1. **To what extent do the methods used by the authors provide a representative picture of burglary?**
2. **Summarize the factors that appeared to make some houses vulnerable to burglary.**

In the USA, William Julius Wilson (1996) has adapted a version of this approach to explain the high levels of offending in deprived neighbourhoods. He argues that there is a high level of social interaction between people, so that it is not true that people are isolated. There are, however, low levels of social control. Wilson suggests that this comes from a sense of powerlessness and a lack of integration into the wider society. People in deprived areas do interact, but not in a way that provides social controls or positive social models for young people, as the adults themselves feel isolated from the broader society.

## Time: the night-time economy

If different places have varying levels of crime and different styles of control, then so do different times. The busy city centre, filled with families shopping during the day, becomes the location for the young seeking pleasure at night. The same location, therefore, changes its meaning and possibilities with the closing of the shops and the coming of the darkness.

An interesting example of the significance of time is what Hobbs *et al.* (2000) call the '**night-time economy**'. They point out that in the last 15 years, there has been a huge growth in pubs and clubs, as Britain's younger people have increasingly embraced the leisure society. This involves, in Britain at least, going out at the weekend to clubs and pubs to consume alcohol (and possibly also drugs) and to enjoy oneself. In 2003, for example, there were over 210 million club admissions to the value of £2.5 billion. Investment in the night-time economy totals around £1 billion a year and is growing at an annual rate of 10 per cent.

The sheer scale of the leisure industry means that there are now huge numbers of young people who come together within a very narrow time-band and in a relatively restricted area, in order to engage in the search for pleasure. Almost three-quarters of all violent incidents in urban areas occur during the weekend between 9 pm and 3 am, usually by and between groups of young males fuelled by drink and/or drugs. Hobbs (2003) illustrates this by pointing out that, in Manchester, an average of 75 000 people are out visiting the clubs, pubs and bars on Friday and Saturday evenings. There are only about 30 police officers to control them, but over 1000 door staff and 'bouncers'. So, the control of the night-time economy has largely been passed from the police to private security companies.

## Key terms

**Concentric zones** widening circles.

**Cultural transmission** values are passed on from one generation to the next.

**Differential association** the theory that deviant behaviour is learned from, and justified by, family and friends.

**Marginalization** refers to socially excluded people living on the edge of society.

**New Right** right-wing thinkers who emerged at the time of Margaret Thatcher's rise to power in the 1970s and 1980s.

**Night-time economy** refers to the way that a leisure industry has developed at night, which provides the location of many offences.

**Realist approaches** approaches that take a more practical view of crime, offering practical suggestions to reduce crime.

**Relative deprivation** awareness of your own disadvantage deriving from comparisons with the more affluent.

**Right-wing** political viewpoint that rejects the idea of state intervention in society

**Social capital** the extent of social networks.

**Social disorganization** a city area that does not have a shared culture.

**Tipping** the process by which an area moves from being predominantly law-abiding to predominantly accepting antisocial behaviour.

**Underclass** term used to describe a group of people dependent on state benefits who live an unstable life based on immediate gratification.

**Zero-tolerance** using the law to ensure that minor incidents of anti-social behaviour are crushed.

**Zone of transition** the cheapest, least desirable zones of the city, into which immigrants are moved.

## Check your understanding

1 Identify and explain the key similarities and differences between right and left realism.

2 What do left realists believe are the causes of crime?

3 Which social groups are most likely to become victims of crime and why?

4 Why do both feminists and Marxists want to extend the boundaries of criminology and victim studies?

5 Shaw and McKay suggested two explanations for the behaviour of the people in the zones they identified. What are these explanations?

6 Explain, in your own words, what is meant by the term 'tipping'.

## Activities

### Research idea

Undertake a small survey among the students at your school or college of fear of crime in your area. Ask a small random selection of students about their fear of being victims of crime. Ask them about whether they go out in the evening and, if so, do they have greater concerns than during the day. What differences, if any, emerge?

### Web.task

Go to **www.neighbourhood.statistics.gov.uk** and input your postcode or that of your school or college. Select the statistics on 'Crime and safety'. Try to explain the patterns of crime in your locality.

## An eye on the exam Realism, victimization and locality

A detailed description of realist approaches is required, using sociological concepts, theories and studies.

Weigh up the strengths and weaknesses of realist approaches in some detail, then present alternative perspectives before reaching a balanced conclusion.

**Outline and assess the usefulness of realist approaches to an understanding of crime and deviance. (50 marks)**

You will need to consider both left and right realism

### Grade booster Getting top marks in this question

The idea of realism will require explanation at the start of this answer, as well as the two different types of realism: left and right. It would be helpful to discuss briefly what 'left' and right' refer to in terms of political viewpoint before discussing the realist perspectives on crime and deviance in more depth. The ideas of Wilson are likely to feature heavily in the account of right realism and Lea and Young in the account of left realism.

The analytical part of the essay should compare the two types of realism on issues such as the causes of crime, policing and the criminal justice system and solutions to crime and deviance – a look forward to Topic 9 will be of use here. The theories will need to be criticized as well, for example Marxists accuse realists of ignoring the crimes of the powerful.

# TOPIC 6

# Feminism, gender and crime

## Getting you thinking

To be a woman in most societies is to experience physical and/or sexual terrorism at the hands of men. Our everyday behaviour reflects our precautions, the measures we take to protect ourselves. We are wary of going out at night, even in our own neighbourhoods. We are warned by men and other women not to trust strangers. But somehow they forget to warn us about the men we know. Many men familiar to us also terrorise our everyday lives in our homes, our schools and workplaces.

At one extreme, and which most men condemn, some males engage in activities of violence and rape against women. However, typical male behaviour is also threatening to women and provides the basis from which the extreme behaviour grows. Typical male behaviour includes the wolf whistle and calls in the street, the obvious staring at the female body, the comments about a woman's body and the brushing up against the female office worker's body in the photocopying room. These expressions are regarded as natural expressions of maleness.

Adapted from Stanko, A.E. (1985) *Intimate Intrusions: Women's Experiences of Male Violence*, London: Routledge

**Offenders found guilty of, or cautioned for, indictable offences: by sex and type of offence, 2006**

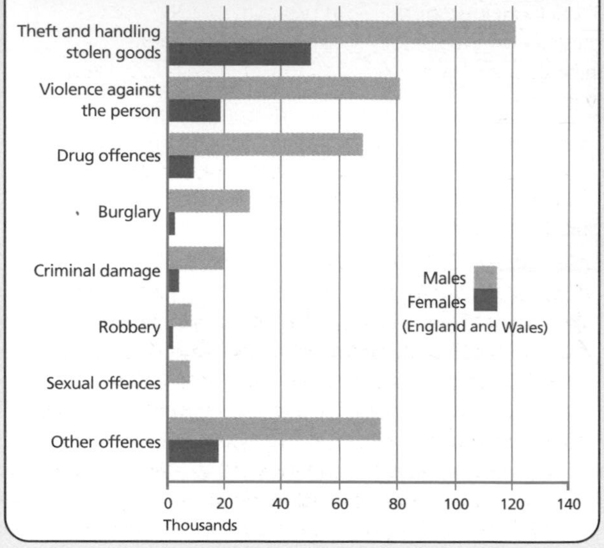


1. **What is your reaction to reading the extract on the way males treat females? Do you think it is true? What implications would it have for the way men ought to behave?**
2. **Identify the main patterns in the chart above.**
3. **What explanations can you suggest for the differences between male and female offending?**

In this topic, we want to explore the relationship that gender has to offending. Official records show an overwhelming predominance of males compared with females committing crime. Self-report studies, too, show a noticeable, if less marked, difference between the offending levels of males and females. Given this, there has to be something in the different construction of femininity and masculinity that can help us to explain these differences. We will try to unravel some of the strands of explanation offered.

Before we do so, however, we need to explain why, surprisingly perhaps, there has been relatively little research that explicitly sets out to explain the links between gender and offending. It seems that most sociologists have started off with the assumption that males commit more crime, and have then moved on to explore why it is that only some males commit crime. Explanations offered by sociologists have, therefore, concentrated mainly on comparing offending males with non-offending males, without explaining why males are more likely to offend in the first instance.

The topic falls into two main areas of discussion:

- the issue of women and crime
- male gender roles and crime.

First, we ask why women have been ignored in the sociology of crime and delinquency, before turning to examine the explanations for lower rates of female offending. In the second part of the topic, we turn things on their head and ask what lessons the exploration of gender roles might have for male offending. The answers we arrive at may be rather surprising, for it seems that the opening-up of criminology by feminists provides us with clues as to why males have such high rates of offending. Indeed, so significant are these insights that much contemporary criminology is heavily influenced by them.

# Feminism and crime

Anyone studying the sociology of crime and deviance will notice after a while that it is mainly about male offending. In fact, it would not be unfair to call it the sociology of male crime and deviancy. Although it is true that the majority of offenders are male – comprising about 80 per cent of all official statistics on offenders – it is surprising that 20 per cent of all offenders are simply ignored.

Frances Heidensohn (1989) has criticized the male dominance of the subject (known as **malestream** criminology) and has suggested that there are four reasons why it is so:

- *Male dominance of offenders* – As the majority of offenders are male, for many sociologists it was therefore most appropriate to study them, rather than the minority of female offenders.
- *Male domination of sociology* – Although the majority of sociology students are women, it has always been the case that the majority of academics have been male. According to Heidensohn, sociological topics of investigation reflect a male view and male interests.
- *Vicarious identification* – This follows from the previous point. Men study what interests them, and, applied to crime, this is most often the lives of the marginal and the exciting, i.e. **vicarious identification**.
- *Sociological theorizing* – Male sociologists constructed their theories without ever thinking about how they could be applied to females. Most traditional theories are 'gender blind'; in effect, that means they ignore the specific viewpoint of women.

# Explaining female crime: women's roles

Most theories that explain crime, as we saw earlier, implicitly accept that males are more likely than females to commit crime. In the process, criminologists have omitted to explain what it is that makes males more likely than females to commit crime. There have, however, been a number of exceptions to this and we explore these approaches in this section. Three major approaches to explaining the relationship between women and offending are:

1. biological explanations
2. socialization and social control
3. changing role or 'liberationist' perspective.

## Biological explanations

This approach has been used by different writers to explain why the vast majority of women do not offend and, conversely, why a small minority do. It starts from the belief that women are innately different from men, with a natural desire to be caring and nurturing – neither of them values that support crime. 'Normal' women are therefore less likely to commit crime. On the other hand, some women writers, such as Dalton (1964), have claimed that hormonal or menstrual factors can influence a minority of women to commit crime in certain circumstances.

## Socialization and social control

Many feminists argue that women are less likely to commit crime than men because there are core elements of the female role that limit their ability and opportunity to do so. There are a number of different versions of this theory, all of which can fit quite comfortably together.

## Socialization

You will recall from the AS course that many feminists and other sociologists have identified gender differences in socialization. From infancy, children are taught that the sexes are different and that there are certain characteristics that males and females ought to have. Female roles contain such elements as attractiveness, softness, caring and domesticity. Male roles, on the other hand, stress elements such as toughness, aggression and sexuality. As a result of socialization, girls could be said to be lacking in the values generally associated with crime and delinquency.

This approach is supported to some extent by the low levels of conviction of females for violent street crime. This is the area where there is the largest difference in the numbers of convictions of men and women. The offences for which females are more likely to be arrested than males are shoplifting and prostitution, and these can be tied in with the different sex-role expectations for females. For example, shoplifting derives from the role of mother and family provider and prostitution from another element of the female role, that of sexual provider in exchange for economic benefits.

## Social control

Another concept that cannot be clearly distinguished from socialization is social control. These processes overlap and reinforce one another. Women are less likely to commit crime, not from any natural streak of goodness, but rather because they spend most of their lives being confined by men in law-abiding roles, particularly within the family. Heidensohn (1996) points to the wide range of informal sanctions to discourage women from straying from 'proper' behaviour, including gossip, fear of a bad reputation and the comments of male companions. Hagan (1987) studied child-raising patterns in Canada and argued that there was significantly greater informal control of daughters' activities in families compared to sons. McRobbie (1994) found that many young women were excluded from subcultures because of parental control. Instead they stayed indoors with their friends, creating a 'bedroom culture'.

Heidensohn (1985) identifies three areas where control of women operates and which means they have fewer opportunities to commit crime.

### *Control of women within the home*

Women are still seen as primarily responsible for domestic life. Caring for children and housework can take up many hours, leaving little time for criminal or deviant activities.

### *Control of women in public*

Many women do not feel comfortable in public places, especially at night. They also limit their behaviour in order to avoid labelling. Lees (1986) has shown how labels such as 'slag' can have major controlling consequences on the way girls behave.

### *Control of women in work*

Most areas of employment feature a majority of male bosses and female subordinates (see Chapter 6 for more detail) and many females at work are subject to sexual harassment such as sexual comments and inappropriate touching.

Carlen (1988) studied a sample of women who had been convicted of one or more crimes. She found that the mechanisms of social control had broken down for many of these women. Their efforts to gain material rewards from the workplace (what Carlen calls the 'class deal') had not been successful, nor had they found satisfaction in the traditional role of wife, mother and homemaker (the 'gender deal').

## The changing role or 'liberationist' perspective

So far, we have characterized female sex-roles as being more passive and less aggressive than those of males. However, a number of writers, including Adler (1975), have suggested that the increasing rates of female crime are linked to their freedom from the traditional forms of social control, discussed earlier, and their acceptance into more 'masculine' roles. More recently, Denscombe (2001) has argued that changing female roles over the last ten years mean that, increasingly, females are as likely as males to engage in risk-taking behaviour. In his research into self-images of 15 to 16 year olds in the East Midlands, in which he undertook in-depth interviews as well as focus groups, he found that females were rapidly adopting what had traditionally been male attitudes. This included such things as 'looking hard', 'being in control' and being someone who can cope with risk-taking. This provides theoretical support for the fact that female crime levels are rising much more quickly than male ones, not just in terms of numbers but also in terms of seriousness of crimes committed.

Westwood (1999) develops similar ideas when she argues that identities are constantly being reconstructed and reframed. The concept of a fixed female identity has limited our understanding of crime, so we need to understand how women are reconfiguring their identity in a more confident, forceful way, and the possible link to the growth of female crime. However, Heidensohn (2002) disputes this argument, citing evidence from a number of other studies which show that convicted offenders tend to score highly on psychological tests of 'femininity', indicating, according to her, that they have not taken on male roles.



# Transgression: a postmodernist critique

The various explanations of female crime put forward were not popular with feminist sociologists, as they felt that they were not really adequate explanations for the differences between male and female causes for offending. Pat Carlen (1992) argued, for example, that these were theoretically weak and represented a sort of 'bolt-on' to existing male criminology.

It was in response to the need for a feminist version of criminology – one that answered the concerns of women – that Carol Smart (1990) introduced the idea of a **transgressive criminology**. By this, Smart was suggesting that criminology itself as a discipline was tied to male questions and concerns and that it could never offer answers to feminist questions. Instead of trying to produce a feminist criminology by asking the question, 'What can feminism offer criminology?', feminists should be arguing, 'What can criminology offer feminists?' The answer to this question lay in looking at a whole range of activities (both legal and illegal) that actually harm women, and asking how these came about and how they could be changed. The term 'transgressive', in this context then, meant to go beyond the boundaries of criminology. This did lead to feminists (and sympathetic male sociologists) looking more closely at things such as:

- the way women stayed in at night for fear of becoming victims
- domestic violence
- how women were treated by the law in issues of rape and harassment (where they form the overwhelming bulk of the victims).

Transgression is a good example of the postmodern influence in sociology, when the traditional boundaries of sociology and the categories used to classify issues are abandoned, and new ways of thinking are introduced.

# Women and the criminal justice system

Despite committing less crime overall, the number of women who receive prison sentences has always been high compared to the numbers prosecuted, with about 34 per cent of women receiving jail sentences for their first offence, compared to approximately 10 per cent of men. This seems to suggest that women are sentenced more harshly than men. But a study by Hedderman and Hough (1994) showed that, when women with similar backgrounds were charged with similar crimes to men, they received more lenient sentences. Heidensohn (2002) also found that women are more likely to receive shorter sentences than men. This has been described as a process of '**chivalry**', by which we mean that the male-dominated legal system treats women differently, seeking to explain away their offending, as males find it difficult to believe that women can be 'bad' – they are merely 'led astray'.

## Focus on research

### Stephen Jones (2008) The influence of men on female offenders

One of the current explanations for the rise in female offending is that it reflects the increased freedom of women from male control. This decline in male social control has allowed women to make choices to offend in the same way that men do. Increasing autonomy for women leads to increasing offending by women. However, this has been criticized by other sociologists, who suggest that women offend precisely because they are under the control of men.

Stephen Jones decided to test the extent to which female offending was of their own choosing or whether they were influenced by men. He did this by interviewing women who had been found guilty of an offence for which they had been charged jointly with a male (the co-defendant) and asking them how much they had been influenced by their male co-defendant. This is how he describes his research methods:

> *<<Between December 2004 and December 2005, all sentenced women aged 21 or over who passed through one English prison were given a letter inviting them to be interviewed about their experience with a co-defendant. It was usually possible for the letters to be delivered by the researcher in person and this proved valuable as it enabled the women to ask questions about the research ... Fifty women with co-defendants agreed to be interviewed. These were conducted in private and tape-recorded. The interviews were of a semistructured nature. Having been asked several background questions about themselves and their co-defendants, the women were then engaged in a more general conversation about the relationship they had with these people and how they came to commit offences together.>>*

Jones, S. (2008) 'Partners in crime: a study of the relationship between female offenders and their co-defendants,' *Criminology and Criminal Justice*, 8

**1 Explain the aims of this research and the reason why it was conducted.**

**2 Why do you think the interviews were conducted in the way described above?**

Farrington and Morris (1983) argue that magistrates and judges distinguish between 'types' of women and that certain 'types' are more likely to receive harsher sentences than men, whilst others receive more lenient sentences. So, when sentencing, judges are more likely to take into account issues of family responsibility, marital status and 'moral background'. So unmarried women without ties and stable relationships may receive harsher sentencing – they are seen as '**doubly deviant**', that is deviating from both the law and the norms of traditional femininity.

# Explaining male crime: male roles and masculinity

Smart's idea of transgressive criminology, linked to the growing importance of postmodern analysis, began to feed back into mainstream criminology. Some sociologists began to go beyond traditional confines and to revisit the issue of why most crime is male crime.

## Normative masculinity

The analysis of masculinity began with the Australian sociologist, Bob Connell (1995). He argued that there were a number of different forms of masculinity, which change over time – in particular, he identified the concept of hegemonic masculinity. Although crime was not central to his analysis, the idea of multiple, constructed masculinities was taken up by Messerschmidt (1993).

Connell argues that a '**normative masculinity**' exists in society, highly valued by most men. Normative masculinity refers to the socially approved idea of what a 'real male' is. According to Messerschmidt, it 'defines masculinity through difference from and desire for women'. Normative masculinity is so prized that men struggle to live up to its expectations. Messerschmidt suggests then that masculinity is not something natural, but rather a state that males only achieve as 'an accomplishment', which involves being constantly worked at.

However, the construction of this masculinity takes place in different contexts and through different methods depending upon the particular male's access to power and resources. So, more powerful males will accomplish their masculinity in different ways and contexts from less powerful males. Messerschmidt gives examples of businessmen who can express their power over women through their control in the workplace, while those with no power at work may express their masculinity by using violence in the home or street. However, whichever way is used, both types of men are achieving their normative masculinity.

So, it is achieving masculinity that leads some men to commit crime – and, in particular, crime is committed by those less powerful in an attempt to be successful at masculinity (which involves material, social and sexual success).The idea that masculinity is the actual basis of crime is reflected in the writings of a number of writers.

Although male sociologists have largely ignored female offending, feminist writers from the various strands within feminism have all sought to include criminological analyses within their approaches.

**Feminist perspectives on crime and deviance**

**Liberal feminism**

This approach to feminism is based on the idea that by bringing women onto the agenda and by demonstrating how women have been ignored in research, there will be greater understanding of female deviance. In particular, new theories can be developed that will cover both males and females.

**Socialist feminism**

This approach stresses that the position of men and women in general – and with reference to crime in particular – can only be understood by locating males and females within the context of societies divided by both sexism and by capitalism.

**Radical feminism**

Radical feminists argue that the only way to understand crime is to see it through a female perspective – and research should be based on the assumption that all men are prepared to commit crimes against women if given the chance. Women should construct their own unique approaches to explaining crime and deviance, and this should incorporate the threat from men.

**Postmodern feminism**

The work of Smart (1990) and Cain (1986) is particularly important, since they argue that the very concerns of criminology (burglary/street crime, etc.) are actually a reflection of male concerns, and that women should be looking beyond these to study how harm comes to women in the widest sense possible. Feminist criminology should not accept the (male) boundaries of criminology, but should look at the way women are harmed by a whole range of processes.

## Katz: seductions of crime

A postmodern twist on the idea of masculinity is the work of Katz (1988), who argues that what most criminology has failed to do is to understand the role of pleasure in committing crime. This search for pleasure has to be placed within the context of masculinity, which stresses the importance of status, control over others and success.

Katz claims that crime is always explained with reference to background causes, but rarely attempts to look at the pleasure that is derived from the actual act of offending. Doing evil, he argues, is motivated by the quest for a 'moral self-transcendence' in the face of boredom. Different crimes provide different thrills, that can vary from the 'sneaky thrills' of shoplifting, to the 'righteous slaughter' of murder.

Katz argues that by understanding the emotional thrills that transgression provides, we can understand why males commit crime. Katz gives the example of robbery, which is largely undertaken, he claims, for the chaos, thrill and potential danger inherent in the act. Furthermore, in virtually all robberies 'the offender discovers, fantasizes or manufactures an angle of moral superiority over the intended victim', such that the robber has 'succeeded in making a fool of his victim'. This idea of the thrill of crime has been used to explain the apparent irrational violence of football 'hooligans', and also the use of drugs and alcohol.

Katz's work is clearly influenced by the earlier work of Matza (1964) (see Topic 2), who has argued that constructing a male identity in contemporary society is difficult. Most youths are in a state of **drift** where they are unsure exactly who they are and what their place in society is. For most young males, this is a period of boredom and crisis. It is in this period of life that any event that unambiguously gives them a clear identity is welcomed, and it could equally be an identity of offender as much as employee. Committing offences provides a break from boredom, pleasure and a sense of being someone – for example, a gang member or a 'hard man'.

## Lyng: edgework

A linked argument can be found in the work of Lyng (1990), who argues that young males search for pleasure through risk-taking. According to Lyng, the risk-taking can best be seen as 'edgework', by which he means that there is a thrill to be gained from acting in ways that are on the edge between security and danger.

This helps explain the attractiveness of car theft and 'joy riding', and of searching for violent confrontations with other groups of males. By engaging in this form of risk-taking, young men are, in Messerschmidt's terms, 'accomplishing masculinity', and also proving that they have control over their lives.

## Masculinities in context

The work of Connell (via Messerschmidt) and the arguments of Katz and Lyng have been very influential in contemporary criminology. However, they have all been criticized for not slotting the notion of masculinities into a context. So Winlow (2004) has asked questions about the conditions in which men demonstrate their aggressiveness, and why it is that young, working-class males are more likely to be violent. The answers, he argues, lie in the changing nature of the economy in late modernity. For generations, working-class masculinity has been linked to manual employment in manufacturing industry. With the huge changes in the economy, most notably the decline in manual work and the increase in low-level, white-collar employment, a significant proportion of the male working-class population has been excluded from the possibilities of regular employment. According to Wilson (1996), this has resulted in the development of an urban underclass who manifest a range of violent and antisocial behaviours. The masculinity they exude, therefore, can only be understood within the context of the changing economic structure of the UK.

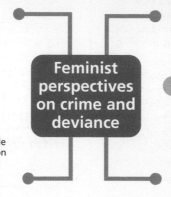

# Activities

## Research idea

Devise a simple 'self-report' questionnaire (see Topic 1) with a maximum of ten questions. The offending behaviour or deviant acts should be fairly minor, but common (e.g. starting a fight, drinking alcohol under age).

Either working in groups or individually, divide your questionnaires into two sets. Give out one set of questionnaires to be completed anonymously (but devise a way of ensuring you know the gender of the person completing each one). Use the other set with interview techniques to complete the questionnaire directly.

1. Are there different results between the two methods?
2. Are there any differences between males and females?

## Web.tasks

1. Go to the Home Office Research and Statistics Publications site. You will find a report on domestic violence, sexual assault and stalking at **www.homeoffice.gov.uk/rds/pdfs04/hors276.pdf**

   What does this report tell you about the relationship between gender and these crimes?
2. Visit the Fawcett Society (an organization to promote the rights of women) at **www.fawcettsociety.org.uk** and then click on the heading 'Crime and Justice'. Explore the up-to-date statistics on women's experience of the criminal justice system.

# Key terms

**Doubly deviant** deviating from both the law and the norms of femininity.

**Chivalry** men treating women in a traditionally polite manner e.g. giving up their seat

**Drift** term used by Matza to describe a state where young men are unsure about their identity and their place in society.

**Malestream** a term used to describe the fact that male ways of thinking have dominated criminology.

**Normative masculinity** the socially approved idea of what a real male is. According to Messerschmidt, it 'defines masculinity through difference from and desire for women'.

**Transgressive criminology** feminist theorists use this term to suggest a need to 'break out' of the confines of traditional criminology.

**Vicarious identification** when people obtain a thrill by putting themselves in the place of another person.

# Check your understanding

1. **Why did criminology traditionally ignore female crime?**
2. **Give two examples to show how social control can lead to low female crime rates.**
3. **What is the evidence for and against the existence of a 'chivalry factor' in the sentencing of women?**
4. **How is the idea of 'transgression' relevant to the debate about gender and crime?**
5. **In your own words, explain the term 'normative masculinity'. How does it help us to understand crime?**
6. **What is 'moral transcendence'?**
7. **Suggest three examples of 'edgework'.**
8. **What implication for the level of female crime is there as a result of the changing role of women in recent years?**

## An eye on the exam Feminism, gender and crime

A detailed description of the different explanations is required, using sociological concepts, theories and studies.

Weigh up the strengths and weaknesses of each explanation in some detail before reaching a balanced conclusion.

**Outline and assess sociological explanations of gender differences in crime rates. (50 marks)**

No need to describe biological or psychological explanations

This will involve a consideration of both male and female crime rates

### Grade booster Getting top marks in this question

Recent patterns and trends in crime rates in relation to gender will need to be outlined at the start of this answer. Then different sociological explanations will need to be described and analyzed. Some of these explanations will focus on the lower crime rates of women (e.g. feminist writers such as Heidensohn and Smart) and others on the higher crime rates of men (e.g. Connell, Messerschmidt and Katz). There may also be an account of explanations for the rising crime rate among younger women. Some explanations accept the official statistics while approaches influenced by labelling theory are more likely to emphasize the ways in which gender stereotypes held by the police and courts may play a part in constructing gender differences in crime rates.

# TOPIC 7

# Ethnicity and crime

## Getting you thinking

### Gang warfare on the streets of London as Asian and Black youths battle outside Julie Christie's house

A WARM LATE summer afternoon on a leafy street in an area colonised by fashionable cafes and shops came to an abrupt end when the peace was shattered by a raw, terrifying eruption of gang violence this week. Armed with spades, screwdrivers, bars and sticks, two gangs clashed and sent locals fleeing into shops for safety.

This running battle between Black and Asian youths – a sickening example of brutal Britain today – was captured by a photographer who had been waiting in the street to take a photo of the actress Julie Christie, who lives nearby.

Daniel Martin & Niall Firth, *The Daily Mail*, 5 Sept 2008

### The silenced majority

*Constant media stories about gang crime create a depressing and unbalanced picture of Black youngsters. So why are their positive achievements ignored?*

SINCE JANUARY, the term 'knife crime' has been used more than 1,500 times by the national press – and it is a fair bet that most media images associated with these figures will be of young Black men. Unsurprisingly, this is leading to a growing sense of frustration among Black community leaders, academics and, not least, Black youngsters themselves, over what they see as blatant misrepresentation.

Black youths who fit this media stereotype represent a tiny fraction of the young Black population as a whole, they argue, and while negative stories about Black teenagers are almost guaranteed headlines, the positive achievements of Black youth go largely ignored.

This trend has consequences beyond creating an unbalanced picture. Numerous studies have shown a clear link between media furore and draconian policy-making, says Kjartan Sveinsson, the author of a Runnymede Trust report on the ways in which popular understandings of race and crime influence media reporting, and vice versa. 'The tragedy is this can increase racial tension on the street and do little to stem the violence,' he says. Which in turn, of course, leads to further reports of violence, and the circle continues.

Eric Allison, *The Guardian*, 25 Aug 2008

**1** **Do you agree with the argument that Black youths only get negative news coverage?**

**2** **Do you think that Black or Asian youths are portrayed differently from White youths in the media?**

**3** **How do you think this could be changed?**

A recurring theme in media reporting of street crime since the mid-1970s has been the disproportionate involvement of young African-Caribbean males. It has partly been on this crime–race linkage that the police have justified the much greater levels of **stop and search** of young, Black males, than of White males.

Images of Asian criminality have, until recently, portrayed the Asian communities as generally more law-abiding than the majority population. However, after the attack on the World Trade Center in New York in 2001 and, more significantly, the bombings in 2005 on the London Underground, a new discourse has emerged regarding Muslim youths. The newer image is of them as being potentially dangerous – a threat to British culture.

Just discussing the relationship between criminality and race is itself a difficult task, and some sociologists argue that making the subject part of the A-level specifications actually helps perpetuate the link. After all, there are no discussions on 'White people and crime'! Despite these reservations, sociologists have set out to examine the argument that there is a higher rate of crime by certain ethnic minorities, and the counterclaim that the criminal justice system is racist.

# Offending, sentencing and punishment

## Offending

There are three ways of gathering statistics on ethnicity and crime: official statistics, victimization studies and self-report studies.

### *Official statistics*

According to Home Office statistics (Ministry of Justice 2008), about 9.5 per cent of people arrested were recorded as 'Black' and 5.3 per cent as 'Asian'. This means that, relative to the arrest rates of the population as a whole, Black people were over three times more likely than White people to be arrested. Asian people's rates were similar to those for White people.

Official statistics tell us the numbers of people arrested by the police. However, they are not necessarily a reflection of offending rates, as they could be seen, equally, as a comment on the actions of the police. If, as some sociologists argue, the actions of some police officers are partly motivated by racism, then the arrest rates reflect that, rather than offending rates by ethnic-minority groups.

A second point to remember is that offenders are most likely to be young males aged between 14 and 25. Any ethnic group with a high proportion of this age group within it will have relatively high arrest rates. The British 'Black' population does, in fact, have a high proportion of young males in this age group and we would therefore expect arrest rates to be higher. A similar demographic profile is emerging amongst 'Asian' British youth.

Finally, the more economically disadvantaged a particular social group is, the higher the crime rates. Once again, young Black British youths tend to be in worse-paid jobs and more likely to be unemployed than White or Asian youths.

### *Victimization studies*

Victim-based studies (such as the British Crime Survey) are gathered by asking victims of crime for their recollection of the ethnic identity of the offender. According to the British Crime Survey, the majority of crime is **intraracial**, with 88 per cent of White victims stating that White offenders were involved, 3 per cent claiming the offenders were Black, 1 per cent Asian and 5 per cent 'mixed'.

About 42 per cent of crimes against Black victims were identified as being committed by Black offenders and 19 per cent of crimes against Asians were by Asian offenders. The figures for White crimes against ethnic minorities are much higher – about 50 per cent, though this figure needs to be seen against the backdrop of 90 per cent of the population being classified as White.

Like official statistics, asking victims for a description of who committed the crimes is shot through with problems. For a start, only about 20 per cent of survey-recorded crimes are personal crimes (such as theft from the person), where the victims might actually see the offender. Bowling and Phillips (2002) argue that victims are influenced by (racial) stereotypes and 'culturally determined expectations' as to who commits crime. Certainly, research by Bowling (1999) indicates that where the offender is not known,

## Focus on research

### Waddington *et al.* (2004)
### Race, the police, & stop and search

Waddington, Stenson and Don were concerned at the way it has become accepted that members of minority-ethnic groups are unfairly stopped by the police. They therefore undertook research in Reading and Slough, two towns to the west of London. The researchers used a variety of methods. These included:

- direct non-participant observation of police officers, including watching CCTV footage
- detailed analysis of the official records of stop and search
- interviews with police officers about their stop and search activities.

The researchers argue that the evidence suggests that police officers do stop a proportionately high number of young members of ethnic-minority groups (and of White groups), but that these figures are in direct proportion to their presence in the central city areas and their likelihood to be out at night. Those groups who are most likely to be out in the evening in high crime areas are most likely to be stopped and, in these areas, young people – and particularly young members of ethnic-minority groups – are most likely to be out. They conclude that police stop and searches in the area they researched reflected the composition of people out on the streets, rather than any ethnic bias.

Waddington, P.A.J., Stenson, K. and Don, D. (2004) 'In proportion – race, and police stop and search', *British Journal of Criminology*, 44(6)

1. **Comment on the range of methods used by the researchers. Are there any other groups that might have been interviewed?**
2. **Explain how the researchers reached their conclusion that 'police stop and searches in the area they researched reflected the composition of people out on the streets, rather than any ethnic bias'.**

African-Caribbean origins having a four-times higher rate of arrest than Whites. Sociologists are split between those who argue that this reflects real differences in levels of offending and those who argue that the higher arrest rates are due to the practices of the police.

## A reflection of reality?

Sociologists all reject the idea that there is an association between 'race' and crime, in the sense that being a member of a particular ethnic group in itself has any importance in explaining crime. However, a number of writers (Mayhew *et al.* 1993) argue that most crime is performed by young males who come from poorer backgrounds. This being so, then there would be an overrepresentation of offenders from minority ethnic groups, quite simply because there is a higher proportion of young males in the ethnic-minority population than in the population as a whole. It is also a well-researched fact that minority ethnic groups overall are likely to have lower incomes and poorer housing conditions. These sociologists would accept that there is evidence of racist practices by certain police officers, but that the arrest rates largely reflect the true patterns of crime.

Phillips and Brown's (1998) study of ten police stations across Britain found that those of African-Caribbean origin accounted for a disproportionately high number of arrests. However, they found no evidence that they were treated any differently during the arrest process, with about 60 per cent of both Blacks and Whites and about 55 per cent of Asians eventually being charged.

## Racist police practices?

A second group of sociologists see the higher arrest rates as evidence of police racism. Within this broad approach there are a number of different explanations.

### *Reflection of society approach*

This approach, often adopted by the police, is that there are some individuals in the police who are racist, and once these 'bad apples' are rooted out, the police force will not exhibit racism. This approach was suggested by **Lord Scarman** (1981) in his inquiry into the inner-city riots of 1981. According to Scarman, the police reflect the wider society and therefore some racist recruits may join.

### *Canteen culture*

The 'canteen culture' approach (see Topic 8) argues that police officers have developed distinctive working values as a result of their job. Police officers have to face enormous pressures in dealing with the public: working long hours, facing potential danger, hostility from significant sections of the public, and social isolation. In response, they have developed a culture that helps them to deal with the pressures and gives them a sense of identity. The 'core characteristics' of the culture, according to Reiner (1992), include a thirst for action, cynicism, conservatism, suspicion, isolation from the public, macho values and racism.

Studies by Smith and Gray (1985), Holdaway (1983) who was himself a serving police officer at the time, and Graef (1989), all demonstrated racist views amongst police officers who, for example, held stereotypical views on the criminality of youths of African-Caribbean origin. Most importantly, it led them to stop and search these youths to a far greater extent than any other group. In fact, African-Caribbean people are six times more likely than Whites to be stopped and searched by the police.

### *Institutional racism*

The key point about institutional racism is that it is not necessarily intentional on the part of any particular person in the organization, but that the normal, day-to-day activities of the organization are based upon racist ideas and practice. This means that police officers might not have to be racist in their personal values, but that in the course of their work, they might make assumptions about young Black males and the likelihood of their offending that influence their attitudes and behaviour as police officers.

# Theorizing race and criminality

## Left-realist approach

Lea and Young (1993), leading writers in the left-realist tradition, accept that there are racist practices by the police. However, they argue that, despite this, the statistics do bear out a higher crime rate for street robberies and associated 'personal' crimes by youths of African-Caribbean origin. They explain this by suggesting that British society is racist and that young ethnic-minority males are economically and socially **marginalized**, with lesser chances of success than the majority population. Running alongside this is their sense of relative deprivation. According to Lea and Young, the result is the creation of subcultures, which can lead to higher levels of personal crime as a way of coping with marginalization and relative deprivation (see Topics 2 and 3 for a discussion of subcultures).

## Capitalism in crisis

A study by Hall *et al.* (1978) of street crime ('**mugging**') illustrates a particular kind of Marxist approach. According to Hall, the late 1970s were a period of crisis for British capitalism. The country was undergoing industrial unrest, there was a collapse in the economy and the political unrest in Northern Ireland was particularly intense. When capitalism is in crisis the normal methods of control of the population may be inadequate, and it is sometimes necessary to use force. However, using obvious repression needs some form of justification. It was in these circumstances that the newspapers, basing their reports on police briefings, highlighted a huge increase in 'mugging' (street robberies).

According to Hall, the focus on a relatively minor problem, caused by a group who were already viewed negatively, served the purpose of drawing attention away from the crisis and focusing blame on a scapegoat – young African-Caribbean males. This 'moral panic' (see Topics 4 and 9) then justified increased numbers of police on the streets, acting in a more repressive manner.

Hall's analysis has been criticized for not making any actual effort to research the motivations and thinking of young African-Caribbean males. What is more, the association between 'criminality and Black youth', made by the police and the media, has continued for over 25 years, and so it seems unlikely that this can be explained simply by a 'crisis of capitalism'.

## Cultures of resistance

A third approach overlaps with the Marxist approach just outlined. According to this approach, linked with Scraton (1987) and Gordon (1988), policing, media coverage and political debates all centre around the issue of 'race' being a problem. Minority ethnic groups have been on the receiving end of discrimination since the first migrants arrived, leaving them in a significantly worse socioeconomic position than the White majority.

In response to this, **cultures of resistance** have emerged, in which crime is a form of organized resistance that has its origins in the **anticolonial** struggles. When young members of minority ethnic groups commit crimes, they are doing so as a political act, rather than as a criminal act.

There are a number of criticisms of this approach. Lea and Young (1993) have been particularly scathing, pointing out that the majority of crimes are actually 'intraracial', that is 'Black on Black'. This cannot, therefore, reflect a political struggle against the White majority. Second, they accuse writers such as Scraton of 'romanticizing' crime and criminals, and thereby ignoring the very real harm that crime does to its victims.

## Exclusion and alternative economies

This approach integrates the previous approaches and relates quite closely to the work of Cloward and Ohlin (1960) (see Topic 2). A good example of this sort of argument is provided by Philippe Bourgois' study (2002) of El Barrio, a deprived area in East Harlem, New York. Bourgois spent seven years living and researching the street life and economy of El Barrio, whose inhabitants were overwhelmingly Puerto Ricans, illegal Mexican immigrants and African-Americans. Bourgois argues that the economic exclusion of these minority ethnic groups, combined with negative social attitudes towards them, has forced them to develop an 'alternative economy'. This involves a wide range of both marginally legal and clearly illegal activities, ranging from kerbside car-repair businesses to selling crack cocaine. Drug sales are by far the most lucrative employment: 'Cocaine and crack … have been the fastest growing – if not the only – equal-opportunity employers of men in Harlem'.

Running alongside this informal economy has developed a distinctive (sub)culture, which Bourgois calls 'inner-city street culture' – as he puts it:

> « *this 'street culture of resistance' is not a coherent, conscious universe of political opposition, but rather a spontaneous set of rebellious practices that in the long term have emerged as an oppositional style.* »

This subculture causes great damage because the illegal trade in drugs eventually involves its participants in lifestyles of violence, substance abuse and '**internalized rage**'. Many of the small-scale dealers become addicted and drawn into violence to support their habit. Furthermore, their behaviour destroys families and the community. The result is a chaotic and violent 'community', where the search for dignity in a distinctive culture leads to a worsening of the situation.

Although this is an extreme lifestyle, even for the USA, elements of it can help us to understand issues of race and criminality in the UK. Exclusion and racism lead to both cultural and economic developments that involve illegal activities and the development of a culture that helps resolve the issues of lack of dignity in a racist society. But both the illegal activities and the resulting culture may lead to an involvement in crime.

## Statistical artefact approach

The **statistical artefact** approach suggests that the higher levels of involvement of young males from an African-Caribbean background in crime is more a reflection of how the statistics are interpreted than of a genuinely higher level. Fitzgerald *et al.* (2003) researched ethnic-minority street crime in London, comparing crime rates against a wide range of socioeconomic and demographic data. They also interviewed a cross section of young, ethnic-minority offenders and their mothers, as well as running focus groups of 14 to 16 year olds in schools. The outcomes of the study were complex, but they throw light upon a number of the other explanations we have discussed so far. They reached the following conclusions:

- Street crime is related to levels of deprivation in an area, as well as to a lack of community cohesion, as measured by a rapid population turnover. This reflects crime levels in Britain as a whole, as we know amongst all ethnic groups that the higher the levels of deprivation in an area, the higher the levels of crime.
- The high rates of ethnic-minority offending were directly linked to the numbers of young, ethnic-minority males. Once again, all statistics point to young males as the highest offending group in the population, whatever their ethnic background. As there are higher proportions of young, ethnic-minority males in the population as a whole, and in London in particular, then we would expect there to be higher rates of crime committed by ethnic-minority males – if only as a reflection of the high percentage they form of all young males.
- There was a statistical link between higher crime levels and lone-parent families. African-Caribbean households are more likely to be headed by a lone parent, so there would be a statistical link here too.
- A subculture had developed amongst certain ethnic-minority children that provided justification for crime. This was very closely linked with school failure and alienation from school. However, similar views were held by White school-age students who were doing poorly at school or who were no longer attending. A disproportionate amount of all crime is performed by young, educationally disaffected children of all backgrounds.

In conclusion, therefore, Fitzgerald and colleagues suggest that there is no specific set of factors that motivates young, ethnic-minority offenders – they are exactly the same ones that motivate White offenders. However, the overrepresentation of young males from African-Caribbean backgrounds is partly the result of their sheer numbers in the age band in which most offending takes place.

# Key terms

**Anticolonial struggles** historically, Black resistance to Western attempts to control and exploit Black people.

**Cultures of resistance** the term used to suggest that ethnic-minority groups in Britain have developed a culture that resists the racist oppression of the majority society.

**Institutional racism** racism that is built into the normal practices of an organization.

**Internalized rage** term used by Bourgois to describe the anger and hurt caused by economic and social marginalization.

**Intraracial** within a particular ethnic group.

**Lord Scarman** in 1981 there were serious inner-city disturbances, particularly in Brixton in London. Lord Scarman led a government inquiry into the causes of these 'riots'.

**Macpherson Inquiry** Sir William Macpherson led an inquiry into the events surrounding the murder of Stephen Lawrence (allegedly) by White racists, and the subsequent police investigation.

**Marginalized** a sociological term referring to those who are pushed to the edge of society in cultural, status or economic terms.

**Mugging** a term used to describe street robbery. It has no status as a specific crime in England and Wales.

**Statistical artefact** the 'problem' emerges from the way that the statistics are collected and understood.

**Stop and search** police officers have powers to stop and search those they 'reasonably' think may be about to, or have committed, a crime; this power has been used much more against ethnic-minority youths than White youths.

## Check your understanding

1. What different interpretations are there concerning the arrest rates of members of ethnic-minority groups?
2. What do we mean when we say that the majority of crime is 'intraracial'?
3. Identify any two problems with the statistics derived from victimization studies.
4. What are self-report studies? Do they confirm the statistics derived from the arrest rates?
5. What two general explanations have sociologists put forward for the higher arrest rates of members of minority ethnic groups?
6. Explain the significance of the terms 'canteen culture' and 'institutional racism' in explaining the attitudes and behaviour of the police towards minority ethnic groups.
7. How do left-realist sociologists explain the relationship between ethnicity and crime?
8. What is the relationship between crises in capitalism and police action against 'muggers'?
9. What does the term 'culture of resistance' mean?
10. How can it be argued that the relationship between ethnicity and crime is a 'statistical artefact'?

# Activities

## Research idea

Your local police force will have an ethnic-minority liaison officer (or similar title). Ask the officer to come to your institution to talk about their work and, in particular, stop and search. Before the talk, get into small groups and sort out a list of questions – ideally, you should then email these to the officer to base their talk on.

## Web.tasks

1. The Ministry of Justice produces an online publication *Race and the Criminal Justice System*, which contains a wide range of up-to-date statistics. Explore the site and make your own mind up about the way that ethnic minorities interact with the criminal justice system. **www.justice.gov.uk/publications/raceandcjs.htm**
2. At the beginning of the topic, we discussed the image of Black youth presented by the media. Visit some of the websites of the main national newspapers. In the 'Search' box, key in terms such as 'Black youth', 'Asian youth', 'White youth', 'Gangs', 'Knife crime'. What picture emerges?

## An eye on the exam Ethnicity and crime

A detailed description of the view is required, using sociological concepts, theories and studies.

Weigh up the strengths and weaknesses of the view in some detail, then present alternative interpretations before reaching a balanced conclusion.

**Outline and assess the view that ethnic minorities are over-represented in criminal statistics. (50 marks)**

Avoid over-generalising – take into account ethnic diversity

This means that they appear more in criminal statistics than their numbers in the population would suggest

### Grade booster Getting top marks in this question

An explanation of the idea of over-represented (disproportionately high) is required at the beginning of this answer, along with some description of patterns of crime in relation to ethnicity. Be careful not to generalise – stress the fact that crime rates are different for different minority ethnic groups.

In fact, many sociologists agree that there is some over-representation of ethnic minorities in official crime statistics due to stereotyping and racism within the criminal justice system. Examples of these sociologists include Reiner on 'canteen culture' and the 'institutional racism' argument of the McPherson Report. Other sociologists accept that there may be over-representation in criminal statistics but also identify reasons why members of minority ethnic groups may be more crime-prone than other groups. These sociologists include left realists, Marxists and 'cultures of resistance' writers such as Gilroy.

Specific criticisms of the views above will be required in addition to a discussion of the view that ethnic minorities are no more prone to crime than any other group, but are simply over-represented in the social categories that are at high risk of offending – that is young, male and working class.

# TOPIC 8

# The social construction of crime and deviance

## Getting you thinking

It is important to understand the relationship between three different definitions of crime: the official, the media and the public definitions of crime. Each of these is socially constructed – each is produced by a distinctive social and institutional process.

The official definition of crime is constructed by the agencies responsible for crime control such as the police and the courts. This definition is the result of the rate of reported crime, the police response to crime and the way patterns and rates of crime are interpreted by judges and magistrates.

The media definition of crime reflects the selective attention of the news media to crime and the routines and practices of news gathering and presentation.

The public definition of crime is constructed by the public with little direct experience or expert knowledge of crime. This makes it very dependent on the other two definitions – the official and media definitions. The selective portrayal of crime in the mass media plays an important part in shaping public definitions of the 'crime problem', and hence its official definition.

Adapted from Cohen, S. and Young, J. (1981) *The Manufacture of News*, London: Constable

Perceptions of likelihood of victimisation and actual risk by individual crime type, 2008/09 BCS

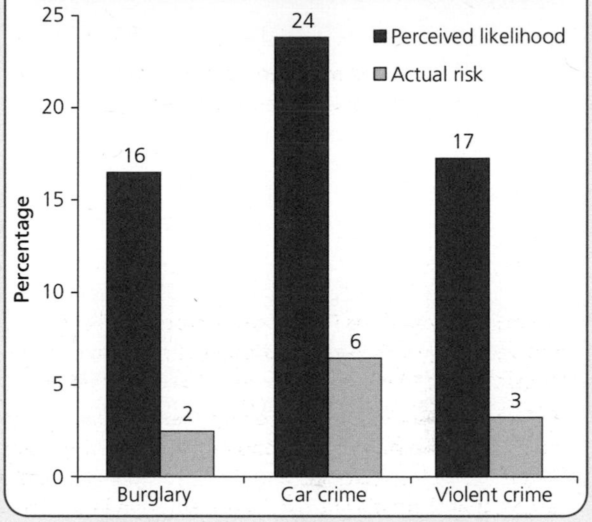


1. **Explain in your own words the differences between the three definitions of crime**
2. **What is the relationship between official, media and public definitions of crime?**
3. **What does the bar chart show about the relationship between public perceptions of risk of victimization and the actual risk of becoming a victim of crime?**
4. **How can the extract about the socially constructed definitions of crime help understand the pattern shown in the bar chart?**

The activity above shows that there is a complex relationship between the agencies of social control, media accounts of crime and deviance and public perceptions of the 'problem' of crime. These relationships are crucial to how we think about crime and deviance and illustrate the way in which crime and deviance are socially constructed. This topic deals with the role of the police, courts and the media in that process but the perspective that has been most influential in understanding the social construction of deviance is labelling theory - the subject of Topic 4. The specific ways in which official statistics of crime are socially constructed are discussed in Topic 1.

We can now move on to look in more detail at the three key agencies involved in the social construction of crime.

## The police

The main agency responsible for the enforcement of social control is the police force. This is the arm of the state whose role is to maintain public order and to enforce the law. In recent years, there have been considerable changes in the styles of policing.

### Styles of uniformed policing in Britain

Traditional 'beat' policing, in which one officer had a geographical area to control, was phased out in the 1960s and replaced by officers in cars who responded to reports of incidents. During the 1980s, on top of ordinary patrol cars, the police introduced a new form of policing in urban areas that involved larger groups of police officers in minibuses ready to respond to disturbances. By the turn of the century, these methods of policing were largely replaced by two approaches – neighbourhood policing and reactive policing:

- *Neighbourhood policing* – Dedicated teams of police and community support officers work in a geographical area. The aim is to get to know members of the community and to respond to their specific concerns. In reality, this means dealing with issues of antisocial behaviour.
- *Reactive policing* – Police respond to emergency calls from the public for help.

## The relationship of the police to society

Although there would appear to be relatively little controversy about these styles of policing, the changes over time have been explored theoretically by different sociological approaches. There are three main positions in understanding the relationship of the police to society: the consensual approach, the conflict approach and the late-modern approach.

### *The consensual approach*

A consensual approach sees the police as having a close relationship with the local area, and the role of the police force being to represent the interests of the majority of law-abiding people, defending them against the minority of offenders. Officers are drawn from the community and reflect its characteristics. Individual offenders are caught as a result of complaints made by the community. Neighbourhood and reactive policing reflect the balance of police work, which is responding to the specific and emergency needs of local communities.

### *The conflict approach*

A very different view of the police is provided by Scraton (1985), who argues that the police can best be seen as an occupying force, imposed upon working-class and ethnic-minority communities. Police officers largely patrol working-class and ethnic-minority areas, where they impose the law and order that reflects the interests of the more powerful groups.

According to Reiner (1997), those who are stopped and searched, or questioned in the street, arrested, detained in the police station, charged and prosecuted, are disproportionately young men who are unemployed or casually employed, and from discriminated-against minority ethnic groups. The police themselves recognize that their main business involves such groups, and their mental social maps delineate them by a variety of derogatory epithets: 'assholes', 'pukes', 'scum', 'slags', 'prigs'.

### *The late-modern approach*

This approach is the one we discussed earlier when we explored the changes in the development of community safety. Writers like Garland, Foucault, Cohen, and Feeley and Simon would all argue that the shift towards neighbourhood policing represents an extension of control over the population, with the police, as representatives of the state, integrating themselves in local communities.




## Discretion, policing and the law

It is the job of the police to enforce the law. However, there are so many laws that could be applied in so many different circumstances that police officers need to use their **discretion** in deciding exactly which laws to apply and in what circumstances. Sociologists have been particularly interested in studying the nature of such discretion, and in seeing the implications for different groups in society. Discretion can also provide evidence to support one or other of the (consensual or conflict) styles of policing we have just discussed.

Reiner (1992) has suggested three ways of explaining the basis of police discretion: individualistic, cultural and structural.

### *Individualistic*

The explanation for police discretion is that a particular police officer has specific concerns and interests, and thus interprets and applies the law according to them. Colman and Gorman (1982) found some evidence for this in

## Focus on research

### Hough and Roberts (2004)
### Perceptions of youth crime

Mike Hough and Julian Roberts conducted research on the public's attitudes to youth offending and the punishment of young people. They inserted additional questions into the Office of National Statistics Omnibus Survey (the ONS is a government department) which takes place every month (on a variety of subjects). Researchers have to buy a block of questions and Hough and Roberts bought a block of 30 questions. Government-trained interviewers then conducted interviews with 1692 people aged over 16. The block of questions took about 15 minutes to complete. The response rate was 67 per cent.

Hough and Roberts found that people have negative perceptions about youth and the youth justice system. People believe that **offending rates** are higher than they are in reality and that young people are unlikely to be punished.

Hough, M. and Roberts J.V. (2004) *Youth Crime and Youth Justice Public Opinion in England and Wales*, Oxford: Blackwell

**Suggest reasons why respondents believed that offending rates are higher than they really are.**

their study of police officers in inner London. In particular, they noted individual racist police officers who would apply the law more harshly on certain ethnic minorities.

### *Cultural*

New recruits enter a world that has a highly developed culture – evolved from the particular type of job that police officers must do. Police officers are overwhelmingly White and male. They work long hours in each other's company and are largely isolated from the public. The result of this is the development of a very specific occupational culture – sometimes referred to as a '**canteen culture**'. According to Skolnick (1966), this has three main components – and we can add a fourth suggested by Graef (1989): that of masculinity.

1. *Suspiciousness* – As part of their job, police officers spend much of their time dealing with people who may have committed a criminal offence. As part of their training, therefore, they are taught to discriminate between 'decent people' and 'potential troublemakers'. According to Reiner (1992), they categorize and stereotype certain people as 'police property'. This involves regarding young males, and particularly youths from ethnic minorities, as potential troublemakers.
2. *Internal solidarity and social isolation* – We have just noted how police officers spend large amounts of time in the company of their peers, isolated from the public. They also rely upon each other in terms of support in times of physical threat and when denying accusations from the public.
3. *Conservatism* – Those who join the police in the first place are rarely politically radical, and while the actual job of policing emphasizes a non-political attitude – police officers must uphold the law – it also upholds traditional values and the very nature of the state. Added to the factors of social isolation and the majority recruitment from White males, this generates a strong sense of conservative values.
4. *Masculinity* – Most police officers are male and drawn from the working class. The culture of police officers very much reflects traditional working-class values of heavy drinking, physical prowess and heterosexuality. Racial stereotyping is also heavily emphasized and linked with assuming the role of a police officer.

### *Structural*

A third approach, derived from Marxist theory, stresses that the very definition of law is biased in favour of the powerful groups in society and against the working class. Therefore, any upholding of the law involves upholding the values of capitalist society. Police officers' definition of crime in terms of street crimes and burglary (as opposed to white-collar or corporate crime) derives from their role as agents of control of a capitalist society. Their internal values simply reflect the job they have been given to do.

Evidence for this view can be found in Tarling's (1988) study, which showed that over 65 per cent of police resources are devoted to the uniformed patrolling of public space – particularly poorer neighbourhoods and central-city areas. The result is that, as Morgan and Russell (2000) found, about 55 per cent of prisoners in police custody were unemployed, and of the rest, 30 per cent were in manual, working-class jobs. Most detainees were young, with 60 per cent being under 25, and 87 per cent of all those arrested being male. Finally, over 12 per cent were from African or African-Caribbean backgrounds – despite these groups forming less than 3 per cent of the population (see Topic 7 for more on detail ethnicity and the police).

# The courts

Once a person has been caught by the police, the decision to press charges will be made by the Crown Prosecution Service and the person will then be taken to court. Less serious offences are judged in magistrates courts (presided over by magistrates) and serious crimes in Crown Courts (presided over by judges).

## Magistrates and judges

Magistrates are volunteers drawn from the local community and are meant to be representative of it. However, when Morgan and Russell (2000) explored the background of the magistrates, they found that, although there was an equal balance from either sex and that, overall, the magistrates reflected the ethnic divisions in the country, 40 per cent of magistrates were over retirement age and 70 per cent held, or had previously held, professional or managerial positions.

When it comes to the more senior judges, their background is overwhelmingly male, White and educated at Oxford or Cambridge Universities. However, for the last 10 years, there has been a significant increase in the proportion of female and ethnic-minority-background judges appointed. Nevertheless, in 2007, of all 3544 judges, 81 per cent were male, 19 per cent were female and 3.5 per cent came from an ethnic-minority background (Hansard 2008). Although the backgrounds of magistrates and judges do not have to reflect the population as a whole, critics have argued that, as they are drawn from such a narrow band of social backgrounds, they are unable to understand the situation of those they are judging – as offenders are overwhelmingly socially marginalized males, with a disproportionate number drawn from the ethnic minorities.

Discussion of gender, ethnicty and the courts can be found in Topics 6 and 7.

# The mass media

## The media

The role of the media in deviancy amplification has been discussed in Topic 4. Here we will focus on the idea of a moral panic. An important aspect of news production is the focus on particular types of news that result in moral panics. The media sometimes focus on certain groups and activities and, through the style of their reporting, define these groups and activities as a problem worthy of public anxiety and official censure and control.

## What is a moral panic?

The term 'moral panic' was popularized by Stanley Cohen (1972) in his classic work Folk Devils and Moral Panics. It refers to media reactions to particular social groups or particular activities that are defined as threatening societal values and thus create anxiety amongst the general population. This anxiety or panic puts pressure on the authorities to control the problem and discipline the group responsible. However, the moral concern is usually out of proportion to any real threat to society posed by the group or activity.

Cohen focused on the media's reaction to youth 'disturbances' on Easter Monday 1964. He demonstrated how the media blew what were essentially small-scale scuffles and vandalism out of all proportion by using headlines such as 'Day of Terror' and words like 'battle' and 'riot' in their reporting. Little time or interest was paid to what actually happened, which was a series of localized scuffles. Cohen argued that not only were the events overreported, but also the coverage awarded them far outweighed their importance.

He argues that the media tapped into what they saw as a social consensus – they assumed that decent law-abiding members of society shared their concerns about a general decline in the morality of the young symbolized by the growing influence of youth culture. Consequently, mods and rockers were presented and analysed in a distorted and stereotyped fashion as a threat to law and order, and the media attempted to impose a culture of control on them by calling for their punishment.

Goode and Ben-Yehuda (1994) note that the moral panic produces a 'folk devil' – a stereotype of deviance that suggests that the perpetrators of the so-called deviant activities are selfish and evil, and steps need to be taken to control and neutralize their actions so that society can return to 'normality'. However, the media also engages in a type of social soothsaying – they often adopt a disaster mentality and predict more problems if the problem group is not kept under surveillance or punished. This increases the social pressure on the forces of law and order to stamp down hard on the problem group.

Goode and Ben-Yehuda note the volatility of moral panics – this means they can erupt suddenly, although they usually subside or disappear just as quickly. Some are dormant but re-appear from time to time. However, the panic usually has some lasting effect – it may have raised public consciousness and, in extreme cases, may have led to changes in social policy or the law.

### *Binge-drinking*

Borsay (2007) notes that the moral panic that focused on binge-drinking in 2008 is very similar to one that gripped Britain in the early 1700s. He therefore argues that media, public and political concern about problem drinking is not new. He suggests that the parallels between the 18th-century gin craze and contemporary binge-drinking are striking. He argues that moral panics characterized both periods, fuelled by pressure groups, the media and perceptions of government complacency. He notes the media-constructed moral panics found in both eras were symbolic of wider anxieties about 'social breakdown'.

**Figure 2.11** Stages of a moral panic

Moral panics go through a number of stages, which some sociologists have termed a 'cycle of newsworthiness'.

**STAGE 1**

The tabloid media report on a particular activity/incident or social group using sensationalist and exaggerated language and headlines.

**STAGE 2**

Follow-up articles identify the group as a social problem. They are demonized as 'folk devils', i.e. the media give them particular characteristics, e.g. focused particularly on dress and behaviour which helps the general public and police to identify them more easily.

**STAGE 3**

The media oversimplify the reasons why the group or activity has appeared, e.g. young people out of control, a lack of respect for authority, a decline in morality.

**STAGE 4**

Moral entrepreneurs, e.g. politicians, religious leaders, react to media reports and make statements condemning the group or activity; they insist that the police, courts and government take action against them.

**STAGE 5**

The reporting of incidents to the police by the general public associated with the group or activity rises as the group or activity becomes more visible in the public consciousness.

**STAGE 6**

The authorities stamp down hard on the group or activity – this may take the form of the police stopping, searching and arresting those associated with the activity, the courts severely punishing those convicted of the activity or the government bringing in new laws to control the activity and group. Other institutions, e.g. shopping centres may ban the group or activity.

**STAGE 7**

The group may react to the moral panic, overpolicing, etc., by becoming more deviant in protest or the activity may go underground where it becomes more difficult to police and control.

**STAGE 8**

More arrests and convictions result from the moral panic and the statistics are reported by the media, thereby fulfilling the initial media prophecy or prediction that the group or activity was a social problem.

Borsey notes that the gin craze of the 1700s was finally brought under control with a combination of increased tax and licensing fees, along with restrictions on retail outlets. He concludes that:

> << *no doubt concerted action by the government and police could bring a similar end to binge-drinking today, but whether this would produce an overall drop in alcohol consumption and other social problems and a more disciplined and conformist youth remains questionable.* >>

### *Hoodies*

Fawbert (2008) examined newspaper reports about so-called hoodies between 2004 and 2008, and notes that there was only one article in the national papers in 2004 that used the word 'hoodie' to describe a young thug. However, a year later, the Bluewater Shopping Centre caused outrage by banning its shoppers from sporting hoodies and baseball caps. This was followed by Tony Blair vowing to clamp down on antisocial behaviour perpetrated by hoodies. The media seemed to seize on this and 'hoodies' became a commonly used term, especially between 2005 and 2007, to describe young people involved in crime. He notes that articles would often use the term in the headline, but there would be no reference in the story about whether the young criminal was actually wearing one, it was just presumed. Hoodies suddenly became a symbol of mischief, and sales of the clothing began to soar as young people realized by wearing them they upset people in authority.

**Figure 2.12** Examples of moral panics since the 1950s

| Period | Example |
|---|---|
| Mid-1950s | • teddy boys |
| 1964 | • mods and rockers |
| Late 1960s | • hippies smoking marihuana<br>• skinhead violence |
| Early 1970s | • football hooliganism;<br>• street crime, i.e. mugging |
| 1976/7 | • punk rock<br>• heroin addiction |
| Mid to late 1980s | • homosexuality and Aids (i.e. 'gay plague')<br>• illegal acid house raves<br>• hippy peace convoys<br>• video-nasties |
| Early to mid 1990s | • child sex abuse<br>• single-parent families, especially teenage mothers<br>• ecstasy use (post Leah Betts)<br>• children and violence (post Jamie Bulger)<br>• dangerous dogs |
| Mid to late 1990s | • welfare scroungers<br>• boys' underachievement in schools |
| 2002/3 | • paedophiles<br>• Black gun culture<br>• asylum seekers |
| 2004–9 | • hoodies, knife and gun crime<br>• binge-drinking |

## Focus on research

### Pampered prisoners

Yvonne Jewkes (2006) carried out a content analysis of British newspapers in order to find out how they reported the activities of inmates in British prisons. Jewkes suggests that there are various 'frames' through which prisoners are viewed. These are: celebrity prisoners, pampered prisoners, sexual relations in prison, lax security and, finally, assaults on prisoners. Of these five frames or themes, four of them involve giving the impression that prisoners lead easy lives in a relatively pleasant environment and only the fifth covers negative aspects of prison life. Jewkes argues that the majority of newspaper readers 'are looking for both confirmation of their existing views – which tend to be punitive – and for further opportunity to be shocked and outraged'. In order to get people to read their articles, therefore, the newspapers will reinforce these views. Jewkes's research is interesting as it partially supports Durkheim's argument that the law-abiding draw together in moral outrage at crime and this helps social cohesion (see Topic 2). The newspapers in her study help maintain high levels of moral outrage.

**1** **How are prisoners typically represented in the mass media?**

**2** **How do Jewkes' findings support Durkheim's arguments about the functions of crime and punishment?**

## Why do moral panics come about?

### *A reaction to rapid social change*

Furedi (1994) argues that moral panics arise when society fails to adapt to dramatic social changes and it is felt that there is a loss of control, especially over marginalized groups such as the young. He notes that in the 1950s and 1960s, British society experienced great social change as younger people acquired more economic and cultural power. This period particularly saw the emergence of distinct youth cultures such as teddy boys (1950s), mods, rockers and hippies (1960s). As a result, the older generation felt they were losing authority and control over the younger generation.

Furedi therefore argues that moral panics are about the wider concerns that the older generation have about the nature of society today – people see themselves (and their families) as at greater risk from a variety of groups. They believe that things are out of control. They perceive, with the media's encouragement, that traditional norms and values no longer have much relevance in their lives. Furedi notes that people feel a very real sense of loss which makes them extremely susceptible to the anxieties encouraged by media moral panics.

Young (1981) suggests that the media's anxiety about the behaviour of particular social groups originates in the consensual nature of the media in the UK today. Journalists assume that the majority of people in society share common values of reality, especially about what is acceptable and not acceptable. Generally, topics outside these so-called shared ideas are deemed wrong or detrimental. The media's focus on so-called problem groups is seen as newsworthy because journalists, editors and broadcasters assume that like-minded decent people share their moral concerns about the direction that society is taking. In this sense, the media believes that it is giving the public what it wants.

### *A means of making a profit*

Some commentators argue that moral panics are simply the product of news values and the desire of journalists and editors to sell newspapers – they are a good example of how audiences are manipulated by the media for commercial purposes. In other words, moral panics sell tabloid newspapers. However, after a while, news stories exhaust their cycle of newsworthiness and journalists abandon interest in them because they believe their audiences have lost interest too. The social problems, however, do not disappear – they remain dormant until journalists decide at some future date that they can be made newsworthy again and attract a large audience.

### *Serving ruling-class ideology*

Marxists such as Stuart Hall see moral panics as serving an ideological function. His study of the moral coverage of black muggers in the 1970s (Hall et al. 1978) concluded that it had the effect of labelling all young African-Caribbeans as criminals and a potential threat to White people. This served the triple ideological purpose of:

1 turning the White working class against the Black working class (i.e. 'divide and rule')
2 diverting attention away from the mismanagement of capitalism by the capitalist class
3 justifying repressive laws and policing that could be used against other 'problem' groups.

The notion that moral panics make it easier for the powerful to introduce control legislation that might be rejected by the general public under normal circumstances has attracted some support. For example, the moral panics aimed at the hippy peace convoys and rave culture that existed in the 1980s resulted in a law banning illegal parties and criminalized trespass. The latter law has since been used by the police to prevent demonstrations and workers' picketing their place of work. It can also be argued that both the installation of surveillance cameras in our city centres and greater film and television censorship are the direct consequences of the moral panic that developed out of the murder of the toddler James Bulger by two children.

### *A reflection of people's real fears*

Left realists argue that moral panics should not be dismissed as a product of ruling-class ideology or news values. Moral panics have a very real basis in reality, i.e. the media often identifies groups who are a very real threat to those living in inner-city areas – portraying such crime as a fantasy is naïve because it denies the very real harm that some types of crime have on particular communities or the sense of threat that older people feel. In other words, moral panics are probably justified in some cases.

## Conclusions

The study of moral panics has drawn our attention to the power of the media in defining what counts as normal and deviant behaviour and the effects of such media labelling on particular social groups. Most importantly, it reminds us continually to question our commonsensical understanding of crime, which is often underpinned by media reporting of crime. However, McRobbie argues that moral panics are becoming less frequent and harder to sustain today as those groups labelled as folk devils by the media can now effectively fight back through pressure groups and new social movements.

## Key terms

**Canteen culture** a term which refers to the occupational culture developed by the police.

**Discretion** the fact that the police have to use their judgement about when to use the force of the law.

**Folk devil** stereotype of deviants which suggests that the perpetrators of the so-called deviant activities are selfish and evil and therefore steps need to be taken to control and neutralize their actions so that society can return to 'normality'.

**Moral entrepreneurs** politicians, religious leaders, etc., who react to sensational media reports and make statements condemning the group or activity and insist that the police, courts and government take action against them.

**Moral panics** media reactions to particular social groups or particular activities which are defined as threatening societal values and consequently create anxiety amongst the general population.

**Socially constructed** produced by social processes.

## Check your understanding

1. How do the media affect public perceptions of crime and deviance?
2. Describe the different ways of looking at the relationship between the police and society.
3. Identify the components of the police occupational culture.
4. Why is an understanding of police discretion important?
5. To what extent do the social backgrounds of judges and magistrates reflect wider society?
6. According to Goode and Ben-Yehuda, what are the effects of (a) 'folk devils' (b) 'moral panics'?
7. Briefly explain one recent example of a moral panic.
8. Outline and explain two explanations for the existence of moral panics.

## Activities

### Research idea

1. Contact your local police and ask if an officer will come in to discuss policing in the local area. Prepare some questions based on the material in this topic.
2. Conduct a small-scale survey at your school or college aiming to find out students' attitudes towards the police.

### Web.tasks

Select one recent moral panic and use online searches to investigate newspaper coverage of that issue in the popular press. Does the coverage match the features of a moral panic?

## An eye on the exam The social construction of crime and deviance

A detailed description of the role of the police in the social construction of deviance is required, using sociological concepts, theories and studies.

Weigh up the role of the police in some detail, then present alternative ways in which crime and deviance are socially constructed before reaching a balanced conclusion.

**Outline and assess the role of the police in the social construction of crime and deviance. (50 marks)**

You will need to included a discussion of the role of the police in relation to gender, ethnicity and social class

This refers to the ways in which crime and deviance can actually created by society and the forces of social control

### Grade booster Getting top marks in this question

An introduction will need to include an explanation of the question, in particular of the idea of 'social construction' in this context. Then the answer can move on to discuss the ways in which police practices and discretion can play a part in the construction of crime. The functionalist view of Durkheim (Topic 1) that the police reflect common values can be contrasted with Marxist positions (see Topic 3). A discussion of relevant aspects of left and right realism could lead on to a discussion of styles of policing, along with different views of the relationship between the police and society and the ways in which police discretion can lead to stereotyping – material from Topic 6 on gender and Topic 7 on ethnicity (for example the idea of 'canteen culture') should be introduced. Analysis marks will be gained according to how well you can assess and link the different views you include.

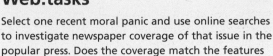

# TOPIC 9

# Solutions to the problem of crime

## Getting you thinking

### Big Brother UK: Police now hold DNA 'fingerprints' of 4.5m Britons

MORE THAN one million people's genetic fingerprints have been added to the police DNA database in only ten months. The 'Big Brother' system, already the biggest in the world, now permanently stores the details of more than 4.5 million individuals. The rise is the equivalent of 150 new entries every hour. The database now covers one in 13 of the population – around 7.5 per cent. In total, 6.5 million people are on the police fingerprint database

Although the database is a crime-fighting tool, producing around 3000 matches a month with samples taken from crime scenes, around a third of all the DNA stored is taken from individuals who were not charged with any offence, and have no criminal record.

Campaigners also fear unscrupulous government agencies could use the database to track political protesters, find out who they are related to, or to refuse jobs or visas to anyone considered 'undesirable'. They have demanded tougher safeguards including time-limits on storing data and an independent regulator.

The Home Office has repeatedly claimed the innocent have 'nothing to fear' from the growth of the database, which police cite as a key tool in modern crime-fighting. But critics fear the Government will eventually link the database to its plans for ID cards, and eventually move to make DNA sampling universal – an approach which civil liberties campaigners view as a nightmare scenario.

At this rate of growth, the database will double in size by 2011, with almost 10 million profiles stored.

Shami Chakrabarti, director of civil rights group Liberty, said: 'The DNA database has become a national disgrace, stuffed with innocent children and a disproportionate number of Black people.'

*Daily Mail*, 5 November 2007

**1** **What do you think about DNA testing – do you think that it is an attack on our civil liberties or a useful way to catch criminals?**

**2** **Would you willingly give your DNA profile to be stored by the police?**

**3** **Do you think that the government intrudes too much into our lives?**



The activity above should have made you think about the ways in which technology is being used to help solve crime while at the same time perhaps threatening our civil liberties. This topic will explore the nature of social control in Britain today and the various approaches to dealing with crime and deviance.

All of the main perspectives previously discussed in this chapter have implications for addressing crime and deviance.

## Functionalism

In Topic 2 we saw that Merton argued that crime and deviance can be a reaction to a mismatch between the goals valued by a society and the means that society provides to achieve those goals. So advertising and the rest of the media may encourage people to judge their success in terms of their wealth, consumer goods and so on. If society cannot provide fair means for achieving these goals then deviance can result. The implication here is that society needs to 'balance' itself by encouraging a wider range of goals and providing fairer opportunities for all. Policies which encourage community service might help change values while providing more opportunities for people in poorer areas and those from minority ethnic backgrounds may enable more people to feel they can succeed.

## Marxism

For Marxists (discussed in Topic 3), the root of all social problems lies in the unequal and exploitative nature of capitalist societies that punish and control the poor while enabling the rich to accumulate wealth without interference. The ultimate way to reduce crime would be to replace capitalism with socialism but, failing this, Marxists would favour policies that redistribute wealth in favour of poorer sections of the community and that clamp down on white-collar and corporate crime.

## Interactionism

Labelling theory sees the process of labelling by agents of social control as creating deviance and deviancy amplification (see Topic 4). Any policies that aim to reduce stereotyping by the police and other agents of social control, as well as the de-criminalization of certain behaviours such as drug taking, could reduce secondary deviance.

## Left realism

Realist approaches have a clear focus on policies to deal with crime and deviance (see Topic 5). From a left realist point of view, a more equitable distribution of wealth and opportunities would reduce relative deprivation and social exclusion. More sensitive neighbourhood policing would improve relationships between the police and young people and those from minority ethnic groups.

## The New Right

For New Right authors such as Murray (see Topic 5) the key to crime reduction lies in dealing with the so-called 'underclass'. This may be achieved by policies such as:

- encouraging traditional values in relation to marriage and families, for example providing tax breaks for married couples,
- adjusting welfare benefits so that young motherhood and unemployment are seen as a 'less attractive' option,
- making punishments more severe so they act as a deterrent to those considering crime and deviance.

## Right realism

The 'broken windows' theory of Wilson and Kelling and resulting 'zero tolerance' policies are described in Topic 5 and again later in this topic.

## Feminism

Policies aimed at protecting women from male violence and routine harassment are likely to be favoured by feminists (see Topic 6). The police need to prioritize the victimization of women in the form of domestic violence, sexual attack and harassment and to deal with these issues in a more sensitive manner. The law needs to do more to protect women.

Now we will move on to look in more detail at the issues of:

- Social control
- Crime prevention and community safety

# Social control

Most societies tend to have a mixture of informal and formal control mechanisms, but the balance depends upon the type of society. For example, smaller and less complex groups with strongly shared values might rely more upon informal methods, whilst large, complex and multicultural societies may have to rely more upon the use of specific organizations. In this section we explore approaches to understanding formal control in complex, contemporary societies.

## The functionalist perspective

Functionalist writers see the criminal justice system as operating to look after the interests of society as a whole. According to this approach, without control and punishment, society would collapse into a state of anomie. As we discussed in Topic 2 Durkheim (1893) believed that societies could only exist if the members shared certain common, core values, (the collective conscience). However, many other values exist too that have rather less general acceptance (ranging from ones generally accepted to those that are openly in dispute). Thus a system of law exists to mark an unambiguous boundary line, identifying actions that trangress the boundary of acceptance into behaviour generally regarded as so deviant as to be illegal. We also saw how the process of prosecution provides a constant means of checking whether the law reflects the views of the majority of society. The role of the law is therefore crucial both in reflecting a consensus and maintaining social solidarity.

For Durkheim, the type of punishment provided by the formal system of control reflects the type of society. In less complex, **mechanistic societies**, punishment is based on **retribution** – in which savage penalties are imposed upon the wrongdoer in order to demonstrate society's abhorrence at the breaking of the commonly shared values. The punishment will be both public and physical in nature – so people are executed, mutilated and branded.

As societies develop and become more complex (**organic societies**), then the punishment shifts away from public punishment to imprisonment, and the aim of the punishment is more to force the person to make amends for their wrongdoing. He called this '**restitutive** law'. This approach is reflected in recent policy innovations such as **restorative justice**, where offenders are made to take responsibility for their actions by listening to victims describe the impact of the crime and to do something to repair the harm they have caused.

## Marxist approaches

Marxist writers, take a very different view of the criminal justice system from functionalists. Writers such as Hall (Hall *et al.* 1978) and Chambliss (Chambliss and Mankoff 1976) argue that the criminal justice system operates solely for the benefit of the ruling class. The criminal justice system – police, judiciary and prisons – is based on controlling the working class and ensuring that any opposition to capitalism is quashed. Indeed, the law, according to Reiman (2006) is itself based upon outlawing certain acts performed by the working class, yet ignoring possibly more harmful acts performed by the ruling class.

Rusche and Kircheimer (1939) agree with the general Marxist argument that laws reflect the interests of the ruling class. However, they go further and argue that the forms of punishment also reflect their interests. As these interests change, so do the forms of punishment. Rusche and Kircheimer claim, for example, that slavery was an early form of punishment because of the need for manual labour, and that in feudalism the state used physical punishment as there was slightly less need for labour, but the peasants still needed to be repressed. With the arrival of capitalism, the prisons served the useful purposes of, first, training workers in the disciplines of long hours of meaningless work (for example, the treadmill) in poor conditions, and second, of mopping up the unemployed.

To support this argument, they pointed out that in times of high unemployment the prison population expands and then contracts in periods of high employment.

## Late-modern perspectives: combining formal and informal control

Late-modern writers provide rather more complex analyses of the criminal justice system and the forms of punishment. Their interests focus more on the changing forms of social control over time. Two writers are particularly well known within this tradition: Foucault and Stanley Cohen.

### *Foucault*

Foucault (1977) uses the term '**discipline**' instead of social control, as his explanation for the changing nature of control combines both informal and formal social control. Foucault argues that there have been key changes in the natures of discipline and punishment over the period of pre-modernity to late-modernity. In pre-modernity, social control was exercised through discipline imposed upon the body – public executions, flogging, cutting limbs and so on. These punishments were performed publicly so that people were frightened by the sheer pain they saw, but also dazzled by the 'majesty of the law' in action. The discipline or nature of formal social control by the state was haphazard and erratic. However, over time, and particularly in late modernity, the nature of discipline and punishment has become much more intertwined and subtle. In particular, Foucault argues, discipline took on two main characteristics:

**1** It became extended and diffused throughout society, no longer haphazard and erratic, with more and more agents of social control (police, PCSOs, wardens, antisocial behaviour coordinators, community safety officers, youth offending workers, and so on).

**2** It moved from being something physical, imposed via punishment upon individuals, to something subtle which people internalized in such a way that, increasingly, they police themselves. Instead of a central state seeking to control people through the threat of violence, the state seeks to control through the minds of the population. Examples of this include the cognitive therapy courses prisoners must do on 'controlling offending behaviour' and curbing violence.

Foucault suggests that the effect is such that people always feel that the state is watching them. For Foucault, these ideas are summarized in the design of a prison which was proposed in the mid-19th century (though never built in its pure form) in which prisoners would sit, isolated in their cells in a circular shaped prison which allowed the prison officer sitting in the centre of the prison to watch all the prisoners, but they were unable to see the officer. This meant that they never knew when they were being watched and, consequently, had to ensure that they always behaved as the prison wanted. Foucault called this form of prison the '**panopticon**'.

### *Cohen*

Stan Cohen, writing at about the same time (1985), provided a fairly similar analysis, summarizing his work into a number of key themes which explain the changing nature of formal control in Western societies.

- *Penetration* – Historically, societies had fairly simple forms of control, with the state passing a law which was then haphazardly enforced by whatever authorities existed at the time. However, Cohen argues that increasingly the law is expected to penetrate right through society, and that conformity and control are part of the job that schools, the media and even private companies are supposed to engage in. Social control has extended throughout society and is performed by many more agencies than in the past. Today, the police are only one of a wide range of 'enforcement agencies'. This leads to his second point.
- *Size and density* – Cohen points out the sheer scale of the control apparatuses in modern society, with literally hundreds of thousands of people working for the state and other organizations involved in imposing control – and over a period of time, millions having that control imposed upon them. For example, approximately one-third of all males under 30 have been arrested for a criminal offence. Cohen points out that the range of control agencies is increasing and 'processing' ever larger numbers of people. Furthermore, the criminal justice system is constantly extending its reach into the population by devising new 'social problems' which require ever more control by the state. A good example of this was the construction of the term 'antisocial behaviour' at the turn of 21st century. This drew a wide range of unrelated acts – such as young people hanging around, noisy neighbours, dropping litter, and prostitution – under the umbrella of antisocial behaviour. A new profession was then introduced to police these acts, that of the antisocial behaviour coordinator and each local authority is required by the government to have at least one of these officials.
- *Identity and visibility* – Cohen argues that control and punishment used to be public and obvious, but more recently there has been a growth in subtle forms of control and punishment. Closed-circuit TV (CCTV), tagging, legally enforceable drug routines for the 'mentally ill' and curfews are all part of an ever-growing and invisible net of control. He also notes that the state has handed over part of its monopoly of controlling people to private organizations. So there has been a growth in private security companies, doorstaff at nightclubs and even private prisons, all of whom exist to police people, but are not members of the police force.

# Crime prevention and community safety

## Situational crime prevention

Crime prevention, in the formal sense, developed from the writings of a group of criminologists, such as Clarke (1992) who focused on what has become known as '**situational crime prevention**'.

Clarke based his ideas on the deceptively simple notion that people will commit offences when the costs of offending (economic or social) are less than the benefits obtained from offending. However, unlike most previous criminologists who argued that the way to make the costs outweigh the benefits was to increase punishment, he argued that it was better to make it more difficult to steal or attack someone. For policy makers, this presented a range of new possibilities and they combined Clarke's ideas with those of an earlier writer, Oscar Newman. As early as the 1970s, Newman (1972) had introduced the idea of '**defensible space**', arguing that, by changing the design of streets and housing estates, it was possible to make them safer.

Situational crime prevention as a policy led to a wide range of initiatives. These included '**target hardening**', which involved making sure that it was more difficult to steal things, for example by improving locks on houses and windows, and by marking valuable objects with owners' postcodes in indelible ink, so that should they be stolen, they would be more difficult to sell. At the same time, areas with high levels of crime would have physical changes made in order to limit the opportunities for crime or benefits from it.

Critics of this approach, such as Garland (2001), have argued that it ignores the *causes* of crime, dealing only with limiting its extent and impact. Furthermore, critics argue, it leads to **crime displacement**, in which the type of crime, or the times of crimes or the place of crimes might all shift in response to the new measures. For example, CCTV may limit crime in areas where it is introduced, but crimes may rise outside this area.

## Community safety/crime reduction

Although situational crime prevention continues to be very influential, since the mid-1990s a rather broader approach, known as **community safety** (or **crime reduction**), has developed. This approach argues that alongside crime prevention measures, two other actions must happen:

1 *Intervention* – It is important to identify the groups most at risk of committing crime and to put into action forms of intervention to limit their offending.
2 *Community* – It is important to involve the local community in combating crime.

### *Intervention*

As we saw earlier with situational crime prevention, policy makers were not interested in the broader causes of crime, but rather with what worked to stop offending. The concept of 'what works' came to dominate thinking on offending in Britain and – influenced by realist approaches – the USA.

In Britain, the work of the Cambridge School of Criminology, for example Farrington (1995) and West (and Farrington 1973), was particularly influential. They took a **positivistic** research approach, using longitudinal studies in which they compared the backgrounds of young males who offended with those young males without any police record. They found clear differences between the two groups. Some of the main '**risk factors'** which were linked to early offending were:

- low income and poor housing
- living in run-down neighbourhoods
- high degree of 'impulsiveness and hyperactivity'
- low school attainment
- poor parental supervision with harsh and erratic discipline
- parental conflict and lone-parent families.

The implications of the research were that intervening to change some or all of these risk factors would lead to lower levels of crime. The importance of this was underlined by the claimed success of the Perry Pre-School Project in Michigan, USA. Two groups of African-American children aged 3 or 4 from disadvantaged backgrounds were chosen. One group was given pre-school educational support and the family received weekly visits from social workers. The results were dramatic. By the age of 27, members of the group which received the interventions had half the number of arrests of the group that did not receive interventions.

This risk-based model of offending has been – and still is – extremely influential. Governments in both the USA and Britain decided where possible to identify the children at risk of offending and to put various interventions in place. Indeed, it has been argued (Rodgers 2008) that many of the social policy interventions that have been introduced since 1998 – to combat poverty, to redevelop run-down housing estates, to improve schools and to support families – can be seen to be as much anticrime measures as social policies to improve the lives of the poor and marginalized.

### *Community*

Running parallel to the risk-based interventions are other policies that emphasize the importance of drawing upon the influence of the community.

Community approaches to crime reduction have been heavily influenced by the **broken windows theory** of the right realists Wilson and Kelling (1982). They argued that high levels of crime occur in neighbourhoods where there has previously been a loss of informal social control over minor acts of antisocial behaviour. They claim that if low-level antisocial behavior can be prevented (such as littering, noise, or youths blocking the pavements), then the escalation to more serious criminal acts can, in turn, be stopped. The analogy that Wilson and Kelling use is of an abandoned building. The point out that once one window gets broken, then all the windows soon get smashed. So, by preventing the breaking of the first window, all the rest are more likely to be saved. In a similar way, stop the minor crimes and the major ones are much less likely to happen.

The policy implications were that the government should find ways of strengthening local communities to 'fight' crime and antisocial behaviour. The ways chosen have been to introduce a range of legal powers through which the police and local authorities can issue antisocial behaviour orders, curfews, street drinking bans and dispersal orders (where you must leave a designated area of a town if a police officer tells you to do so). Exactly what is to be targeted as 'antisocial behaviour' depends upon local crime and antisocial perception surveys that local authorities have to carry out.

## Theoretical perspectives on community safety/crime reduction

### *Managing crime in the culture of control*

Garland (2001), in *The Culture of Control,* argues that the development in crime prevention and community safety just described is part of much wider shifts in the nature of the criminal justice system in late-modern societies. He provides a theoretical framework to explain these changes.

He suggests that the traditional method of dealing with crime, which he calls **penal welfarism**, has been overtaken by a much more complex model that is less concerned about *preventing* crime than *managing* crime by reassuring communities. Penal welfarism is the term Garland uses to describe how the criminal justice system in Britain sought to catch and punish offenders, but also to rehabilitate them so that they could be reintegrated in society. According to Garland, this approach has been seen as a failure by policy makers, as more than 60 per cent of those sent to prison reoffend.

Replacing this traditional model is the new '**culture of control**', which has two elements: adaptive and expressive. The point of both elements is to change society's attitude to crime and the role of the state in combating offending:

1 *The adaptive response* leads governments to identify certain groups that represent a danger to society and then to intervene in their lives at an early stage in order to change the way these risk groups think and act. Examples of this include Home Start, where volunteers help parents who are deemed to have problems, and family intervention projects where experts work with 'problem families'.
2 *The expressive strategy*, according to Garland, represents a complete change in the way that crime is viewed by society. Increasingly, he argues, crime has come to be seen as central to politics and to winning elections. It is more important to politicians to create the *perception* that crime is declining than to effect any real changes in the levels of crime. Therefore, much government intervention centres on changing perceptions rather than effective measures to limit crime.

### *Actuarialism*

Feeley and Simon (1992) have developed a similar analysis to that of Garland. They argue that a 'new penology' has developed in crime control. The criminal justice no longer operates on the basis of catching offenders in order to punish or rehabilitate them, but instead seeks to 'identify and manage unruly groups'. Feeley and Simon call this **actuarialism**. The term derives from the insurance industry, where the people who work out the chances of a particular event happening (and therefore the price to charge for insurance) are known as actuaries. Feeley and Simon argue that, in contemporary society, the stress of social control has changed from controlling deviant behaviour, to controlling potentially deviant people. Therefore, agencies of social control work out who is likely to pose the greatest risk of deviance and then act against them. The police patrol working-class and ethnic-minority areas, while the private security companies police the shopping developments, monitor people who enter and exclude the potential troublemakers – defined as the poor, the young and the homeless.

### *Penetration into society*

The final theoretical approach to understanding the growth of community safety has been provided by Foucault (1977) and, separately, by Stanley Cohen (1985). According to Foucault and to Cohen (see above), community safety policy is just one example of the way that governments seek to diffuse their power throughout the community. Public concern over crime allows governments to intervene in an ever-broader range of social activity, as new areas of social life, such as the family, the community and the school, are redefined as potential causes of crime.

### *Davis: control of space*

Davis, in the very influential book, *City of Quartz* (1990), studied Los Angeles and pointed out that there is an increasing division between the affluent, living in segregated and (privately) protected areas, and the areas lived in by the poorer majority. The role of the police is to contain the poor, segregating them in their ghettos.

# Key terms

**Actuarialism** Feeley and Simon's view that modern governments look for risk factors and then focus all their energies on the group(s) identified as most likely to commit crime (see Risk factors).

**Broken windows theory** the idea that if less serious crimes are allowed, more serious ones are likely to occur later.

**Community safety** refers to any preventive measure designed to stop crime from happening.

**Crime displacement** where effective crime prevention in one place has the unfortunate result of moving it elsewhere or onto different victims.

**Crime reduction** *see* **Community safety**.

**Culture of control** Garland claims that modern governments have given up trying to stop crime; they now merely wish to manage it and to manage people's attitudes towards it.

**Defensible space** architectural design that makes it more difficult to commit crime.

**Discipline** a term used by Foucault, merging the notions of formal and informal social control.

**Mechanistic societies** technologically and socially simple societies, as identified by Durkheim, in which people are culturally very similar.

**Offending rates** statistics referring to the number of crimes committed, and by whom.

**Organic societies** culturally and technologically complex societies, as identified by Durkheim, in which people are culturally different from each other.

**Penal welfarism** Garland's name for the traditional approach of the criminal justice system, which sought to punish and rehabilitate offenders.

**Panopticon** a design of prison in which the prisoners can be observed at all times, but never know whether or not they are being observed. The term is now used as a means of describing a society where this happens.

**Postitivistic** using natural scientific methods, adapted to sociology.

**Restitutive** a model of law based upon trying to repair the damage done to society.

**Restorative justice** approach to justice where offenders are made to take responsibility for their actions by listening to victims describe the impact of the crime and to do something to repair the harm they have caused.

**Retributive** a model of law based upon revenge.

**Right realism** approach to crime deriving from the rightwing theories of James Q. Wilson and emphasizing 'zero tolerance'.

**Risk factors** the family and social factors which are statistically most likely to predict future offending.

**Situational crime** prevention making it more difficult to commit crime and to benefit from it.

**Target hardening** ways of making objects more difficult to steal and people less likely to be victims.

**Underclass** term used by Charles Murray to describe a distinctive 'class' of people whose lifestyle involves taking what they can from the state and living a life involving petty crime and sexual gratification.

# Check your understanding

1. **According to Durkheim, how does the type of punishment vary between societies?**
2. **How do Rusche and Kirchheimer argue that forms of punishment reflect the interests of the ruling class?**
3. **What is 'discipline' and how does Foucault argue it has changed over time?**
4. **Explain the key concepts used by Cohen to explain the changing nature of social control.**
5. **Give two examples of crime prevention.**
6. **Briefly explain what is meant by the term 'community safety'.**
7. **What does Garland mean when he writes about the 'culture of control'?**
8. **Explain the term 'actuarialism'. Why is it different from traditional policing practices?**

# Activities

## Research idea

Conduct a small survey to find out young people's views about how best to address crime in Britain today.

## Web.tasks

1. Learn about the Criminal Justice System by going to: **www.cjsonline.gov.uk**
2. Go to the website of the Judiciary for England and Wales. There are a number of learning resources there. Try 'The Crime Survey Quiz' (and explain why it is biased), 'The Myth Busting Quiz' and 'Lifeline of Joe X' **www.judiciary.gov.uk/learning_resources/index.ht**
3. Search online for the policies on crime and justice of the main political parties. What are their views? Do their policies relate to any sociological perspectives?

## An eye on the exam Solutions to the problem of crime

A detailed description of the various solutions is required, using sociological concepts, theories and studies.

Weigh up the strengths and weaknesses of each solution in some detail before reaching a balanced conclusion.

**Outline and assess solutions to the problems of crime and deviance. (50 marks)**

This refers to the various attempts that have been made to reduce the amount of crime and deviance

It is worth considering this concept: a problem in what way? For whom?

### Grade booster Getting top marks in this question

The implications of left and right realism need to be discussed, especially their relationship to social policies such as neighbourhood policing and zero tolerance. Broader theories are also relevant here. Functionalists such as Merton see the need for societies to ensure that the aspirations of their members are realistic, Marxists argue strongly for the need to end capitalism while interactionists focus on ending stereotyping and the criminalization of certain groups. In fact, most key writers and theorists have something to say about how to deal with crime and deviance so you will need to plan this answer very carefully.

The different theories will need to be evaluated, compared and contrasted.

## Exam Practice

**Outline and assess sociological explanations of the relationship between social class and crime.** ***(50 marks)***

Social class is an issue which has a wide impact on everyone in society, including in relation to crime. Many sociological perspectives look into the link between the lower classes and crime, one of which is functionalism. One functionalist in particular who looks into this is Merton. After studying patterns of class and crime, Merton developed strain theory. This states that everyone in society wants to achieve the same goals, however for the lower classes this is more of a struggle. Therefore they experience a strain between socially achievable goals and socially acceptable means of achieving them. There are five ways Merton sees the lower classes as reacting to this. The first is conformity, whereby people continue to strive for the goal, despite the highly limited likelihood that it will be achieved. Another is ritualism whereby the person works but is under-motivated and therefore reaps less of the rewards e.g. bonuses and there are also retreatism whereby the person gives up and is no longer involved in society, for example alcoholics and rebels who reject the means and goals of society and want to change these. The final is innovators, who Merton sees as finding new ways to achieve the goals, which is how he explains criminal behaviour. Whilst Merton's strain theory has been very influential, it has also experienced high levels of criticism. Some sociologists argue that stating there is a value consensus is not true, and that people's values are individual. It is also criticised for only explaining crime as a reaction to structural strain, ignoring other reasons, such as for thrills. Another criticism is the over-emphasis on working class crime and ignoring other types of crime.

Is there an introduction here? If so, it consists of the first sentence which does not contribute much to the essay. This is a shame as an introduction would have been an appropriate place to explain how most of the classic theories on crime can be applied to the issue of class and crime.
The account of Merton is adequate but fails to spell out how the 'innovation' response leads to criminal activity. The influence of Merton is referred to but this point would have had far more impact if one or two examples were provided e.g. his influence on subcultural theorists and Bourgois. The last few sentences evaluate Merton – it is a very good idea to evaluate as the essay progresses as a significant proportion of marks are available for this skill. However, the point should have been made that Merton was writing in the 1930s.

Other theorists who place a high emphasis on working-class crime are left realists. They have three key concepts in relation to crime: relative deprivation, marginalisation and subcultures. Relative deprivation can be a cause of crime as blatant class divides can cause resentment leading to the working class committing crime in order to get what the upper classes have. One recent example of this is the working classes purchasing of 'Burberry' items, previously known as a brand specifically worn by the wealthiest members of society. Marginalisation refers to how the poorest people are on the edge of society and experience the worst economic, social and political positions, also leading to resentment. The final key point is subcultures, which left realists see as forming as a result of the relative deprivation and marginalisation, in order to show resistance to society. The combination of all these points is seen to lead to crime, in particular street crime and burglary. However left realism has been criticised for failing to explain the precise causes of street crime as well as failing to explain why not everyone who experiences relative deprivation and marginalisation turn to crime. As with functionalism, they are seen by some to place too higher emphasis on working-class crime and ignore corporate crimes.

Left realism is a very relevant theory to include and three key concepts of this theory are identified although examples of each could have been further developed in terms of the wording of the question. The introduction of contemporary examples is good practice as it shows the examiner you are using your subject knowledge to understand the social world. However, the reference to Burberry is not that effective as its link to the idea of relative deprivation is not clear – is the essay suggesting that working-class people need to steal Burberry items!

From the age of four or five, for six or so hours per day, over a period of at least 11 years, young people are bombarded with a vast amount of knowledge, attitudes and skills. These may be acquired in formal lessons or informally through what is known as the **hidden curriculum** – the accidental or deliberate messages communicated by schools through rules, organization and the behaviour of teachers and students. By the time they finish compulsory education, most pupils will have spent over 15 000 hours in lessons. It is no surprise that sociologists see the education system in modern societies as a really important agent of socialization.

The introductory activity should have provided you with some ideas about the sorts of attitudes and values communicated by the hidden curriculum. Competition, discipline and respect might have featured among your answers. Do these values benefit everyone or are they about controlling young people so they can be more easily exploited in later life? As you can probably guess, different sociological perspectives will take very different positions on this and these contrasting ideas are discussed later in this topic.

Students achieve very differently in education – there is certainly not **equality of outcome** – but does our education system provide **equality of opportunity**, in other words, are the chances of success the same for every student? Is education like the running race shown in the photograph above where the most talented are the most successful or is achievement closely linked to social characteristics such as class, ethnicity and gender? Unsurprisingly sociologists disagree about this too and the debate between different perspectives on this issue provides a key theme that runs throughout this chapter.

The question above relating to the control of schools reflects another key debate of the last 25 years – what is the most effective way to organize the education system? Is the best way of improving standards to encourage **marketization** – that is, to allow schools to compete with each other so the best get larger whilst the least successful have to improve, close or be taken over? And who should control schools? Do teachers and the government have too much say? Should employers be able to dictate the curriculum so that subjects and lessons are more closely linked to the world of work (the subject of Topic 5)? And what about students and parents? After all, they are the 'consumers' of education. Should there be a **parentocracy**, where parents have control of their local schools?

The debate about the best way to organize the education system and about the effects of recent government policies is the subject of Topic 6.

In 2009 Britain spent over £80 billion on education. Why do modern societies invest so much in schooling the next generation? Sociologists agree that education is important, both in teaching skills and knowledge and in encouraging certain attitudes and values, but they disagree about why this occurs and who benefits from it. We now move on to look at the different perspectives on these issues.

## Functionalist approaches

Functionalists argue that education has three broad functions:

1 *Socialization* – Education helps to maintain society by socializing young people into key cultural values, such as achievement, competition, **equality of opportunity**, social solidarity, democracy and religious morality. Durkheim was particularly concerned that education should emphasize the moral responsibilities that members of society had towards each other and the wider society. In his view, the increasing tendency towards **individualism** in modern society could lead to too little social solidarity and possibly anomie (a state of normlessness or lack of shared norms). This emphasis can be seen today through the introduction of citizenship and the maintenance of religious education as compulsory subjects. Parsons also recognized the social significance of education. He suggested that it forms a bridge between the family and the wider society by socializing children to adapt to a **meritocratic** view of achievement. In the family, **particularistic standards** apply – a child's social status is accorded by its parents and other family members. However, in wider society, **universalistic standards** apply – the individual is judged by criteria that apply to all of society's members. Education helps ease this transition and instil the major value of achievement through merit.

2 *Skills provision* – Education teaches the skills required by a modern industrial society. These may be general skills that everyone needs, such as literacy and numeracy, or the specific skills needed for particular occupations. As the division of labour increases in complexity and occupational roles become more specialized, increasingly longer periods in education become necessary. The need for an increasingly skilled workforce is reflected in many aspects of education. It is why politicians are so concerned about the teaching of numeracy and literacy in primary schools, why the school leaving age has been rising throughout recent years and why so many new vocational courses such as **Diplomas** have been introduced.

3 *Role allocation* – Education allocates people to the most appropriate job for their talents, using examinations and qualifications. This ensures that the most talented are allocated to the occupations that are the most functionally important for society. This is seen to be fair because there is equality of opportunity – everyone has the chance to achieve success in society on the basis of their ability. Davis and Moore (1945) argue that societies need to ensure that the most talented people occupy the most important positions. In modern societies, education plays a key role in this process.

## Criticisms of functionalist approaches

Functionalist approaches have come under attack in recent years.

1 As modern societies have become more complex many sociologists recognize an increasing diversity of values rather than the shared values described by functionalists. For example, ethnic diversity has brought

with it a range of values in relation to gender, religion and the family for example.

2 Marxists have suggested that the values and skills passed on through the education system favour the rich and powerful rather than society as a whole. For example, the emphasis on conformity and discipline in schools encourages people to be passive and accept authority in later life, while the emphasis on skills for employment directly benefits the capitalist class by providing them the workers they require to maximize their profits. More details of Marxist approaches are provided below.

3 British society is still a long way from the meritocracy described by functionalists such as Parsons and Davis and Moore. Social class remains a massive influence on educational achievement and gender and ethnicity also play a significant role in students' patterns of attainment. These influences are discussed in detail in Topics 2, 3 and 4.

## Marxist approaches

For Marx, education is seen as an important part of the superstructure of society. Along with other institutions (e.g. the mass media, family, religion and the legal system), it serves the needs of the economic base, which contains everything to do with production in society (bosses, workers, factories, land and raw materials). This base shapes the superstructure, while the superstructure maintains and justifies the base (see Fig. 3.1).

For Marx then, education performs two main functions in capitalist society:

1 It reproduces the inequalities and social relations of production of capitalist society.
2 It serves to legitimate (justify) these inequalities through the myth of meritocracy.

The neo-Marxist Althusser (1971) also disagrees that the main function of education is the transmission of common values. He argues that education is, rather, an ideological state apparatus (ISA). Its main function is to maintain, legitimate and reproduce, generation by generation, class inequalities in wealth and power, by transmitting ruling-class or capitalist values disguised as common values. Along with other ISAs, such as the media and the legal system, education reproduces the conditions needed for capitalism to flourish without having to use force, which would expose it as oppressive. Instead, **ideology** gets the same results exerting its influence subconsciously. Althusser argues that

## **Focus** on **research**

### The British Cohort Study – evidence on education and social mobility

The British Cohort Study is a longitudinal piece of research which takes as its subjects all those living in England, Scotland and Wales who were born in one particular week in April 1970. Data were collected about the births and families of just under 17200 babies; since then, there have been five more attempts to gather information from this group. With each successive 'sweep', the scope of enquiry has broadened and it now covers physical, educational, social and economic development.

Data have been collected in a variety of ways. In the 1986 research, 16 separate methods were used, including parental questionnaires, school-class and head-teacher questionnaires and medical examinations. The sample completed questionnaires, kept two diaries and undertook some educational assessments. In both 1975 and 1980, immigrants to Britain who were born in the target week in 1970 were added to the sample. Over the period of the research, the sample has reduced to 15500.

Jo Blanden, Paul Gregg and Steve Machin have used data from The British Cohort Study to compare the life chances of British children with those in other advanced countries, and the results are disturbing. In a comparison of eight European and North American countries, Britain and the United States have the lowest social mobility (movement between classes). Social mobility in Britain has declined, whereas in the USA it is stable. Part of the reason for Britain's decline has been that the better off have benefited disproportionately from increased educational opportunity

Comparing surveys of children born in the 1950s and the 1970s, the researchers went on to examine the reason for Britain's low, and declining, mobility. They found that it is partly due to the strong and increasing relationship between family income and educational attainment.

For these children, additional opportunities to stay in education at age 16 and age 18 disproportionately benefited those from better-off backgrounds. For a more recent group born in the early 1980s, inequality of access to higher education has widened further: while the proportion of people from the poorest fifth of families obtaining a degree has increased from 6 per cent to 9 per cent, the graduation rates for the richest fifth have risen from 20 to 47 per cent.

Sources: Blanden, *et al.* (2005); The Centre for Longitudinal Studies (www.cls.ioe.ac.uk)

1 **Explain how the British Cohort Study is a longitudinal piece of research.**

2 **Suggest reasons why the sample size was increased in 1975 and 1980.**

3 **What reasons might there be for the reduction in sample size over the period of the study?**

4 **What does this research by Blanden *et al.* tell us about the functionalist view of education?**

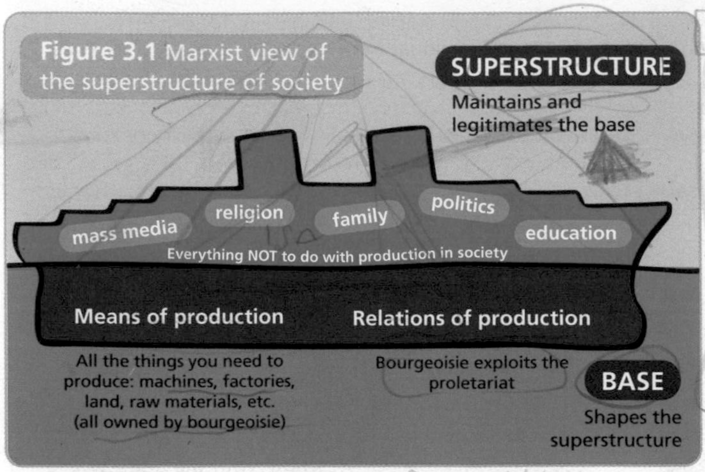

**Figure 3.1** Marxist view of the superstructure of society

this is done through the hidden curriculum: the way that schools are organized and the way that knowledge is taught means that working-class people are encouraged to conform to the capitalist system, and accept failure and inequality uncritically.

Bourdieu (1977) has called the means by which the working classes are effectively duped into accepting their failure and limited social mobility as justified, 'symbolic violence'. Their cultural attributes are rejected because the system is defined by, and for, the middle classes who, in turn, succeed by default rather than greater ability. Their cultural assets are seen as worthy of investment and reward and hence have greater value as **cultural capital**. This is discussed more fully in the next topic.

## Correspondence theory

Bowles and Gintis (1976) argue that education serves to reproduce directly the **capitalist relations of production** – the hierarchy of workers from the boss down – with the appropriate skills and attitudes. Education ensures that workers will unquestioningly adapt to the needs of the system. Bowles and Gintis's '**correspondence theory**' suggests that what goes on in school corresponds directly to the world of work. Teachers are like the bosses, and pupils are like the workers, who work for rewards (wages or exam success). The higher up the system the individual progresses, however, the more personal freedom they have to control their own educational or working experiences, and the more responsibility they have for the outcomes.

Bowles and Gintis point out, however, that success is not entirely related to intellectual ability. Those pupils who fit in and conform, rise above those who express attitudes or display behaviour which challenge the system. Bowles and Gintis go as far as to say that this is irrespective of ability, some of the most creative and talented being among the latter group. Schools, therefore, reproduce sets of workers with the appropriate ways of being for the position that they come to occupy. This explains why White middle-class pupils tend to do better whatever their ability. The education system disguises this injustice through the myth of meritocracy, whereby those denied success blame themselves rather than the system. The hidden curriculum of the school not only reproduces the relations of production, it makes inequality in society appear legitimate and fair.

## Criticisms of Marxist approaches

Many writers have criticized Bowles and Gintis for their failure to recognize a lack of correspondence between schools and the needs of the economy, in particular in terms of the content of the formal curriculum. Reynolds (1984) claims that the curriculum does not seem designed to teach either the skills needed by employers or uncritical passive behaviour that makes workers easy to exploit. He points out that the survival of liberal humanities-based subjects and limited emphasis on science and applied knowledge suggest a lack of correspondence. How, for example, can Sociology itself be such a popular A-level subject if schools and colleges are all about developing unthinking workers?

Employers are highly critical of the low level of employability skills possessed not only by school leavers, but even graduates. Brown (1997) points out that modern businesses require shared creativity and teamwork. However, the exam system in which people are judged and compete with one another as individuals discourages the development of these skills.

Furthermore, numerous studies show that many pupils have little regard for the rules of the school, and little respect for the authority of the teacher. Paul Willis's research *Learning to Labour* (1977) showed that working-class 'lads' learned to behave at school in ways quite at odds with capitalism's supposed need for a docile workforce. Willis, however, supported the principle that schools reproduce the relations of production by demonstrating that the boys in the antischool subculture he observed, shared a similar outlook to the workers in the factories they were likely to end up in. They accepted the inevitability of educational failure and so developed strategies ('having a laff') to deal with the boredom of school which would also serve them well in the boring jobs they were destined for.

While the work of Bowles and Gintis has been criticized for failing to live up to its claims of direct correspondence on a number of levels, recent developments are causing some writers to revisit their work. For example, the freedom of teachers has been restricted by the introduction of a national curriculum, and education has become more explicitly designed to meet the needs of employers – not only in curriculum terms, with the introduction of more vocational education such as BTECs and the Diplomas, but also through the influence of the work-oriented ethos characteristic of many **specialist schools** and **academies**. Employers also have more direct say in the organization and curriculum of such schools. These issues are more fully discussed in Topics 5 and 6.

# Interactionist approaches

The close and detailed observations of Willis serve to remind sociologists that it is important to move beyond the theorizing of many Marxists and functionalists to look at what actually goes on in schools. In this sense, Willis is influenced by interactionist perspectives (see Chapter 1). Interactionist sociologists focus on small-scale interaction in the classroom. They study the relationships between pupils themselves and between pupils and teachers rather than making the broad generalizations about the education system favoured by Marxists and functionalists.

Key concepts for interactionists are **labelling** and stereotyping. For example, teachers may hold stereotypes about certain groups of pupils and these stereotypes lead them to treat different groups in different ways. This treatment affects the way pupils see themselves – their **self-concepts** – and this can have positive or negative effects on their educational progress and self-esteem. For example, Gillborn (1990) has shown how teachers' stereotypical beliefs can cause them to interpret the behaviour of African-Caribbean behaviour as 'unruly' and that this 'label' can cause those boys to 'live up' to that label.

## Criticisms of interactionist approaches

Interactionist approaches have been criticized in a number of ways.

- Often interactionist research is based on small-scale studies of classrooms. Data collected by this type of research is based on small samples and cannot be checked, so its reliability and representativeness have been questioned.
- Interactionists' emphasis on the negative effects of labelling give the impression that only one type of response is possible to teacher labelling. In fact many pupils may want to prove their teachers wrong and increase their efforts as a result of labelling.
- The focus on classroom processes has left interactionists vulnerable to the criticism that they ignore wider issues of power and inequality in society. In other words, they ignore 'the big picture' of social structure which provides the context in which classroom processes operate and which influences the actions of both pupils and teachers.

More detail and more examples of interactionist approaches can be found in Topics 2, 3 and 4.

Unlike interactionism, the final two approaches discussed in this topic – social democratic and the New Right – look at the education system as a whole. They have both been influential in the development of educational policies since the Second World War and the specific details of their influence are discussed in Topic 6.

# Social democratic approaches

In two key ways, social democratic approaches to education resemble those of functionalists.

1. Like Davis and Moore, social democrats see education as the key method by which modern societies can provide the equality of opportunity necessary to create a meritocratic society where the most important positions are filled by the most talented people, regardless of their social class, gender, ethnicity or any other characteristic.
2. As societies become more complex, education needs to expand and develop to make sure that the next generation are equipped with the appropriate skills knowledge and attitudes to create economic growth and increase wealth.

Unlike many functionalists however, social democrats believe that inequalities in society prevent the kind of meritocratic society based on equality of opportunity described above. If poverty or racism, for example, prevents an individual from having the same chances as those from more privileged backgrounds, then this is not helping create a meritocracy and the government should take measures to bring about greater equality of opportunity. Similarly, governments need to keep spending high on education and to ensure that this spending is used by schools and colleges to develop the knowledge and skills needed for economic growth.

## Criticisms of social democratic approaches

Social democratic approaches have been criticized by both Marxists, who believe that social democrats are not radical enough, and by the New Right, who believe that they are too radical.

Marxists believe that 'tinkering' with the education system will not threaten the dominance of the capitalist class so will not help bring about genuine equal opportunities in society.

The New Right believe that there is not necessarily a link between high expenditure on education and economic growth. For example, Woolf (2002) argues that Switzerland spends relatively little on education but is still one of the most wealthy countries in the world. Also, the New Right do not believe that spending on education is always used efficiently. Often the views of the 'consumers' of education – pupils, parents, businesses – are ignored and power ends up in the hands of educational professionals and government officials. This leads on directly to their own ideas regarding the organization of education.

# New Right approaches

New Right thinkers believe that the education system should operate on the same principles as the market for goods and services. Individuals and their families should be able to make choices about education in the same way as they make choices about soap powder and clothes. In this way schools will have to respond to what consumers want and more resources will go to the most successful in attracting 'customers'. The least successful will have to improve, shut or be taken over by the more successful. A market-led system will make education more accountable and save taxpayers' money. To make all this work, parents will need information about the quality of schools so students will need to be tested on a regular basis and the results made freely available.

## Criticisms of New Right approaches

Market-led approaches lead to greater inequalities. Middle-class parents are more able to manipulate the system and use their cultural capital to get the best education for their children. Ball *et al.* (1994) illustrate this process (see Topic 2).

Schools want to appear successful in 'league tables' so there is a temptation for over-subscribed schools to select the best pupils, leaving others to attend less successful schools. What is more, in order to get the best test results teachers end up 'teaching to the test' and ignoring the broader education of their pupils.

More details about the influence of social democratic and New Right approaches on recent educational policies can be found in Topic 6.

# Key terms

**Academies** type of secondary school partly sponsored by an organization such as a business and partly funded by central government. Academies have more control than other state schools over what they teach and how they teach it.

**Capitalist relations of production** how members of the workforce are organized in relation to each other under capitalism. (In capitalist industrial societies, this is usually hierarchical, with a few at the top making all the decisions and giving out orders, while the majority do what they are told.)

**Correspondence theory** Bowles and Gintis's theory that various aspects of economic production (work) have corresponding features in the education system.

**Cultural capital** cultural skills, such as knowing how to behave, speak and learn, passed on by middle-class parents to their children. These skills give middle-class pupils educational advantages.

**Equality of opportunity** every person having the same chances.

**Equality of outcome** Every person achieving the same level.

**Hidden curriculum** the informal learning of particular values and attitudes in schools.

**Ideology** a set of interconnected ideas that serve the interests of a particular group.

**Individualism** the belief that individuals are far more important than social groups.

**Labelling** treating an individual or group on the basis of a stereotype.

**Marketization** organizing education according to supply and demand.

**Meritocracy** system where people are rewarded on the basis of ability and talent.

**Parentocracy** control by parents.

**Particularistic standards** judgements based on the exclusive views of a particular group.

**Schooling** the process of compulsory education.

**Self-concept** the way we see ourselves.

**Specialist schools** schools that have a particular focus within their curriculum and links to specialist areas of work, e.g. arts and media, business, languages, healthcare and medicine. They can select 10 per cent of their intake on the basis of ability.

**Universalistic standards** standards that apply to all members of society.

# Check your understanding

1 Explain the difference between equality of outcome and equality of opportunity.

2 According to functionalists, what are the main functions of schools?

3 For functionalists, what is the role of education in creating a meritocracy?

4 What does Althusser consider to be the main purpose of education, and how is it achieved?

5 Why do you think the theory of Bowles and Gintis is sometimes called 'correspondence' theory? Give examples.

6 Why, according to Bowles and Gintis, do White, middle-class pupils do better in education?

7 How does Willis's work appear to support the views of Bowles and Gintis?

8 In what ways might it be claimed that Bowles and Gintis' theory has relevance today?

9 What is the key difference between interactionist approaches and those of Marxism and functionalism?

10 Contrast the approach taken to education by social democratic and New Right thinkers.

# Activities

## Research idea

1 Interview a range of your teachers. Ask them to explain the values which they consider are encouraged by the following aspects of school organization and routine: assemblies, sports days, school uniform, registration, house competitions, school rules, prefects, detention.

Evaluate the extent to which their responses subscribe to functionalist, Marxist, interactionist, social democratic or New Right views of education.

2 Organize a small research project to discover what people consider to be the primary purpose of education. Compare class, gender and age patterns in terms of the extent to which the wider social purposes are recognized. Which groups see school as most beneficial to individuals – for example, as helping someone to get a better job?

## Web.tasks

Search for government educational policy documents and statements at www.education.gov.uk. What are the government's stated aims? How do these aims relate to the sociological views you have been introduced to in this chapter?

## An eye on the exam — The role and function of education in society

A detailed description of functionalist explanations is required

Weigh up the strengths and weaknesses of functionalist explanations in some detail, then present alternatives before reaching a balanced conclusion

**Outline and assess functionalist explanations of the role and function of education in society. (50 marks)**

Other theories only need to appear as part of an evaluation of functionalist views

Be careful to focus on the education system as a whole

### Grade booster — Getting top marks in this question

It is worth using the introduction to provide a brief explanation of the key ideas of functionalism and their application to education. The contribution of writers such as Durkheim, Parsons and Davis and Moore is likely to figure in the central part of the answer. There is no need to distinguish between the role and function of education.

Criticisms of the functionalist view will need to be included and other perspectives such as Marxism can be introduced briefly as further evaluation – but avoid getting sidetracked into describing alternative theories in any detail.

# TOPIC 2

# Social class and educational achievement

## Getting you thinking

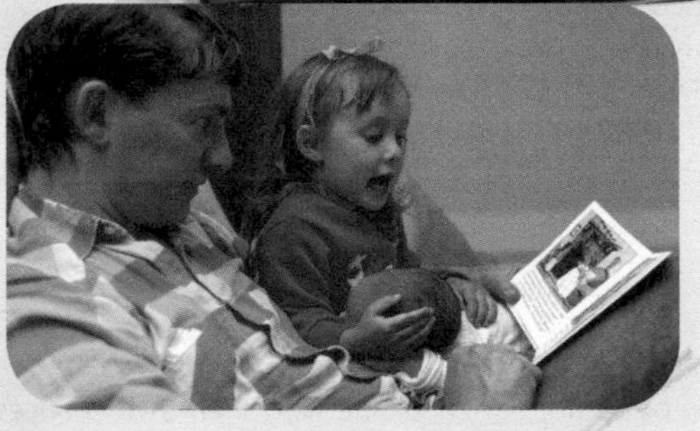

- Smaller percentages of children in Sure Start (more deprived) areas achieved a 'good' level of development by the end of the 'foundation' stage in school (3 to 5 year olds) than in non-Sure Start (less deprived) areas (DfES 2006).
- Analysis of 2006 Key Stage 2 results – for 11 year olds achieving Level 4 – reveal an attainment gap of 22 percentage points in children receiving free school meals compared to those not doing so.
- 38.5 per cent of children from the quarter of UK districts with the lowest incomes achieve five or more GCSE passes at Grade C or above; 72.5 per cent of children from the quarter of UK districts with the highest incomes achieve five or more GCSE passes at Grade C or above.
- More than half of young people who were NEET (not in education employment or training) or in jobs without training were from routine or manual backgrounds compared with only around 18 per cent who were from higher professional backgrounds (DfES 2006).

In addition, children from working-class backgrounds:

- are less likely to be found in nursery schools or pre-school playgroups
- are more likely to start school unable to read
- are more likely to fall behind in reading, writing and number skills
- are more likely to suffer from ill health, which can affect their attendance and performance at school
- are more likely to be placed in lower sets or streams
- are more likely to leave school at the age of 16
- are less likely to go on to sixth form and university.

It seems obvious: our educational success or failure is simply the result of our ability and motivation. When sociologists look at educational achievement, however, they find that there are distinct patterns. It seems that ability and motivation are closely linked to membership of certain social groups.

**Differential educational achievement** refers to the tendency for some groups to do better or worse than others in terms of educational success. The issue was initially considered by sociologists solely in terms of class. Differences between boys and girls and between different ethnic groups are a more recent focus, which will be explored in later topics.

Much of the government's focus over the last decade has been about raising the standards of teaching and learning in schools, and many reports suggest that school quality does have an impact on achievement across all social classes. Such research, however, needs to be put into context. According to DfES research (2004):

- The effectiveness of teaching only contributes to an 8 per cent difference in achievement.
- However, the proportion of pupils receiving free school meals has a 19 per cent impact, whereas the most significant impact is made by the SATs scores on entry to secondary school, at 73 per cent impact.

A recent large-scale study of over a million secondary-school pupils by Butler and Hamnetta (2007) has shown that a school's performance directly corresponds to the number of middle-class pupils that attend it, as evidenced by their postcode.

Sociologists have developed a range of explanations for the relationship between social class and educational achievement. These explanations emphasize different factors in searching for causes and each has links with particular sociological perspectives.

We will now look at these explanations and perspectives in more depth.

## Material explanations: Marxist and social democratic perspectives

Some explanations focus on the home background of students, for example the impact of living in a low-income household on educational opportunities. This sort of explanation sees the cause of educational inequality as lying in the way society works – its social structure – which makes some people wealthy while others are left in poverty. For this reason, the view is often associated with Marxist or social democratic perspectives (see Topic 1).

Certain groups have less money than others and so are not able to make the most of their educational opportunities. For example, in a study of the effects of poverty on schooling, Smith and Noble (1995) list the 'barriers to learning' which can result from low income. These include the following:

- If families are unable to afford school uniforms, school trips, transport to and from school, classroom materials and, in some cases, school textbooks, this can lead to children being isolated, bullied and stigmatized. As a result, they may fall behind in their school work.
- Low income reduces the likelihood of a computer with internet access, a desk, educational toys, books, space to do homework and a comfortable well-heated home.
- The marketization of schools means that there will be better-resourced, oversubscribed schools in more affluent areas, while socially disadvantaged children are concentrated in a limited number of increasingly unpopular schools.

Furthermore, older working-class children are more likely to have to work part time to support their studies, or to have to care for younger siblings if informal childcare networks break down, affecting their attendance at school, whereas middle-class parents can more easily afford to pay for childcare.

**Material deprivation** has been shown to impact upon the selection of a higher-education institution, whereby choice can be severely limited by low income. According to Reay *et al.* (2005), many working-class students intended to apply for the nearest university, not for reasons of educational quality, but because they felt they could not afford the costs of travel and/or accommodation away from home. Only 32 per cent of the working-class students in the study were considering moving out of the family home to attend university, compared to over 70 per cent of the middle-class students.

Once at university, students from poorer backgrounds suffer material disadvantages that affect their capacity to study. A survey was conducted to examine the effect of term-time working on academic attainment (Universities UK 2005). The survey found that students from the poorest homes were most likely to be working and to be working the longest hours. As a result, they often missed lectures, handed in work late and produced poor-quality assignments.

### *Evaluation of material explanations*

While there can be little doubt that poverty will affect educational achievement for the lowest-income groups, standards of living have been rising in the UK and most families are now able to afford the basics for their children. The New Labour government after 1997 (influenced by social democratic perspectives) also put into place a series of measures aimed at providing assistance for those experiencing material deprivation. These included the introduction of **Educational Maintenance Allowances** for post-16 students and the Excellence in Cities programme (see Topic 6 for more detail).

Increases in income and wealth for the majority of the population led sociologists looking for explanations of working-class underachievement to turn their attention towards the influence of cultural factors.

## Cultural explanations

These types of explanation also focus on home background but emphasize the importance of cultural factors, for example values, beliefs, attitudes, knowledge and language. The explanations come in two forms:

1. **Cultural deprivation** – a view associated with functionalist and New Right perspectives
2. **Cultural capital** – a view associated with neo-Marxist perspectives

### Cultural deprivation: functionalism and the New Right

The culture of some working-class families, it is argued, is just not suited for educational success. For example, if students do not see the value of doing homework or revision or do not communicate well, then their chances of educational success are likely to be limited.

This view is sometimes associated with the functionalist perspective because the functionalist emphasis on a harmonious and balanced society implies that there is something at fault with its members if things go wrong.

One of the first sociologists to identify 'cultural deprivation' was Hyman (1967). He argued that a significant section of the working class did not value education and did not believe they had realistic opportunities to better themselves. Hyman's research was based on American evidence but his key themes were picked up by Sugarman (1970) who argued that working-class subcultures developed four 'attitudes and orientations' that presented serious barriers to working-class children's educational progress.

1. *Fatalism* – accepting things as they are because you cannot change them
2. *Immediate gratification* – enjoy yourself now, don't worry about tomorrow

3 *Present-time orientation* – focus on the present, there's no point in planning for the future
4 *Collectivism* – be loyal to the wider group rather than focusing on yourself

It is not difficult to see how socialization into these values will make it difficult to succeed educationally – there would be little point in paying attention, doing homework, revising, applying to university and so on.

You may have noticed that the above research took place over 40 years ago. More recently, ideas about cultural deprivation have been picked up by the New Right. They believe that an **underclass** has developed characterized by values and a lifestyle that are just not conducive to educational success.

Underclass theorists such as Marsland (1996) and Murray (1994) have long argued that the unstable family life, inferior socialization and lack of discipline experienced by the poor, result in increased levels of crime, educational underachievement, and higher levels of single parenthood. The journalist Melanie Phillips, in her critique of the comprehensive system, *All Must Have Prizes* (1997), further argues that working-class educational underachievement arises as a result of teachers being too willing to blame poverty for underachievement, when the real reason is poor teaching and parenting. Phillips and Murray (2001) further argue that the increase in children's rights introduced by liberal social policy makers, has led to parents taking less responsibility for the parenting process and pupils taking less responsibility for themselves, further undermining educational achievement.

### *Evaluation of cultural deprivation explanations*

Cultural deprivation arguments have been criticized for over-emphasizing differences in values between classes. In fact, working-class subcultures may simply be a realistic method of responding to material and structural disadvantages. Opportunities for the working-class are blocked off so they develop subcultures as a response. In another situation their values and norms would appear similar to the rest of society.

## The home and the school: parental interest

Early studies of the relationship between the home and the school, such as that of Douglas (1964), suggested that a significant influence on pupil's attainment was parental interest in their child's education, as evidenced by the extent to which they visited the school and discussed progress with teachers. Douglas concluded that this was much higher among middle-class parents and hence helped explain differences in achievement. More recently, Feinstein (2003) has used longitudinal data to argue that parental interest and support explains social-class differences in achievement.

### *Evaluation*

Other sociologists have cast doubt on the claim that working-class parents are less interested in their child's education. Sharpe and Green (1975) found that parents who had been defined by teachers as being uninterested were very ready to talk about their children's education and very articulate about their reasons for holding their views. Blackstone and Mortimore (1994) point out that working-class parents may have less time to become involved in their children's education and may be put off school by the way teachers communicate with them.

## Language, social class and educational success

Research into language use and social class by Bernstein (1971) has been very influential in the sociology of education. He identified class differences in spoken and written language which, he argued, disadvantage working-class children. The middle classes succeed not because of greater intelligence but merely because they use the preferred way of communicating.

In examining the link between language and learning, Bernstein distinguished between two codes:

1 The **restricted code** – sentences are short, vocabulary is limited and few adjectives are used. As a result, such language is context-bound, i.e. has to be interpreted in the context in which it is used and assumes the listener shares the same set of experiences.
2 The **elaborated code** – characterized by long sentences, a rich vocabulary and a complicated structure of phrases that depend upon and link with each other. This form of language use is context-free and so is better suited to the more formal, impersonal communication required by the education system.

Berstein argued that the restricted code is the language form most commonly adopted by working-class children, while the elaborated code is typically used by the middle class and therefore is the form generally accepted in school by teachers and in examinations.

This has obvious implications for the learning experience of working-class children who, attending school, are entering into a world where they have less experience of the language used. Not only are they less able to express themselves in ways deemed acceptable, but they are also less likely to feel at home in the kind of environment that the middle-class child has become already used to, through their preschool socialization. In this way, the school system plays a part in reproducing social inequality. By having to become familiar with and use the language of the middle class, working-class children are disadvantaged

### *Evaluation*

Bernstein's work has proved controversial. Some commentators have seen his ideas as implying that the working class are culturally deprived in their language use although this was never his intention. He has also been criticized for lack of evidence and an over-simplified view of social class (Gaine and George, 1999). Rosen (1974) agrees with these criticisms and adds that it is simply not the case that the restricted code is in any way superior to the elaborated code. This point has led sociologists (including Bernstein) to explore the ways in which the culture of the middle classes appears to dominate education. We now move on to consider these views.

## Cultural capital: neo-Marxism

An alternative version of the culture argument focuses on the domination of middle-class culture rather than the deficiencies of working-class culture. This view suggests that the middle classes possess cultural advantages –

known as cultural capital – when it comes to education. They are more able to manipulate the education system to get the best for their children and share a culture with the majority of people who work in education. This viewpoint reflects a Marxist perspective in so far as it pays attention to class inequalities built into social structure. However, because it emphasizes the importance of culture it is more associated with neo-Marxism (see Chapter 1).

Bourdieu and Passeron (1977) suggest that middle-class culture (cultural capital) is as valuable in educational terms as material wealth (economic capital). Schools are middle-class institutions run by the middle class. The forms of knowledge, values, ways of interacting and communicating ideas that middle-class children possess are developed further and rewarded by the education system. Working-class and ethnic-minority children may lack these qualities and so do not have the same chances to succeed. Bourdieu's theory of cultural capital was tested in research by Alice Sullivan. Her research is discussed below (see Focus on research).

Ball *et al.* (1994) showed how middle-class parents are able to use their cultural capital to play the system so as to ensure that their children are accepted into the schools of their choice. The strategies they use include attempting to make an impression with the headteacher on open day, and knowing how to mount an appeal if their child is unsuccessful in their application to a particular school.

Later research by Ball (2003) showed how middle-class parents are able to use a variety of forms of capital to benefit their children. For example, they can use their material capital to buy extra tuition and their social capital in the form of contacts and networks to provide information and create relationships with important people such as governors and headteachers.

In *Education and the Middle Class* (2003), Power *et al.* note that, once middle-class parents had secured a place in the school of their choice, 'travelling time, homework and the schools' perceived exclusiveness made it difficult for children to maintain an "external" social life, thus focusing peer-group activity within the school territories and in the company of academically able and often ambitious students like themselves'. They conclude that an important aspect of cultural capital is the pursuit of 'conspicuous academic achievement' by both middle-class parents and children.

## The curriculum

Some sociologists have argued that what is taught in schools – the curriculum – actually disadvantages the working class. The knowledge that they encounter at school does not connect with their own cultural

## Focus on research

### Alice Sullivan (2001)
### A test of Bourdieu's theory of cultural capital

Although many sociologists have used Bourdieu's concept of cultural capital to understand and explain inequality of educational achievement, there have been few attempts to test Bourdieu's theory directly. One such attempt is provided in a study by Alice Sullivan (2001). In 1998, Sullivan carried out survey research on children approaching school-leaving age in four schools in England and received questionnaire data from a total of 465 pupils. The occupation of the parent in the highest-status job was used to determine the class of the children, and parents' educational qualifications were used to measure their cultural capital. A number of measures of pupils' cultural capital were used. Pupils were asked about the books they read, the television programmes they watched, the music they listened to, whether they played a musical instrument, and attendance at art galleries, theatres and concerts; they were also tested on their knowledge of cultural figures and on their vocabulary.

The research then examined which of these factors affected educational performance in GCSEs. Sullivan found that pupils were more likely to be successful if they read more complex fiction and watched TV programmes such as arts, science and current affairs documentaries and more sophisticated drama. Watching programmes such as soap operas and game shows did not improve GCSE performance. Attendance at cultural events and involvement in music had no significant effect, suggesting that these should not be considered important aspects of cultural capital. Pupils who read widely and watched sophisticated television developed wider vocabularies and greater knowledge of cultural figures, and this was reflected in exam performance. Sullivan found that pupils' cultural capital was strongly correlated with parental cultural capital (i.e. their educational qualifications), which in turn was closely linked to their social class. Graduate parents in higher professions had children with the most cultural capital and who were most successful in exams.

Adapted from Haralambos, M. and Holborn, M. (2008) *Sociology: Themes and Perspectives (7th edn)*, London: Collins Educational

1. **How was the concept of social class operationalized in Sullivan's research?**
2. **What indicators were used to measure cultural capital?**
3. **Which cultural factors correlated with educational performance? Suggest reasons why this might be the case.**

*How does this cartoon illustrate the idea of cultural capital?*

experience. Working-class experience is almost invisible in the school curriculum. History, for example, tends to deal with the ruling classes – such as kings, queens and politicians – rather than with the vast majority of ordinary people. The study of Shakespeare is still a compulsory component of English GCSE specifications.

### *Evaluation of cultural capital explanations*

Explanations of educational success and failure based on the idea of cultural capital have been very influential, especially in explaining the ways the middle classes have benefitted from the marketization of education (see Topics 1 and 6). However, for Marxists, differences in cultural capital derive from the fundamental economic inequality between social classes that is the basis of capitalism. Focusing on cultural factors should not distract from an analysis of the impact of structural inequalities on educational achievement.

All of the explanations we have been considering up to this point have placed home and cultural background at the centre of the relationship between social class and educational achievement. A key element in the process of education has been ignored: the school itself.

## In-school explanations: interactionism

In-school explanations concentrate on the role of factors within schools for creating class inequalities in achievement, in particular the way in which teacher stereotypes lead to the labelling of many working-class children as likely failures. This explanation is associated with interactionism due to its focus on the importance of relationships within the classroom and their effect on students' view of themselves – their self-concept (see Topic 1).

### Labelling, stereotypes and teacher expectation

Interactionist explanations of differential educational achievement – based on 'labelling theory' (see Chapter 2 Topic 4) – look at what goes on in schools themselves, and, in particular, teacher–pupil relationships. Labelling theories suggest that teachers judge pupils not by their ability or intelligence, but by characteristics that relate to class, gender and ethnicity, such as attitude, appearance and behaviour. Becker (1971) showed how teachers perceive the 'ideal pupil' to be one who conforms to middle-class standards of behaviour. Middle-class teachers are more likely to perceive middle-class behaviour as evidence of commitment to study, and working-class cultural demeanour as evidence of indiscipline, lower ability or motivation. They may hold different expectations of eventual achievement, which in turn can affect pupils' progress according to the ways in which they are labelled and sorted into ability groups. In other words, a **self-fulfilling prophecy** can be seen to occur, whereby teachers' expectations are translated into actual outcomes. The ideas of labelling and the self-fulfilling prophecy concentrate on effects on the individual. Ball (1981) in his study of 'Beachside Comprehensive' argued that the same effects can be observed in whole groups. Pupils at this school were put into three 'bands' on the basis of information about their ability given by primary schools: band 1 mostly contained pupils from non-manual backgrounds; those in band 2 were socially mixed; while those in band 3 were mostly from manual backgrounds.

Ball argues that all students entered the school eager to learn but due to the effects of teacher attitudes and expectations, band 1 'warmed to education' and did well in school, whereas bands 2 and 3 'cooled down' and underachieved.

Recent research in nine state secondary schools by Dunne and Gazeley (2008) confirms the view that teachers tend to perceive the 'ideal pupil' as middle class. Dunne and Gazeley found that most pupils identified as 'underachievers' came from working-class backgrounds and that teachers used social-class stereotypes when discussing pupils, for example associating working-class parents with unemployment, deviance and predicting negative outcomes such as early pregnancy and crime for working-class pupils. Most middle-class pupils were expected to enter higher education. Gillborn and Youdell (2001) conducted research in two London secondary schools and found that teachers used the idea of 'ability' to categorize pupils. Although research suggests that 'ability' is not fixed, teachers believed that it was and saw Black and working-class pupils as having less 'ability' and so lower achievement.

### *Evaluation of interactionist explanations*

The interactionist perspective has the advantage of focusing directly on small-scale interaction situations in schools and colleges. In doing so, it provides detailed evidence of what actually happens within educational institutions. However, critics contend that this focus can lead researchers to ignore wider cultural and structural factors. Some interactionist research appears to 'blame' teachers for working-class and other underachievement while ignoring the way in which teachers' behaviour is controlled and limited by the forces that shape educational policy.

Interactionist approaches are also criticized for being **deterministic**. They imply that labelling and stereotyping has the inevitable effect of causing pupils to rebel, give up and so underachieve. They ignore the fact that pupils can respond in a variety of ways, for example with a determination to prove their teachers wrong.

## Conclusion

Class is still considered by far the most significant factor influencing educational attainment – thought to have twice the effect on educational achievement of ethnicity and five times the effect of gender (Gillborn and Mirza 2000). However, these other dimensions are still important and will be explored in the following two topics.

# Key terms

**Compensatory education** making more resources available to schools in poorer areas in order to compensate (make up) for deprivation.

**Cultural deprivation** 'cultural deprivation' theory suggests that some pupils' backgrounds are in some way deficient or inferior.

**Deterministic** in this context, making it appear inevitable that people will react in a particular way.

**Differential educational achievement** the extent to which educational achievement differs between social groups.

**Educational Maintenance Allowance (EMA)** a means-tested sum of up to £30 per week given to post-16 students to support them in meeting the daily costs of coming to school.

**Material deprivation** lack of money leading to disadvantages such as an unhealthy diet and unsatisfactory housing.

**Self-fulfilling prophecy** a prediction that causes the outcome it predicts.

**Underclass** term used by the New Right to describe group below the working class with unstable domestic lives, reliance on benefits and fatalistic values.

# Check your understanding

1. **How can material factors influence working-class students' experience of school?**
2. **How can material factors influence working-class students' experience of higher education?**
3. **Give three examples of ways in which differences in class culture might affect achievement in education.**
4. **How have cultural deprivation theories been criticized?**
5. **What are the arguments for and against the view that working-class parents are less interested than middle-class parents in the education of their children?**
6. **How can language affect the relationship between class and educational success?**
7. **How does Ball argue that cultural capital helps middle-class children to gain a place in the school of their choice?**
8. **Why might the formal curriculum appear less relevant to working-class children?**
9. **How are explanations that emphasize teacher stereotyping and labelling linked to interactionist perspectives?**
10. **Using examples, explain how labelling can affect educational success.**

# Activities

## Research idea

1. Interview other people in your class to find out their experiences of setting and banding. Compare their experiences with Ball's views.
2. Conduct a survey to establish the most popular secondary schools in your area. Use the internet and the local press to investigate relative house prices for similar styles of property.

## Web.tasks

Visit the website of Action Access at www.actiononaccess.org. What is the organization trying to achieve and what is it doing? Can you access some statistics about the relationship between university applications and socio-economic status? What do they show?

## An eye on the exam Social class and educational achievement

A detailed description of the view in the question is required, using sociological concepts, theories and studies.

Weigh up the strengths and weaknesses of cultural explanations in some detail, then present alternative views before reaching a balanced conclusion.

**Outline and assess the view that social-class differences in educational achievement are the result of cultural factors. (50 marks)**

Cultural refers to attitudes, norms and values

It would help to know some statistical patterns to illustrate these

### Grade booster Getting top marks in this question

An introduction should provide some examples of the patterns of differential achievement between social classes. Then a detailed account of explanations which emphasize cultural factors is needed. These should include those influenced by functionalist and New Right ideas that stress cultural deprivation as well as those influenced by Marxism that point to the influence of cultural capital. These different types of explanation need to be contrasted and evaluated as the answer progresses. Alternative explanations that focus on material factors and in-school factors can be used to assess the cultural view.

# TOPIC 3

# Ethnicity and educational achievement

## Getting you thinking

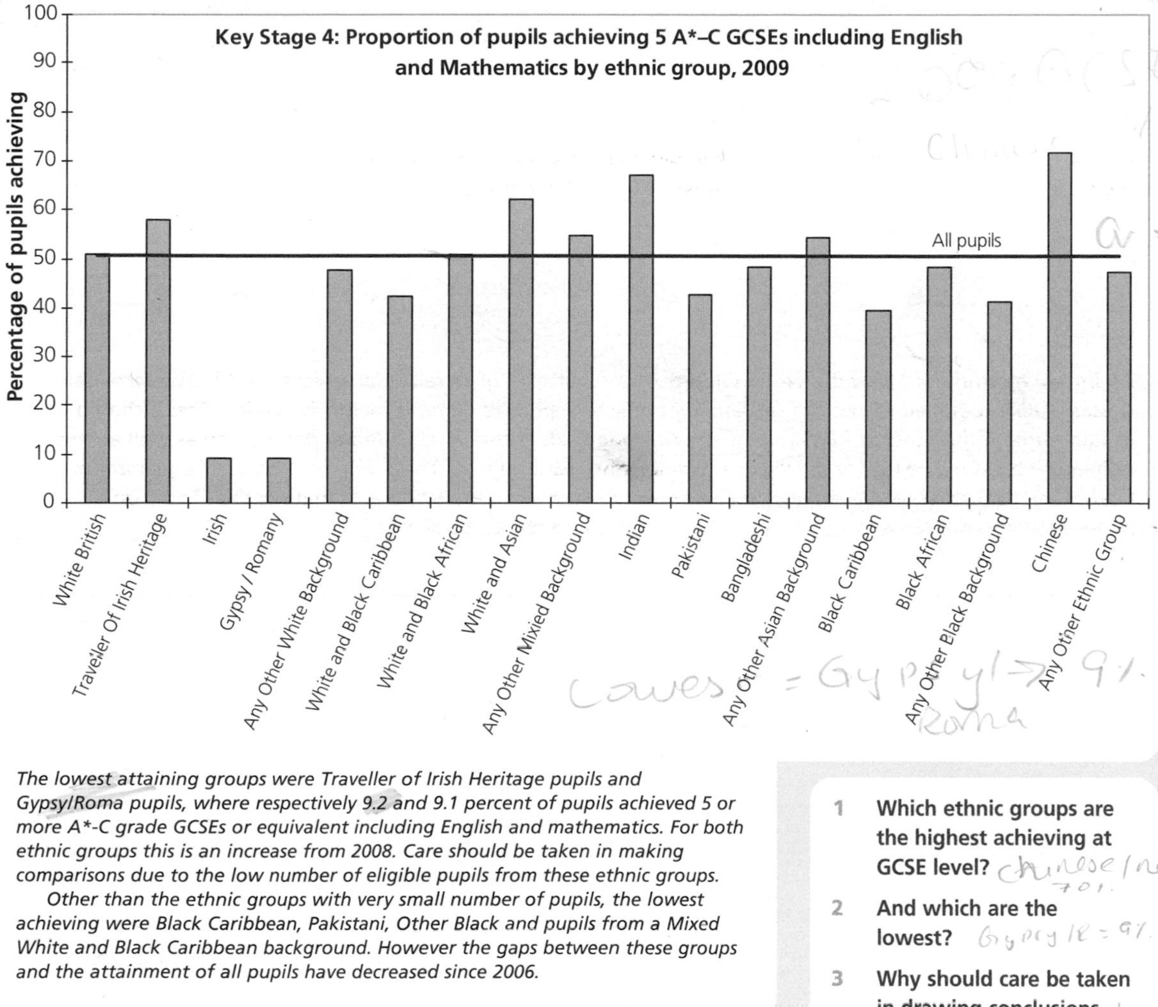


*The lowest attaining groups were Traveller of Irish Heritage pupils and Gypsy/Roma pupils, where respectively 9.2 and 9.1 percent of pupils achieved 5 or more A*-C grade GCSEs or equivalent including English and mathematics. For both ethnic groups this is an increase from 2008. Care should be taken in making comparisons due to the low number of eligible pupils from these ethnic groups.*

*Other than the ethnic groups with very small number of pupils, the lowest achieving were Black Caribbean, Pakistani, Other Black and pupils from a Mixed White and Black Caribbean background. However the gaps between these groups and the attainment of all pupils have decreased since 2006.*

According to a report by Babb *et al.* (2004), children who are most likely to be low educational achievers in England are:

- male
- from a low socio-economic background
- with parents who have low or no qualifications
- living in a single-parent household
- having many siblings
- attending a state school rather than an independent school
- attending a school with a high rate of free-school meal eligibility.

1 **Which ethnic groups are the highest achieving at GCSE level?**

2 **And which are the lowest?**

3 **Why should care be taken in drawing conclusions about the two lowest achieving ethnic groups?**

4 **How many of the factors listed by Babb do you think apply to ethnic minorities?**

5 **Why do you think these factors have such a significant impact on educational achievement?**

# Material and cultural factors affecting underachievement

## Ethnic diversity and achievement

Material and cultural explanations of educational disadvantage referred to in the previous topic also apply to the experience of ethnic minorities, because a higher proportion than White British pupils tend to be working-class.

It is clearly not possible to argue that the worst case systematically happens to every minority ethnic child. The interplay between class, gender and ethnicity is highly complex and is affected by a multitude of factors both inside and outside school. However, as we saw from the 'Getting you thinking' exercise, relative deprivation is a key factor and higher proportions of people from ethnic minorities, than White British, are from lower-income households (see Table 3.1).

There are clearly noteworthy differences from the norm for certain ethnic categories. African-Caribbean males are near the bottom of each class group in terms of attainment. However, working-class African-Caribbean females, although they suffer from initial disadvantages in school, tend to do significantly better than working-class White pupils by the time they take their GCSEs. Fuller (1984) suggests that they may appear 'cool' in order to present a positive self-image to boys and teachers, but that they recognize the importance of getting good qualifications.

Children of Indian, Chinese and African-Asian origin also do very well within the education system. There is a strong emphasis on self-improvement through education in these cultures, and many of the children come from professional backgrounds, providing support, appropriate role models and material advantages. Their culture is perceived more positively by teachers than that of, for example, African-Caribbean males. In addition to all of the points listed in the previous topic (for children from working-class backgrounds), many pupils from particular ethnic-minority groups are relatively disadvantaged within the education system.

According to a recent report commissioned for the DfES (Wanless Report 2007), Black pupils:

- are significantly more likely to be permanently excluded and routinely punished more harshly
- are praised less and told off more often
- are 1.5 times as likely as White British pupils to be identified with behaviour-related special needs
- outperformed White pupils in school entry tests (but when these were changed to teacher observations, the pattern was reversed)
- are disproportionately put in bottom sets – due to behaviour rather than ability
- are much less likely than the average to be identified as gifted and talented.

While some Pakistani and Bangladeshi children still do relatively badly in school, recent research has shown these groups to be catching up. Bangladeshi pupils have made the greatest gains since 2000 with a gain of 28 percentage points, which brings them to the national average,

**Table 3.1** Percentage of pupils entitled to a Free School Meal (FSM) by ethnicity

| *Ethnic group* | *per cent entitled to FSM* |
|---|---|
| White British | 12.8 |
| Mixed heritage | 25.2 |
| Indian | 13.7 |
| Pakistani | 38.2 |
| Bangladeshi | 58.5 |
| African-Caribbean | 26.2 |
| Black African | 41.4 |
| Any other group | 29.6 |

Source: Strand, S. (2007)

followed by Pakistani pupils with a gain of 22 percentage points.

However, the length of time Asian immigrant groups have lived in Britain varies. A study by Haque and Bell (2001), showed that recent arrival into the UK had a significant negative effect on performance (by the equivalent of more than one level in each core subject). Like social class and recent arrival, as we saw in Topic 2, parental education is a significant influence on their children's achievement, in particular the level of the mother's education. However, while 83 per cent of Bangladeshi parents have no qualifications, compared with 16 per cent of White British parents, the children of those who have been here longer achieve more highly in the education system. This is because older siblings, educated here, are able to help their younger brothers and sisters. Also, as we have seen, reflecting changes within the White community, females generally tend to perform better than males within each ethnic group (see Topic 4).

However, when compared to Whites, minority ethnic groups have a larger proportion of members with working-class backgrounds in higher education. This is particularly true for Pakistanis and Bangladeshis – nearly two-thirds of the entrants to higher education from these groups came from households headed by manual workers or the unemployed (Modood 2004).

Some African-Caribbean pupils have very high attainment and make excellent progress. On the other hand, some White British pupils have extremely low attainment, particularly those from economically disadvantaged groups, and make poor progress. For example, national statistics highlight the fact that only 24 per cent of White British boys entitled to FSM achieved 5 or more GCSE grades at A* to C compared to 27 per cent of African-Caribbean boys entitled to FSM (DfES 2007). Also, White British working-class pupils in inner-city areas have recently emerged as the group making the least progress over the secondary phase.

### Strand: Indian and African-Caribbean pupils

Highlighting a relatively long-term trend, Strand (2007) focuses on two ethnic groups of particular interest, as both vary considerably in terms of progress throughout the first four years of secondary school, relative to their White

British peers. Indian pupils widen the gap by achieving significantly better than their White peers, whereas African-Caribbean pupils do so by achieving considerably less progress. According to Strand, Indian pupils' relative progress can in part be explained by positive factors such as:

- high parental and pupil educational aspirations
- undertaking high levels of homework
- low levels of truanting, exclusion, or social services/ Educational Welfare Service involvement
- high resource provision at home (computers and private tuition)
- high parental monitoring of their children's whereabouts.

However, his research can not fully account for the poor progress of the African-Caribbean group. Relative to White British pupils generally, African-Caribbean pupils on average experience greater poverty (entitlement to FSM), are more likely to live in rented accommodation and to attend schools that are more deprived, as well as live in more deprived neighbourhoods, as is the case for Indian pupils. In terms of social class and mother's educational qualifications, however, African-Caribbean pupils do not differ markedly from White British pupils. In addition, African-Caribbean pupils (and their parents) have higher educational aspirations, have a more positive attitude to school, a higher academic self-concept and are more likely to be actively planning for the future. Despite this, African-Caribbean pupils, especially boys, are (in addition to their lower level of achievement) much more likely to have identified special educational needs and to be temporarily excluded from school, and are less likely to do homework. Given the similar socio-economic background and, if anything, more favourable balance of advantage/disadvantage relative to Indian pupils, Strand concludes that it is difficult to explain the poor progress of the African-Caribbean group.

It is, therefore, necessary to look at wider explanations of ethnic group differences, beyond those described above.

### Cultural factors

African-Caribbean underachievement has been blamed on the high numbers of one-parent families in African-Caribbean communities (57 per cent compared with 23 per cent for White British families). Some politicians have suggested that, because many of these families are female-headed, African-Caribbean boys, in particular, lack the discipline of a father-figure, which they suggest may account for the high percentage of African-Caribbeans in special schools. For girls, on the other hand, the role model provided by a strong, independent single mother is a motivating influence, and this helps to explain their relative success in education. Living in a single-parent household is not necessarily a cause of low attainment where it occurs, but according to Strand, it is a significant risk factor. Single-parent households have, on average, lower income, greater levels of parental stress and less time for educational input to the child, all of which may impact negatively on educational attainment. However, although a higher number of African-Caribbeans do live in one-parent families, it should be noted that most children of African-Caribbean origin live in nuclear families.

Many working-class and ethnic-minority pupils may feel undervalued and demotivated by an educational system that does not recognize their qualities, which are based on their class and ethnic culture.

Language has also been seen as a problem for children of African-Caribbean origin, who may speak different dialects of English, and for children from other ethnic groups who come from homes where a language other than English is spoken. This language difference may cause problems in doing schoolwork and communicating with teachers, leading to disadvantage at school.

Ball (2002) shows how ethnic-minority parents are at a disadvantage when trying to get their children into the better schools. The parents, especially if born abroad, may not have much experience of the British education system and may not be able to negotiate the system. This may be compounded by a lack of confidence in their English-language skills.

Issues such as uniform (which markets a school well and fosters an impression of discipline) may disrupt teacher–pupil relationships, particularly between teachers and ethnic-minority pupils whose cultural influences may exert more pressure on them to subvert the formal dress codes of the school, e.g. by refusing to remove baseball caps. This may provoke more antischool behaviour, truancy and the constructive exclusion of 'problem children'. Gewirtz (2002) identifies further socially exclusive practices, such as the creation of complex application forms requiring high levels of literacy and often available only in English.

## In-school factors

The above section shows how difficult it is to generalize about ethnicity and educational achievement and reveals some of the complex links between social class, gender and ethnicity. But the factors identified above only focus on the home environment and culture of ethnic groups. We need to look at the processes and relationships that occur within schools to gain a fuller picture. Once again, these are often influenced by interactionist perspectives although many also take into account patterns of racism and ethnic inequalities in wider society.

### Labelling, racism and subcultures

*Ethnic-minority boys*

Boys of African-Caribbean origin often have the label 'unruly', 'disrespectful' and 'difficult to control' applied to them. Gillborn (1990) found that African-Caribbean pupils were more likely to be given detentions than other pupils. This was because the teachers interpreted (or misinterpreted) the dress and manner of speech of African-Caribbean pupils as representing a challenge to their authority. In perceiving their treatment to be unfair, the pupils responded, understandably, in accordance with their labels. Tony Sewell (1996) claimed that many teachers were fearful of Black boys in school, the result of socialization into stereotypical assumptions. Jasper (2002) goes further to suggest that the expectations that White female teachers have of Black boys' behaviour dictate the form and style of the teaching that they offer them, a style less conducive to learning than they offer to other groups. O'Donnell (1991) showed how the various ethnic

# Focus on research

## Tony Sewell
### Black masculinities and schooling

Tony Sewell (1996) conducted research in comprehensive schools in London. The bulk of the study took place in what Sewell refers to as 'Township School'. This school was a boys' comprehensive for children aged 11 to 16. There were 61 students of Asian origin, 63 of African origin, 140 of African-Caribbean origin, 31 mixed race students, 127 White boys and 23 'others'.

Sewell gathered his material through an ethnographic approach using semi-structured interviews and observation. At the time, he was in his early 30s and describes himself as Black. He is careful to point out that he was able to make very good relationships with the boys and was able to mix with them socially. He describes this process as being able to 'chill'.

Sewell found that some Black pupils were disciplined excessively by teachers who were socialized into racist attitudes and who felt threatened by these students' masculinity, sexuality and physical skills. Furthermore, the boys felt that their culture received little or no positive recognition.

Adapted from Blundell, J. and Griffiths J. (2002) *Sociology since 1995 vol. 2*, Lewes: Connect Publications

1. **Why do sociologists such as Sewell often change the names of the schools in which they conduct research?**
2. **Why was it important for Sewell to make good relationships and 'chill' with the boys?**
3. **To what extent did Sewell's own social identity help his relationships with the boys?**
4. **Do you think the boys would have been completely honest with Sewell? Explain your answer.**
5. **What are the dangers for a researcher in identifying too strongly with the group being studied?**



subcultures have distinctive reactions to racism, prejudice and discrimination, which may have different effects on educational performance. African-Caribbean males often react angrily to and reject the White-dominated education system, gaining status and recognition through other means. Indians show their anger, but do not tend to reject the education system. Instead, they succeed because they use the education system to their advantage.

According to Sewell (1996) and O'Donnell and Sharpe (2000), in responding to teacher's labels, racism and poor economic prospects, Black males construct a form of masculinity that earns respect from peers and females. This macho response may have little relevance for males in general with the decline in manual work and increasing opportunities within the **service sector**. However, for young Black men, with more limited employment prospects, opposition to schooling still has some relevance in highlighting their masculinity and alternative attributes of success. Despite the fact of their relatively high academic self-concept (Strand 2007), educational success is seen as a feminine thing. The way for them to get respect is through the credibility of the street. In Sewell's words, the young man wants to be a 'street hood'. Success in the school room marks the Black boy out from his peers or classmates and is likely to make him the target of ridicule or bullying. According to Sewell, educational failure becomes a badge to wear with pride. Aspects of this view have been reflected in concerns about the development of 'gangsta' culture and the absence of positive Black male role-models at home as well as in schools. The current moral panic over gun and knife crime is in part supported by such assertions.

A similar response has been identified among some Asian youths – in particular, Bangladeshi boys, whose economic prospects are generally bleaker than those of other Asian groups. O'Donnell and Sharpe (2000) recognized that this macho 'warrior' perception by peers existed alongside perceptions of other Asian youths as 'weaklings' conforming to demands of the school or 'patriarchs', whose loyalty lay with the prescriptions of the male-dominated Asian family.

Connolly (1998) also examined the treatment in school of boys of South Asian origin. He found that teachers tended to see some South Asian boys as immature rather than as seriously deviant. Much of their bad behaviour went unnoticed by teachers and was not punished to the same extent as that of Black boys. The South Asian boys, therefore, had difficulty in gaining status as males, which made it more difficult for them to enjoy school and feel confident. However, teachers did have high expectations of their academic potential and they were often praised and encouraged.

### *Ethnic-minority girls*

Connolly (1998) found in his recent investigation of three classes of 5 to 6 year olds in a multi-ethnic, inner-city primary school that some negative stereotypes are not just confined to boys. Like Black boys, girls were perceived by teachers as potentially disruptive but likely to be good at sports. The teachers in one school tended to 'underplay' the Black girls' educational achievements and focus on their

① exam Q.) In School process result in different attainment for Bm =
1) Intract - labelling
2) Black boys / conforming - Black girls indexes x
3) NO) outside factors more important
4) theory:
att = mon
5) Conclu

social behaviour'. Like their male counterparts, they were quite likely to be disciplined and punished, even though their behaviour did not always seem to justify it.

While few would argue that teachers display overt racism, Wright (1992) found considerable discrimination in the classroom. She observed Asian and African-Caribbean children in primary schools and found that teachers paid Asian pupils, especially girls, less attention. They involved them less in discussion and used simplistic language, assuming that they had a poor command of English. Teachers also lacked sensitivity towards aspects of their culture and displayed open disapproval of their customs and traditions. Teachers also made little effort to ensure that they pronounced names correctly, causing embarrassment and unnecessary ridicule. This had the effect of making the girls feel less positive towards the school. It also attracted hostility from other pupils, who picked up on the teachers' comments and attitude towards the Asian pupils. Despite this, teachers did have high expectations of Asian pupils with regard to academic success. According to Connolly (1998), South Asian girls, though generally successful in the education system, may be overlooked because of their perceived passivity, or they may feel marginalized and left out of **discourses** relating to intimacy, love and marriage because of stereotypical assumptions about Asian family life. Connolly also challenged the stereotypical assumptions many teachers made, noting that the behaviour of South Asian girls pointed towards a similar mix of work and avoidance of work and obedience and disruption, making their behaviour largely indistinguishable from that of their female peers. It would appear, therefore, that high expectations may to some extent be responsible for creating a self-fulfilling prophecy in terms of Asian girls' relative success.

Some evidence indicates that Black girls are antischool, but pro-education. They resent low teacher expectations and labelling, but are more determined to succeed than many other groups, especially Black boys. Both Fuller (1984) and Mirza (1992) have noted how Black girls respond to the failure of the school to address their needs by rejecting the help of teachers, which they regard as patronizing and, though sometimes well-meaning, misguided. For example, the girls were entered for fewer subjects 'to take the pressure off' or given ill-informed, often stereotypical careers advice. The girls respond outwardly by appearing to reject the values of the school through their dress, attitudes and behaviour. In terms of academic achievement, however, Fuller is more optimistic than Mirza about the outcomes and suggests that the strategies that they adopt in working with and helping each other enable them to succeed academically and prove their teachers wrong. In Mirza's study, on the other hand, rejection of teachers' help and limited involvement in lessons were seen to place them at a disadvantage academically, even though they preserved high self-esteem. They were not victims of overt racism or labelling, they were simply held back by the well-meaning but misguided behaviour of most of their teachers.

While teachers may have certain expectations of ethnic-minority groups, some of which may have been detrimental to their success, pupils of both Asian and African-Caribbean origin are, according to Connolly (1998), often victims of racism from White pupils. The impact of

# Focus on research

## Tikly *et al.* (2006)
## Aiming high

In 2003, the government set up a programme called 'Aiming High' to help raise the achievement of African-Caribbean pupils. It provided extra resources to 30 schools where African and Caribbean pupils were performing below the average for all pupils between the ages of 11 and 16. In 2006, a team of sociologists led by Leon Tikly evaluated the success of the project.

Tikly's team used postal questionnaires to produce quantitative information about setting, examination tiers and rates of exclusion. The questionnaires were returned by only 18 schools at the start of the project and 11 at the end. One third of the sample (10 schools) were subsequently involved in semi-structured interviews with, for example, governors, headteachers, pupils, parents and teachers. These produced qualitative data about the extent to which schools recognized and valued ethnic diversity and the ways they treated ethnic-minority pupils in relation to behaviour and discipline. Those that did most appeared to have fewer behavioural problems and lower exclusion rates.

Tikly, L. *et al.* (2006) *Evaluation of Aiming High: African Caribbean Achievement Project*, Bristol: University of Bristol

1 Identify the quantitative and qualitative methods used in this research.

2 What are the advantages and disadvantages of using postal questionnaires?

3 To what extent do you think the results of this research can be generalized to other schools?

4 What was the benefit for the schools who valued ethnic diversity?

this on educational commitment and performance is inevitably negative.

Other authors argue that racism, at least in the overt sense, cannot be a complete explanation for ethnic-group differences in attainment. Modood (2003) argues: 'If racism leads to the victim being turned off school and dropping out, why do Asian men and women have such high staying-on rates and make academic progress?' This does not discount the possibility of social stereotyping or **institutional racism** against some ethnic groups, but does highlight the importance of being sceptical with regard to generalized explanations.

### The curriculum

Some sociologists have argued that the curriculum – what is taught in schools – actually disadvantages ethnic minorities. The knowledge that they encounter at school may not connect with their own cultural experience, while **ethnocentrism**, resulting from the use of out-of-date material, could be potentially offensive by reflecting old colonial values and racial stereotypes. Coard (1971) showed how the content of education also ignored Black people. The people who are acclaimed tend to be White, while Black culture, music and art are largely ignored. Coard argued that this led to low self-esteem among Black pupils. However, this assertion was refuted by both the Swann Report (1985) and Stone (1981), who noted that, despite feeling discriminated against by some teachers, African-Caribbean children had been able to maintain an extremely positive self-image.

Since the 1970s, some effort has been made to address the neglect of other cultures in the curriculum. **Multicultural education**, which acknowledges the contribution of all of the world's cultures, has become more common, although it has been criticized for focusing only on external factors ('saris and samosas') and failing to address the real problem of racism. Ethnic-minority languages still do not have the same status as European languages, and schools are still required to hold Christian assemblies. The National Curriculum itself has also been criticized for being ethnocentric – especially in its focus on British history and literature. Geography also emphasizes Britain's positive contribution to the rest of the world, rather that the negative consequences of unfair trade and employment practices. Tikly *et al.* (2006), in their study of 30 comprehensive schools (see also Research methods, p. 217), found that a significant number of African-Caribbean pupils noted their invisibility in the curriculum and were exasperated by the White European focus. Moreover, when Black history was acknowledged within the curriculum, many pupils reported their frustration with the tendency to focus on slavery. However, while the curriculum may be ethnocentric, it is unlikely that this, in isolation, is a major factor in the underachievement of ethnic minorities, as it is not the case that all pupils from ethnic-minority backgrounds underachieve to similar degrees. Indian and Chinese pupils' achievement, for example, is above the national average.

### Institutional racism?

Gillborn (2002) argues that schools are institutionally racist as teachers interpret policy in a way that disadvantages Black pupils. For example, setting, schemes for gifted and talented pupils, and vocational schemes for the less academic all underrate the abilities of Black children, relegating them to low-ability groups, a restricted curriculum and entry for lower-level exams. The increased marketization of schools (see Topic 6), has led to what some writers have called an 'A to C economy'. According to Gillborn and Youdell (1999) this creates a rationing of education, whereby teachers are forced to focus on those in danger of not realizing their potential for an above C grade. They thus neglect the no-hopers and high achievers, leaving them to their own devices. Many ethnic-minority pupils are judged, often subjectively, to belong to the former group. Hatcher (1996) examined the role of school governing bodies and found that they gave low priority to race issues, failing to deal adequately with pupil racism. Furthermore, formal links with ethnic-minority parents tended not to exist, which meant that little was done to address their concerns. Ethnic-minority pupils' needs therefore tended to be low priority or disregarded. Ranson (2005) highlights the unrepresentativeness of school governing bodies which are 'disproportionately White, middle-aged, middle-class, middle-income, public/community service workers'.

## Problems of categorization

Classifying according to ethnic origin is by no means simple. The term 'ethnic minorities', for example, includes many different groups and does not take account of class and gender differences within those groups. Gillborn and Gipps (1996) argue that terms such as 'White', 'Black', 'Asian' and 'other' actually prevent any real understanding of differences in achievement. Postmodernists go further; they argue that the increasingly diverse nature of contemporary societies makes it impossible to explain educational achievement (or anything else) in terms of broad categories such as class or ethnicity, and that the generalizations that are made actually do more harm than good. They suggest that a conscious attempt needs to be made to understand the complexities of cultural difference and identity in modern society.

## Key terms

**Anomaly** an odd, peculiar, or strange condition, situation, quality, etc.

**Discourse** a set of ideas that tell us how to make sense of the world, what kind of questions to ask, what counts as a problem and how to solve problems.

**Ethnocentric** emphasizing White middle-class culture at the expense of other cultures.

**Institutional racism** racism that is built into the normal day-to-day practices of an organization.

**Multicultural education** education that recognizes cultural diversity.

**Service sector** a group of economic activities loosely organized around finance, retail and personal care.

# Activities

## Research idea

Analyse the content of a sample of text books at your school or college. Focus on visual images, examples and case studies. To what extent do they recognize the variety and contribution of ethnic groups in contemporary Britain?

## Web.tasks

Visit 'Talking Race' at www.multiverse.ac.uk/attachments/TalkingRaceSite/si.html.

Browse through the information here. What problems are created by making generalized statements about minority ethnic underachievement?

## Check your understanding

1. Briefly describe some of the material disadvantages that might be faced by ethnic minorities from working-class backgrounds (see also previous topic).
2. What are the possible reasons for differences in educational achievement between Asian groups?
3. What has recently become a concern in relation to White British working-class pupils?
4. Why do you think a higher proportion of members of ethnic minorities than White students attend university?
5. Explain how Indian pupils and African-Caribbean pupils demonstrate a widening of the achievement gap in relation to White pupils.
6. Give three examples of ways in which cultural differences may affect ethnic achievement in education. Include some reference to Tony Sewell's research.
7. How do pupil subcultures illustrate aspects of ethnic-minority experience of school?
8. How may the labelling of Black boys have a negative impact upon their achievement?
9. How, despite generally high expectations, does the behaviour of teachers towards Asian children impede their success?
10. How might the curriculum itself disadvantage ethnic-minority pupils?

## An eye on the exam Ethnicity and educational achievement

A detailed description of the view is required, using sociological concepts, theories and studies.

Weigh up the strengths and weaknesses of home background explanations in some detail, then present alternative views before reaching a balanced conclusion.

Include both material and cultural factors

**Outline and assess the view that home background is the main cause of differential educational achievement between ethnic groups. (50 marks)**

This can be measured in different ways

Be careful to avoid over-generalizations

### Grade booster Getting top marks in this question

An introduction should be used to show the marker that you are aware of ethnic diversity and are able to use statistical patterns and trends to illustrate this diversity in educational achievement patterns. Explanations that emphasize the role of material and cultural features will need to be discussed and then compared and evaluated as the answer progresses. Further evaluation can take the form of presenting alternative explanations, notably the significance of in-school factors such as labelling and stereotyping in schools. A conclusion could note the importance of taking into account the relationships between ethnicity, gender and class rather than analyzing their impact on educational achievement separately.

# TOPIC 4

# Gender and educational achievement

## Getting you thinking

The table below highlights the extent to which girls outperform boys at GCSE and at A-level in a range of subjects, with girls outperforming boys in every subject.

**Girls' achievement of A*–C grades in GCSE subjects relative to boys' in 2006**

| | No. sat ('000s) | | % diff A* to C | | No sat ('000s) | | % diff A* to C |
|---|---|---|---|---|---|---|---|
| | M | F | | | M | F | |
| Art | 86 | 126 | +19 | Information technology | 50 | 40 | +8 |
| Design & technology | 203 | 168 | +16 | Geography | 104 | 83 | +7 |
| English | 306 | 305 | +15 | History | 106 | 102 | +6 |
| Drama | 35 | 59 | +14 | Science single award | 36 | 35 | +5 |
| English literature | 255 | 271 | +13 | Business studies | 46 | 33 | +4 |
| French | 93 | 116 | +13 | PE | 91 | 61 | +3 |
| Religious studies | 63 | 81 | +12 | Science double award | 220 | 223 | +3 |
| All GCSE subjects | 3180 | 3110 | +9 | Mathematics | 310 | 305 | +2 |

**Girls' achievement of A–E grades in A-level subjects relative to boys' in 2006**

| | No. sat ('000s) | | % diff A to E | | No sat ('000s) | | % diff A to E |
|---|---|---|---|---|---|---|---|
| | M | F | | | M | F | |
| Law | 5.4 | 8.1 | +2.7 | Sociology | 5.7 | 18.6 | +1 |
| Psychology | 12.4 | 35.2 | +2.7 | Mathematics | 30.6 | 19.1 | +0.9 |
| Music | 5 | 4 | +2.2 | Drama | 4.5 | 10.5 | +0.8 |
| Physics | 18.7 | 5 | +2 | Media Studies | 10 | 13 | +0.8 |
| ICT/Computing | 12.5 | 4.7 | +1.9 | History | 20.5 | 20.1 | +0.8 |
| Design & technology | 9.7 | 7 | +1.9 | Geography | 15.5 | 12.7 | +0.7 |
| PE | 12.5 | 9 | +1.6 | Economics | 9.5 | 4 | +0.5 |
| English | 24 | 54 | +1.3 | Religious Studies | 4.7 | 10.2 | +0.4 |
| Art | 11 | 26 | +1.1 | Spanish | 1.7 | 3.5 | +0.2 |
| Chemistry | 17.7 | 16.8 | +1.1 | German | 2 | 3.5 | +0.1 |
| Biology | 19.3 | 27.3 | +1 | Politics | 5.7 | 3.8 | 0 |
| All A-level subjects | 328 | 387 | +1.2 | French | 3.9 | 8.3 | 0 |

1. **What is the general pattern of female achievement at GCSE and A-level?**
2. **Why do you think more girls than boys enter for A-levels even though they take fewer GCSEs?**
3. **Significant differences in entry numbers at A-level are highlighted above. How would you account for the variation in entry numbers between males and females in each subject? Share your explanations with your peers.**

Until the late 1980s, there was considerable concern about the underachievement of girls. They did not do quite as well as boys in exams, and were also less likely to take A-levels and enter higher education. However, since the early 1990s, girls have begun to outperform boys at most levels of the education system. For example, they do better at every stage of the National Curriculum SAT results in English, Maths and Science, and in all subjects at GCSE and A-level. In 2006, 48 per cent of females progressed to higher education, compared with 38 per cent of males.

With regard to the number achieving first-class and second-class degrees, the gender gap has remained consistent, with women outperforming men by about 7 per cent (Higher Education Statistics Agency 2007).

However, there are still concerns about the subject choices made by girls. Boys dominate in maths, science and technology at A-level and far more men than women study these subjects in higher education. This has significant implications for men's and women's career choices and future earnings: 60 per cent of working women are clustered in only 10 per cent of occupations.

## Why has girls' achievement improved?

### The job market

There are increasing job opportunities for women in the service sector of the economy, while the availability of traditional male manual work has reduced considerably. About half of all women of working age were in employment in 1960. By 2006, the proportion had risen to three-quarters, with many more in higher-status, relatively well-paid positions. Many girls have mothers in paid employment providing positive role models and contributing, often equally, to the household economy. As a result, girls recognize that the future offers them more choices – they are provided with the incentive to seek economic independence, and careers are now a real possibility.

### Female expectations

Many women are now looking well beyond the mother/housewife role. In a 1976 survey, Sue Sharpe discovered that girls' priorities were 'love, marriage, husbands, children, jobs and careers, more or less in that order'. When the research was repeated in 1994, she found that the priorities had changed to 'job, career and being able to support themselves' above all other priorities. Studies of girls in primary and secondary schools illustrate this change in emphasis. According to Francis and Skelton (2005), 'The majority (of primary and secondary school female pupils) appear to see their chosen career as reflecting their identity and as a vehicle for future fulfilment, rather than as simply a stopgap before marriage'. The growth in employment opportunities, along with the rise in young women's occupational ambitions, have increased their incentives to gain educational qualifications. Studies of both primary and secondary school pupils show that many girls are now looking forward towards jobs that require degree-level qualifications (Francis and Skelton 2005).

### Feminism

The work of feminist sociologists in the 1970s and 1980s led to a greater emphasis on equal opportunities in schools. Teaching approaches and resources were monitored for sex bias to ensure more 'girl-friendly schooling', especially in the sciences. Consequently, teachers are now more sensitive about avoiding gender stereotyping in the classroom. Various antisexist initiatives have raised both teachers' and girls' consciousness. Single-sex classes in some subjects, the exploration of sexism through **PSE**, and citizenship classes have all made a difference. Boys, especially in mixed schools, are more aware of equal opportunities and of the unacceptability of sexist behaviour. Weiner (1995) has argued that teachers have more forcefully challenged stereotypes since the 1980s and many sexist images have been removed from learning materials. However, research by Best (1993) and Abraham (1996) found that women continue to be presented as passive or in a narrow range of often domestic jobs (shopping or buying domestic appliances) whilst men are shown as active, running a business or investing.

### Behaviour

There is mounting evidence that girls work harder and are more motivated than boys. On average, girls put more effort into their work and spend more time on homework. They take more care with presentation of their work, are better organized and, consequently, meet deadlines more successfully than boys. Many boys believe school work should be done at school and, unlike girls, are not prepared to draft and redraft assignments (Burns and Bracey 2001).

Research shows that, from the age of 6, girls read more books than boys, and this trend continues through their lives. Girls are three times more likely than boys to borrow books from a public library (Book Marketing Limited 2000).

### Changes in the organization of education

Before the introduction of the GCSE examination, the gender gap at age 16 was either slightly in favour of girls or non-existent. From 1988, when GCSEs replaced O-levels, the gender gap steadily widened. Pirie (2001) has argued that the old O-level was a boy's exam with its 'high-risk, swot it all up for the final throw' approach to assessment. By contrast, the coursework involved in GCSE and some A-levels requires organizational skills and sustained motivation – skills that girls seem to be better at than boys. However, Debra Myhill (1999) has pointed out that shifts in assessment to increase the proportion of unseen examinations in English have actually been paralleled by an increase in the extent to which girls outperform boys in that subject. Recent changes in the assessment of GCSE and A-level, reducing the level of coursework may not, therefore, make any significant difference to the gender gap.

### Better socialization for schooling

Research by Hannan (2000) shows that girls spend their leisure time differently from boys. Whereas boys relate to their peers by doing (i.e. being active in a range of ways), girls relate to one another by talking. This puts girls at an advantage, because school is essentially a language experience – most subjects require good levels of comprehension and writing skills. Among boys, peer-group pressure is often very strong. It is noticeable from research that boys who do well at school are often helped at home, away from the view of the peer group. Boys often consider it weak to request help from a teacher and it is also especially difficult for a boy to accept help from another boy. Girls, on the other hand, are happy to help each other. It is an acceptable part of being female. (Look at the photos on p. 113 and think about the questions beneath.)

Kirby (2000) has suggested that communicative play through organized social games has been replaced with TV, DVD and computer games. In addition, there has been a decline in family discussion time, through occasions such as mealtimes. Both changes have reduced opportunities for boys to catch up with girls in terms of language development. He points out that, while modern computer games (more popular with boys than girls) may exercise already advanced spatial and visual abilities, they do little to address language deficiency.

# Focus on research

## Becky Francis
### Gender and learning

Becky Francis studied the ways in which gender affects students learning in school and ambitions once they finish compulsory education. The project involved research in three different London secondary schools. Observation was used to record classroom interaction and student behaviour during GCSE lessons as well as individual interviews. The schools were all mixed-sex comprehensives with a large majority of working-class pupils. Approximately one third of the sample were from African-Caribbean origin, one third were White and one third from other ethnic groups.

The observation was conducted in English lessons (a traditionally feminine subject) and Maths lessons (a traditionally masculine subject) – both important for acceptance to certain levels of post-compulsory education and for future employment. A top set and a lower set lesson were observed, so four lessons were observed at each school (12 classes in all). Each class had three lessons observed. A limitation of the classroom observation was an inability to faithfully record all the interaction, due to the sheer noise levels in some of the classes.

In terms of power, boys gained status by taking up 'laddish' or 'class clown' roles. Many used these roles to dominate the classroom interaction, marginalizing girls and other boys. In eight of the twelve lessons observed, boys dominated the classroom interaction by being louder than girls, making greater use of the classroom space, shouting out questions and answers, being disruptive, and/or taking up more of the teachers' attention.

However, the research also showed how the view of femininity as 'sensible' fits more easily with the qualities required for educational success such as concentration and hard work.

Girls' choices of future occupations were as diverse and ambitious as those of boys. They did, however, believe that gender discrimination at work still exists. Their ambition for a 'good job' and the need to compete with men may be motivating them to perform well at school.

Francis, B. (2005) *The Impact of Gender Constructions on Pupils' Learning and Educational Choices: Final project report*, London: ESRC

1. **To what extent is Francis' sample representative of secondary pupils across the UK?**
2. **Why did Francis choose to observe GCSE lessons in English and Maths?**
3. **How might the presence of an observer in the classroom have affected the validity of the data collected?**
4. **What problem did Francis encounter when observing in classrooms?**
5. **What does the research suggest might be the cause of some girls' educational success?**
6. **What does the research suggest might be the cause of some boys' educational underachievement?**

## What are the concerns about boys' achievement?

The increased success of girls relative to boys has caused considerable alarm and, some would argue, overreaction, with some politicians going as far as to warn of the prospect of 'a wasted generation of boys' (Gordon Brown in 2006). Evidence, however, shows that the achievement of both boys and girls has increased over the last 20 years; it is just that girls have improved at a faster rate, resulting in a significant widening of the gender gap. This applies to boys and girls from *all* social classes. Whether this should be seen as 'boys' underachievement' is a matter of opinion. One might well ask why girls are not being enthusiastically applauded for their accomplishments. Some of the concerns over boys are these:

- Boys are behind girls at reading and writing by the age of 6.
- At age 11, the average boy is nine months behind the average girl in development of speaking skills, 12 months behind in literacy and six months behind in numeracy.
- Traditionally, boys have matured later than girls, who have always been ahead in language at primary level, but boys no longer appear able to catch up, remaining, for example, 15 per cent behind at GCSE in English with half the number choosing the subject at A-level.
- White working-class boys are for the first time the lowest achieving group.
- There is a view that less-able boys are virtually unemployable because they lack interest, drive, enthusiasm and social skills (Burns and Bracey 2001), and this increases government anxiety over future generations' dependency on the state.
- Young men are much more likely than young women to be excluded from school (DfES 2006) and, it is feared, increasingly likely to be exposed to deviant and antisocial behaviour.

# Why are boys making slower progress?

## Changes in the job market/status frustration

Some commentators, notably Mac an Ghaill (1994), suggest that working-class boys are experiencing a 'crisis of masculinity'. They are socialized into seeing their future male identity and role in terms of having a job and being a 'breadwinner'. However, the decline of **manufacturing industry** and the rise in long-term unemployment make it increasingly unlikely that males will occupy these roles. Moreover, new jobs in the service sector are often part-time, desk-based, and suited to the skills and lifestyles of women. In some families, females may be the primary breadwinners. Consequently, traditional masculine roles are under threat. Working-class boys' perception of this may influence their motivation and ambition. They may feel that qualifications are a waste of time because there are only limited opportunities in the job market. They may see their future as bleak and without purpose. Consequently, they don't see any point in working hard at school and seek other ways of defining their masculinity.

1 What features of schooling might seem more in line with girls' experiences outside school?
2 What features of schooling might seem to conflict with boys' experiences outside school?

## 'Laddish' behaviour and peer-group status

Early research into **peer-group status** highlighted the development of antischool subcultures that tended to be developed by some working-class boys, particularly those placed in lower streams, bands and sets. Studies by Hargreaves (1967) and Willis (1977), for example, showed how such boys were either fatalistic in accepting school failure as inevitable and so developed anti-educational **coping strategies,** or sought to compensate for status frustration by gaining credibility in the eyes of their peers. However, studies now indicate that 'laddish' behaviours have spread to most boys – both working-class and middle-class – and to some extent to girls (see Focus on Research on 'lads and ladettes').

## Social control differences

According to Mitsos and Browne (1998), teachers are not as critical with boys as with girls. They may have lower expectations of boys, expecting work to be late, rushed and untidy, and expecting boys to be disruptive. Some research suggests that boys are less positively influenced than girls, or even turned off, by primary-school environments, which are female dominated and may have an emphasis on neatness and tidiness.

## Unrealistic attitudes

There are signs that boys' overconfidence may blind them to what is actually required for educational success. Research indicates that they are surprised when they fail exams and tend to put their failure down to bad luck rather than lack of effort. On the other hand, girls are more realistic, even self-doubting, and try that much harder in order to ensure success. However, according to Francis (2000), boys are no longer likely to consider themselves more able than girls, as was the case in the 1970s and 1980s. Also, Francis notes that boys are more likely to have career aspirations that are not only unrealistic, but less likely to require academic success, e.g. professional footballer, whereas girls' career ambitions more often require academic success, e.g. doctor, and hence a commitment to schoolwork.

# What about the future?

According to a number of writers, the solutions to boys' underachievement are couched within a number of discourses, some of which are sympathetic to boys' predicament while others are more critical:

- Epstein (1998) refers to the 'poor boys' discourse that blames schools for failing to cater for boys. Teachers, the exam system, and female concerns and interests ignore boys' learning needs and fail to appreciate and understand their masculinity, especially during primary school. To resolve this, proponents argue that schools should be made more 'masculine', and attention and resources should be directed from girls to boys. However, recent research by Carrington *et al.* (2007) suggests that the gender of the teacher has little or no impact on boys' or girls' learning.
- Second, the 'boys will be boys' discourse suggests that, while boys may be naturally clever, they also tend to be lazy and difficult to motivate, slap-dash, noisy, competitive and demanding. The solution lies with setting clear targets for boys and strong discipline while respecting their masculinity.
- Francis and Skelton (2005) identify two further discourses. The first sees boys themselves as the barrier. The so-called 'problem boys discourse' suggests that

boys are to blame for their own underachievement. They get involved in behaviour that is troublesome to themselves and society. The solution lies with strong discipline and more social control.

- They finally recognize a more sympathetic view – the 'boys at risk' discourse – which sees boys as vulnerable, confused, insecure, and with low self-esteem. They suggest that while the underachieving boy may appear tough on the outside, seeking to impress and boost his self-image, on the inside he is insecure and has low self-esteem. Schools need to be sensitive to and appreciate this and provide opportunities for such boys to rebuild their sense of worth.

Some feminist researchers are concerned that girls are still underachieving because of disruptive boys. Teachers may be so tied up with controlling boys that girls don't get the attention they deserve. Recent research shows that girls' educational achievement has improved despite continuing male dominance of the classroom, curriculum content (for example History's focus on the lives of men) and greater demands on teacher time (Francis 1998). By implication, without boys holding them back, it could have improved even more.

Feminists are also still concerned about the narrow subject choices that females are making at further and higher education level. Females are still more likely to take arts subjects, and males are more likely to take scientific and technological subjects. Such gender stereotyping may be the result of gender socialization in early childhood (e.g. different toys and activities around the home), teacher advice on subject choice, and a continuing perception that the sciences are masculine subjects.

Many feminists believe that the current concern about boys and achievement is simply a 'moral panic'. Weiner *et al.* (1997) argue that the media see the underachievement of Black and working-class boys as a problem because it may lead to the creation of a potentially dangerous underclass, and failure to celebrate girls achievement is merely part of a backlash against female success.

Some critics have argued that the whole question of equality of educational opportunity has now been reduced to gender and the focus on boys. A number of costly government measures aimed at raising boys' educational attainment have been initiated. However, as noted earlier, class has over five times the effect on educational attainment as gender, and ethnicity has twice the effect (Gillborn and Mirza 2000). According to some researchers, the focus on boys has diverted attention from not only underachieving girls but from pupils disadvantaged by their class and/or ethnic background. Osler (2006) picks up on this. She highlights one key area which the Report

# Focus on research

## Carolyn Jackson (2006)

### Lads and ladettes in school

Carolyn Jackson's research investigates a growing culture of 'laddishness' among girls at school. She calls these girls 'ladettes'.

Jackson used a variety of methods, including self-completion questionnaires and interviews. Year 9 pupils completed three questionnaires. The first two concerned their educational goals and behaviour; the third, their views about 'laddishness' and popularity. Pupils were required to respond to statements on a five-point scale according to levels of agreement, and there were slightly different questionnaires for girls and for boys.

Semi-structured interviews were also used. Jackson herself interviewed 153 pupils: 75 girls and 78 boys. The audio tapes were transcribed and then analysed with the help of computer packages which identified key themes: academic pressure, academic self-presentation, SATs, 'lads', 'ladettes'. Some of the key themes were further subdivided into ability, aggression, loudness, language, drinking and dress.

According to Jackson, laddish behaviour can have important advantages from the perspectives of many boys and girls. First, it makes them appear 'cool' if they have a laugh and mess about in class. This aspect of laddishness was accepted by the vast majority of boys and girls, whatever their social-class background. Second, there is so much academic pressure due to teachers' concerns about their school's league table that there is a fear of failure and of being regarded as stupid. Being laddish allows pupils to appear workshy and unconcerned with failure. If they do succeed, they are seen to be 'a genius' because they have apparently done so without doing any work.

Jackson claims that there are no quick fixes for laddish behaviour, but she suggests that it could probably be reduced if the culture of competition in schools was replaced with a more supportive atmosphere where developing ideas was more important than passing tests.

Sources: Jackson, C. (2006) *Lads and Ladettes in School: Gender and a Fear of Failure*, Buckingham: Open University Press ; and Blundell, J. and Griffiths, J. (2008) *Sociology since 2000*, Lewes: Connect Publications

1. **What are the advantages and disadvantages of using self-completion questionnaires to find out about 'laddishness'?**
2. **What are the advantages and disadvantages of using interviews to find out about 'laddishness'?**
3. **How does Jackson operationalize the concept of 'laddishness' when analysing interview data?**
4. **What does Jackson identify as the advantages of 'laddishness' for both boys and girls?**

identifies as a priority for action, namely 'reducing school exclusions among boys and certain ethnic minorities'.

She points out that the current focus on boys' exclusion (and underachievement) is masking a serious problem of exclusion and underachievement among girls, which is increasing at a faster rate than that of boys. African-Caribbean girls are often hailed as one of education's success stories. Yet girls classified as African-Caribbean are more vulnerable to disciplinary exclusion than their White female peers. Despite this, mentoring schemes and other support systems are targeting Black boys. Furthermore, girls who are excluded from school are less likely than their male counterparts to access appropriate support or secure places in pupil referral units or other alternative schemes. Not only do they fail to access the appropriate resources but their right to education is also denied. The research also revealed that official disciplinary exclusion rates mask a wider problem of exclusion from school among girls, which is expressed in a number of hidden ways, including self-exclusion, withdrawal from learning, and truancy. The report advocates a move away from the 'gender see-saw' (in both exclusions and achievement), where we focus on girls for a while and then on boys, to a more integrated approach.

## Key terms

**Coping strategies** ways of 'getting by' in an unpleasant situation.

**Manufacturing industry** industries that actually make goods. Most of the work in such industries is manual and based in factories.

**Peer-group status** being seen as 'big' or important in the eyes of friends and other people around you.

**PSE** Personal and Social Education. Sometimes known as PSHE (including Health Education) or PSME (including Moral Education).

## Check your understanding

1. What have been the overall trends in male and female achievement in the last 20 years?
2. How might changes in the economy affect both female and male attitudes towards education?
3. How have changes in girls' aspirations given them more ambition to succeed academically?
4. What effects might gender stereotyping have on female subject choice at school and university?
5. How may aspects of boys' socialization explain why they underachieve at school?
6. How do boys' aspirations sometimes fail to match up with commitment to study?
7. What solutions have been proposed to address boys' underachievement?
8. (a) Why do male and female students adopt 'laddish' behaviour?
   (b) What form does it take?
   (c) How is increased academic pressure contributing to laddish behaviour?
   (d) What is the solution proposed?
9. Explain how class and ethnicity may be just as important as gender in explaining the current achievement patterns of boys.
10. What does Audrey Osler see as the main problem being caused by the exclusive focus on boys' so-called underachievement?

# Activities

## Research idea

1. Locate achievement data at your school or college (often available on the school or college website). Are there gender patterns in achievement and in subject choice?
2. Interview a sample of boys and girls. Try to find out if they have different expectations about future success. Are there differences in the amount of time they spend on homework?

## Web.tasks

Go to www.teachernet.gov.uk/wholeschool/equality/genderequalityduty/thegenderagenda/. This will give you access to a range of information and research findings about gender and education. Find out what schools are doing about the 'gender gap'.

A detailed description of the various explanations is required, using sociological concepts, theories and studies.

*as you go along* ✓
*along*
*AO2 throught* 😊

Weigh up the strengths and weaknesses of each explanation before reaching a balanced conclusion.

No need to discuss biological or psychological explanations

Outline and assess sociological explanations of the relationship between gender and educational achievement.

(50 marks)

This can be measured in different ways

Include both males and females

## Grade booster  Getting top marks in this question

Examples of the statistical patterns and trends linking gender and educational achievement are worth including in an introduction. Then the various explanations that have been used to explain the relationship between gender and achievement will need to be discussed. Some of these will relate to the improving achievement of female students while others will apply to the underachievement of some boys. The feminist perspective is likely to feature. The explanations will need to be compared and evaluated as the answer progresses. A conclusion could note the importance of taking into account the relationships between ethnicity, gender and class rather than analyzing their impact on educational achievement separately.

*theory, fem, new, JD + label*

*Into:*

# TOPIC 5

# The relationship between education and the economy

## Getting you thinking

1. Which of your experiences, both in and out of school, have been helpful in developing knowledge and skills that may prove useful in working life?
2. Do you think that vocational education (teaching the skills required for jobs) is thought of less positively than traditional academic education? Why do you think this may be the case?
3. Do you think the low status of vocational education and training may have played a part in Britain's lack of economic success relative to other countries?
4. In your opinion, is the perception of Oxbridge and other elite universities as the pinnacle of success in any way to blame for the lower status of other routes to jobs in British society? If so, how?

Ever since the introduction of compulsory education, successive governments have recognized that the low status of work-related (or **vocational**) education is a problem. It is claimed that many members of the British workforce lack appropriate technical skills, adequate literacy and numeracy and the values of hard work and self-discipline required by employers. Schools and colleges have lost touch with the needs of industry, promoting an academic curriculum at the expense of vocational courses with their students aspiring to careers in law and medicine rather than engineering or manufacturing. Consequently, Britain is seen at a disadvantage when compared to its European competitors in particular.

These fears have led recent governments to develop a vast range of vocational schemes, initiatives and qualifications aimed to bring education closer to the world of work. This topic will outline some of these developments before discussing the different ways sociologists have interpreted them.

## Developments in vocational education and training

### Conservative work-based education and training initiatives 1979-97: 'the new vocationalism'

#### *National Vocational Qualifications (NVQs)*

In 1986, the National Council for Vocational Qualifications was set up to introduce standardized vocational qualifications for particular occupations. These were job-specific qualifications which demonstrate 'on-the-job' competencies, such as 'production machine sewing', and are often studied part time in college in the evening, or on day release, alongside full-time work. They now cover about 88 per cent of all occupations.

### General National Vocational Qualifications (GNVQs)

GNVQs were studied in school as an alternative to academic courses and cover wider areas – for example, leisure and tourism and health and social care; GNVQs have now been replaced by vocational GCSEs and A levels.

### Apprenticeships

From 1995, these programmes combined training at work with part-time attendance at college with the aim of achieving an NVQ qualification at Level 3 (equivalent to an A-level) as well as other accreditation and skills.

### Training schemes

A Youth Training Scheme (YTS) was a one-year training scheme combining work experience with education for school leavers. In 1986, YTS was extended to a two-year scheme. YTS was replaced in 1990 with Youth Training. The only requirement in this scheme was for employers to ensure that trainees followed some sort of training programme which led towards a Level 2 NVQ.

## New Labour work-based education and training initiatives 1997–2010

### New Deal for Young People (NDYP)

In 1998, Labour introduced the DNYP, with the aim of reducing youth unemployment. The programme was designed for 18 to 24 year olds who had been unemployed and claiming Jobseeker's Allowance for six months. They were provided with Personal Advisors to guide them through the various options: (1) full-time education or training for up to 12 months; (2) work for six months in either the Environmental Task Force or the voluntary sector; (3) a subsidized job with at least one day a week of training; (4) loss of benefits if they refused to take part in the programme. From April 1998 to the end of May 2005, 567900 (46 per cent) of those leaving the programme entered employment (Social Trends 2006). Most jobs were relatively short term.

### Apprenticeships

Labour also expanded the Apprenticeship scheme. More NVQs at Level 2 or 3 were offered, as well as a technical certificate and Key Skills to complete a full framework. Young apprenticeships at Level 1 for 14 to 16 year olds in schools and colleges have also been introduced.

### Vocational GCSEs/A levels

These replaced GNVQs in an attempt to create parity of esteem with academic courses.

### Increased Flexibility programme

Pupils at Key stage 4 (14 to 16) were allowed to attend college for one or two days per week to follow vocational qualifications not available at school. Most schools used the IFP to re-engage disaffected young people.

### Diplomas

A combination of vocational and academic learning studied alongside other complementary qualifications and 'functional' skills in literacy, numeracy and IT. The aim is to engage all 14 to 19 year olds in education and further study. Diplomas are delivered in partnerships between schools, colleges and employers. Diplomas are available at different levels and in different vocational areas.

### Work-related learning

A range of initiatives to encourage schools to do more vocational education such as an entitlement to work experience at Key Stage 4, work shadowing and mock interviews.

## Perspectives on education and work

Most of these perspectives are described and evaluated in Topic 1. Here we will focus on their views of the relationship between education and the economy.

## Functionalism

Back in the 19th century Durkheim (1893) argued that modern societies are based on a specialized division of labour that requires a great number of occupational roles, each needing specialized skills. As modern societies become more complex, the skills they require will become more diverse and education and training will need to develop and adapt to meet these requirements. Developing Durkheim's point, Parsons and Davis and Moore put forward the view that education is important in allocating roles in society, examinations and qualifications functioning to place people into their most appropriate roles.

### Evaluation

Marxists have suggested that the skills passed on through the education system favour the rich and powerful rather than society as a whole. For example, the emphasis on conformity and discipline in schools encourages people to be passive and accept authority in later life, while the focus on skills for employment directly benefits the capitalist class by providing them the workers they require to maximize their profits.

The idea that modern societies require increasing levels of specialized skills is challenged by the Braverman (1974). He argues that computerization has actually **deskilled** some white-collar and professional jobs, reducing their pay and status.

Finally, British society is still a long way from the meritocracy described by functionalists such as Parsons and Davis and Moore. Social class remains a massive influence on educational achievement (see Topic 2) and gender and ethnicity also play a significant role (see Topics 3 and 4).

## Social democratic

Social democratic approaches to education and the economy resemble those of functionalists. As societies become more complex, education needs to expand and develop to make sure that the next generation are equipped with the appropriate skills knowledge and attitudes to create economic growth and increase wealth.

Education is the key method by which modern societies can provide the equality of opportunity necessary to create a meritocratic society where the most important positions are filled by the most talented people, regardless of their class, gender, ethnicity or any other social characteristic.

Unlike many functionalists however, social democrats believe that inequalities in society prevent the kind of meritocratic society based on equality of opportunity described above. If poverty, for example, prevents an individual from having the same chances as those from more privileged backgrounds, then this is not helping create a meritocracy and the government should take measures to bring about greater equality of opportunity. Similarly, governments need to keep spending high on education and to ensure that this spending is used by schools and colleges to develop the knowledge and skills needed for economic growth.

### Evaluation

Social democratic approaches have been influential in the development of vocational education and training. These developments can be seen as attempts to make education respond to the changing needs of a modern economy.

However, social democratic views have been criticized by both Marxists, who believe that they are not radical enough, and by the New Right, who believe that they are too radical.

Marxists believe that 'tinkering' with the education system will not threaten the dominance of the capitalist class so will not help bring about equal opportunities in society.

The New Right agree that education should be more directly focused on the needs of the economy (see below) although they do not believe that there is necessarily a link between high expenditure on education and economic growth. For example, Woolf (2002) argues that Switzerland spends relatively little on education but is still one of the wealthiest countries in the world.

## New Right

The view of the New Right is that the education system should serve the needs of the economy and provide workers with the skills and attitudes required by employers. New Right views of the relationship between education and work became prominent during the 1980s and were favoured by the Conservative government of Margaret Thatcher. During this period youth unemployment steadily rose – in 1986 three million people were unemployed, many of them school leavers. Trowler (2003) argues that the government were concerned about youth unemployment for three main reasons.

1. The costs of paying out benefits to the unemployed and their families.
2. The social costs of unemployment, such as rising crime and social disorder.
3. The long-term effects of unemployment on young people themselves. There was a real danger that they would lose the '**work ethic**' and become unemployable in the future.

This last point ties in with the arguments of New Right thinkers such as Murray (see Chapter 6 Topic 4) that the long-term unemployed would become dependent on benefits, lose the desire to work, become detached from mainstream social values and become part of a growing 'underclass'.

The New Right believed that education had become dominated by liberal, academic thinking that was out of step with the needs of industry. Influenced by New Right thinking, the Conservative government set about rationalizing and strengthening vocational education and training in schools and further education colleges to more successfully meet the needs of employers for young workers with the 'right' skills and disciplines. A variety of schemes and initiatives were introduced that became known as the '**new vocationalism**' (see above). A key aim of these was to prevent young people from moving straight from school to unemployment.

Tomlinson (2005) argues that the broad thrust of the 'new vocationalism' has been built on by more recent New Labour governments which have accepted uncritically the principle that a primary aim of education is to serve the needs of employers (see above for New Labour work-based and training initiatives).

### Evaluation

The new vocationalism has come under attack in several ways.

- It has been seen as an attempt to reduce unemployment figures rather than provide real opportunities for young people.
- It has been criticized for implying that unemployment is the fault of young people themselves when in fact, there were simply not sufficient jobs available in the right areas.
- Dale (1985) argued that the new vocationalism was aimed only at lower-ability young people and effectively trained them only for low-skilled, insecure employment.

Sociologists influenced by both social democratic and Marxist ideas have attacked vocational education and training for reproducing social inequalities of class, ethnicity and gender. Lee (1990) conducted a six-year project studying a training scheme in the south of England and concluded that the influence of New Right thinking on the scheme led to a 'free-market' philosophy that left too much power in the hands of employers. This led to the exploitation of trainees and their use as cheap labour, magnifying the effects of social inequalities.

Marxists have gone further in their criticisms, which we now move on to consider.

## Marxism

The neo-Marxist Finn (1987) argues that there is a hidden political agenda to vocational training:

- It provides cheap labour for employers and keeps the pay rates of young workers low.
- It undermines the bargaining power of the unions (because only permanent workers can be members).
- It reduces politically embarrassing unemployment statistics.
- It may also be intended to reduce crime by removing young people from the streets.

Critics such as Phil Cohen (1984) argued that the real purpose of vocational training is to create 'good' attitudes and work discipline rather than actual job skills. In this way, young people come to accept a likely future of low-paid and unskilled work. Those young unemployed who view training schemes as cheap labour, and refuse to join them, are defined as irresponsible and idle, and are 'punished' by the withdrawal of benefits. It is not proven that young people lack job skills. Many have already gained a lot of work experience from part-time jobs. Youth unemployment is the result not of a shortage of skills, but of a shortage of jobs. Critics also point out that the sorts of skills taught to trainees are only appropriate for jobs in the secondary labour market. This consists of jobs that are unskilled, insecure, and pay low wages – such jobs offer little chance of promotion, employer investment is very low, and labour turnover is consequently very high. In practice, it is lower-ability students who tend to be channelled into vocational courses. The new vocationalism thus introduced another form of selection, with working-class and ethnic minority students being disproportionately represented on these courses.

### *Evaluation*

Marxist approaches are extremely negative in the ways they analyze vocational schemes. They ignore the genuine opportunities that some of these initiatives have provided students and the ways in which successive governments have attempted to improve the quality of vocational education and training.

## Feminism

Training schemes have also been criticized for failing to break down the traditional patterns of sex stereotyping found in employment and education and for failing to encourage girls to move into non-traditional areas. In fact, according to Buswell (1987), they are structured so as to reproduce gender inequality. She points out that the types of schemes into which girls are channelled, such as retail work, lead to occupations where they are low paid when young, and work part time when older, reflecting women's position in the labour market. This problem has remained up to the present day. For example, according to official figures, in 2006, six per cent of Apprenticeships in hairdressing were taken up by males compared with 94 per cent by females. Retail fares slightly better with a 38/62 split, whereas in construction crafts, the male-to-female ratio is 99 to1.

See also the Focus on Research below.

## **Focus** on **research**

### Becky Francis, Louise Archer, Jayne Osgood and Jacinta Dalgety, 2005

### Gender equality in work experience placements for young people

The authors of this study used a range of methods to study the relationship between gender and work experience placements in schools.

Work-experience co-ordinators in schools recognised that work placements were overwhelmingly gender-stereotypical. Males were assigned to traditionally masculine areas of work such as engineering, semi-skilled manual labour and information technology, while girls were assigned to traditionally female jobs such as retail work and childcare.

Female pupils reported that their choice of work placements was restricted by the fact that more male-dominated (and therefore stereotypically masculine) places were available. Females often found that their placements were restricted to hair and beauty, childcare and retail. Consequently, girls often found themselves in stereotypically feminine work placements which many were not particularly interested in as a career.

There were also some signs of social-class bias in the allocation of pupils to placements. Pupils who aspired to university were generally given high-status placements in the legal profession, media production, medicine, education, and so on. However, often it was they or their parents who were instrumental in arranging these placements. Students who did not aspire to higher education often found themselves placed in shops, nurseries, garages, and factories. However, despite these class differences, allocation to work placements, whether high or low status, were still gender stereotyped in most cases.

Pupils were asked about their aspirations with regard to future occupations and these turned out to be highly gender-stereotypical. Girls focused on the caring and creative while boys aspired to scientific, technical and business jobs. Boys tended to hold more strongly stereotypical views than girls. However, the majority of the pupil sample stated that they did not want non-traditional jobs and expressed the stereotypical belief that men and women are simply better at different jobs.

Sources: Adapted from Chapman, S. and Langley, P. (2010) *Key Studies in Education*, Lewes: Connect Publications

1. **What was the relationship between gender and work-experience placements?**
2. **What was the relationship between social class and work-experience placements?**
3. **How did parents' social and cultural capital give their children advantages in work-experience placements?**
4. **What was the relationship between gender and the pupils' career aspirations?**

## Key terms

**Deskilled** removal of the skilled element from a job

**New Vocationalism** series of youth training and vocational schemes set up in the 1980s

**Vocational** relating to jobs

**Work ethic** positive attitude to hard work

## Check your understanding

1. Give examples of two work-related initiatives introduced in the 1980s that have become known as part of the new vocationalism.
2. Explain the 'New Deal for Young People' and the 'Increased Flexibility' programme in your own words.
3. How did New Right ideas influence the new vocationalism?
4. What do you consider to be the three most serious criticisms of the new vocationalism?
5. How have feminists criticized vocational schemes?

## Activities

### Research idea

1. Survey a group of students at your school or college. Choose a sample that includes students following both academic and vocational courses. Why did they stay on at 16? What is motivating them and what do they hope to achieve from their qualifications? Are there different motivations for students following academic and vocational courses?
2. Conduct semi-structured interviews with students who have been on work experience. Find out about their experiences and whether or not they feel that these have made them better equipped for a future job.

### Web.tasks

Go to a job vacancy website such as www.jobsearch.co.uk. Look up a sample of jobs and note the skills and qualities required. Where are young people likely to develop these skills and how? What is the role of the education system in teaching these skills?

## An eye on the exam The relationship between education and the economy

A detailed description of Marxist explanations is required, using sociological concepts, theories and studies.

Weigh up the strengths and weaknesses of Marxist explanations in some detail, then present alternative perspectives before reaching a balanced conclusion.

**Outline and assess Marxist explanations of the relationship between education and work. (50 marks)**

Other theories only need to appear as part of an evaluation of Marxist views

Include vocational education and training

### Grade booster Getting top marks in this question

It is worth using the introduction to provide a brief explanation of the key ideas of Marxism and their application to education. The broader theoretical position of Marxism on the relationship between education and the economy (e.g. Bowles and Gintis) can be discussed before moving on to Marxist critiques of vocational education and training. Assessment of the various Marxist views needs to occur throughout the answer. Alternative positions such as those taken by functionalists, the New Right and social democrats can be used to evaluate further.

# TOPIC 6

# Social policy and education

## Getting you thinking

**SECONDARY SCHOOL PERFORMANCE T**

| BOLTON | KEY STAGE 3 RESULTS: PUPILS AGED 14 | (% achieving level 5 or above in test) ENGLISH | MATHS | SCIENCE | GCSE/GNVQ RESULTS: PUPILS AGED 15 | 5 or more Grades A*-C | 5 or more Grades A*-G | % in age group with no passes |
|---|---|---|---|---|---|---|---|---|
| Al Jamiah Al Islamiyyah | 22 | 55% | 59% | 36% | 23 | 0% | 22% | 26% |
| Bolton Muslim Girls' School | 65 | 95% | 71% | 54% | 61 | 54% | 97% | 0% |
| Bolton School Boys' Division | - | - | - | - | 139 | 96% | 96% | 4% |
| Bolton School Girls' Division | - | - | - | - | 120 | 99% | 99% | 1% |
| Canon Slade CofE School | 270 | 90% | 90% | 88% | 246 | 81% | 98% | 0% |
| The Deane School | 154 | 46% | 53% | 47% | 175 | 27% | 80% | [illegible] |
| George Tomlinson School | 123 | 41% | 42% | 42% | 85 | 22% | 91% | [illegible] |
| Harper Green School | 288 | 68% | 59% | 59% | 258 | 36% | 92% | [illegible] |
| Hayward School | 260 | 63% | 58% | 56% | 232 | 31% | 91% | [illegible] |
| Little Lever School Specialist Language College | 210 | 64% | 70% | 63% | 231 | 47% | 97% | [illegible] |
| Lord's College | - | - | - | - | 9 | 44% | 89% | [illegible] |
| Mount St Joseph RC High School, Bolton | 183 | 63% | 67% | 69% | 205 | 42% | 92% | [illegible] |
| Rivington and Blackrod High School | 310 | 70% | 71% | 69% | 303 | 52% | 94% | [illegible] |
| St James's Church of England Secondary School | 200 | 80% | 83% | 84% | 178 | 56% | 98% | 1% |
| St Joseph's RC High School and Sports College | 174 | 73% | 85% | 78% | 154 | 69% | 98% | 1% |
| Sharples School | 214 | 48% | 56% | 66% | 203 | 42% | 90% | 4% |

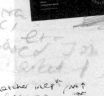

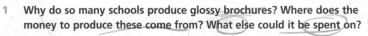

1 **Why do so many schools produce glossy brochures? Where does the money to produce these come from? What else could it be spent on?**

2 **Why have recent governments been keen to produce education 'league tables'?**

3 **Apart from improving quality, what can schools do to improve their position in league tables?**

4 **Why do you think the developments discussed here are sometimes referred to as the 'marketization' of education?**

5 **What arguments can be put forward:**

(a) **in favour of marketization?** (b) **against marketization?**

The questions above should have encouraged you to think about the effects of what sociologists have called the '**marketization**' of schools. The idea behind marketization is that schools compete for pupils; the best schools attract the most pupils and the weaker schools have to improve. As you may have noticed from your own experiences, the idea of marketization is still very much alive. This topic traces the origins of this and other key themes in social policy on education. It should be used in conjunction with Topic 5, which also deals with social policy on education, focusing on work-related education and training.

## Perspectives on social policy

Two key perspectives have influenced social policy on education since the Second World War.

1 Social democracy
2 The New Right

### 1. Social democratic perspectives on educational policy

From a social democratic perspective, society should be based on justice and fairness; everyone should have an equal chance to succeed. In other words, society should be meritocratic – based on equality of opportunity. Education has an important part to play in this meritocracy, as it acts as be the mechanism through which individuals are given equal chances to develop their talents.

Policies influenced by social democratic perspectives will emphasize providing equal opportunities for all pupils and investing resources in education to develop skills and help the economy grow. The influence of social democratic views can be seen in some New Labour policies between 1997 and 2010 (see below).

### 2. New Right perspectives on educational policy

New Right policies became increasingly influential during the Conservative governments of 1979 to 1997 although they have also influenced some New Labour policies as we will see later. New Right policies favour the use of market forces as a method of distributing resources. In a free market, consumers choose between a range of products. Producers compete to produce the best product at the best price. In this way, schools compete to attract pupils and educational standards improve as a result.

First, let's look at the origins of the different types of secondary schools in Britain.

## Types of school

### Grammar and secondary modern schools

After the Second World War the government introduced a new system where all pupils would be entitled to secondary education. This was known as the **tripartite system**. The system reflected social democratic principles as its aim was to abolish class inequalities in access to schools and to provide equality of opportunity. All children would take an IQ test at the age of 11 in order to discover which kind of school most suited their abilities. 'Academically able' pupils (about 20%) would attend grammar schools, students with practical skills technical schools and the rest secondary modern schools. In reality, few technical schools were built so the vast majority of pupils attended grammar or secondary modern schools.

The problem was that the system reproduced social-class inequalities. Two thirds of grammar school places were taken by middle-class pupils. The mainly working-class pupils in secondary moderns were effectively labelled as failures and so lacked the means and motivation to succeed.

This system still has its supporters. It served middle-class families very well and still survives today in some parts of the country. It must also be remember that it did virtually guarantee social mobility for those working-class pupils who made it to grammar schools. Some recent research has gone so far as to suggest that the system gave working-class pupils more chance than they have today (see Focus on research, p91).

### Comprehensive schools

The tripartite system failed to bring about the social democratic ideal of equality of opportunity. What might bring that ideal closer was to educate all children in the same school, regardless of class, gender, ethnicity and ability. In 1965 the Labour government introduced comprehensive schools. Facilities were upgraded so that the new schools could provide a broad curriculum and more sporting and recreational activities.

Most state schools today still operate along comprehensive principles, although these are coming under increasing pressure as a result of marketization. Comprehensives are criticized by social democrats for their failure to eliminate class differences and by the New Right for their lack of discipline, failure to prepare students for the world of work and their uniformity. These criticisms have led governments to attempt to create more choice and diversity in secondary education by introducing specialist schools and academies.

### Specialist schools and academies

These are discussed later in the Topic.

### Fe[illegible]schools

char[illegible] obliga[illegible]ools have been left largely untouched by [illegible] state education system. They have no Curricul[illegible] children or to follow the National Roker (19[illegible] of private education by writers such as [illegible] curriculum g[illegible] that these schools transmit a hidden leadership roles [illegible]ierarchy, elitism and future [illegible] schools and, whi[illegible]zes tend to be half those in state [illegible] attend private scho[illegible]out 7 per cent of students and Cambridge Univ[illegible]st half the students at Oxford [illegible]

Individuals who atte[illegible]e privately educated. [illegible] higher positions in British [illegible]vate schools dominate the [illegible] of MPs were educated privat[illegible] for example about a third [illegible] Reid (1998) found that 84 per ce[illegible] Sutton Trust, 2005). [illegible] of bank directors and 49 per cent [illegible]f judges, 70 per cent [illegible]p civil servants went to private schools.

### Faith schools

Churches have played a role in education for hundreds of years, long before the state became involved. In fact, it was churches that first provided education for poorer people. Since 1944 religious organizations have been able to set up schools within the state system if there is parental demand. Around a third of state schools in Britain today are faith schools.

Faith schools have to comply with testing and the National Curriculum. However, they can appoint up to 20 per cent of teachers on the basis of their ability to provide religious education in line with the principles of the particular set of beliefs. Faith schools can select pupils on the basis of their religious beliefs but have to take other pupils if the school is not filled. Almost all (98%) of faith schools in Britain are Roman Catholic or Church of England.

## The New Right and education 1979–1997

The Conservative government of this period, led by Margaret Thatcher, used education policy to put into practice many of the market principles of the New Right. The key legislation of the 1980s was probably the 1988 Education Reform Act although their policies on vocational education and training were also very significant - these are discussed in Topic 5.

### The 1988 Education Reform Act

The influence of the New Right is clearly seen in this Act, the most influential in education since 1944. It introduced a new emphasis on competition and choice in education. Its key elements consisted of the following.

#### *Marketization*

Competition between schools was to be encouraged. The greater the competition, the greater the incentive for schools to improve. Successful schools could expand; unsuccessful schools would have to improve or face t[illegible] possibility of funding cuts and, ultimately, closure. P[illegible] would be given a real choice between schools.

### Testing

Parents would need a way of judging the ... onal schools. It was decided that all pupils w... draw up tests – 'SATs' – at the ages of 7, 11 an... formed with GCSE and A-level results, woul... league tables so that parents could ... choice of school.

### The National Curriculum

In order to develop meaningf... rds for comparison and to ensure that all pupils ... teaching in appropriate knowledge and skills, a Na... **curriculum** was introduced. This prescribe... ledge in a range of subjects that every school woul... to teach. In addition, the influence of local auth... s on education was reduced. Schools could decide ... to manage their own budgets and even opt out o... cal authority control altogether, enabling them to make their own decisions about which pupils to admit, even ... troducing selection if they wished.

### *Criticisms of ... e Education Reform Act*

1. Concerns were expressed over the damaging, stressful effects of testing children so often – also, that testing could distort what was taught so that schools would 'teach to the test'.
2. League tables were felt to be counterproductive. They meant that some schools might not admit low achievers and difficult pupils or enter them for exams. Competition might also force schools to spend large amounts of money on marketing rather than on the education of pupils (see 'Getting you thinking'). Also, schools would be tempted to 'teach to the test' in order to boost their league table position.
3. Very few extra places were available in popular schools, so many parents had very little or no choice of school.
4. Class differences were reinforced by the Act. Middle-class parents were able to use their cultural capital (see Topic 2) to make sure that their children got into the best schools. Research by Ball *et al.* (1994) showed that middle-class parents were better able to impress at interview, write convincing letters and manipulate the system, for example by making multiple applications to schools. They could also use their economic capital (money) to pay transport costs if better schools were further away and even move nearer their favoured school if necessary.

## New Labour: 1997–2010

### New Labour: New Right influences

New Right thinking continued to influence the New Labour government elected in 1997. Many of the policies begun by the Conservatives were continued and developed. One example was the expansion of **specialist schools**.

#### *Specialist schools*

...hools were encouraged to specialize in particular subjects. ... aim was to increase choice, encourage competition, ... standards and allow schools to excel at their ...lisms. No longer did school pupils have to attend what ...cation secretary of the day David Blunkett referred to ...g standard' local comprehensive school.

State secondary schools could apply to become a specialist school in one of ten specialisms – art, business and enterprise, engineering, humanities, languages, mathematics and computing, music, science, sports and technology. They had to raise £50 000 from sponsors, which was matched by government funding. Once a specialist school, they could select up to 10 per cent of their pupils who showed an aptitude for their specialism.

In 1997, New Labour inherited 196 specialist schools from the Conservatives. Ten years later, there were 2500 – about 80 per cent of all secondary schools in England.

### New Labour: social democratic influences

By no means all New Labour's educational policies have reflected New Right thinking, however. The influence of social democratic viewpoints were also apparent. Here are some examples of policies which aimed to reduce **social exclusion** and promote equality of opportunity.

- *Academies* – In 2001, it was proposed that Academies should be established in partnership with employers and other sponsors to replace failing schools and provide high-quality education for all in deprived areas. The best teachers would be encouraged to work in these schools and there would be a high level of resourcing. Sponsors could have a say in how the school is run and what curriculum is on offer. In the sense that Academies represent private companies becoming involved in state education, there is also a New Right influence visible in this policy.
- *Sure Start* – This term describes a wide range of programmes targeted at giving young children a better start in life. Free nursery education was made available, and Sure Start children's centres brought together a range of educational and other support services in disadvantaged communities.
- *Educational Maintenance Allowances* – Students between the ages of 16 and 19 who are in full-time education and training could apply for Educational Maintenance Allowances of up to £30 a week. These were available to families on lower incomes and aimed to encourage young people to stay in education.

### Evaluation of New Labour policies

The influence of New Right ideas on government thinking meant that competition and choice continued to be seen as the key way to improve educational standards. However, as Sally Tomlinson has pointed out, in practice, the middle classes gained most from these policies (Tomlinson 2005). In addition, the focus on exams and league tables meant that much education became, as she puts it, 'examination techniques, rote learning and revision'.

Social democratic influences on educational policy resulted in the directing of resources towards deprived groups and areas. This may have resulted in some improvements although these are not yet clear (McKnight *et al.* 2005).

It appears that New Right and social democratic approaches will continue to influence the coalition government of 2010. The 'pupil premium' involves directing resources towards poorer pupils while the expansion of academies and encouragement of 'free schools' reflect New Right concerns of choice an...

New Labour policy on higher education presents an interesting case study of the way in which New Labour tried to increase opportunities.

### Higher education

A stated aim of the government was to increase the numbers of students in higher education. The target was that 50 per cent of young people would be entering higher education by 2010. To meet this target, university facilities were expanded, funded by the replacement of student grants with loans, to be repaid once the graduate's salary has reached a certain level. Also, students now had to meet some of the cost of their tuition fees. Financial support for less affluent applicants was available.

So, did the government's plan to encourage a wider range of young people to apply to university work? In one sense it did: the percentage of young people from manual working-class backgrounds going to university increased from 11 per cent to 19 per cent between 1991/2 and 2001/2 (*Social Trends 34*). However, over the same period, the percentage from middle-class backgrounds increased from 35 to 50 per cent. Recent statistics from the Higher Education Statistics Agency show that only 28.7 per cent of young entrants to university in 2004/5 came from lower socio-economic groups. If anything, class inequalities in higher education have increased (McKnight *et al.* 2005).

What is more, a range of research evidence shows that university students from a working-class background are more likely to:

- study at local institutions with limited course options
- live at home while studying
- study part time
- have family or work commitments
- incur high levels of student debt
- drop out from their initial choice of course.

See also the Focus on research on 'Fear of debt' below.

### Conclusion

The changes in higher education under New Labour reflect the overall pattern of their policies on education: opportunities have increased for everybody, but class inequalities remain stubbornly present. Back in 1971, Basil Bernstein wrote that 'education cannot compensate for society' – in other words, education will tend to reflect social inequalities rather than eliminate them. That seems to be the story of education under New Labour.

## Focus on research

### Callendar and Jackson (2004)

### Fear of debt

One policy of the Labour Government elected in 1997 was to increase numbers going to university. At the same time, the cost to students of a university education has been going up. Student grants have been replaced as the main source of funding by loans that have to be repaid once they graduate and are earning a reasonable income.

Callendar and Jackson's study investigates whether students from poorer families were more likely than those from better-off backgrounds to be deterred from applying to university by concerns about cost and debts, especially the student loan debt.

The research involved a survey of prospective higher-education students producing quantitative data. 101 school sixth forms and further education colleges agreed to take part, and 3582 questionnaires were sent out. A national stratified random sample of schools and colleges was used. Responses were received from 1954 students in 82 schools and colleges; a 55 per cent response rate was achieved.

Self-completion questionnaires were handed out to students in classes by teachers. Three questions were asked to gather information on general level of debt aversion; students were asked to what extent they agreed or disagreed with these statements:

- 'Owing money is basically wrong.'
- 'There is no excuse for borrowing money.'
- 'You should always save up first before buying something.'

Students were then asked their attitudes towards statements about the costs and benefits of going to university, e.g. 'Borrowing money to pay for a university education is a good investment.'

Callendar and Jackson's conclusion is that, 'Debt aversion is a class issue'. Those from lower income groups were more debt averse (more likely to see debt as negative, to be avoided) than the other classes. This was true even holding constant the type of institution they attended (college or state or independent school), gender, ethnicity and age. The lower income group was also more likely to see more costs than benefits in going to university.

Adapted from Blundell, J. and Griffiths, J. (2008) *Sociology since 2000*, Lewes: Connect Publications

1. **Explain how the researchers attempted to make their sample representative of prospective university applicants.**
2. **What is meant by a 'response rate'?**
3. **What are the advantages and disadvantages of using a quantitative approach to investigate fear of debt and its influence on university application?**
4. **What problems may have been caused by the method used to distribute the questionnaires?**
5. **What are Callendar and Jackson's conclusions?**

## Key terms

**11+** IQ test taken at the age of 11 to determine what sort of school you would attend under the tripartite system.

**Academies** schools set up in partnership with sponsoring organizations in order to replace failing schools. They have more freedom in what and how they teach.

**IQ tests** supposedly objective tests that establish a person's 'intelligence quotient' (how clever they are).

**Marketization** the move towards educational provision being determined by market forces.

**National Curriculum** what every pupil in every state school must learn, decided by the government.

**Secondary education** education between ages 11 and 16.

**Social exclusion** the situation where people are unable to achieve a quality of life that would be regarded as acceptable by most people.

**Specialist schools** schools which have a particular focus within their curriculum and links to specialist areas of work, e.g. arts and media, business, languages, healthcare and medicine. They can select 10 per cent of their intake on the basis of ability.

# Activities

### Research idea

Interview an experienced member of your school or college staff. Ask them to describe the impact that the following changes had upon their educational career and experiences: the introduction of the National Curriculum, school/college inspections, league tables, competition between schools/colleges, parental choice and Educational Maintenance Allowances.

### Web.tasks

Visit the Teachernet site at www.teachernet.gov.uk and find information on different types of schools and key educational initiatives.

## Check your understanding

1. What key principles lie behind the social democratic approach to education?
2. What key principles lie behind the New Right approach to education?
3. What are grammar and secondary modern schools?
4. What criticisms have been made of comprehensive schools?
5. What is the relationship between private education and elite positions in British society?
6. How did the Education Reform Act 1988 attempt to create a more unified and accountable education system?
7. How can it be argued that the Act failed to achieve this?
8. Give one example of a New Labour educational policy influenced by New Right thinking. Explain your answer.
9. Give one example of a New Labour educational policy influenced by social democratic thinking. Explain your answer.
10. Explain the phrase 'Education cannot compensate for society' using New Labour's higher education policy as an example.

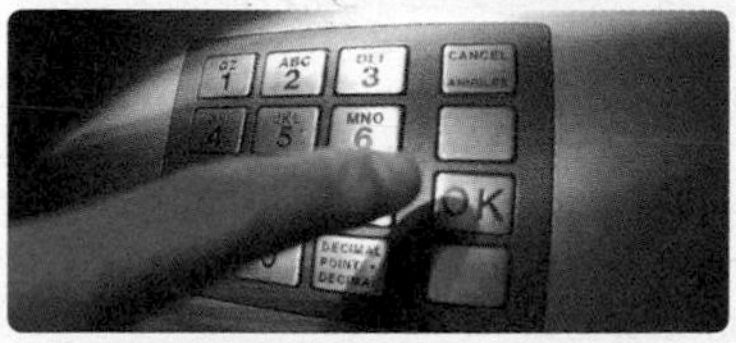

## An eye on the exam Social policy and education

A detailed description of the view is required, using sociological concepts, theories and studies.

Weigh up the strengths and weaknesses of the view in some detail before reaching a balanced conclusion.

Can include class, gender and ethnicity

**Outline and assess the view that educational policies since 1988 are reinforcing social inequality. (50 marks)**

Select a few that illustrate the points you wish to make

No need to discuss the period before

### Grade booster Getting top marks in this question

The introduction could provide an overview of some of the key changes in educational policy during the relevant period. Then some of these will need to be analyzed in terms of their impact on inequality – social class, gender and/or ethnic inequality. Key perspectives in supporting the view in the question are likely to be Marxist, neo-Marxist and social democratic, while New Right views can be used to evaluate these interpretations. Suggested policies which lend themselves to an analysis in terms of inequalities are those relating to marketization as well as New Labour policies such as the introduction of Educational Maintenance Allowance and academies. Try to include an analysis of some of the policies introduced since the coalition govenment came to power in 2010 such as the 'pupil premium'.

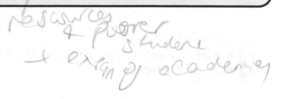

# Exam Practice

**Outline and assess the view that differential educational achievement is caused by teacher labelling.** ***(50 marks)***

Educational achievement depends on a number of different factors. It is usually operationalised by the level of achievement in exams. The concept of labelling was developed by interactionists who believe that the cause of behaviour is based around how you are judged or labelled by others. In relation to educational achievement, this refers to teachers judging pupils by characteristics to do with their class, gender or ethnicity, like their attitudes and behaviour rather than by their ability to perform at school. The theory of teacher labelling was developed by Becker, who believed teachers had a perception of the 'ideal pupil' which is someone who conforms to middle-class standards of behaviour. Those who didn't conform to this were labelled by teachers negatively, which led to either the pupils internalising these labels and believing they had low ability and therefore underachieving, or reacting against these labels and exhibiting poor behaviour, which also leads to underachievement.

> The idea of differential educational achievement needs to be explained more clearly at the start of the answer. It is a good idea to establish the link between teacher labelling and the interactionist perspective although the perspective could be explained in a bit more detail.

Becker believed that social class has a large impact on teacher labelling. Most teachers are middle class and white, which can lead to teachers holding the view that middle-class values are evidence of a commitment to study whereas working-class demeanour is taken to be a sign of indiscipline. This has an effect on the pupil's ability to perform well and can lead to a self-fulfilling prophecy whereby the teacher's assumptions cause the pupil to underachieve.

Whilst Becker mainly looked into the effect of teacher labelling on the individual, Ball studied teacher labelling on groups and found similar results. He carried out research as 'Beachside Comprehensive', where pupils were placed in groups based on information on ability they had received from the students' primary schools. This led to pupils being placed into three different bands – band one contained mostly pupils from non-manual backgrounds, band two contained pupils from mixed backgrounds and band three mainly from manual backgrounds. Whilst all three bands entered the school enthusiastic about learning, the teachers' different attitudes and expectations led to band one doing the best, whilst bands two and three underachieved. These two pieces of evidence suggest that social class has a large impact on teacher labelling and this labelling can lead to underachievement.

> These paragraphs concern the link between social class and teacher labelling. The work of Becker and Ball is linked well and the explanation is clear. Although both these studies still have relevance today, it would have been nice to see some recognition that they were written some time ago – Becker in the 1960s and Ball in the 1980s.

Ethnicity is seen to affect teacher labelling in a similar way to class. African Caribbeans are more likely to be seen as unruly, disrespectful and hard to control. Evidence for this comes from Gillborn's research, which found that African Caribbean pupils were more likely to be given detentions than any other pupils. He saw teachers misinterpret the African Caribbean pupils' dress and way of speaking as challenging their authority, which then led to pupils behaving in the way the teachers had labelled them. The idea of ethnicity being a factor in teacher labelling is also supported by Jasper's study. This suggested that the expectations that white female teachers, who make up the majority of teachers, have of black boys' behaviour can dictate the style of teaching they give to them, which is less helpful than they offer to others and therefore leads to underachievement. However interactionists do not believe that the way teachers label by ethnicity is caused by racism, instead by ignorance and a lack of understanding of how to respond to them as they were socialized differently from themselves.

> This paragraph concerns ethnicity and teacher labelling. It is clear by now that the answer is going to consider class, ethnicity and gender in terms of teacher labelling. This represents a sound interpretation of the question which does ask about underachievement generally rather than any one social characteristic. Perhaps the candidate could have signposted this approach more directly in the introduction.

# Exam Practice

The other way in which interactionists believe teachers can label pupils is by gender. Mitsos and Browne found that teachers were not as critical with boys as they labelled them as less likely to achieve, expecting their work to be late, untidy and them to be more disruptive than girls. Again this can lead to a self-fulfilling prophecy, whereby boys then go on to be less likely to achieve.

However there are a number of ways in which the theory of teacher labelling can be criticized. It is difficult to state exactly whether labelling is a cause of underachievement, or whether the underachievement causes the negative labelling, although the trends in gender, ethnicity and class suggest the former. Also whilst interactionists focusing on small-scale interaction situations in schools and colleges can allow them to gather detailed evidence, it also means they dismiss other factors of wider society. This is a crucial flaw in their theories as wider society has a large impact on a child's ability to achieve in school. For example the Marxist theory of cultural capital states that children in the middle classes have the resources to achieve better in schools, like middle-class parents. Their parents will usually have the education to be able to help their children when they are struggling or will have the economic resources to provide them with a private tutor. They are also more likely to be able to skilfully articulate their views to the school and are much more likely to complain to the school if they feel it necessary. This suggests it is more than just teacher labelling which affects pupils' ability to succeed.

Whilst the interactionist theory of teacher labelling can provide a good insight into differences in educational achievement, the lack of insight into wider areas of the effect of social structure on achievement means it is limited and cannot provide a full understanding of differences in educational achievement.

The paragraph on gender is more limited in terms of evidence, with points not really developed in sufficient detail to convince the examiner of in-depth knowledge and understanding. The candidate is also leaving virtually all the evaluation until the last part of the answer – a dangerous tactic when time is short.

This paragraph contains the vast majority of the answer's critical evaluation. It is better to spread evaluation throughout the answer so marks for this skill can be gathered more consistently. There could also be more discussion of the influence of home background as a contrast to the in-school factors that are the subject of the title. However, the critical points here are explained clearly and do bring in an alternative theory – Marxism.

This conclusion is too brief but it does make a good point.

$\frac{41}{50}$  A*

## An examiner comments

The evidence included in this answer would benefit from some chronological evaluation (pointing out that the research was conducted some time ago) and some points, such as those relating to gender, could do with further development. In terms of analytical skills, points are generally linked together well but evaluation, although sound, is confined to one paragraph. However, this is a well-organised answer that interprets the question well.

# TOPIC 1

# Defining and researching the mass media

## Getting you thinking

1 **How do you think communication and access to information has changed over the last 25 years?**

2 **What are the advantages of these changes?**

3 **What are the disadvantages of these changes?**

4 **Do you think these changes have helped to reduce inequalities or make them worse? Explain your answer.**

## Defining the media

Traditionally, the **mass media** were defined as those agencies of communication that transmit information, education, news and entertainment to mass audiences. Until recently, there were broadly two types of mass media:

1 *The print media* – newspapers, magazines, comics, books and some forms of advertising – most of these types of media are commercially owned and produced in order to generate profit for the publishing companies that own them.

2 *The audio-visual media* – terrestrial and satellite television, radio, cinema, DVDs and music. Most of these types of media are owned and produced by commercial broadcasters whose main aim is to make profit, usually through subscriptions and/or advertising revenue. However, in the UK a significant proportion of the audio-visual media are publicly or state-owned – the BBC is controlled by a board of governors appointed by the government and is funded by a state broadcasting tax (the television licence). Channel 4, too, is publicly owned and has no shareholders. However, it receives no funding from government, but is financed entirely by its commercial activities such as advertising revenue.

The 1990s saw the emergence of a third type of media – the cyber-media – focused on the increasing use of personal computers, laptops and computer game consoles such as the PS3 and Xbox, and access to the super information super-highway, i.e. the internet or world-wide web. This type of media, however, has continued to evolve. Some sociologists have suggested a new 21st century media has evolved in which cyber-media has converged with other types of media, particularly the audio-visual and telecommunications, and mobile phone technology.

# Defining the new media

This type of media is generally the result of two trends that have occurred over the past 30 years:

1. The evolution of existing media delivery systems – If we examine the media of moving images, we can see that they have been around since the turn of the 20th century, but the way they have traditionally been delivered has been transformed, particularly in the last 20 years. For example, only a decade ago most people received television pictures through aerials and analogue-signal television sets, and there were a mere five terrestrial television channels. Today, however, people are increasingly buying digital, high-definition, flat-screen televisions and subscribing to digitalized satellite and cable television that offer a choice of hundreds of television and radio channels. Moreover, these new television sets offer the consumer a greater set of services, including sending emails, paying bills, shopping and game-playing.
2. The emergence of new delivery technologies – Cheap personal computers and mobile-phone technology, and especially texting, are relatively novel forms of communication. However, the most innovative technology that has appeared in the last 20 years is probably the internet or worldwide web – a global multimedia library of information and services in cyberspace made possible by a global system of interconnected computers. Moreover, in the past five years, we have seen the emergence of even newer technology that has improved society's access to the internet such as the introduction of high-capacity broadband wireless networks.

# The characteristics of new media

The new media – whether evolved from traditional media delivery systems or new in their own right – share a number of important characteristics that mean they differ enormously from the media delivery systems that dominated 20 years ago.

## The digital revolution

The growth of digital technology in the 1990s resulted in changes in the way information is stored and transmitted. The development of digitalization led to the translation of all information, regardless of format (images, texts, sounds), into a universal computer language. The new media all share this common digital format.

## Convergence

Most importantly, digitalization resulted in the realization that different ways of presenting a variety of types of information – text, photographs, video, film, voices and music – could all be combined into a single delivery system or media. This process is known as 'convergence'. As Boyle (2005) notes, digitalization allows information to be delivered across a range of media platforms; what were once separate and unconnected technologies are 'now part of a converging media landscape that blurs the lines about how we use these technologies'. Theoretically, it is now possible to watch television through a personal computer or on a mobile phone as well as on MP3 players such as the iPod, to send e-mails through television and to download music from the Internet.

Technological convergence has also led to economic and social convergence. This means that media and telecommunication industries that had previously produced separate and distinct systems of communication, such as the telephone, television programmes or computers, began to make alliances with each other because digitalization reduces the boundaries between media sectors. This cross-fertilization of ideas and resources underpinned by digitalization produces new forms of multimedia or converged media delivery systems. The mobile phone is an excellent example of this. Jenkins (2008) documents these changes with regard to mobile phone technology:

> *<<Call me old fashioned. The other week I wanted to buy a cellphone – you know, to make phone calls. I didn't want a video camera, a still camera, an MP3 player, or a game system. I also wasn't interested in something that could show me movie previews, would have customizable ring tones, or would allow me to read novels. I didn't want the electronic equivalent of a Swiss army knife. When the phone rings, I don't want to have to figure out which button to push. I just wanted a phone. The sales clerks sneered at me; they laughed at me behind my back. I was told by company after mobile company that they didn't make single function phones anymore. Nobody wants them. This was a powerful demonstration of how central mobiles have become to the process of media convergence.>> (pp.4–5)*

## Compression

Digital technologies enable the compression of signals. This has led to a proliferation of radio and television channels because it means that many signals can be sent through the same cable, telephone line, etc. This has resulted in the development of new markets organized around the concept of 'narrowcasting' – the transmission of particular types of media content to niche or even individualized consumers. For example, digital television providers have attempted to target young audiences by setting up channels aimed at their interests. As Boyle (2007) notes, the focus of many media companies is now on creating a personalized media experience.

## Interactivity

The new media are interactive media that are responsive in 'real time' to user input through clicking on links or selecting menu items with a mouse. The internet epitomizes such interactive media because it lets users select the stories that they want to watch in the order that they want to watch them. They can also mix and match the information they want – for instance, people may access news from several different sources.

Jenkins argues that interactivity has been brought about by convergence. He notes that media audiences today will go almost anywhere in search of the kinds of entertainment experiences they want. He suggests that interactivity and convergence have produced a '**participatory culture**'. In other words, media producers and consumers no longer occupy separate roles – they are now participants who interact with each other according to a new set of rules which are constantly evolving. This has produced more control at the user end compared with the past. For example, Jenkins notes that the print fanzine magazines of the 1980s have now migrated to the online digital world of bloggers because these websites have greater accessibility and the speed of feedback is almost instant.

The internet provides the main means through which people can interact with each other in a participatory culture and build up a collective intelligence. They can engage in on-line discussions or play on-line live games with each other through media such as Xbox Live. They may simply be interested in networking with others through sites such as Facebook and Twitter. Some of this interactivity will be creative – people may live alternative simulated lives on internet sites such as Second Life, or they may wish to convey their thoughts, feelings and opinions through the setting up of their own websites or the online diaries known as blogs. They may produce their own films and music and post them on sites such as YouTube and MySpace. User-generated content and information sites such as Wikipedia and IMDB are a popular source of knowledge.

Boyle (2005) sees similar trends in television media because we have now evolved from a system of supply-led television, available free to the whole population, to a demand-led television, organized around the idea that the viewers or subscribers should decide what they want to watch and when. We are no longer restrained by television schedules. The development of Sky+ and Freeview are good examples of how consumers of new media are encouraged to take an active role in the construction of their own television schedules. We can now pause live television. We can interact with particular shows such as Strictly Come Dancing or Big Brother by 'pressing the red button'. If we miss the programme, we can catch up by using our personal computer to access those programmes using BBC iPlayer or 4oD.

## Determinism

The increasing presence of the mass media in our daily lives has led to a sociological debate about the power of the media to determine, i.e. to shape and influence, our attitudes and behaviour. On the positive side, media sociologists claim that members of society are more educated and informed than ever about the important issues that underpin the organisation of British society today. Moreover, it is claimed that the evolution of the mass media in the UK has resulted in unprecedented consumer choice being available to the British people in terms of entertainment and lifestyle.

However, on the negative side, many sociologists claim that the mass media have become the most important secondary agent of socialisation, and that particularly, for young people, the influence of mass media far exceeds both education and religion. Some media commentators, most notably Sue Palmer in 'Toxic Childhood' (2006) suggest that the family's role as the primary agent of socialization may be under serious threat from the media because parents are using the media, particularly, television and computer games, as a substitute for parenting. Palmer suggests that many of the social problems of contemporary society, especially increasing violence and anti-social behaviour among the young, may a product of the 'toxic' influence of the media. These concerns are explored in more depth in Topic 6.

## Focus on research

### Helen Haste (2005)
### Joined-up texting

**Helen Haste conducted a survey to investigate the use of mobile phones by young people. She took a random sample of 200 schools and colleges and used self-completion questionnaires to collect data.**

**Haste found that many young people owned mobile phones for reasons of personal safety and security. Possession of a mobile phone ensured that parents could contact them quickly. Young women and younger children were most concerned with reassuring parents and personal safety. Some 73 per cent of respondents had used phones in emergencies and nearly a quarter had dialled 999.**

**Young people used their phones to organize their social lives. A whole range of different rules emerged over the way phones were used in certain situations. Text messaging was most commonly used in seeking information. More complex social negotiations, such as maintaining or ending relationships, were achieved through a phone conversation. Females were more likely to use a landline for arranging to meet friends. Females were also more likely to use letters to say thank you and to use email to keep in touch with their parents. Males were happy to use a mobile phone conversation to flirt, whereas only 10 per cent of girls were comfortable with this. Females preferred to flirt using text messaging. Serious disagreements were conducted using landline telephones.**

Haste, H. (2005) 'Joined-up texting: mobile phones and young people', *Young Consumers*, Quarter 2, 6(3), pp.56–67

1 **Identify three ways in which young people used mobile phones.**

2 **Give two examples of gender differences in the use of mobile phones.**

# Censorship

One by-product of the debate about potential media determinism has been the call for more censorship of the mass media in order to protect 'vulnerable' individuals, especially children, from its content. There are a number of different types of censorship.

- **Official or state censorship focused on the security of the nation** – concerns about national security may result in the security services asking the government to impose **DA Notices** (Defence Advisory Notices) on newspapers or television programmes to prevent the publication or screening of sensitive material which is thought to be in breach of national security or the Official Secrets Act. Failure to abide by such notices can result in the arrest of journalists and broadcasters.
- **Legislative censorship** – the state has passed legislation in order to protect children from exposure to violent or sexual imagery, bad language, deviant or criminal behaviour. For example, in 1984 the government passed the Video Recordings Act which stated that video (now DVD and Blu-Ray) recordings must be classified as suitable for viewing in the home. The British Board of Film Classification (BBFC) was charged with this responsibility. Local authorities too have the power to ban films or to demand cuts to them, even if these have been passed by the BBFC.
- **Voluntary censorship** – the British Board of Film Censors was set up in 1912 by the film industry as an independent, non-governmental body in order to bring about a degree of uniformity to the classification of films. In 1984, this organisation was renamed the British Board of Film Classification in order to reflect the fact that classification plays a far larger part in the Board's work than censorship. Another example of voluntary censorship is the nine o'clock watershed introduced by the television companies – this is the agreement that no sex, violence or swearing will be broadcast before 9pm.
- **Self-censorship** – programme makers and journalists may impose restrictions on themselves because of public anxiety, political pressures, pressures from owners and shareholders, or after discussion with fellow media professionals.

The debate about censorship is hugely controversial in a country like the UK which prides itself on freedom of speech and self-expression. Some sociologists argue that there is no need for censorship because the relationship between media content and social problems like violence is unproven. Censorship is regarded by these critics as a dangerous subversion of human rights as well as an insult to audiences who, it is argued, are actively and intelligently engaged with media content rather than being victims of it. These arguments too are examined in further detail in Topic 6.

# Researching the media

During the last thirty years, there has been a steady growth of interest in mass media reports, both textual and visual, as a source of secondary data, especially as the influence of the mass media has been seen to grow as a secondary agency of socialization. Early research into the media mainly originated with supporters of the **hypodermic syringe model** (see Topic 6) and feminist research which has led to what McNeill and Chapman (2005) termed an 'academic representations industry' concerned with examining all sorts of media content for signs of patriarchy, racism, homophobia, ageism, etc. This 'industry' is further explored in Topics 4 and 6. Moreover, in the field of crime and deviance, sociologists such as Stan Cohen and Jock Young explored media documents relating to so-called deviant groups and activities, and established moral panic theory (explored further in Topic 3).

Research groups such the Glasgow University Media Group and Goldsmiths College have been engaged in the monitoring and analysis of media reports of politics, economic affairs, industrial disputes and world events and argue that such reporting is often biased and responsible for determining public opinion on issues such as strikes and public perceptions of politicians and of the less-developed world.

## Researching media content

The main method used by sociologists for the analysis of media content, whether textual or visual, has been **content analysis**, which in its simplest form, simply involves counting up the frequency of particular words, images or category of articles. Content analysis often uses a table or grid known as a content analysis frame or schedule in order to log the number of times language, images and so on appear, in order to build up a quantitative picture of media representation. For example, the feminist media researcher Marjorie Ferguson conducted a study 'Forever Feminine' (1983) that involved counting up the number of feminine themes that appeared in three popular women's magazines between 1949 and 1974. The Glasgow University Media Group conducted a close analysis of the language used in television news reports in the 1980s and concluded that it was biased in favour of certain powerful groups.

## The strengths and weaknesses of content analysis

Quantitative content analysis has been popular because it is a relatively straightforward method to use. Media reports exist in a variety of forms and are relatively easy and cheap to access and use. It is regarded as a reliable method because members of a research team can use the same content analysis schedule to record and analyse media content independently of each other. Results can then be compared and discussed to check and verify that both researchers are recording the same content.

Content analysis is seen as representative if it is properly organized. For example, if print media is being examined, a range of media might be analyzed across a number of weeks or months or even years. Different themes within magazines and newspapers can be explored. A study of television advertisements might focus on a number of different channels at different times of day.

Another strength of content analysis is that it is a non-reactive and **unobtrusive method**. The media document is not affected by the sociological analysis and no human sample is directly involved in the research.

However, content analysis is seen to have some limitations with regard to validity. First, the content analysis schedule is the product of human interpretation which may be unconsciously influenced and biased by the personal or ideological prejudices or the experiences of the researcher. For example, Ferguson used a 'happy family' category in her analysis of magazines but her idea of 'a happy family' might have differed from the definitions used by other sociologists. Second, simply counting images, words and phrases tells us very little about the actual effects of these on audiences or why the media report was produced and presented in the way it was in the first place.

## Semiology

Some sociologists have adopted a more qualitative version of content analysis influenced by the study of signs and codes known as **semiology**, which argues that symbolic signs and codes underpin all forms of behaviour and language. For example, the colour red in UK society symbolizes a number of things – danger, stop (e.g. traffic lights), promiscuity (e.g. red light district), passion etc. Such signs, signals and codes are part of our culture and their meanings are learnt and communicated through the process of socialization.

Media sociologists suggest that hidden meanings lie behind the media's use of particular words and images. For example, the Glasgow University Media Group employed semiology in their analysis of the text and images used in television news reports of industrial disputes. They observed that journalists used positive words like 'offer' or 'proposals' when discussing management and negative words like 'demand' and 'rejected' when discussing workers. This gave the impression that managers were more reasonable than the trade unions and workers. This was confirmed by the visual images of managers being interviewed in offices whilst workers were interviewed outside on picket lines or after confrontation with police officers. Moreover images of the 'inconvenience' caused by the strike strengthened the view that the strike was the fault of the strikers rather than the management.

However, critics of semiology claim that this approach lacks objectivity and reliability because it is too reliant on the researcher's subjective and selective interpretations of the text or image. This may differ from that of other researchers or that of the audience. It is therefore difficult to repeat in order to verify findings because of differences in interpretation.

Secondly, semiology is a time consuming method. Each semiological analysis takes time and consequently it is not a very representative method. Thirdly, semiology tells us little about how and why the text was manufactured in the first place or how it actually affects the audience.

## The laboratory experiment

Some sociologists and psychologists have conducted **laboratory experiments** to investigate the potential effects of mass media. Laboratory experiments are mainly used by natural scientists such as chemists to gather evidence in order to establish scientific laws of cause and effect.

Experiments involve a great deal of control over the laboratory environment in order to establish a relationship between an independent variable or cause (e.g. the content of a specific type of media) and a dependent variable or effect (e.g. a violent reaction or imitation). Experiments usually involve setting up groups whose characteristics should be as identical as possible. Some groups are exposed to the independent variable and their behaviour is then compared to a control group who have not been exposed. Any difference in behaviour between the two groups is assumed to be the result of the independent variable.

Bandura (1963) is the most well known laboratory experiment being employed to conduct media research. His research team showed three groups of children real, film and cartoon examples of a self-righting doll ('bobo doll') being attacked with mallets, whilst a fourth group saw no violent activity. After being introduced to a room full of exciting toys, the children in each group were made to feel frustrated by being told that the toys were not for them. They were then led to another room containing a bobo doll, where they were observed through a one-way mirror. The three groups who had been shown the violent activity – whether real, film or cartoon – all behaved more aggressively than the fourth group. Bandura concluded on the basis of this data that media content could have an **imitative effect**.

### *Criticisms of laboratory experiments*

However, there are practical, ethical and theoretical reasons why sociologists are not keen on using laboratory experiments. The main practical difficulty with such experiments is that people do not behave under laboratory conditions as they do in their natural environment. For example, Bandura's experiment did not replicate the conditions that the children would experience in the home when normally watching television. There were no parental controls present and the films the children saw did not resemble the sorts of programmes or films they would normally be watching at home or at the cinema in terms of plot, character or moral themes. Moreover, the nature of the central object of the experiment – the bobo doll – invited a violent reaction in that they were designed to be knocked about. The children (who were the sons and daughters of university workers) could have known what was expected of them simply because they were aware of the nature and purpose of the dolls.

Experiments may also suffer from the **Hawthorne effect** – people may behave in the way they do because of the presence of the researchers. This researcher effect was first noted by Mayo in the 1920s who was conducting research at the Hawthorne plant of the General Electric Company in the USA into worker productivity. He concluded that the increases in worker productivity that he observed were quite simply the result of people being anxious about being watched and compensating by working harder. In other words, behaviour in contexts like laboratory experiments can be caused by the research subjects' knowledge that they are being researched.

There is also the practical problem of the expectancy effect. This refers to the possibility that the researcher's expectations can influence the outcome of the research in that they may see what they want to see. For example,

Bandura may have interpreted any difference between the behaviour of the control and experimental groups' behaviour as evidence of imitation quite simply because he expected it to be so.

Laboratory experiments on human beings are also undermined by **ethical issues**. Sociological research should seek informed consent but this would alert the research subjects to the nature of the research and could influence their behaviour. Sociological research needs to avoid causing psychological damage to its subjects and consequently this makes any long-term experimental research on the effects of media violence virtually impossible.

Finally, there are theoretical objections to researching people under laboratory conditions. Interpretivist sociologists point out that humans do not share the same characteristics as the usual laboratory subjects such as chemicals and animals because human beings have consciousness and free will. It is consequently almost impossible to find control and experimental groups that are exactly alike because people are unique and have their own individual interpretation of the social world. For example, a pair of twins may be physically exactly alike but it does not mean they experienced and interpreted their childhood in the same way. Interpretivists point out that our behaviour is not caused by exposure to external factors such as independent variables. Rather it is caused by how we interpret the world around us. We may behave in the way we do in a laboratory set-up quite simply because we interpret the research event in a particular way and choose from a variety of experiences how we are going to react.

## Field or social experiments

Some interpretivist sociologists have carried out experiments in naturally occurring settings. This type of sociological research aims to examine the way people behave in everyday, small social groups and is referred to as a **social or field experiment**. The researcher sets up a situation in a familiar social context such as a classroom and manipulates particular variables (i.e. influences) to test out the reactions of the research subjects (who, of course, are not aware that a social experiment is taking place).

These social experiments allow the sociologist to unravel the often hidden processes and rules of everyday life and allow researchers to get very close to people's interpretations of everyday life. In this sense, they are thought to be high in validity. However, most social experiments do not involve the informed consent of those being experimented upon and they have been consequently criticised for their unethical use of deception and manipulation.

## Check your understanding

1. What has caused the growth of the new media?
2. Explain the characteristics shared by the new media.
3. What concerns have been expressed about the effects of the mass media?
4. Explain the different types of censorship.
5. Why is the debate about censorship controversial?
6. In what way is content analysis an example of an unobtrusive method?
7. How can content analysis be both quantitative and qualitative?
8. How has content analysis been criticized?
9. How have laboratory experiments been used to study the mass media?
10. How has the use of laboratory experiments to investigate the mass media been criticized?

## Activities

### Research idea

Design a questionnaire and conduct a survey within your school or college to assess the differences in access to and consumption of the new media in relation to class, gender, ethnicity and age. Consider both household ownership and personal consumption of the various forms of the new media.

### Web.task

Go to the student section of the website of the British Board of Film Classification at **www.sbbfc.co.uk**. Select 'Timelines' and draw a timeline to trace the history of legislation on film censorship. Then select two of the issues covered and find out the key moments in the history of censorship on those issues.

# Key terms

**Censorship** the suppression of information or other media content.

**Content analysis** examination of the content of the mass media.

**DA Notices** Defence Advisory Notices are requests from the government to news outlets not to publish certain information for reasons of national security.

**Determinism** view that behaviour and actions are caused by outside forces, in this context the mass media.

**Ethical issues** moral issues of right and wrong

**Hawthorne effect** research participants changing their behaviour due to the presence of researchers.

**Hypodermic syringe model** the view that the media are very powerful and the audience very weak. The media can 'inject' their messages into the audience, who accept them uncritically.

**Imitative effect** people copying what they see or hear in the media.

**Laboratory experiment** a method of discovering causal relationships in a setting where the variables can be controlled.

**Mass media** agencies of communication that transmit information, education, news and entertainment to mass audiences.

**New media** range of new digital communication technologies, often characterized by the potential for interactivity.

**Participatory culture** the potential for interaction between media producers and consumers created by new media.

**Semiology** the study of the signs and codes that make up communication.

**Social or field experiment** experiments that take place in naturally occurring settings.

**Unobtrusive methods** methods which involve no contact between the researcher and the individual or group being studied so there is no possibility of researcher imposition.

## An eye on the exam Defining and researching the mass media

Provide a detailed description of the methods including concepts, studies and any relevant theories

Several methods of researching the media will need to be discussed

**(a) Outline and assess the methods used by sociologists to investigate the influence of the media. (50 marks)**

Weigh up the strengths and weaknesses of the methods in some detail before reaching a balanced conclusion

Consider how effective each method is in investigating media influence

### Grade booster Getting top marks in this question

An introduction could consider the problems involved in researching the influence of the media given its diversity and the range of ways in which the media might affect its audiences. The main part of the answer is likely to consist of a discussion of quantitative and qualitative content analysis, semiology and the use of experiments. These methods will need to be explained and examples of their use provided (Topics 4, 5 and 6 may provide extra material). Each method will also need to be evaluated – it is probably better to evaluate them as the answer progresses rather than in a separate concluding section.

# TOPIC 2

# Ownership and control of the media

## Getting you thinking

1. Explain the main trend in the graph on the right.
2. What effect do you think this trend might have on the content of the media?
3. Are you concerned about the trend shown in the graph? Explain your answer.

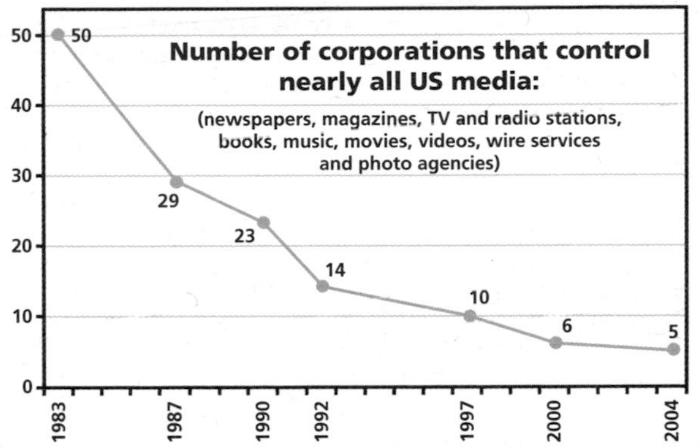


Some sociologists have expressed concern about recent trends in media ownership and control. On the surface, the number of media outlets available to the general public has increased dramatically. Thirty years ago, there were only four television channels – today hundreds of television channels are available via digital and satellite services such as Sky and Virgin. The number of national newspapers has remained fairly stable over the last 30 years, but the number of free papers and magazines has grown enormously. Thirty years ago, the internet did not exist.

All these changes in the availability of media seem to imply a greater degree of choice. However, sociologists who have examined recent trends in the ownership of such media suggest that this increased choice may be an illusion. Some even suggest that, despite this media expansion, consumer choice has actually declined. There are a number of trends which are seen as contributing to this contraction of choice.

## Concentration of ownership

Bagdikian (2004) points out that, in 1983, 50 corporations controlled the vast majority of all news media in the USA. However, by 1992, 22 companies owned and operated 90 per cent of the mass media – controlling almost all of the USA's newspapers, magazines, TV and radio stations, books, records, movies, videos, wire services and photo agencies. Bagdikian argues that if the USA's media were owned by separate individuals, there would be 25 000 owners; instead, by 2004, media ownership in the USA was concentrated in seven corporations: Time Warner, Disney, News Corp, Sony, Bertelsmann of Germany, Viacom (formerly CBS) and General Electric NBC.

Many of these companies have now started to move into **cybermedia**, which until recently were dominated by four major companies: Microsoft, Apple, Google and Yahoo. We are now seeing concentration in terms of ownership of internet companies, as the traditional media companies compete with cybermedia organizations to control social networking sites, which are extremely lucrative in terms of advertising revenue. For example, NewsCorp now owns MySpace, Microsoft owns a significant stake in Facebook; and Google has bought into YouTube.

### The British print media

Curran (2003) suggests that concentration of ownership of British newspapers is not a new phenomenon. In 1937, four men – Lords Beaverbrook, Rothermere, Camrose and Northcliffe, known as the 'press barons' – owned nearly one in every two national and local daily newspapers sold in the UK. Today, seven individuals dominate the ownership and content of UK national daily and Sunday newspapers:

1. News Corp (owned and controlled by the Australian-American Rupert Murdoch and his family) produces *The Times, Sun, News of the World* and *Sunday Times*.
2. Associated Newspapers (owned by Lord Rothermere) owns the *Daily Mail, Mail On Sunday, Metro* and London's biggest selling newspaper, the *Evening Standard*, as well as 54 regional papers.
3. United Newspapers is owned by Richard Desmond and produces the *Daily* and *Sunday Express*, the *Daily Star* and *OK!* magazine.
4. The *Telegraph* group (*Daily* and *Sunday*) is owned by the Barclay Brothers.

5 The *Independent* and *Independent on Sunday* are owned by the entrepreneur Alexander Lebedev.
6 Viscount Cowdray has a £570 million stake in the Pearson group, which owns the *Financial Times*, Penguin Publishing and *The Economist*.

Only two national newspaper groups are controlled by companies rather than individuals. Trinity Mirror owns the *Daily Mirror, Sunday Mirror, Sunday People* and *Daily Record* (Scotland's biggest selling paper), as well as over 150 regional daily newspapers. The Guardian Media Group is controlled by a board of trustees – the Scott Trust – which owns both the *Guardian* and the *Observer*.

By 2006, just three publishers controlled two-thirds of national newspapers sold in the UK. The top five publishers also controlled 69 per cent of regional evening papers and 75 per cent of free sheets such as *Metro*.

The UK magazine market is dominated by two major companies. Almost two in every three UK women and over 45 per cent of UK men read an IPC magazine, i.e. 27 million UK adults. IPC produces 80 magazines including *What's on TV, Marie Claire, Woman, Nuts* and *Country Life*. IPC is owned by Time Warner. In 2008, the Bauer Publishing Group, controlled by the Bauer family, published 80 magazines including *FHM, Empire, Grazia* and *Elle* with an estimated readership of 26 million.

## The broadcasting media

The content of commercial terrestrial television is mainly controlled by one company, ITV plc, which is the result of a merger in 2004 between the two biggest owners of commercial television franchises, i.e. Granada (which controlled most of the regional television stations in the North of England) and Carlton Communications (which controlled most of the terrestrial stations in Southern England and Wales). This company currently owns 11 of the 15 regional commercial television franchises. Channel 5, on the other hand, is owned by three companies – United Business Media, Bertelsmann and Pearson.

Access to satellite, cable and digital television in the UK is generally controlled by two companies – News Corp, which owns BSkyB, and Virgin Media (formerly NTL), owned by Richard Branson.

The British music industry is owned and controlled by six major companies, but only one of these – EMI – is British. In 2007, EMI was acquired by the private equity group Terra Firma controlled by the financier, Guy Hands. The cinema industry is also dominated by American media – three of the five largest cinema owners in the UK, particularly of the multiplexes, are American subsidiaries. Even those chains which are British in origin, e.g. Odeon, Virgin and ABC, are contracted to strong links with US distributors.

The UK media industry is therefore dominated by 13 companies. Ten of these companies are owned and controlled by wealthy and powerful individuals rather than shareholders. Considerable parts of the British media industry are owned and controlled by global corporations.



## Horizontal integration

**Horizontal integration** is also known as **cross-media ownership** and refers to the fact that the bigger media companies often own a diverse range of media. For example, News Corp, in addition to newspapers in Britain and Australia, owns the publisher HarperCollins as well as US interests, including the *New York Post*, Fox TV and 20th Century Fox film studios. It also owns Sky and the biggest Asian satellite channel, Star TV. Associated Newspapers also has stakes in several radio stations, and owns 20 per cent of ITN and 40 per cent of Teletext.

## Vertical integration

Some media companies are increasingly trying to control all aspects of their industry in order to maximize their profits, e.g. Time Warner makes its own films and distributes them to its own cinema complexes. News Corp owns television and film studios as well as the satellite television channels that show them. **Vertical integration** therefore gives media companies greater economic control over their operating environment.

## Diversification

**Diversification** is also called 'lateral expansion' and occurs when firms diversify into new business areas in order to spread risk. Losses made in one area may be compensated for by profits in another. Virgin is a good example of a diversified corporation – it has major media interests in music, publishing, cinemas, digital television and internet access. However, it also sells insurance and banking services as well as running an airline and a train service.

## Global conglomeration

Media companies have also taken advantage of the erosion of traditional boundaries surrounding media markets. Globalization has opened up national markets and created international competition between media companies. The result is that many of these companies have become **global conglomerations** – transnational corporations with a presence in many countries, operating in a global market. News Corp, for example, owns newspapers in Australia, the UK and USA. Many of these corporations are also conglomerates – business corporations that control dozens of media companies with wide interests across a wide range of products and services.

## Synergy

Increasingly, media companies are using their different interests to package their products in several different ways, e.g. *Spiderman 2* was not only a movie – it was a soundtrack album, computer game and ring tone. It was also turned into toy action figures and marketed through fast food outlets, newspaper, radio and television coverage. Often, the media company producing the film will own the companies that produce the music, computer game, etc., or that distribute the franchise (the licence that lets other companies do it). Another variation on **synergy** is that the media company producing a product often owns newspapers and magazines through which it can be advertised and promoted, for example the *Sun* newspaper often promotes Sky products.

## Technological convergence

**Technological convergence** is a fairly new concept and refers to the trend of putting several technologies into one media product – for example, through the personal computer, mobile phones and digital television, we can now access the internet, telecommunication services, games, etc., as well as paying bills, buying films, downloading music and so on. Consequently, companies that normally work in quite separate fields are joining up or converging – for instance, Orange have linked up with Sony to explore ways of improving mobile-phone technology by giving access to media services, such as music, the internet and video.

# Why should we study media ownership and control?

Doyle (2002) suggests that we need to study media ownership and control for two reasons:

1 She suggests that there is a need for societies to have a diverse and pluralistic media provision so that all points of view can be heard and abuses of power and influence by elites can be avoided.
2 She notes that ownership and control over the media:

> *<<raise special concerns that do not apply to other sectors of industry.* **Media concentrations** *matter because ... media have the power to make or break political careers ... Control over a substantial share of the more popular avenues for dissemination of media content can, as politicians are well aware, confer very considerable influence on public opinion.>>* (pp.6–7)

However, Doyle's views have attracted some criticism from those sociologists who call themselves pluralists, who argue that these concerns are exaggerated. They argue that media owners generally manage their media in a responsible fashion, because content is largely determined by the demands of the consumer market and, even if they did not, the professional ethics of journalists and editors, as well as the commonsense of the general public would undermine any attempt by owners to use their media as a mouthpiece for their own views.

# The pluralist theory of media ownership

From a **pluralist** viewpoint, modern capitalist societies are democratic – all interest groups, whether they are right-wing, centrist or left-wing, are given a platform to express their views to the electorate, and the most persuasive arguments will result in their representatives being voted into power. The mass media are seen to be an essential component of this democratic ideal, because most people obtain their knowledge about politics from newspapers and television. Pluralists, therefore, argue that media owners are objective, responsible and impartial facilitators of this political process.

## The economics of media ownership

Moreover, pluralists also point out that the behaviour of media owners is constrained by the market – in free-market economies, media owners compete against each other in order to attract people to their product. Readers, viewers and listeners are the real power-holders because they exercise the right to buy or not to buy. In other words, they have freedom of choice. If they did not like the choices that media owners are making available to them, or if they suspected the media product was biased one way rather than another, the media audience would probably respond by not buying the product and the media company would go out of business. Power, then, according to pluralist thinkers, lies with the consumer or audience rather than with owners. The media, therefore, give the public what the audience wants rather than what the owner decides.

Pluralists argue that the rationale for media concentration is essentially economic rather than political or ideological. They argue that media products are costly to produce. Concentration of ownership is aimed at the maximization of audience size in order to reduce costs and to attract advertising revenue. The globalization of the media and the conglomerates that have resulted from this are also merely attempts at finding new audiences in order to increase profits, rather than some sort of cultural imperialism.

Vertical and horizontal integration, as well as synergy, reduce costs because media companies no longer have to contract services out to other media companies who might be competing with them. Profits are also enhanced because they are no longer subjected to the fluctuating prices charged by other companies. Moreover, the main rationale for diversification is spreading risk and possible loss, e.g. EMI can afford to sustain losses across its record labels because its music publishing company is so successful.

Pluralists argue that it is practically impossible for owners to interfere in the content of newspapers and television programmes because their businesses are economically far too complex for them to take a regular interest. Whale (1977), for example, argues that 'media owners have global problems of trade and investment to occupy their minds' and so do not have the time to think about the day-to-day detailed running of their media businesses.

## Media diversity

Pluralists argue that the range of media products available is extremely diverse and that, as a result, all points of view in a democratic society are catered for. If some viewpoints have a greater range of media representing them, this is not necessarily biased. It merely mirrors what the audience wants or sees as important. For example, if the majority of newspapers raise concerns about young people carrying knives, they are mirroring the concerns of the majority of citizens. If women's magazines seem to focus disproportionately on features about slimming, beauty, babies and weddings, this is because this is what the majority of women want to read about.

## Public service broadcasting

Pluralists point out that a significant share of the media market in the UK is taken up by **public service broadcasters** (PSB), i.e. media outlets controlled by the state, which have a world-wide reputation for impartiality, and which cater for every conceivable taste and opinion. The British Broadcasting Corporation (BBC) is the most obvious example of this, although Channel 4 is also a public service broadcaster.

The BBC was set up by a Royal Charter in 1926, which clearly states that the BBC has a legal obligation to provide specific services – to inform, to educate and to entertain the full audience spectrum (i.e. all social groups in society must be catered for). In 1999, the government outlined what it saw as the functions of the BBC:

- to provide quality programming with particular emphasis on giving the audience access to the 'arts', i.e. drama, opera, classical music
- to protect vulnerable programme types, such as news, documentaries, children's programming and drama
- to accurately and impartially report news
- to educate audiences so that they can make informed decisions about political issues
- to ensure that programming is pluralistic and diverse, and consequently caters for all segments of society
- to protect consumers, especially children, from harmful material.

Pluralists therefore see PSB as the epitome of impartial and objective media and a counterweight to any potential bias in the private sector.

## Focus on research

### The Campaign for Press and Broadcasting Freedom (CPBF)

### Media ownership in the age of convergence

*In January 2007, the Campaign for Press and Broadcasting Freedom launched its media ownership project to research the changing patterns of ownership in our rapidly converging media, and to develop new policy initiatives.*

Long-standing concerns about the power and influence of media moguls in traditional media (film, television, radio, newspapers, books and magazines) remain central to our work on media ownership. The distorting impact of excessive media power on politics is vividly exemplified by Silvio Berlusconi's election victory in Italy and his subsequent actions, or by the global role Rupert Murdoch plays. As the *Wall Street Journal* pointed out when it was still owned by the Bancroft family, Murdoch 'has blurred a line that exists at many other US media companies ... a line intended to keep the business and political interest of owners from influencing the presentation of news'.

We need to develop our analysis to take in the big policy implications of converged media and the transition to multimedia and multiplatform (PC, mobile, interactive TV) systems and the internet. Whereas 'old media' still has some regulatory scaffolding governing programming obligations, new media programme providers and businesses are keen to limit traditional regulation.

Consolidation is occurring at an alarming rate, with $30 billion spent in 2007 in mergers and acquisitions by Microsoft, Time Warner (AOL), Yahoo! and WPP on interactive advertising companies. ... Growing consolidation will also undermine diversity of both content and ownership, and the transformation of the internet from an open, global means of communications into one designed primarily to serve the interests of corporate brands and commercialism.

Privacy also will be eroded as massive databases of information on internet users become more intrusive. For example, the recent Google/DoubleClick merger formed an information colossus that combines information about consumers that Google collects through its search engine with the tracking data that DoubleClick collects about users as they surf the net. Also new ad-targeting systems are being developed which determine users' interests by monitoring the websites they visit.

The outcomes of the Media Ownership project will be to:

- chart the patterns of ownership which span converged communications media
- produce a clear set of relevant policies on media ownership for the UK and Europe
- identify the kind of regulation which is required to protect public service content (news, children's programmes, documentaries, etc.) in the digital age
- produce a chart, popular campaigning pamphlet and book with the facts, arguments and analysis on media ownership
- hold a major conference to launch our polices in autumn 2009
- ensure that in the run-up to the next election our policy proposals are at the centre of political debate.

Source: www.cpbf.org.uk/body.php?subject=media%20ownership

1. **List the issues that the CPBF are concerned about in relation to ownership and control of the media.**
2. **Suggest reasons for the various proposed outcomes of the project.**

## State controls

Pluralists note that the power of media owners is also restricted by state or government controls. For example, in some societies, owners are not allowed to own too much media or different types of media, in order to reduce the possibility that one person's or group's views or products can become too dominant. For example, in the USA, the huge film studios have been prevented from owning film production, film distribution and cinemas at the same time. Many countries have cross-ownership rules preventing companies from owning more than one media form in the same area – for example, owners are only able to own one television station rather than several.

Another state constraint on media ownership is the fact that both the BBC and ITV have some formal legal requirements imposed upon them by a powerful regulator – the Office for Communications (Ofcom) – which was set up in 2003. Ofcom's function is to monitor the content and quality of television and radio output on both the BBC and the commercial channels, and to investigate viewer and listener complaints. Pluralists argue that this combination of audience and regulator prevents unscrupulous media owners imposing biased content upon the general public.

## Media professionalism

Pluralists stress the professionalism of journalists and editors, arguing that editors would never allow owners to compromise their independence. They argue that journalists have too much integrity to be biased regularly in favour of one particular perspective. Pluralists also point out that the media have a strong tradition of **investigative journalism**, which has often targeted those in power. For example, two reporters on the *Washington Post* forced the President of the USA – Richard Nixon – to resign after they exposed him for authorizing the bugging of his opponent's offices at Watergate in 1972. Newspapers in the UK have also uncovered corruption in high places and forced politicians to resign from office.

## Media audiences

Pluralists also suggest that audiences do not passively accept what is being fed to them. They argue that audiences are selective and often critical of media content. Audiences are very diverse, and interpret and use the media in different ways.

# The Marxist critique of media ownership and control

Marxists argue that the economic system of the UK, i.e. capitalism, is deeply unfair because it generally benefits a minority – the capitalist class – at the expense of the majority. Marxists believe that inequalities in wealth and income and, therefore, poverty are the direct result of the way capitalism is organized. They argue that the wealth of the capitalist class is obtained by exploiting the labour power of the working class. Moreover, the capitalist class is able to ensure that class inequality is transmitted down through the generations through inheritance and private education.

## The role of ideology

Marxists suggest that the capitalist class uses '**ideology**' – a false but influential set of ideas, values and norms – to make sure that the working class accept capitalism and do not threaten its stability. In order to this, the capitalist class uses its cultural power to dominate institutions such as the education system, religion and the mass media. The role of these ideological agencies is to transmit ruling-class ideology by persuading the majority that capitalist society is meritocratic. This is the view that if people work hard, they can be materially successful. These agencies, therefore, aim to convince people of the benefits of capitalism. Consequently, working-class people experience '**false class-consciousness**' – they come to believe that capitalism is a fair system which benefits us all equally. They are told that if they fail to get on then it is their fault for not working hard enough to achieve qualifications. Therefore, they fail to see the reality of their situation – that they are being exploited by a system that only benefits a powerful minority.

## The media and ideology

Marxists believe that media owners aim to transmit a conservative and conformist ideology in the form of news and entertainment. They argue that the main function of the media is to convince the general public that ruling-class ideology is 'truth' and 'fact'. In other words, as Miliband (1973) argued, the role of the media is to shape how we think about the world we live in. We are rarely informed about important issues such as why people continue to live in poverty. We are never encouraged to be critical of the capitalist system. Marxists argue that owners ensure that we only get a narrow range of 'approved' views and knowledge, with the result that 'alternative', critical points of view are rarely heard. Marxists argue that the media is happy to transmit ruling-class ideology through television and newspapers because media owners are part of the ruling capitalist class and have a vested interest in it not being criticized or dismantled. The last thing they want is equality for all, because this would mean less wealth for them.

Tunstall and Palmer (1991) argue along these lines with regard to government regulation of **media conglomerates**. They suggest that governments are no longer interested in controlling the activities of media owners. Rather 'regulatory favours' are the norm – newspapers owned by a conglomerate will directly support a government or neglect to criticize government policy or even withhold information from the general public in return for governments failing to enforce media regulation or even abolishing it altogether.

## Evidence for the ideological nature of ownership and control

The problem with this Marxist account is that it implies that media owners, wealthholders and the political elite are united in some sort of ideological conspiracy to brainwash the population. There is some evidence for this cooperation in other societies – for example, in Italy, it has been demonstrated that Silvio Berlusconi's control of three television stations (which reached 40 per cent of the Italian audience) was instrumental in his party winning the general election in 1994 and Berlusconi becoming Prime Minister. However, on the whole, sociologists generally only have anecdotal evidence to confirm their suspicions that concentration of media ownership is damaging democracy.

However, Curran's (2003) detailed systematic examination of the British press does suggest that the evidence for owner interference in and manipulation of UK newspaper content is strong. He suggests that four distinct periods can be seen with regard to owner intervention and the consequent undermining of journalistic and editorial integrity.

### *1920 to 1950*

Curran notes the rise of the 'press barons' and suggests that proprietorial control was a norm in this period. He notes that Lord Beaverbrook (who owned the *Express* newspaper group) and Lord Northcliffe (who owned Associated Newspapers) exercised detailed control over their favourite newspapers in terms of both content and layout. These owners were quite open in their purpose – Beaverbrook famously said: 'I run the *Daily Express* merely for the purpose of making propaganda and with no other motive.'

However, although false class-consciousness was probably not the ideological motive of the media barons in this period, Curran notes that there was an ideological effect of owner interference in media content:

> *<<Their main impact lay in the way in which their papers selectively represented the world. This tended to strengthen the mainly conservative prejudices of their readers and reinforce opposition, particularly within the middle class, to progressive change.>>* (p.47)

### *1951 to 1974*

Curran argues this period was the great pluralist phase in terms of newspaper reporting because there was a greater delegation by owners to editorial authority and autonomy. This period saw investigative reporting (especially into the activities of powerful groups) at its height. Curran argues that a group consensus emerged among journalists and editors that proprietorial influence should be resisted. However, this did not mean that interventionism by owners disappeared; most were still able to insist that their newspaper supported a particular political party.

### *1974 to 1992*

Curran argues that a new type of interventionist proprietorship appeared in this period, as symbolized by Rupert Murdoch – 'a businessman first and foremost' – who acquired both the *Sun* and *The Times*. Murdoch was oriented towards what sold rather than what furthered a party interest or ideological viewpoint. Curran notes that Murdoch shifted his newspapers to the right because he believed that right-wing economic policies were the key to making vast profits.

Murdoch introduced a new personalized style of management to the production of newspapers in the UK – he read proofs, wrote leaders, changed content and layout. Most importantly, he handpicked compliant editors and managing directors. Between 1979 and 1992, Murdoch was a strong supporter of Mrs Thatcher's Conservative government because it pursued economic policies he agreed with and actively encouraged, to such an extent that he was dubbed the 'phantom prime minister'. There is little doubt that this interference produced both overt and covert forms of censorship – for example, during the 1984/5 miners' strike, *Times* journalists found that stories that were critical of the miners' employers were rejected by Murdoch. After a while, self-censorship became the norm as journalists decided there was no point in submitting such stories.

Other proprietors followed suit in this period. For example, Lord Matthews, proprietor of the Express group between 1977 and 1985, said: 'By and large editors will have complete freedom as long as they agree with the policy I have laid down.' Lord Stevens, who succeeded Lord Matthews, said: ' I would not be happy to be associated with a left-wing paper. I suppose the papers echo my political views ... I do interfere and say enough is enough'.

### *1997 to the present day*

Curran has noted that media ownership in the past ten years has been based on a 'global conservatism', as British newspaper groups have moved into the global marketplace. The most successful media entrepreneur in this period has been Rupert Murdoch, who Bagdikian dubbed 'lord of the global village'. Curran notes how, in 1997, Murdoch instructed his newspapers to abandon support for the Conservative Party and to support Tony Blair's New Labour. However, this was not due to Murdoch's sudden conversion to social democracy. Rather, it was a hard-nosed business decision because Blair was willing to lift state controls that prevented cross-media ownership. Curran argues that Murdoch was right-wing, but perceived Blair to be 'the only credible conservative worth supporting in 1997. In effect, a tacit deal was made between two power-holders – one a market-friendly politician and the other a pragmatic businessman – in a form that sidelined the public' (p.75). As Curran concludes, 'the Murdoch press thus changed its political loyalty but not its politics' (p.74).

Curran's analysis of British newspapers suggests that both pluralist and Marxist theories may be mistaken in the way they look at media owners. First, the pluralist view that media owners do not intervene in media content is evidently false. Curran argues that the last ten years have seen even greater intervention because owners have undermined newspaper independence and balance in subtle ways by choosing the editors they want and getting rid of editors that 'fail'. As Curran notes:

> *<<Editors' freedom of action is curtailed by ... budgetary controls, management guidelines, and an implicit understanding of how the paper should develop ... Journalists tend to be selected in the first*

*place on the grounds that they will 'fit' in. Conforming to hierarchical requirements brings rewards in terms of good assignments, high exposure, promotion and peer group esteem. Resistance invites escalating sanctions. Dissident reporters who do not deliver the goods suffer professional death.* >> (p.85)

Moreover, there are signs that the general public are well aware that these processes are undermining the pluralist view that journalists are first and foremost the objective seekers of truth. In 1993, only 10 per cent of the general public believed that journalists could be trusted to tell the truth, and in 2002, a Eurobarometer survey conducted across several European nations concluded that the British general public was the least likely to trust the media, particularly the print media.

Curran's analysis also belies the Marxist notion that there is a deliberate capitalist conspiracy to subvert working-class consciousness. There is little evidence of this. Curran suggests media owners are not united in an ideological quest, but are primarily motivated by economics rather than capitalist ideology. Moreover, their actions are not collectivized; they pursue their economic goals in a ruthlessly individualized way in an attempt to obtain a bigger share of the market than their capitalist competitors. For example, Murdoch's instructions to Fox News to be a cheerleader for the Iraq War, and his decision that Sky News should not cover pro-democracy protests in China were motivated simply by his economic relationships with the USA and China respectively. However, there is sufficient evidence to suggest that the actions of media owners produce media content which in the long term benefits capitalism. In this sense, Curran's analysis fits in with the analysis of the Glasgow University Media Group, which takes a **hegemonic** approach to media ownership and control.

# The Glasgow University Media Group

The Glasgow University Media Group (GUMG) suggests that media content does support the interests of those who run the capitalist system but this is an accidental byproduct of the social backgrounds of journalists and broadcasters. These tend to be overwhelmingly White, middle-class and male. A Sutton Trust report in 2006 (see 'Focus on research', on p146) found that leading news and current affairs journalists are more likely than not to have been to independent schools, which educate just 7 per cent of the population. Of the top 100 journalists in 2006, 54 per cent were independently educated – an increase from 49 per cent in 1986. The Sutton Trust asks the important question: is it healthy that those who are most influential in determining and interpreting the news agenda have educational backgrounds that are so different from the vast majority of the population?

The GUMG claims that these journalists and broadcasters tend to believe in 'middle-of-the-road' (consensus) views and ideas, which are generally unthreatening and which, they believe, appeal to the majority of their viewers, listeners and readers. Such journalists and broadcasters tend to see anyone who believes in ideas outside this media consensus as 'extremist', and consequently such people are rarely invited to contribute their opinion in newspapers or on television. When such alternative views are included in newspapers or television broadcasts, they are often ridiculed by journalists.

## Economic pressures

The GUMG argues that this journalistic desire not to rock the boat is mainly motivated by profit. The media is generally a profit-making business – it makes those profits by attracting advertising, and advertisers are attracted to a specific type of media by the number of readers and viewers. If, for some reason, those viewers or readers are put off the television programme or newspaper or magazine because its content is interpreted as offensive or upsetting, then profits decline. Those who commission and plan programmes or decide newspaper or magazine content usually play safe by excluding anything that might offend or upset.

Curran agrees with the GUMG and argues that, at best, journalists are now only a moderating influence. Their objectivity and impartiality have been undermined by the fact that journalists are not immune to the way the labour market has changed in the UK over the past ten years. Curran notes that unemployment has grown considerably among journalists and there is an increasing tendency for media employers to take on staff on temporary contracts. Compliancy with the ethos of the owner is therefore more likely to secure a journalist a permanent position.

## Agenda setting

The result of this journalistic consensus, says the GUMG, is that the media decide what issues should be discussed by society and which ones should be avoided. This is known as '**agenda setting**'. The GUMG argues that the media present us with a fairly narrow agenda for discussion. We talk about the size and shape of a female singer's bottom, but don't often discuss the massive inequalities that exist in society. We are more likely to be outraged by the latest events in Albert Square or Coronation Street than by the number of people living in poverty. In this way, ordinary members of the public never really question the workings of capitalist society. The GUMG consequently argues that we do not get presented with the really important information that would help ordinary members of society make real choices about how society should be run. Agenda setting therefore results in 'cultural hegemony', with the basic principles of capitalism – private enterprise, profit, the 'free market' and the rights of property ownership – being presented by the media as 'normal' and 'natural'.

# The fallacy of choice

We saw earlier that pluralists are keen to focus on public service broadcasters as proof of media integrity. However, a number of commentators have suggested that the BBC is increasingly abandoning its PSB aims because it is losing its audience to commercial and satellite television. As a result, the BBC has become more commercialized and populist in its programming in an attempt to hang on to its audience.

# Focus on research

## The Sutton Trust: The educational background of leading journalists

As their starting point, the researchers determined who were the 100 leading journalists working in news and current affairs. They did this by consulting senior figures in the media industry. The journalists on their list fell into four categories:

1 newspaper editors
2 newspaper columnists
3 broadcast presenters
4 broadcast editors.

These four groups together shape the news stories presented to the public through newspapers, radio and television – they are the gatekeepers for the news media. The researchers then drew up a list for 1986 in order to track changes over time. As far as possible, the 1986 list comprised the people in the same or equivalent roles to those in 2006, but with some changes to reflect the changing nature of news media (for example, Sky TV's senior journalists appear in the 2006 list but not the1986 version). On both lists, the organization with the most journalists is the BBC, which, despite falling shares of viewers and listeners, remains the dominant force in news.

Information on the journalists' backgrounds was gathered by a variety of means: contacting the journalists directly, using official sources such as *Who's Who* and profiles on websites and publications. The schools attended were classified as comprehensive, grammar or private at the time the journalist joined the school. The universities attended were classified into Oxbridge, the Sutton Trust top 13 (those consistently ranked high in the average of major league tables) and other universities.

The researchers also attempted a broader survey into the educational backgrounds of a much wider range of journalists, to see whether the pattern at the top of the profession was constant throughout the profession, and especially for those entering journalism now. However, the response of those approached was unhelpful. Information on the educational background of journalists was requested from the BBC under the Freedom of Information laws, but the BBC said that it would be too time consuming and costly to produce the information. Editors in other news organizations said that such information was not collected.

Finally, the researchers attempted a survey on recruitment procedures, asking a wide range of people, including editors, producers, course directors, students and trainees, how recruitment was carried out.

Source: Blundell, J. and Griffiths, J. (2008) *Sociology since 2000*, Lewes: Connect Publications

1 **How did the Sutton Trust identify who were 'leading journalists'?**
2 **How did the Trust find out about the journalists' educational backgrounds?**
3 **Why did the Trust try to conduct a broader survey involving a wider range of journalists?**

Some pluralists argue that this is not a problem because PSB and ITV have had to offer more choices to their audiences in order to compete with Sky and Virgin, e.g. the setting up of the BBC digital channels and an internet news site are a rational response to this increased competition, which pluralists claim can only be good for audiences.

However, critics such as Barnett and Weymour (1999) have argued that the quality of television has been undermined by these commercial pressures. They argue that the main aim of all television companies, including the BBC, is to achieve the largest possible audience. This is because commercial television needs to attract the maximum advertising revenue whilst the BBC needs to justify the licence fee. Large audiences are achieved by targeting the lowest common denominator – content based primarily on entertainment – because this aspect of media is least likely to alienate or bore viewers.

Barnett and Weymour argue that such decisions have had a hegemonic cultural effect in the sense that education, information and news have been increasingly sidelined. They compared television schedules in 1978, 1988 and 1998 and argued that the evidence suggests that television in the UK has been significantly dumbed down. For example, the number of single dramas and documentaries has halved over the last 20 years, while soap operas and cheap reality shows have increased fivefold. We also now get more repeats and cheap American imports. Time allocated to news programming has fallen dramatically, and more time is devoted on serious news programmes to celebrity news and human-interest stories. Barnett and Weymour note that even the BBC is succumbing to these commercial pressures. Furthermore, they conclude that despite hundreds of television channels, we do not have more choice, just more of the same thing. Ironically, the dramatic expansion in the number of television channels may have led to less choice overall.

Curran notes the same pressures in the popular press as the rising costs of newsprint in the 1990s led to a major decrease in serious and political news stories and a corresponding increase in stories with lowest-common-denominator appeal, such as human-interest stories or those focused on celebrities. Curran argues that this led to a fall in journalistic standards because it resulted in intrusive cheque-book journalism and the rise of the paparazzi photographer. In addition, Curran argues that there is little choice for audiences in the printed media. There is no radical alternative to the mainstream newspapers, and the press has failed to reflect the growing diversity of public opinion on issues such as the Euro and the abolition of monarchy.

## Conclusion

In conclusion, pluralist theories of media ownership and concentration seem increasingly out of touch with the modern global world. As a theory, it has failed to acknowledge that journalistic or editorial integrity no longer has a great deal of influence in the global marketplace. However, some Marxists are guilty of over-simplifying the relationship of owners both within the media world and with the political elite. Marxist conclusions about the ideological motives of media owners can also be questioned, although the GUMG is probably right to stress that the way the media is organized and journalists are recruited has resulted in the cultural hegemony of capitalist values and ways of seeing the world. All the indicators suggest this will continue to be the norm and that it is likely to spread even further. The territories of 21st century media owners are no longer restricted by time or space. As Coleridge (1993) notes, as they move into acquiring chunks of the internet and online services, they will have subjugated more territory in a decade than Alexander the Great or Genghis Khan did in their lifetimes.

## Key terms

**Agenda setting** controlling which issues come to public attention.

**Cross-media ownership** occurs where different types of media – e.g. radio and TV stations – are owned by the same company.

**Cybermedia** the internet and worldwide web.

**Diversification** the practice of spreading risk by moving into new, unrelated areas of business.

**Global conglomeration** the trend for media corporations to have a presence in many countries and operate in a global market.

**False class-consciousness** coming to believe (wrongly) that capitalism is a fair system which benefits us all equally. Associated with Marxism.

**Hegemony** domination by consent (used to describe the way in which the ruling class project their view of the world so that it becomes the consensus view).

**Horizontal integration** also known as cross-media ownership. Refers to the fact that the bigger media companies often own a diverse range of media.

**Ideology** a set of ideas used to justify and legitimate inequality, especially class inequality.

**Investigative journalism** journalism that aims to expose the misdeeds of the powerful.

**Mass media** agencies of communication that transmit information, education, news and entertainment to mass audiences.

**Media concentration** the result of smaller media companies merging, or being bought up by larger companies, to form a small number of very large companies.

**Media conglomerate** a company that owns various types of media.

**Pluralism** a theory that society is made up of many different groups, all having more or less equal power.

**Public service broadcasting** media outlets controlled by the state.

**Synergy** a mutually advantageous combination of distinct elements, as where two or more related businesses work together, e.g. to promote and sell a film, computer game and toys more effectively than they could individually.

**Technological convergence** the tendency for once diverse media forms to combine as a result of digital technology.

**Vertical integration** owning all the stages in the production, distribution and consumption of a product.

## Check your understanding

1. **What types of media are usually thought to make up the mass media?**
2. **Give examples to illustrate the concentration of ownership in the press and broadcasting media in Britain.**
3. **What is the difference between horizontal and vertical integration?**
4. **Why does Doyle argue that it is important to study the ownership and control of the media?**
5. **What evidence do supporters of the pluralist position use to argue the case that all groups have a voice in the contemporary mass media?**
6. **How do Marxists use the term 'ideology' to understand the content of the mass media?**
7. **What is Curran's conclusion about the influence of media owners?**
8. **Why is the term 'agenda setting' useful when discussing the work of the Glasgow Media Group?**
9. **How do Barnett and Weymour argue that the quality of television has been undermined?**
10. **Identify one criticism of Marxist views of ownership and control of the media, and one of pluralist views.**

## Activities

### Research idea

Conduct a small-scale survey to discover to what extent people of different ages and/or ethnic and/or class backgrounds believe that the content of the media reflects the wide variety of views present in British society.

### Web.tasks

Use the internet to investigate the synergy in the marketing of the Harry Potter stories.

## An eye on the exam Ownership and control of the media

Provide a detailed description of Marxist explanations including concepts, studies and any relevant theories

A discussion of Marxist explanations will take up the main part of the answer

**(a) Outline and assess Marxist explanations of ownership and control of the mass media (50 marks)**

Weigh up the strengths and weaknesses of Marxist explanations in some detail, then present alternative views before reaching a balanced conclusion

Focus on these aspects of the mass media only

### Grade booster Getting top marks in this question

An introduction could be used to provide a brief summary of the key ideas of Marxism and an explanation of how these apply to an analysis of the mass media. Doyle's views are helpful in explaining why issues of ownership and control are important.

The main part of the answer will need to discuss Marxist interpretations of the increasing concentration of ownership of the media in the hands of a few global corporations. The work of Bagdikian is likely to feature here, along with the concepts of horizontal and vertical integration. Neo-Marxist views can be represented by the work of the Glasgow University Media Group and the concept of ideology is important here. The main criticisms of Marxist positions come from those favouring a pluralist position who point to the diversity of media, the independence of public service broadcasting, state controls and the professionalism of journalists.

# TOPIC 3

# The social construction of news

## Getting you thinking

**Which of the following news providers do you trust most and which do you trust least? Explain your answer: Sky, BBC, ITV, broadsheet newspapers, tabloid newspapers.**

News is presented in many different forms in the 21st century. However, despite the growth of new media, particularly the internet and 24-hour rolling news channels on satellite television channels, the majority of the population still rely on traditional methods of news coverage. In 2005, 72 per cent of people indicated that television was their primary source of news coverage. In contrast, only 10 per cent relied upon newspapers to obtain their news, and a further 9 per cent relied upon radio.

An Ofcom survey conducted in 2005 indicated that 94 per cent of the UK population believed that it is important for television news to be impartial. Sixty-seven per cent regarded television news as the most trusted news medium and saw it as a 'window on the world' offering the audience fair and unbiased 'evidence' of events as they happened. In contrast, despite sales of about 10 million daily, only 7 per cent saw newspapers in the same light. Most of those surveyed recognized that their newspapers acted as cheerleaders for particular political ideologies and that many newspapers' editorial lines identified with a particular political party – the *Daily Mirror* has traditionally supported Labour, whilst the *Sun, Mail, Express, Times* and *Telegraph* have traditionally supported the Conservatives.

In 2007, most of the news services in the UK were concentrated in the hands of a very small number of organizations. The primary news providers to terrestrial television channels are:

- the BBC – which attracts two-thirds of the UK audience for news
- Independent Television News (ITN) – which provides news to the ITV network as well as Channel 4
- BSkyB – which not only produces its own Sky News and Five News but is also the main conduit (along with FreeView and Virgin) by which people gain access to 24-hour rolling satellite news programmes such as BBC News, CNN, Fox News and Al Jazeera.

The print news media is dominated by those newspapers owned by News Corp (see Topic 1), through News International, which, in 2007, had over 50 per cent of the market of daily and Sunday newspaper sales.

In the past ten years, the UK has seen an increase in new ways in which people can access the news, such as satellite television, the internet, blogs and text news to mobile phones. The internet has been hailed as leading a cultural revolution in terms of giving the population access to alternative sources of news. However, as of 2009, the

**Table 3.1** UK news provision by television channel

| Channel | News provider | Share of UK news audience |
|---|---|---|
| BBC | BBC | 64% |
| ITV1 | ITN | 22% |
| Sky News | BSkyB | 5% |
| Channel 4 | ITN | 5% |
| Five | BSkyB | 3% |

Source: Broadcasters' Audience Research Board, May 2006 – April 2007

established television news providers (BBC, ITV, Sky News) and newspaper publishers (e.g. News International, Guardian Media Group) dominated internet 'hits' on their news websites. There is little sign that the alternative news websites or blogs are attracting a significant audience. Couldry *et al.* (2007b) found that 85 per cent of people regularly watched television for news – at least three times a week – as opposed to only 23 per cent of people who used the internet in that way.

However, Couldry *et al.* (2007a) note that newspaper sales, in particular, have fallen dramatically in the last 30 years, whilst young people's viewing of terrestrial channels in general, and their news bulletins in particular, is also in decline. Despite the fact that accessing news websites is still a minority activity, there are signs that online use, especially by the young, may increasingly grow in importance; this may be one of the main reasons why conventional news sources, such as the BBC and newspapers like the *Sun* and the *Guardian,* are spending millions of pounds developing sophisticated news websites.

# Television news: a window on the world?

Chandler (1994) suggests that the way television news is presented results in it being regarded as the most reliable source of news by its audience. He notes that:

- Newsreaders are presented as 'neutral' observers in the way they read the scripted news, dress with sober formality and make eye contact with the viewer.
- The body language of newscasters is reduced by seating them behind a desk (which in itself denotes authority) or by having them stand clipboard in hand.
- The content of the news may be far from reassuring, but the newsreader's manner is always friendly, reliable and reassuring. As Peace (1998) argues, this factor creates the idea that the newsreader is the viewer's trustworthy and reliable 'friend'.
- The orderly high-tech studio symbolizes the scientific lengths to which the broadcaster has gone to find the 'truth' and reinforces the image of formal and objective authority.

Overall, then, the presentation of the news by television appears to convey objective truth. Buckingham (1996) carried out research based on interviews and discussions with 12 to 15 year olds about television news, and concluded that the status and credibility of the news was hardly ever challenged by them. Rather, the news was perceived to be an honest and trustworthy reflection of the real world. Moreover, they were happy to accept implicitly the validity of news items that were beyond their own experience. Survey evidence suggests that many mature adults treat their daily diet of television news in precisely the same way. However, sociological critics of the way news is presented suggest that television news actually presents its audience with an *illusion* of objectivity.

## The construction of reality in the news

McQuail (1992) argues that 'news' is not objective or impartial. Events happen, but this does not guarantee that they become news – not all events can be reported because of the sheer number of them. The reality is that news is actually a socially manufactured product because it is the end result of a selective process – **gatekeepers** such as editors and journalists, and sometimes proprietors, make choices and judgements about what events are important enough to cover and how to cover them. As McQuail notes, 'news' is not simply a collection of facts that happen, but a special form of knowledge made up of information, myth, fable and morality. In this sense, it is 'loaded' information and often reflects the perspective or interpretation of particular interest groups, particularly powerful groups, rather than being an objective report of events as they occur.

Critics point out that the process of news selection is biased because it is generally dependent upon three broad influences:

1. organizational or bureaucratic constraints/routines
2. the news values held by media organizations
3. ownership, **ideology** and bias.

## Organizational or bureaucratic routines

Newspapers and television news programmes do not react spontaneously to world events – news coverage is shaped by the way television news companies and newspapers are organized and which audiences they are aimed at. The logistics of collecting news may bias what news is gathered or how it is actually presented and reported. This can be illustrated in a number of ways.

### *Sources of news*

Many of us rather naively believe that news stories are generated by reporters trekking the streets and interviewing witnesses to particular events. However, this is largely untrue. Many newspapers and TV news producers purchase most of their news items from press agencies such as the Press Association (PA) or Reuters – companies who sell brief reports of world or national news 24 hours per day – because they can no longer afford to employ hundreds of journalists. They also receive press releases from pressure groups, government agencies, public-relations companies, private companies and individuals, all of whom wish to publicize their activities. Many stories appear on the news or in print quite simply because a press agency deems it important or because a spin doctor or public-relations officer wants to plant a positive story about the government or a celebrity.

### Financial costs

Sending personnel overseas and booking satellite connections can be very expensive and may result in the BBC or ITN giving us 'news' reports even if very little is actually happening, in order to justify such heavy costs. This is also partly the result of the fact that news organizations will have reporters already stationed in European countries and in the USA, so that when a story arises there is someone there to cover it. However, this often leads to a superficial treatment of events in developing countries because news organizations have very few journalists on duty in Africa or Asia. The last ten years have actually seen a decline in expensive forms of news coverage such as investigative reporting or foreign affairs coverage (apart from conflict in which the UK is involved) because news organizations are cutting costs.

### Time or space available

News has to be tailored to fit either the time available for a news bulletin or the column space in a newspaper. For example, the BBC's *9 O'Clock News* and ITN's *News at Ten* contain, on average, 15 items transmitted over a 30-minute period. Similarly, a newspaper has a fixed amount of space for each news category. Sometimes stories are included or excluded merely because they fit or don't fit the time or space available.

### Deadlines

Television news has an advantage over newspapers because it can bring us news as it happens – it is not affected by deadlines, especially now we have 24-hour rolling news on television. A good example of news as it happened was the destruction of the World Trade Center in 2001. On the other hand, newspapers do have deadlines (usually about 10pm, if the news is to be included in the morning edition) and consequently they focus more on yesterday's news. This is why broadsheet newspaper coverage of stories generally tends to be more detailed and analytical than most television news coverage.

### Immediacy and actuality

Events are much more likely to be reported, especially on television, if they can be accompanied by sound bites of speech and film footage, especially live background pictures from an actual location. Journalists reporting 'live' from the street are thought to add dramatic actuality; stories that have this footage are therefore more likely to be selected than those that do not.

Recent technological advances in newsgathering – particularly in the form of new media such as internet sites – have also made possible a level of immediacy unimagined a few decades ago. For example, BBC News 24 is now able to inform the UK about news events through live streams – 'breaking news' – on all the BBC websites, by texting to mobile phones and through the BBC's digital interactive service. This new technology has also been used to encourage interaction between news organizations and their audiences/readerships.

A plane crash-lands in the Hudson River in the middle of New York in January 2009. Photos taken on mobile phones by 'citizen journalists' appeared in the news media within minutes. This photo was taken by Janis Krums, a ferry passenger.

Viewers are encouraged to text information or send pictures and video clips of news events direct to the BBC Newsroom on their mobile phones. Pictures and copy of breaking news can therefore reach the newsroom long before professional journalists and camera operators reach the scene. Most of the 'live' pictures from the London bombings of 7/7 came from the mobile phones of '**citizen journalists**'.

Spencer-Thomas (2008) uses the example of Burma to illustrate the growing influence of citizen journalists. He notes that the mass antigovernment demonstrations in Burma in 1988 failed to receive much media attention because the military regime banned overseas journalists from the country. By contrast, the mass demonstration in 2007 received far more attention because civilians themselves had the technology, in the form of modern mobile phones and camcorders, to send instant messages and pictures out of the country to waiting international media such as Reuters, BBC and CNN.

### The audience

The content of the news and the style in which news is presented are very much a reaction to the type of audience that is thought to be watching or the social characteristics of a newspaper's readers. For example, *Five News* is characterized by short, snappy bulletins because it is aimed at a young audience. The *Sun* is aimed at a working-class youngish readership and so uses simple language because it believes this is what its readership wants. It also reflects the educational level of its target audience. Newspapers such as the *Guardian*, on the other hand, are aimed at the more qualified professional middle classes (as is Channel 4 News).

Who is perceived to be watching a news broadcast at particular times of the day also influences the selection of news. A lunchtime broadcast is more likely to be viewed by women, and so an item relating to a supermarket 'price war' might receive more coverage than it would in a late-evening news bulletin.

## News values

Spencer-Thomas (2008) notes that **news values** are general guidelines or criteria that determine the worth of a news story and how much prominence it is given by newspapers or broadcast media. Specifically, they refer to what journalists, editors and broadcasters consider as 'newsworthy', i.e. interesting enough to appeal to and attract a significant readership or audience. What is regarded as newsworthy will vary from newspaper to newspaper because they may be aimed at different types of readership. What television editors and journalists regard as newsworthy may also differ between channels – for example, Channel 4 tends to focus on more social-policy issues than do the BBC or ITV. News values are of crucial importance because news producers are under great commercial pressure to increase their audience or readership in order to generate the advertising revenue that makes up most of a media organization's profit.

One of the best known lists of news values is supplied by Johan Galtung and Marie Holmboe Ruge. Although their research was conducted in 1965, virtually any media analyst's discussion of news values will always refer to their list, which was initially intended for the coverage of international events. Galtung and Ruge (1970) identified the following set of news values used by journalists.

### *Extraordinariness*

Unexpected, rare, unpredictable and surprising events have more newsworthiness than routine events because they are out of the ordinary, e.g. the tsunami that hit South East Asia in 2004 or the unexpected death of Diana, Princess of Wales in 1997. As Charles A. Dana famously put it: 'if a dog bites a man, that's not news. But if a man bites a dog, that's news!'

### *Threshold*

The 'bigger' the size of the event, for example war or natural disaster, the more likely it will be nationally reported. There is a threshold below which an event will fail to be considered worthy of attention, and will not be reported. A good example of this is the death of Princess Diana, where we saw almost 24-hour television news coverage of the event being 'filled- out' with items that would not normally reach national television, such as primary schools commemorating her life.

### *Unambiguity*

Events that are easy to grasp are more likely to be reported than those which are open to more than one interpretation, or where understanding of the news depends on first understanding the complex background to the event. A survey of 300 leading media professionals across the USA, conducted by *The Columbia Journalism Review* (2000), revealed that the most regular reason why stories don't appear is that they are 'too complicated for the average person'.

### *Reference to elite persons*

The famous and the powerful – those at the top of the socio-economic hierarchy – are often seen as more newsworthy to the general public than those who are regarded as 'ordinary'. For example, pictures of Prince William on the cover of news magazines can increase sales by tens of thousands. Famous people like Barack Obama therefore get more coverage than your local councillor. If the Queen's finger is nipped by a royal corgi, that is news – for the rest of us it would take a life-threatening savaging by a rabid Rottweiler. Media sociologists have noted that, in the past ten years, the cult of celebrity that exists in the UK has extended our definition of who counts as worthy of public interest, so that celebrity gossip, such as Britney Spears' 'breakdown' is increasingly front-page news, especially in the tabloid newspapers.

On the other hand, members of minority-ethnic groups, the underprivileged, the young – that is, ordinary people living ordinary lives in ordinary towns and cities outside London (where most of the main news centres are located) – are likely to receive limited news coverage, unless they pose a threat to the core values of society.

### *Reference to elite nations*

This relates to cultural proximity, i.e. stories about people who speak the same language, look the same, and share the same preoccupations as the audience receive more coverage than those involving people who do not. Events happening in cultures very different from our own will not be seen as being inherently meaningful to audiences here.

A disaster which involves loss of life will not automatically qualify as important news – its reporting often depends on a kind of sliding scale of importance given to the number of deaths, measured against the country in which they occur. The loss of a few lives in a Western country may achieve recognition, whereas a considerable number of deaths in a developing country would have to occur to achieve similar recognition. This is the so-called 'McLurg's Law', named after a legendary British news editor, who once claimed that 1 dead Briton was worth 5 dead Frenchmen, 20 dead Egyptians, 500 dead Indians and 1000 dead Chinese in terms of news coverage. Consequently, events in distant parts of the world may only be reported when they involve Westerners, for example the headline 'Disco Fire in Thailand injures Brits' may be accompanied by an article that reports that 60 other foreigners died in the same fire.

### *Personalization*

Events may be 'personalized' by referring to a prominent individual or celebrity associated with them. Complex events and policies are often reduced to conflict between personalities. This is because journalists and editors believe that their audiences will identify with a story if social events are seen as the actions of individuals. For example, British politics is often presented as a personal showdown between the two party leaders, especially if there is footage of the two engaged in a parliamentary slanging match, complete with cheers and jeers. International affairs, too, are often reported in this way – for example, the invasion of Iraq in 2003 was often presented as Bush and Blair versus Saddam Hussein.

### *Frequency*

This refers to what Dutton (1997) calls 'the time span taken by the event'. Murders, motorway pile-ups and plane crashes happen suddenly and their meaning can be established quickly. However, more long-term structural social trends are often outside the 'frequency' of the daily papers; for example, inflation or unemployment tend to be reported when the government releases figures on them. Therefore, events which occur suddenly and fit in well with the newspaper or news broadcast's schedule are more readily reported than those which occur gradually or at inconvenient times of day or night. Political parties' news-management techniques often take advantage of this news value – for example, in the run-up to an election, they will hold press conferences or arrange photo opportunities at times which do 'fit in'.

### *Continuity*

Once a story has achieved importance and is 'running', it will continue to be covered for some time. This is partly because news teams are already in place to report the story, and partly because previous reportage may have made the story more accessible to the public. **Moral panics** are sometimes the result of such continuity, as journalists and editors enter a cycle of newsworthiness. However, journalistic interest in the story may wane when they assume their audiences are losing interest.

### *Narrative*

Journalists prefer to present news in the form of a story with heroes and villains, and a beginning, middle and end, in order to make it more interesting. If an event can be presented in this way, it is more likely to be reported.

Think about how the Iraq war, for example, has been presented as a newsworthy **narrative**. According to the news narrative, Iraq was being led by a brutal unelected leader who did not care about killing his own people and who was threatening the world with weapons of mass destruction, as well as financing and harbouring terrorist groups. The USA and UK invaded in order to remove the problem, to destroy the weapons of mass destruction and to restore democracy to the people of Iraq. These valiant efforts are currently being disrupted by insurgents, who are a threat to the Iraqi people and need to be removed by the brave efforts of 'our boys' in the army. This narrative forms the basis of much news reporting about Iraq. The 'truth' is a lot more complicated than this, but this narrative underpins much news coverage because it is easier for audiences and readerships to understand.

### *Negativity*

Bad news is regarded by journalists as more exciting and dramatic than good news and is seen as attracting a bigger audience. Generally, good news, such as 'there were no murders today', is regarded as less interesting and entertaining than 'three people were shot to death today'. Stories about death, tragedy, bankruptcy, violence, damage, natural disasters, political upheaval or simply extreme weather conditions are therefore always rated above positive stories. Often, journalists will go looking for bad news. For example, Fiske (1987) refers to an American journalist arriving in the Belgian Congo during the war there, running up to a group of White women waiting for a plane to leave and shouting out: 'Has anyone here been raped and speaks English?'

The threshold for reporting bad news is lower than that for reporting good news because it usually incorporates other news values: it is often unambiguous; it occurs in a short space of time; it is often unexpected; and it may be big, for example a disaster.

Use the concept of news values to explain why the death of Princess Diana in a car crash in Paris was the biggest news story of the 1990s.

### *Composition*

Most news outlets will attempt to 'balance' the reporting of events, so that if for example there has been a great deal of bad or gloomy news, some items of a more positive nature will be added. If there is an excess of foreign news, for instance, the least important foreign story may have to make way for an inconsequential item of domestic news. Balance may also be achieved if news happens to come overwhelmingly from one source over a certain period.

An interesting news story will, therefore, contain some of these news values, but it is unlikely it will contain them all. Research conducted in the USA by Buckley gave 12 television editors 64 news stories, which they were asked to classify for newsworthiness. All classified them in a similar manner and those items with the greatest number of news values made it to the highest position on the list of stories they would have definitely reported.

## Ownership, ideology and bias

The implication in many studies of news values seems to be that they are virtually objective factors, to which journalists and editors react reflexively. The gatekeeping process, which leads to the selection of some news stories and the exclusion of others, is seen to be apolitical and unbiased, especially by pluralist sociologists and media professionals themselves.

## Neo-pluralism

Pluralists have traditionally argued that journalists are professionals who are disinterested, impartial and objective pursuers of truth. However, some media commentators, who we shall call **neo-pluralists**, suggest that, in the modern world of journalism, these goals are increasingly difficult to attain. Davies (2008) argues that the most basic function of journalism is to check facts. However, he argues that in practice, contemporary journalism has been corrupted by an endemic failure to verify news stories.

Davies was alerted to this practice by what he calls the appearance of 'flat-earth' news stories. This is a type of news story that appears to be and is universally accepted as 'true'. As an example, he cites the millennium bug stories that appeared in 1999, suggesting that there would be a universal breakdown in computerized systems as we entered 2000. Davies concludes that the millions of words written about the bug were written by journalists who had no idea whether what they were writing about was true.

Davies argues that modern-day British journalism is characterized by what he calls '**churnalism**' – the uncritical overreliance by journalists on 'facts' produced by government spin doctors and public-relations experts. He notes that: 'where once journalists were active gatherers of news, now they have generally become mere passive processors of unchecked, second-hand material, much of it contrived by PR to serve some political or commercial interest'. Davies argues they are no longer journalists, but churnalists.

Research by Davies aimed to quantify churnalism in the serious broadsheet press, e.g. *The Times*, and also the *Daily Mail* over a period of two weeks in 1997. He found that 80 per cent of the 2207 stories examined consisted of material which was taken from the PA or public-relations companies. Only 12 per cent of stories were generated by the reporters themselves. He also found that where a story relied on a specific statement of fact, in 70 per cent of them, the claimed fact passed into print without any corroboration at all. Only 12 per cent of 'factual stories' had been thoroughly checked by journalists using investigative techniques.

Davies argues that journalism is forced into churnalism because of commercial pressures that have resulted in more space to fill but with added pressure to do this quickly and at the lowest possible cost. Consequently, facts from official sources are used because they are so cheap. He notes too there are active commercial pressures to pursue stories that tell people what they want to hear, e.g. to give them lots of celebrity stories because this attracts large audiences and therefore advertising revenue. However, he also suggests that journalists today are simply indifferent to the truth and reality. He argues that they prefer to sermonize about the world rather than objectively report it.

However, Davies has attracted some criticisms from Marxist sociologists who suggest that he fails to recognize the role of owners and advertisers in these processes. Edwards and Cromwell (2008), writing on the website Media Lens, argue that newspapers 'are in the business of selling wealthy audiences to advertisers. This is not an apolitical stance. This marketplace naturally favours facts, ideas, values and aspirations that are popular with elite audiences, elite advertisers and elite journalists'. Flat-earth stories underpinned by churnalism provide a cheap supportive environment in order to attract advertising revenue, which makes up most of the profits made by media conglomerates. Monbiot (2004) agrees and notes that 'the falsehoods reproduced by the media before the invasion of Iraq were massive and consequential: it is hard to see how Britain could have gone to war if the press had done its job'.

Marxists are also critical of Davies' view that truth-telling is the primary function of Davies' profession. McChesney (2002) argues that the notion that the media are professional is an ideological myth invented by media owners in order to present the corporate media monopoly as a 'neutral' and unbiased contributor to democracy, so increasing their potential to be profitable. Consequently, some media researchers suggest that news content is manufactured or socially constructed in a way that benefits powerful groups and has negative consequences for the rest of society.

## Concentration of ownership of news organizations

Couldry *et al.* (2007a) note that only six corporations operate the majority of major websites, commercial broadcasting/cable casting and newspapers worldwide.

Sociologists have identified a number of ways in which a media owner might influence the editorial priorities, fairness, transparency and impartiality of the news:

- They may issue direct instructions or the media owner may be directly involved in setting the editorial approach or policy of the news media.
- The owner may influence the way in which the news is gathered and presented – in terms of resources available and which stories they consider worthy of investment (e.g. whether to station correspondents in Iraq or to rely on agency coverage).
- The owner's political or business ideology may directly or indirectly impact on the choice of stories pursued by their editors and the way in which those stories are presented. In other words, an owner does not have to exercise day-to-day control – compliant editors who value their jobs know what their employer expects. For example, a number of national newspapers (the *Independent,* the *Guardian, Daily Mail, Mirror* and *Daily Telegraph*) carried a story on 19 July 2007 concerning Rupert Murdoch's contacts with Tony Blair in the run-up to the Iraq war. The story was not featured at all in either the *Sun* or *The Times*.

Couldry and colleagues note that editors and journalists are subjected to increased commercial pressures in a global multimedia market. This has led to the cutting of newsroom budgets, the undermining of journalistic integrity, and the danger of greater advertiser and sponsor influence over news agenda. Resource pressures mean journalists have to appeal to even bigger audiences and so have to compete with the entertainment sector for consumers. This often leads to the tabloidization of news as it is becomes increasingly underpinned by entertainment values: coverage of sports, crime, entertainment and celebrity becomes the central focus of news reporting. In contrast, the coverage of political debate and social problems declines because it is not entertaining enough.

Couldry *et al.* (2007a) argue that these trends have led to a decline in public trust in the media profession, especially among the young and minority audiences. Public opinion polls (for example, Ipsos MORI 2005) put journalists behind doctors, teachers, scientists, business executives and civil servants and on a par with politicians in terms of public esteem and trust. Couldry and colleagues conclude that the general public is aware that, as a result of market forces, the news lacks balance and relevance, and that it generally serves corporate interests rather than society as a whole.

## The power elite

Bagdikian (2004), in his critique of the American news media, suggests that almost all media leaders in the USA are part of a wider **power elite** made up of a powerful industrial, financial and political establishment. Consequently, media owners ensure that the content of news is politically conservative and that their news outlets promote corporate values. He notes how such values often imperceptibly permeate news; for example, most newspapers have sections dedicated to business news, which present corporate leaders as heroes or exciting combatants, and they uncritically and frequently report corporate and stock-market information. In contrast, very little attention is paid to ordinary Americans and the economic pressures that they face; for example, the news media seem uninterested in the growing gap between the rich and poor in the USA.

Bagdikian notes that reporters are expected by the public to act like independent, fair-minded professionals. However, he notes that reporters are also employees of corporations that control their hiring, firing and daily management, as well as dictating what stories they can cover and which part of their reporting will be used or discarded. Bagdikian suggests that seeing their journalists as obedient workers on an assembly line has produced a growing incidence of news corporations demanding unethical acts, such as chequebook journalism and intrusion into people's privacy, as symbolized by paparazzi photographers.

Bagdikian also argues that the commercial pressure on journalists has meant the neutralization of information and a reduction in objectivity because of fears that it might offend part of the audience and so reduce circulation. Bagdikian concludes that, as a result of these processes, the news in the USA – and increasingly in the UK – reflects an official, but bland, establishment view of the world.

There is some evidence for Bagdikian's assertions. For example, 274 out of 275 News Corp editors around the world came to exactly the same conclusion as their proprietor, Rupert Murdoch, on the war in Iraq. The only one that did not was in Borneo, a predominantly Muslim country, in which support for the war would have resulted in a major decline in circulation. There is some concern that the recent large BSkyB investment in ITV may have similar effects on ITN (40 per cent of which is owned by ITV plc), which produces news for all ITV channels and Channel 4. Sky News already produces news for Five. This means that the BBC is the only news broadcaster in the UK not privately owned by a media transnational conglomerate.

## The propaganda model of the media

Herman and Chomsky (1988) argue that the media participate in propaganda campaigns helpful to elite interests. They suggest that media performance is largely shaped by market forces and that built into the capitalist system is a range of filters that work ceaselessly to shape media output.

They note that media businesses are profit-seeking businesses, owned by very wealthy companies (or other companies) and they are funded by advertisers who are also profit-seeking entities and who want their advertising to appear in a supportive selling environment. The media are also dependent on government and major businesses as information sources. These overlapping interests mean there is a certain degree of solidarity between government, major media and other corporate businesses. Government and large non-media business firms are also best positioned (and sufficiently wealthy) to be able to pressure the media with threats of withdrawal of advertising or TV licences, and therefore control the flow of information.

However, Herman and Chomsky suggest that the media are also constrained and their content is shaped by the dominant politically conservative ideology, which extols the virtues of free-market capitalism and is critical of any alternative point of view. McChesney (2000) notes that, as a result, the media sees official sources of information as legitimate, but he notes that:

> *<<if you talk to prisoners, strikers, the homeless, or protesters, you have to paint their perspectives as unreliable, or else you've become an advocate and are no longer a 'neutral' professional journalist.>>*

Edwards and Cromwell (2006) argue that particular subjects – US/UK government responsibility for genocide, vast corporate criminality, threats to the very existence of human life – are distorted, suppressed, **marginalized** and ignored by the British mass media. Leaders of developing countries of whom the West disapproves are uncritically demonized whilst the USA is lauded as the champion of democracy and the benign military occupier of Iraq.

## The hierarchy of credibility

Stuart Hall (1973) agrees that news is supportive of capitalist interests because those in powerful positions have better access to media institutions than the less powerful. Hall argues that this is a result of the news values employed by most journalists. In particular, most journalists rank the views of politicians, police officers, civil servants and business leaders (Hall calls these groups '**primary definers**') as more important (or credible) than those of pressure groups, trade unionists or ordinary people. Hall calls this the 'hierarchy of credibility'. News often reports what prominent people say about events rather than the events themselves; indeed, what such people say may constitute an event in itself – powerful people 'make news'.

# Focus on research

## Greg Philo

### Bad news from Israel: media coverage of the Middle East conflict

If you don't understand the Middle East crisis, it might be because you are watching it on TV news. This scores high on images of fighting, violence and drama but is low on explanation. The Glasgow University Media Group interviewed 12 small audience groups (a total of 85 people) with a cross section of ages and backgrounds. They were asked a series of questions about the conflict and what they had understood from TV news. The same questions were then put to 300 young people (aged between 17 and 22) who filled in a questionnaire. We asked what came to their mind when they heard the words 'Israeli/Palestinian conflict' and then what was the source of whatever it was. Most (82 per cent) listed TV news as their source and these replies showed that they had absorbed the 'main' message of the news, of conflict, violence and tragedy, but that many people had little understanding of the reasons for the conflict and its origins. Explanations were rarely given on the news and when they were, journalists often spoke in a form of shorthand which assumed quite detailed knowledge of the origins of the conflict. For example, in a news bulletin which featured the progress of peace talks, a journalist made a series of very brief comments on the issues which underpinned the conflict: Journalist: 'The basic raw disagreements remain – the future, for example, of this city Jerusalem, the future of Jewish settlements and the returning refugees.' (ITN 18.30, 16 October 2001)

Adapted from the Glasgow University Media Unit website at www.gla.ac.uk/departments/sociology/units/media

1 **How did the Glasgow University Media Group try to achieve a representative sample?**

2 **Why does Greg Philo write that 'if you don't understand the Middle East crisis it might be because you are watching it on TV news'?**

Some sociologists have drawn attention to the appearance of spin doctors as primary definers of information in recent years. Jones refers to the Labour Government 1997–2010 as the 'sultans of spin'. He notes that spinning a story on behalf of the government or other powerful institution is a form of news management aimed at putting a favourable bias on information presented to the general public via the media in order to gain the most support.

The media's focus on primary definers means that minority groups are often ignored by the media or are portrayed negatively as threats to society. Manning (2001) notes that less-powerful groups have to tone down anything extreme or radical in their message in order to get their message heard by the media.

## The social background of media professionals

However, the Glasgow University Media Group (1981) argue that the way the news is gathered and presented has nothing to do with the rich and powerful. Rather, they argue that news is the product of the social backgrounds of journalists and editors, who are usually White, male and middle-class. The lifestyle that most journalists and editors lead results in them seeing very little wrong with the way society is presently organized (despite inequality) and, as a result, they are rarely critical. They unconsciously side with the powerful and rich quite simply because they have more in common with them, and do not welcome the sorts of radical change proposed by the representatives of the poor and powerless.

## Semiotic analysis

The GUMG have studied news broadcasts and have used a technique called **semiotic content analysis** which involves detailed analysis of the language and visual images used by the media. They have found that the language and images used by the media are more sympathetic to the interests of the powerful and often devalue the points of view of less powerful groups. For example, in some news programmes, trade unions are typically presented as 'demanding' whereas management make 'offers'. Fiske (1987) argues that:

> *« the word 'offer' suggests its agents ... are generous ... and are comfortably in control, whereas 'demand' suggests that its agents are greedy ... and having to struggle to gain control of the situation. Demand is a disruptive word which places 'demanders' with the negative forces that make news. »* (p.285)

In their analysis of industrial disputes such as strikes, the GUMG discovered that managers were often interviewed in the orderly, calm environment of their offices, whilst strikers were interviewed above the noise of the picket lines. The former were seen as the representatives of order and reason, the latter as shouty and unreasonable.

Individuals may also be labelled by the media as 'scroungers', 'terrorists' or 'extremists' – these labels serve to undermine the credibility of the powerless. In foreign news reports, the media often make the ethnocentric and ideological distinction between 'terrorists', who are seen as disrupting friendly regimes, and 'freedom fighters', who are resisting regimes hostile to the West.

The research of the Glasgow Media Group shows that the media do not just reflect public opinion. They also engage in agenda setting, i.e. they provide the framework (or agenda) in which issues are discussed, so that people think about issues in a way that benefits the ruling class. Certain assumptions are built into news programmes, such as that we all want strikes to end, that we oppose 'extremism' and favour 'moderation', and so on. Agenda setting also refers to the exclusion or marginalization of issues that need to be discussed, such as the causes of inequality and poverty. Hall argues that, over time, news actually creates the illusion that consensus characterizes debate in modern capitalist societies.

### Criticisms

However, Schlesinger (1990) is critical of theories that focus on the power of elites or owners because the media do not always act in the interests of the powerful – contemporary politicians are very careful what they say to the media because they are aware that the media can shape public perceptions of their policies and practices and perhaps influence voting behaviour, as well as putting them under considerable pressure to resign. Media owners too are engaged in competition with each other, as illustrated by newspaper price wars and the fact that some media owners, most notably, Rupert Murdoch and Richard Branson, have engaged in some public conflicts with each other over matters of media ownership. Schlesinger argues that this does not suggest a unified media, never mind a unified establishment elite.

Pluralists, too, would argue that the news contains many different points of view. They note that certain views may dominate in particular situations, but the direction that bias takes is not consistent, and so there is no overall slant towards the rich and powerful.

### Conclusions

The news may not be as impartial as we like to think it is. Critics of news gathering suggest that a range of influences – bureaucratic constraints, news values, churnalism, the concentration of ownership, commercial pressures, primary definers and the social backgrounds of journalists – mean that the news is a socially manufactured product which may end up reflecting the interests and ideology of powerful groups. This may undermine democracy, as audiences are not being exposed to a range of facts and information and, as a result, are unable to make informed choices about how society should be organized or about how to deal with the social and economic inequalities that might eventually destabilize such societies.

## Moral panics

An important aspect of news production is the focus on particular types of news that result in moral panics. The media sometimes focus on certain groups and activities and, through the style of their reporting, defines these groups and activities as a problem worthy of public anxiety and official censure and control.

### What is a moral panic?

The term 'moral panic' was popularized by Stanley Cohen (1972) in his classic work *Folk Devils and Moral Panics*. It refers to media reactions to particular social groups or particular activities that are defined as threatening societal values and thus create anxiety amongst the general population. This anxiety or panic puts pressure on the authorities to control the problem and discipline the group responsible. However, the moral concern is usually out of proportion to any real threat to society posed by the group or activity.

Cohen focused on the media's reaction to youth 'disturbances' on Easter Monday 1964. He demonstrated how the media blew what were essentially small-scale scuffles and vandalism out of all proportion by using headlines such as 'Day of Terror' and words like 'battle' and 'riot' in their reporting. Little time or interest was paid to what actually happened, which was a series of localized scuffles. Cohen argued that not only were the events overreported, but also the coverage awarded them far outweighed their importance.

He argues that the media tapped into what they saw as a social consensus – they assumed that decent law-abiding members of society shared their concerns about a general decline in the morality of the young symbolized by the growing influence of youth culture. Consequently, mods and rockers were presented and analysed in a distorted and stereotyped fashion as a threat to law and order, and the media attempted to impose a culture of control on them by calling for their punishment.

Goode and Ben-Yehuda (1994) note that the moral panic produces a '**folk devil**' – a stereotype of deviance that suggests that the perpetrators of the so-called deviant activities are selfish and evil, and steps need to be taken to control and neutralize their actions so that society can return to 'normality'. However, the media also engages in a type of social soothsaying – they often adopt a disaster mentality and predict more problems if the problem group is not kept under surveillance or punished. This increases the social pressure on the forces of law and order to stamp down hard on the problem group.

Goode and Ben-Yehuda note the volatility of moral panics – this means they can erupt suddenly, although they usually subside or disappear just as quickly. Some are dormant but reappear from time to time. However, the panic usually has some lasting effect – it may have raised public consciousness and, in extreme cases, may have led to changes in social policy or the law.

However, both the publicity and social reaction to the panic may create the potential for further crime and deviance in the future. Thornton (1995), for example, notes that the 'Just Say No' drug campaign of the early 1990s probably attracted more young people to the use of ecstasy as they realized adult society disapproved of their membership of the e-generation. There is also evidence that the police reaction to illegal rave parties in the 1980s – using riot gear, dogs, horses, etc. – led to young people violently confronting police officers' attempts to close down these parties. Consequently, arrests for violent conduct rose dramatically in those parts of the country where these parties were popular.

**Figure 3.2** Stages of a moral panic

Moral panics go through a number of stages, which some sociologists have termed a 'cycle of newsworthiness'.

**STAGE 1**

The tabloid media report on a particular activity/incident or social group, using sensationalist and exaggerated language and headlines.

**STAGE 2**

Follow-up articles identify the group as a social problem. They are demonized as 'folk devils', i.e. the media give them particular characteristics, focused particularly on dress and behaviour, which helps the general public and police to identify them more easily.

**STAGE 3**

The media oversimplify the reasons why the group or activity has appeared, e.g. young people out of control, a lack of respect for authority, a decline in morality.

**STAGE 4**

**Moral entrepreneurs**, e.g. politicians and religious leaders, react to media reports and make statements condemning the group or activity; they insist that the police, courts and government take action against them.

**STAGE 5**

There is a rise in the reporting to the police by the general public of incidents associated with the group or activity as the group or activity becomes more visible in the public consciousness.

**STAGE 6**

The authorities stamp down hard on the group or activity – this may take the form of the police stopping, searching and arresting those associated with the activity, the courts severely punishing those convicted of the activity or the government bringing in new laws to control the activity and group. Other institutions, e.g. shopping centres may ban the group or activity.

**STAGE 7**

The group may react to the moral panic, overpolicing, etc., by becoming more deviant in protest, or the activity may go underground where it becomes more difficult to police and control.

**STAGE 8**

More arrests and convictions result from the moral panic and the statistics are reported by the media, thereby fulfilling the initial media prophecy or prediction that the group or activity was a social problem.

## Contemporary examples of moral panics

### *Ravers and ecstasy use*

Redhead (1993) notes that a moral panic in regard to acid house raves in the late 1980s led to the police setting up roadblocks on motorways, turning up at raves in full riot gear and eventually led to the passing of the Criminal Justice Act (1990), which banned illegal parties. Thornton notes that the moral panic that surrounded rave parties in the late 1980s and early 1990s had the effect of attracting more young people to the rave culture, quite simply because it had been labelled deviant by disapproving media coverage.

### *Refugees and asylum seekers*

In 2003, there was a moral panic focused on the numbers of refugees and asylum seekers entering the UK and their motives. Elements of the tabloid press, particularly the *Daily Mail* and the *Sun,* focused on the alleged links between asylum seekers and terrorism to create public anxiety. In the case of asylum seekers, the moral panic of 2003 reduced the motives for people wanting to enter the UK to either terrorism, crime or taking advantage of the UK's generous welfare system. The very complex and genuine reasons why people come to the UK were neglected or ignored altogether.

### *Binge drinking*

Borsay (2007) notes that the moral panic that focused on binge drinking in 2008 is very similar to one that gripped Britain in the early 1700s. He therefore argues that media, public and political concern about problem drinking is not new. He suggests that the parallels between the 18th-century gin craze and contemporary binge drinking are striking. He argues that moral panics characterized both periods, fuelled by pressure groups, the media and perceptions of government complacency. He notes the media-constructed moral panics found in both eras were symbolic of wider anxieties about 'social breakdown'. Borsay notes that the gin craze of the 1700s was finally brought under control with a combination of increased tax and licensing fees, along with restrictions on retail outlets. He concludes that:

> *<< no doubt concerted action by the government and police could bring a similar end to binge drinking today, but whether this would produce an overall drop in alcohol consumption and other social problems and a more disciplined and conformist youth remains questionable. >>*

### *Hoodies*

Fawbert (2008) examined newspaper reports about so-called hoodies between 2004 and 2008, and notes that there was only one article in the national papers in 2004 that used the word 'hoodie' to describe a young thug. However, a year later, the Bluewater Shopping Centre caused outrage by banning its shoppers from sporting hoodies and baseball caps. This was followed by Tony Blair vowing to clamp down on antisocial behaviour perpetrated by hoodies. The media seemed to seize on this, and

**Table 3.2** Examples of moral panics since the 1950s

| Period | Example |
|---|---|
| Mid-1950s | teddy boys |
| 1964 | mods and rockers |
| Late 1960s | hippies smoking marihuana<br>skinhead violence |
| Early 1970s | football hooliganism<br>street crime, i.e. mugging |
| 1976/7 | punk rock<br>heroin addiction |
| Mid to late 1980s | homosexuality and Aids (i.e. 'gay plague')<br>illegal acid-house raves<br>hippy peace convoys<br>video-nasties |
| Early to mid 1990s | child sex abuse<br>single-parent families, especially teenage mothers<br>ecstasy use (post Leah Betts)<br>children and violence (post Jamie Bulger)<br>dangerous dogs |
| Mid to late 1990s | welfare scroungers<br>boys' underachievement in schools |
| 2002/3 | paedophiles<br>Black gun culture<br>asylum seekers |
| 2004–9 | hoodies, knife and gun crime<br>binge drinking |

'hoodies' became a commonly used term, especially between 2005 and 2007, to describe young people involved in crime. He notes that articles would often use the term in the headline, but there would be no reference in the story about whether the young criminal was actually wearing one; it was just presumed. Hoodies suddenly became a symbol of mischief, and sales of the clothing began to soar as young people realized they upset people in authority by wearing them.

## Why do moral panics come about?

### *A reaction to rapid social change*

Furedi (1994) argues that moral panics arise when society fails to adapt to dramatic social changes and it is felt that there is a loss of control, especially over powerless groups such as the young. He notes that in the 1950s and 1960s, British society experienced great social change as younger people acquired more economic and cultural power. This period particularly saw the emergence of distinct youth cultures such as teddy boys (1950s) and mods, rockers and hippies (1960s). As a result, the older generation felt they were losing authority and control over the younger generation.

Furedi therefore argues that moral panics are about the wider concerns that the older generation have about the nature of society today – people see themselves (and their families) as at greater risk from a variety of groups. They believe that things are out of control. They perceive, with the media's encouragement, that traditional norms and values no longer have much relevance in their lives. Furedi notes that people feel a very real sense of loss, which makes them extremely susceptible to the anxieties encouraged by media moral panics.

Cohen and Young (1981) suggest that the media's anxiety about the behaviour of particular social groups originates in the consensual nature of the media in the UK today. Journalists assume that the majority of people in society share common values of reality, especially about what is acceptable and not acceptable. Generally, topics outside these presumed shared ideas are deemed wrong or detrimental. The media's focus on so-called 'problem groups' is seen as newsworthy because journalists, editors and broadcasters assume that like-minded decent people share their moral concerns about the direction that society is taking. In this sense, the media believes that it is giving the public what it wants.

### *A means of making a profit*

Some commentators argue that moral panics are simply the product of news values and the desire of journalists and editors to sell newspapers – they are a good example of how audiences are manipulated by the media for commercial purposes. In other words, moral panics sell tabloid newspapers. However, after a while, news stories exhaust their cycle of newsworthiness and journalists abandon interest in them because they believe their audiences have lost interest too. The social problems, however, do not disappear – they remain dormant until journalists decide at some future date that they can be made newsworthy again and attract a large audience.

### *Serving ruling-class ideology*

Marxists such as Stuart Hall see moral panics as serving an ideological function. His study of the moral coverage of black muggers in the 1970s (Hall *et al.* 1978) concluded that it had the effect of labelling all young African-Caribbeans as criminals and a potential threat to White people. This served the triple ideological purpose of:

1. turning the White working class against the Black working class (i.e. 'divide and rule')
2. diverting attention away from the mismanagement of capitalism by the capitalist class
3. justifying repressive laws and policing that could be used against other 'problem' groups.

The notion that moral panics make it easier for the powerful to introduce control legislation that might be rejected by the general public under normal circumstances has attracted some support. For example, the moral panics aimed at the hippy peace convoys and rave culture that existed in the 1980s resulted in a law banning illegal parties and criminalized trespass. The latter law has since been used by the police to prevent demonstrations and workers picketing their place of work. It can also be argued that both the installation of surveillance cameras in our city centres, and greater film and television censorship are the direct consequences of the moral panic that developed out of the murder of the toddler James Bulger by two children.

### *A reflection of people's real fears*

Left realists argue that moral panics should not be dismissed as a product of ruling-class ideology or news values. Moral panics have a very real basis in reality, i.e. the media often identifies groups who are a very real threat to those living in inner-city areas – portraying such crime as a fantasy is naive because it denies the very real harm that some types of crime have on particular communities or the sense of threat that older people feel. In other words, moral panics are probably justified in some cases.

## Conclusions

The study of moral panics has drawn our attention to the power of the media in defining what counts as normal and deviant behaviour and the effects of such media labelling on particular social groups. Most importantly, it reminds us continually to question our commonsensical understanding of crime, which is often underpinned by media reporting of crime. However, McRobbie (1999) argues that moral panics are becoming less frequent and harder to sustain today, as those groups labelled as folk devils by the media can now effectively fight back through pressure groups and new social movements.

## Check your understanding

1. **What evidence is there that the public trust TV news reports more than those in newspapers?**
2. **Give three reasons why the public regard TV news as a 'window on the world'.**
3. **Give four examples to illustrate how organizational or bureaucratic routines affect news reporting.**
4. **Explain how news values are important in the selection of news, providing examples to illustrate the points you make.**
5. **What evidence does Davies provide to illustrate the importance of what he calls 'churnalism'?**
6. **How might media owners influence news coverage?**
7. **Explain how Bagdikian can argue that 'media owners ensure that the content of news is politically conservative and that their news outlets promote corporate values'.**
8. **How can Hall's idea of a 'hierarchy of credibility' help to explain why news coverage tends to reflect capitalist interests?**
9. **According to Goode and Ben-Yehuda, what are the effects of:**
   **(a) 'folk devils'** **(b) 'moral panics'?**
10. **Briefly explain one recent example of a moral panic.**
11. **Outline three explanations for the existence of moral panics.**

## Activities

### Research ideas

1. List the first ten news items from an edition of the BBC evening news. Do the same for ITN news on the same evening. What are the differences? Can they be explained in terms of 'news values'?
2. Record one news programme. Analyze the lead story in terms of the sources that are used, e.g. newscaster's script, live film footage, location report from a reporter at the scene, interview – taped, live or by satellite – archive footage (old film), amateur film, etc. Then brainstorm a list of all the people who must have been involved, e.g. reporters, photographers, editors, companies buying and selling satellite time, drivers, outside broadcast crews, film archivists, etc. Discuss how practical problems may have served to structure the story in a particular way.

### Web.tasks

1. Look at the websites of the following newspapers on the same day: *Sun, Daily Mail, Daily Telegraph, Guardian*. Compare the presentation of their main stories.
2. Find out about the recent work of the Glasgow University Media Group at **www.glasgowmediagroup.org**

# Key terms

**'Churnalism'** uncritical over-reliance by journalists on 'facts' produced by government spin doctors and public-relations experts.

**Citizen journalists** members of the public who record news events, for example using mobile-phone cameras.

**Content analysis** a research method that analyses media content in both a quantitative and qualitative way.

**Folk devil** stereotype of deviants which suggests that the perpetrators of the so-called deviant activities are selfish and evil and therefore steps need to be taken to control and neutralize their actions so that society can return to 'normality'.

**Gatekeepers** people within the media who have the power to let some news stories through and stop others, e.g. editors. They therefore decide what counts as news.

**Ideology** a set of ideas used to justify and legitimate inequality, especially class inequality.

**Marginalizing** making a group appear to be 'at the edge' of society and not very important.

**Moral entrepreneurs** politicians, religious leaders, etc., who react to sensational media reports and make statements condemning the group or activity and insist that the police, courts and government take action against them.

**Moral panics** media reactions to particular social groups or particular activities which are defined as threatening societal values and consequently create anxiety amongst the general population.

**Narrativization** transforming real events into easily digestible stories with causal agents, (heroes and villains) and a sense of closure.

**Neo-pluralism** view that journalists are professional, objective pursuers of truth who face obstacles in living up to these principles in the modern world.

**News values** assumptions about what makes an event newsworthy (i.e. interesting to a particular audience) that guide journalists and editors when selecting news items.

**Power elite** the wealthy minority who control economic and political power.

**Primary definers** powerful groups that have easier and more effective access to the media, e.g. the government, the rich and powerful.

**Semiotics** the sociological study of signs and symbols contained in languages and images such as advertisements. *See also* **content analysis**.

## An eye on the exam The social construction of news

Provide a detailed description of the view including concepts, studies and any relevant theories

This includes coverage in newspapers, TV, radio and online

**(a) Outline and assess the view that the news is a socially constructed media product. (50 marks)**

Weigh up the strengths and weaknesses of the view in some detail, then present alternative views before reaching a balanced conclusion

Created by social processes and influenced by social structure

### Grade booster Getting top marks in this question

An introduction needs to explain the idea of a 'social construction' and contrast it with the dominant idea of news as a 'window on the world'. Then the main part of the answer can discuss the social processes and influences that are involved in the making of news in the various media. This section of the answer is likely to refer to the role of gatekeepers such as editors and journalists and the pressures of organizational routines. A key concept is news values and this idea will need to be explained and the main news values identified. Marxist explanations focus on the reasons why news tends to reflect the interests of the powerful. These reasons include the direct and indirect influence of media owners as well as the more ideological explanations favoured by sociologists such as Stuart Hall.

# TOPIC 4

# Media representations of gender

## Getting you thinking

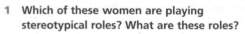

1. **Which of these women are playing stereotypical roles? What are these roles?**
2. **To what extent do you think that representations of women in the media are changing? Give examples to support your answer.**





Bob Connell (1995) argues that cultural expectations about gender roles in the UK in the 20th century were dominated by **hegemonic definitions** of masculinity, femininity and sexuality. These cultural ideas stressed two broad traditional ideas with regard to gender:

1. Paid work was central to men's identity and role. Men were expected to be breadwinners and heads of households responsible for the economic security of their dependants. Masculinity was perceived to be individualistic, competitive, ambitious and aggressive. Men were not expected to openly demonstrate emotion.
2. Females were culturally categorized primarily as home-makers, mothers and carers. Women were confined to a life defined by the family, the home and personal relationships. They were expected to be less rational and more emotional and neurotic than men.

Connell argues that these ideas about gender constituted a patriarchal ideology, which assumed that masculinity was dominant and femininity was subordinate because males exercised economic, social and physical power over females. This ideology was transmitted from one generation to the next through the process of gender-role socialization that mainly occurred in the family. However, the mass media, a secondary agent of socialization, were also seen as playing a key role in teaching and reinforcing these cultural expectations about how each gender was supposed to operate in the social world. Consequently, a great deal of sociological effort and analysis has been expended in the last 30 years examining media representations of gender roles and how these contributed to the dominance of masculinity and the subordination of femininity. However, media research has also focused on how these representations may be responding to the profound economic and social changes that have occurred in the fields of education and employment, which some argue have transformed the power relationship between males and females.

Almy *et al.* (1984) argue that media representations are important because they enter 'our collective social understandings, constituting our sense of ourselves, the positions we take up in the world, and the possibilities we see for action in it' (p.19). In other words, these media representations not only stereotype masculinity and femininity into fairly limited forms of behaviour, but they also provide role models that members of each gender are encouraged to aspire to.

However, Gauntlett (2008) points out that sociological analysis of media representations need to be cautious, because of the sheer diversity of media that exist in the UK. The mass media constitute a range of audio-visual, written and new media. Moreover, media audiences are also wildly diverse. Gauntlett suggests therefore that it would be folly to assume that the ideological messages that are transmitted reflect similar perspectives on gender. Moreover, it is highly likely that, as a result of media and audience diversity, media messages about gender will be contradictory and possibly irreconcilable.

# Traditional media representations of femininity

## Limited roles

It is often argued by feminist sociologists that women are generally represented in a narrow range of social roles by various types of media, whilst men are shown performing a full range of social and occupational roles. Tunstall (1987) is typical of this perspective. He argues:

> *<<The presentation of women in the media is biased because it emphasizes women's domestic, sexual, consumer and marital activities to the exclusion of all else. Women are depicted as busy housewives, as contented mothers, as eager consumers and as sex objects. This does indeed indicate bias for family status because, although similar numbers of men are fathers and husbands, the media has much less to say about these male roles; men are seldom presented nude, nor is their marital or family status continually quoted in irrelevant contexts. Just as men's domestic and marital roles are ignored, the media also ignore that well over half of British adult women go out to paid employment, and that many of their interests and problems are employment-related.>>*

Furthermore, feminist analyses often see media representations of working women as a problem in two ways:

1. They are portrayed as unfulfilled, unattractive, possibly unstable and unable to sustain relationships.
2. It is implied that working mothers are guilty of the emotional neglect of their children. Working fathers are rarely portrayed in this way.

## Symbolic annihilation

Tuchman *et al.* (1978) used the term '**symbolic annihilation**' to describe the way in which women's achievements are often not reported, or are condemned or trivialized by the mass media. Often their achievements are presented as less important than their looks and sex appeal.

### *Women (hardly) in the news*

Gallagher (1980) reviewed the portrayal of women by the media across different continents and found that the activities of women were rarely seen as newsworthy compared with the activities of men. The Global Media Monitoring Project (GMMP) published a snapshot of gender in news media on one day across 76 countries in 2005 and suggested that little has changed since Gallagher's observations. The GMMP found that women appeared in, or were the subject of British television news stories much less than men: when they did appear they were usually there as celebrities or in some kind of decorative role, and the stories they appeared in tended to be 'softer' news features, e.g. women were interviewed as consumers. There were very few stories about their professional abilities or expertise, and most press coverage continues to rely on men as experts in the fields of business, politics and economics. In 2000, the Association of Women Journalists studied news coverage of women and women's issues in 70 countries. It reported that only 18 per cent of stories quote women, and that the number of women-related stories came to barely 10 per cent of total news coverage. Moreover, Gill (2007) argues that female issues and news are often marginalized by newspapers, in that newspaper editors see the need to have 'women's pages' which focus on women as a special group with special – often emotional – needs.

### *Coverage of women's sport*

A good example of the symbolic annihilation of women's activities is the media coverage of women's sport in newspapers and on television. Research into TV sport presentation shows that what little coverage of women's sport there is tends to sexualize, trivialize and devalue women's sporting accomplishments (Women's Sport and Fitness Foundation 2006). Evidence collected by the Bristol Fawcett Society (2008) suggests this limited coverage is still the case, even in broadsheet quality newspapers such as the *Observer*. Their analysis of the *Observer Sports Monthly* in 2008 found that 177 men were featured, compared with only 13 women.

Duncan and Messner (2005) note that commentators, (97 per cent of whom are men), use different language when they talk about female athletes. Men are described as 'big', 'strong', 'brilliant', 'gutsy' and 'aggressive', whereas women are more often referred to as 'weary', 'fatigued', 'frustrated', 'panicked', 'vulnerable' and 'choking'. Commentators are also twice as likely to call men by their last names only, and three times as likely to call women by their first names only. Furthermore, women in sports are often described as 'girls', whereas males are rarely referred to as 'boys'. Duncan and Messner argue that this reduces female athletes to the role of children, while giving adult status to white male athletes. The media also subject women in sport to the **male gaze** (see p. 164) because female athletes are increasingly photographed in hyper-sexualized poses.

### *Women's invisibility in the media*

Another aspect of symbolic annihilation is the invisibility of women in various parts of the media. Recent studies suggest that the male-to-female ratio in speaking parts in prime-time drama is about 60/40. Even children's television is dominated by males. The Bristol Fawcett Society (2008) analysed a day's output from CBeebies and found that only 30 per cent of main characters were female, all the story narrators were male and a very clear majority of anchors and presenters were also male.

Females are also invisible in new types of media. A content analysis by Dietz (1998) of 33 popular Nintendo and Sega Genesis video games found that there were no female characters in 41 per cent of the games; in 28 per cent of them, females were portrayed as sex objects, while 21 per cent of the games portrayed women as victims of male violence. An Ofcom survey in 2008 found that boys of all ages were more likely than girls to access such games through games consoles. However, on a more positive note, the survey also concluded females were more likely to use social network internet sites that involved creative online activities, particularly those related to communicating or sharing content with other people.

## Ideological ideals

Apart from television, the most popular type of media that women mainly access is women's magazines. These magazines have attracted a great deal of attention from feminist sociologists over the last 25 years, who suggest that they strongly encourage women to conform to ideological patriarchal ideals that confirm their subordinate position compared with men.

### *A cult of femininity?*

Ferguson (1983) conducted a content analysis of women's magazines from between 1949 and 1974, and 1979 and 1980. She notes that such magazines are organized around '**a cult of femininity**', which promotes a traditional ideal where excellence is achieved through caring for others, the family, marriage and appearance. She argues that, although modern female magazines, especially those aimed at teenagers, are gradually moving away from these stereotypes, they still tend to focus narrowly on 'him, home and looking good (for him)'. Contemporary evidence suggests that not much has changed. The Bristol Fawcett Society analysed 521 covers of magazines in 2008 that featured people, and discovered that 291 (56 per cent) featured idealized images of men and women, of which 84 per cent were women. The other 44 per cent of magazine covers, which focused on subjects such as sport, politics and music, featured a mere 15 per cent of women.

However, Ferguson's ideas were challenged by Winship (1987), who argued that women's magazines generally play a supportive and positive role in the lives of women. She argues that such magazines present women with a broader range of options than ever before, and that they tackle problems that have been largely ignored by the male-dominated media, such as domestic violence and child abuse.

### *The sexual objectification of women*

Wolf (1990) suggests that the images of women used by the media, especially the print media and advertising, present a particular '**beauty ideal**' through which they transmit the strong ideological message that women should treat their bodies as a project in constant need of improvement. Cumberbatch (2004) found that being 'attractive' fitted the description for nearly two-thirds of females featured in television advertising but only one-quarter of males. He concluded that women generally occupy a passive 'decorative' role in television advertising.

This media beauty ideal, especially when it is found in pornography, national newspapers and lads' magazines such as *Nuts*, essentially views women as **sex objects** to be consumed by what Mulvey (1975) calls the 'male gaze', whereby the camera lens essentially 'eyes up' the female characters, providing erotic pleasure for men. According to Kilbourne (1995), this media representation presents women as mannequins: tall and thin, often size zero, with very long legs, perfect teeth and hair, and skin without a blemish in sight. Kilbourne notes that this mannequin image is used to advertise cosmetics, health products and anything that works to improve the appearance of the body for the benefit of the male gaze (rather than for female self-esteem).

This beauty ideal makes an appearance in a variety of media. Mulvey notes that physical looks, sex appeal and youth seem to be necessary attributes for women to be successful in television and in the cinema. In news presentation, in particular, with its increasingly intimate mode of presentation, good-looking young women are used to improve ratings, employing at times a flirtatious relationship with their more mature male co-presenter.

### *Slimness = happiness?*

Magazines for teenage girls also concentrate heavily on beauty and slimming. For example, content analysis of teenage magazines in the UK indicates that almost 70 per cent of the content and images focus on beauty and fashion, compared with only 12 per cent focused on education or careers.

Some feminist commentators, such as Orbach (1991), have suggested that such media can create anxieties in young females with regard to their body image and identity. She notes that the media, especially those magazines that focus on fashion and celebrity, as well as the tabloid newspapers, perpetuate the idea that slimness equals success, health, happiness and popularity. She accuses the media of overemphasizing this aspect of the beauty ideal and for encouraging young girls to be unhappy with their bodies. She notes that they create the potential for eating disorders in several ways:

- by constantly exhorting females to be concerned with their weight, shape, size, looks
- by using pictures of size-zero supermodels to illustrate articles
- by running features that criticize so-called 'overweight' celebrities
- through adverts encouraging dieting and cosmetic surgery.

Orbach argues that exposure to such ideal images coincides with a period in girls' lives where self-regard and self-efficacy is in decline, where body image is at its most fragile because of physical changes of puberty, and where the tendency for social comparison is at its peak.

Hamilton and Waller (1993) take a slightly different view of media effects than Orbach. They suggest that the media

Do you think there is a 'causal link between media images of super-thin women and eating disorders in young women'?

may act as a negative reinforcer of body-size overestimation – the media does not make women feel a need to be thinner *per se*, but the media focus on thinness may assist them in feeling bigger than they already feel themselves to be.

In 2003, *Teen* magazine reported that 35 per cent of girls aged 6 to 12 have been on at least one diet, and that 50 to 70 per cent of normal-weight girls believe they are overweight. Overall, research indicates that 90 per cent of women are dissatisfied with their appearance in some way. Tebbel (2000) reports that women's magazines have ten-and-a-half times more advertisements and articles promoting weight loss than men's magazines do, and over three-quarters of the covers of women's magazines include at least one message about how to change a woman's bodily appearance – by diet, exercise or cosmetic surgery. Television and cinema reinforce the importance of a thin body as a measure of a woman's worth. Fouts (1999) reports that over three-quarters of female characters in television situation comedies are underweight, and only one in 20 are above average in size.

There is no scientific proof of a direct causal link between media images of super-thin women and eating disorders in young women, but all the research points to a direct impact on teenage girls. It is a fact that in societies where there are no established media, there is no culture of thinness and eating disorders are very rare. However, there is evidence that the introduction of Western-style media has led to an increase in eating disorders in several cultures, e.g. Becker *et al.*'s (2003) study of the appearance of eating disorders in Fiji after the introduction of Western television.

## Do the modern media empower women?

Gill (2008) argues that the depiction of women in advertising has changed from women as passive objects of the male gaze, to active, independent and sexually powerful agents. She examined advertisements on television, in magazines and on billboards over a ten-year period and suggests that three stereotypes of women can be seen:

1. the young physically toned and smart heterosexual who uses her sexual power to control a man
2. the vengeful heterosexual beautiful woman set on punishing her ex-lover
3. the 'hot lesbian' entwined with another beautiful woman.

However, Gill argues that, although these advertisements claim to **empower** young women, 'the toned, beautiful, heterosexual women featured in these ads come straight out of the most predictable templates of male sexual fantasy, and embody very narrow standards of female beauty and sex appeal'. In other words, the images contained in these advertisements are contradictory.

She concludes:

> <<*Instead of passive, 'dumb' or unintelligent sex objects, women in advertisements are now active, beautiful, smart, powerful sexual subjects. In some respects, this shift is a positive one, offering modern representations of femininity that give women power and agency, and not exclusively defining women as heterosexual. However, these limited representations of female desire in the media may also be influencing women to feel that they should fit a mould and look and act in a certain way; that they should not only be beautiful, but sexy, sexually knowledgeable and always 'up for it' – and we must question whether this is how women should be represented – and sold to.*>>

In other words, Gill agrees that there are elements of Wolf's beauty ideal in these representations, which may have the negative side-effect of encouraging ordinary women to pursue the impossible. Orbach notes that, as a result, numerous surveys indicate that a majority of young women are constantly dissatisfied with their bodies and likely to be experiencing low self-esteem.

## Positive role models?

Other sociologists have noted the increasing number of positive female roles, which, they claim, are emerging especially in television drama and films. It is argued that these reflect the social and cultural changes that females have experienced in the last 25 years, especially the feminization of the economy, which has meant that women are now more likely to have careers and an independent income. Moreover, there has been a fundamental change in women's attitudes – Wilkinson (1994) calls this a 'genderquake' – which means that their aspirations have dramatically changed, with education and career replacing marriage and family as priorities.

These cultural changes started to seep into British television culture through American series such as *Sex in the City, Ally McBeal, Buffy the Vampire Slayer* and *The X-Files*. Westwood notes how many of these series subverted hegemonic definitions of gender by having female lead characters who were just as confident and powerful as the male character. She also argues that we are now seeing more 'transgressive' (i.e. going beyond gendered expectations) programming on television. Traditional gender roles are constantly being experimented with. She cites the example of *The X-Files*, in which the female character, Scully, represents the 'masculine' world of science, rationality and facts, whilst the male character, Mulder, is emotionally open and vulnerable – traits normally associated with femininity. There are signs that British television series are now well down this path – think of the ways in which femininity was represented by the female characters in dramas such as *Dr Who*,

*Prime Suspect* and *Gavin and Stacey*. Some cultural commentators have suggested that soap operas, such as *Coronation Street* and *Eastenders,* also promote independent and assertive female characters compared with weaker male characters. Women often use their sexuality as a source of power over men.

However, Fiske (2003) argues that despite positive changes in media representations of women, there are also contradictions reflecting those faced by women in their attempt to assert feminine values within a society where patriarchal values dominate. Soaps focus on domestic issues – the domestic setting may be regarded as the only legitimate (accepted) area for female authority in patriarchal societies. Therefore, while soap operas do portray women in a more positive way than advertising and other forms of television, they still ultimately respect and conform to hegemonic definitions of femininity. Soaps often show women as having jobs, but rarely pursing their careers, and if they do, more often than not, they are unsuccessful. Thus we can see how even a form of television programming aimed at a majority female audience contains subliminal messages reinforcing the dominant male ideology.

Gauntlett (2008), however, has drawn attention to 21st-century media aimed at young women, which, he claims, differ in character from the media of 20 years ago. He argues that magazines:

> *<<are emphatic in their determination that women must do their own thing, be themselves, and/or be as outrageously sassy and sexy as possible. Several recent movies have featured self-confident, tough, intelligent female lead characters. Female pop stars sing about financial and emotional independence, inner strength, and how they don't need a man.>>*

This set of media messages from a range of sources suggest that women can be tough and independent whilst 'maintaining perfect make-up and wearing impossible shoes'. He claims that surveys of young women and their lifestyles suggest that these media messages are having a positive and significant impact on the way young women construct their identities today.

# Traditional media representations of masculinity

Until fairly recently, there has been little analysis of how the media construct, inform and reinforce cultural expectations about men and masculinity. Tunstall (1987) points out that the media rarely focus on men's marital and domestic roles, or claim that fathers' lack of contact with their children (because of their jobs) leads to social problems such as juvenile delinquency. On the other hand, working and single women are often seen as blameworthy for such problems. Tunstall also observed that men are seldom presented as sex objects in the same way as females or judged by the media in terms of how well they conform to a feminine definition of an ideal male physical form.

In 1999, the research group Children Now asked boys between the ages of 10 and 17 about their perceptions of the male characters they saw on television, in music videos and in movies (Children Now 1999). Their results indicate that media representations of men do not reflect the changing work and family experiences of most men today. The study found the following:

- on television, most men and boys usually keep their attention focused mostly just on women and girls
- many males on TV are violent and angry
- men are generally leaders and problem-solvers
- males are funny, confident, successful and athletic
- it is rare to see men or boys crying or otherwise showing vulnerability
- male characters on TV could not be described as 'sensitive'
- male characters are mostly shown in the workplace, and only rarely at home
- more than a third of the boys had never seen a man on TV doing domestic chores.

These images support the idea that hegemonic images of masculinity generally continue to dominate mass media coverage of boys and men.

## The masculine myth

Easthope (1990) argues that a variety of media, especially Hollywood films and computer games, transmit the view that masculinity based on strength, aggression, competition and violence is biologically determined and, therefore, a natural goal for boys to achieve. He argues that the Hollywood action hero is the embodiment of this view. Easthope argues that, while most men cannot hope to achieve such a masculine image, i.e. it is an ideological myth, they internalize the notion that men have physical, cultural and emotional power and that this is part and parcel of their male identity.

## Men and magazines

### *The 'new man'*

The 1980s saw the emergence of a new breed of glossy magazines aimed at middle-class young men, such as *GQ, Maxim* and *FHM*. Interestingly, their content focused on the masculine experience rather than specifically on interests or hobbies. The content of such magazines often suggested that:

- men are emotionally vulnerable
- they should be more in touch with their emotions or feminine side
- they should treat women as equals
- they should care more about their appearance
- active fatherhood is an experience worth having.

These magazines were seen by some commentators as evidence of a new type of masculinity – the 'new man'. Television advertising in the 1980s and 1990s also focused on this phenomenon, presenting us with a series of commercials peopled with caring sharing men.

### *The 'metrosexual male'*

Media representations of this new type of masculinity led to postmodern sociologists speculating that masculinity was responding to the growing economic independence and assertiveness of women. Frank Mort (1988), for example, argued that the rise in men's fashion magazines, and the advertising and consumption of male toiletries and designer-label clothing for men, reflected changes in masculine social attitudes and, in particular, the emergence of the 'metrosexual' male. Rutherford (1998) suggests media images of the new man were an attempt – partly in a response to feminism – to express men's repressed emotions and aimed at revealing a more feminized image. However, Tim Edwards (1997) argues that the new man was quite simply a product of advertisers, who invented the concept in order to sell products to both men and women.

Gauntlett (2008) is particularly supportive of men's magazines such as *FHM*, which, he claims, have an almost obsessive relationship with the socially constructed nature of manhood. He argues that such media are positive because they stress that 'the performance of masculinity can and should be practised and perfected'. His study of the content of *FHM* concludes that the masculine values it transmits are 'fundamentally caring, generous and good humoured'. Gauntlett argues that these magazines are often centred on 'helping men to be considerate lovers, useful around the home, healthy, fashionable, and funny – in particular, being able to laugh at themselves'.

### *Retributive masculinity*

Collier (1992) notes that men's magazines are often contradictory in their representations of masculinity. He notes that these magazines continue to define success in traditional terms, i.e. in terms of work, salary and materialism, whilst women are objectified in an explicitly sexual fashion. These magazines continue to relegate women to the background. Gauntlett agrees that images of the 'conventionally rugged, super-independent, extra-strong macho man still circulate in popular culture'. Sharples (1999) argues that some of the newer magazines, such as *Zoo* and *Nuts*, have actually rejected metrosexuality. Rutherford suggests they are symbolic of what he calls '**retributive masculinity**' – an attempt to reassert traditional masculine authority by celebrating traditionally male concerns in their content, i.e. 'birds, booze and football'. Some feminist sociologists have seen these traditional representations as part of an antifeminist backlash. However, as Sharples notes, it is unlikely that these magazines set out to be misogynist – rather they simply promote masculinity in what their editors and journalists see as positive ways. Gauntlett suggests that media sociologists tend to be obsessed with the traditional aspects of men's media and consequently fail to understand that 'men's magazines are not perfect vehicles for the transformation of gender roles, by any means, but they play a more important, complex and broadly positive role than most critics suggest'.

Gary Whannel's observations on David Beckham (2002) note that mass media stories about and images of David Beckham are also contradictory, in that they stress Beckham as representative of both metrosexual and retributive versions of masculinity. Whannel notes that media representations of Beckham are fluid – his good looks, his football skills, competitive spirit and his commitment mark him out as a traditional 'real man'. However, this image has been balanced with alternative media representations that stress his metrosexuality, particularly his emotional commitment to his family and the fact that he spends a great deal of time, effort and money on his image.

There are, then, signs that media representations of masculinity are moving away from the emphasis on traditional masculinity, to embrace new forms of masculinity that celebrate fatherhood and emotional vulnerability. In the past 20 years, the media have also become more accepting of homosexuality, as major celebrities have come out and declared themselves gay. However, there are still contradictions in the media representation of homosexuality. Similarly, it is important not to exaggerate changes in representations of masculinity, as the overall tone of media representations still strongly supports hegemonic versions of what it is to be a man.

Do you agree with Gauntlett that men's magazines have a positive influence on modern men?

## Theoretical perspectives and media representations

Feminists are the main sociologists working in this field. They have been very critical of the representations of men and women in the media. However, they differ in their emphasis.

### Liberal feminism

Liberal feminists are concerned about media representations because they believe that the mass media play a major role, alongside the family and education, in the social construction of gender roles, i.e. how children learn to be feminine or masculine. The media emphasis on females as domestic goddesses and sex objects is seen as a problem because it is believed to have a limiting effect on young females' behaviour and aspirations, especially in adolescence.

Liberal feminists believe that media representations are slow to change in response to women's achievements in society. This 'cultural lag' is due to the fact that attitudes and ideas change more slowly than social and economic conditions. Women are still ignored or trivialized by the media, although liberal feminists accept that this is happening to a lesser degree than in the past as the number of female journalists, editors and broadcasters increases.

However, liberal feminists are concerned that women's progress in media professions has considerably slowed. The majority of media owners are male, as are the higher position holders within media conglomerates. For example:

- In 2009, out of 20 national daily and Sunday newspapers, only three editors were female (ironically of tabloid newspapers, the *Sun, Star* and *Sunday Mirror*).
- In 2006, only 26 per cent of the boards of television and film production companies in the UK were women.
- Women made up 50 per cent of the advertising workforce in 2006, but only 26 per cent of managers and 15 per cent of top executives.
- A spot survey carried out by the pressure group Women in Film and Television into 10 prime-time UK dramas during one week's transmissions showed that only 15 per cent of directors and only 25 per cent of writers were female.
- Women continue to dominate areas in the film and television industries such as costume, make-up and hair, which have less status and are paid less than male-dominated technical areas such as camera, sound and lighting.
- In 2002, the BFI analysed UK feature-film productions of the previous two years (including those in production). Out of the total of 350 films, only eight were directed by women.

## Socialist and Marxist feminism

Marxist or socialist feminists believe that the roots of the stereotypical images of men and women in the media are economic. They are a by-product of the need of media conglomerates in capitalist societies to make a profit. The male-dominated media aim to attract the largest audience possible, and this leads to an emphasis on the traditional roles of men and women in sitcoms, game shows and soap operas. The alternative images of women encouraged by feminism, such as the assertive career woman, do not fit easily into this type of media content and consequently such women are ignored, devalued or treated critically.

A great deal of the content of women's magazines is shaped by advertising. These types of media make profits from advertising rather than sales, and therefore it is in the interests of these magazines to promote 'false needs' around beauty, size and shape, in order to attract advertising revenue from the cosmetics, diet and fashion industries. By presenting an ideal difficult to achieve and maintain, the cosmetic and diet product industries are assured of growth and profits. It is estimated that the diet industry alone is worth $100 billion a year in the USA.

Marxists note that another media marketing strategy that encourages women to invest in the beauty market is an increasing emphasis in media content on retaining youth and resisting ageing. Marxists argue that women are therefore not only exploited by the media as mother/housewives and sex objects, but their anxieties about weight and age are also deliberately manipulated by the media so that they can be exploited as consumers of body-related products.

## Radical feminism

Radical feminists feel strongly that the media reproduce patriarchy. In patriarchal societies, men dominate positions of power and control and have a vested interest in keeping women in subordinate positions. Radical feminists argue that traditional images are deliberately transmitted by male-dominated media to keep women oppressed into a narrow range of roles.

Radical feminists believe that the media deliberately dupe women into believing in the 'beauty myth', i.e. that they should conform to a male image of what it is to be a 'proper' woman in terms of good looks, sexiness, ideal shape, weight, size. Women are strongly encouraged by the media to see these goals as central to their personal happiness, rather than competing with men for positions of power. This creates a form of **false consciousness** in women and deters them from making the most of the opportunities available to them.

Radical feminists claim that men's magazines that celebrate and encourage retributive masculinity are examples of a social backlash directed against the gains made by women because of the feminization of the economy, and attempts to compensate for a 'crisis in masculinity' as men's economic and social power declines. They suggest it is no coincidence that, at the same time as women are achieving greater social, political and professional equality, these magazines symbolically relegate them to subordinate positions as sex objects.

## Popular feminism

McRobbie (1999) argues that much of young women's media today constitutes a form of '**popular feminism**' expressed through young women's magazines that promote the concept of 'girl power'. McRobbie argues that young women in the 21st century are promoting a new form of feminism that, on the surface, looks like it is a rejection of the feminism of previous generations that focused on patriarchal forms of exploitation. She argues that:

> *<<to these young women, official feminism is something that belongs to their mothers' generation. They have to develop their own language for dealing with sexual inequality; and they do this through a raunchy language of 'shagging, snogging and having a good time'.>>* (p.122)

McRobbie argues that the key difference in the language used by traditional and popular feminists is that the latter is now in the mainstream of commercial culture, whereas the former was marginalized and often ignored by the mainstream media. Hollows (2000) suggests popular

Girls Aloud: female stereotypes or symbols of popular feminism?

culture in the form of women's magazines is a site of a cultural struggle, in which new forms of femininity and feminism are being defined and negotiated. As Gill (2007) notes: 'the fact that magazines are commercial ventures does not mean that they can not also be spaces for progressive ideas or cultural contestation' (p.204).

## Postmodernism

Gauntlett (2008) focuses on the relationship between the mass media and identity. He argues that the mass media today challenge traditional definitions of gender and are actually a force for change, albeit within limits, for encouraging a diversity of masculine and feminine identities. He notes that: 'the traditional view of a woman as a housewife or low-status worker has been kick-boxed out of the picture by the feisty, successful "girl power" icons'. There has also been a new emphasis in men's media on men's emotions and problems, which has challenged masculine ideals such as toughness and emotional reticence. As a result, the media are now providing alternative images and ideas, which are producing a greater diversity of gender identities.

Gauntlett argues that, as far as identity goes, the media provide consumers with a greater degree of choice as they provide the tools for the social construction of identity. However, he also acknowledges the contradictory nature of modern media and notes that, 'like many toolkits, it contains some good utensils and some useless ones'. In particular, Gauntlett suggests that media role-models, alongside parents, friends, teachers, etc., serve as 'navigation points' to assist individuals in making decisions and judgements about their own lifestyles. Gauntlett rejects the view that young men are attracted to magazines that focus on retributive forms of masculinity because they are experiencing a crisis of masculinity. He notes that young men in the 21st century have adapted to the modern world and have grown up with women as their equals. They therefore do not feel threatened or emasculated by the way femininity has changed.

Gauntlett argues that the power relationship between the media and its audience is complex. Both media producers and consumers subscribe to traditional ideas about gender as well as new ideas. However, he notes that in contrast with the past, we now no longer get singular and straightforward media messages that suggest that there is only ideal type of masculinity or femininity. In response, the audience borrows bits and pieces from media content in order to help them to construct their own identities. Gauntlett suggests, therefore, that media content, despite its contradictions, should be seen as a resource that people can use to think through their identities and how they might present themselves to the world. The media, in turn, will be influenced by these myriad new forms of identity and lifestyle that result from consuming media messages.

## Pluralism

Pluralists claim that critiques of the media representations found in modern media underestimate women's ability to see through gender stereotyping and manipulation. They believe that feminists are guilty of stereotyping females as impressionable and easily influenced. They claim that there is no real evidence that girls and women take any notice of media content or that it profoundly affects their attitudes or behaviour.

Pluralists believe that the media simply reflect social attitudes and tastes – in other words, public demand. They argue that the media are meeting both men and women's needs and that if women were really unhappy at the way they were being represented, they would not buy media products such as women's magazines. However, in criticism of pluralism, the question remains: to what extent are the media actually creating those needs in the first place?

## Check your understanding

1. **Why does Gauntlett argue that sociological analysis of media representations should be 'cautious'?**
2. **Give two examples of the 'symbolic annihilation' of women.**
3. **What evidence is there that teenage girls' magazines overconcentrate on beauty and slimness?**
4. **According to Gill, to what extent are modern women empowered by the increasing number of positive female role-models in the media?**
5. **Give three pieces of evidence that suggest the depiction of men in magazines is changing.**
6. **Compare the views of two types of feminism on women's representations in the media.**
7. **How does Gauntlett argue that 'the power relationship between the media and its audience is complex'?**

# Activities

## Research idea

Compare the views of young men and young women about the representations of men and women in the media. You could do this by conducting in-depth interviews or by using a questionnaire. Try showing respondents examples of men's and women's magazines to get them talking.

## Web.task

David Gauntlett is the author of *Media, Gender and Identity: An Introduction*. Go to his book's website at **www.theoryhead.com/gender**

Select 'Bonus discussions and interviews' and read his articles and the discussions about men's and women's magazines. To what extent do you agree with Gauntlett's views?

Also, it is well worth exploring some of the 'related features', including links to other websites.

## Key terms

**Beauty ideal** the idea that women should strive for beauty.

**Cult of femininity** the promotion of a traditional ideal where excellence is achieved through caring for others, the family, marriage and appearance.

**Empower** make powerful.

**False consciousness** Marxist term used to describe the way in which people's values are manipulated by capitalism.

**Hegemonic definitions** the dominant ways of defining something.

**Male gaze** the camera 'inspecting' women in a sexual way in films and TV.

**Popular feminism** term used to describe the promotion of 'girl power' in women's magazines.

**Retributive masculinity** the attempt to reassert traditional masculine authority by the celebration of traditionally male concerns such as football.

**Sexual objectification** turning into objects of sexual desire.

**Symbolic annihilation** the way in which women's achievements are often not reported, or are condemned or trivialized by the mass media.

## An eye on the exam Media representations of gender

Provide a detailed description of feminist explanations including concepts, studies and any relevant theories

Include different types of feminist explanations

This includes all the various forms of media such as TV, newspapers and magazines

**(a) Outline and assess feminist explanations of the representation of women in the mass media. (50 marks)**

Weigh up the strengths and weaknesses of feminist explanations in some detail, then present alternative views before reaching a balanced conclusion

Avoid discussion of representations of masculinity

### Grade booster Getting top marks in this question

A brief explanation of the main ideas of feminism and its different branches might be useful in an introduction. The main part of the answer needs to consider the main feminist criticisms of the representation of women in the media, including the ideas of limited roles and of 'symbolic annihilation' Feminist perspectives that need to be considered include liberal feminism, Marxist feminism, radical feminism and 'popular feminism'. The views of these perspectives need to be evaluated - postmodern and pluralist perspectives provide alternative perspectives that stress the increasing diversity of gender representations

# TOPIC 5

# Representations of ethnicity, age and social class

## Getting you thinking

1. How do you think most people would interpret what is happening in this photograph?
2. Why will they think this?
3. What other possible interpretations can you think of?

According to the 2001 UK Census, ethnic-minority groups represent 7.9 per cent of the UK population. The UK, therefore, is a multicultural society. Moreover, the majority of the main ethnic-minority groups – African-Caribbeans, Pakistanis, Indians and Bangladeshis – are British-born and British citizens. An Ofcom survey conducted in 2008 suggests that members of these ethnic-minority groups are at the forefront in terms of their use of new media such as mobile phones, the internet and multichannel television take-up. For example, members of ethnic minorities in the under-45 age group are more likely to own a mobile phone and access digital TV and the internet than the average person under 45.

Furthermore, adults from ethnic-minority groups are more likely to be confident about using interactive functions on digital devices such as televisions than the general UK population. They are more likely to have downloaded music, video clips, films and television programmes than the UK population as a whole. For example, between 65 and 79 per cent of ethnic-minority groups say that they use the internet to listen to or download music online, compared to 57 per cent of the UK population. Indians and Pakistanis spend more time online than any other adults in the UK (13.5 hours per week compared to the UK average of 12.1 hours per week).

The take-up of media technology among ethnic-minority groups is, therefore, well developed. With this in mind, you might assume that mainstream media institutions and agencies such as newspapers, magazines, advertisers, television, film-makers, record labels and internet providers would be constructing media content that reflected the everyday experiences of all sections of society and bore their media needs in mind. However, this is not the case.

Evidence suggests that media representations of ethnic-minority groups may be problematic because these are shaped by what media professionals believe the majority White audience want to read, see and hear. These media representations may also be contributing to the maintenance – and even reinforcement – of negative racist stereotypes. In this sense, media representations of ethnic minorities may be undermining the concept of a tolerant multicultural society and perpetuating social divisions based on colour, ethnicity and religion.

## Representations of ethnic minorities

Evidence suggests that, despite some progress, ethnic minorities are generally under-represented or are represented in stereotyped and negative ways across a range of media content. In particular, newspapers and television news have a tendency to present ethnic minorities as a problem or to associate Black people with physical rather than intellectual activities, and to neglect and even ignore racism and the inequalities that result from it.

## Stereotypical representations

Akinti (2003) argues that television coverage of ethnic minorities overfocuses on crime, Aids in Africa and Black underachievement in schools, whilst ignoring the culture and interests of a huge Black audience, diverse in interests and age, and their rich contribution to UK society. In other words, news about Black communities always seems to be 'bad news'.

Van Dijk (1991) conducted a content analysis of tens of thousands of news items across the world over several decades. He noted that news representations of Black people could be categorized into several types of stereotypically negative news, as outlined below.

## Ethnic minorities as criminals

Black crime and violence is the most frequent issue found in media news coverage of ethnic minorities. Van Dijk found that Black people, particularly African-Caribbeans, tend to be portrayed as criminals, especially in the tabloid press – and more recently as members of organized gangs that push drugs and violently defend urban territories. Akinti (2003) suggests that television often reflects an inaccurate and superficial view of Black life, focusing almost exclusively on stereotypical issues such as gun crime.

Agbetu (2006) suggests that 'a Black person constructed in the media has three attributes: they are involved in criminality, involved in sports or involved in entertainment'. He suggests that anything that lies outside those classifications is not of interest to the media. He notes that the media frequently focus on Black people as the perpetrators of crime rather than as victims. The word 'Black' is often used as a prefix if an offender is a member of an ethnic minority, e.g. 'a Black youth'. The word 'White' is rarely used in the same way. Furthermore, African-Caribbean people are portrayed as 'only interested in carnival and dancing and, of course, they all come from Jamaica, and they're all yardies'. He argues that 'Black people are troublesome but exciting for the media'. In other words, they are newsworthy because they almost always constitute 'bad news'.

### *Ethnic minorities and moral panics*

Watson (2008) notes that moral panics often result from media stereotyping of Black people as potentially criminal. This effect was first brought to sociological attention by Stuart Hall's classic study of a 1970s moral panic that was constructed around the folk devil of the 'Black mugger' (Hall *et al.* 1978). Hall argues that some sections of the right-wing newspaper media colluded with the state and its agents, such as the police, to create a moral panic around the criminal offence of 'mugging'. Sensationalist news stories in the tabloid press were based on information fed to them by the police. The result of these stories was the labelling of all young African-Caribbeans as criminals and as a potential threat to White people. Hall claims that this served the ideological purpose of turning the White working class against the Black working class. He argues that this classic 'divide and rule' strategy diverted attention away from the mismanagement of capitalism. Moreover, the subsequent demands from the media and general public for an increased policing of Black communities because of the fear of being mugged led to the introduction of more repressive laws, which eventually ended up restoring ruling-class hegemony, i.e. domination.

Back (2002) notes that the reporting of inner-city race disturbances involving members of ethnic-minority groups in the UK over the last 25 years, often stereotypes them as 'riots'. This implies that such disturbances are irrational and criminal, and conjures up images of rampaging mobs that need to be controlled by justifiable use of police force. Journalists very rarely use the word 'uprising', because this suggests that members of ethnic-minority groups may have a genuine grievance in terms of being the victims of racial attacks, discrimination by employers and police harassment. The idea that people are angry enough to take to the streets because they want to rebel against injustice very rarely forms part of the media coverage of such events.

### *Moral panics and rap music*

Further moral panics have developed around 'Black crime', which is seen by the media as characterized by drugs, gangs and gun culture. In 2003, 'gangsta rap' lyrics came under attack for contributing to an increase in gun crime. Zylinska (2003) notes that this moral panic was initiated by the then Home Secretary, David Blunkett, who announced that he was 'appalled' by some lyrics in rap and hip-hop music, whilst the Culture Secretary, Kim Howells, claimed that the London garage collective So Solid Crew were glorifying gun culture and violence. In 2005, a poster of rapper 50 Cent's film *Get Rich or Die Tryin'* featuring the rapper holding a gun and baby was criticized by the UK Advertising Standards Authority (ASA) for glamorizing gun crime. The ASA noted that 50 Cent had such cultural credibility, especially among young people, that his association with gang culture and criminal behaviour was likely to be seen as glamorizing and condoning the possession and use of guns.

There were also calls for stores in the UK to withdraw 50 Cent's computer game *Bulletproof*, in which players follow 50 Cent from crack-dealing gangsta to superstar by gunning down, stabbing and strangling rivals. Gun-crime campaigners were particularly angered by graphics that allow a bullet's-eye view of a gunshot as it ploughs into a rival's exploding head and the fact that 50 Cent's bullet

wounds miraculously heal. More controversy followed 50 Cent's television commercials for Reebok that showed him counting to nine – the number of times he has been shot.

In 2006, the leader of the Conservative Party, David Cameron, criticized BBC Radio 1 for playing gangsta rap because in its lyrics, such music 'encourages people to carry guns and knives' and consequently become more violent, sexist and intolerant. This is not a new debate. The African-British pressure group Ligali protested at the 2003 Music of Black Origins Awards (MOBO) about the music industry's support, promotion and awarding of artists who promote the ownership of illegal firearms and the ideology of shooting others in order to gain respect, and who have previously engaged in criminal activity and refuse to show remorse for their crimes. Furthermore, Ligali highlighted the **misogynist** nature of rap lyrics and videos, which it claimed devalue, disrespect and damage women by treating them as inanimate objects who exist purely for the purpose of male sexual gratification.

A number of themes are worth exploring with regard to the relationship between rap/hip-hop and gun crime:

- *A form of cultural identity* – Best and Kellner (1999) argue that rap articulates the experiences and conditions of young Blacks living on the margins in inner-city areas or deprived council estates who feel that they are being stereotyped and stigmatized. They argue that rap provides the means through which they can communicate their anger and sense of injustice. It also shapes their lifestyles and gives them an identity. As Best and Kellner note, 'rap is thus not only music to dance and party to, but a potent form of cultural identity'.
- *Ambivalent effects* – Best and Kellner argue that rap 'is a highly ambivalent cultural phenomenon with contradictory effects'. On a positive note, it highlights racism and oppression, and describes the hopelessness of the inner-city and deprived experience. It is a symbol of Blackness in that it celebrates Black culture, pride, intelligence, strength, style, and creativity. It supplies a voice for people excluded from mainstream society and mass media and enables White people to better understand the everyday experiences of the Black community. However, Best and Kellner note that at its worst, it is 'racist, sexist, and glorifies violence, being little but a money-making vehicle that is part of the problem rather than the solution. Many of its images and models are highly problematic, such as the gangsta rap celebration of the outlaw, pimp, hedonistic pleasure seeker, and drug dealer'. Best and Kellner, therefore, argue that rap music is complex and many-sided with contradictory effects. It attracts a large White audience who can gain some insight into the Black experience. They argue that 'rap music makes the listener painfully aware of differences between Black and White, rich and poor, male and female. Rap music brings to White audiences the uncomfortable awareness of Black suffering, anger, and violence'. However, successful male rap artists undermine this potential awareness by expressing misogyny, violence towards women and homophobia in their lyrics. Ironically, some rappers direct their rage towards other members of their community, i.e. women and homosexuals, rather than those who are responsible for their oppression and subordination.

## Focus on ...

### Rap music and role models

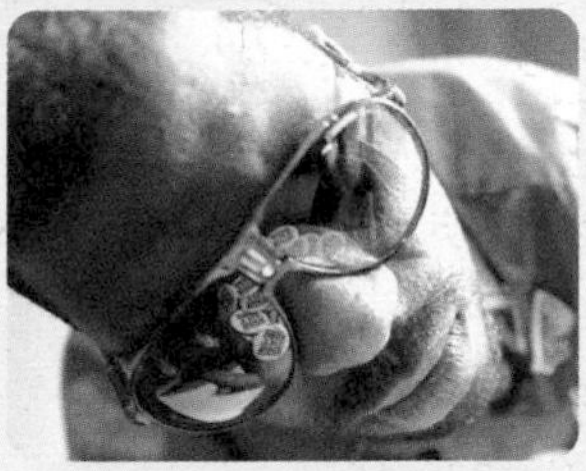

Grammy Award winner Rhymefest (pictured here) wrote this response to David Cameron's comments on rap music.

*<<I agree that rap music and urban music depicts a life in the inner cities and poor communities that is often violent. I also agree that by glorifying and promoting violence via radio, TV and videos, it does give an acceptance for that behaviour that is then negative for the community. As a Grammy Award-winning artist, who has worked and written with many other rap artists such as Kanye West and ODB, I myself on occasion am guilty of contributing to the culture. I believe that the hip-hop community is definitely in a state of denial about our complicity with the glorification of drugs and violence... However, although I agree with you that we are role models that affect our community and our music does play a role in people's behaviour, beneath the surface there are artists making changes and making the difference and there is more to rap than what you see ...>>*

**Do you agree with these comments? Give your reasons.**

- *Negative role models* – In 2007, the REACH report commissioned by the government suggested that violence within the Black community was partly the result of the media's failure to portray the image of Black boys and young Black men positively (REACH 2007). The report suggested that where children are without positive role models, 'they will seek them from the world of fantasy and the media'. Young Black participants in the research specifically cited the negative media portrayals of young Blacks, focused around criminality, guns and gangs as having a detrimental effect on their aspirations. Some even suggested that their teachers give up on them too easily because of these stereotypes. Moreover, these portrayals negatively influenced their self-image, lowered their expectations and resulted in low self-esteem and low confidence.
- *Role of education and family life* – The REACH report does not solely blame the media; it also suggests that the education system and Black family life are partly to blame for why some young Black men may turn to negative role models in their communities. Sewell (2004), too, identifies three major risk factors, which he claims are responsible for the relatively high levels of crime among African-Caribbean boys. One of these is

media culture, particularly MTV, rap music and advertising, which encourages the idea that status or respect can be achieved by adopting a consumer street culture that views material things such as designer labels, trainers and jewellery ('bling') as more important than education. This street culture often takes its lead from deviant or questionable role models, such as 50 Cent, who boast about their sexual conquests and gun-centred lifestyles. However, Sewell also notes that Black family life – especially the absence of fathers – young Black's experience of the White education system, institutional racism and, especially, aggressive policing, are just as important as the media in shaping Black subcultures on the street.

- *Reinforcing capitalist ideology* – Cashmore (1996) suggests that it is not media representations of violence that are responsible for shaping the identities of Black youth, but the lifestyle that is promoted and promised by media culture. Media messages about the lifestyles that can be achieved only reflect the dominant ideology of capitalist societies, which suggests that material success in meritocratic societies is within the reach of anyone if they are intelligent and prepared to work hard. However, the experience of racism convinces young Blacks that legitimate ways of achieving such success are impossible. As Mitchell (2007) argues, the real message that young Blacks pick up from rap is 'that if you're not loaded, you're not happening'. Mitchell argues that the real problem with rap is that far from undermining society's values it's reinforcing them, and the most fundamental of all our society's values at the moment is that 'you are what you own'. The videos show the stars by the swimming pool, in a fast car, wearing designer clothes and jewellery, and surrounded by attractive available young women. Mitchell notes that these images do not do any harm to middle-class youth because they have access to materialism via their parents, higher education and decent jobs and pay. However, he notes:

  *<<For working-class youngsters, taught by our culture since the 1970s that they're losers and failures, it's part of a profoundly poisonous cocktail of attitudes. Pride and self-respect are at the heart of this debate and it's the lack of those, or the wrong sort, that's really driving the violence on our streets.>>*

It is probably too simplistic to suggest that rap and hip-hop lyrics are responsible for gun and knife crime in British cities. As Sewell and Cashmore point out, socio-economic factors, are a far more reliable explanation for gang activity than the music teenagers are listening to. In any case, Rhymefest (see 'Focus on ... rap music and role models') and Mitchell point out that hip-hop is about much more than violence – artists rap about a wide spectrum of issues, including politics and race awareness. Also, according to social historians such as Pearson (1983), gang violence existed well before rappers started talking about it. Critics of rap music conveniently ignore the violent content of other music genres, e.g. a moral panic did not arise when the popular Country and Western singer, Johnny Cash, sang 'I shot a man just to watch him die'. Finally, some commentators suggest that music, along with films, television and recently computer games have always been a convenient scapegoat to blame for social problems which are both complex and most probably the result of structural inequalities.

## Ethnic minorities as a threat

Van Dijk's (1991) content analysis suggested that a common news stereotype was the idea that ethnic minorities are posing a threat to the majority White culture. The concept of 'threat' is central to both news values (i.e. it is an essential component of bad news) and moral panics. In recent years, three groups seem to constitute the greatest threat in the UK, according to newspapers and television. Moral panics have, therefore, been constructed around:

- *immigrants* – who are seen as a threat in terms of their 'numbers', and because of the impact they supposedly have on the supply of jobs, housing and other facilities
- *refugees and asylum seekers* – who are often portrayed as coming to Britain to abuse the welfare state and take advantage of a more successful economy than their own
- *Muslims* – who both before and since 9/11 have been subjected to **Islamophobic** media coverage.

### *Race, migration and media*

Philo and Beattie (1999) argue that moral panics often arise focused on immigrants and asylum seekers. They traced how one such panic developed in the wake of a government trade minister resigning in 1995 because he was unhappy about a lack of European border controls which, he claimed, made the UK vulnerable to mass illegal immigration. Philo and Beattie note that this resignation set off media hysteria about immigration. Television journalists, in particular, presented their stories about immigration in an extremely negative and alarmist way; they focused on borders being 'dangerously' underpoliced, and presented immigration as a 'threat' to the UK way of life, using sensationalist language such as 'flood' and 'tidal wave'. Moreover, the media used the terms 'illegal immigrant' and 'immigrant' interchangeably. Philo and Beattie suggest this coverage also had racist overtones in that journalists focused on illegal immigrants from Africa. Furthermore, the media presented estimates as to the extent of possible immigration as facts.

Philo and Beattie argue that this coverage created fear and concern among the general UK population. No consideration was given by television journalists to the fact that immigrants to the UK had made a substantial contribution to the economy, nor were the complex reasons why people might want to come to the UK explored. The notion that the vast majority of such refugees may be genuinely escaping political persecution, torture and poverty in their home country was neglected or ignored. In fact, it was broadly hinted that immigrants wished to take advantage of the UK's benefit and health systems. Philo and Beattie conclude:

> *<<the result was a news which was sometimes xenophobic in tone, which reinforced our identity and their exclusion and, perhaps more importantly, provided a rationale for the apparent need for exclusion.>>* (p.196)

The Information Centre about Asylums and Refugees (ICAR) notes that studies of media coverage of asylum seekers have shown that the media have constructed an image of this group as problems or threats (Greenslade 2005). The ICAR study found the British media often repetitively used certain terms and types of language. Asylum seekers are described as a 'flood' or 'wave' and as 'bogus' or 'fraudulent'. ICAR argues that there is often a link between media coverage and community tensions. They conducted research in London and discovered that unbalanced and inaccurate media images of asylum seekers made a significant contribution to their harassment by local residents.

### *Media representations of Islam and Muslims*

Poole (2000), pre 9/11, argued that Islam has always been demonized and distorted by the Western media. It has traditionally been portrayed as a threat to Western interests. Representations of Islam have been predominantly negative and Muslims have been 'homogenized as backward, irrational, unchanging fundamentalists and misogynists who are threatening and manipulative in the use of their faith for political and personal gain'. Poole's content analysis of broadsheet British newspapers between 1993 and 1996 found that representations of British Muslims suggested that they were a threat to UK security and mainstream values. Patel (1999) suggests that Islam is purposely misrepresented because it commands an allegiance that goes beyond boundaries of wealth, nationality, sex, race or culture and consequently is seen to challenge Western cultural power.

Richardson's (2001) empirical study of representations of British Muslims in the broadsheet press suggests that:

- British Muslim communities are almost wholly absent from the news.
- When they do appear, it is usually in a predominantly negative context.
- British Muslims are very rarely called upon as providers of informed commentary on news events.
- The everyday issues and concerns of Muslim communities in the UK are not being addressed.

In his analysis of Muslims and Islam in the British press, Whitaker (2002) notes the existence of four very persistent stereotypes in news stories and features: Muslims are presented as 'intolerant, misogynistic, violent or cruel, and finally, strange or different'. Nahdi (2003), too, argues the Western news agenda is dominated by hostile, careless coverage of Islam that 'distorts reality and destroys trust amongst Muslim readerships and audiences'. He argues that the general decline in the standards of Western media and journalism, with the move towards sound bites, snippets and quick and easy stories, has actually legitimized the voice of extremist Islam. Nahdi argues that this way of newsgathering focuses on extreme minority or fringe groups, which represent a very small minority of the Muslim population and which are often unacceptable to other Muslims. Most importantly, it disguises the vast diversity and range of perspectives amongst Muslims and equates the outlook and actions of a few individuals to over one billion people worldwide.

However, positive or balanced stories about Islam and Muslims do exist. Both the BBC and Channel 4 have websites that explain Islam in a balanced fashion, whilst the *Guardian*, *Observer* and *Independent* have sympathetically focused on Muslim Britain. Even the *Sun* ran a two-page editorial in 2005 declaring 'Islam is not an evil religion'. However, despite these positive representations, surveys of the Muslim population in the UK suggest that they see the British media generally as unsympathetic towards Islam. Many media sociologists argue that certain negative images and stereotypes about Islam and Muslims (referred to as Islamophobia) propagated by the British mass media over the past

## Focus on research

### Ameli *et al.* (2007)

### The ideology of demonization

Ameli *et al.* (2007) analysed the mainstream news programmes of *BBC News*, *Newsnight*, *ITV News* and *Channel 4 News* before and after the events of 7 July 2005. They particularly examined the language used by journalists to discuss that event. They found that 'asylum-seekers' and 'immigration' were frequently focused on, despite the fact that the suspected bombers were British born and raised. The researchers argue that this had the effect of reinforcing the view that all Muslims are of the same mind and that they should be suspected of being 'others', i.e. not integrated into British society. Moreover, the media also focused on the issues of 'loyalty' and 'belonging' and it was generally accepted that, despite a British upbringing, Muslim youth had the potential to develop extremist views and be led away from 'normality'. They had now become 'the enemy within'. In fact, this media portrayal strongly implied that *any* Muslim, especially any young male, had the potential to become an extremist. Ameli and colleagues conclude that despite the good intentions of these news networks, issues regarding Islam were discussed within a very narrow ideological framework.

Adapted from Ameli, S., Marandi, S., Ahmed, S., Kara, S. and Merali, A. (2007) *The British Media and Muslim Representation: The Ideology of Demonisation*, London: Islamic Human Rights Commission

**What evidence does the passage contain to support the researchers' conclusion that 'issues regarding Islam were discussed within a very narrow ideological framework'?**

30 years are now deeply embedded in journalistic practices and the popular consciousness.

## Ethnic minorities as abnormal

Sections of the British media may be guilty of creating false cultural stereotypes around the value systems and norms of other cultures. A survey of ethnic-minority audiences conducted by the BBC in 2002 found that Asian audiences were unhappy at the way that the media failed to differentiate between different Asian groups, which have very distinctive cultures. They did not want to be labelled as 'Asian' and they called for their own distinct cultural identities to be shown. They were also concerned that some of their cultural practices were called into question by the media, and were labelled as deviant or abnormal.

Many of the Asian sample felt that the treatment of arranged marriages was often inaccurate and did not reflect the way that the system had changed over time. The distinction between 'forced' marriage – an extremely rare occurrence, strongly disapproved of by Asian communities – and arranged marriage, which is based on mutual consent, is rarely made by the media. A survey of Asian viewers, by the market research company Ethnic Focus (2004), cited the most common complaint 'was that the media divided Asians into two camps; either miserable folk being forced into loveless marriages or billionaires who had come to Britain with nothing and had now made a fortune'.

Ameli *et al.* (2007) note that media discussion around the issue of the wearing of the hijab and the veil is also problematic, often suggesting that it is somehow an inferior form of dress compared with Western female dress codes – and that it is unnecessary. It is often portrayed as a patriarchal and oppressive form of control that exemplifies the misogyny of Islam and symbolizes the alleged subordinate position of women in Islam. Ameli and colleagues note that the underlying questions being asked by the media include: 'Why must Muslim women insist on wearing hijab when other women don't?' and 'Why is it that Muslims have so much trouble accepting and adopting our values and dressing accordingly?' As Watson (2008) notes, the general media theme is that the wearing of such apparel symbolizes divisiveness, which Watson argues further encourages suspicion and distrust of Muslim people.

## Ethnic minorities as unimportant

Van Dijk (1991) notes that some sections of the media imply that the lives of White people are somehow more important than the lives of non-White people. News items about disasters in other countries are often restricted to a few lines or words, especially if the population is non-White. The misfortunes of one British person tend to be prioritized over the sufferings of thousands of foreigners.

It is argued by the British-African pressure group, Ligali (2006), that Black victims of crime are not paid the same degree of attention as White victims of crime. This view was especially developed after Sir Ian Blair, the ex-Metropolitan police commissioner, claimed that institutionalized racism was present in the British media in the way they reported death from violent crime. He highlighted the discriminatory nature of media coverage given to the murder of the Asian taxi driver Balbir Matharu and that of the White solicitor Tom ap Rhys Pryce on the same day in 2006. He noted 'that the death of the young lawyer was terrible, but an Asian man was dragged to his death, a woman was chopped up in Lewisham, [an African] chap shot in the head in a Trident murder – they got a paragraph on page 97'. A BBC survey of the coverage of the Matharu and Rhys Price murders, showed that Tom ap Rhys Pryce received 87 per cent coverage in the tabloid press compared with 13 per cent for Balbir Matharu. Both the *Independent* and the *Mirror* are reported to have not covered the Matharu story at all.

Piers Morgan, editor of the *Daily Mirror* from 1995 to 2004, described decision-making by newspaper and television editors as influenced by 'subliminal racism':

> «*[there is] a perception that the public would be more interested in, for example, five young 'White' teenagers dying in a car crash than they would be if they were five Asian or 'Black' teenagers dying in a car crash, and I remember decisions like that coming along and feeling somehow that we were making the wrong decision here and it was by any sense a racist view to down play one against the other.*»

However, some sections of the media have been very positive in their exposure of problems such as racism. The murder of the Black teenager Stephen Lawrence by White racists in 1993 received high-profile coverage, both on television and in the press. Even the right-wing *Daily Mail* presented a front-page story highlighting police racism, and attempted to 'name and shame' the racists who had allegedly committed the murder. However, critics suggest that such coverage is actually quite rare. For example, Sir Ian Blair's comments about institutional racism in the media resulted in a hailstorm of media criticism, focusing on his ability rather than engaging with the debate he was attempting to initiate.

## Ethnic minorities as dependent

> «*Africa is helpless, Africa is poor. Africa is a world of dread and fear.*» *Do they know it is Christmas?* written by Bob Geldof and Midge Ure

The government report *Viewing the World* (Glasgow University Media Group 2000) points out that stories about less developed countries tend to focus on a 'coup-war-famine-starvation syndrome'. The implication of such stories, both in newspapers and on television, is that the problems of developing countries are the result of stupidity, tribal conflict, too many babies, laziness, corruption and unstable political regimes. It is implied that the governments of these countries are somehow inadequate because they cannot solve these problems. Such countries are portrayed as coming to the West for help time and time again. Live Aid and Comic Relief are portrayed by the Western media as the only way the people of these countries, which are nearly always African, can survive the calamities and disasters that allegedly characterize their everyday lives.

Pambazuka (2005), an African organization working to increase understanding of African issues makes a number of criticisms of British news coverage of Africa:

- The media constructs myths about Africa, such as Africa's current situation is the fault of African people,

which means that people of the West need not feel a sense of responsibility about African issues. Pambuzuka notes a media overemphasis on African corruption and inefficiency and a reluctance to discuss the West's role in keeping some parts of Africa poor by:
  - propping up corrupt regimes for political reasons
  - failing to give African producers a fair price for their goods
  - not controlling the illegal and immoral activities of Western transnational companies.
- Informed African experts are ignored in favour of Europeans who talk from a Eurocentric perspective about African affairs, ultimately to the benefit of their respective nations.
- Media reporting about Africa is too dominated by Western campaigns such as Make Poverty History and Live 8. The agenda of Bob Geldof is highlighted at the expense of Africans themselves.
- There are signs that the media are now suffering from 'Africa fatigue', which reinforces their usual apathy about Africa.

There is some sociological evidence for Pambazuka's observations. The Glasgow University Media Group (2000) found that there has been a drastic reduction in factual programming (50 per cent in ten years) about the developing world. A third of media stories about the developing world were focused on bad news, such as war, conflict, terrorism and disasters. Much of the remaining coverage was devoted to sport or visits by Westerners to developing countries – for example, some countries were only featured because Richard Branson's balloon had floated over them! Little time was devoted to analysis of why countries were underdeveloped and poor, and the role of the West with regard to domination of world trade, debt and multinational exploitation was very rarely explored. It can be concluded that British news reporting is ethnocentric, i.e. shaped by the view that British White culture is superior in its values and norms compared with other cultures. As a result, the activities of other cultures are likely to be generally reported as deficient, inferior, strange.

## Ethnic minorities as invisible

A survey by the BBC (2002) asked the question: 'Are ethnic minorities better represented on TV than they were 10 years ago?' The answers are shown in Table 3.3. Although the responses were generally positive, members of ethnic-minority groups were less likely to respond positively to the statement. However, since 2002, surveys do indicate that there has been some perceived improvement in the way that television dramas, such as soap operas, deal with race.

**Table 3.3** Responses in BBC survey: Are ethnic minorities better represented on TV than they were 10 years ago?

| | Total | White | Black | Asian |
|---|---|---|---|---|
| Yes | 78% | 80% | 73% | 67% |
| No | 8% | 7% | 12% | 16% |
| Don't know | 13% | 12% | 15% | 17% |

In 2005, a BBC News Online survey noted that Black and Asian people were better represented as newscasters and television journalists, as well as in comedy and children's television. However, it was also clearly stated by the same sample that things still have some way to go before the UK's multicultural character is fully represented in the media. A number of problem areas still exist:

1 *Limited roles* – In popular drama, the perception of ethnic-minority audiences is that when actors from ethnic minorities appear, the range of roles they play is very limited and often reflects low status, e.g. Africans may play cleaners or Asians may play shopkeepers. This may reflect the fact that ethnic groups are more likely to be found in low-status, low-paid semi-skilled and unskilled work. It fails to be a true representation of the range of jobs that members of ethnic minorities have, e.g. as successful business people and media professionals.

2 *Cultural irrelevance* – Research carried out by the Open University and British Film Institute (Bennett *et al.* 2006) found that the UK's main ethnic-minority communities do not relate to much of the nation's TV culture and do not identify with television programmes that have strongly White, middle-England associations. A central problem identified by the report was not that minority groups failed to integrate with the national culture, but rather that aspects of the national film and television culture offer little space for ethnic-minority interests or identities.

3 *Invisibility* – One area of the media that has attracted considerable criticism for excluding Black and Asian images, and thus rendering ethnic-minority groups invisible, is the advertising industry, and especially the beauty industry. Gill (2007) has noted that images of feminine beauty in women's media tend to over-emphasize Whiteness. Naomi Campbell (a famous model) has long complained about the relative lack of Black and Asian models. Gill argues this is caused by the assumption that Anglo-Saxon blondes have the ideal feminine look.

4 *Tokenism* – Ethnic-minority audiences are hostile towards **tokenism**, where television programmes, such as soap operas, include characters from ethnic-minority groups purely because they 'should'. The characters themselves are often so unimportant that they are rarely in a series for very long; dramas set in workplaces seem to be a convenient place to include an ethnic-minority actor for cosmetic purpose without being obliged to look at their culture or what happens in their homes. Such tokenism is often the result of positive discrimination or equal opportunities practices by television companies such as the BBC. An ex-BBC executive, Shah (2008) argues that broadcasters overcompensate for the lack of executives, producers, directors and writers from ethnic minorities by putting too many Black and Asian faces on screen regardless of whether they authentically fit the programmes they are in. In this sense, they are 'props'. For example, a Black character will pop up incongruously in a drama like *Emmerdale*, despite the fact that the racial profile of the Yorkshire Dales is overwhelmingly White.

5 *Realism* – Ethnic-minority audiences complain that Black and Asian people are rarely shown as ordinary

citizens who just happen to be Black or Asian. More often they play 'Black' roles, in which their attitudes, behaviour and interaction with other social groups are shaped by their ethnic identity. Research suggests that ethnic-minority audiences want to see more realistic representation of ethnic-minority people, in areas and situations that occur in their real world, enjoying life in very similar ways to the White majority and facing similar problems often unrelated whatsoever to race.

6 *Ghettoization* – Other critics have suggested that television programmes dedicated to minority issues effectively **ghettoize** such issues by scheduling them at times (i.e. very early or late) or on channels that ensure small audiences. This has two effects. First, it means that White audiences, who may not have direct contact with ethnic-minority groups, are unlikely to access and increase their understanding of minority culture – if programming is labelled as being 'for minorities', the positive representations within them end up simply being preached to the converted. Second, the mainstream media assumes certain issues are being dealt with by minority programming, so mainstream news and documentaries may be less likely and willing to report them.

7 *Media personnel* – Audience research suggests that members of ethnic-minority groups believe that media institutions produce a media content geared to the interests of White people because, as Shah has noted, it is dominated by a metropolitan, liberal, White, male, public-school and Oxbridge-educated, middle-class cultural elite. There has been some acknowledgement of this problem from inside the profession. For example, Greg Dyke, ex-Director-General of the BBC, said in 2002 that the BBC was 'hideously White' in terms of both management and creative types. A survey of media advertising and marketing (Institute of Practitioners in Advertising 2006) found that fewer than 7 per cent of people working in these fields were from ethnic-minority backgrounds.

## Conclusions

Despite these problems, media professionals from ethnic-minority backgrounds have responded to these inequalities and prejudices by developing media institutions and agencies that specifically target the interests and concerns of ethnic-minority audiences. Some have chosen to work within the established system by developing aspects of institutional media, such as the BBC Asian digital network and (despite the risk of ghettoization described above) programmes such as Ebony and Café 21.

Other ethnic-minority media originate from outside the UK, e.g. Bollywood and Asian satellite channels such as Asia TV and Zee TV, that keep people in touch with Indian, Pakistani and Bangladeshi culture and news.

Finally, there is a range of homegrown media agencies that are owned, managed and controlled by ethnic minorities themselves, including:

- newspapers and magazines – e.g. *Eastern Eye, Snoop, The Voice, The Indian Times, New Nation, Desi Xpress*
- radio stations – e.g. Sunrise Radio, Asian FX

What are the arguments for and against having media agencies that specifically target ethnic-minority groups, as this website does?

- new media websites – e.g. www.brasian.co.uk, www.asianlite.co.uk and www.easterneyeonline.co.uk.

# How does the media represent social class?

Mass media representations of social classes rarely focus on the social tensions or class conflict that some critical sociologists see as underpinning society. In fact, as previous topics have indicated, some neo-Marxist sociologists suggest that the function of the media is to ensure the **cultural hegemony** of the dominant capitalist class and to ensure that inequality and exploitation are not defined as social problems so that they do not become the focus of social debate and demand for social change.

## Representations of the monarchy

Nairn (1988) notes that the monarchy has successfully converted much of the modern mass media to its cause, so that, until fairly recently, it was rare to see any criticism of this institution or the individuals in it.

Nairn argues that this is because, after the Second World War, the monarchy, with the collusion of the media, reinvented itself as a 'Royal Family' with a cast of characters, not unlike our own families, who stood for national values such as 'niceness', 'decency' and 'ordinariness'. Members of this 'family' were presented as `like us' but `not like us'; for example, the Queen was just an 'ordinary' working mother doing an extraordinary job. This successful make-over resulted in a national obsession with the Royal Family, reflected in media coverage that has focused positively on every trivial detail of their lives, turning the Queen and her family into an on-going narrative or soap story, but with a glamour and mystique far greater than any other media personality.

Mass-media representations of the Queen are also aimed at reinforcing a sense of national identity, in that she is portrayed as the ultimate symbol of the nation. Consequently, the media regards royal events, such as weddings and funerals, as national events. It was not until the death of Diana, Princess of Wales, in 1997 that the Queen started to receive some criticism from the media for misjudging the popularity of Diana. However, the media's very positive reaction to the Queen's Golden Jubilee in

2002 suggests that the Royal Family has again succeeded in convincing the media and the general public that British identity is wrapped up in the Queen continuing to be the Head of State.

Recent media coverage has continued this process, with Prince William being portrayed as the 'pin-up prince' and Prince Harry as the 'hero prince' after his stint in Afghanistan. Consequently, this royal populism, which is simultaneously created and fed upon by a ravenous tabloid media, celebrity magazines such as *Hello,* and even the BBC and ITV with its 'Royal correspondents', can also engage in damage limitation when members of the Royal Family make mistakes. In 2009, for example, both Prince Harry and Prince Charles were accused of casual racism, but this controversy was quickly defused by a forgiving media, that, only two years previously, had crucified the working-class celebrity, Jade Goody, for similar remarks.

## Representations of the upper class and wealth

Neo-Marxists argue that mass-media representations of social class tend to celebrate hierarchy and wealth. Those who benefit from these processes – i.e. the monarchy, the upper class and the very wealthy – generally receive a positive press as celebrities who are somehow deserving of their position. The UK mass media hardly ever portray the upper classes in a critical light, nor do they often draw any serious attention to inequalities in wealth and pay or the overrepresentation of public-school products in positions of power.

Sociological observations of media representations of the upper classes suggest that popular films and television costume drama tend to portray members of this class either in an eccentric or nostalgic way. In films such as *Gosford Park* and *The Queen*, and television costume dramas, a rosy, idealized picture is painted of a ruling elite characterized by honour, culture and good breeding.

### *Representations of wealth*

Reiner (2007) and Young (2007) have recently argued that the media tend to represent the UK as a meritocratic society, in which intelligence, talent and hard work are rewarded. Marxists point out that this is an ideological myth because the evidence suggests wealth is more important than ability in opening up access to Oxbridge and top jobs. Moreover, Cohen and Young (1981) suggest that British culture is a monetary culture characterized by a 'chaos of rewards', whereby top businessmen are rewarded for failure and celebrities are overrewarded for their 'talents'. In contrast, ordinary people in functionally important jobs struggle to get by. However, the media very rarely focus on these issues. Rather, they celebrate celebrity culture and its excesses, and encourage their audiences to engage in a popular culture underpinned by materialism and conspicuous consumption.

Newman (2006) argues that the tabloid media dedicate a great deal of their content to examining the lives of another section of the wealthy elite, i.e. celebrities and their lavish lifestyles. These media representations invite media audiences to admire the 'achievements' of these celebrities. However, very little of this is critical or, if it is, it is superficially focused on issues such as weight or taste.

Newman argues that the media focus very positively on the concerns of the wealthy and the privileged. He notes that the media overfocus on consumer items such as luxury cars, costly holiday spots and fashion accessories that only the wealthy can afford. In the UK, the upper class have magazines exclusively dedicated to their interests and pursuits such as *Country Life, Horse and Hound* and *The Tatler*. Newman also notes the enormous amount of print and broadcast media dedicated to daily business news and stock market quotations, despite the fact that few people in the UK own stocks and shares. He notes that 'international news and trade agreements are reported in terms of their impact on the business world and wealthy investors, not on ordinary working people'.

## Representations of the middle classes

Some sociologists argue that the middle classes (i.e. professionals, managers, white-collar workers) and their concerns are overrepresented in the media. There is not a great deal of British sociological research in this area, but four broad sociological observations can be made:

1. In general, the middle class are overrepresented on TV (whilst the working class are underrepresented). In dramas, apart from soaps and situation comedies, middle-class families are predominant. They are generally portrayed as concerned about manners, decency and decorum, social respectability, etc.
2. A substantial percentage of British newspapers, e.g. the *Daily Mail* and *Daily Telegraph*, and magazines are aimed at the middle class and their consumption, tastes and interests, such as computers, music, cars, house and garden design, that can only be afforded by those with a good standard of living.
3. The content of newspapers such as the *Daily Mail* suggests that journalists believe that the middle classes of middle England are generally anxious about the decline of moral standards in society and that they are proud of their British identity and heritage. It is assumed that their readership feels threatened by alien influences such as the euro, asylum seekers and terrorism. Consequently, newspapers like the *Daily Mail* often crusade on behalf of the middle classes and initiate moral panics on issues such as video-nasties, paedophilia, asylum seekers and so on.
4. Most of the creative personnel in the media are themselves middle-class. In news and current affairs, the middle classes dominate positions of authority – the 'expert' is invariably middle-class.

## Representations of the working class

Finally, it can be argued that some mass-media representations of the working class are also part and parcel of capitalist ideology. Newman notes that there are very few situation comedies, television dramas or films that focus on the everyday lives of the working class, despite the fact that this group constitutes a significant section of society. Newman argues that when working-class people are featured, the media depiction is often either unflattering or pitying. Blue-collar heads of households on prime-time television have typically been portrayed as well-intentioned but dumb buffoons (e.g. Homer Simpson) or as immature macho exhibitionists (e.g. Phil Mitchell in *Eastenders*). Research by Butsch (1992) argued that working-class men were more likely to be portrayed as flawed individuals compared with middle-class individuals. Moreover, these flaws are highlighted by the portrayal of working-class women as more intelligent, rational and sensible than their husbands.

Newman argues that when news organizations focus on the working class, it is generally to label them as a problem, – as welfare cheats, drug addicts or criminals. Working-class groups, e.g. youth subcultures such as mods or skinheads, are often the subject of moral panics, whilst reporting of issues such as poverty, unemployment or single-parent families often suggest personal inadequacy is the main cause of these social problems, rather than government policies or poor business practices. Studies of industrial relations reporting by the Glasgow University Media Group (2000) suggest that the media portray 'unreasonable' workers as making trouble for 'reasonable' employers.

Other representations are more sympathetic. The 'kitchen-sink' British cinema of the 1960s, represented by films such as *Saturday Night and Sunday Morning* and *Kes*, television drama such as *Our Friends in the North* and films such as *The Full Monty* and *Brassed Off* have portrayed working-class life and problems in a dignified, sensitive and supportive way, and even commented upon and challenged social inequality, class exploitation and racial intolerance.

Curran and Seaton (2003) note that newspapers aimed at working-class audiences assume that they are uninterested in serious analysis of either the political or social organization of UK society. Political debate is often reduced simplistically to conflict between personalities. The content of newspapers such as the *Sun* and the *Star* assume that such audiences want to read about celebrity gossip and lifestyles, trivial human interest stories and sport. Marxists see such media content as an attempt to distract the working-class audience from the inequalities of capitalism (see cultural effects in Topic 4).

## Representations of poverty and underclass

Newman argues that when the news media turn their attention to the most destitute, the portrayals are often negative or stereotypical. Often, the poor are portrayed in statistical rather than in human terms by news bulletins that focus on the numbers unemployed or on benefits rather than the individual suffering and personal indignities of poverty. Some sociologists note that the dumbing-down of television has led to a decline in serious dramas and documentaries highlighting the personal costs of poverty and degradation.

A very recent development in media interest in the poor has been the labelling of some sections of the poor as 'chavs' or 'charvers', which Shildrick and MacDonald (2007) suggest is another way of suggesting that the poor are undeserving of public sympathy. As Hayward and Yar (2006) argue, the label 'chav' is now used by newspapers and websites as a familiar and amusing term of abuse for young poor people. Lawler (2005) notes that 'though the term chav now circulates widely in Britain as a term of disgust and contempt, it is imposed on people rather than being claimed by them'. He argues that the media use this discriminatory and offensive form of language to vilify what they depict as a peasant **underclass** symbolized by stereotypical forms of appearance (e.g. tracksuits, bling). This 'dangerous class' is portrayed by the media as consisting of irresponsible parents with 'out of control' children, living in council housing, welfare-dependent and probably criminal. As Webster (2007) argues, these media representations of the poor as 'chavs' define them as 'social scum' and hence neutralize any public concern or sympathy for their social and economic plight.

Swale (2006) notes the conservative social and moral agenda that underpinned some of the media's reporting of the poor in 2005. She notes that newspapers such as the *Sunday Times* started using the term 'Neet' meaning 'Not in Education, Employment or Training' to describe youth whom the paper described as antisocial and feckless. The paper alleged that many of the young poor were responsible for their own poverty because they had dropped out of school, refused work and training when it was offered, and, in the case of girls, become single mothers. Swale argues that this type of coverage negatively stigmatizes sections of the poor as an 'out group', encouraging readers to label those on benefits as the undeserving poor.

McKendrick *et al.* (2008) studied a week's output of mainstream media in 2007 and concluded that coverage of poverty is marginal in the UK media, in that the causes and consequences of poverty were very rarely explored across the news, documentaries or drama. Dramas such as *Shameless* presented a sanitized picture of poverty, despite featuring characters who were economically deprived, whilst family issue-based programmes such as *Jeremy Kyle* treated poverty as an aspect of entertainment.

Cohen (2009) argues the UK mass media was so concerned about 'trumpeting the good fortune' of British capitalism that it paid less attention to its 'casualties'. Cohen argues that journalists, entertainers and artists were hopeless at realistically reporting or dramatizing the plight of the poor. He argues that some sections of the media revelled in the suffering of the poor. He notes that:

*Little Britain* character Vicky Pollard. What stereotypes of poverty and the underclass does this character exemplify?

# Focus on research

## McKendrick *et al.* (2008)

### The media, poverty and public opinion in the UK

Interviews were conducted with nine key informants involved in producing media coverage of poverty – journalists, editors and press officers. Three aspects of media output were examined. First, a systematic content analysis of news content over a study week (30 July to 5 August 2007) sampled over 150 newspapers, 100 radio news programmes, 75 television news programmes, a selection of news magazines and a range of new media. Second, the varying treatment of six poverty-related news reports was examined across a range of media. Third, interpretive analysis was undertaken of the portrayal of poverty in selected drama, documentary and 'reality TV' broadcasts. To explore audience responses to media coverage, eleven focus groups were conducted with different socio-demographic groups across a range of geographic areas in Britain. The key findings were as follows:

> Coverage of poverty is peripheral in mainstream UK media. The causes of poverty and the consequences of poverty were rarely explored. Non-news broadcasts rarely mentioned poverty, although they often featured those experiencing deprivation. Coverage tended to focus on extreme cases, highlighting the inherent 'failings' of undeserving people. Some documentaries explored the inequities of poverty and complex circumstances of those experiencing it, but reached limited audiences.
>
> In news media, poverty in the developing world received as much coverage as poverty in the UK, but was reported differently. Depictions of extreme poverty outside the UK correspond with and may influence how the public perceive and define poverty.
>
> Audiences tend to interpret representations of poverty and its causes in accordance with their beliefs and understandings. A key limitation of media coverage is the tendency to marginalize accounts that confront negative public attitudes.

Adapted from McKendrick, J.H., Sinclair, S., Irwin. A., O'Donnell H., Scott, G. and Dobbie, L. (2008) *The Media, Poverty and Public Opinion in the UK*, York: Joseph Rowntree Foundation

1 **What do you think the aims of this research were?**
2 **What three main methods of research were used?**
3 **Explain why each method was used.**
4 **What perceptions of poverty are the British public likely to develop?**

> «*Media executives commissioned shows such as* Little Britain *and* Shameless, *in which the White poor were White trash; stupid teenagers who got pregnant without a thought; alcoholic fathers with delinquent children who wallowed in drugs and sex … The poor were the grasping inhabitants of a parasite paradise, scrounging off the … middle classes in television comedy, or freaks to be mocked on the British versions of the* Jerry Springer Show.»

The media therefore reinforced the popular view that the poor were poor because of their own depravity and weakness. Most importantly, says Cohen, the media failed to see the connection between deprivation and wealth.

### Conclusions

Despite the lack of empirical research in this area, it can be argued that media representations of the powerful tend to be more positive than representations of the less powerful working class and poor.

## Representations of age

Media representations of different groups of people based on age (children, adolescents and the elderly), also generalize and categorize people on the basis of stereotypes. The media encourage audiences to assume that specific representations in terms of image and behaviour can be applied wholesale to particular age groups.

### Childhood

British children are often depicted in the UK media in fairly positive ways. Content analyses of media products suggest that seven stereotypes of children are frequently used by the media:

1 *As victims of horrendous crimes* (e.g. Madeleine McCann, James Bulger, Holly Chapman and Jessica Wells) – Some critics of the media have suggested that White children who are victims of crime get more media attention than adults or children from ethnic-minority backgrounds. Note, too, that the media ethnocentrically portrays foreign children in quite a different way from British children; for example, African children are often represented as emaciated and dying, whilst 2009 saw many sections of the British media publishing pictures of the dead bodies of Palestinian children in Gaza.
2 *As cute* – This is a common stereotype found in television commercials for baby products or toilet rolls.
3 *As little devils* – Another common stereotype especially found in drama and comedy, e.g. Bart Simpson.
4 *As brilliant* – Perhaps as child prodigies or as heroes for saving the life of an adult.
5 *As brave little angels* – Suffering from long-term or terminal disease or disability.
6 *As accessories* – Stories about celebrities such as Madonna, Angeline Jolie or the Beckhams may focus on how their children humanize them.

**7** *As modern* – The media may focus on how children 'these days' know so much more 'at their age' than previous generations of children.

Heintz-Knowles' (2002) study of children on television found that children are often portrayed as motivated primarily by peer relationships, sports, and romance, and least often by community, school-related, or religious issues. They are rarely shown as coping with societal issues such as racism or with major family issues such as child abuse and domestic violence. However, most representations of children are positive and show them engaged in prosocial actions such as telling the truth and helping others. About 40 per cent of television drama depicted children engaged in antisocial actions, such as lying or bullying. However, one very noticeable feature of children's television that has occurred in the last 15 years has been the move to more realistic drama featuring issues from a child's rather than an adult's point of view.

Children are also represented in television commercials in ways that socialize them to become active consumers. They are encouraged by television advertising and film merchandizing to have an appetite for toys and games. Some family sociologists note that this has led to the emergence of a new family pressure: 'pester power', the power of children to train or manipulate their parents to spend money on consumer goods that will increase the children's status in the eyes of their peers. Evans and Chandler (2006) suggest that pester power is creating great anxiety among poorer parents, who will often go into debt to provide for their children's needs.

## Youth

There are generally two very broad ways in which young people have been targeted and portrayed by the media in the UK. On the one hand, there is a whole media industry aimed at socially constructing youth in terms of lifestyle and identity. Magazines are produced specifically for young people. Record companies, internet music download sites, mobile telephone companies and radio stations all specifically target and attempt to shape the musical tastes of young people. Networking sites on the internet, such as Facebook, Bebo and MySpace, allow youth to project their identities around the world.

However, youth are often portrayed by news media as a social problem, as immoral or anti-authority, and consequently constructed as folk devils as part of a moral panic. The majority of moral panics since the 1950s have been manufactured around concerns about young people's behaviour, such as their membership of specific 'deviant' subcultures (e.g. teddy boys, hoodies) or because their behaviour (e.g. drug-taking or binge drinking) has attracted the disapproval of those in authority.

Research by Wayne *et al.* (2007) confirms this overwhelmingly negative portrayal of youth in the UK. Their analysis looked at 2130 news items across all the main television channels during May 2006 and found 286 stories that focused specifically on young people. Of these, 28 per cent focused on celebrities, but 82 per cent focused on young people as either the perpetrators or the victims of violent crime. In other words, young people were mainly represented as a violent threat to society. Wayne and colleagues also found that it was very rare (only 1 per cent) for news items to feature a young person's perspective or opinion. They note that the media only delivers a one-dimensional picture of youth, one that encourages fear and condemnation rather than understanding. Moreover, they argue that it distracts from the real problems young people face in the modern world – such as homelessness, not being able to get onto the housing ladder, unemployment, mental health, etc – that might be caused by society's or the government's failure to take the problems of youth seriously.

## The elderly

Research focusing on media representations of the elderly suggests that age is not the only factor that impacts on the way the media portrays people aged 65 and over. For example, Newman (2006) notes that upper-class and middle-class elderly people are often portrayed in television and film dramas as occupying high-status roles as world leaders, judges, politicians, experts, business executives, etc. Leading film stars such as Harrison Ford and Clint Eastwood are well beyond retirement age. Moreover, news programmes seem to work on the assumption that an older male with grey in his hair and lines on his face somehow exudes the necessary authority to impart the news. However, female newscasters, such as Anna Ford, have long complained that these older men are often paired with attractive young females, while older women newsreaders are often exiled to radio. Leading female film and television stars are also often relegated to character parts once their looks and bodies are perceived to be on the wane, which seems to be after the age of 40.

Alastair Stewart (born 1952) and Katie Derham (born 1970) were paired by ITN for various news bulletins. How do they illustrate the point made by Anna Ford above?

It can be argued that old age is generally devalued by the media industry. This is particularly apparent in the advertising of beauty products aimed at slowing down the ageing process or hiding it altogether. On the whole, however, research into media representations of the elderly shows that the elderly are largely invisible across a range of media and, when they do appear, they are often negatively stereotyped.

### *The invisible elderly*

Age Concern (2000) argue that the elderly are under-represented across a variety of mass media. For example, in 2000, 21 per cent of the population was aged 65+, yet only 7 per cent of representations on television were of that age group. Older men constituted 70 per cent of these representations despite making up only 43 per cent of the 65+ population. Landis (2002) conducted an analysis of media representations in popular magazines. She found that in *Family Circle* only 8 per cent of stories and images focused on people aged 55+, whilst in *Good Housekeeping* only 6 per cent of the magazine was focused on the elderly. She found that, in most popular magazines aimed at women, only 9 per cent of features or images were focused on elderly people.

### *Stereotypes of the elderly*

When the elderly do appear in the media, they tend to be stereotyped as having specific characteristics, many of which are negative and one-dimensional:

- *Grumpy* – This stereotype paints elderly women as shrews or busybodies and males as curmudgeons who spend their time waxing lyrical about the past, bemoaning the behaviour of young people and complaining about the modern world, e.g. Victor Meldrew in *One Foot in the Grave*. These characters tend to be portrayed as conservative, stubborn and resistant to social change.
- *Mentally challenged* – This stereotype ranges from those elderly who are forgetful or befuddled to those who are feeble-minded or severely confused, i.e. suffering from senility. This stereotype suggests that growing old involves the loss of or at least, the decline of people's mental functions.
- *Infantile* – Media representations of the elderly portray them as children, who need to be treated as such, or as helpless and dependent on other younger members of the family or society. The 'sweet little old lady' stereotype is typical of this representation.
- *As a burden* – The elderly are portrayed as an economic burden on society (in terms of the costs to the younger generation of pensions and health care) and/or as a physical and social burden on younger members of their families (who have to worry about or care for them).
- *As enjoying a second childhood* – Sometimes films or television show the more affluent elderly attempting to relive their adolescence and engaging in activities that they have always longed to do before they die, as, for example, in the film *The Bucket List*.

Research in the early part of the 21st century generally suggests that the contribution of the elderly to society is not appreciated by media agencies, who rarely consult them as experienced or wise elders with a wealth of experience to pass on to younger members of society. Furthermore, the emphasis in television, film and advertising on youth and beauty imply that ageing should be avoided at all costs, which in itself strongly implies that to be old is a stigmatized identity.

However, recent research suggests that media producers may be gradually reinventing how they deal with the elderly, especially as they realize that this group may have disposable incomes.

Lee *et al.* (2007) note that representation of the elderly in advertisements is still fairly low, i.e. 15 per cent, but the majority of these advertisements (91 per cent) portray the elderly as 'golden agers', who are active, alert, healthy, successful and content. However, this research suggests that this stereotype may be unrealistic in that it does not reflect the wide range of experiences that people have as they age, including loss of status, poverty, loneliness and loss of their partner.

Robinson *et al.* (2008) compared how older adults and college students perceived the stereotypes of the elderly found in magazine adverts. They found that the elderly sample liked those adverts that showed them as clever, vibrant and having a sense of humour. Interestingly, neither the elderly nor the student respondents liked those adverts that poked fun at the elderly or presented them as out of touch or as unattractive.

## Conclusions

Media representations of age, alongside other agencies of socialization such as family experience and education, are important in shaping our attitudes towards other age groups and perhaps to our own futures as we go through the ageing process. However, research in this field, especially with regard to the very young and the elderly, is fairly limited. Perhaps this fact, too, is illustrative of the low status that society generally accords to these age groups.

## Key terms

**Cultural hegemony** the interests of the ruling class being accepted as 'common sense' by the mass of the population.

**Ghettoization** in this context, scheduling programmes aimed at minority ethnic groups at times or on channels which ensure small audiences.

**Islamophobia** fear of Muslims.

**Misogyny** hatred of women.

**Tokenism** including a limited number of minority group members only because it is felt that this is expected.

**Underclass** group below the working class, dependent on benefits and unlikely to secure employment.

# Activities

## Research idea

**Interview a sample of over-60s about their feelings about representations of the elderly in the media. Focus the discussion by showing participants some well-known personalities. To what extent are they concerned about stereotyping in the media?**

## Web.task

**Read the following web column about the links between rap music and gun crime.**

**www.spiked-online.com/Articles/00000006DBBE.htm**

**To what extent do you agree with the columnist in 'Spiked'?**

## Check your understanding

1 What evidence is there that 'the take-up of media technology among ethnic minority groups is ... well developed'?

2 According to Agbetu, what are the three attributes of a Black person constructed in the media?

3 How did Hall argue that the moral panic over mugging served an ideological purpose?

4 What are the arguments for and against the view that rap music has a negative influence on young Black men?

5 Give evidence to show how media coverage can represent asylum seekers and refugees as 'a threat'.

6 What evidence is there for Islamophobia in the British media?

7 How has media reporting of less-developed countries been criticized?

8 How do ethnic-minority audiences perceive race issues are dealt with in dramas?

9 How have media professionals from ethnic-minority backgrounds responded to inequalities and prejudices?

10 How has the use of the term 'chav' been criticized by sociologists?

11 Identify and explain three examples of often-used stereotypes of children in the media.

12 In what ways are youth are often represented as a problem in the media?

13 Explain how it can be argued that 'old age' is generally devalued by the media industry.

## An eye on the exam — Media representations of ethnicity, age and social class

Provide a detailed description of the view including concepts, studies and any relevant theories

This includes coverage in various forms of media such as TV, newspapers, films and magazines

Reflecting commonly held beliefs that are not necessarily accurate

**(a) Outline and assess the view that mass media representations of ethnic minorities are stereotyped. (50 marks)**

Weigh up the strengths and weaknesses of the view in some detail, then present alternatives before reaching a balanced conclusion

Bear in mind ethnic diversity

### Grade booster — Getting top marks in this question

An introduction could consider both the idea of a stereotype and the diversity of ethnic groups in Britain. The main part of the answer needs to discuss stereotyped representations of ethnic minorities and will need to consider the different types of stereotypes that are presented in the mass media. These include ethnic minorities as deviant, as a threat, as abnormal, as unimportant and as invisible. Evaluation of these ideas needs to focus on the development of more positive and diverse representations, using examples from various types of media such as TV and films. The development of ethnic-minority media such as Asian satellite channels can also be used as evidence of change.

# TOPIC 6

# The effect of the media on society

## Getting you thinking

### Still Too Much Violence on TV

A new public opinion poll has found that a clear majority, 64 per cent, of people agree that there is too much violence portrayed in entertainment programmes on television.

Speaking in November 2008, ahead of a major conference on violence in the media, John Beyer, director of mediawatch-uk, said:

*'The results of this independent poll are very significant. It is clear that the majority of people want action taken to reduce screen violence but the crucial question now is how broadcasters, film and game producers will respond to this latest expression of public concern about violence in entertainment. At a time of rising social and criminal violence, manifested in the shocking level of gun and knife crime, we know there is widespread support for standards to be raised generally, especially on television.'*

Source: mediawatch (www.mediawatch.org.uk)

1. **Have you or any of your friends ever played computer games such as Grand Theft Auto? Did you or they enjoy it? What was enjoyable about it?**
2. **Suggest reasons why the director of mediawatch-uk is concerned about screen violence.**
3. **Do you agree with him? Explain your view.**

## The effect of mass media content on audiences

Many people believe that the media influence behaviour and what we think or believe. Influential psychologists, pressure groups such as mediawatch UK, religious leaders and politicians have suggested that there is a fairly direct causal link between violence in films, television programmes and computer games, and violent real-life crime. It is argued that such media content exerts an overwhelmingly negative effect on mass audiences, and particularly the impressionable young. These beliefs have led to increasing government attempts to control particular types of media, to the extent that many media sociologists believe that Britain is the most heavily censored country in the Western world.

However, sociologists too have argued that media content can have a direct effect upon their audiences and trigger particular social responses in terms of behaviour and attitudes. These sociological contributions to the debate about media effects come from a wide range of perspectives and make for a strange set of bedfellows:

- Some sociologists, e.g. Gerbner *et al.* (1986), have focused on representations of violence in certain types of media and suggest that these contribute to violent crime and antisocial forms of behaviour in real life, especially those committed by the young.
- Some feminist sociologists, e.g. Dworkin (1990), Morgan (1980) have suggested that the consumption of pornography, which is easily accessed through newspapers and magazines, and particularly through the internet, is harmful in terms of encouraging sexual violence and negative attitudes towards women.
- Other feminists, e.g. Orbach (1991) and Wolf (1990), have expressed concerns about the representations of young women, particularly size zero models in magazines and newspapers, which they claim may be producing a generation of females who suffer from eating disorders.
- Interactionist sociologists, such as Stanley Cohen (1980) and Jock Young (1981), have pointed to the influence

of the media in the creation of moral panics which increase social anxiety and fear among the general population and have even led to changes in social policy and the law (see Topic 3).

- Some sociologists have focused on the power of advertising and how it may have an instant effect on the sales of a product, especially if it is promoted by a popular celebrity. A great deal of concern has recently been expressed at advertisements aimed at children which result in 'pester power' and pressure on parents to 'buy' their children's love.
- Feminist critics of the media have focused on the subtle effects of media representations of masculinity and femininity. As Gunter (2008) has noted:

  *<<Exposure to individual advertisements showing men promoting cars, and women promoting washing-up liquids might not be regarded as particularly noteworthy. However, repeated over time, such depictions could cultivate the idea that decisions about cars are the preserve of men and decisions about washing-up liquids are best taken by women.>>* (p.7)
- Some sociologists, e.g. Norris (1999), claim that media coverage of political issues can influence voting behaviour.
- Some early Marxist commentators, particularly those belonging to the Frankfurt School, such as Marcuse (1964), believed that the media transmitted a 'mass culture' which was directly injected into the hearts and minds of the population making them more vulnerable to ruling-class propaganda. More contemporary Marxists suggest that the way the media are organized and operate in capitalist societies may be influencing sections of the population to believe in cultural values that are a reflection of ruling-class ideology. They argue that media representations of women, ethnic minorities, homosexuality, young people, the elderly, the mentally ill and the disabled may also be creating and reinforcing negative stereotypes of these groups and others.

As we can see, the media effects debate is both complex and crowded. However, this topic intends to focus on two important aspects of this debate:

1. We need to distinguish between effects on *behaviour* and effects on *attitudes*. As we shall see, it is the former that is the most controversial and contested part of the media **effects approach**.
2. The claims that the media have an effect upon their audiences can also be divided into those who assume audiences are passive, **homogeneous** and vulnerable, and those who see audiences as actively interacting with the media and hence evolving into citizens who use media content in a responsible fashion to help them make choices about their identities and lifestyles.

## The hypodermic model of media violence

This model believes that a direct **correlation** exists between the violence and antisocial behaviour portrayed in the media and violence and antisocial behaviour. The model suggests that children and teenagers are vulnerable to media content because they are still in the early stages of socialization and therefore very impressionable. Consequently, they are seen to be in need of protection from this powerful secondary agency of socialization. Believers in this **hypodermic syringe model** point to a number of films which they claim have resulted in young people using extreme violence. The most notorious examples cited in recent years are the Columbine High School massacre and the killing of the Liverpool toddler James Bulger by two young boys.

In 1993, the tabloid press claimed that watching *Child's Play 3* caused two 10-year-old boys to murder a toddler when there was no evidence that they had even seen it. Why do you think papers like the *Sun* and *Daily Mirror* have taken this view?

In April 1999, two students took guns and bombs into their school – Columbine in Colorado – and killed 13 people. A number of media influences have been cited by supporters of the hypodermic syringe model as being primarily responsible for the boys' actions such as playing the computer game *Doom,* listening to the 'violent' lyrics of Marilyn Manson and watching violent videos, most notably *The Basketball Diaries*.

On the 12 February 1993, two 10-year-old boys abducted toddler James Bulger from a shopping mall in Liverpool. They tortured and killed him, according to the tabloid press, by mimicking scenes from a video – *Child's Play 3*. Later that year, the judge, in sentencing the boys, speculated on the significant role that violent videos had played in influencing the boys, although he made no specific reference to *Child's Play 3*. However, tabloid newspapers, particularly the *Sun*, led an emotional campaign to get *Child's Play 3* and other violent films (dubbed 'video nasties') banned. This has been presented by followers of the hypodermic syringe model as a straightforward illustration of the relationship between screen violence and violence in real life. However, the facts are not that simple. The police investigation team stated that there was no evidence at all that either of James's killers had seen *Child's Play 3* or that they had been copying particular scenes. At best, the 'evidence' is speculative.

## Imitation or copycat violence

Early studies of the relationship between the media and violence focused on conducting experiments in laboratories. For example, Bandura *et al.* (1963) looked for a direct cause-and-effect relationship between media content and violence. They showed three groups of children real, film and cartoon examples of a self-righting doll ('bobo doll') being attacked with mallets, whilst a fourth group saw no violent activity. After being introduced to a room full of exciting toys, the children in each group were made to feel frustrated by being told that the toys were not for them. They were then led to another room containing a bobo doll, where they were observed through a one-way mirror. The three groups who had been shown the violent activity – whether real, film or cartoon – all behaved more aggressively than the fourth group. On the basis of this experiment, Bandura and colleagues concluded that violent media content could lead to imitation or **'copycat' violence**.

In a similar vein, McCabe and Martin (2005) argued that imitation was a likely outcome of media violence, because the latter is portrayed as an heroic problem-solving exercise that not only goes unpunished but also brings rewards to its perpetrators. Consequently, it is argued that such media violence has a '**disinhibition effect**' – it convinces children that in some social situations, the 'normal' rules that govern conflict and difference can be suspended, i.e. discussion and negotiation can be replaced with violence.

## Desensitization

The most influential hypodermic syringe commentator in recent years has been the psychologist, Elizabeth Newson, who, as a consequence of the murder of James Bulger, was commissioned to investigate the effect of violent films and videos. She concluded that sadistic images in films were too easily available and that films too easily encouraged viewers to identify with violent perpetrators rather than victims (Newson 1994). Moreover, she noted that children and teenagers are subjected to thousands of killings and acts of violence as they grow up through viewing television and films. She suggested that such prolonged exposure to media violence may have a 'drip-drip' effect on young people over the course of their childhood and result in their becoming **desensitized** to violence – they become socialized into accepting violent behaviour as normal, especially as a problem-solving device. She concluded that, because of this, the latest generation of young people subscribe to weaker moral codes and are more likely to behave in more antisocial ways than previous generations.

## Censorship

Newson's conclusions had a great impact on society and politicians. Her report led directly to increased censorship of the film industry with the passing of the Video Recordings (Labelling) Act 1985, which resulted in videos and DVDs being given British Board of Film Classification (BBFC) age certificates. The BBFC also came under increasing pressure to censor films released to UK cinemas by insisting on the film-makers making cuts relating to bad language, scenes of drug use and violence.

Television too was affected by this climate of censorship. All the television channels agreed on a nine o'clock watershed, i.e. not to show any programmes that used bad language or contained scenes of a sexual or violent nature before this time. Television channels often resorted to issuing warnings before films and even edited out violence themselves or beeped over bad language.

This assumption among the political elite that violent movie content can affect people in real life continues into the 21st century. For example:

- In 2006, an advertising campaign for a film starring the American rapper 50 Cent was criticized for glamorizing gun crime.
- In 2007, the government launched a review of the impact of media violence on children, with the emphasis on the supposedly excessive violence and graphic sexual images found on children's television, on the internet and in computer games such as Grand Theft Auto.
- In 2008, an Ofcom survey of children added to this debate by reporting that two-thirds of their sample of children aged 12 to 15 years claimed that violence in computer games had more impact on their behaviour than violence in film or on television.

## A feminist perspective on the hypodermic syringe model

Some feminists see a direct causal link between pornography and sexual violence in real life. Morgan (1980) for example, suggests that 'pornography is the theory, rape is the practice', whereas Dworkin (1990) suggests that pornography trivializes rape and makes men 'increasingly callous to cruelty, to infliction of pain, to violence against persons, to abuse of women' (p.205). Studies by others show that exposure to X-rated material makes both men and women less satisfied with their partners, less supportive of marriage, more interested in emotionless sex, and more accepting of female servitude.

However, there is also evidence that suggests that pornography can be a positive influence on behaviour. For example, a study conducted by Hald in Denmark (2007) concluded that men and women generally considered pornography a positive influence in their lives. They credited it with improving their sex lives, their sexual knowledge, their attitudes toward the opposite gender, and even their general quality of life. Malamuth's American study (1984) found that in certain people who were already inclined to be sexually aggressive, pornography worsened their attitudes and actions towards women. However, for the majority of men, Malamuth found no negative effects.

## Critique of the hypodermic syringe model

A number of critiques have developed of the imitation–desensitization model of media effects.

### *Preventing real-life violence*

Some media sociologists claim that media violence can actually prevent real-life violence:

- **Catharsis** – Fesbach and Sanger (1971) found that screen violence can actually provide a safe outlet for people's aggressive tendencies. This is known as catharsis. They looked at the effects of violent TV on teenagers. A large sample of boys from both private schools and residential homes were fed a diet of TV for six weeks. Some groups could only watch aggressive programmes, whilst others were made to watch non-aggressive programmes. The observers noted at the end of the study that the groups who had seen only aggressive programmes were actually less aggressive in their behaviour than the others. It was suggested by Fesbach and Sanger that media violence had had a cathartic effect – watching an exciting film releases aggressive energy into safe outlets as the viewers immerse themselves in the action.
- **Sensitization** – Similarly some media sociologists, such as Jock Young (1981), argue that seeing the effects of violence – and especially the pain and suffering that it causes to the victim and their families – may make us more aware of its consequences and so less inclined to commit violent acts. When filmed in a certain way, (i.e. ever more graphically), violent scenes can be so shocking as to put people off violence. Sensitization to certain crimes therefore may make people more aware and responsible so that they avoid getting involved in violence.

### *Methodology*

The methodology of hypodermic syringe studies, such as Bandura's, have been questioned.

- Gauntlett (2008) notes that most effects studies have been conducted in the artificial context of the laboratory. He argues that this makes their findings questionable because people, especially children, do not behave as naturally under laboratory conditions as they would do in their everyday environment. For example, children's media habits are generally influenced and controlled by parents, especially when they are very young.
- Such studies are not clear how 'violence' should be defined. There exist a number of different types – cartoons; authentic violence as seen in images of war and death on news bulletins; sporting violence, such as boxing, and fictional violence. Moreover, it is often unclear in media effects studies whether these different types of violence have the same or different effects upon their audiences or whether different audiences react differently to different types and levels of violence. The effects model has been criticized because it tends to be selective in its approach to media violence, i.e. it only really focuses on particular types of fictional violence.
- The effects model fails to put violence into context – for example, it views all violence as wrong, however trivial, and fails to see that audiences interpret it according to narrative context. This point is supported by Morrison (1999) who showed a range of clips – including scenes from *Brookside*, news footage, and excerpts from violent films – to groups of women, young men, and war veterans. All of the interviewees felt that the most violent and disturbing clip was a man beating his wife in *Ladybird, Ladybird*, a film by Ken Loach. It caused distress because of the realism of the setting, the strong language, the perceived unfairness, and also because viewers were concerned about the effect on the child actors in the scene. By contrast, a clip from *Pulp Fiction* – in which a man is killed out of the blue during an innocent conversation, spraying blood and chunks of brain around a car – was seen as 'humorous' and 'not violent', even by women over the age of 60, because there was lighthearted dialogue. Morrison's research, therefore, suggests that the context in which screen violence occurs affects its impact on the audience.
- Many hypodermic syringe model studies tackle social problems like violence backwards. For example, Belson (1978) showed violent teenagers violent videos and claimed that, because they reacted positively to them, this type of viewing had obviously caused the violence in the first place. Gauntlett points out that such studies merely tell us about the viewing preferences of teenage boys rather than the effects of such habits on their behaviour.

### *Children as sophisticated media users*

Some sociologists believe that people, and particularly children, are not as vulnerable as the hypodermic syringe model implies. For example, research indicates that most children can distinguish between fictional/cartoon violence and real violence from a very early age, and generally know that it should not be imitated. Two research studies illustrate this criticism:

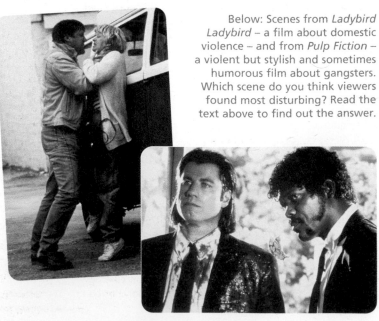

Below: Scenes from *Ladybird Ladybird* – a film about domestic violence – and from *Pulp Fiction* – a violent but stylish and sometimes humorous film about gangsters. Which scene do you think viewers found most disturbing? Read the text above to find out the answer.

- Buckingham (1993) looked at how children interpret media violence. His findings illustrated that children are much more sophisticated in their understanding of media content and much more **media literate** than previous researchers have assumed, e.g. Buckingham's sample could clearly differentiate between fictional violence and real violence.
- Julian Wood (1993) conducted a small-scale study of boys' use of video. He attended an after-school showing of a horror video in the home of one of the boys whilst the boy's parents were away. Wood describes the boys' comments in detail, and is able to demonstrate that, in this situation, the horror film is used almost as a rite of passage. The boys can prove their heterosexuality to each other, behave in a macho way, swear and, above all, demonstrate their fearlessness. He concludes that this notion of 'terror as pleasure' is not a corrupting influence. Rather, the violence of horror films is merely a part of growing up.

### *Audiences are not homogeneous*

Sociologists are generally very critical of this model because they believe that it fails to recognize that audiences are not homogeneous – they have very different social characteristics in terms of age, maturity, social class, education, family background, parental controls, etc. These characteristics will influence how people respond to and use media content. Active audience research suggests that, because of these characteristics, the audience have a much more active relationship with the media than the hypodermic syringe model assumes.It also suggests that audiences are not the cultural dopes that the hypodermic syringe model makes them out to be.

### *Scapegoating the media*

The hypodermic syringe model focuses almost entirely on media content as the scapegoat for society's ills; it fails to account for other social and psychological factors that may be causing violent or antisocial behaviour, such as peer-group influences, drugs, childhood trauma or mental illness. As Michael Moore points out in his documentary film *Bowling for Columbine*, blaming one cause – the media – for the Columbine massacre makes as much sense as blaming bowling, which both the killers were very keen on!

## Conclusions about the hypodermic syringe model

Overall, the evidence claimed for the hypodermic syringe model is really quite weak. For example, most of the studies that have looked at how children are affected when television first arrives in a society have found little change. The last study was in St Helena, a British Colony in the South Atlantic Ocean, which received television for the first time in 1995. Before-and-after studies showed no change in children's social behaviour (Charlton *et al*. 2000).

Guy Cumberbatch (2004) looked at over 3500 research studies into the effects of screen violence, encompassing film, TV, video and more recently, computer and video games. He concluded that:

> *<<If one conclusion is possible, it is that the jury is still not out. It's never been in. Media violence has been subjected to a lynch mob mentality with almost any evidence used to prove guilt.>>*

In other words, there is still *no* conclusive evidence either way that violence shown in the media influences or changes people's behaviour.

# Active audience approaches

**Active audience approaches** see the media as far less influential. They believe that people have considerable choice in the way they use and interpret the media. There are various versions of this view, outlined below.

## The two-step flow model

Katz and Lazarsfeld (1965) suggest that personal relationships and conversations with significant others, such as family members, friends, teachers and work colleagues, result in people modifying or rejecting media messages. They argue that social networks are usually dominated by 'opinion leaders', i.e. people of influence whom others in the network look up to and listen to. These people usually have strong ideas about a range of matters. Moreover, these opinion leaders expose themselves to different types of media – newspapers, television news, documentaries, soap operas – and form an opinion on their content. These interpretations are then passed on to other members of their social circle. Katz and Lazarsfeld suggest that media messages have to go through two steps or stages:

1. The opinion leader is exposed to the media content.
2. Those who respect the opinion leader internalize their interpretation of that content.

Consequently, media audiences are not directly influenced by the media. Rather, they choose to adopt a particular opinion, attitude and way of behaving after negotiation and discussion with an opinion leader. The audience is, therefore, not passive, but active.

However, critics of this model point out two problems:

1. There is no guarantee that the opinion leader has not been subjected to an imitative or desensitizing effect; for example, a leader of a peer group such as a street gang might convince other members that violence is acceptable because he has been exposed to computer games that strongly transmit the message that violence is an acceptable problem-solving strategy.
2. People who may be most at risk of being influenced by the media may be socially isolated individuals who are not members of any social network and so do not have access to an opinion leader who might help interpret media content in a healthy way.

## The selective filter model

In his **selective filter model**, Klapper (1960) suggests that, for a media message to have any effect, it must pass through the following three filters:

1. **Selective exposure** – The audience must choose to view, read or listen to the content of specific media.

Media messages can have no effect if no one sees or hears them! However, what the audience chooses depends upon their interests, education, work commitments and so on. Hollywood makes specific types of genre film with this in mind – most horror movies are aimed at a teenage audience. Moreover, the BBFC certificate system prevents the access of some audiences to specific types of media content.

2 **Selective perception** – The audience may not accept the message; some people may take notice of some media content, but decide to reject or ignore others. For example, a heavy smoker may choose to ignore the content of a television programme that stresses the link between smoking and lung cancer. Festinger (1957) argues that people will only seek out information that confirms their existing attitudes and view of the world.

3 **Selective retention** – The messages have to 'stick' in the mind of those who have accessed the media content. However, research indicates that most people have a tendency to remember only the things they broadly agree with. Berry's (1986) research into knowledgeable, well-motivated, grammar-school sixth formers, found that they only retained 60 per cent of the news information that they were tested on minutes after viewing. Postman (1986) argued that we now live in a 'three-minute culture', i.e. the attention span of the average member of society is only three minutes or less!

Klapper therefore suggests that these three filters involve a degree of active choice on behalf of the audience.

## The uses and gratifications model

Blumler and McQuail (1968) and Lull (1995) see media audiences as active; their **uses and gratifications model** suggests that people use the media in order to satisfy particular needs that they have. Blumler and McQuail argue that these needs may be biological, psychological or social. Moreover, these needs are relative – the way the audience use the media to gratify its needs will depend upon influences such as social position, age, gender, ethnicity and so on. For example, Wood (1993) illustrated how teenagers may use horror films to gratify their need for excitement.

Blumler and McQuail identify four basic needs which people use television to satisfy:

1 *Diversion* – As Watson (2008) notes, 'we may use the media to escape from routines, to get out from under problems, to ease worries or tensions'. People may immerse themselves in particular types of media to make up for the lack of satisfaction at work or in their daily lives. For example, women may compensate for the lack of romance in their marriages by reading Mills and Boon romantic novels. Some people even live alternative lives and identities as avatars on websites such as Second Life. With regard to soap opera characters, Watson notes:

<< *These people have become our friends and neighbours. If not friends, they are our companions. What is more, they are our friends' and companions' friends and companions. We go to college or to work, and the topic of conversation may well be what has happened in last night's soap. If you are not a fan you may find yourself an outsider in the dominant social communication of the day.* >> (p.74)

It could be argued today that reality shows such as *Big Brother* may be gratifying similar needs.

2 *Personal relationships* – Watson notes that we often know more about characters in soap operas than we do our own neighbours. The media may, therefore, provide the means to compensate for the decline of community in our lives. For example, socially isolated elderly people may see soap opera characters as companions they can identify with and worry about in the absence of interaction with family members. Cybercommunities on the web may also be seen by users as alternative families.

3 *Personal identity* – People may use the media to 'make over' or to modify their identity. For example, teenagers who suspect they are gay may use the experience of a gay character in a teenage soap opera such as *Hollyoaks* or *Skins* to help them make decisions about how they might deal with their own sexuality. Sites like Facebook, MySpace and Bebo allow people to use the

## Focus on research

### Andrea Millwood Hargrave (2003)
### How children interpret screen violence

Millwood Hargrave found that children (aged 9 to 13) could clearly distinguish between fictional violence and violence that is 'real'. They made clear judgements about the justified use of violence, and this could affect how 'violent' an image was perceived to be in the first place. This research found no evidence of confusion in children's minds between fictional and real-life violence. The children also proved to be very sensitive to cues provided by production techniques: they responded to changes in music, aural cues and visual images to build expectations of how violent a scene might be. Crucially, expectations of violence in various programme genres were clearly differentiated: dramas and soaps were recognized as fictional representations of the 'real' world, while the news was known to be 'real' and always treated seriously. Similarly, clear distinctions were made between cartoon-like film violence – even if the characters were played by actors rather than animated – and film violence that shows human emotions and pain, even though it may be set within a fantastical storyline.

Adapted from Buckingham, D. (2004) *The Media Literacy of Young People: A review of the research literature*, London: Ofcom

**Why might the findings of this research reassure those concerned about the effects of media violence on children?**

media to present their particular identities to the wider world in a way that they can control.

4 *Surveillance* – People use the media to obtain information and news about the social world in order to help them make up their minds on particular issues. In recent years, the gratification of this need is increasingly taking on an interactive quality with the growing popularity of online blogging and websites to which people can add their own knowledge, e.g. Wikipedia.

Lull (1995) carried out a participant observation study of families' use of television and agreed with Blumler and McQuail that the audience actively uses the media in a social way. He noted five uses of the media:

1. *Relational* – The media is used as a currency of communication, i.e. it gives people, especially families, something to talk to each other about. This may compensate for the fact that many families no longer sit down together for dinner.
2. *Affiliation* – Television may reinforce family community as some families, parents and children, sit down to watch a popular show that transcends age differences together.
3. *Avoidance* – People may use television to escape from others.
4. *Social learning* – People may use the media to solve problems, to seek guidance, to access information and learning, and to find role models.
5. *Competence dominance* – Members of families, usually the father, may demonstrate their power by controlling the family's access to television – for example, by taking charge of the remote control. An unqualified family member may also gain intellectual validation and status by watching quiz shows and impressing other family members and friends by successfully answering the questions.

However, Watson notes the trend towards children possessing their own privatized new-media technology within the confines of their bedrooms, e.g. iPods, DVD and CD players, televisions, personal computers, access to the internet, mobile phones and games consoles. He argues that this trend may lead to the obsolescence of those social needs relating to social interaction and community because the availability of such gadgets probably means less communication and interaction between family members. The young may see these new forms of media communication as lessening the need for face-to-face forms of communication. A good example of this is the fact that Facebook members do not have to meet someone in person to be their friend.

Marxists are critical of this model because they suggest that needs may be socially manufactured by the media. Marxists argue that the mass media in capitalist societies, especially the advertising industry, promote the ideology that consumption and materialism are positive goals to pursue. This may mean that people mistake 'false needs' for personal or social needs. The concept of false needs refers to an outcome of media that convinces people that a consumer item is vital to their social wellbeing. For example, people may be persuaded to wear particular brands or logos because these will supposedly make them feel better about themselves.

## The reception analysis model

This view suggests that the way people interpret media content differs according to their class, age, gender, ethnic group and other sources of identity. Sociologists who subscribe to this model are interested in analyzing how different groups interpret media content. The **reception analysis model**, therefore, suggests that media content is interpreted in a variety of ways.

Morley's (1980) research into how audiences interpreted the content of a well-known 1970s evening news programme called *Nationwide* examined how the ideological content of the programme (i.e. the messages that were contained in the text and images) were interpreted by 29 groups made up of people from a range of educational and professional backgrounds. Members of these groups were subjected to an in-depth interview in order to see how they had decoded the messages they had received, to see whether they accepted such messages or whether they had modified or rejected *Nationwide's* version (i.e. the preferred reading which media professionals subscribed to) of events and issues relating to strike action taken by a group of workers.

Morley found that audiences were far from passive in their reading of media content; instead, audiences made up their own minds, and there was significant opposition to the views contained in the news programme, both between groups with common characteristics and between people within those groups. Even when the sample agreed with the ideological position of the programme, this was not a result of a blind acceptance that journalists are objective pursuers of truth – rather their acceptance was more to do with personal knowledge and experience.

The reception analysis model concluded that people choose to make one of three readings or interpretations of media content:

1. **Preferred (or dominant) reading** – This is a reading of media content that is based on consensus, i.e. that most people are likely to go along with it because the subject matter is widely accepted as legitimate. For example, the British people generally approve of the Royal Family, so very few people are likely to interpret stories about them in a critical fashion. The dominant reading is also very likely to be shared by journalists and editors, and is likely to underpin news values.
2. **Oppositional reading** – A minority may oppose the views expressed in media content. For example, people who are anti-monarchy or Republicans may be critical of stories about Royal celebrities.
3. **Negotiated reading** – The media audience may reinterpret media content to fit in with their own opinions and values. For example, they may not have any strong views on the Royal Family but enjoy reading about celebrity lives.

Morley suggests all three interpretations or readings of media content can be generated within one social group. For example, let's say the news contains a report about the Glastonbury Festival, focusing on arrests for drug use. A preferred (or dominant) reading might be that young people cannot enjoy themselves without breaking the law. An oppositional reading might be that the police or the media focus on drug-related crime unnecessarily. After all, a few arrests are nothing, considering the thousands who attend. A negotiated reading might be that there is probably a lot of drug use among young people, but that it is mostly cannabis use, which should, in the viewer's opinion, be legalized anyway.

Morley argues that the average person belongs to several subcultural groups and this may complicate a person's reading of media content in the sense that they may not be consistent in their interpretation of it. For example, a young British Jewish person may respond to the Israeli–Palestinian problem in a number of ways:

- As a socially aware, educated person, they may feel that the Palestinians have not been given a fair deal by the Israelis.
- As a British person, they may feel that this conflict has very little impact on them.
- As a Jewish person, they may feel a strong sense of identification with Israel.
- As a young person, they may feel that politics is fairly boring and consequently not show much interest.

These subcultural characteristics are not predictable in the way they influence responses to media content – for example, belonging to a Jewish subculture does not bring about automatic identification with media stories sympathetic to Israel.

The point of reception analysis theory is to suggest that audiences are not passive, impressionable and homogeneous. They act in a variety of subcultural ways and, for this reason, media content is '**polysemic**', i.e. it attracts more than one type of reading or interpretation.

However, Morley did concede that his research could have been compromised by the fact that his sample did not see the *Nationwide* programme in their natural environment. The investigation into the response of the audience to media messages should have been conducted where the audience normally watches television, i.e. in the home, in the company of family members or flatmates.

## The cultural effects model

The Marxist **cultural effects model** sees the media as a very powerful ideological influence that is mainly concerned with transmitting capitalist values and norms. There is disagreement about why this process occurs. As we saw in Topics 2 and 3, some suggest it is because of the influence of media owners, some suggest that it is due to capitalist market conditions in which the imperative is to make profit, whilst others suggest that it is an accidental byproduct of the social and educational backgrounds of most journalists, who are happy to subscribe to a consensus view of the world.

In its focus on audiences, the cultural effects model, like the reception analysis model, recognizes that the media audience is made up of very different types of people from a variety of social backgrounds who have had very different experiences. This means that they interpret what they see, read and hear in many different ways. For example, a programme about life in an inner-London borough may be interpreted as evidence of racial conflict and deprivation, or as evidence of interesting cultural diversity, depending on who is doing the watching.

However, Marxist cultural effects theory argues that media content contains strong ideological messages that reflect the values of those who own, control and produce the media, whether they be newspapers, magazines, television, pop music or film. Consequently, media producers expect audiences (who often lack direct experience of an issue) to interpret media content in a particular way, i.e. to agree with their own preferred reading.

The cultural effects model argues that media coverage of particular issues results in most people coming to believe that media perspectives on particular issues are correct – and that these perspectives reflect a consensus perspective that generally fails to challenge or actually reinforces ruling-class ideology. For example, media coverage of unemployment and single-parent families gives the general impression that these situations are often the result of choice and so the claiming of benefits by these groups is probably unjustified. This leads to many people seeing claiming benefits as a form of scrounging. There is evidence that many elderly people are taken in by this media portrayal and that, as a result, they do not claim the benefits that they are rightfully entitled to.

Marxists believe that audiences have been exposed over a long period of time to a 'drip-drip' effect process in which media content has become imbued with ideological values. Cultural effects theory believes that television content, in particular, has been deliberately dumbed down and this has resulted in a decline of serious programmes such as news, documentaries and drama that might made audiences think critically about the state of the world. Instead, reality shows such as *Big Brother* abound, celebrating celebrity, consumption and dubious forms of behaviour.

Curran (2003) argues that the popular tabloid newspapers are also guilty of these ideological practices. He notes that ideological values are embedded in the entertainment features of the tabloid newspaper industry. He notes:

> <<*Above all, its greatly enlarged human interest and entertainment content tends to portray tacitly society as a structure of individuals, explain events in individual terms, and to offer individual-moral rather than collective solutions to problems. The press's support for a conservative, 'common-sense' view of the world may have contributed more towards maintaining an inegalitarian and social order than its explicitly political content.*>> (p.103)

Marxists argue that the long-term effect of the preferred reading of media content is that the values of the rich and powerful come to be unconsciously shared by most people – people come to believe in values such as 'happiness is about possessions and money', 'you must look like the models in magazines', 'most asylum seekers are just illegal immigrants', 'black people are potential criminals', 'being a celebrity is really important', etc.

However, it is important to understand that the cultural effects model does not simply suggest that the media is a brainwashing apparatus. Instead it suggests that some media content helps those who manage (and benefit from) capitalist society to obtain the active consent of the majority (who do not particularly benefit from the organization of capitalist society). The cultural effects model recognizes that audiences interpret media messages in different ways but within certain confined limits. As Curran notes above, the frequent reading of particular newspapers means the immersion of the reader into a particular ideological way of seeing and interpreting the world. Consequently, it is argued that this view of the world is bound to affect the reader, who may come to see such ideology as common sense or as a product of their own choices. Cultural effects theory argues that most types of media probably have these ideological effects in the long term.

### GUMG research

Research by the Glasgow University Media Group (GUMG) suggests that varied audience groups do have a very clear understanding of the intended ideological message found in media content and a section of that audience often accurately reproduce it in terms of their own attitudes. The GUMG's research into public perceptions of the 1984/5 miners' strike involved giving small groups of people press photographs and asking them to write their own news story. They were then questioned about what they believed about the strike. There were a number of findings:

- The sample quickly recognized the ideological messages contained in the photographs that the strike was violent and that the miners were to blame.
- People who were sympathetic to the miners' cause were weakened in their support by what they saw on the news.
- The majority of the sample who had not directly experienced the strike interpreted it as violent and illegitimate.
- However, some members of the audience rejected the ideological message (although these tended to be in the minority).

Philo (2001), who conducted the research, notes that this version of cultural effects theory shows that, if there is no direct experience or other knowledge of a particular issue, the ideological power of the media message will be strong and likely to shape an individual's view of the social world. However, alternative sources of knowledge based on direct experience were sometimes used by audiences to evaluate and counter the media message (although they can also be used to justify the acceptance of them). The main point made by Philo and the GUMG is that the cultural effects model needs to be dynamic – internalization or rejection of media messages needs to be understood as a product of the relationship between changing media messages and personal experience.

### Criticism of the cultural effects model

However, in criticism of the cultural effects model, it has to be said that these 'cause' and 'effects' are very difficult to operationalize and measure. It also suggests that Marxists are the only ones who can see the 'true' ideological interpretation of media content, which implies that the rest of us are 'cultural dopes'. Pluralists too question the idea that the views of the capitalist elite make up the main constituents of that ideology – they argue that this underestimates the role of professional and objective journalism in constructing media content.

### Postmodernism and reception analysis

Later postmodern perspectives on media content are essentially an extension of reception analysis. Whereas the reception analysis model focuses on how there exist subcultural differences in how audiences might respond to media messages, the postmodern model focuses on how individual members of audiences create their own meanings from a **media text**. As Philo (2001) argues, postmodernists see media content as producing one particular definition of reality, which has the same degree of importance as any other definition of reality. Moreover, these interpretations of media reality are constantly changing and being modified. They are not fixed. Philo notes that postmodernists argue that:

> *<<All definitions of reality are just that – mere definitions which are constantly changing with each new interpretation of what is real or what has occurred. There is, therefore, no 'fixed' way of describing anything – it all depends on what is seen and who is describing it. There is no way of saying that reality is distorted by media images since there is no fixed reality or truth to distort. It is all relative to who is looking; 'truth' and 'reality' are in the eye of the beholder.>>* (p.27)

In other words, rather than seeing the audience as an undifferentiated mass, or as divided into cultural or other groupings, postmodernists argue that generalizations about media effects and audiences are impossible, since the same person may react to the same media message in different ways in different situations.

## Conclusions

All of these 'active audience' approaches see the audience as interpreting media messages for themselves and, consequently, this makes it difficult to generalize about the effects of the media. What is apparent is that the media does have the potential power to influence public belief, but the role of audiences in interpreting and modifying media messages cannot be underestimated.

# The effect of the mass media on wider society

According to Curran and Seaton (2003), two perspectives dominate the debate about the effects of the media on UK society;

1. The 'neophiliacs' are optimistic about the spread and influence of media technologies, which they see as offering consumers more choice and the opportunity to participate more interactively and effectively in the democratic process.
2. The 'cultural pessimists' suggest that new media are not really that new, that interactivity is an illusion because ownership of the media is still overwhelmingly concentrated in the hands of powerful corporations and that new media content has generally led to a decline in the quality of popular culture.

## The neophiliac perspective

Neophiliacs (who are essentially postmodernists) argue that new media is beneficial to society for several reasons, outlined below.

### *Increased consumer choice*

Neophiliacs argue that the convergence, compression and interactivity that characterize media technology and delivery today have increased consumer choice. There are now literally hundreds of entertainment and news channels on television which allow people to see the same events from different angles. It is suggested that the competition between media institutions will result in more quality media output. Moreover people can choose from a number of media delivery systems, e.g. people may choose to buy music in CD form or to download it from iTunes.They may listen to it by playing a CD, or through a television, personal computer, a MP3 player or a mobile phone.

Moreover, the internet has led to a revolution in ecommerce in recent years. E-retailers such as Amazon and Play.com have been great economic successes and actually undermined high-street sales of books and music. Most major commercial companies now have their own websites. It is claimed that this e-commerce trend has resulted in more choice to consumers because it increases competition, leads to lower prices and puts consumers in control as they can compare prices from a huge range of products and services.

### *Revitalizing democracy*

It is argued that new media technologies offer opportunities to people to acquire the education and information required to play an active role in democratic societies and to make politicians more accountable to the people. The Internet is a means of communicating information that the giant corporations who own and control the world's traditional media are unlikely to want to report. The internet, in particular, has been highlighted in this respect because it is a public sphere that anybody can access usually at no or little cost. It provides people with the opportunity to access a wide range of information and alternative interpretations and viewpoints, which are unlikely to be found in the conventional mainstream media that traditionally have set the agenda for debate in wider society. Some commentators have referred to this as 'citizen journalism'.

Seaton (1993) notes that many believe that the internet is advancing progressive politics:

> <<*'internet technology converts the desk into a printing press, broadcasting station and place of assembly. This enables "many-to-many communication", which allegedly is changing the way we do politics. In this view, the net is rejuvenating civil society, generating political activism and launching exciting experiments of popular participation in government. Established centres of power and monopolies of communication are being bypassed … and a process of progressive mobilization is under way that will empower the people.*>> *(p.264)*

Some media sociologists, therefore, have suggested that the internet can revitalize democracy because it gives a voice to those who would otherwise go unheard. It allows like-minded people to join together and take action which may lead to social change.

Some neophiliacs who are part of the anti-global capitalism movement have used the internet to challenge power-elites. As Itzoe (1995) argues, the Internet is 'a loose and anarchic confederation of millions of users around the world who communicate in perhaps the freest forum of speech in history'. The internet has, therefore, been used in a variety of political ways by these activists:

- to monitor the illegal or immoral activities of big businesses
- to harness mass support for causes such as Make Poverty History
- to coordinate protests and activism ranging from hunt saboteurs and anti-vivisection to disrupting G8 meetings about climate change and third world debt.

Any political point of view, no matter how extreme, can therefore be found on the internet.

## The cultural pessimist perspective

Cultural pessimists believe that this revolution in new media technology has been exaggerated by neophiliacs. There are a number of strands to their argument.

### *'Not-so-new' media*

Cornford and Robins (1999) argue that new media are not so new. They argue that media today is an accommodation between old and new because to use a game console, a television is required, while to connect to the internet, a telephone line is still needed. They suggest further that interactivity is not something new because people have written to newspapers and phoned in to radio and television for many years. The only thing that is new about new media is its speed – information, news and entertainment can be accessed in 'real time'. The most convincing example of this is still the plane hitting the second World Trade Center tower. Cornford and Robins suggest that what the new technologies permit is the refinement, extension and embellishment of traditional media. They suggest we might consider the relationship of new media to old as:

> <<*being like that between an old Hollywood movie and its re-make: the characters are the same, the story is the same, but the special effects are more spectacular, and the marketing budget is much larger.*>> *(p.124)*

### *Domination by media conglomerates*

Cultural pessimists criticize idea that new media are increasing the potential for ordinary people to participate more fully in the democratic process and cultural life. They point to the role of the transnational media conglomerates in the development and control of the new media.

Jenkins notes that new media developed as a result of investment by the big media corporations. In particular, he argues that the cross-media ownership that began in the 1980s was the first phase of media concentration and technological convergence. Owning different types of media made it more desirable for companies to develop content across a variety of media platforms and delivery systems. As Jenkins notes, 'digitalization set the conditions for convergence; corporate conglomerates created its imperative'.

The internet, in particular, is dominated by a small number of media corporations – for example, Microsoft has developed most of the software required for accessing the net as well as being an Internet Service Provider (ISP).The USA's main ISP is AOL, which is owned by Time- Warner. These ISPs enable people to log on in the first place, direct users to particular commercial services and play a key role in on-line advertising. Most of the internet's commercially viable content is, therefore, controlled by, or commissioned by the big entertainment, press, telecommunications, advertising and software companies.

These media superpowers had many advantages over individuals in setting up websites – they have back catalogues, funds for investment, technical expertise, close links with the advertising industry, brand visibility and cross-ownership that meant that it was relatively easy for them to cross-promote products – for example, Time-Warner produces computer games, websites, films, television, popular music, toys, amusement parks, books, newspapers, magazines and comics. Over three-quarters of the 31 most visited news and entertainment websites are affiliated with the largest media corporations according to Curran.

### *Commercialization*

As a result, the internet is now extremely commercialized. Moreover, there have been recent signs that e-commerce has now taken off. Millions of people manage their bank accounts, pay bills and buy services such as insurance and consumer goods over the internet. In short, the last five years have seen a major shift in internet activities from educational use to commercial use.

Cornford and Robins (1999) agree that these new technologies may produce more choice for the consumer, but there are also some dubious side-effects. For example, many companies that sell products and services on the internet engage in consumer surveillance. New technologies, e.g. in the form of cookies, can monitor and process the data generated by interactive media usage so they can segment and target potential future audiences, and thus enhance profits. Some Marxist sociologists have grown alarmed at this commercialization of the internet and other new media such as mobile phones and digital television, claiming that it encourages materialism, consumerism and false needs. It consequently furthers capitalist domination and control.

### *Reinforcing elite power*

Cornford and Robins are sceptical of the view that new media will lead to a more democratic communications structure which will bring about a new political and social order. They note that through a series of assertive tactics – alliances, mergers, takeovers, licensing deals, patents and copyright restrictions – media corporations seek to monopolize key strategic links within the new media.

Jenkins, too, notes that not all the participants in the new media are created equal. Corporations – and even individuals within corporate media – still exert greater power than any individual consumer or even aggregates of consumers. Political elite power-holders too, such as government departments and agencies, political parties, and the security services, have not been slow to see the power of new media delivery systems and have constructed sophisticated and elaborate websites to make sure their view of the world dominates the internet. Media technologies are, therefore, mainly strengthening the power of the existing elites rather than promoting alternative ideas, free speech or democracy. The digital class divide also contributes to this inequality because it is probably those who are unable to access the web who have the most genuine political grievances.

However, Seaton reports that on-line political involvement probably mirrors the level of ordinary people's political involvement in the real world. Studies conducted by Hill and Hughes (1997) found that only 6 per cent of web pages were devoted to political issues. They also challenged the view that cyberspace is more likely to contain web content that supports alternative minority political issues or views. Seventy-eight per cent of political opinions expressed on the American websites were mainstream. Seaton remarks 'when the net was a marginal experimental sphere in which counter-cultural movements were especially active, the net had a different significance, but those halcyon days are over' (p.265–6). Even when the net was used to plan and mobilize the anti-globalization protests, it was only one of number of strategies used that included leaflets, posters, graffiti, mainstream news reports and cheap air travel. As the media corporations successfully colonized most of the net with their news, entertainment, business and sport sites minority political views and civic discourse were shifted to the margins.

### *Decline in quality of popular culture*

Cultural pessimists argue that increased choice of media delivery systems, and particularly the digitalization of television, has led to a decline in the quality of popular culture. Harvey (2008), for example, suggests that digital television may have dramatically increased the number of channels for viewers to choose from, but this has led to a dumbing-down of popular culture as television companies fill these channels with cheap imported material, films, repeats, sport, reality television shows and gambling.

Harvey argues that increasingly television culture transmits a 'candy floss culture' that speaks to everyone in general and no one in particular. ITV, especially, underwent a process of 'tabloidization' in the late 1990s in an attempt to compete with Sky. This resulted in a decline in its current affairs and news coverage and an increase in softer crime, human interest and consumer features.

A survey conducted by the British Broadcasting Standards Commission (BBSC) in 2003 indicated that television viewers agreed that more channels had led to a decline in the standard of television programmes.

Moreover, having to compete with both the commercial television channels, and satellite and cable television puts pressure on the BBC to fill its schedules with similar content. Consequently, choice becomes more of the same.

### *Lack of regulation*

It is argued by sociologists, politicians and cultural commentators that new media, particularly the internet, is in need of state regulation. All points of view are represented on the net but it is argued that easy access to pornography, and homophobic, racist and terrorism-inciting sites is taking free speech too far. An Ofcom survey in 2006 found that one in six children questioned reported coming across 'worrying' material on the internet, while more than seven out of ten parents of children aged 12 to 15 worried about their offspring seeing inappropriate material.

Some commentators, however, believe that the irresponsible use of the internet is a price worth paying for the free expression and exchange of information that it provides. However, the control of information on the web is largely outside the government's control because many ISPs operate outside UK territory. So far, the British government has confined its efforts to monitoring and controlling paedophilia, although in 2008, it announced plans to discuss with ISPs policies that would close down sites which promote race hate and terrorism.

While neophiliacs are very upbeat about the future role of new media technologies, cultural pessimists remind us that we need to be cautious about how the new media may be employed. Both perspectives probably exaggerate how far the media is being transformed. The last two decades have probably seen continuity and at the extreme, evolutionary rather than revolutionary change. Television is still the most popular medium and the print media, despite fears that it was going to be replaced by the internet, still sells extremely well. A small number of media companies are still very much in control of both traditional and new media.

## Postmodernism and the media




It is argued by postmodernist sociologists that UK society has undergone fundamental change in the last decade, so that we are now living in what they call a 'postmodern age'. They argue that this change is caused by a number of economic and social factors:

- Postmodernists have argued that industrialization and the manufacture of goods is in decline in postmodern societies. In the postmodern age, service industries concerned with the processing and transmission of information, knowledge and servicing consumption, e.g. the mass media, government, finance and retail, have become more important than the factory production of manufactured goods.
- In particular, postmodernist sociologists have argued that the rapid expansion in media technologies in the last decade has led to postmodern societies becoming 'media saturated'.
- As a result, the media – and the popular culture that they generate – now shape our identities and lifestyles much more than traditional influences such as family, community, social class, gender, nation or ethnicity.
- The media has also changed and shaped our consumption patterns by making us more aware of the diversity of choices that exist in the postmodern world. This is because the media provides us with most of our experience of social reality.
- The globalization of media means that we now have more globalized cultural influences available to us in terms of lifestyle choices and consumption.
- Postmodernists argue that the media generally define our lifestyles and identity for us – media such as lifestyle magazines, television documentaries and advertising now shape all aspects of our lives, such as how we should dress and look, how we should organize our homes and gardens, what we should think, how we should be feeling, and so on. If we don't like ourselves, all sorts of media can advise us on how we can 'make over' our bodies or lives.
- The media now inform us that the consumption of images, logos and brands for their own sake (i.e. conspicuous consumption) should be a central aspect of our identities. In other words, fashion, style and image are often more important than substance. We buy the designer labels rather than the clothes and goods themselves, with the result that people are no longer judged on the basis of ability, skill or personality but on how 'cool' they look or behave.
- Many people now feel that they no longer belong to real communities – the proto-communities of internet chat-rooms, blogging and on-line fantasy gaming such as SecondLife and the imagined communities of television soap operas are increasingly replacing the role of neighbours and extended kin in our lives. We may know the characters from soap operas better than we do the people living in our street.
- In the postmodern world, it is suggested that we no longer look to grand theories or meta-narratives such as science, Marxism, etc., to explain the world and its problems. An increasingly media-literate society is now aware that knowledge is underpinned by diversity, plurality and difference and, consequently, all knowledge is relative. All points of view have some relevance.

## The critique of postmodernism

Postmodernists have been criticized for exaggerating the degree of social change. Evidence from attitude surveys indicates that many people see social class, ethnicity, family, nation and religion as still having a profound influence over their lives and identities. Media influence is undoubtedly important, but it is not the determining factor in most people's lifestyle choices.

There is also a rather naïve element to postmodernist analyses in that they tend to ignore the fact that a substantial number of people are unable to make consumption choices because of inequalities brought about by traditional influences such as unemployment, poverty, racial discrimination and patriarchy. Traditional forms of inequality remain a crucial influence as access to the internet, digital television and so on is denied to many people in the UK.

## The globalization of media

In relation to the mass media, globalization takes a number of forms:

- *Ownership of mass media* – As we have already seen, when looking at the ownership and control debate, media companies are no longer restricted by national boundaries. Most Western countries have relaxed ownership controls. As a result, media moguls such as Rupert Murdoch and media conglomerates such as NewsCorp own hundreds of media companies spread throughout the world.

- *Satellite television* – This new medium has opened up the world to the television viewer. You can sit in a hotel anywhere in the world and watch programmes with which you are familiar on channels such as Sky, Fox, CNN and Al-Jazeera.
- *The internet* – Access to the worldwide web via the internet, global web-servers (such as AOL, Google, etc.) and new technology (such as wireless broadband) mean that we can access information and entertainment in most parts of the world. However, China (with the help of a Western new media corporation, Google) forbids the access of its citizens to some parts of the worldwide web, especially sites that it believes support the pro-democracy movement in China, because the Chinese authorities believe access to such information is politically dangerous.
- *Advertising* – Advertising occurs on a global scale and particular brands have become global as a result. For example, Coca-Cola, Levis and McDonalds are global household names. Coca-Cola is now the most widely known (and used) consumer product in the world. Its advertising message is simple, its product immediately recognizable wherever you are in the world and its taste the same in every part of the world.
- *Entertainment* – Entertainment has become globalized via satellite television, global marketing and advertising, and the internet. The world's population engages with much the same popular culture – i.e. the same films (mainly Hollywood produced), the same television programmes (e.g. Friends was a global phenomenon), and the same music (e.g. Coldplay, Madonna and Britney Spears, are all global icons). Sport has been globalized through global media events such as the Olympic Games, the World Cup and the African Nations Cup.

## What are the possible consequences of globalization?

Supporters of globalization, such as postmodernists, suggest that it brings about more choice with regard to identities and lifestyles. They see the global media as a positive influence in that they can inject the developing world with modern ideas and therefore kick-start economic and cultural ideas and behaviour that will help develop those societies. Global media are also seen as beneficial because they are primarily responsible for diffusing different cultural styles around the world and creating new global hybrid styles in fashion, music, consumption and lifestyle. It is argued that, in the postmodern global world, this cultural diversity and pluralism will become the global norm.

However, in contrast, Marxists argue that choice is restricted because transnational media companies and their owners, such as Rupert Murdoch, have too much power. Marxists are particularly concerned that local media and cultures may be replaced by a global culture. As Rosenau observed:

> *<<Coca-Cola, Disney and McDonalds, from Moscow to New York, from Tiananmen Square to Papua, it is the same culture that is present everywhere.>> (p.306).*

Cultural pessimists refer to this trend as the 'Disneyfication' of culture because it is claimed that this global culture is overwhelmingly an American entertainment culture, focused on sitcoms, reality television, soap operas, celebrity gossip and consumerism. Kellner (1999) suggests that this global media culture is about sameness and that it erases individuality, specificity and difference.

It is also suggested that global media and culture are 'dumbing down' real and authentic local cultures, and perhaps even killing off the nation state. A good example of this argument is Schiller's (1976) observation of Brazilian television, which, he claims, is a spiced up copy of Western values, norms and lifestyles.

Putnam (1995) argues that one of the side-effects of a global culture organized around television and the internet is civic disengagement – people are no longer willing to get involved in their communities. They would rather stay at home and watch television.

However, postmodernists disagree with this Marxist argument. They argue that globalization is good for both the developed and developing worlds because it offers their citizens more choices and opportunities. Postmodernists argue that British cultural identity is now influenced in a positive way by a range of cultures from around the world –for example, fashion and music – brought to us by global media. Postmodernists also argue that local cultures are not swallowed up by global media culture; rather, local culture adapts to global culture. In India, for example, Bollywood films are produced by a local film industry that is organized around both Hollywood and Indian entertainment values.

Cohen and Kennedy (2000) suggest that cultural pessimists underestimate the strength of local cultures – they note that people do not generally abandon their cultural traditions, family duties, religious beliefs and national identities because they listen to Madonna or watch a Disney film. Rather they appropriate elements of global culture and mix and match with elements of local culture in much the same way as the citizens of the USA and UK.

Lull (1995), who studied the impact of television in China, notes how television opened up localized ways of thinking and seeing the world and made available new perspectives, lifestyles and ways of thinking and responding to the world. Seeing other global experience allows people to think critically about their own place in the world. However, Thompson notes that the interaction between global media and local cultures can also create tensions and hostilities. For example, the Chinese authorities have attempted to control and limit the contact that the Chinese people have with global media whilst some Islamic commentators have used global media to convince their local populations of the view that Western culture is decadent and corrupt.

# Key terms

**Active audience approaches** theories that stress that the effects of the media are limited because people are not easily influenced.

**Catharsis** the process of relieving tensions – for example, violence on screen providing a safe outlet for people's violent tendencies.

**'Copycat' violence** violence that occurs as a result of copying something that is seen in the media.

**Correlation** a relationship between two or more things, where one characteristic is directly affected by another.

**Cultural effects model** the view that the media are powerful in so far as they link up with other agents of socialization to encourage particular ways of making sense of the world.

**Cultural pessimists** commentators who are pessimistic about the spread and influence of new media technologies.

**Desensitization** the process by which, through repeated exposure to media violence, people come to accept violent behaviour as normal.

**Disinhibition effect** effect of media violence, whereby people become convinced that in some social situations, the 'normal' rules that govern conflict and difference, i.e. discussion and negotiation, can be replaced with violence.

**Effects approach** an approach based on the hypodermic syringe model which believes that the media have direct effects on their audience.

**Homogeneous** the same throughout, undifferentiated.

**Hypodermic syringe model** the view that the media are very powerful and the audience very weak. The media can 'inject' their messages into the audience, who accept them uncritically.

**Media literate** an intelligent, critical and informed attitude to the media.

**Media text** any media output – written, aural or visual, e.g. magazine article, photo, CD, film, TV or radio programme.

**Negotiated reading** an interpretation of a media text that modifies the intended (preferred) reading so that it fits with the audience member's own views.

**Neophiliacs** commentators who are optimistic about the spread and influence of new media technologies.

**Oppositional reading** an interpretation of a media text that rejects its intended (preferred) reading.

**Polysemic** attracts more than one type of reading or interpretation.

**Preferred (dominant) reading** the intended messages contained within the text.

**Reception analysis model** the view that individuals make meanings from media messages.

**Selective exposure** the idea that people only watch, listen or read what they want to.

**Selective filter model** the view that audience members only allow certain media messages through.

**Selective perception** the idea that people only take notice of certain media messages.

**Selective retention** the idea that people only remember certain media messages.

**Sensitization** the process of becoming more aware of the consequences of violence.

**Uses and gratifications model** the view that people use the media for their own purposes.

# Check your understanding

1. **Identify and explain three concerns sociologists have expressed about the effects of the mass media.**
2. **Explain why the model of media effects described on p. 186 is known as the 'hypodermic syringe model'.**
3. **In your own words, explain three criticisms of the hypodermic syringe model.**
4. **What are the 'two steps' in the 'two-step flow' model?**
5. **In your own words, explain the key ideas of the 'uses and gratifications' model.**
6. **Give your own example to illustrate Morley's three readings of media content.**
7. **Give one example of a sociologist who subscribes to cultural effects theory and explain their work.**
8. **How can the cultural effects model be criticized?**
9. **According to 'neophiliacs', what are the main benefits of the new media?**
10. **What are the main points raised by the 'cultural pessimist' critics of the new media?**
11. **What role does the media play in postmodern societies?**
12. **How have postmodern approaches to the media been criticized?**
13. **Give three examples of ways in which globalization has affected the mass media.**
14. **List points for and against the argument that globalization is having positive effects on the media and culture.**

# Activities

## Research idea

Conduct a content analysis of part of one evening's TV programmes on any one major terrestrial channel. Add up the number of times acts of violence are depicted. After noting down each act of violence, explain the type of programme (e.g. news, cartoon, drama) and the type of violence (e.g. real, humorous).

What do your results tell you about the amount and type of violence on television?

## Web.tasks

1 Watch Gerbner talk about violence in the media at **http://uk.youtube.com/watch?v=2PHxTr-59hE&feature=related**

To what extent do you agree with the views expressed?

2 Read David's Gauntlett's assessment of the 'effects model' at **www.theory.org.uk/effects.htm**

## An eye on the exam The effect of the media on society

Provide a detailed description of sociological explanations including concepts, studies and any relevant theories

Weigh up the strengths and weaknesses of different explanations in some detail, before reaching a balanced conclusion

Will need to include those that suggest there is a direct effect and others with a more cultural view

**(a) Outline and assess sociological explanations of the relationship between the mass media and its audiences.** **(50 marks)**

Note the plural, suggesting that media audiences are diverse

### Grade booster Getting top marks in this question

This is a broad question that will require careful planning. The main body of the answer is likely to consider the different theories of media effects but broader issues of consumer choice, culture, globalization and the influence of postmodernism are also relevant.

The main theories of media effects need to be explained using examples and then evaluated. These include the hypodermic model as well as active audience approaches such as the uses and gratifications model and cultural effects theory. Wider issues about the relationship between the media and audiences that could be covered include ideas about consumer choice and democracy, and less positive views about commercialization and elite power. A discussion and evaluation of postmodern views is also relevant.

# Exam Practice

**Outline and assess the view that all points of view in a democratic society are fairly represented by the media**

A democratic society is where all interest groups are able to represent their views to the public, and the public decide on who will get into power based on who they believe presents the most persuasive argument. A theory which believes in the power of a democratic society is pluralism.

Introductions to essays should always try to 'set the scene' of the argument represented by the essay title. This candidate explains what is meant by the statement in the title fairly well and correctly identifies the appropriate sociological theory.

Pluralists believe that the media is essential in democracy as most people obtain their political knowledge from newspapers and television. They believe media owners to be objective and impartial. Pluralists say that media owners are governed by the market, as they need to compete against one another in order to attract consumers to their product. Therefore the consumers hold the power and have a freedom of choice to choose products free from bias and so biased media products will not be bought and the companies will go out of business. They believe that media presents the public with what they want to see as this makes financial sense for the companies in order for them to maximise profits as media products are costly to produce. Pluralists argue that it is basically impossible for media owners to interfere in the content of newspapers and television programmes as it is too economically risky for them.

This paragraph demonstrates a very good level of knowledge and understanding of pluralism. It focuses on the 'market forces' aspect of pluralism in a slightly fussy way but uses concepts like 'objectivity', 'impartiality', 'choice' and 'bias' reasonably well.

Another belief of pluralists is that due to the wide range of media products, all views are catered for, due to the diversity of the media. They acknowledge that some views are more widely represented than others but say that this is because of an interest in these issues. One recent representation of this in our society is the television coverage of the election debates. Some would argue that these do not fairly represent all parties as only the Conservatives, Labour and Liberal Democrats were represented. However Pluralists would take the view that the choice to represent these political parties is due to the fact that this is what the majority of audiences want to see.

This paragraph continues to show that the candidate demonstrates a very good level of knowledge and understanding. This time the emphasis is on the concept of 'media diversity' which is articulated fairly well. The candidate also demonstrates a good ability to interpret sociological knowledge and to apply it to concrete examples as shown by the reference to the election television debates.

Pluralists argue that it would be difficult for the media to show bias even if they wanted to, as a large amount of the market is taken up by public service broadcasters, which are under the control of the state, for example the BBC. These are very carefully regulated to make sure they are impartial and cater to all social groups. The rest of the media market is regulated as the state only allows media owners to have control of a certain amount of the market, in order that the public are presented with only one view as well as OFCOM who operate to maintain high quality television and radio output and to investigate consumer complaints which prevents bias. Therefore pluralists deny that there is any content bias or benefitting of the powerful.

This is an excellent paragraph which lays out how pluralism views the role of public service broadcasters and OFCOM in a very convincing way.

However Marxists reject the Pluralist notions of equality in the media. They believe that in every aspect of society the ruling class try to use their power to dominate, including the media. Their view is that the media is used to push upon them their ideology of what they should believe and so the working class experience a false class consciousness and believe that capitalism is fair and equal, when in fact it only benefits the rich and powerful members of society.

The candidate recognises that some evaluation of the pluralist position should be constructed around the Marxist theory of the media. However, the content of this paragraph is extremely generalised because the candidate is trying to say too much too quickly. It required some type of theoretical context, e.g. why do the ruling class need to use the media in this way? What exactly is 'ideology'? What is 'false class consciousness'? How is capitalism linked to media content? In what way does capitalism benefit the rich and powerful? This paragraph therefore raises more questions than answers.

# Exam Practice

Marxists believe that the main function of the media is to convince the subject class that their ideology is true. One Marxist who looked into this is Miliband. He believes that the role of the media is to shape our views of the world and that we are rarely informed about important issues such as poverty and are never offered a critical view of the capitalist class. However this could be denied, using examples such as the recent MP's expenses scandal, which was widely covered by the press.

> This is better and more focused because for the very first time the candidate has cited a study, i.e. Miliband. A2 essays should contain frequent references to the studies and/or the names of sociologists. These illustrate the theoretical points of view by providing the empirical evidence that either supports or challenges aspects of the debate. This paragraph is still a bit vague especially with regard to 'ideology'. Moreover, although the attempt to apply these ideas to the expenses scandal is creditable, it too suffers from vagueness.

Marxists state media owners ensure that we only receive a limited view of events and that they are happy to conform to this as they make up part of the ruling class and that equality for all would result in less wealth for themselves. McQuail is a Marxist who looked specifically into the news. He found that the news isn't objective or impartial at all as due to the wide breadth of news stories there are much too many to be covered. Therefore it is a socially manufactured product as a number of people make choices and judgements about what can be published and can reflect the perspective of particular powerful interest groups rather than being objective. As news is passed to media owners through press agencies many stories are in the news as they have been pushed by spin doctors to plant positive stories about members of the ruling class.

> There are some excellent points raised in this paragraph especially with regard to the idea that news is a socially manufactured product and the role of press agencies and spin doctors. The paragraph demonstrates good sociological knowledge but the candidate fails to make a convincing link between Marxist theory and news construction. The notion that the motive of media owners is 'equality for all would result in less wealth for themselves' is over-simplistic.

It is difficult to understand precisely how much of the media is controlled by the state as most of the evidence is anecdotal. However the ruling class obviously have an impact on what is and isn't reported. Despite this, in a democratic society it is clearly important for the media to offer the audience what they want to see and therefore pluralism is something which cannot be dismissed.

28/50

> This is a rather pointless conclusion that adds nothing new to the overall essay. Marxist sociologists have actually marshalled a range of evidence regarding ownership and control of media conglomerates that point to the real possibility of either direct or indirect interference by media owners of media content. A more sophisticated version of Marxism by the Glasgow University Media Group (GUMG) focuses on how media content might still benefit the ruling capitalist class without recourse to direct interference. Unfortunately this candidate fails to recognise these aspects of Marxism. Conclusions are usually an opportunity to pick up extra marks. It is recommended that you attempt to come up with an evaluative rather than a summative conclusion. Perhaps leave some of your sociological knowledge in reserve so that you can insert original material into your conclusion.

### An examiner comments

This candidate showed a good knowledge and understanding of pluralist ideas although it was a shame that no studies were cited in support of it. However, concepts were reasonably well dealt with and there was some attempt at interpretation and application. Knowledge and understanding of Marxist theory was less successful. The candidate obviously had a reasonable level of knowledge but it was often vague and key concepts were not developed. More studies such as the GUMG and/or empirical evidence needed to be referenced.

Finally, the evaluation was disappointing. This essay was a classic example of evaluation by juxtaposition – i.e. by placing two very different theories side-by-side. There was no specific and explicit criticism of either pluralist or Marxist ideas. This candidate was therefore awarded 16 marks for knowledge and understanding, 6 marks for interpretation and application and 6 marks for evaluation, making a total of 28 marks out of a possible 50.

| OCR specification | | Coverage |
|---|---|---|
| **Defining and exploring political action in society** | | |
| Key concepts | • Political parties<br>• Pressure groups<br>• New Social Movements<br>• Direct and indirect action<br>• Terrorism<br>• Riots<br>• Demonstrations and strikes<br>• Lobbying<br>• Cyber-networking | Covered in Topic 1 |
| **Participation in, and emergence of, new social movements** | | |
| Role in society | • Membership and participation | Covered in Topics 1 & 2 |
| Theoretical explanations | • Marxism<br>• Post-modern views<br>• Collective behaviour/identity<br>• Globalization | Covered in Topic 2 |
| **The changing patterns of political action** | | |
| Theoretical explanations of political action | • Marxism<br>• Postmodernism<br>• Feminism<br>• Globalization<br>• Pluralism<br>• Collective behaviour/identity | Covered in Topic 2 |
| **Political ideologies and their relationship to political action** | | |
| Ideologies and their role in political action, such as: | • Conservatism/neo-conservatism<br>• Fundamentalism<br>• Liberalism<br>• Marxism/neo-Marxism<br>• Anarchism<br>• Feminism | Covered in Topic 1 |
| **The nature and distribution of political power** | | |
| Power held by: | • The state<br>• Government<br>• Media<br>• Trans-national corporations<br>• Individuals<br>• Businesses | Covered in Topic 3 |
| Theoretical explanations | • Weberian<br>• Elite theories<br>• Neo-liberalist<br>• Pluralism<br>• Marxism<br>• Neo-Marxism<br>• Postmodern views | |

# The Sociology of Power and Politics

# TOPIC 1

# Defining and exploring power and political action in society

## Getting you thinking

**All of the people shown above exercise some sort of power.**

1. **What type of power do you think they exercise?**
2. **How do these types of power differ from each other?**
3. **Rank these individuals in hierarchical order on the basis of how much power they exert over your life.**
4. **How might Madonna's success have equipped young females today with more power than their mothers?**



## Defining power

In the most general sense, power refers to any kind of influence exercised by individuals or groups on others. For example, Max Weber defined power as the chance or probability of an individual or group of people imposing their will on others despite resistance, i.e. where A has power over B to the extent that A can get B to do something that B would not otherwise do. This conception of power – the **zero-sum view of power** – implies that the exercise of power involves negative consequences for some individuals and groups because it involves repression, force and constraint. Weber believed that such power could be exercised in a range of social situations as Lukes illustrates:

> <<*Positions of power can emerge from social relations in a drawing room as well as in the market, from the rostrum of a lecture hall as well as the command post of a regiment, from an erotic or charitable relationship as well as from scholarly discussion or athletics.*>> (Lukes 1986)

Weber distinguished between two main types of power implied here – coercion and authority:

- *Coercion* is force, usually in the form of violence or military resources.
- *Authority* depends upon consent – that is, people believe that the power is **legitimate**. For example, students generally obey their teachers because they accept their authority. This type of power is often wielded by institutions – we accept the power or authority of individuals such as doctors, teachers, judges, tax inspectors, police officers because they belong to an institution which we recognize as having legitimate power. However, as Allen (2000) points out, we also accept authority of which we are not always aware, such as that represented by CCTV which subjects us to daily scrutiny and control, because we accept the idea that the benefits of such a system outweigh the costs. In other words, we accept that the authority of such a surveillance system is legitimate.

Some sociologists have highlighted other forms of power halfway between coercion and authority, such as influence (where people are persuaded to change their minds) and manipulation (where individuals are cynically deceived, perhaps through control over education, knowledge, information and news).

# Sources of legitimate power

Weber argues that legitimate power is derived from three sources:

- *Charisma* – Some individuals are able to direct the behaviour of others because they have exceptionally powerful personalities that inspire strong feelings of devotion and loyalty. These may be political leaders such as Adolf Hitler, religious leaders such as Gandhi or the Reverend Jim Jones and sporting personalities such as Sir Alex Ferguson. Note how some of your teachers may use their charisma to motivate you.
- *Tradition* – Power can be derived from historical precedent, such as that embodied in the succession of the Royal Family in the UK. Many people in the UK believe that the Queen has inherited the 'right' to rule and so consider themselves as loyal subjects.
- *Rational–legal* – Most authority in Britain, whether that of the prime minister, a police officer or a teacher, derives from formal rules which often take the form of laws. Such authority is thought to be impartially applied to everyone and enforced without bias. Consequently, people consent to obey this type of power, which is usually administered by a hierarchical **bureaucracy**. Morgan (1999) refers to this as 'the routinization of obedience'. The option of force still exists but it is used only as a final resort.

# Defining politics

Crick (2000) suggests that politics is essential to genuine freedom because it is the only possible solution to the problem of how societies establish social order. He argues that politics is the only means whereby different and often conflicting interest groups are able to live alongside each other in relative harmony.

Jones *et al* (2004) note that that 'politics is difficult to define yet easy to recognise'. They suggest that modern-day politics has the following characteristics:

- It is a universal activity.
- It is concerned with the governance of states.
- It involves a conciliation or harmonisation process.
- It is about the management of conflict.

Jones *et al* note: 'People or groups of people who want different things – be it power, money, liberty etc – face the potential or reality of conflict when such things are in short supply. Politics begins when their interests clash.' (p.9)

Politics is, therefore, a process that attempts to manage conflict in a peaceful fashion through debate, discussion and negotiation. It normally refers to the complex relationship that exists between state institutions particularly the government and the rest of society who are represented by political parties and other interest groups.

Political processes –the pursuit and exercise of power – are usually peaceful, (e.g. the democratic process involves rational argument, debate and persuasion to convince people to vote in a particular way), but they can also involve violence or the threat of it embodied by more direct forms of political action such as demonstrations, riots, terrorism, or military coups.

### Ideologies

Morgan (1999) defines **ideology** as a 'set of ideas about society and politics which describe how things are and prescribe how things should be' (p.18). Ideologies guide behaviour and consequently they have practical consequences for the social world. Morgan argues that there are three aspects to ideology:

- All thinking is ideological in that everyone has a unique view of the world.
- Some individuals subscribe to a distinctive set of political ideas and beliefs that they act upon by forming political parties and pursuing power.
- Some sets of beliefs can become closed, fixed and rigid. Such beliefs are often oppressive in that they result in groups with less power such as women experiencing subordination and exploitation.

## Political parties and ideologies

Politics is the site of a power struggle between belief systems or ideologies represented by political parties. In Britain, this struggle has generally been between ideologies associated with liberalism and socialism at one extreme (the so-called 'left' with their emphasis on equality for all and social change) and conservatism and nationalism at the other extreme (the so-called 'right' associated with **individualism**, **free enterprise**, respect for tradition and Britishness).

### Liberalism

One of the first and most influential political ideologies to develop in Britain was liberalism. Marshall (1998) notes that classical liberalism developed as a set of ideas opposed to political absolutism in all its forms. Liberals oppose all forms of totalitarian power, whether that power is monarchist or communist in origin. Liberalism believes in the preservation and protection of personal freedoms such as the rights to private property, the free exercise of religion and freedom of speech.

Liberalism emphasises a social contract between society and the individual in which society through institutions like the government and the law guarantees personal liberty in return for people's commitment to society, law and order, democracy etc. Furthermore, liberalism encourages the meritocratic ideal – it argues that societies should be characterized by social justice and consequently members of society should be rewarded on the basis of merit (talent, achievement, hard work etc.) rather than ascribed characteristics such as the inheritance of wealth or titles. Liberals believe in reducing inequality and bringing about social improvements, particularly through education and welfare reform. Finally, liberalism also stresses tolerance for others and is critical of those societies that suppress minority groups or which ban all criticism or opposition.

The government of Lloyd George from 1918–1922 was the last time that this liberal ideology was put into practice by a Liberal administration although the 2010 coalition government of Conservatives and Liberal Democrats finds liberal values at the centre of power again. However, there are some fears that such values may inevitably collide with some aspects of Conservative ideology.

## The Conservative party and Conservative ideology

The **right-wing belief** system or ideology that characterizes the Conservative party (which has held power on and off for 47 years since 1922) is generally focused on preserving tradition and established institutions. Giddens (1994) suggests that conservatism is about conserving the 'inherited wisdom of the past'. In other words, Conservatives value the status quo and generally oppose radical change.

Conservatives are particularly concerned with defending the concept of social hierarchy, i.e. the division of society into different ranks of status. Moreover, Conservatives stress the benefits to society of a ruling class. They argue that the majority needs to be guided and restrained by a powerful and wise minority or ruling elite. They also believe that inequality is a good thing because it motivates people to adopt **entrepreneurial skills** and to work hard. From a Conservative perspective, then, inequality is an inescapable and necessary fact of life.

However, Conservatives also believe that one role of government is to provide help for those who are unable to help themselves. This paternalistic streak in Conservative thought led to post-1945 Conservative governments committing themselves to the concept of the welfare state and the maintenance of full employment as an aspect of economic policy.

## Neo-Conservatism or New Right

An ideological struggle amongst politicians and thinkers on the right led to the emergence and dominance of a New Right ideology in the late 1970s.

This neo-conservative approach was based on a zealous belief in laissez-faire ('leave alone') economic policies of free trade or market, the minimum intervention of the state in people's lives and individual self-reliance, i.e. standing on one's own feet rather than being dependent on state welfare benefits. Neo-conservatives see the welfare state as a threat to individual liberty because its costs are borne by those in work and the affluent. This position is nicely summed up by Festenstein (1998) who said 'We may not remove an eye from a sighted person to give to a blind one, nor redistribute friends from the popular to the lonely'.

Neo-conservative arguments (often called 'New Right') were adopted and practised by Margaret Thatcher's government (1979–90). Her administration preached minimum state intervention, the promotion of free enterprise and individual choice. In the pursuit of these ideological goals, she challenged the power of organizations such as the trade unions, which she claimed exerted too much authority over their members, employers and the British people. However, after Mrs. Thatcher's removal as Conservative Party leader in 1990, the emphasis in Conservative ideology shifted back to the paternalistic Conservatism that dominated the party before she took power.

## Nationalism

Traditionally, Conservative ideology has tended to be nationalistic in the sense that it is concerned with protecting traditional British interests from a European community perceived as wanting to force rapid social change on an unsuspecting British public. Conservatives tend to be Euro-sceptics and oppose threats to the 'British way of life' such as replacing the Pound with the Euro. Conservatives also tend to be in favour of limiting immigration.

However, this Conservative ideology is not seen as going far enough for some politicians committed to the ideology of nationalism. For example, the UK Independence Party (UKIP) stresses the need for the UK to leave the European Union in order to return power to British citizens. Their manifesto in 2010 also stressed the need to end immigration and the 'abuse' of the UK asylum system.

The British National Party (BNP) is also an example of a political party that pursues an aggressively nationalistic agenda in that it aims to restore the overwhelmingly white ethnicity of Britain through voluntary incentives for immigrants and their descendants to return to the country of their origin. It also wants the repeal of anti-discrimination legislation. During the 2010 election the BNP received 1.9% of the vote but failed to win any parliamentary seats.

## Ultra-nationalism

Some societies have seen the emergence of authoritarian ultra-national movements that have resulted in fascist states, such as Nazi Germany. Ideologies with an ultra-nationalistic or fascist character promote national collectivism and a totalitarian state. Fascism stresses the subservience of the individual to the state, and especially the need for absolute and unquestioned loyalty to an authoritarian ruler. It also promotes ethnic purity and often uses war to expand its territories and to ethnically cleanse (using massacres and forced removal) ethnic groups seen to be 'impure'.

## Fundamentalism

A variation on neo-conservatism is fundamentalism. This ideology is mainly associated with the religious right, particularly in the USA, although both Hinduism and Islam have fundamentalist wings. Fundamentalism involves attempts to convince societies to return to the fundamentals or basic teachings of original religious texts and/or traditional values associated with the nuclear patriarchal family. It often involves a rejection of the social change associated with liberalism such as the improvement in women's and gay rights.

Fundamentalism has not had a great influence over British politics although politicians on the right are fond of suggesting that Britain is 'broken' because of the alleged decline of traditional family life and increasing immorality. They sometimes suggest that there needs to be a 'return to basics' morality in how families and society are organized.

Some fundamentalists in the USA have promoted their cause through conventional democratic politics and their influence is such that it is a brave (and possibly foolish) American politician who professes that he or she does not believe in God, is pro-abortion etc.

Some fundamentalists have used direct political action in the form of violence to promote and further their cause. For example, US fundamentalists have attacked and murdered doctors who work in abortion clinics whilst Islamic fundamentalists have engaged in terrorist activities against Western interests.

## The Labour party

The **left-wing belief** system associated with the Labour Party has undergone radical change since 1979. From 1945 to the 1970s, the Labour party was generally seen as the party of the working class, and its ideology was predominantly socialist in principle. Nationalization of key industries such as coal, steel and the railways, the setting-up of the welfare state (especially the NHS), and the introduction of the comprehensive system in education, can all be seen as socialist ideology (**socialism**) put into practice.

## Socialism

This is a set of political and economic beliefs that developed as a reaction to capitalism in the late 19th century. For many years, this ideology underpinned the political goals of the Labour Party, in particular Clause IV, which advocated common ownership of the means of production, distribution and exchange. Socialists believed that the only way they could prevent the inequality and exploitation that seemed to be a natural product of the way the capitalist system was organized was to take chunks of it into public ownership. During the 20th century, the Labour Party nationalized large sections of the economy including coal mining, iron and steel, and the railways.

Socialists also stress the need for equality of opportunity as well as social justice in the distribution of income and wealth. The comprehensive education system and many aspects of the welfare state such as national insurance and the National Health Service were introduced by the Labour Party in an attempt to create a more egalitarian society.

## The third way

However, the party reacted to the election defeat of 1979 by embarking on a re-evaluation of its ideology and a revamp of its image. This resulted in Labour jettisoning many of the overtly socialist principles embodied in its constitution, especially Clause IV, and describing itself as a party aiming to work for all sections of the community, rich and poor. Tony Blair's election to the Labour leadership in 1994 saw a major shift to the centre in terms of ideology, as Labour politicians made statements about New Labour being a **social democratic** party rather than a socialist one. Labour presented itself as forging a 'third way' towards a common good. Labour politicians such as Gordon Brown presented themselves as trustworthy and competent, particularly with regard to managing the economy. This rebranding of the Labour party as a 'safe pair of hands' was ultimately successful, as Labour won three successive general elections in 1997, 2001 and 2005.

## Marxism

Socialism is to some extent influenced by the political and economic theories of Karl Marx. Marx argues that power arises out of the social **relations of production** that characterize the economic system of production found in **capitalist societies**. These social relations exist between two groups characterized by their access (or lack of access) to economic resources:

- The **bourgeoisie** or ruling class – a minority group who own and control the **means of production**, such as capital, land, factories, technology and raw materials
- The **proletariat** or working class – the majority group who have only their labour power, which they hire out to the bourgeoisie in return for a wage.

This class inequality is further deepened by the bourgeoisie's exploitation of the proletariat's labour power, in that the wealth of the dominant class is increased by the fact that the value of the goods produced by the worker always far exceeds the wage paid. This surplus value is pocketed by the bourgeoisie in the form of profit. Marx argues, therefore, that inequalities in ownership and control – along with exploitation – lead to economic inequality, and this is the source of political and social power in society. In other words, power derives from class relationships.

## Neo-Marxism

Modern-day Marxists, i.e. Neo-Marxists argue that class domination and economic power are maintained through coercion (although this tends to be used as a last resort) and ideological **hegemony** (the control of ideas). Marxists argue that this latter concept is much more effective than force in controlling a proletariat that has the potential to be very disruptive if it decides that the organization of the capitalist infrastructure is unfair and unjust in how income and wealth are distributed. Hegemony or cultural dominance by the ruling class is needed in order to make sure that the working class regard bourgeois power as legitimate, and so reduce the potential for revolutionary protest.

According to Bocock (1986), hegemony occurs when the intellectual and moral ideas of the ruling class provide the dominant cultural outlook for the whole of society.

Neo-Marxists such as Althusser (1971) argue that the bourgeoisie achieve this cultural dominance by using its economic power to define what counts as knowledge, ideas, art, education, news and so on. Social institutions such as the education system, the legal system, the political system, the mass media and religion, which Marxists see as making up the '**superstructure**' of capitalist society, play an important role in transmitting ruling-class ideology so that it is accepted by the mass of the population as 'normal' or 'natural'.

Westergaard (1996) argues that the result of hegemonic power is that workers fail to understand their own structural position correctly – that is, they fail to realize their true interests as exploited workers. This false class-consciousness means that they rarely realize their potential power for bringing about revolutionary change.

The Frankfurt School of Marxism in a similar analysis argue that the working class has become 'ideologically incorporated' into capitalist society. Marcuse (1964) argued that this incorporation takes the form of encouraging 'one-dimensional thought': the general population is encouraged to indulge in uncritical and sterile forms of entertainment or mass culture that reduce their appetite for critical and creative thought and action that might challenge hegemonic power. Following on from Marcuse, White (2004) argues that Western culture today is dominated by a 'Middle Mind' – a mainstream consensus that is shaped by consumer culture that pleases everyone but moves, challenges or shocks no one. He notes:

> << *When we accept the Middle Mind as our culture (or, worse yet, when we demand it as consumers), we are not merely being stupid or unsophisticated or "low brow". We are vigorously conspiring against ourselves. We murder our own capacity for critique and invention as if we were children saying, 'Can you do this for me?'.*>>

According to Gramsci (1971), hegemony, and the resulting consent of the people, has enabled the ruling class to deal with any threats to its authority without having to use force. However, Gramsci argues that hegemony does not mean that subordinate classes will always lack power or that the power of the dominant class is absolute. He argues that power is potentially available to the subordinate classes if they become sufficiently class-conscious and politically organized to seize or to challenge the control of the means of production. Importantly, Gramsci argues that people in capitalist societies experience 'dual consciousness' – their beliefs are only partly shaped by capitalist ideology because they are also influenced by their personal day-to-day experiences of society. These sometimes contradict or challenge dominant ideology and so encourage some resistance and opposition to it. This 'resistance' might take an overtly political form (for instance, active campaigning or taking to the streets to oppose G8 talks) or a 'symbolic' form (such as setting out to challenge dominant institutions and beliefs through the use of 'shock', e.g. through fashion statements or simply substituting a hedonistic lifestyle for the 9-to-5 lifestyle demanded by capitalism).

Neo-Marxists such as Stuart Hall (Hall and Jefferson 1976) have developed **relational conceptions of power** – that is, they recognize that power is a process which involves **ideological struggle** between the capitalist class and groups such as working-class youth. The capitalist class is normally able to impose cultural hegemony and so obtain the consent of most of the people to rule.

However, pockets of **symbolic resistance** among sections of the working class indicate that power is not a one-way process. Gilroy (1982a) suggests that working-class crime may well be political – a means by which subordinate groups can enjoy some power through hitting back at the symbols of capitalist power such as wealth and property. The work of the Birmingham Centre for Contemporary Cultural Studies similarly suggests that working-class deviant youth subcultures may be symbolically resisting hegemonic definitions of respectability by adopting forms of style and behaviour that set out to shock. For example, the Punk subculture of the late 1970s incorporated conformist symbols, such as the Queen and Union Jack, as well as deviant symbols, such as Nazi insignia, into its dress codes in a deliberately provocative way.

## Criticisms of Marxism

Abercrombie *et al.* (1980) are dismissive of Marxist claims that a dominant ideology characterizes contemporary society. They make the following arguments:

- Capitalism today is characterized by conflicts between capitalist interests such as small businesses, finance capital, industrialists, multinational companies and state corporations. This conflict undermines the idea that the capitalist class is transmitting strong and unified ideological messages.
- The subordinate class often rejects the so-called dominant ideology – as can be seen in surveys of working-class people who recognize that we live in a class society characterized by inequality. Such workers may express resistance through strikes and membership of trade unions.
- It is the simple fact that workers have to work in order to preserve their standard of living that leads to their cooperation and participation. People conform, not because of ideological hegemony but quite simply because they fear unemployment and poverty.

## Feminism

Feminists argue that the most important type of power originates in the relationship between men and women. They focus on the concept of '**patriarchy**', which they define as the power that men have over women. Millett (1970) argued that patriarchal power and ideology has resulted in male dominance and female subordination. She suggests that patriarchy is the most powerful ideology of our culture, arguing that it is more important than social class because it has been around for a lot longer. Millett argues that patriarchy is the result of a number of factors:

- *Biology* – Males have been able to use their superior physical strength to dominate women. The socialization of children encourages qualities, e.g. aggression that reinforce the coercion of women.
- *Ideology* – Powerful institutions such as the government, the civil service, businesses and the mass media are dominated by males and consequently these

transmit the view that men are better suited than women to high-status jobs and roles.

- *The family* – Millett argues that this institution is the source of patriarchy which it transmits from generation to generation.
- *Caste* – Millett argues that gender is a type of caste that operates independently of class, e.g. she points out that upper-class women are generally regarded as subordinate to men.
- *Education* – Women are not encouraged to study high-status subjects.
- *Economic dependency* – Women are segregated in the job market – they are denied entry to top jobs by a '**glass ceiling**' and often end up in low-paid and low status women's work.
- *Religion and myth* – Religion often legitimates women's low status in society.
- *Psychology* – Women develop an inferiority complex as a result of the above influences. Many believe that their role is to have children and a family rather than a career.
- *Physical force* – Patriarchy is backed up by force or the threat of it, e.g. domestic violence, rape.

Millett's conception of male power has been criticized. Rowbotham (1982) is sceptical of Millett's claim that all men exploit women and that all men benefit from patriarchy. She points out that this claim is exaggerated because it implies that men and women cannot have loving or friendly relationships without some form of male exploitation being present. Rowbotham suggests that the relationship between men and women is not always characterized by power inequalities.

## Anarchism

Marshall notes that anarchism is a set of philosophical and political ideas that suggests that societies function best without government or authority. It suggests that the natural state of human beings is to live together harmoniously and freely without intervention in the form of a state. Such a situation, it is argued, does not lead to chaos and social breakdown but rather to 'spontaneous order'.

In the 19th century, Proudhon developed 'syndicalism' – a type of anarchism which argued that the ideal ordered society was made up of small self-contained units of people that interacted with each other on the basis of 'mutualism', i.e. an equal exchange of goods and services.

Some anarchists have advocated violence to destroy state and elite power. The anti-globalization and the environmental movements contain anarchist elements which have used illegal and violent forms of action such as squatting in homes in Central London owned by wealthy individuals and corporations to protest against inequalities in the housing market, whilst Reclaim the Streets have organized street parties to block traffic. Anarchist groups affiliated to the anti-capitalist movement have been at the forefront of violent confrontations with the police at global conferences such as the G8 economic summits of world leaders.

# Indirect and direct action

## Indirect forms of political action

Indirect political action refers to that which occurs within the existing political framework. Traditionally this means that members of society express their political views through the electoral system by voting for the political party of their choice at general elections.

However, there are signs that voter apathy is becoming a problem, especially among young people. In 2001 and 2005, only 60 and 61 per cent of the electorate respectively voted in the General Elections compared with 71 per cent in 1997. Some commentators argue that conventional two-party politics are a turn-off, particularly for the younger generation who see very little difference between the messages propagated by Labour and Conservatives. For example, in 2001, it is estimated that fewer than 40 per cent of 18 to 24 year olds voted in the General Election.

Some sociologists, particularly Wilkinson and Mulgan (1997), argue that young people now make up a politically disaffected or 'switched-off generation'. There is some evidence for this; Fahmy (2004) notes that young people, compared with older citizens, are less likely to attend party-political rallies, to contact their MP or local councillor, to join a political party or put themselves up for public office. Many studies indicate that young people's political knowledge of both political philosophy and process is poor, whilst surveys indicate that young people are less willing to trust politicians. This last point is important because it suggests that young people are cynical about politics rather than apathetic. Surveys indicate that they believe that politicians and political parties are 'out of touch' with their needs and that their views are not taken seriously.

The turn-out for the 2010 General Election which produced the UK's first coalition government since the Second World War also indicates considerable voter apathy and disillusionment which may be undermining the efficacy of indirect political action. Only 65 per cent of the electorate voted. Moreover, disillusion with voting may be reinforced by the first past the post voting system which meant that it took 284, 566 votes to elect one Green MP, about 119,000 votes to elect each Liberal Democrat, about 34,000 votes to elect each Conservative and 33,000 to elect each Labour MP. Critics of this system argue that electoral reform is needed to truly reflect what the electorate want.

## Other forms of indirect political action

In addition to voting in elections, other forms of indirect action include:

- Taking issues and concerns to MPS by meeting with them at constituency surgeries.
- Collecting signatures for petitions to be presented to political leaders.
- Publishing concerns by producing leaflets or bringing issues to the attention of the local or national media.
- Joining pressure groups

## Pressure groups

Pressure groups are organized bodies that aim to put pressure on decision-makers, such as government ministers, Members of Parliament, representatives in the European Union and local government. This pressure may take the form of mobilizing public opinion and/or lobbying behind the scenes in order to encourage policymakers either to make no change to existing policies and practices, or, more likely, to insist on reform and even radical innovation. Pressure groups seek to influence rather than to get elected.

### *Types of pressure group*

It is generally accepted by sociologists that two broad types of pressure group exist:

1. *Interest or sectional pressure groups* aim to protect the interests of their members or a section of society. This category would include the following:
   - Trade unions representing workers
   - Employer and trade associations, such as the Confederation of British Industry (CBI) and Institute of Directors
   - Professional associations, such as the British Medical Association and the Law Society
   - Organizations such as the National Trust and Automobile Association.

   All of these protect the interests of particular social groups.
2. *Promotional pressure groups* focus on specific issues or causes that members feel strongly about. Examples would include:
   - Greenpeace and Friends of the Earth, which aim to protect the environment
   - Oxfam, which aims to promote greater understanding and sensitivity towards issues such as poverty and debt in developing countries
   - Gingerbread, which seeks to alleviate the problems and poverty of single-parent families.

However, this distinction is not watertight. For example, some interest pressure groups, such as trade unions, may also pursue causes that are in the wider public interest, such as the need for greater corporate responsibility in terms of health and safety. Professional associations such as the British Medical Association have drawn attention to the need to increase public spending to reduce health risks, such as specific types of cancer.

In addition, Morgan (1999) identifies the following types of pressure groups:

- Ad hoc or 'fire brigade' groups – formed to deal with specific new proposals, such as the building of a motorway. These are often disbanded once their aims and objectives are achieved.
- 'Idea' or think-tank groups – aiming to provide an ideological rationale or to carry out research for the aims and objectives of specific causes or issues. For example, the Fabian Society has provided the intellectual rigour that has underpinned socialism and the actions of trade unions, whilst the Adam Smith Institute has provided much of the New Right philosophy underpinning those organizations in favour of free-market government policies. Groups such as the Joseph Rowntree Foundation often provide the research and evidence in antipoverty campaigns.
- 'Political cause' groups – seeking to change the organization of the political system. For example, Charter 88 aimed to change the nature of democracy in the UK. It can be argued that the Human Rights Act in 2001 was a direct consequence of their campaign.
- 'Latent' groups – those which have not yet fully evolved in terms of organization, representation and influence. There are some social groups, such as the poor and minority ethnic groups, who experience a 'poverty of politics or protest' in that they have no formal organizations to speak out on their behalf. However, their 'representatives' may be consulted by the government or media, especially when moral panics develop around 'problems' perceived to be associated with such groups.

Morgan's typology is by no means comprehensive or watertight. In recent years, we have seen the evolution of the 'celebrity' pressure group, with rock stars such as Sir Bob Geldof, Sting and Bono using their celebrity status to raise the public profile of issues such as famine, the degradation of the Amazonian jungle and debt in the developing world, in order to influence governments to change or modify their policies.

## Insider and outsider status

Another useful way to look at pressure groups is to work out whether they have 'insider' or 'outsider' status when it comes to exercising power over the decision-making process.

### *Insider pressure groups*

Pressure groups with insider status are often invited to send representatives to sit on official committees and to collaborate on government policy papers. Civil servants and ministers regularly consult with them. Such groups tend to use 'political brokers' or professional lobbyists who have inside knowledge of how the political process works and/or have official and non-official access to influential politicians and public servants. Such groups prefer to keep a low profile. This is not surprising because, as Duverger (1972) notes, some of these pressure groups, especially those representing the interests of capital, have 'unofficial power' – 'they actually have their own representatives in governments and **legislative bodies**, but the relationship between these individuals and the groups they represent remains secret and circumspect'.

### *Outsider pressure groups*

Outsider groups, on the other hand, do not enjoy direct access to the corridors of power. Such groups attempt to put government under pressure by presenting their case to the mass media and generating public opinion in their favour. Their campaigns are likely to involve demonstrations, boycotts and media campaigns, writing to those with influence and occasionally giving evidence to government committees. Some pressure groups have gone further than this and either disobeyed the law or challenged the law through the courts.

## Lobbying

This refers to the process of trying to influence MPs with regard to their stance on particular issues. Pressure groups and trade unions approach MPs who they believe would be

**Table 5.1** Ideal types of old and new social movements

| Characteristics | Old social movement – Labour movement | New social movements |
|---|---|---|
| Principal objective | Control of state | To change aspects of state policy |
| Type of movement | Political | Cultural, but redefines the political, e.g. the personal is political |
| Key issues | Eradication of inequality | Identity, liberation, protection of nature and the maintenance of peace |
| Organization | Centralized and hierarchical parties and unions | Loose networks of affiliated individuals |
| Tactics | Participation in elections and industrial action | Sporadic mass demonstrations and protests, cultural expressions of alternative lifestyles and identities |
| Link to international | International solidarity | Awareness of connections between the global and the local – act local, think global |
| Main social base | Working class and socialist intellectuals from other social classes | Middle class, especially professional and public-sector workers, and university-educated working class |

Adapted from Faulks, K. (1999) *Political Sociology: A Critical Introduction*, New York University Press

sympathetic to their cause and keep them up to date on these issues so that their interests would be represented in parliamentary debates.

However, in recent years, this type of lobbying has been superceded by the rise in professional lobbying companies, which are often set up by ex-politicians or civil servants who offer to influence policy by selling the contacts they have made during their careers. Such companies have employed MPs (who supposedly represent their constituents' and party's interests first and foremost) as advisers.

There are signs too that lobbying has increased both voter apathy and disillusion with indirect political action as allegations of MP sleaze emerged in the 1990s when MPs were accused of taking money from both lobbying organisations and wealthy individuals in return for asking questions in parliament on behalf of clients.. In 2010, three prominent Labour ex-ministers were forced to stand down as MPs when they were caught on camera offering their political influence for money.

## New Social Movements

Marshall (2005) defines social movements as organised efforts by significant numbers of people to change (or resist change) in some aspect of society. Marshall argues that social movements would include those supporting civil rights, gay rights, trade unionism, environmentalism and feminism. Social movements normally operate outside regular political circles but as interest groups, they do exert political pressure. However, the variety of such movements has led to some sociologists attempting to differentiate between 'Old Social Movements' (OSMs) and 'New Social Movements' (NSMs).

The term OSM is used to refer to older, more established political organizations, such as the socialist movement, or organizations representing working-class alliances, such as trade unions, or employers' associations. OSMs mainly focus on bringing about economic change and tend to be class-based with formal and centralized organization.

In contrast, the followers of NSMs tend to be young middle-class and educated, and are focused on less materialist issues such as quality of life, identity and self-expression. The membership of NSMs tends to be quite loose and the movements themselves tend to be less formalized, hierarchical and bureaucratic than OSMs. Participation in NSMs is voluntary whilst decision-making is more bottom-up than top-down as in OSMs. Members of NSMS are encouraged to take an active part in constructing their own forms of political action which often takes the form of direct action such as demonstrations and criminal damage. (NSMs are examined in more depth in Topic 2).

## Direct political action

Direct action is political action which operates outside the formal political framework of parliamentary democracy. It takes several forms, many of which are obstructive, focused on gaining maximum publicity and which are often illegal, including demonstrations, sit-ins, anarchic stunts, riots and acts of violence.

Jones *et al* note that such direct action is not necessarily the result of politicians or governments failing to listen to people's concerns (although it often is). Rather it is the result of a passionate belief in a cause symbolised by identification with a new social movement. Often passion turns to frustration with the realization that the slow-moving machine of government means that social change is not likely to occur in the immediate future. Direct action is usually concerned with speeding up that change.

### Demonstrations and protests

Organizing peaceful demonstrations and protest marches has long been part of the democratic process in that governments in the UK have generally recognized the right to peaceful assembly in order to bring the concerns of the people to the attention of politicians. For example, in 1936, the Jarrow March (in which thousands of unemployed miners from the North East walked to London) highlighted the economic and social suffering caused by unemployment.

However, although such protests are legitimate, there has been a tendency in recent years for demonstrations to evolve into violent confrontation with the police. Consequently they can be seen as a form of direct action in that they often result in anti-social and anti-authoritarian behaviour which causes maximum disruption to everyday life. The transformation of demonstrations into deliberate forms of direct action of this obstructive and violent nature is probably due to two fairly recent developments:

- Halloran *et al* (1970) note that policing of such demonstrations became increasingly aggressive from the 1960s. Tougher policing methods including snatch squads, mounted police and the employment of riot gear such as shields were seen more frequently throughout the 1970s and 1980s, whilst the 1994 Criminal Justice and Public Order Act attempted to impose stricter controls on political protest. Such military-style policing led to the view that police officers were being used politically to suppress dissent, that politicians were uninterested in listening to the grievances of the people and that more radical measures needed to be adopted to get their attention.
- Button (1995) suggests that the 1960s saw a shift from an old style of politics, mainly organized around conventional class and industrial issues and indirect political action to a 'new' radical style of political action in the 1980s often focused on empowerment and rights. He claims that a new 'fearlessness' gradually evolved organized around 'people power' which aimed to resist centralised power (which was interpreted as oppressive) and which involved new forms of political activity based on civil disobedience. Often such political activists were loosely linked by a common identity with others in a new social movement.

Direct action in the form of civil disobedience demonstrations took a number of new forms from the 1980s. Protesters against new roads and airport runways often used their own bodies as shields by physically placing themselves on building sites at great risk to their own personal safety. Anti-genetically-modified crop protesters destroyed fields of crops whilst environmental protesters hijacked coal trains and dumped their cargo on railway lines. Those who opposed laboratory testing on animals physically attacked researchers whilst disabled wheelchair users chained themselves to the railings outside Downing Street. (See Topic 2 for many more examples of direct action carried out by members of NSMs).

## Riots

Riots are a form of direct action which usually involves some degree of violence, especially against property, and confrontation with the police. They are a type of collective urban disorder which tends to be focused in inner-city areas characterized by high levels of social and economic deprivation. Some sociologists believe that rioting can be perceived as the only option available to some groups who lack access to legitimate means of political protest and who see mainstream political parties, pressure groups and trade unions as failing to represent their interests. Bachrach and Baratz (1970) suggest that in this sense riots are the 'ballot boxes of the poor' and are attempts to force onto a political agenda demands that would otherwise be neglected or ignored. The poor have no other way of being heard.

Conservative writers and commentators, on the other hand, argue that urban riots are the product of moral corruption, criminality – signs that some elements of the urban population – the underclass – see themselves as outside the moral and legal constraints of wider society. Moreover, conservative thinkers have often racialized urban disorder by suggesting that riots arise out of the unique confrontational nature of ethnic-minority culture rather than being a legitimate or understandable reaction to poor social conditions.

The radical view of urban disorder sees it as a conscious and deliberate form of direct action by groups who have no other opportunities to bring their grievances to public attention. Marxists see urban riots as 'uprisings' by a disenfrachized urban poor and consequently as a legitimate form of resistance and revolutionary protest.

Beynon (1986) sees a number of factors influencing the potential for rioting as a form of direct action:

1. *Structural factors* – rioters experience inequalities in power, resources and life-chances. Inner-city residents may feel relatively deprived and frustrated because the government seems uninterested in or unwilling to relieve their problems.
2. *Political/ideological factors* – rioters lack political representation. They feel that no-one cares and that they have little to lose.
3. *Cultural factors* – the police and other agencies of social control may not be able to relate to young people's culture such as hanging around in the street. If the groups have different or incompatible definitions of a situation, then the potential for conflict is increased.
4. *Contextual factors* – those who riot may be responding to a past history of conflict between themselves and the authorities.
5. *Situational factors* – riots may evolve spontaneously in response to a particular situation such as a 'wrongful' arrest.
6. *Interactional factors* – the quality of interaction between police and members of a community may be poor. 'Flashpoints' may occur as the community perceive police action as breaking unwritten rules with regard to, for example, unfair arrests or excessive police violence.

Cashmore (1989) argues that riots have four constructive consequences for communities:

- They provide a spontaneous outlet for built-up emotional energies. They are occasions for symbolic revenge against a system that deprived groups despise.
- They draw attention to the social and economic deprivation that triggered off the protest. Deprived groups are often denied access to conventional means of protest. Riots are an alternative means of grabbing the attention of politicians.
- They often lead to educational reform because it is recognised that urban violence is partially the result of

unemployment, which in turn is partly due to educational underachievement.

- They often result in the economic revitalization of the inner cities as governments pour funds into them in order to attract businesses and jobs.

## Terrorism

Terrorism aims to inspire fear through the use of violence which is often aimed at civilian populations in order to force governments to make concessions or to give up policies entirely. Terrorism is strongly opposed by the general public but it has been frequently used by extremist political groups. For example, the Irish Republican Army (IRA) carried out bombings and assassinations in Northern Ireland and on the British mainland between 1975 and1996, whilst the 9-11 attack on the Twin Towers in New York in 2001 was carried out by fundamentalist Islamic terrorists. However, it is important to understand that such terror tactics can also actually attract considerable support among those who believe in the cause. These supporters will interpret the perpetrators of terror acts as freedom fighters rather than as terrorists. Moreover radical sociologists note that the US and UK governments routinely define acts of violence committed by Islamic fundamentalists as terrorism but are unwilling to interpret the violence perpetrated on Muslims by Western armed forces in Iraq and Afghanistan in a critical way.

Some political activists in NSMs in the UK have adopted terror-like tactics. The Animal Liberation Front (ALF) have threatened the lives of scientists who experiment on animals and placed bombs under their cars. They have firebombed laboratories where experiments on animals take place and department stores that sell fur products.

## Cyber-networking

One of the biggest differences in the political actions taken by old social movements and new social movements is the use by the latter group of information technology or **cyber-networking**. Global NSMS have harnessed the world wide web – the internet and e-mail – to bypass traditional centres of power (i.e. the government) and traditional means of communication (i.e. the print media, television and radio) to empower their members. It is suggested that NSM use of the internet to mobilise support has revitalized democracy because it has given a voice to those who would otherwise go unheard.

Itzoe (1995) notes that the internet is a 'loose and anarchic confederation of millions of users around the world who communicate in perhaps the freest forum of speech in history'. The internet has, therefore, been used in a variety of political ways by these activists:

- to monitor the illegal or immoral activities of big businesses
- to harness mass support for causes such as Make Poverty History
- to coordinate protests and activism ranging from hunt saboteurs and anti-vivisection to disrupting G8 meetings about climate change and third world debt.

Giddens (2006) notes that cyber-networking is producing a 'migration of power' away from governments and transnational corporations into new non-governmental alliances and coalitions. Giddens suggests that it may even result in 'netwars' – large-scale global conflicts over information and public opinion. Castells (1997) suggests that three social movements have effectively used cyber-networking to attract international attention to their cause. The Mexican Zapatista movement, US right-wing militias and the Japanese Aum Shinrikyo religious cult have all used the internet to publicise their opposition to globalization. Castells notes that all these movements would still be isolated and obscure without the power of the internet.

Giddens also notes that authoritarian governments such as those in China and Burma are finding it increasingly difficult to control the flow of information available to their populations because we now live in an 'open informational world'. Cyber-networking encourages debate and dissent and therefore challenges the traditional forms of power that exist in authoritarian societies that expect unquestioned respect and support. For example, in Burma, supporters of the imprisoned pro-democracy leader Aung San Suu Kyi have successfully used cyber-networking to build up a global resistance to the military elite that runs the country by persuading global corporations like Pepsi-Cola not to invest in the country.

Klein (2000) has noted how the global anti-capitalist movement has used technology, particularly cyber-networking and computer hacking to oppose corporate branding through a strategy known as '**culture jamming**'. This refers to the practice of hacking into corporate web-sites to leave cyber-graffiti which humorously distort corporate messages and images such as logos into anti-globalization messages and parodies.

Cyber-networking is constantly evolving. For example, social networking sites such as Facebook and Twitter now host a diversity of political forums that are dedicated to political campaigns. Most political parties and new social movements also use these sites to generate support and to propagate their policies and opinions. There is also some evidence that pro-democracy protests in Iran and Moldova were co-ordinated through Twitter. In some cases, even the mainstream news media have used Twitter to source their 'information' on certain political upheavals. Cyber-networking may therefore be producing a new type of politics and a new type of citizen activism.

# Check your understanding

1 How does the 'zero-sum of power' model define power?

2 What is the difference between coercion and authority?

3 What type of power is exercised by the prime minister?

4 Define what is meant by ideology.

5 Why can liberalism be regarded as a left-wing ideology?

5 What are the main differences between Conservatism and Neo-Conservatism?

6 How does nationalism in the UK differ from the ultra-nationalism found in some other countries?

7 What was the 'third way'?

8 What is the relationship between the superstructure and ideology according to Marxists?

9 How can ordinary people resist ruling class ideology according to Gramsci?

10 Identify five ways in which patriarchal ideology is transmitted and reinforced according to feminists.

11 What is anarchism?

12 Identify three types of indirect action.

13 Identify and explain five different types of pressure groups.

14 How has the nature of lobbying changed?

15 Why are demonstrations now regarded as a direct form of action?

16 How do Marxists view riots?

17 What terror tactics have been adopted by some members of new social movements?

18 How does cyber-networking challenge ruling class power?

19 How has the internet globalized protest and dissent?

20 What is culture-jamming?

# Key terms

**Bourgeoisie** Marxist term describing the ruling (or capitalist) class in capitalist society.

**Bureaucracy** form of organization associated with modern societies, consisting of a hierarchy of formal positions, each with clear responsibilities.

**Capitalist** societies where one social class owns the means of production, while another class does the work.

**Culture jamming** hacking into corporate websites to subvert corporate branding and publicity.

**Cyber-networking** using the internet to mobilize support.

**Glass ceiling** work-based situation in which women are prevented from accessing top jobs because of discrimination by male employers.

**Hegemony** situation where the ideology of the dominant class becomes accepted as the shared culture of the whole of society.

**Ideological struggle** cultural conflict between the capitalist and subordinate classes.

**Legitimate** justified and accepted.

**Means of production** Marxist term referring to the material forces that enable things be produced, e.g. capital, land, factories.

**Meritocracy** a society in which people are rewarded on the basis of merit, i.e. intelligence and ability, usually via examinations and qualifications.

**Patriarchy** male power over women.

**Proletariat** in Marxist terms, the working class, who hire out their labour to the bourgeoisie in return for a wage.

**Relations of production** Marxist term referring to the allocation of rules and responsibilities among those involved in production.

**Superstructure** Marxist term used to describe the parts of society not concerned with economic production, such as the media, religion and education.

**Symbolic resistance** rebellion which takes an indirect form.

**Zero-sum view of power** idea that power involves one person or group gaining and another person or group losing.

# Activities

## Research idea

1 Construct a spider chart with a box in the centre symbolizing yourself. Draw lines to other boxes containing the names of significant people in your life, e.g. friends, brothers and sisters, parents, other relatives, teachers, employers, workmates. Use a different colour pen to symbolize the type of power relationship you have with these people – for example, if the relationship is based on authority draw a red line, as you would from you to your teacher.

Some of your relationships may be based on coercion, persuasion, influence, manipulation, even ideology – use different colour lines to symbolize these. You may have to add categories or adapt existing ones.

2 Ask a small sample of other people (try to include people of different ages, gender, ethnic and class backgrounds) to construct similar diagrams. Compare the diagrams. What similarities and differences do you find?

## Web.tasks

Search the worldwide web for lists of powerful men and/or women in Britain. What is the basis of the power of those who make up these lists?

## An eye on the exam — Defining and exploring power and political action in society

Provide a detailed description of the explanations including concepts, studies and any relevant theories

Weigh up the strengths and weaknesses of explanations in some detail before reaching a balanced conclusion

**(a) Outline and assess sociological explanations of the relationship between ideology and political action** **(17 marks)**

Political action takes many forms, e.g. political parties, voting, demonstrations, direct action

There are a range of ideologies that could be examined

### Grade booster — Getting top marks in this question

The introduction should focus on clearly defining the concept of ideology and identifying the major ideologies e.g. liberalism, conservatism, nationalism, socialism, Marxism, feminism. The introduction should also identify the range of political actions available to people in the UK. Most of this essay will explore the links between ideologies and the major political parties, e.g. how are the actions of the Labour Party and Conservative Party shaped by the ideologies of socialism and conservatism respectively? However, a section of the essay should explore how ideologies such as Marxism, feminism and anarchism have shaped the direct action tactics of new social movements.

# TOPIC 2

# The emergence of and participation in new social movements

## Getting you thinking

### Mission statement

Greenpeace is an independent, campaigning organization that uses non-violent, creative confrontation to expose global environmental problems, and force solutions for a green and peaceful future. Greenpeace's goal is to ensure the ability of the Earth to nurture life in all its diversity.

Greenpeace does not solicit or accept funding from governments, corporations or political parties. Greenpeace neither seeks nor accepts donations that could compromise its independence, aims, objectives or integrity. Greenpeace relies on the voluntary donations of individual supporters, and on grant support from foundations. Greenpeace is committed to the principles of non-violence, political independence and internationalism. In exposing threats to the environment and in working to find solutions, Greenpeace has no permanent allies or enemies.

### Animal liberation

*The ultimate struggle.* All too often animal liberation is seen, by those who do not understand, as a radical form of animal welfare. It's not about welfare, it's about freedom from oppression, it's about fighting abuses of power and it's about achieving a world in which individuals – irrespective of gender, race or species – are at liberty to be themselves. The state, the establishment and the multinationals seek to control our lives and imprison or kill us when we resist.

They seek to profit from the imprisonment or murder of those from the other species. They seek to own and control the land, the oceans and the skies which should be free to all. Animal Liberation is the struggle – indeed the war – against such tyranny in all its forms. We must fight this tyranny in all its forms. We must fight for the defenceless and the innocent. We must fight for a more compassionate world. We can, we must and we will win the ultimate struggle. When Animal Liberation is achieved, we shall all be free... free to enjoy the true liberty that has been denied us for far too long!

### Compassion in World Farming (CIWF)

CIWF campaigns to end the factory farming of animals and long-distance transport, through hard-hitting political lobbying, investigations and high profile campaigns.

CIWF was started in 1967 by dairy farmer Peter Roberts. Peter and his wife Anna were becoming increasingly concerned with the animal welfare issues connected to the new systems of intensive factory farming that were becoming popular during the 1960s.

CIWF campaign through peaceful protest and **lobbying** and by raising awareness of the issue of farm animal welfare. We also produce fully referenced scientific reports. Our undercover teams provide vital evidence of the suffering of farm animals.

### North West Hunt Saboteurs Association

18th February 2005 saw a day that many decent people had thought may never come – the day that hunting with hounds was relegated to the history books.

The North West Hunt Saboteurs Association (NWHSA), is an organization that is dedicated to the saving of the lives of hunted animals. Whilst the 18th February marked a very special day, it did not signal the end of that fight. There is still much work to do to ensure that the hunters do indeed desist with their sick pastime, make the switch to drag hunting, or face the consequences of breaking the law.

The ban is workable, can be enforced and bring an end to hunting as we know it. And this is where the continued role of hunt saboteurs comes in ... We do know that some blatant infringements of the law are taking place. And it's in cases such as these that hunt sabs are possibly best placed to gather evidence, as after all we are the people who have always been in the field with the hunts, know what constitutes illegal hunting and aren't afraid to get in amongst the action to get what is required. This of course doesn't mean that we won't intervene to save the life of the hunted animal – after all, that remains our sole aim as hunt saboteurs.

**Examine the manifestos (statement of beliefs) of the four organizations above.**

1. **Allocate these organizations to the following categories:**

   **A Those that conform to mainstream political rules and work within the law to achieve their aims.**
   **B Those that use both politically acceptable and unlawful means of drawing attention to their cause(s).**
   **C Organizations that are generally in confrontation with the authorities.**

   **Under each category, clearly state why the organization's beliefs and tactics may be acceptable or unacceptable forms of political action.**

2. **Are any of these organizations influential enough to shape their members' sense of personal identity?**

You will have noticed that the organizations above occupy very different positions on a continuum of political protest. Two of these organizations operate within the conventional political world – Greenpeace and Compassion in World Farming (CIWF) – but reserve the right to work outside the democratic process in order to draw attention to particular causes. For example, CIWF uses undercover agents in factory-farming enterprises to gather evidence for animal cruelty. Both these organizations qualify as '**new social movements**', because membership usually involves a type of dedication to a cause which shapes the identity of the member. We can see this more clearly in the case of social movement organizations and groups that lie *outside* the political mainstream. Membership of groups like the Hunt Saboteurs Society and especially the Animal Liberation Front (ALF) involve their members in actively opposing the democratic mainstream. Moreover, the fact of their membership tends to lie at the very heart of the identity of their members – in other words, an Animal Liberationist is likely to see membership of the ALF as a central defining component of their existence.

# New social movements

Hallsworth (1994) defines the term new social movement as:

> *<< the wide and diverse spectrum of new, non-institutional political movements which emerged or (as in the case of feminism) which re-emerged in Western liberal democratic societies during the 1960s and 1970s. More specifically, the term is used to refer to those movements which may be held to pose new challenges to the established cultural, economic and political orders of advanced (late-20th-century) capitalist society. >>*

Storr (2002) notes that NSMs are a form of extra-parliamentary politics, i.e. they tend to operate outside the formal institutions of parliament or government. Faulks (1999) suggests that the most distinctive feature of NSMs is their rejection of the state and their determination to highlight the limitations of a state-centred system of governance.

Diani (1992) argues that the key characteristics of a new social movement are:

- an informal network of interactions between activist groups, individuals or organizations
- a sense of collective identity
- a sense of opposition to or conflict with mainstream politics with regard to the need for social change.

Using Diani's definition, we can see that NSMs focus on broad issues such as environmentalism, animal rights, antiglobalization, anticapitalism, anarchism, human rights, gay rights, travellers' rights. If we examine the NSM of environmentalism, we can see that it includes a wide diversity of groups and organizations, including pressure groups such as Greenpeace and Friends of the Earth, eco-warriors and anarchist groups such as Reclaim the Streets. The Reclaim the Streets group is also an excellent example of the interconnection of NSMs. The group was originally formed by a group of squatters in protest at the extension of the M11 in East London in the early 1990s, so it was originally an anti-road group. However, its activities have expanded to take in action in support of sacked Liverpool dock workers, organizing global carnivals 'against capital', as well as being heavily involved in antiglobalization protests in cities where the World Trade Organization hold meetings. Reclaim the Streets also protest using environmental actions such as 'guerilla gardening', whereby activists plant trees in unexpected places.

Foulks suggests that the main reason for the appearance of NSMs is disillusionment with the policies of both left-wing and right-wing governments. NSMs symbolize an awareness, especially among young people, that state solutions have failed and perhaps even worsened problems such as racism and global pollution. They are a reaction to the failure of politicians to achieve social justice and to be accountable for this failure. Moreover, NSMs have also evolved to confront the coercive practices of other social movements that are perceived to be fascist and racist – for example, the anti-Nazi League and Rock Against Racism were part of a NSM that aimed to counter the influence of racist organizations such as the British National Party and Combat 18.

An NSM can also be composed of ideas and informal networks, rather than a specific organization pursuing particular goals. A good example of this is feminism – it is difficult to identify a particular campaign group or set of influential women that works either defensively or offensively in the pursuit of a feminist or antipatriarchal agenda. Rather there exists a network of female academics who identify themselves as liberal, Marxist or radical feminists, pressure groups such as Gingerbread and the English Collective of Prostitutes, and voluntary groups such as Rape Crisis, that recognize a common theme – that most women in the UK share similar experiences in terms of how a patriarchal society views and treats them.

## Types of NSM

Hallsworth (1994) argues that if we examine the ideological values underpinning the activities and philosophy of NSMs, we can see two broad types: defensive NSMs and offensive NSMs.

### *Defensive NSMs*

These are generally concerned with defending a natural or social environment seen as under threat from unregulated industrialization and/or capitalism, impersonal and insensitive forms of state bureaucracy and the development of **risk technology** such as nuclear power or genetically modified (GM) crops. Examples of such organizations include animal-rights groups such as the Animal Liberation Front, environmental groups such as Friends of the Earth and the anti-nuclear movement. Such groups call for an alternative world order built on forms of **sustainable development** in tune with the natural world, as well as social justice for all.

A variation on defensive NSMs is a form of association that Hetherington (1998) calls the '**Bünde**', made up of vegetarian groups, free-festival goers, dance culture, squatters, travellers, and so on. This social network of groups has characteristics similar to defensive NSMs. They generally resist the global marketplace, are anticapitalist, and oppose the rituals and conventions that modern societies expect their members to subscribe to, such as settling down in one permanent place or abiding by social standards of hygiene. The Bünde therefore create their own spaces, such as 'Teepee valley' in Wales, and gather in 'tribes' at key events and places, such as Stonehenge and Glastonbury, to celebrate symbolically their alternative lifestyles. The Bünde can experience intense hostility from society. For example, the police have been accused of singling out traveller convoys for regular surveillance and harassment.

### *Offensive NSMs*

These aim to defend or extend social rights to particular groups who are denied status, autonomy or identity, or are marginalized and repressed by the state. The concept of difference, therefore, is central to these movements. Hallsworth argues that such NSMs are concerned with exposing institutional discrimination and advancing the social position of marginalized and excluded groups such as women, gay men and lesbians, minority ethnic groups, refugees and those denied human rights. They are also involved in bringing about the emancipation of social groups such as women and Black people from the ideas promoted by right-wing movements such as pro-family, pro-life and racism.

## NSMs and identity

Whether defensive or offensive, NSMs are generally concerned with promoting and changing cultural values and with the construction of identity politics. People involved in NSMs see their involvement as a defining factor in their personal identity. NSMs provide their members with a value system which stresses 'the very qualities the dominant cultural order is held to deny' (Hallsworth 1994). This value system embodies:

- *active participation* – people genuinely feeling that they can help bring about change, as opposed to feeling apathy and indifference towards formal politics
- *personal development* – wanting personal as opposed to material satisfaction
- *emotional openness* – wanting others to see and recognize their stance
- *collective responsibility* – feeling social solidarity with others.

## The organization of NSMs

Hallsworth notes that the internal organization of NSMs is generally characterized by low levels of bureaucracy, the encouragement of democratic participation at all levels of decision-making for all members, and few, if any, full-time officials. Such organizations are usually underpinned by local networks and economic self-help, both of which deliberately aim to distance their activities from traditional political institutions and decision-making. Mainstream politicians are mainly concerned with raising economic standards and improving standards of living. However those actively engaged with NSMs are more likely to be

## Focus on research

### Kate Burningham and Diana Thrush (2001)

### The environmental concerns of disadvantaged groups

**NSMs mainly attract a middle-class clientele, so how do disadvantaged people perceive environmentalism and organizations such as Greenpeace? These researchers carried out focus-group interviews with 89 members of disadvantaged groups in Glasgow, London, North Wales and the Peak District. It found that the poor were more interested in local issues, such as the rundown state of the areas they lived in, rather than national or global environmental concerns. This stemmed from real anxieties about meeting basic economic needs, which left little time for them to think or worry about wider or more abstract concerns. They gave priority to their most immediate problems, and so environmental concerns were viewed as too distant. They knew little about environmental organizations or eco-warriors beyond the media stereotypes, and generally perceived activists as too extreme. No one in the sample belonged to an environmental NSM, although this was put down to the lack of a local presence from such organizations rather than lack of interest. Finally, the sample expressed confusion about green consumerism, particularly about the merits of organic food and non-genetically modified foods. Most felt that buying environmentally friendly food was too expensive anyway.**

Burningham, K. and Thrush, D. (2001) *Rainforests Are a Long Way from Here: The Environmental Concerns of Disadvantaged Groups*, York: Joseph Rowntree Foundation

1. **What problems of reliability and validity might arise in the use of focus-group interviewing?**
2. **Using evidence from the above study, explain why working-class people appear to be less interested than middle-class people in the goals of NSMs.**

motivated by postmaterialist values – for example, they may wish to improve quality of life for animals and people, or encourage lifestyles that are more in harmony with the environment.

## The social characteristics of the members of NSMs

Research into the social basis of support for NSMs suggests that members and activists are typically drawn from a restricted section of the wider community, specifically from the youth sector. Typical members of NSMs are aged 16 to 30 and tend to be middle class in origin; they are likely to be employed in the public and service sector of the economy (teaching, social work, and so on), or born to parents who work in this occupational sector. Other typical members are likely to be peripheral to (i.e. on the margins of) the labour market, such as students and the unemployed. However, Scott (1990) points out that it is difficult to make accurate generalizations about the membership of NSM groups. For example, many of the anti-veal export campaigners at Brightlingsea in Sussex in the late 1990s were middle-aged or retired.

Cohen and Rai (2000) are critical of those sociologists who distinguish between OSMs and NSMs. They point out that organizations such as Amnesty International, Greenpeace and Oxfam are not that new, and have often used very traditional methods such as lobbying ministers, MPs and civil servants to pursue their interests. Moreover, it is too narrow to say that political parties and trade unions are mainly concerned with class politics or sectional economic interests. Political parties, particularly those of a socialist and liberal tendency, have been involved in identity politics, promoting and protecting the legal and social rights of women, minority ethnic groups, refugees, asylum seekers, and gay men and lesbians, as well as campaigning for human rights and democracy abroad. Both the Green and Liberal Democratic parties have long been involved in environmental campaigns.

Foulks has highlighted the danger of lumping together groups that have very different ideological perspectives, levels of commitment to the 'cause', varied organizational forms and a variety of political as well as cultural objectives. He notes that it may not be appropriate to group together formal groups such as Greenpeace and Friends of the Earth, in which there is very little opportunity for participation by ordinary supporters, with more radical groups such as Earth First and Justice, which promote anarchic activism. For example, these latter groups have been extremely critical of Greenpeace because it is supposedly too close to the formal political establishment.

However, Cohen and Rai do acknowledge that the way NSMs communicate with their members differs from that of old social movements or pressure groups in two crucial respects:

1 New media technology, particularly the internet and e-mail, have improved the ability of social movements to get their message across to much larger audiences than in the past. This has put greater pressure on politicians to bring about social change.

2 Some social movements have taken advantage of this new media technology to globalize their message. For example, Greenpeace has members in over 150 countries.

## NSMs and political action

The type of political action adopted by some NSMs deliberately differs from the activities of OSMs and pressure groups. The latter generally work within the existing framework of politics, and their last resort is the threat of withdrawal of whatever resource they control – for example, labour or capital investment. Many NSMs tend to operate outside regular channels of political action and tend to focus on 'direct action'. This form of political action includes demonstrations, sit-ins, squatting, street theatre, publicity stunts and other obstructive action. Much of this action is illegal, but it often involves fairly mild forms of mass civil disobedience, such as anti-road protestors committing mass trespass in order to prevent bulldozers destroying natural habitats, the Reclaim the Streets movement disrupting traffic in the centre of London, and Greenpeace supporters destroying fields of GM crops. The British gay and lesbian group, Outrage, has involved its supporters in mass gay weddings and 'kiss-ins'. However, there have been instances of action involving more serious forms of illegal and criminal action – for example, damaging nuclear-weapons installations or military hardware, fire-bombing department stores that sell fur goods, breaking into animal-testing laboratories and attacking scientists with letter and car bombs.

Faulks notes that NSM political action may not look successful but it is all about winning small battles and creating confidence. He notes that supporters of NSMs see the sum of these small battles as eventually transforming society because, bit by bit, they lead to the coercive state being destabilized. Doherty (1998) agrees and argues that the anti-road groups that were set up in the 1980s as a form of environmental protest against the government's road-building programme failed to halt that particular state policy. However, the tactics employed by these eco-warriors, as they called themselves, led to lots of publicity for their cause and great expense for the government in terms of increased security costs. Doherty suggests that these effects led to the Conservative government cutting the size of its road-building programme by two-thirds.

## The nature of politics

The emergence of NSMs in the 1960s indicates that the nature of political debate and action has undergone fundamental change. It is suggested that up to the 1960s, both political debate and action were dominated by political parties and pressure groups that sought either to protect or challenge the economic or material order. In other words, politics was dominated by class-based issues. However, the emergence of the women's movement and the civil-rights movement led to a recognition that wider social inequalities were of equal importance and resulted in a concern to protect, and even celebrate, the concept of 'social difference'. It was argued that affluence in Western societies meant than economic issues became subordinated to wider concerns about long-term survival, reflected in increased interest in social movements related to antinuclear technology, peace, the environment and global issues such as debt.

# Theories of NSMs

## Collective behaviour theory

This theory is mainly concerned with how collective or group behaviours emerge to deal with problematical circumstances and situations. It sees collective behaviour as existing on a continuum. At one end, collective behaviour may be coordinated and organized and take the form of distinct social movements. At the other end of the continuum is spontaneous collective behaviour such as outbreaks of mass hysteria. Marshall notes that between these two extremes can be found collective responses to natural disasters, riots, demonstrations, crazes, fads, fashions, rumours, panics and even rebellions and revolutions.

Smelser (1962) suggests that social movements as collective behaviour appear when the following conditions are in place:

- *Structural conduciveness* – this means that the society must be organised in such a way that collective behaviour is encouraged or permitted, and regarded as legitimate. For example, democratic societies permit freedom of speech and peaceful assembly whilst totalitarian states generally do not.
- *Structural strain* – the society may be undergoing economic or social problems leading to deprivation and inequality or the spread of beliefs that some social groups have advantages over others.
- *Precipitating factors* – there may be a dramatic event, e.g. a racial incident, massacre or scandal that confirms the inequality/deprivation or the belief that it exists.
- *Mobilization to action* – a group of like-minded people react to the event by forming or joining a social movement.
- *Social control* – the authorities react to the collective behaviour by attempting to deal with the strains that led to the behaviour and/or by attempting to shape and control the actions of the social movement, e.g. by making sure that its actions are constrained by the legal and democratic process. More direct forms of action such as demonstrations may be met by force and coercion.

## Resource mobilization theory

This approach to social movements emphasizes that the success of a social movement is dependent on the resources available to them. In particular, resources such as wealth, facilities, the effort or labour that the membership is happy to expend on the movement, the ability to acquire the necessary knowledge and information, access to publicity and advertising, and particularly support from and access to the ruling elite are essential if a social movement is to achieve its goals.

**Resource mobilization theory** (RMT) argues that social movements develop when individuals with grievances are able to mobilize sufficient resources to take action. It suggests that people rationally weigh up the costs and benefits of being involved with social movements. They base their decision to get involved with such movements by judging whether the movement's aggregated or total resources in terms of:

- economic capital,
- social capital (access to political contacts and media, links to other groups etc.) and
- cultural capital (the strategic skills of the leadership, the information and knowledge available to the group etc.) are sufficient to bring about success in terms of achieving its goals.

RMT therefore argues that the amount of activity directed towards accomplishing goals is dependent on the resources controlled by the organization. For example, a social movement that is resource-poor in terms of cash may be less successful than one that can afford to pay salaries to full-time employees or to pay lobbying companies to represent their interests.

However, critics of this theory suggest it puts too much emphasis on material resources. Some social movements such as the women's movement and the civil rights movement have been very effective despite not having access to large funds and having to face a very hostile media and ruling elite. Some critics have suggested that RMT may under-estimate the commitment to ideology that results in members of some social movements giving considerable time, labour and commitment to the movement, and even, on occasion, going as far to put lives on the line for the cause.

## Marxist theories

The Marxist, Habermas (1979), saw membership of NSMs as arising out of the nature of postcapitalism, in which the majority of people enjoy a good standard of living and are supposedly, therefore, less interested in material things. In such societies, priorities change – economic matters are of less importance than issues such as protecting human rights and democracy from an ever-encroaching state bureaucracy. NSMs, therefore, are a means by which democratic rights are protected and extended.

Touraine (1982), another Marxist, agrees, arguing that NSMs are a product of a postindustrial society that stresses the production and consumption of knowledge rather than materialism, consumerism and economic goals. The focus on knowledge has led to a critical evaluation of cultural values, especially among the young middle class, who have experienced greater periods of education. NSMs are therefore concerned with the promotion of alternative cultural values encouraging quality of life, concern for the environment and individual freedom of expression and identity. Touraine sees NSMs as at the heart of a realignment of political and cultural life. He suggests that they are in the process of replacing political parties as the major source of political identity.

Marcuse (1964) argued that NSMs are the direct result of the **alienation** caused by the capitalist mode of production and consumption. He suggested that capitalism produces a superficial **mass culture** in order to maximize its audience and profits. However, the emptiness of this culture has led some middle-class students whose education has given them critical insight, to reject materialism. NSMs, therefore, are a form of **counterculture** that encourages people to focus on unselfish needs, such as concern for other people or the environment.

## Postmodern theories of NSMs

Other writers believe that NSMs are the product of a search for identity rather than the product of common political ideology or shared economic interests. Alberto Melucci (1989) argues that the collective actions and political campaigns associated with NSMs are not organized in a formal sense. It is this informality or looseness that appeals to its membership. This belonging to a vast unorganized network is less about providing its members with a coherent and articulate political manifesto or ideology than about providing a sense of identity and lifestyle. In this sense, Melucci argues that NSMs are a cultural rather than political phenomenon. They appeal to the young, in particular, because they offer the opportunity to challenge the dominant rules, whilst offering an alternative set of identities that focus on fundamentally changing the nature of the society in both a spiritual and cultural way.

Melucci suggests that NSMs have made a significant cultural contribution to society because direct action, even if unsuccessful in conventional terms, reveals the existence of unequal power structures and makes people aware that these require challenging. In fact, Melucci argues 'that to resist is to win' – in other words, the mere fact of a protest action is a kind of success, because it is a challenge to existing power structures. Road protesters might fail to prevent a road being built, but, as Field (quoted in Storr 2002) notes:

> *<< resistance to road-building is not just about stopping one particular project. Every delay, every disruption, every extra one thousand pounds spent on police or security is a victory: money that is not available to spend elsewhere. 'Double the cost of one road and you have prevented another one being built' is an opinion often expressed by activists. In such an unequal struggle, to resist is to win.>>*

Postmodernists argue that the meta-narratives that were used to explain the world are in decline, as the modern world evolves into a postmodern world. Meta-narratives are the 'big theories' – science, religions and political philosophies (e.g. socialism, conservatism, nationalism, liberalism and social democracy). The search for truth, self-fulfilment and social progress through these meta-narratives has largely been abandoned as people have become disillusioned by the failure of these belief systems (as seen in the fall of communism) and/or the damage caused by them in terms of war, genocide, environmental destruction and pollution. The postmodern world is characterized by global media technology, which has led to knowledge becoming relative, i.e. accepting that all knowledge has some value. Moreover, in the postmodern world, knowledge is also an important source of power and personal identity. Access to the knowledge marketplace allows people a greater degree of choice about how they should consume knowledge in order to shape their personal identity. Postmodernists see NSMs as offering nuggets of relative knowledge that contribute important dimensions to personal identity. For example, people may partly define themselves by making statements that involve membership of causes such as vegetarianism, the anti-globalization movement or the Make Poverty History campaign.

## The decline of social class?

Crook *et al.* (1992) argue that in postmodern society, sociocultural divisions (e.g. differences in consumption and lifestyle) are more important than socioeconomic divisions (e.g. differences between social classes). Consequently, the traditional 'them-versus-us' conflict between employers and the working class has gone into decline and politics is now concerned with more universal moral issues. This has led to the emergence of new political organizations – NSMs that generally appeal to people's moral principles as well as their lifestyles. For example, we may be convinced by the moral arguments advanced by environmental organizations to consume in an ecologically responsible fashion and to dispose of our waste by recycling. Getting involved in NSM activities, therefore, is both a political statement and a lifestyle choice.

## Risk and reflexivity

Commentators such as Ulrich Beck (1992) and Anthony Giddens (1991) note that in a postmodern world dominated by global media and communications, there is a growing sense of risk – people are increasingly aware of the dangers of the world we live in. In particular, there is a growing distrust of experts such as scientists, who are seen as being responsible for many of the world's problems. Giddens uses the concept of 'increasing **reflexivity**' to suggest that more and more people are reflecting on their place in the world and realizing that their existence and future survival increasingly depend on making sure that key political players, such as governments and global corporations, behave in a responsible fashion.

However, not all sociologists agree that we have entered a postmodern age. Meta-narratives still seem important. Religious meta-narratives, in particular, have re-emerged as important explanations of terrorism and suicide bombings in the UK. Crook and colleagues have been criticized for overstating the decline of social class, and for suggesting that sociocultural differences in consumption and lifestyle are not connected to socioeconomic differences. As Marxist critics have noted, the poor do not enjoy the same access to cultural consumption or NSMs as other sections of society.

## Global social movements

There is evidence that NSMs are becoming increasingly globalized. Callinicos (2003) argues that an anti-capitalist social movement emerged in the late 1990s which brought together campaigns concerned with the negative effects produced by global or transnational corporations. For example, this movement is focused on how developing countries are exploited by transnationals with regard to the prices they receive for their cash crops and raw materials. Moreover, the anti-capitalist movement is critical of the exploitation of labour in sweatshops in the developing world as well as the damage transnationals are doing to the environment of developing countries.

Callinicos notes that the anti-capitalist movement is made up of some strange bedfellows who occupy a range of ideological positions. Some are Marxists and socialists who have quite radical demands which mainly focus on the dismantling of the global capitalist system, others are anarchists, whilst some just seek moderate reform to the global free market.

Callinicos identifies three factors which he believes led to the appearance of the anti-capitalist movement:

- It is a response to the growing importance of global political and economic institutions such as the World Bank, the International Monetary Fund, G8 group and European Union.
- Specific global campaigns such as Live Aid, Jubilee 2000 and Make Poverty History highlighted the importance of global issues and reinforced international links between new social movements across the world. Cyber-networking led to a rapid dissemination of anti-capitalist ideas and campaigns across the world.
- The global capitalist system experienced some major problems in the early 21st century such as the global banking crisis of 2009 and the financial crises of countries such as Greece in 2010. These types of problems attract people to the anti-capitalist movement as they become aware of the potential grave damage that global capitalism can do to local economies and livelihoods.

Callinicos suggests that the anti-capitalist movement works effectively because it lacks an overall leader, a coherent ideology and a formal organisational machinery. Anti-capitalist campaigners cooperate with each other, despite their diverse ideologies, because they generally share the same aims. Ideology takes second place to action.

Klein, in her book *No Logo* (2001), suggests that global capitalism, with its strategy of **global branding** and marketing, is responsible for the alienation fuelling an emerging global anticorporate movement. She identifies five aggressive branding and marketing strategies adopted by global corporations that have resulted in the superficial mass culture that has led to this alienation:

1. *Logo inflation* – The wearing of logos such as the Nike swoosh or FCUK on clothing has become a universal phenomenon.
2. *Sponsorship of cultural events* – Rock festivals are increasingly sponsored by global corporations. Even the visit of Pope John Paul II to the USA in the late 1990s was sponsored by Pepsi.
3. *Sport branding and sponsorship* – Corporations such as Nike and Adidas have attempted to turn sport into a philosophy of perfection by recruiting sports icons such as Michael Jordan and David Beckham to promote their products.

*Designer labels: corporate branding or individual choice?*

4. *The branding of youth culture* – Youth trends such as snow-boarding, hip-hop and skate-boarding have been hijacked by corporations in order to make brands 'cool' and 'alternative'.
5. *The branding of identity politics* – Some corporations, most notably Nike and Benetton, have identified their products with liberal issues that young people are likely to identify and sympathize with, e.g. antiracism.

Klein argues that young people are disillusioned with capitalism. This, she claims, is the result of their increasing realization that what counts as youth identity in modern society is often a product of corporate branding rather than individual choice. Moreover, people are beginning to understand that excessive branding has led to corporate censorship – the elimination and suppression of knowledge that does not support corporate interests – as well as the restriction of real choice, as two or three corporations dominate particular markets. The antiglobalization social movement has also drawn people's attention to how the activities of global corporations in the developing world sustain debt, subsistence wages and child labour. Consequently, people see governments of all political persuasions as colluding with global corporations or as ineffective in the face of corporate global power. Klein argues that what unites all these people as they join a loose network of antiglobalization groups and organizations is their desire for a citizen-centred alternative to the international rule of these global brands and to the power that global corporations have over their lives. Examples of this alternative in action include consumer boycotts of environmentally unfriendly goods and goods produced by child labour or regimes that regularly engage in human-rights abuse. The global anticorporate movement has also provided networks in which high-profile organizations such as Greenpeace and Oxfam have been able to collaborate and exert pressure on governments and transnational companies.

## The social and political significance of NSMs

Faulks (1999) suggests that NSMs have had a significant effect on British politics for several reasons:

- They have mounted a significant challenge to the power of the state.
- They have introduced innovative methods of protest and put new issues on the political agenda, e.g. women's rights, environmental issues, globalization.
- They have helped increase political participation in Europe and the USA among young people who had previously felt alienated by bureaucratic and the increasing similarity of political parties.
- Many of the issues championed by NSMs have been taken up by governments and political parties.
- They have considerably improved sociological understanding of the multifaceted nature of power – in particular, highlighting the ways in which a supposedly neutral state can actually contribute to real inequalities.

However, Faulks does conclude that NSMs have mainly served to highlight the problems of the state rather than significantly diminish its power.

## NSMs – the end of class politics?

There has undoubtedly been a huge surge of interest in NSMs in the past 30 years, but it is a mistake to conclude that this indicates the end of class politics. An examination of the distribution of power, studies of voting behaviour and the activities of pressure groups indicate that class and economic interests still underpin much of the political debate in Britain. It is also important not to exaggerate the degree of support that NSMs enjoy. Most people are aware of such movements but are not actively involved in them. However, conventional political parties and pressure groups can still learn a great deal from such movements, especially their ability to attract the educated, articulate and motivated young.

## Check your understanding

**1** **What are the main differences between defensive NSMs and offensive NSMs?**

**2** **How does a NSM such as feminism differ from a NSM such as Reclaim the Streets?**

**3** **What is the 'Bunde'?**

**4** **What internal organizational characteristics do NSMs generally have in common?**

**5** **What sort of personal characteristics do people who get involved in NSMs generally have?**

**6** **In what ways might membership of NSMs be related to anxieties about postindustrial society?**

**7** **How do Marxists like Marcuse explain the emergence of NSMs?**

**8** **How is the notion of 'increasing reflexivity' related to membership of new social movements?**

**9** **What evidence is there that NSMs have become globalized?**

**10** **How does Callinicos explain how the anti-capitalist movement came about?**

# Activities

## Research idea

Choose an issue, such as vivisection, testing drugs on animals or using animals in testing perfumes, and research one or more of the following:

1. the depth of feeling about the issue in your school or college – find this out either by conducting a brief questionnaire or by asking people in your school or college to sign a petition asking for it to be banned
2. the plans of conventional political parties with regard to the issue
3. what social movements exist in regard to your issue and what tactics are they adopting to bring the issue to public attention?

## Web.task

**www.resist.org.uk/** is the coordinating site for most of the organizations that make up the antiglobalization social movement. Click on their website and go to the 'Links' page. This lists all the organizations/ issues that are affiliated. Choose a sample of organizations and find out their aims and tactics.

# Key terms

**Alienation** an inability to identify with an institution or group to which you might belong.

**Bunde** term used by Hetherington to describe a new form of association made up of vegetarian groups, free-festival goers, dance culture, travellers, and so on.

**Collective behaviour theory** theory concerned with how collective or group behaviours emerge to deal with problematical circumstances and situations.

**Counterculture** a culture that is in opposition to authority.

**Global branding** attempts by global corporations to make their image and products recognizable worldwide.

**Legislative bodies** the state, parliament, the judiciary, i.e. agencies that have the power to make laws.

**Lobbying** a means by which pressure groups and NSMs inform politicians and civil servants of their concerns and/or pass on information that will assist their cause; pressure groups often employ lobbyists to promote their cause in parliament.

**Mass culture** a superficial entertainment culture propagated by the mass media undermining people's capacity for critical thinking.

**New social movements** loosely organized political movements that have emerged since the 1960s, based around particular issues.

**Neo-pluralists** writers who have updated the idea of pluralism.

**Reflexivity** the ability to reflect on your experiences.

**Risk technology** technology that poses dangers to society, such as nuclear power.

**Resource mobilisation theory** approach to social movements that emphasizes that the success of a social movement is dependent on the resources available to them.

**Sustainable development** strategies for modernizing the developing world that result in a fairer distribution of wealth and resources.

## An eye on the exam — The emergence of and participation in new social movements

Provide a detailed description of explanations including concepts, studies and any relevant theories

Weigh up the strengths and weaknesses of sociological explanations in some detail, then present alternative views before reaching a balanced conclusion

**(a)** **Outline and assess sociological explanations of new social movements** **(50 marks)**

There should be a balanced discussion of a range of theoretical explanations

These organisations should be clearly defined, described and illustrated with examples

### Grade booster — Getting top marks in this question

The first part of this essay should clearly define and describe what is meant by a new social movement. Clearly explain and describe how their goals, internal organization, membership and tactics differ from political parties and pressure groups.

The second half of the essay should focus on outlining and evaluating the major theoretical positions on new social movements. Begin with collective behaviour theory and resource mobilisation theory. The theories of the Marxist writers Habermas and Touraine should be explored as well as postmodernists such as Melucci, Crook and Beck. Finish with some reference to Callinicos and Klein and the impact of globalization on the anti-capitalist movement.

# TOPIC 3

# The nature and distribution of political power in society

## Getting you thinking

**Read through the following fictional scenario and then answer the questions that follow.**

**Imagine you are attending a Public Inquiry into whether a new road should be built between the port of Grimsby and the A1. There are two proposed routes. Route A will cost £210 million and will run straight through the only known habitat in the north of England of the rare wide-mouthed frog. It will also involve the blasting of a tunnel through the Lincolnshire Wolds, an area of outstanding natural beauty. Route B will cost £160 million but will run through the greenbelt around the historic city of Lincoln, as well as involve great disruption to traffic in the area while a bypass is especially built to take traffic away from the city centre. Five groups will give evidence to the Inquiry.**

### A Lincoln Chamber of Commerce

We favour Route B. The motorway will bring extra business and trade to the city which is good for our members. Hauliers and builders will especially benefit. In particular, it will increase the tourist trade to the city. The motorway will affect the surrounding countryside but there is plenty of it to enjoy that will not be affected. (Report prepared by John Smith of Smith Road Haulage Ltd and Stephen Brook of Brook Building Quarries Ltd.)

### B Department of the Environment, Food and Rural Affairs

We approve of Route B for cost reasons. It will also attract foreign investors to the area because of the fast road-links to London. It will increase the status of the area and attract commuters in from London who can take advantage of rail links from Lincoln. Employment opportunities will increase, leading to full employment and higher wages. However, the department is also content with Route A because the Ministry of Defence requires a fast road from the Grimsby area to facilitate the efficient movement of nuclear waste in and out of RAF Binbrook. (This information is highly confidential and should not be disclosed to the Inquiry.)

### C Friends of the Earth

We oppose both routes on the grounds that wildlife and the countryside will suffer. We are particularly concerned about the survival of the wide-mouthed frog, which is in danger of extinction across the country. Both roads will be a blot on the landscape. Existing rail services can easily deal with the container traffic from the port of Grimsby.

### D North Lincolnshire Ramblers' Association

We oppose both routes. We are concerned that the natural beauty of the area will be ruined. We are concerned about the danger to children from more traffic, especially in terms of accidents and pollution. There may be an influx of new people into the area. Some of these may be undesirables and bring crime to the area. The value of our properties may fall considerably.

### E National Farmers' Union

We favour Route A. This route involves less damage to the environment compared with Route B. The danger to the wide-mouthed frog is over-estimated. It can be moved to another habitat. The land around Route B currently attracts about £200 million in EU subsidies – the NFU estimates that we would only receive about £70 million from the Ministry of Transport if the land is compulsorily purchased whereas our members would receive approximately £90 million for the less fertile land around Route A.

**1 Look carefully at the five briefs. If you were representing these organizations, what information would you disclose to the Inquiry? What would you hold back and why?**

**2 What does this exercise tell you about the decision-making process?**

The point of this exercise is to demonstrate that decision-making is not a straightforward process. You will have noticed that four of the groups have a vested interest in either one or both routes. Moreover, they probably made decisions not to divulge all of the information they had because it might have prejudiced the Inquiry against them. The Inquiry, then, is basing its conclusions on incomplete information. There are three groups who would benefit enormously whichever road is built. Only one group has nothing to hide. Ironically, this group, Friends of the Earth, is most likely to lose.

What this exercise tells us is that decision-making is not an open process. Rather, there are hidden dimensions to it that we rarely see. It is important to examine the distribution of power if we want to gain insight into the decision-making process in modern societies.

# Pluralism

Robert Dahl (1961) carried out an **empirical** study of decision-making in New Haven, USA, on three contentious issues. He employed a range of methods which he believed would precisely measure the exercise of power. These included:

- looking at changes in the socio-economic background of those who occupied influential political positions in the community
- measuring the nature and extent of the participation of particular socio-economic groups
- determining the influence of particular individuals
- randomly sampling community-based activists and voters
- analyzing changing voting behaviour.

Dahl's research concluded that:

1. Power in modern societies is **diffused** and distributed among a variety of community elites who represent specific interests in fairly unique areas. No one group exerts influence in general.
2. Each group exercises **countervailing** power – that is, each serves as a check on the others thus preventing a monopoly of power.
3. Power is also **situational**, tied to specific issues. If one group does succeed in dominating one area of policy, it will fail to dominate others.
4. All elites are **accountable** because they rely on popular support and must constantly prove they are working in the public interest rather than in their own.

Dahl concludes, therefore, that societies are characterized by democratic **pluralism**. Power is open to all through political parties and pressure groups. No interest group or individual can have too much of it.

## Elite pluralism

Grant (1999) is an elite pluralist, meaning that he accepts that power in the UK is in the hands of **elites** or leaders of pressure groups, political parties and government departments, rather than all members of society having equal access to power. He argues the following:

- Power is widely dispersed between a greater range of pressure groups than ever before.
- Most interest groups in the UK are now represented.
- There now exist multiple arenas in which these pressure groups can influence policy on behalf of their clients, such as Parliament, regional assemblies in Scotland and Wales, the European Union, the mass media and the courts.

As well as lobbying politicians, many of these pressure groups use direct action, such as demonstrations, blockades, advertising, boycotts of consumer goods, internet canvassing and sometimes even violence. Grant acknowledges that some groups have more influence than others, but argues that pressure-group politics is generally a just way of managing the democratic process.

## The role of the state

The function of the state, according to pluralist theory, is to act as a neutral, independent referee or 'honest broker', whose role is to reconcile and accommodate the competing interest groups. Aron (1967) saw the state as in the business of compromise. Resources such as power and capital are primarily in the hands of the state, and its role is to distribute such resources to deserving causes on the basis of public or national interest. The state therefore regulates competing interest groups and operates to ensure that no one group gets its own way all of the time. Aron argued that the state and its servants, such as the civil service, are neutrally serving the needs of all by ensuring that all competing interest groups have some influence on government policy.

## Pluralism: the critique

Dahl was criticized by Newton (1969), who notes that about 50 to 60 per cent of the electorate fail to vote in US presidential elections. It is therefore not enough to assume that inclusion within a community is evidence of sharing in the power process. Newton suggests that Dahl overstates the 'indirect influence' that voters have over leaders for five reasons:

1. Votes are often cast for packages of policies and personnel rather than leaders, and it is extremely difficult for a sociologist to work out what a vote actually stands for. Consider, for example, votes for the Labour Party in the 2005 election. Could the Labour leader, Tony Blair, regard these as support for the Iraq War? Some people voting Labour may have been against the war, but voted the way they did because Labour's other policies – on the economy, poverty, and so on – remained attractive or because they were not attracted to the policies of the other political parties.
2. Indirect influence via the medium of voting assumes voters' interests are similar and that these are clearly communicated to politicians. However, the motives of a stockbroker working in the City of London voting for Labour are going to be different to those of a traditional trade unionist.
3. It is also assumed that voters are represented by selfless politicians. There is a failure to recognize that power

may be wielded in self-interest or on behalf of powerful groups that have little in common with the electorate.

4 The needs of groups such as the poor, the unemployed, the young, single mothers and asylum seekers can be ignored because they lack the economic and cultural power to be heard.

5 The power of elected officials may be severely constrained by permanent officials such as civil servants. Ambitious plans to bring about great social change may be slowed down or watered down because of advice and pressure from those responsible for the day-to-day implementation of such policy. The television comedy series *Yes, Minister* is both a realistic and humorous illustration of this process.

However, in his defence, Dahl did acknowledge that political apathy, alienation, indifference and lack of confidence among the poor and ethnic-minority sections of US society did create obstacles to effective participation in political life.

### *The critique of the pluralist view of the state*

However, the pluralist theory of the state has been criticized by Abercrombie and Warde (2000), who point out that many aspects of the state are secret, which makes it is difficult, if not impossible, to assess whether or not the state is an honest broker. They note that civil servants rarely appear in public to explain or to justify their actions. Judges and senior police officers are generally not accountable for their decisions or actions. The security or intelligence services also largely operate outside the law. They note that the elected parts of the state have little idea of the activities of the security services, or of the scale of their operations.

Moreover, some commentators have become concerned with the concentration of political power in the hands of those who manage the state, i.e. the prime minister and a core of close advisers. Many of the latter are not elected officials or civil servants. Tony Blair was criticized for his 'presidential' approach between 1997 and 2005, when the huge majority Labour enjoyed in parliament allegedly led to Labour MPs merely rubberstamping his executive decisions.

In addition, powerless groups complain that the state ignores or neglects their concerns. Some interest groups representing ethnic minorities have accused the state of **institutional racism**. The immigration laws are the most obvious example, but sociological evidence indicates that institutional racism may be embedded in the everyday practices of the police, the judiciary, the prison service, the NHS – especially the mental-health sector – and in education.

Feminist sociologists, too, argue that the state is patriarchal. State agencies have, until fairly recently, been dominated by male personnel. Feminists argue that state policy is also patriarchal, especially in the fields of family welfare and in its failure to get to serious grips with gender inequalities.

### *Second and third dimensions of power*

Bachrach and Baratz (1970) note that Dahl only looked at what Lukes (1974) calls the 'first dimension of power' – decisions that can be seen and observed. They argue that Dahl neglected the second dimension of power – the ability to prevent issues from coming up for discussion at all. Power, then, is not just about winning situations but confining decision-making to 'safe' issues that do not threaten powerful interests. In short, power may be expressed through '**non-decision-making**'. Bachrach and Baratz note that non-decision-making can work in two ways:

1 The powerful can ignore the demands of the less powerful. If these demands are put on the political agenda, they can effectively be undermined via fruitless discussion in endless committees and public inquiries.

2 Some issues may not be raised simply because opposition is anticipated.

Lukes takes this critique of Dahl further by identifying a third dimension of power. He suggests some groups exercise power by deliberately manipulating or shaping the desires of less powerful social groups so that they are persuaded that the agenda of the powerful is in their interests. As Faulks (1999) notes, this form of power: 'involves thought control and the creation of a "false consciousness" amongst the powerless, who come to identify with and support what may in reality be the exact opposite of their true interests'.

However, Lukes also acknowledges that powerful groups may pursue policies that they genuinely believe will benefit the whole community, but which in the long term actually benefit the interests of the powerful more than others. He argues, therefore, that we need to identify who benefits in the long term from particular decisions. For example, a couple may make a joint decision that the

## Focus on ...

### Pluralism

Abercrombie and Warde (2000) argue that the pluralist view of power in Britain is undermined by four processes:

1 Many interests are not represented by pressure groups and political parties. For example, less than half the workforce is represented by trade unions. Sections of society such as the poor, single mothers, women in general, ethnic minorities and young people lack specific groups that represent their interests in the political arena.

2 Some interests (in particular finance capitalism and employers) are overrepresented in terms of powerful interest groups working on their behalf.

3 Many campaigning groups are undemocratically organized and dominated by self-perpetuating **oligarchies**.

4 There is evidence that key institutions in the UK are run by elites who share similar economic, social and educational backgrounds.

**What is meant by the pluralist view of power?**

female will stay at home to raise the children, but the male may benefit in the long term from this decision in terms of career development, income, influence over decision-making, etc. Lukes argues that this third dimension of power is the most potent type of power because it is rarely questioned or challenged.

A study by Saunders (1979) of two policies in a rural community illustrates Lukes' point about the third dimension of decision-making. The two policies were the preservation of the environment and the maintenance of low rates (a form of property tax). These would appear to be in everybody's interests, but the reality was different:

- Preserving the environment ensured that private housing was scarce and expensive, and council house-building was restricted. Farm labourers were forced into tied housing and therefore dependence upon their employers. No new industry was allowed to develop and this resulted in farmers being able to maintain the low wage levels paid to their employees.
- Low rates meant that little was spent on services that would benefit the poor, such as public transport, welfare and education provision.

However, Lukes' concept of the third dimension of power has been criticized by Hay (1997), because it involves making subjective ethical judgements about how power is being used. Lukes is assuming that power should be equally distributed. Hay argues that such a conception of power would make it impossible to construct and administer any political community, for example the state requires more power than other institutions in order to maintain social order. Moreover, in Lukes' account of power, the uses and consequences of power are interpreted entirely negatively. Hay suggests that these flaws in Lukes' analysis of power indicate that Lukes subscribes to an unrealistic view of human relations.

Hay suggests an alternative model of power which, he argues, has two dimensions.

1. Power involves 'conduct shaping' – in which A directly alters the behaviour of B through coercion or manipulation.
2. Power involves 'context shaping', in which A acts in a way that accidentally and/or indirectly impacts on B's actions. In this sense, moral judgements are removed from the equation of power because we need not blame A for any effect on B because they were never intended. For example, the husband in Lukes' example above, did not intend for his career to benefit from the decision for the couple to have children.

# Elite theory

Classical elite theory stresses that power is concentrated in the hands of an elite – a closed minority group. Pareto (1935) argued that concentration of power is an inevitable fact of life. In any society, power is exercised by the active few, who are supposedly better suited to such a role than the passive masses because they possess more cunning or intelligence, or because they have more organizational ability. Some elite theorists simply suggest that some elites are 'born to rule'.

Pareto saw power as a game of manipulation between two dominant elites who compete with each other for power:

- *the foxes* (who used cunning and guile) – e.g. politicians and diplomats
- *the lions* (who exercise power through force) – e.g. military dictators.

Pareto argued that all states are run by these elites and all forms of government are forms of elite rule. Political change is merely the replacement of one elite by another, as the elite in power becomes either decadent (soft and ineffective) or complacent (set in their ways). In fact, Pareto argues that history is simply a 'circulation of elites'.

Similarly, Mosca (1939) argued that the masses will always be powerless because they don't have the intellectual or moral qualities to organize and run their societies. He suggested that a minority were more cultured, rational, intellectual and morally superior compared with the masses and were more suited to rule over them. He argued that elections are merely mechanisms by which members of this elite have themselves elected by the masses. Mosca believed in government *for* the people, and dismissed the idea that government could ever be government *by* the people. Mannheim (1960) agreed, but went further, arguing that democracy could not work because the masses were 'irrational'. 'Cultured' and 'rational' elites, he claimed, were essential to maintain civilization.

Some critics have suggested that this is a very simplistic view of power and politics because real differences between governments are dismissed. Both socialism and democracy are seen to conceal elites. However, no criteria are provided by which we can measure the so-called superior qualities of elites. It is merely assumed that the masses are inferior and that the elite is superior.

## C. Wright Mills: the power elite

The American sociologist C. Wright Mills (1956) regarded the USA as a society characterized by elite rule. He argued that three key elites monopolize power in modern societies like the USA:

1. the economic or business elite, symbolized by the growth of giant corporations controlling the economy
2. the political elite, which controls both political parties and federal and state governments
3. the military elite.

Mills argued that the activities of each elite were interconnected to form a single ruling minority or 'power elite' dominating decision-making in the USA. The cohesiveness of this group is strengthened by their similarity of social background, i.e. White, male, Protestant, urban and sharing the same educational and social-class background. Moreover, there is interchange and overlap between these elites, in that company directors sit on government advisory committees, retired generals chair business corporations, and so on. Such unity, argues Mills, means that power elites run Western societies in their own

# Focus on research

## Hywel Williams
### Power elites in the UK

Williams (2006) is very influenced by C. Wright Mills' concept of the power elite. He identifies three groups of elites in the UK – the political elite, the professional elite and the financial/business elite – and argues they constitute a UK power elite.

Williams argues that democracy in the UK is largely illusory because the ideological differences between political leaders have virtually disappeared and government ministers have tenuous control over an increasingly globalized free market economy. However, he notes that the political elite are 'conduits of power' in that, through mechanisms such as patronage, they are able to appoint members of the professional and financial/business elites to positions of power and influence in government organizations. Moreover, financial/business elites repay this debt by appointing politicians and ex-civil servants to the boards of their companies.

Williams argues that the financial/business elite is the most influential part of the power elite and the political elite often defers to them. In particular, financiers in the City of London shape the economic decisions of governments because their vast wealth is the foundation stone of the British economy and the political elite dare not risk this financial elite moving this wealth abroad.

Williams points out that the power elite has flourished because other sources of power, such as the Church and trade unions, have declined. These may have once acted as a check on the power elite. Williams notes too that the power elite has been successful in manipulating the language of national interest in order to convince society that they are working in all our interests.

*Source:* Williams, H. (2006) *Britain's Power Elites*, London: Constable

**1** **What sorts of groups do you think make up Williams' professional elite?**

**2** **In your opinion, what has been the effect of the worldwide banking crisis on the power elite, and especially their argument that everything they do is in the public or national interest?**

interests; the bulk of the population is manipulated by the elite through their control of education and, particularly, the newspaper and television news media.

Moore (2001, 2003) and Phillips (2004) have both documented the 'special relationship' between what Phillips calls the 'American dynasty' of the Bush family, the American political **establishment**, economic corporations such as Haliburton and Enron, military incursions in both Afghanistan and Iraq, and an uncritical mass media, especially symbolized by Fox-News. Both authors generally agree that the power elite dominates American politics today and the brand of 'crony capitalism' that it attempts to impose on the rest of the world is alienating vast sections of the world's population, particularly in the Islamic world. Moore's film *Fahrenheit 9/11* is a particularly interesting critique of this power elite.

# Marxism and the distribution of power

Marxists believe that elites constitute a ruling class whose major aim is the preservation of capitalist interests. Marxists argue that exploitation of the working class has led to the concentration of wealth in the hands of the few. For example, in the UK, the wealthiest 1 per cent of the population own about 22 per cent of total wealth, and the wealthiest 10 per cent own 56 per cent of all wealth – mainly in the form of company shares (Inland Revenue 2004). This economic elite is united by common characteristics, such as inherited wealth and **public school** and **Oxbridge** connections. Marxists argue that the class structure is of central significance because those who own what Abercrombie and Warde (2000) call 'property for power' – the means of production such as **finance capital**, land, technology and factories – are able to exert power over everyone else.

## Direct and indirect rule

Miliband (1970) argued that the capitalist class rules both directly and indirectly in the UK:

- *Direct rule* – The capitalist class rules directly by forming Conservative governments. Miliband argued that direct and open rule by the ruling class is common in history, as is their willingness to confront working-class dissent and protest.
- *Indirect rule* – The ruling class also rule indirectly by occupying powerful positions in the **civil service** and **judiciary**. The upper levels of the civil service (responsible for advice and policy) are mainly drawn from the same background as the economic elite. Like other members of this elite, their outlook tends to be conservative and suspicious of change.

Miliband argued that the groups that constitute the political elite (i.e. members of the government, politicians in general, top civil servants, judges and so on) and the economic elite share similar educational backgrounds. Research by the Sutton Trust (2005) reported that 59 per cent of Conservative MPs had attended private schools compared with 18 per cent of Labour MPs. Most importantly, those MPs holding political offices were more likely to have been to public school (42 per cent) compared with MPs on the backbenches (29 per cent), and are also more likely to have attended Oxbridge (34 per cent compared to 24 per cent). In particular, Labour MPs who serve as members of the government are more likely to have been to private school (25 per cent) than Labour backbenchers (16 per cent), and are more likely to have been to Oxbridge (23 per cent compared to 15 per cent). Sixty-two per cent of officeholders within the Conservative opposition were from independent schools, and 46 per cent were Oxbridge graduates. No less than 14 Conservative frontbench spokesmen were educated at one school: Eton. In the past 18 years, the proportion of privately educated high court judges has barely shifted: in 1989, it was 74 per cent; in 2007, it was 70 per cent (see Table 5.2). Moreover, of the 10 most senior staff in each armed service, nine out of 10 Army officers, six out of 10 Royal Navy officers, and three out of 10 Royal Air Force officers were educated in independent schools.

Miliband notes this political elite often have family connections and are members of the same London clubs. Moreover, elite members often 'swap' roles. For example, top civil servants on retiring often take up directorships in business, whilst prominent businessmen often appear on government committees. He therefore argues that they are similar enough to constitute a ruling class.

### *Economic power and ideological power*

Marxists also suggest that economic power results in ideological power. The ruling class exerts influence over the ideas transmitted through a range of social institutions. Miliband, for example, focused on the role of the media in promoting the view that the national interest is best served by capitalist interests. This can be seen in advertising campaigns that promote companies such as BP as symbolizing 'security, reliability and integrity'. Television programmes and tabloid newspapers reinforce capitalist values by encouraging people to see the way to fulfilment as being through the acquisition of material goods. Such ideological power leads to hegemony or cultural domination. People accept that the culture of capitalism (based on consumerism, materialism and individualism) is good for them and so consent to power being held by the capitalist class or its representatives, who are seen to manage the economy effectively and thus maintain their standard of living.

## Divisions within the capitalist class

Miliband argued that the ruling class rules but does not necessarily govern – instead it rules the government by the fact of common background and hence class interest. If we examine the statistical evidence in regard to social and educational backgrounds, it does seem to support Miliband's argument that those in elite occupations do share characteristics and there is considerable overlap between these groups. Scott (1991) refers to this overlap




## Focus on research

### The Sutton Trust: Educational backgrounds of UK's leading people

**Table 5.2** Percentages of 500 leading people educated in the UK at different types of schools

| | Year | %Ind. | %State | %State selective | %State comp |
|---|---|---|---|---|---|
| Judges | 2007 | **70** | **30** | 28 | 2 |
| | 1989 | **74** | **26** | 20 | 6 |
| Politicians | 2007 | **38** | **62** | 27 | 36 |
| | 1974 | **46** | **54** | 32 | 22 |
| Journalists | 2006 | **54** | **46** | 33 | 14 |
| | 1986 | **49** | **51** | 44 | 6 |
| Medics | 2007 | **51** | **49** | 32 | 17 |
| | 1987 | **51** | **49** | 32 | 17 |
| Chair/CEO of companies, banks, etc. | 2007 | **54** | **46** | 26 | 20 |
| | 1987 | **70** | **30** | 20 | 10 |
| TOTALS | Now | **53** | **47** | 29 | 17 |
| | Then | **58** | **42** | 30 | 12 |

Source: Sutton Trust (2007

**Table 5.3** Percentages of 500 leading people who have been to university in the UK educated at Oxbridge

| | Year | %Oxbridge | | Year |
|---|---|---|---|---|
| Judges | 2007 | **78** | **87** | 1989 |
| Politicians | 2007 | **42** | **62** | 1974 |
| Journalists | 2006 | **56** | **67** | 1986 |
| Medics | 2007 | **15** | **28** | 1987 |
| Chair/CEO of companies, banks, etc. | 2007 | **39** | **67** | 1987 |
| TOTALS | Now | **47** | **61** | Then |

Source: Sutton Trust (2007)

1. **Which occupations have experienced the most increase in the percentage of state-educated leaders?**
2. **How might the trends between 1987 and 2007 support the Marxist contention that there exists a unified capitalist elite which pursues the same interests?**
3. **Why might critics of the Marxist position be sceptical?**

as 'the establishment' and claims it monopolizes the major positions of power and influence.

However, in criticism of this Marxist argument, other sociologists have pointed out that government economic policy has generally failed to benefit those groups who dominate capitalism. Some actually suggest that the economic elite is characterized by conflict and division. Scott points out that the interests of industrialists may be different from those of finance capital. He notes the existence of 'power blocs' within the capitalist class which form alliances to promote their interests. He notes how different power blocs dominate the political and economic decision-making process at different points in history in Britain. For example, **manufacturing capital** was dominant in the 1950s, while in the 1980s and 1990s, finance capital (i.e. the City) was dominant. It could be argued that power today is dominated by transnational companies and currency speculators, as economies become increasingly globalized. However, Marxists argue that it does not matter which power bloc dominates, the overlap between them guarantees that capitalist interests are generally promoted before the interests of the rest of society.

## Poulantzas: power and the capitalist system

Poulantzas (1973) suggested that the common social background of the ruling class is less important than the nature of capitalism itself. It does not matter whether elite groups rule directly or indirectly because the ruling class will always benefit as long as capitalism exists. Most governments across the world, whether on the right or left of the political spectrum, accept that management of their economies involves the management of capitalism in such a way that they do not lose the confidence of international investors or The Stock Exchange. Moreover, legislation in favour of subordinate groups, such as pro-trade union or health and safety laws, benefit the capitalist class in the long term because it results in a healthy, fit and possibly more productive workforce.

Poulantzas argued that the capitalist class will always ultimately benefit unless the whole system is dismantled. The capitalist class does not have to interfere directly in decision-making – the fact that the decision-making process is happening within a capitalist framework will always benefit it.

The observations of Abercrombie and Warde (2000) support Poulantzas' argument. They note that no elected government in Britain has ever attempted to abolish or even modify the capitalist economy. In general, British economic policy has been mainly devoted to protecting capitalism by maintaining the strength and value of the pound sterling. No government has seriously tried to reorganize industry so that companies are managed by their workers. There has been little attempt by British governments to extend the welfare state so that it provides adequate provision for everyone from the cradle to the grave. Finally, no government has ever seriously threatened the dominance of the public school system in providing access to top jobs.

The work of Westergaard (1995) suggests that the state, even when managed by Labour governments, has done very little to challenge the inequality inherent in modern capitalist Britain. Economic inequalities, in terms of the distribution of income and wealth, continue to persist, whilst health inequalities have actually widened in recent years. For example, the incomes of the richest 1 per cent have risen sharply since 1997; the wealthiest 10 per cent of the population now own 56 per cent of the UK's wealth; and the gap in life expectancy between the bottom fifth and the general population has widened by seven to eight years. From a Marxist perspective, these are indications that state social policy is generally benefiting the bourgeoisie. As Hastings (2005) notes:

> << *Until the 20th century, disease was no respecter of purses. The wife of a Victorian financial colossus was almost as vulnerable to the perils of childbirth as a maid in his household. The tombstones of the great reveal how many died before their natural spans were exhausted. Today, medical science can do many extraordinary things for people able to pay. There has never been a wider gulf between the remedies available to the rich and those on offer to most of the poor, even in societies with advanced public healthcare systems.*>>

# Conclusion: pluralism or elitism?

### *Evaluating Marxism*

Despite differences of interpretation, all Marxist positions agree that the state serves the interests of the dominant class. However, this is a difficult assertion to prove. We can see economic and social connections between the political elite and members of the economic elite, but this does not necessarily mean that they are using the mechanisms of the state to advance ruling-class interests.

Concepts such as 'ideology' and 'hegemony' are difficult to operationalize and to use as a means of measuring degrees of power. It is also unlikely that hegemony is experienced universally. Over the past 30 years, the state has consistently faced opposition in the form of urban riots by the powerless, strikes, new social movements and terrorism, and it has been forced to use coercion and force on a number of occasions.

The view that the British state is an instrument of the capitalist class can also be criticized because a great deal of economic policy has been unsuccessful. The state has been unable to prevent events such as stock market and banking crashes, devaluation of sterling and the decline of heavy industry and manufacturing. If the state is an agent of the ruling class, its success is far from complete.

The overall evidence seems to support the view that elites dominate decision-making in both Britain and the USA. There is no doubt that these elites share some elements of a common social background and culture. However, this is not the same as suggesting that these elites constitute a unified ruling class working to promote its own economic and political interests. At best, the evidence for this is speculative.

# Key terms

**Accountable** those in power can be held responsible for their decisions and actions.

**Civil service** paid officials who work in government.

**Countervailing power** an alternative source of power that acts as a balance to the prevailing power source.

**Diffused** spread widely.

**Elite** small, closed, dominant group.

**Empirical** based on first-hand research.

**Establishment** informal network of the powerful, linked by shared social, economic and educational backgrounds.

**Finance capital** financial investment institutions.

**Judiciary** judges.

**Manufacturing capital** businesses that make products.

**Non-decision-making** the power to prevent some issues from being discussed.

**Oligarchy** control by a small elite.

**Oxbridge** the universities of Oxford and Cambridge.

**Pluralism** the theory that power is shared amongst a range of different groups in society.

**Public school** the top private, fee-paying schools, e.g. Eton, Harrow, Roedean.

**Situational** holders of power vary from issue to issue, no one individual or group is dominant.

# Check your understanding

1. **What does Dahl mean when he says that power is diffused?**
2. **What does Lukes identify as the three dimensions of power?**
3. **What is the most potent type of power, according to Lukes?**
4. **Outline the contribution of 'foxes' and 'lions' to our understanding of power.**
5. **What is the power elite?**
6. **In what ways does a ruling class rule both directly and indirectly according to Miliband?**
7. **How does the term 'the establishment' assist an understanding of the distribution of power?**
8. **Why are the common social backgrounds of elites not that important, according to Poulantzas?**

# Activities

## Research idea

Interview a small sample of teachers about the distribution of power at your school or college. You could ask them to explain one or two recent decisions and how they were taken. To what extent does the evidence you have collected support pluralist or elite theories?

## Web.task

Find out the names of the politicians who make up the Cabinet and Shadow Cabinet. Examine the biographical data available on some of these people by looking at their websites. Investigate the educational and occupational backgrounds of the elite to see whether they share any common ground.

## An eye on the exam

## Defining and exploring power and political action in society

Provide a detailed description of the view including concepts, studies and any relevant theories

Weigh up the strengths and weaknesses of the view in some detail, then present alternative views before reaching a balanced conclusion

**(a)** **Outline and assess the view that power in the UK is concentrated in the hands of a ruling elite. (50 marks)**

Be aware that there are different dimensions of power.

Two theories – elite theory and Marxist theories – argue from this position.

### Grade booster

**Getting top marks in this question**

The idea that power is concentrated in the hands of a ruling elite is held by several sociologists. However, they often do not share the same ideological position so you need to be careful to distinguish between them. Begin with elite theory and the work of Pareto, Mosca and Mannheim before moving on to describe the power elite ideas of C. Wright Mills and Williams. Marxists also argue that there is a ruling elite – the ruling or capitalist class. Note that there are two Marxist positions on the distribution of power. The instrumental Marxist position of Miliband suggests that the capitalist class rules both directly and indirectly in the UK – illustrate these ideas with reference to empirical evidence, e.g. studies of the social and educational backgrounds of those who occupy top jobs. You should contrast this approach with the hegemonic Marxist approach of Poulantzas which suggests that ruling elites do not necessarily need a concentration of power to rule because the continued existence of capitalism (whoever runs it) with benefit them.

# Exam Practice

**Outline and assess the usefulness of elite theory in understanding the distribution of power in modern Britain** ***(50 marks)***

The distribution of power is a concept which is important across modern Britain, as it impacts on all members of society. It is mainly operationalised in terms of who has control, economically and politically. Elite theorists believe that power is concentrated in the hands of an elite who are a closed minority group who dominate control of modern Britain.

The candidate has rightly decided to begin this essay by defining the concepts in the title. Introductions should always focus on setting the scene in this way. The explanation of the distribution of power isn't very successful but the concept of elite is reasonably well defined.

One elite theorist is Pareto, who believes that this powerful minority is inevitable and that those who rule do so because of their superior skills or intelligence. He believes that power is a game of manipulation between two dominant elites who are competing against one another. He describes these as the 'foxes' and the 'lions'. The foxes are so named due to their cunning and guile and are mainly politicians and diplomats whereas the lions take their power through force and are mainly military dictators. Pareto believes that all types of government are forms of elite rule and that even political change is just a replacement of one elite with another. Political history is just a 'circulation of elites'.

The candidate demonstrates excellent knowledge and understanding of Pareto's ideas in this paragraph. The knowledge is detailed and deals with the concepts of 'foxes' and 'lions' in an articulate and confident fashion.

Another elite theorist is Mosca. He believes that masses will never be in control as they lack the intellectual and moral qualities to organize and run their societies. It is his belief that the minority rule because they are superior in a multitude of ways, including culturally, rationally, intellectually and morally and these qualities are needed to rule. He believes in a government for the people, rather than a government of the people. However this theory has been dismissed for being simplistic by ignoring the differences between governments. It is also criticized for not giving specific criteria to measure these 'superior qualities' that the elite are supposed to hold and instead it is just assumed that these qualities exist.

The candidate's knowledge and understanding of Mosca's ideas are excellent. The evaluation is welcome but it is a little vague. It is unclear what is meant by 'differences between governments'.

Wright Mills believed that the USA was characterised by elite rule. He found three key elites, similar to those found by Pareto, who controlled power in modern societies which were; the economic elite who were in charge of the huge corporations who control the economy, the political elite who controlled all aspects of the government and the military elite. These were all interconnected to form a single ruling minority, which he called the 'power elite'. Part of the reason these are so strong is their shared social background as they were most likely to come from the same class and have been similarly educated, as well as being male and white. The fact that they three groups' roles often overlapped only increase their unity. Wright Mills believed that this power elite control the majority of the population through the mass media and education.

This is another strong detailed paragraph with regard to knowledge and understanding. The candidate summarises the theory intelligently and succinctly and confidently deals with the concept of 'power elite'. However, the candidate needs to apply these ideas to modern Britain.

# Exam Practice

However not all sociologists believe that the elite works for the good of the majority and are superior to that majority. Marxists also believe in a ruling-class minority, but believe these are working to preserve capitalist interests and exploit the working class in order to concentrate wealth in their own hands. In modern Britain the wealthiest 10% of the population own 56% of wealth, mainly through company shares. They believe this ruling minority to be united by common characteristics such as their inherited wealth and public schooling. They also argue that the wealthiest members of society have the control and therefore hold power over everyone else.

This is a very good introduction to Marxism and shows that the candidate understands these ideas. However it would have benefitted from some contextualisation: there is a need to describe how capitalism is organised according to Marxism and some explanation as to why the ruling class is so concerned to protect its interests.

One Marxist is Miliband, who wrote about how the capitalist class rule both directly and indirectly in the UK. He states that they rule directly via forming Conservative governments and argued that this direct open rule has existed throughout history. However he also believes that the ruling class occupy powerful positions in the civil service and judiciary, allowing them to rule indirectly. The upper levels of these jobs have often been drawn from the same background of the ruling minority and so support them in their decisions. Marxists believe that, rather than having the interests of the entire population of modern Britain in mind, the ruling class only work to support their own interests.

This is an excellent summary of Miliband's ideas and consequently demonstrates a very good level of knowledge and understanding.

Pluralists also do not believe in the elite theory of the distribution of power, but look at it in a different way from Marxists. One significant pluralist was Dahl who carried out a study of decision making in New Haven, USA on three particular issues. He used a range of methods to measure the exercise of power including looking at changes in the socio-economic background of those who occupied powerful political positions in the community, investigating the nature and extent of participation of particular socio-economic groups, understanding the influence of individuals and analyzing changes in voting behaviour. He found power to be distributed among a variety of community elites who represented specific interests in unique areas with no one particular person exerting excessive influence. Each group seemed to make sure that power was spread out in order for no one person to control all power and as they relied on public support it was important for them to prove they were working in the public interest.

This is again a very detailed and accurate summary of Dahl's ideas and shows a strong level of knowledge and understanding. However, the candidate seems to have lost sight of the need to focus on modern Britain.

Elite theory does offer an influential view of how power is distributed in modern Britain. However all of these theorists can be described as leaning too strongly in one direction. Elite pluralism combines elite theory and pluralism and believes that, whilst power is concentrated in the hands of pressure groups, political parties and government departments, the multitude of these means that most interest groups in the UK are now represented and there are a multitude of places where pressure groups can influence policy on behalf of their clients. They accept that not everyone has equal access to power, but believe everyone can express their views. Therefore elite pluralism could be a more useful way of understanding the distribution of power than only using elite theory.

The candidate finally acknowledges 'modern Britain'. This paragraph demonstrates a good knowledge and understanding of theory and concepts but it was a shame that the ideas were not applied using specifically British examples of pressure groups, political parties, government departments etc.

33/50

## An examiner comments

This candidate has a very good level of knowledge and understanding relating to this debate. It is obvious that they understand the theoretical positions and are capable of interpreting and applying quite complex concepts. However, it is only in the final paragraph that the reference to modern Britain in the essay title is acknowledged. There also needs to be far more empirical evidence in the answer. Moreover, apart from a couple of brief references to Mosca, there is no specific evaluation – this skill is mainly confined to juxtaposition. The candidate therefore was awarded 17 marks for knowledge and understanding, 7 marks for interpretation and application and 9 for evaluation.

# CHAPTER 6

# Social inequality and difference


TOPIC 1 Introduction: Defining and measuring social class **238**

TOPIC 2 Theories of inequality and stratification **245**

TOPIC 3 Life-chances and social class **253**

TOPIC 4 Changes in the class structure **262**

TOPIC 5 Gender and stratification **270**

TOPIC 6 Ethnicity and stratification **280**

TOPIC 7 Age and stratification **291**

Exam practice **299**


| OCR specification | | | Coverage |
|---|---|---|---|
| Patterns and trends of inequality and difference related to: | • social class<br>• gender | • ethnicity<br>• age | Social class inequalities covered in Topic 3, gender inequalities in Topic 5, ethnic inequalities in Topic 6 and age inequalities in Topic 7. |
| Theoretical explanations of the patterns and trends: | • functionalist<br>• Marxist<br>• Neo-Marxist | • feminist<br>• Weberian<br>• postmodern views | Explanations of social class inequality covered in Topic 2, gender inequalities in Topic 5, ethnic inequalities in Topic 6 and age inequalities in Topic 7. |
| Sociological explanations of the changing class structure | | | Covered in Topic 4 with definitions and measurements in Topic 1. |
| Explanations for inequality through the intersection of: | • class<br>• gender | • ethnicity<br>• age | Covered in Topics 2, 5, 6 and 7. |

# TOPIC 1

# Introduction: defining and measuring social class

## Getting you thinking

1 Look at the photo on the right. All these children enjoy equal access to education, but does this mean that they will enjoy similar lifestyles when adults?

2 What social factors may create barriers for them?

3 Look at the two photographs below. What ways of measuring class do they indicate?

4 How do the photographs below relate to the criteria listed in the table?

5 Which of the criteria suggested in the table would you use to judge a person's social class and why?

When a random group of respondents were asked to identify the criteria they would use to assess a person's class, the results were as shown in the table below (figures are %).

| | |
|---|---|
| Neighbourhood | 36 |
| How they talk | 17 |
| Job | 31 |
| What they wear | 15 |
| Pay | 29 |
| Parental background | 13 |
| Educational background | 27 |
| Use of leisure time | 11 |
| Wealth (assets such as property and **material** goods) | 22 |
| Political party support | 11 |

Adapted from Hadford, G. and Skipworth, M. (1994) *Class*, London: Bloomsbury, p.19

It is generally believed that modern societies provide their citizens with the opportunities to better themselves. We all enjoy access to education and the chance to obtain formal qualifications; we all have access to a job market that offers decent incomes and promotion opportunities; we all enjoy the possibility of acquiring wealth. Or do we? The exercise above suggests that these opportunities may not exist for all social groups, or if they do, that some social groups have greater or easier access to these opportunities. In other words, inequalities between social groups are a fact of life in modern societies. The job of sociologists working in the field of stratification is to identify which social groups enjoy unfettered access to economic and social opportunities, and which are denied them, and why.

# Differentiation and stratification

All societies **differentiate** between social groups – men and women, the young and the old, the working class and the middle class, and ethnic groups such as Whites, Asians and African-Caribbeans are often perceived to be socially different in some way. When these differences lead to greater status, power or privilege for some over others, the result is **social stratification**. This term – borrowed from geology – means the layering of society into strata, from which a hierarchy emerges reflecting different ranks in terms of social influence and advantage. The degree to which a society has a fixed hierarchy is determined by the degree of opportunity its members have to improve their social position.

The sociological term for a person's social importance is **social status**. Status can be gained in two ways:

- **Ascribed status** is given at birth either through family (e.g. the Queen inherited her right to rule over the UK) or through physical, religious or cultural factors (e.g. in some societies, women and girls are regarded as second-class citizens simply because they are female) – see Table 6.1 below.
- **Achieved status** is the result of factors such as hard work, educational success, marriage, special talent or sheer good fortune (e.g. winning the lottery).

Societies that allow for and reward achievement are called **open societies**, whereas those that ascribe social position are known as **closed societies**. Politicians tend to see the degree of openness in society as a measure of the freedoms they have helped to create, but they often overemphasize the extent to which society is open. Modern Britain, for example, may have free education for all up to the age of 18 or 19, but, as we shall see in Topic 3, those who are rich enough to attend a top public school generally enjoy greater advantages in life.

In reality, few societies are totally open or closed and each could be placed somewhere along a continuum (see Fig. 6.1). Traditional societies tend to be more closed because of the greater influence of religion and tradition, which means that people can only play a limited range of roles and these tend to be fixed at birth. Modern societies, which seem more fluid and open, may actually experience significant levels of closure, in that some groups face social barriers and obstacles when attempting to improve themselves, e.g. racism and sexism.

**Figure 6.1** Open or closed: the continuum of social status

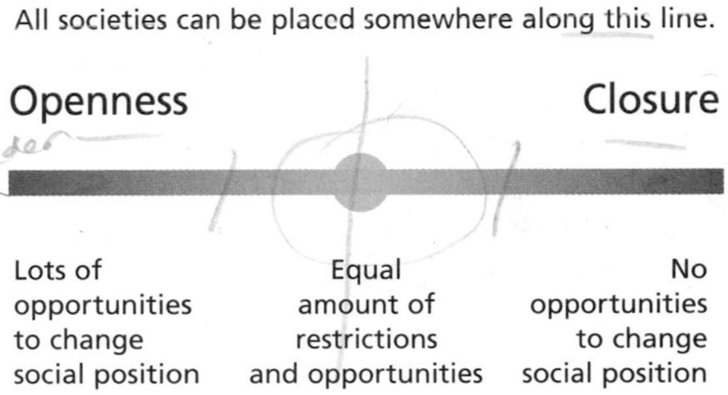


**Table 6.1** Examples of traditional societies based on ascribed status

| | The caste system | The feudal estate system |
|---|---|---|
| **Place and time** | Although officially banned in India today, the Hindu **caste system** of stratification is still enormously influential. | The **feudal estate system** was found in medieval Europe. |
| **Structure** | There are four basic castes or layers, ranging from the Brahmins (religious leaders and nobles) at the top, to the Sudras (servants and unskilled manual workers) at the bottom. 'Untouchables' exist below the caste system and are responsible for the least desirable jobs, such as sewage collection. | The king owned all the land and, in return for an oath of loyalty and military support, he would allocate the land to barons who, in turn, would apportion parts of it to knights. The majority (95%) were peasants or serfs who had to work the knight's land and, in return, were offered protection and allowed to rent land. |
| **Restrictions** | People are born into castes and cannot move out of them during the course of their lives. There are strong religious controls over the behaviour of caste members – for example, you cannot marry a member of another caste, nor can you do certain jobs because these are assigned exclusively to certain castes. | Feudal societies, too, were mainly closed societies – people's positions were largely ascribed and it was rare for people to move up. Marriage between groups was rarely allowed and feudal barons even restricted the geographical movement of the peasants. |
| **Possibility of social mobility** | The system is based upon religious purity – the only way people can be promoted to a higher caste is by living a pure life and hoping that they will be reincarnated (reborn) as a member of a higher caste. | On rare occasions, exceptional acts of bravery could result in a gift of land. |

# Social class

Social class is the stratification system found in modern industrial societies such as Britain. **Social classes** are groups of people who share a similar economic position in terms of occupation, income and ownership of wealth. They are also likely to have similar levels of education, status and power. Class systems are different from previous systems in the following ways:

- They are not based on religion, law or race, but on economic factors such as occupation and wealth.
- There is no clear distinction between classes – it is difficult to say where the working class finishes and the middle class begins, for example.
- All members of society have equal rights irrespective of their social position.
- There are no legal restrictions on marriage between the classes.
- Social-class societies are generally open societies – you can move up or down the class structure through jobs, the acquisition of wealth or marriage.
- Such systems are usually **meritocratic** – that is, people are not born into ascribed roles. Individuals are encouraged to better themselves through achievement at school and in their jobs, by working hard and gaining promotion.

Just how meritocratic social-class societies really are, and the extent to which factors such as race, gender and age can affect access to opportunity, will be a key focus of this chapter.

## Measuring social class

Question 3 in the 'Getting you thinking' activity should have shown that measuring social class is not an easy exercise. People define social class in different ways and some even deny its existence altogether.

### *Why is there a need to measure class?*

Various groups, such as sociologists, advertisers and government agencies, have vested interests in **operationalizing** and measuring the concept of social class in a consistent way for a number of reasons:

- Sociologists want to address class differences in all areas of social life in order to identify reasons why inequalities come about.
- Advertisers want to target particular social groups in order to maximize sales.
- Governments need to formulate social policies in order to address inequalities and future trends.

Each interest group has tended to operationalize the concept of social class in a different way. For example, governments and sociologists tend to approach social class as an objective reality that results in observable patterns of behaviour and inequality in areas such as health, life expectancy and education. Advertisers are more interested in how people subjectively interpret their class position, because this may affect their consumption patterns and their leisure pursuits.

### *Occupation as an indicator of social class*

The single most objective measurable factor that corresponds best with social class is occupation. It is something that the majority of the population has in common. It also governs other aspects of their life, such as income, housing and level of education. Occupation, therefore:

- shapes a significant proportion of a person's life
- is a good indicator of income and consequently wealth and lifestyle
- is a good indicator of similar educational (i.e. skill and knowledge) levels
- is an important influence on a person's sense of identity.

However, this approach to social class still leaves out those who do not work, such as the extremely rich and the long-term unemployed. While such objective measures using occupation have enabled social class to be measured statistically, getting such measures right has proved to be more of a problem. The various occupational scales that have been constructed have all been criticized for failing to present a true picture of the class structure.

# Scales of social class

## The Registrar General's scale

This occupational scale was used by the government from 1911 until 2000 and involved the ranking of thousands of jobs into six classes based on the occupational skill of the head of household:

- Class I: Professional, e.g. accountants, doctors
- Class II: Lower managerial, professional and technical, e.g. teachers
- Class IIINM: Skilled non-manual, e.g. office workers
- Class IIIM: Skilled manual, e.g. electricians, plumbers
- Class IV: Semi-skilled manual, e.g. agricultural workers
- Class V: Unskilled manual, e.g. labourers, refuse collectors.

This scheme differentiated between middle-class occupations (non-manual jobs were allocated to classes I to IIINM) and working-class occupations (manual jobs were allocated to classes IIIM to V). The Registrar General's scheme has underpinned many important social surveys and sociological studies, particularly those focusing on class differences in educational achievement and life expectancy.

### *Criticisms of the Registrar General's scale*

The Registrar General's scale was the main way in which class was measured in official statistics. Most sociological research conducted between 1960 and 2000 uses this classification system when differentiating between different classes. However, it does have disadvantages:

- Assessments of jobs were made by the Registrar General's own staff – hence, there was a bias towards seeing non-manual occupations as having a higher status than manual occupations. However, as we shall see later in this chapter, Marxists argue that the working conditions of some white-collar workers, particular those found in workplaces such as call-centres, is remarkably similar to that of manual workers employed in factories.

- It failed to recognize those people who do not work – the unemployed were classified according to their last job. However, the number of never-employed unemployed has dramatically increased and undermined the idea that jobs underpin social class.
- Feminists criticized the scale as sexist – the class of everyone in a household was defined by the job of the male head of household. Women were assigned to the class of their husbands (or their fathers, if unmarried).
- It glossed over the fact that workers allocated to the same class often had widely varying access to resources such as pay and promotion.
- It failed to distinguish between the employed and self-employed – this distinction is important because evidence shows that these groups do not share similar experiences. For example the **black economy** is much more accessible to the self-employed – they can avoid paying tax and VAT by working at a cheaper rate 'for cash', which cannot be traced through their accounts, or by not fully declaring all the work they do.

**Table 6.2 The Hope-Goldthorpe Scale**

| | |
|---|---|
| **Service class** | |
| 1 | Higher professionals<br>High-grade administrators; managers of large companies and large proprietors |
| 2 | Lower professionals<br>Higher-grade technicians; supervisors of non-manual workers; administrators; small-business managers |
| **Intermediate class** | |
| 3 | Routine non-manual (clerical and sales) |
| 4 | Small proprietors and self-employed artisans (craftspersons) |
| 5 | Lower-grade technicians and supervisors of manual workers |
| **Working class** | |
| 6 | Skilled manual workers |
| 7 | Semi-skilled and unskilled manual workers |

Source: Goldthorpe, J.H. (1980) *Social Mobility and Class Structure in Modern Britain*, Oxford: Clarendon Press

## The Hope-Goldthorpe scale

Sociologists were often reluctant to use government-inspired scales as they lacked sufficient sociological emphasis. John Goldthorpe created a more sociologically relevant scale that has proved very popular with social researchers. Goldthorpe recognized the growth of middle-class occupations – and especially the self-employed – and based his classification on the concept of **market position**, i.e. income and economic **life-chances**, such as promotion prospects, sick pay and control of hours worked. He also took account of **work** or **employment relations**, i.e. whether people are employed or self-employed, and whether they are able to exercise authority over others. The Hope-Goldthorpe scale also acknowledged that both manual and non-manual groups may share similar experiences of work and, for this reason, Goldthorpe grouped some of these together in an **intermediate class**. Instead of the basic non-manual/manual divide used by the Registrar General's scale, Goldthorpe introduced the idea of three main social divisions into which groups sharing similar market position and work relations could be placed: he referred to these as the **service class**, the intermediate class and the working class (see Table 6.2).

Goldthorpe's scale was first used in studies conducted in 1972, published in 1980. The scale more accurately reflected the nature of the British class system, but it was still based on the male head of household. He defended this position by claiming that, in most cases, the male worker still determines the market situation and lifestyle of a couple, i.e. the male is still the main breadwinner. However, many feminists remained unconvinced by this argument. They argued that scales based on the idea of a male 'head of household':

- overlook the significance of dual-career families, where the joint income of both partners can give the family an income and lifestyle of a higher class
- ignore situations where women are in a higher-grade occupation than their husbands
- overlook the significance of the increasing number of single working women and single working parents, who were classified by Goldthorpe according to the occupation of their ex-partners or fathers.

## A feminist alternative: the Surrey Occupational Class Schema

This scale was developed by the feminist sociologists Arber, Dale and Gilbert (1986) in an attempt to overcome what they saw as the **patriarchal** bias inherent in the Hope-Goldthorpe scale. In this scheme, women are classified on the basis of their own occupations, whether they are married or not. The gendered nature of work in contemporary society, especially the growing service sector of the economy, is also taken into account. This is most evident in class 6 which is divided into 6a (sales and personal services – female dominated) and 6b (skilled manual – overwhelmingly male) (see Table 6.3).

However, the inclusion of women in such occupational classifications does present some difficulties because women's relationship to employment is generally more varied than that of men. More women work part time or occupy jobs for short periods because of pregnancy and childcare. It is, therefore, difficult to know whether the class assigned provides a meaningful insight into their life experience as a whole or whether it merely reflects a short-term or temporary experience that has little impact on lifestyle and life-chances.

**Table 6.3** The Surrey Occupational Class Schema

| | |
|---|---|
| 1 | Higher professional |
| 2 | Employers and managers |
| 3 | Lower professional |
| 4 | Secretarial and clerical |
| 5 | Supervisors, self-employed manual |
| 6a | Sales and personal services |
| 6b | Skilled manual |
| 7 | Semi-skilled |
| 8 | Unskilled |

Source: Arber *et al.* (1986)

## A new scale for the 21st century: the National Statistics Socio-Economic Classification (NS-SEC)

The NS-SEC scale, which essentially is a variation on the Hope-Goldthorpe scale, fully replaced the Registrar General's scale for government research and statistics, and was used for the first time to classify data from the 2001 census (see Table 6.4).

Like the Hope-Goldthorpe scale, the NS-SEC is based on:

- employment relations – whether people are employers, self-employed or employed, and whether they exercise authority over others
- **market conditions** – salary scales, promotion prospects, sick pay, how much control people have over the hours they work, and so on.

### *Strengths of the NS-SEC*

- It no longer divides workers exclusively along manual and non-manual lines. Some categories contain both manual and non-manual workers.
- The most significant difference between the Hope-Goldthorpe scale and the NS-SEC is the creation of Class 8, i.e. the long-term unemployed and never-employed unemployed. Some sociologists, most notably from New Right positions, have described this group of unemployed as an 'underclass' (see Topic 4).
- Feminist arguments have been acknowledged and women are now recognized as a distinct group of wage earners. They are no longer categorized according to the occupation of their husbands or fathers.

### *Potential weaknesses of the NS-SEC*

- The scale is still based primarily on the objective criteria of occupation. This may differ from what people understand by the term 'social class' and their subjective interpretation of their own class position.
- Those who do not have to work because of access to great wealth are still not included.
- Some argue that the scale still obscures important differences in status and earning power, e.g. headteachers are in the same category as classroom teachers.
- Some critics have suggested that ethnicity and gender may be more important in bringing about social divisions and shaping identity.

## Subjective measurements of social class

Social surveys suggest there is often a discrepancy between how objective measurements of social class classify jobs and how people who actually occupy those jobs interpret their social status or class position. For

**Table 6.4** The National Statistics Socio-Economic Classification (NS-SEC)

| Occupational classification | % of working population | Examples |
|---|---|---|
| 1 Higher managerial and professional | 11.0 | Company directors, senior civil servants, doctors, barristers, clergy, architects |
| 2 Lower managerial and professional | 23.5 | Nurses, journalists, teachers, police officers, musicians |
| 3 Intermediate | 14.0 | Secretaries, clerks, computer operators, driving instructors |
| 4 Small employers and self-accountable workers | 9.9 | Taxi drivers, window cleaners, publicans, decorators |
| 5 Lower supervisory, craft and related | 9.8 | Train drivers, plumbers, printers, TV engineers |
| 6 Semi-routine | 18.6 | Traffic wardens, shop assistants, hairdressers, call-centre workers |
| 7 Routine | 12.7 | Cleaners, couriers, road sweepers, labourers |
| 8 Long-term unemployed or the never-worked | | |

Source: Rose, D. and Pevalin, D. (with K. O'Reilly) (2001) *The National Statistics Socio-economic Classification: Genesis and Overview*, London: ONS

example, many teachers like to describe themselves as working-class despite the fact that both the Registrar-General's classification of occupations and the NS-SEC objectively categorise them as middle-class. This is because many teachers have experienced upward mobility through educational qualifications from working-class origins and feel that their perspective on the world is still shaped by working-class values and experience. This subjective awareness of class position often conflicts with official objective interpretations.

More important, it is the subjective interpretation of class position that is responsible for the sharp boundary lines that exist between the social classes in the UK. In other words, there is some evidence (which will be explored in more detail in later sections) that those people who interpret themselves as 'working-class', 'middle-class' and 'upper-class' have very clear ideas about what characteristics people who 'belong' to their class should have. Moreover, they tend to have very strong views about the characteristics of other social classes. These subjective interpretations may have little or nothing in common with official and objective attempts to construct broad socioeconomic classifications based on employment. Reay (1998) agrees with these observations and argues that class analysis should move away from the large-scale quantitative analyses of the past based on occupational classifications. She suggests that small-scale **ethnographic** studies of how class is 'lived' and experienced alongside gender and ethnicity may give us greater insight into class position and inequality.

Studies of subjective class identities confirm Reay's observation. Marshall *et al.* (1988) found that 53 per cent of their sample saw themselves as 'working-class' despite the fact that the majority of their sample were in white-collar, non-manual jobs. However, Savage *et al.* (2001) are not convinced that identification with such class categories has any real meaning beyond the need to feel normal and ordinary. They argue that people identify with the term 'middle-class' because they see it as the least **loaded** of the terms offered to them by sociologists. In fact, Savage and colleagues argue that, by saying they are middle-class, people are actually saying they are typical, ordinary people, who are neither particularly well off nor particularly badly off. Bradley (1999) notes, too, that when people identify themselves as working-class, this does not involve a strong sense of group or collective loyalty or attachment to traditional working-class institutions such as trade unions. Again, it is more likely to indicate a claim to be an ordinary and typical working person. In other words, subjective interpretations of social class may have very little to do with the characteristics allocated to social class by objective official classifications.

## Focus on research

### Savage, Bagnall and Longhurst (2001)

### Class identities

Mike Savage and his colleagues carried out in-depth interviews with 178 people living in four sites in and around Manchester. They identified three groups of people in terms of subjective class identity:

- First, there was a small minority of their sample who strongly identified themselves as belonging to a specific class. These were often graduates who had the cultural confidence to express their class position in an articulate fashion.
- The second group was also well educated, but did not like to identify with a particular class position. Rather, this group tended either to reject the notion of social class, because they saw themselves as individuals rather than a product of their social-class background, or they preferred to debate the nature of social class rather than acknowledge their belonging to any particular group. Some felt happier differentiating themselves from other social classes rather than focusing on their own membership of a particular social class.
- The third group, which made up the majority of the respondents, actually identified with a social class, but did so in an ambivalent, defensive and uncommitted way. Some of this group prefaced their 'belonging' with remarks such as 'I suppose I'm …' or 'Probably, I'm …'.

Savage and colleagues concluded that identification with the concepts of 'working class' and 'middle class' for this part of their sample was based on a simple desire to be seen as normal and ordinary, rather than any burning desire to be flag-wavers for their class. They conclude that, in general, the notion of class identity was 'relatively muted'.

Savage, M., Bagnall, G. and Longhurst, B. (2001) 'Ordinary, ambivalent and defensive class identities in the North West of England', *Sociology*, 35(4),

1 **Summarize the study's conclusions about the strength of class identity**

# Check your understanding

1. What is the difference between social differentiation and social stratification?

2. Why might those at the bottom of the caste system accept their lot? *seen as reincarnation - spiritual dharma*

3. What determined a person's position in the hierarchy in the feudal estate system? — *birth: royalty or in extreme cases by bravery!*

4. Why are most modern societies more open than most traditional societies? *lack of → religion / culture t...*

5. Why is occupation considered to be the most defining characteristic for the measurement of social class? *subjective class ident vs objective official back classifica*

6. What problems are created by using occupation as the key indicator of social class? *→ gender - ethnicity mate*

7. What were the strengths and weaknesses of each of the scales used before 2000?

8. How does the NS-SEC scale address the weaknesses of the other scales? *→ recognises women + self - employed*

9. How might the NS-SEC scale still be said to be inadequate? *- does not regard extra rich!*

# Key terms

**Achieved status** the degree of social honour and prestige accorded to a person or group because of their achievements or other merits.

**Ascribed status** the degree of social honour and prestige accorded a person or group because of their origin or inherited characteristics.

**Black economy** illegal ways of increasing income.

**Caste system** Hindu system of stratification, now officially banned in India but still influential.

**Closed societies** societies with no social mobility.

**Differentiation** perceived social differences between people, e.g. along lines of gender, age or race.

**Employment relations** see 'Work relations'.

**Ethnographic** research which focuses on the everyday life of the group being studied, usually using observation and/or unstructured interviews.

**Feudal estate system** stratification system of medieval Europe.

**Intermediate class** according to Goldthorpe, a lower grouping of the middle class containing those with poorer work and market situations than the service class, e.g. clerical workers.

**Life-chances** opportunities for achieving things that provide a high quality of life, such as good housing, health and education.

**Loaded** questions that suggest or encourage a particular answer. *Are you → MC?*

**Market position or conditions** income and economic life-chances, such as promotion prospects, sick pay, and control over hours worked and how work is done.

**Material** physical, often economic, things such as money and consumer goods.

**Meritocratic** rewarding hard work or talent, rather than inherited wealth or position.

**Open societies** societies with a high degree of social mobility, where status is usually allocated on the basis of achievement and merit.

**Operationalize** define something in such a way that it can be measured.

**Patriarchal** male-dominated.

**Service class** according to Goldthorpe, those with the highest work and market situations: the upper-middle class, e.g. large proprietors as well as administrators, managers and professionals. *HG scale 1980+ - 2000, doctors + lawyers + bankers*

**Social class** hierarchically arranged groups in modern industrial societies based on similarities in status, wealth, income and occupation. *socio-economic, modern society*

**Social status** degree of social honour, prestige and importance accorded to a person or group.

**Social stratification** the hierarchical layering of a society into distinct groups with different levels of wealth, status and power. *layers*

**Work relations** whether people are employed or self-employed, and are able to exercise authority over others.

# Activities

## Research ideas

1. Imagine you are conducting sociological research on social class at a horse-racing track or a cricket match, using observation only – you are not allowed to distribute questionnaires or conduct interviews. What sorts of things might you listen or look out for that might give you clues as to a person's social class? *money, dress, accent,*

2. Undertake a piece of research using a structured interview to measure the class distribution of students on various school or college post-16 courses. Pilot it with a random sample of ten students across the institution. After each interview write down any issues that may affect the validity, representativeness or reliability of the evidence gathered. For example:

   - Did respondents understand the questions, answer truthfully or exaggerate aspects of lifestyle/income?
   - Did they find the questions too intrusive or personal? Were they confused by the terminology you used?
   - Identify the main problems you encountered in trying to operationalize social class.
   - Did you note any differences between people's subjective interpretations of their social class position and how the NS-SEC ranks them?
   - What, if any, conclusions can you draw from your findings?

## Web.task

1. Search the worldwide web to find out about the caste system in India. How did it work and how influential is it today? Does it have influence in the UK?

2. Use a careers service on the worldwide web – such as www.prospects.ac.uk – to compare occupations in different social classes. Find out about pay, working conditions and the skills and qualifications needed. Can these explain differences in their position on social-class scales?

# TOPIC 2

# Theories of inequality and stratification

## Getting you thinking

Look at the photo of a richer and a poorer person.

1   Using your knowledge of sociological theory, suggest how the following perspectives might explain the relative class position of the people in the picture:

   (a) Marxism → exploited proletariat

   (b) functionalism. → part of the human body

2   What do you think are the advantages and disadvantages for societies of having:

   (a) a high level of social inequality? Competition/inequality

   (b) a low level of inequality? equality! / lack competition & more complacency

In the broadest terms, you may have been able to work out that Marxists explain class differences in terms of exploitation – the rich owners of large businesses pay as little as possible to their workers, while benefiting from the existence of a group of poor and unemployed people, who help keep the general level of wages low and who can do some low-paid work when necessary. For functionalists, however, inequality can actually benefit society by motivating people to work hard and fulfil their potential. It is this latter view that we consider first.

## Functionalism

The founding father of functionalism, Emile Durkheim (1858–1917), argued that class stratification existed because it was functional or beneficial to social order. He saw modern societies as characterized by a specialized occupational **division of labour**, in which people have very different jobs, skills and abilities. Some of these jobs are more beneficial to society than others. Consequently, they attract more rewards. This is the origin of social divisions. However, Durkheim argued that members of society are happy to take their place within this division of labour because they believe in its moral worth, i.e. there is common agreement or consensus about how society and its institutions, such as work, should be organized. This **value consensus** also means that members of society accept that stratification, and therefore inequality, are good for society. They consequently accept that occupations should be graded in terms of their value to society and that those occupying the more functional or valued positions should receive greater rewards for their

efforts. Durkheim, therefore, saw the stratification system as a moral classification system embodying and reflecting common values and beliefs.

   He also argued that stratification is beneficial because it sets limits on competition and people's **aspirations**, in that it clearly links criteria such as skills and qualifications to particular roles so that people do not become overly ambitious and therefore disappointed and resentful if they fail or don't do as well as they had hoped. Rather, because the system is regarded as fair and just, members of society are relatively contented with their lot, and thus social order is the norm.

   Durkheim did acknowledge some potential problems with this system that might cause conflict and, therefore, possible breakdown in social order. He noted that if people are unable to compete freely for jobs or roles – if they are forced into certain types of work – then moral consensus and solidarity could break down. Durkheim believed that ascription (the arrangement whereby roles are allocated on the basis of fixed inherited criteria such as gender and ethnicity) could lead to conflict because those allocated to particular roles or jobs would have had no choice in the matter. On the other hand, Durkheim believed that the possibility of acquiring skills and qualifications, which is normally found in open societies, gave people an element of choice and so reaffirmed their moral commitment to society. However, he also believed that this moral order could be disturbed by sudden shifts in a society, such as economic recession or the accumulation of too much power in the hands of one individual or group, because these shifts could destabilize what people expected from the stratification system. For example:

- Recession could lead to a rapid and sudden rise in unemployment and deflation in wages.
- A dictatorship could lead to people being put into functionally important and highly rewarded roles on the basis of **patronage** rather than ability, thus fuelling resentment and potential conflict.

Talcott Parsons (1902–79) noted that achievement and skills are the most highly valued qualities in contemporary Western societies. Parsons argues that stratification is therefore the outcome of general agreement in society about how jobs should be ranked in terms of their functional importance or value to society. Those most highly valued are consequently more highly rewarded. As Bottero (2005) notes:

> *<<People have little choice but to accept the general value placed on the different positions in a hierarchy. They may not like it, but – if they want to get on – they have to live with it and play by the rules.>>* (p.49)

Durkheim's and Parson's theories of stratification were built upon by Davis and Moore in the 1950s. Table 6.5 below outlines both their views and those of their critics.

### Is stratification really good for society?

A similar view to that of Davis and Moore has been proposed by the New Right thinker, Peter Saunders (1996). He points out that economic growth has raised the standard of living for all members of society, and social inequality is thus a small price to pay for society as a whole becoming more prosperous. Saunders is influenced by Hayek (1944), who argued that capitalism is a dynamic system that continually raises everybody's standards of living, so the poor in society today are much better off than they were in the past. Moreover, **capitalist societies** offer incentives to those with talent and enterprise in the form of material wealth. If these incentives did not exist, Saunders argues, then many of the consumer goods that we take for granted today, such as cars, computers and iPods, would not exist, because talented people would not have been motivated to produce them. However, this perspective, like functionalism, downplays the argument that social and economic inequality may create resentment and dissatisfaction that could eventually lead to deviance, disaffection and social disorder.

## Marxism

According to Marx (1818–83), the driving force of virtually all societies is the conflict between the rich and powerful minority who control the society, and the powerless and poor majority who survive only by working for the rich and powerful. These two classes are always in conflict as it is in the interests of the rich to spend as little as possible in paying their workers.

### Causes of conflict

The heart of this class conflict is the system of producing goods and services – what Marx called the **mode of production**. This is made up of two things:

1. the **means of production** – the resources needed to produce goods, such as capital (money for investment), land, factories, machinery and raw materials
2. the social **relations of production** – the ways in which people are organized to make things, i.e. the





**Table 6.5** The functionalist theory of stratification

| Davis and Moore (1955) | Criticisms |
|---|---|
| All societies have to ensure that their most important positions are filled with the most talented people. They therefore need to offer such people high rewards. | Does this really happen? Lots of occupations can be seen to be essential to the smooth running of society but are not highly rewarded, such as nursing. There are also plenty of idiots in high places! |
| Class societies are meritocracies – high rewards in the form of income and status are guaranteed in order to motivate gifted people to make the necessary sacrifices in terms of education and training. Educational qualifications (and hence the stratification system) function to allocate all individuals to an occupational role that suits their abilities. People's class position is a fair reflection of their talents. | Some groups may be able to use economic and political power to increase their rewards against the will of the majority. High rewards sometimes go to people who play no functionally important roles but who simply live off the interest generated by their wealth. Do the three to five years of training at college and/or university merit a lifetime of enhanced income and status? Isn't higher education a privilege in itself? |
| Most people agree that stratification is necessary because they accept the meritocratic principles on which society is based. | There is a substantial level of resentment about the unequal distribution of income and wealth, as illustrated by the controversy over bankers' levels of pay and bonuses. Unequal rewards may be the product of inequalities in power. |
| Stratification encourages all members of society to work to the best of their ability. For example, those at the top will wish to retain their advantages whilst those placed elsewhere will wish to improve on their position. | The **dysfunctions** of stratification are neglected by Davis and Moore. For example, poverty is a major problem for people and negatively impacts on mortality, health, education and family life. |

way in which roles and responsibilities are allocated among those involved in production.

Marx described modern Western societies as capitalist societies and suggested that such societies consist of two main classes:

1 the **bourgeoisie** – the capitalist or ruling class, who own the means of production; they are the owners or, today, the large shareholders in businesses, and control decisions about employment, new investment, new products, and so on.
2 the **proletariat** – the working or subordinate class, who sell their ability to work (labour power) to the bourgeoisie; most people make a living by working for a profit-making business, but they have no say in business decisions or how they are put to work, and rely on the success of the company they work for.

Marx argued that the social relations of production between the bourgeoisie and proletariat are unequal, exploitative and create class conflict. Capitalism's relentless pursuit of profit means that wages are kept as low as possible and the bourgeoisie pockets the difference between what they pay their workers and the value of the goods produced by workers. This '**surplus value**' forms the basis of their great wealth. Moreover, workers lose control over their jobs as new technology is introduced in order to increase output and therefore profits. Workers become **alienated** by this process and are united by a shared exploitative class experience. This common class experience means that the working class is a **class-in-itself**.

So, according to Marx, capitalism is a pretty dreadful kind of society. However, if this is the case, why do most people happily accept it – even believing it to be superior to other kinds of societies? Marx had an answer for this, too. Workers very rarely see themselves as exploited because they have been 'duped' by **ideological apparatuses**, such as education and the media, into believing that capitalism is fair and natural. The working class are consequently 'suffering' from **false class consciousness**.

Marx believed that the conflict inherent in the capitalist system would come to a head, because the increasing concentration of wealth would cause the gap between rich and poor to grow and grow, i.e. to become **polarized**, so that even the most short-sighted members of the proletariat would see that the time for change had come. Marx predicted that, eventually, the proletariat would unite, overthrow the bourgeoisie, seize the means of production for themselves and establish a fairer, more equal society – known as **communism**. For Marx, then, radical social change was inevitable as the working class was transformed from a class-in-itself into a revolutionary **class-for-itself**.

## Evaluation of Marx

Marx's ideas have probably been more influential than those of any other political thinker and have had a huge impact in the 20th century. They inspired communist revolutions in many countries, such as China and Russia. However, his ideas have also come in for a great deal of criticism, especially since the communist regimes of Eastern Europe crumbled in the 1990s.

- Marx is accused of being an economic **determinist** or **reductionist**, in that all his major ideas are based on the economic relationship between the bourgeoisie and proletariat. However, many contemporary conflicts, such as those rooted in nationalism, ethnicity and gender, cannot be explained adequately in economic terms.
- Marx is criticized for underestimating the importance of the middle classes. He did recognize a third (in his view, relatively minor, class) made up of professional workers, shopkeepers and clerks, which he called the **petit-bourgeoisie**. However, being outside the system of production, they were deemed unimportant to the class struggle. In his view, as the two major camps polarized, members of this class would realign their interests accordingly with either one. Some **neo-Marxists** have argued that the upper middle class have aligned themselves with the bourgeoisie in that they act as agents for that class in their role of managers and professionals – in other words, the service class 'service' their employers by managing their businesses. Other Marxists, most notably Braverman (1974), argue that white-collar workers have more in common in terms of their working conditions with the proletariat. These issues are explored further in Topics 3 to 4.
- In particular, Marx's prediction that the working class would become 'class conscious' because they would experience extreme misery and poverty, and therefore seek to transform the capitalist system, has not occurred. As we saw in Topic 1, the class identity of working-class people today is not overtly political.. Most people who see themselves as working-class do so not because they recognize their exploited status but because they wish to claim their typicality in terms of being working people. Furthermore, although Western capitalist societies may have problems such as poverty and homelessness, they do have a reasonably good record in terms of democracy and workers' rights. Moreover, the living standards of the working class have risen. It may be, then, that working-class people are sensibly reconciled to capitalism rather than being 'falsely conscious'. In other words, they appreciate the benefits of capitalism despite being aware of the inequalities generated by it.

## Neo-Marxism

Neo-Marxists have tended to focus on the relationship between the **infrastructure** (i.e. the capitalist economy and particularly the social relationships of production characterized by class inequality, exploitation and subordination) and the **superstructure** (i.e. all the major social institutions of society, such as education, the mass media, religion, the law and the political system). Neo-Marxists argue that the function of the superstructure is the reproduction and legitimation of the class inequality found in the infrastructure. In other words, the superstructure exists to transmit ruling-class **ideology** and, in particular, to make sure that the mass of society subscribes to ruling-class ideas about how society should be organized and does not complain too much about the inequality that exists, e.g. in income and wealth. The function of the superstructure, therefore, is to encourage acceptance of class stratification and to ensure that false class consciousness continues among the working class.

Education is seen by neo-Marxists as a particularly important ideological apparatus working on behalf of the capitalist class. Marxists, such as Althusser (1971), suggest that education transmits the idea that capitalist society is a meritocracy – i.e. that ability is the major mechanism of success. However, this disguises the reality of the stratification system: that those born into ruling- or middle-class backgrounds are much more likely to achieve, because what goes on in the educational system, in terms of both the academic and **hidden curriculum**, is the product of bourgeoise values. The **cultural capital** of the children of the upper and middle class (along with the material advantages they enjoy, such as private education) ensure that class inequality is reproduced in the next generation. The children of the working class, on the other hand, lack this cultural capital and so are condemned to a life of manual work, as they are ejected from the educational system at the age of 16. However, these working-class children rarely blame the capitalist system for their 'failure'. Rather, the ideology of meritocracy ensures that they blame themselves, with the consequence that the working class rarely challenge the organization of capitalism or see stratification and inequality as a problem.

Other neo-Marxists have focused on the ideological power of the mass media and how the bourgeoisie might be using this to their advantage. The Frankfurt School of Marxists, for example, writing since the 1930s, have focused on the role of the media in creating a popular culture for the masses that has diverted working-class attention away from the unequal nature of capitalism towards consumerism, celebrity culture and trivia. Marcuse (1964), for example, noted that capitalism has been very successful in bedazzling the working class with what he saw as 'false needs' to buy the latest consumer goods. Neo-Marxists argue that the latest soap storylines, and the lifestyles of the rich and famous, are now given more priority by the media, especially the tabloid newspapers and commercial television, than political and economic life. As Lawrence Friedman (1999) argues, the lifestyle of the rich and famous is now the modern **opium** of the masses.

Consequently, the mass of society is now less knowledgeable about how society is politically and economically organized. The result of this ideological barrage is that the working class is less united than ever, as people compete with each other for the latest material goods. As a result, stratification and class inequality are rarely challenged. This has led to Reiner (2007) arguing that the 'class war' has been won to devastating effect by the capitalist class.

However, in criticism of neo-Marxism, Saunders (1990) argues that such writers suffer from the same two problems:

1 How is it that they know the truth when it is hidden from everybody else? The answer, says Saunders, smacks of arrogance. He points out rather sarcastically 'Marxists know the true situation because Marxist theory is true' (p.19).
2 Marxist theory does have the unfortunate habit of dismissing what working-class people say and think about their situation as the product of ideology and false class consciousness. As Parkin (1972) notes, there is a haughty assumption in Marxist ideology theory that the working class cannot ever appreciate the reality of their situation because they are experiencing a kind of collective brain damage.

## Max Weber

Another classical theorist, Max Weber (1864–1920), disagreed with Marx's view on the inevitability of class conflict. Weber also rejected the Marxist emphasis on the economic dimension as the sole determinant of inequality. Weber (1947) saw 'class' (economic relationships) and 'status' (perceived social standing) as two separate but related sources of power that have overlapping effects on people's life-chances. He also recognized what he called '**party**' as a further dimension. By this, he meant the political influence or power an individual might exercise through membership of pressure groups, trade unions or other organized interest groups. However, he did see class as the most important of these three interlinking factors.

Like Marx, Weber saw classes as economic categories organized around property ownership, but argued that the concept should be extended to include 'occupational skill' because this created differences in life-chances (income, opportunities, lifestyles and general prospects) among those groups that did not own the means of production, namely the middle class and the working class. In other words, if we examine these two social classes, we will find status differences within them. For example, professionals are regarded more highly than white-collar workers, whilst skilled manual workers are regarded more highly than unskilled workers or the long-term unemployed. These differences in status lead directly to differences in life-chances and therefore inequality.

### The significance of status in inequality

People who occupy high occupational roles generally have high social status, but status can also derive from other sources of power such as gender, race and religion. Weber noted that status was also linked to consumption styles (how people spend their money). For example, some people derive status from conspicuous consumption – e.g. from being seen to buy expensive designer products. This idea has been taken further by postmodernists, who suggest that in the 21st century, consumption and style rather than social class will be the biggest influence on shaping people's identity.

Weber defined social classes as clusters of occupations with similar life-chances and patterns of mobility (people's opportunities to move up or down the occupational ladder). On this basis, he identified four distinct social classes:

1 those privileged through property or education
2 the petty-bourgeoisie (the self-employed, managers)
3 white-collar workers and technicians (the lower middle class)
4 manual workers (the working class).

Weber's ideas have influenced the way in which social class is operationalized by sociologists such as Goldthorpe (1980) and by the government through the recent NS-SEC scale – as discussed in Topic 1. Goldthorpe's concepts of market situation and work relations are based on the notion that status differences (and, therefore, life-chances) exist between particular occupational groups.

Weber was sceptical about the possibility of the working class banding together for revolutionary purposes – i.e. becoming class conscious – because differences in status would always undermine any common cause. Social classes were too internally divided into competing status groups, and this undermined any potential for common group identity and action.

The concept of 'status groups' rather than social classes is central to Weber's theory of stratification. Status groups, then, are made up of people who share the same status position, as well as a common awareness of how they differ from other status groups. In other words, their identity is bound up with their exclusiveness as a group, and this shapes their lifestyle in terms of how they interact with others – for instance, they may only socialize with people like themselves.

## Evaluation of Weber

### *Class, status and wealth*

Marxists argue that Weber neglected the basic split between capitalists and workers, and argue that class and status are strongly linked – after all, the capitalist class has wealth, high status and political power. Weber recognized that these overlap, but suggested that a person can have wealth but little status – like a lottery winner, perhaps – or, conversely, high status but little wealth – such as a church minister. He suggested that it is very rare that high-status groups allow wealth alone to be sufficient grounds for entry into their status group. He noted that such groups may exclude other wealthy individuals because they lack the 'right' breeding, schooling, manners, culture, etc. This practice of 'social closure' will be explored in more depth in later topics. Conversely, someone may be accepted as having high status by the wealthy, despite being relatively poor in comparison, such as the aristocrat who has fallen on hard times. Weber rightly points out that high status and political power can sometimes be achieved without great economic resources.

### *Party*

Party or power plays a role in this too. Weber saw this third type of inequality as deriving from membership of any formal or informal association that sets out to achieve particular goals. Such associations might include political parties, trade unions, the freemasons, old boy networks and even sports clubs. Membership of these can influence the social status a person has in the community. For example, membership of the freemasons might increase a person's potential to make social and business contacts, and, therefore, their wealth, whilst many middle-class men may be keen to join the local golf club because of the prestige that such membership may confer on them.

### *Gender and ethnicity*

Weber's analysis helps explain why some groups may share economic circumstances but have more or less status than others, for example, due to gender or ethnic differences. Weber saw gender and ethnicity as status differences which have separate and distinct effects on life-chances compared with social class. In other words, the working class might have less status than the middle class, but working-class Black people and working-class women may have less status than working-class White men.

### *Status and identity*

However, Savage *et al.* (2001) take issue with the importance of 'status' in terms of shaping people's identity or giving us insight into the nature of inequality. Savage notes that people rarely make status claims, and suggests that they are wary of 'appearing to demonstrate openly their cultural superiority'. Savage's research suggests that people are more concerned with stressing how ordinary or how mainstream they are. Very few social groups assert that they are a special case. However, Savage does acknowledge that as a general rule, class, status and party do go together. As Bottero (2005) notes:

> «*The rich tend to be powerful, the powerful to be wealthy, and access to high-status social circles tends to accompany both.*» (p.41)

### *Conflict and stability*

Bottero concludes that Weber provides an adaptable 'history-proof' model of stratification which may be more valid than Marxism in analyzing the variety of stratification arrangements that exist across the world. However, she notes that both Marx and Weber fail to explain why societies organized around conflict or difference are so stable, orderly and reasonably free of major conflict between the social groups who occupy them.

*Gate Gourmet supplies in-flight meals for airlines. Its workers went on strike in August 2005, disrupting British Airways flights. Many of its workers at Heathrow Airport are from ethnic minorities – in particular, the West London Sikh community. Discuss the Gate Gourmet workers in terms of Weber's categories of class, status and party.*

# Interpretive sociology

Most of the accounts that we have examined – especially functionalism and Marxism – are **structural theories**. This type of stratification theory is often accused of over-determinism: reducing all human behaviour to a reaction to either social or economic structure, and presenting people as puppets of society, unable to exercise any choice over their destiny. Interpretivist sociologists suggest that the social actions of individuals are more important than the social structure of society. Interpretivists argue that how people subjectively view the world and their place in it is important because such interpretations make us aware that we have choices in how we behave. For example, we might decide that our ethnicity is more important to us than our social class and act accordingly.

However, Bottero notes that this focus on **agency** or action assumes that social life is patternless. She argues that interpretivists often ignore the very real constraints on people's behaviour caused by structured social inequalities in income, wealth, education, ethnicity, gender, etc. She notes that the organization of society still sets 'substantial limits on choice and agency for all and creates situations in which some are more free to act than others' (p.56). She notes that Marx recognized the role of choice and agency when he stated that 'men make their own history', but he also recognized that social structure shaped action when he said that 'they do not make it under circumstances chosen by themselves'.

## Giddens and structuration

Giddens (1973) attempted to combine structure and action in his theory of structuration, in which he argued that individuals create structural forces, such as social class, by engaging in particular actions. For example, he noted that class advantages can be passed on to the younger generations through family interaction. He also noted that consensus about the status or standing of occupations, as well as our acceptance that some people have the authority to tell us what to do at work, creates a hierarchy of occupations and, therefore, a stratification system based on social class. Giddens also notes that we judge people by the type of house or area they live in, by the car they drive, by the clothes or logos they wear, by the consumer goods they buy. He argues that this consensus about consumption also contributes to stratification and therefore inequality.

However, in 1990, Giddens decided social class was no longer as significant as it had been in the past. Rather, he argued that the major social division in society was between the employed and the unemployed or socially excluded. Social class inequalities no longer constrained the activities and lifestyle of a whole mass of people such as the working class or poor – it was now individuals and families that experienced constraints and opportunities. Moreover, Giddens set himself on the postmodernist road when he argued that lifestyle and taste were now more significant than social class in the construction of identity.

# Postmodernism

Postmodernists reject what they see as the **grand narratives** of the stratification theories discussed so far. They focus instead on the concepts of 'identity' and 'difference'. They argue that the increasing diversity and plurality found in postmodern social life has led to the break-up of collective social identity, and especially class identity. It is argued that the group categories of 'social class', 'ethnicity', and 'gender' no longer exist in an homogeneous form. Subjective individual identity is now more important than objective collective identity.

Postmodernists, such as Waters (1995), argue that social class is in terminal decline as a source of identity and that consumption – how we spend our money – is now central in terms of how we organize our daily lives. As Best (2005) notes, 'we are all cast into the roles of consumers'. Postmodernists argue that increasing affluence and standards of living have led to individuals being faced with a variety of consumer choices about their lifestyle rather than being forced into particular forms of cultural behaviour by forces beyond their social control, such as social class. In particular, they argue that people now use a variety of influences, particularly those stemming from globalization and popular mass media culture, to construct personal identity. For example, Waters suggests that, as a result, postmodern stratification and inequality are about lifestyle choices, fragmented association (we never belong to or identify with one group for very long), being seduced into conspicuous consumption by advertising, and constant change in terms of what we are supposed to be interested in, the choices available to us and how we are supposed to feel.

Topic 3 examines social class and its relationship to future life-chances and identity and, consequently, it is recommended that you use the evidence from that section to judge the validity of this postmodernist view of the influence of social class.

# Key terms

**Agency** social action.

**Aspirations** ambitions.

**Alienation** lack of fulfilment from work.

**Bourgeoisie** the ruling class in capitalist society.

**Capitalist societies** societies based on private ownership of the means of production, such as Britain and the USA.

**Class-for-itself** a social class that is conscious of its exploited position and wishes to change its situation.

**Class-in-itself** a social group that shares similar experiences.

**Communism** system based on communal ownership of the means of production.

**Cultural capital** attitudes, ways of thinking, knowledge, skills, etc., learnt in middle-class homes that give middle-class children advantages in education.

**Determinist or reductionist** the view that phenomena can be explained with reference to one key factor.

**Division of labour** the way the job system is organized.

**Dysfunctions** the negative effects of social actions, institutions and structures.

**False class consciousness** where the proletariat see the society in a way that suits the ruling class and so pose no threat to them.

**Grand narratives** postmodernist term for big structural theories, such as functionalism and Marxism.

**Hidden curriculum** the rules and regulations that underpin schooling in order to produce conformity.

**Ideological apparatuses** social institutions that benefit the ruling class by spreading the ideas that help maintain the system in their interests, e.g. the mass media, education system.

**Ideology** set of beliefs underpinning any way of life or political structure. Used by Marxists and neo-Marxists to refer specifically to the way powerful groups justify their position.

**Infrastructure** in a Marxist sense, the capitalist economic system that is characterized by class inequality.

**Means of production** the material forces that enable things to be produced, e.g. factories, machinery and land.

**Mode of production** economic base of society that constitutes the entire system involved in the production of goods.

**Neo-Marxists** those who have adapted Marx's views.

**Opium** a popular drug of the 19th century that supposedly helped people forget their troubles.

**Party** term used by Weber to describe political influence.

**Patronage** giving jobs or positions of power/privilege to reward loyalty or membership of kinship or political groups.

**Petit-bourgeoisie** term used by Marx to describe the small middle class sandwiched between the proletariat and bourgeoisie.

**Polarization** at opposite ends of the spectrum.

**Proletariat** the working class in capitalist societies.

**Relations of production** the allocation of roles and responsibilities among those involved in production.

**Structural theory** those explanations that generally see the organization of society as more important than individual actions.

**Superstructure** social institutions such as education, mass media, religion, which function to transmit ruling-class ideology.

**Surplus value** term used by Marx to describe the profit created by the work of the proletariat but taken by capitalists.

**Value consensus** moral agreement.

# Activities

## Research idea

Conduct a piece of research to discover how young people explain inequality. Design an interview schedule to assess the ways in which your sample explain inequality. Do they take a functionalist position and see inequality as beneficial, motivating and meritocratic? Alternatively, do they agree with Marxists that inequality is damaging, unfair and demotivating?

## Web.task

Go to the following sites and investigate the writings on class of the classical sociologists:

- **www.intute.ac.uk/socialsciences/sociology/** – use the search engine on this marvellous site to access archives on Durkheim and Marx as well as Verstehen – Max Weber's Home Page
- **www.anu.edu.au/polsci/marx/marx.htm** – an Australian website with some excellent materials on Marx.

# Check your understanding

1. Why is social stratification acceptable, according to Durkheim?
2. In what circumstances might stratification be dysfunctional to society, according to Durkheim?
3. Why, according to Davis and Moore, do some people deserve more rewards than others?
4. Why do functionalists like Davis and Moore see social stratification as good for society?
5. What, according to Marx, determines a person's social class?
6. What is false class consciousness and how does it aid stratification?
7. Marx is accused of being an economic reductionist – what does this mean?
8. What is the role of the superstructure with regard to stratification?
9. What three sources of inequality does Weber identify as important in modern societies?
10. How does the concept of status help explain gender and ethnic differences?
11. How do postmodernists view class identity?

## An eye on the exam — Theories of inequality and stratification

*Stratification pereeved sova standng = CLASS by othes gcse*

Describe only – no need for evaluation

Status inequalities are based on how a person's social position is judged. They might include inequalities based on factors such as gender, ethnicity, religion and age

*weber*

**(a)** Outline the evidence that status inequalities exist in modern Britain. **(20 marks)**

*strany = dyferena sau*

Statistical trends and patterns, research findings and contemporary examples from any module studied and/or your wider sociological knowledge

Describe Marxist theories of stratification in detail using appropriate concepts and writers

Consider the strengths and weaknesses of Marxist theories in comparison with other theories of stratification before reaching a balanced conclusion

*rayes*

*vs: / vs: funct webe post mod fem*

**(b)** Outline and assess Marxist theories of stratification. **(40 marks)**

This also includes neo-Marxist perspectives

Marxists believe that capitalist societies stratify by social class

### Grade booster — Getting top marks in question (b)

It is important to clearly outline the Marxist theory of stratification in depth and detail, and this means accurately using Marxist concepts such as infrastructure, means of production, social relations of production, surplus value, class-in-itself, class-for-itself, alienation, exploitation, superstructure etc. to illustrate Marx's ideas. You should also be willing to explore how neo-Marxists such as Althusser, Bourdieu, Gramsci and the Frankfurt School have built upon Marx's original ideas with references to ideology, false needs and hegemony. Evaluation should be both specific, i.e. focused on problems like over-determinism, and by juxtaposition – outline alternative theories of stratification such as Davis and Moore's functionalist version or Weber, and clearly show how these challenge Marxism. Finally, include evidence relating to class inequalities in income and wealth etc. – does this support or challenge the Marxist case?

# TOPIC 3

# Life-chances and social class

## Getting you thinking

1. **Look at the photographs. How do they show that consumption and lifestyle may be becoming increasingly important as sources of identity?**
2. **How available are the lifestyle choices illustrated here to all social groups? Who may be denied access and why?**

You may have concluded from the exercise above that **consumption**, especially of designer goods and labels, is increasingly important to lifestyle in 21st-century Britain. As we saw in Topic 2, some sociologists have seen these trends as evidence that the UK is no longer a class society, and that our occupational status and the market rewards attached to it are no longer the main source of identity and inequality today. Rather, these sociologists note that social divisions such as those between neighbourhoods, regions and ethnic groups, are now far more important. Other sociologists do not accept the validity of this picture of the United Kingdom. They argue instead that, although the nature of social class in the UK is changing, it is still the most important influence on all aspects of our lives.

## Social exclusion and inclusion

Savage (2000) argues that since 1979, when it suffered the first of four successive election defeats, the Labour party has deliberately avoided talking about class and has focused instead on the concept of '**social exclusion**'. Consequently, political debate has focused on the idea that groups such as the long-term unemployed, single mothers and the residents of socially deprived areas are somehow excluded from the living standards that most of us take for granted. In response, social policy has been devised in the fields of education, training and welfare with the concept of '**social inclusion**' in mind – that is, it has aimed to target these groups so that they can become part of mainstream society again.

However, Savage argues that the concepts of 'social exclusion' and 'social inclusion' are deliberately 'bland and inoffensive' – they reflect the New Labour or **Blairite** view that social-class divisions are no longer important because we allegedly now live in a society 'where most social groups have been incorporated into a common social body, with shared values and interests'. It has been argued by Labour politicians that Britain in the 21st century is a classless society, or if social class is to be acknowledged at all, a society in which the vast majority of us share in middle-class lifestyles and aspirations – as Tony Blair once said, 'we are all middle-class now'.

Sociologists have also taken up this baton of classlessness. New Right sociologists such as Peter Saunders, as well as postmodernists such as Pakulski and Walters, have argued that social class is no longer important as a source of personal identity for people in the 21st century. These sociologists, despite their theoretical differences, have suggested that consumption patterns and '**cleavages**' are far more important than social class in shaping lifestyle and life-chances today.

## Is the UK a meritocracy?

In order to assess whether social class has any relevance in modern Britain today, it is useful to examine the concept of meritocracy. Many of those who argue that social class as a source of inequality no longer matters base this idea on the view that the UK is a meritocracy, i.e. that social origin and background are no longer important in shaping educational and occupational success. They argue that meritocratic institutions such as education and businesses are only interested in rewarding individual merit – hard work, effort, talent, ability, achievement, and so on. In a meritocracy, then, success and failure, and hence inequality, are the product of the individual and not their social-class background.

Sociologists such as Giddens and Diamond (2005) have become known as the '**new egalitarians**'. They suggest that Britain is a fair and open society in which all social groups are given the potential to unlock their talents and to realize material rewards. However, sociologists such as Roberts, Bottero and Young and research organizations such as the Sutton Trust – who we can collectively call the '**new traditionalists**' – suggest that Britain is still a class society in which social background and structural inequalities in income, wealth, power, education and health mean that working-class people rarely have their talents unlocked and, consequently, experience great inequality in material rewards and life-chances.

### The new egalitarian view

Giddens and Diamond (2005) argue that social class is no longer an important source of inequality or identity in the 21st century. They suggest that the UK is a meritocratic society in that **equality of opportunity** is now the norm, i.e. all members of society are objectively and equally judged on their talent and ability. Social background, and therefore social class, is now less important than ever before. Consequently, if people fail to achieve, the implication is that this must be due to an individual failing, e.g. they are not motivated enough or they have been demotivated by, for example, an overgenerous welfare benefit system to work hard.

They argue that the decline of class and the associated rise in meritocracy are the result of a number of social changes that have taken place over the past 30 years, such as:

- The decline of the primary and secondary sectors of the economy has led to a dramatic decline in the number of traditional manual workers and the identity politics associated with them, such as trade union membership. Moreover, the Labour party, which was traditionally seen as the party of the working class, has moved to distance itself from such class-based politics in recent years.
- The service sector of the economy – the public sector, financial services, retail and personal services – has greatly expanded. Many of the jobs in this sector are better paid and more secure than manual work. Furthermore, many workers in this sector, especially women who dominate these jobs in terms of numbers, have been upwardly mobile from the working class. They are now able to invest in a better lifestyle, e.g. owning their own home, and as a result this has undermined traditional patterns of class identification and loyalty.
- The majority of young people in Britain now experience further education, and the opportunities for going into higher education have increased tremendously for all social groups.
- Work contexts are less likely to be socially exclusive, i.e. made up of people from similar class backgrounds, because young people often combine education with work and take longer to establish their careers. As Furlong *et al.* (2006) note, in call centres, students often work, temporarily, next to same-age peers who lack advanced qualifications.

Giddens and Diamond conclude that these trends have resulted in the working class becoming just one more group among many that may be experiencing some type of economic and social deprivation in the UK. They argue that there exist a number of distinctive cleavages or disparities between the social experiences of particular social groups that require addressing by social policy, such as:

- between different types of families, i.e. single-parent families do not experience the same opportunities as dual-career families
- between homeowners and those who live in council housing
- between those living in neighbourhoods with high levels of crime and antisocial behaviour, and little community spirit, and those living in ordered and well integrated communities
- between those with secure well-paid jobs and those in insecure casual or temporary low-paid work and those who are long-term unemployed. Hutton (1996) argues that society is now divided into segments (he also avoids the use of the term 'social class'!) based on inequalities in income and wealth. He argues that the top 40 per cent of society comprises all those with secure jobs, whilst the bottom 30 per cent comprises the disadvantaged – the unemployed and the poor. The middle 30 per cent comprises the **marginalized** – those workers who are not well paid and who often occupy insecure jobs
- between the disabled and the able-bodied
- between ethnic minority groups and the White majority
- between the elderly and younger members of society
- between male pupils and female pupils – female pupils consistently do better at school than male pupils at key stages 1–3 as well as GCSE. Some new egalitarians, therefore, suggest that the talents of boys are not being unlocked compared with girls.

Giddens and Diamond, therefore, reject the notion of an overarching class inequality and argue instead that 'social exclusion' is a more accurate term for 'the range of deprivations' (e.g. low wages, child poverty, lack of educational and training opportunities, low levels of community belonging, and the lack of integration into a unified national identity) that prevent a diverse range of groups from taking their 'full part in society'.

They argue that such deprivations can only be tackled if the following conditions are met:

1 The economy is dynamic, competitive, flexible and efficient – they consequently reject the idea of increasing taxation on the wealthy entrepreneurs whose companies dominate the economy because they argue that the UK can only attract the best businessmen and managers in the world and, therefore, produce a healthy economy if salaries and rewards are attractive. In addition, high rewards encourage talented people to have high aspirations and to work hard to achieve them. As Hazel Blears, the Labour cabinet minister, said in 2008, 'an attack on wealth and income distribution is an attack on aspiration'. However, new egalitarians do acknowledge that some of the practices of the very wealthy, such as tax avoidance, tax evasion and irresponsible corporate behaviour, need to be addressed in order to bring about a fairer society.
2 The excluded are provided with educational and training opportunities, tax breaks and minimum wages so that their talents and abilities can be more effectively unlocked – this should enable them to take meritocratic advantage of the jobs being created by the expansion of the global economy and, therefore, to experience upward social mobility and greater economic rewards.
3 The welfare state is reformed so that those who currently do not want to work can be 'encouraged' to unlock their potential through compulsory training schemes and employment.

Giddens and Diamond argue that the New Labour government of 1997-2010 adopted four measures of social exclusion:

1 the number of people not in employment, education or training
2 the number of those earning below 60 per cent of the average wage
3 the number of those experiencing low levels of social interaction
4 the number of those who believe that they live in an area characterized by high crime, vandalism or material dilapidation.

Using these indicators, Giddens and Diamond argue that less than 1 per cent of the UK population experience social exclusion on all four counts. They also conclude that deprivation affects a very diverse range of disconnected groups. Often, the only thing these groups have in common is one of the above indicators of social exclusion and deprivation. Consequently, they do not constitute a working-class group as a whole.

Giddens and Diamond conclude that social class in the UK has been undermined by a process of 'individualization', meaning that the experiences of young people, in particular, have become more varied and no longer predictable on the basis of social class. They now have access to a diverse set of pathways, making it harder to identify groups of individuals who have the same set of experiences. Class identity and inequality are, therefore, dismissed as things of the past that have very little influence on people's experiences and life-chances in the modern UK.

### The traditionalist view

The 'new traditionalists' are sociologists who argue that class divisions and conflict are still the key characteristics of British society today. They believe that New Labour politicians have abandoned their commitment to equality and social justice for those exploited by the organization of capitalism, namely the working class. These 'traditionalists' believe that New Labour has betrayed its working-class roots because it has done nothing to redistribute wealth and income from rich to poor, nor to address the fundamental flaws that they see as inherent in the capitalist system. Traditionalists accuse the government of tinkering with policies under the banner of social exclusion that raise the opportunities of groups such as the poor and single parents without addressing what traditionalists see as the main cause of their inequality: the concentration of vast amounts of wealth in the hands of an obscenely rich few. They suggest that the concept of social exclusion has three consequences:

1 It implies that the cause of deprivation lies in several factors unrelated to the economic organization of society.
2 By implying that individual effort is the key to economic success, little is done to change existing structural arrangements that have traditionally benefited the economic elite.
3 It shifts the blame for inequality, poverty, etc., very firmly onto the shoulders of those on the bottom rungs of society.

So, who is correct: the traditionalists or the new egalitarians? We need to examine the evidence in more detail before we can come to any firm conclusions.

## Trends in income, wealth and poverty

A number of observations can be made about the distribution of income, wealth and poverty between 1945 and now.

### Income

Between 1979 and 1997 (during an unbroken period of Conservative government), income inequality between the rich and poor in Britain widened until it was at its most unequal since records began at the end of the 19th century. No other Western industrialized country, apart from the USA, had experienced this level of inequality.

Average income rose by 36 per cent during this period, but the top 10 per cent of earners experienced a 62 per cent rise, whilst the poorest 10 per cent of earners experienced a 17 per cent decline. In 2000, those in the service class (professional, managerial and administrative employees) earned well above the average national wage, whereas every group of manual workers (skilled, semi-skilled and unskilled) earned well below the national average. In 2002/03, the richest 10 per cent of the population received 29 per cent of total disposable income (compared with 21 per cent in 1979), whilst the poorest 10 per cent received only 3 per cent (compared with 4 per cent in 1979).

Since 1997, when Labour took power, income inequality has widened even further: in 2007, the top 0.1 per cent (47 000 people in all) received 4.3 per cent of all income – this was three times greater than their share in 1979. The top 10 per cent of individuals in the UK now receive 40 per cent of all personal income (21 per cent in 1979), whilst the poorest 10 per cent still received only 3 per cent (4 per cent in 1979). The Institute for Fiscal Studies study of 2007 tax records concluded that income inequality between the rich and the poor is now at its highest level since the late 1940s (Brewer *et al.* 2008).

## *Income inequality and market forces*

Roberts (2001) notes that the new egalitarian explanation for income inequality is market forces. It is argued that income inequalities have widened because skill requirements have been rising, and workers with the right skills, most notably finance professionals working in the City of London, have benefited. New egalitarians, such as Giddens and Diamond, suggest that the economically successful often bring benefits to the wider society in terms of drive, initiative and creativity, and should not be penalized in the form of excessive taxes. However, Roberts notes that the facts do not support the market-forces view. He points out that pay rarely corresponds with labour shortages or surpluses. Roberts shows that universities today produce more graduates compared with 30 years ago and, logically, average graduate pay should have fallen. However, in practice, graduate pay has actually risen – pay differentials between graduates and non-graduate employees have widened.

Roberts also argues that only class theory can explain income inequalities. He notes that upper-middle-class occupations, such as company executives and senior managers, generally fix their own salaries. They also often supplement their salaries with other financial incentives, such as being given stock options, bonuses and profit-sharing deals, as they have overall day-to-day operational control over corporations and, in some cases, actually own the majority of shares in the company. The reduction in tax rates for top earners from 83 per cent to 40 per cent in 1979 enormously benefited this group. However Roberts notes that whilst some middle-class professionals can negotiate their salaries, the vast majority of lower-middle-class and working-class occupations either have to negotiate collectively as part of trade unions or they are told how much they will earn.

## *Corporate moral responsibility*

In recent years there been some concern about the salaries of so-called 'fat-cat' executives especially in banking following the financial crisis that beset this sector in 2009. It has been suggested that corporations should be more morally responsible in the context of a society in which poverty, deprivation and debt is a norm for many people. For example, in October 2005, Philip Green, the chief executive of Arcadia, was criticized for being greedy in paying himself £1.4 billion in salary. Moreover, there are signs that society is increasingly unhappy because top executives are not only rewarded for success, but seemingly also for failure, in that many executives are paid off with 'golden goodbyes' often totalling hundreds of thousands of pounds. Orton and Rowlingson (2007) conducted a survey into public attitudes to wealth inequality and found deep social unease, especially about the pay of the highest earners. In addition, people were more likely to think that people at the top of the pay scale are paid too much rather than people at the bottom are paid too little.

## *Poverty*

These arguments about corporate moral irresponsibility and executive greed become more acute when we consider that the Low Pay Unit estimated in 2000 that 45 per cent of British workers (overwhelmingly semi-skilled and unskilled workers) were earning less than two-thirds of the average wage. Furthermore, many low-paid workers are often caught in a **poverty trap**. This means they earn above the minimum level required to claim benefits, but the deduction of tax, etc., takes them below it. Similarly, many on benefits actually end up worse off if they take low-paid work because they are no longer eligible for state support.

Low pay has particularly impacted on levels of poverty. While levels of absolute poverty have fallen in the UK, especially since 1997, relative poverty has continued to rise steeply. As Savage (2000) notes, relative poverty in 1997 was twice the level it reached in the 1960s and three times what it had been in the late 1970s. Children have been particularly affected. Forty per cent of children are born into families in the bottom 30 per cent of income distribution. Treasury figures in March 1999 estimated that up to 25 per cent of children never escape from poverty and that deprivation is being passed down the generations by unemployment and underachievement in schools.

Feinstein *et al.* (2007), in a study of 17 000 children born in 1970, found that a child born to a labourer was six times more likely to suffer extreme poverty by the age of 30 than one born to a lawyer. The study also showed that, despite billions of pounds of government funding to cut child poverty, the gap between the poorest and richest children is probably wider today than it was three decades ago. Feinstein points out that the three most influential factors in predicting poverty at the age of 30 were parental occupation, low income and housing – all prime symbols of social-class position.

## Wealth

The 20th century did see a gradual redistribution of wealth in the UK. In 1911, the most wealthy 1 per cent of the population held 69 per cent of all wealth, yet by 1993, this had dropped to 17 per cent. However, this redistribution did not extend down into the mass of society. Rather it was very narrow – the very wealthy top 1 per cent distributed some of its wealth to the wealthy top 10 per cent via trust funds in order to avoid paying taxes in the form of death duties. The result of this redistribution within the economic elite is that in 2003, the top 1 per cent and top 10 per cent owned 18 per cent and 50 per cent of the nation's wealth respectively. The wealth of the most affluent 200 individuals and families doubled by 2000. This polarization of wealth in the UK has also been encouraged by a soaring stock market (investments in stocks and shares) and property values, which as Savage notes 'have allowed those who were already wealthy to accumulate their wealth massively'. In contrast, half the population shared only 10 per cent of total wealth in 1986, and this had been reduced to 6 per cent by 2003.

Things look even worse if property ownership is removed from this wealth analysis and the focus is exclusively on wealth in the form of cash, stocks and shares, art and antiques, etc. In 2003, the top 1 per cent of the population owned 34 per cent of all personal wealth, whilst the bottom 50 per cent owned just 1 per cent.

The privatization of public utilities such as British Telecom and British Gas in the 1980s widened share ownership, so that by 1988, 21 per cent of people owned shares. However, the evidence suggests this was a short-term phenomenon as people who had never owned shares before sold their shares quickly as their value rose. Today, although about 17 per cent of all people own shares, the richest 1 per cent of the population still own 75 per cent of all privately owned shares. As Roberts (2001) notes:

> « *We are certainly not all capitalists now. In 1993, the least wealthy half of the population owned just 7 per cent of all personally-held wealth; around 30 per cent of adults do not own the dwellings in which they live; a half of all employees do not have significant occupational pensions. In fact, a half of the population has near-zero assets, and many are in debt when account is taken of outstanding mortgages, bank overdrafts, hire-purchase commitments, loans on credit cards, store cards and all the rest. It is only roughly a half of the population that has any significant share in the country's wealth.* » (pp.178–9)

The fact that nearly half the population have a share in the country's wealth may sound impressive, but Roberts points out that most of these people will liquidate assets such as savings and pension funds in old age in order to safeguard the standard of living they have enjoyed in the latter half of their life. As Roberts notes, it is only the extremely wealthy who can expect to die with most of their wealth intact. A lot of wealth that people have is also tied up with property in which people live. Homeowners can make money out of their property but this is not the main reason most people buy their houses. Most people own one house, whilst the extremely wealthy may own several houses as well as land bought for its future investment value. Finally, Roberts notes that the proportion of the population with enough wealth that they do not have to work for others is still less than 1 per cent. This elite group employ others to work for them. On the other hand, the life-chances of the vast majority of the population depend on the kinds of jobs they can obtain. Roberts concludes:

> « *Despite the spread of wealth, this remains a clear class relationship and division. It is, in fact, the clearest of all class divisions, and it still splits the population into a tiny minority on the one side, and the great mass of the people on the other.* » (p.180)

## Health

Bottero (2005) claims that 'social inequalities are written on the body' and 'hierarchy makes you sick'. She notes that if illness was a chance occurrence, we could expect to see rates of **morbidity** (i.e. illness and disease) and **mortality** (i.e. death) randomly distributed across the population. However, it is clear from Department of Health statistics that the working class experience a disproportionate amount of illness. In general, health across the population has improved over the last 30 years but the rate of improvement has been much slower for the working class. Generally, the working class experience worse mortality rates and morbidity rates than the middle classes. For example, 3500 more working-class babies would survive per year if the working-class infant mortality rate was reduced to middle-class levels. Babies born to professional fathers have levels of infant mortality half that of babies born to unskilled manual fathers.

### *Class and death rates*

If we examine death rates we can see that, between 1972 and 1997, death rates for professionals fell by 44 per cent, but fell by only 10 per cent for the unskilled. Bartley *et al.* (1996) note that men in Social Class I (using the old RG scale) had only two-thirds the chance of dying between 1986 and 1989 compared with the male population as a whole. However, unskilled manual workers (Social Class V using the old RG scale) were one-third more likely to die compared with the male population as a whole. Despite the NHS providing free universal health care to all, men in Social Class V were twice as likely to die before men in Social Class I.

Bottero notes that:

> « *There is a strong socio-economic gradient to almost all patterns of disease and ill-health. The lower your socio-economic position, the greater your risk of low birthweight, infections, cancer, coronary heart disease, respiratory disease, stroke, accidents, nervous and mental illnesses.* » (p.188)

Moreover, she points out that there are specific occupational hazards linked to particular manual jobs which increase the risk of accidental injury, exposure to toxic materials, pollution, etc. Poor people are more likely to live in areas in which there are more hazards, such as traffic and pollution, and fewer safe areas to play.

# Focus on research

## Andy Furlong *et al.* (2006) Social class in an 'individualized' society

The research aimed to identify the main routes that describe the transitions of young people from school into work. Using data from a longitudinal study carried out in the west of Scotland, the research studied the experiences of over 1000 young people aged between 15 and 23. The research identified eight transitional routes:

1. long higher education – university
2. short higher education – shorter courses such as HND
3. enhanced education – highers (equivalent to A-levels), then employment
4. direct job – leave school at 16 to go to work
5. assisted – on government training schemes
6. unemployment
7. domestic – time out of the labour market to have and/or care for children
8. other – usually made up of chronically sick or disabled people.

Furlong and colleagues found that these transitional routes can largely be predicted on the basis of educational achievement, which, in turn, is predicted by social class. Some 58 per cent of those following the long higher education route had parents in the professional and managerial classes (i.e. classes 1 and 2). Only 18 per cent of children from this class had taken the assisted route, 16 per cent the unemployed route and 14 per cent the domestic route. In contrast, only 9 per cent from semi-skilled and unskilled backgrounds had made it through the higher education route. However, 27 per cent from these backgrounds had taken the assisted route, 27 per cent the unemployed route and 24 per cent had taken the domestic route. Furlong and colleagues conclude that although the social experiences of young people may appear to be more fluid today, concepts such as social class still help sociologists to understand the distribution and persistence of socioeconomic inequalities.

Furlong, A., Cartmel, F., Biggart, A., Sweeting, H. and West, P. (2006) 'Social class in an 'individualised' society', *Sociology Review*, 15(4), pp.28–32

**Explain how the research described above shows that inequalities are persistent. Use examples from the research in your answer.**



Consequently, poor children are more likely to be run over and to suffer asthma.

### *The health gradient*

Some studies have suggested that there exists a **health gradient**, in that at every level of the social hierarchy, there are health differences. Some writers, most notably Marmot *et al.* (1991), have suggested that social position may be to blame for these differences. They conducted a study on civil servants working in Whitehall, i.e. white-collar staff, and concluded that the cause of ill health was being lower in the occupational hierarchy. Those low in the hierarchy had less social control over their working conditions, greater stress and greater feelings of low self-esteem. These psychosocial factors triggered off behaviour such as smoking and drinking, poor eating habits and inactivity. The net result of this combination of psychosocial and lifestyle factors was greater levels of depression, high blood pressure, increased susceptibility to infection and build-up of cholesterol. If we apply Marmot's findings to society in general, it may be the fact that working-class occupations are the lowest in the hierarchy that may be causing their disproportionate levels of morbidity and mortality.

Other sociologists, most notably Wilkinson (1996), argue that the health gradient is caused by income inequality. He argues that relative inequality affects health because it undermines **social cohesion** – the sense that we are all valued equally by society, which affirms our sense of belonging to society. Wilkinson argues that inequality disrupts social cohesion because it undermines self-esteem, dignity, trust and cooperation, and increases feelings of insecurity, envy, hostility and inferiority, which lead to stress. As Wilkinson notes:

> ≪ *To feel depressed, cheated, bitter, desperate, vulnerable, frightened, angry, worried about debts or job and housing insecurity; to feel devalued, useless, helpless, uncared for, hopeless, isolated, anxious and a failure; these feelings can dominate people's whole experience of life, colouring their experience of everything else. It is the chronic stress arising from feelings like these which does the damage. It is the social feelings which matter, not exposure to a supposedly toxic environment.* ≫ (p.215)

Wilkinson notes that egalitarian societies have a strong community life, in that strong social ties and networks exist in the wider society to support their members. In other words, members of these societies have access to '**social capital**' – social and psychological support from others in their community which helps them stay healthy. It is argued that in societies characterized by extreme income inequality, social capital in the form of these networks is less likely to exist and health inequalities continue to grow. We can see this particularly in the UK in residential areas characterized by high levels of council housing.

## Education

Kynaston (2008) argues that most studies of meritocracy recognize that education is the prime engine of social mobility. However, he points out that meritocracy in the UK is undermined by the existence of private schools, which generally reproduce the privileges of the economic elite, generation by generation. Only about 7 per cent of all children are educated at private schools, but these pupils take up 45 per cent of Oxbridge places and a disproportionate number at other top UK universities. As ex-Labour leader Neil Kinnock once observed, public schools are the 'very cement in the walls that divide British society'.

Empirical evidence supports this view. For example, The Sutton Trust (2007) ranked the success of schools, over a five-year period, at getting their pupils into Oxbridge. Top was Westminster public school, which got 50 per cent of its students into Oxbridge and which charges annual boarding fees of £25 956 for the privilege. This means that the wealthy parents of Westminster pupils have a 50/50 chance of their child making it into Oxbridge. Altogether, there were 27 private schools amongst the top 30 schools with the best Oxbridge record; 43 in the top 50; and 78 in the top 100. The Sutton Trust concluded that the 70th brightest sixth-former at Westminster or Eton is as likely to get a place at Oxbridge as the very brightest sixth-formers at a large comprehensive school. Kynaston concludes that these figures suggest that private education is a 'roadblock on the route to meritocracy'. Other Sutton Trust studies show quite clearly that those in high-status jobs, such as senior politicians, top business leaders, judges, etc., are often privately and Oxbridge educated. Moreover, the 'old school tie' network ensures important and valuable social contacts for years to come, particularly in the finance sector of the economy. This is, almost certainly, still the most influential pathway to the glittering prizes of top jobs and super-salaries. This educational apartheid means that only the talents of the children of the wealthy elite are genuinely being unlocked.

### *Cultural capital*

The evidence suggests that middle-class children are more advantaged than working-class children. Studies show that they benefit from living in better areas (with better schools). This, of course, is assisted by the better incomes earned by their parents, which means they can afford to buy into areas which have schools with good league-table standings. Income increases educational choices, so, for instance, parents can choose to send their children to private schools or to hire personal tutors. Middle-class parents are also able to use their knowledge, expertise, contacts and greater confidence in expressing themselves and in dealing with fellow professionals – their cultural capital – to ensure that their children are well served by the educational system. All of these factors undermine the view that the UK is a meritocracy.

### The underachievement of working-class children

Working-class children perform much worse in education than all other social groups at all levels of the education system. For example, more working-class children leave school at the age of 16 with no qualifications than middle-class 16 year olds, and while the number of working-class 18 year olds entering university has increased, the number of middle-class undergraduates still far exceeds them. Moreover, Furlong and Cartmel (2005) found that children from disadvantaged backgrounds were more likely to be found in the 'new universities' rather than elite institutions and they were less likely to secure graduate jobs on leaving. Moreover, as Savage and Egerton (1997) found, ability does not wipe out class advantage. For example, their study found that less than half of the 'high-ability' working-class boys in their study made it into the service class (compared with three-quarters of the 'high-ability' boys with service-class fathers). Furthermore, 65 per cent of their 'low-ability' service-class boys were able to avoid dropping down into manual work.

Feinstein (2007) suggests that class inequalities are a significant influence on the underachievement of working-class children. Feinstein notes that the children of skilled manual workers may not do as badly at school as the children of welfare dependants or unskilled workers, but they still underachieve and there are many more of them. Children from these backgrounds have already fallen behind their more advantaged peers by the age of 3. This process continues throughout childhood, and it operates both ways: less-able and initially low-achieving middle-class children generally improve their position, but the position of initially high-achieving working-class children generally declines. Consequently, more than half of the children from skilled working-class homes (45 per cent of the child population) who are in the top 25 per cent in reading skills at the age of 7 will fall out of this top quarter by age 11. By contrast, if a child from a professional home is in the top quarter at 7 years, he or she is highly likely still to be there four years later. Hirsch (2006) argues that many working-class children fall behind because their homes – however loving and well-intentioned – don't and often can't provide the same support for formal learning as more affluent homes because they lack the material resources, such as income, computers, internet access and so on.

## Conclusions

The new egalitarians are undoubtedly correct in drawing our attention to the fact that a diversity of social groups, such as the long-term unemployed, single mothers and asylum-seekers, are socially excluded from mainstream society and so experience a range of social and economic deprivations. However, their reluctance to acknowledge the role of social class and its indicators (such as inequalities in income, wealth, housing, health and education) is incomprehensible given the weight of the evidence available. As Savage (2000) concludes:

*<<In recent years, whatever people's perceptions of their class might be, there is no doubting that class inequality has hardened. People's destinies are as strongly affected and perhaps more strongly affected, by their class background than they were in the mid-20th century.>>*

The evidence in this section also challenges the postmodernist view that social class has ceased to be the primary shaper of identity and that people exercise more choice about the type of people they want to be, especially in terms of lifestyle and consumption. Postmodernists and New Right thinkers, such as Saunders, neglect the fact that lifestyle choices and consumption depend on educational qualifications, the jobs we have and the income we earn. Unfortunately, members of the working class are less likely to qualify on all three counts for the postmodern lifestyle. Moreover, they are well aware that it is their social class more than any other social factor that is holding them back from making the sorts of choices that are taken for granted by social classes above them.

## Key terms

**Blairite** ideas uniquely associated with Tony Blair or New Labour.

**Cleavage** a term used by Saunders to describe differences in the spending patterns of social groups.

**Consumption** spending on goods and services.

**Equality of opportunity** the idea that social groups should have the same opportunities to succeed.

**Health gradient** the fact that the chances of dying or becoming ill progressively increase or decline the lower or higher you are on the occupational hierarchy.

**Marginalization** powerlessness, i.e. the inability to overcome social and economic injustices.

**Material deprivation** the lack of physical resources needed in order to lead a full and normal life.

**Morbidity rate** reported ill health per 100 000 of population.

**Mortality rate** number of deaths per 100 000 of population.

**New egalitarians** a group of sociologists and politicians who believe that social-class divisions are in decline and that policies to socially include deprived groups are working.

**New traditionalists** sociologists who argue that class divisions and conflict are still the key characteristics of British society today.

**Poverty trap** the fact that after taxation and national insurance contributions, the wages paid by some jobs fall below the official poverty line.

**Social capital** social relationships that benefit people, e.g. in finding a job.

**Social cohesion** the idea that people feel a sense of belonging to society because they feel valued and wanted.

**Social exclusion** the fact that some people are excluded from what everyone else takes for granted, usually because of poor educational, family or economic circumstances.

**Social inclusion** being part of the mainstream because of the opportunities offered by government policies, e.g. training, education.

# Activities

## Research idea

Get an A to Z of your local area. Enlarge a residential area that you know to be a high-demand area. Similarly, enlarge an area in low demand. Annotate each as far as possible to highlight differences in facilities/resources. Conduct a survey of residents in each area to discover the level of services and facilities on offer there.

Compare and contrast the two areas to test the extent to which people in low-demand areas suffer a variety of social exclusions.

## Web.task

Go to the government statistics site at **www.ons.gov.uk**

Select Neighbourhood statistics. Choose your own postcode or the district or postcode where your school or college is situated. You will be able to investigate a variety of indicators of wealth and deprivation. How does your area compare with other parts of the region or with Britain as a whole?

## Check your understanding

1. **What groups are typically socially excluded according to the new egalitarians?**
2. **What is the main difference between new egalitarians and new traditionalists?**
3. **What is the new egalitarian attitude towards the rich?**
4. **Why have income inequalities widened in the UK over the last thirty years?**
5. **What have been the main trends with regard to wealth redistribution in the UK over the past 30 years?**
6. **Give three statistical examples of health differences between classes.**
7. **What effect has the health gradient had on the social make-up of some residential areas?**
8. **What evidence is there that council housing is becoming increasingly the domain of the socially deprived?**
9. **What problems do those living on council estates face?**
10. **How do educational inequalities support the view that social class may still be important?**

## An eye on the exam Life-chances and social class

Describe only – no need for evaluation

Socio-economic differences (see Topic 1)

**(a) Outline the evidence that social class affects life chances. (20 marks)**

Statistical trends and patterns, research findings and contemporary examples from any module studied and/or your wider sociological knowledge

Opportunities to acquire aspects of social life that most people aspire to, such as good health, housing, education, family and employment

### Grade booster Getting top marks in this question

Begin with a brief explanation of the idea of social class. Include evidence of social class differences from other modules you have studied as well as 'Social inequality and difference', for example the family, crime or education. The evidence might be in the form of statistical patterns or trends (e.g. those on income, wealth and poverty) or the findings of particular studies (e.g. Wilkinson, the Sutton Trust). Try to cover a range of points in reasonable detail. Don't be tempted to evaluate any of the points you make as the majority of marks for this question are for knowledge and understanding.

# TOPIC 4

# Changes in the class structure

## Getting you thinking

1 What do you think are the main differences between the people in the photographs above?

2 Which would you call 'posh' and why?

3 Why do you think Victoria Beckham was often referred to as 'Posh' when she performed with the Spice Girls?

4 With which social class do you most associate the Beckhams? Explain your answer.

5 What do the terms 'working class', 'middle class' and 'upper class' mean to you?

6 What factors other than class affect the way people are perceived today?

Your answers to the above questions may demonstrate that class is a difficult thing to define nowadays and that status is no longer a matter of being on the right side of the class divide. The old idea of the class structure was that it comprised a triangular shape, with numbers increasing towards the base, which was composed of a vast number of unskilled manual workers providing a strong industrial-based manufacturing sector. This model implied a strict hierarchy, with higher levels of income, status and power towards the top. Although this was never actually the true shape (because manufacturing jobs have never accounted for the majority of the workforce), there has been a dramatic shift in Britain's industrial structure, with only about 18 per cent of the population working in manufacturing today. At the same time, numbers of those working in **tertiary** or **service-sector jobs** (those providing services such as transport, retailing, hotel work, cleaning, banking and insurance) have increased dramatically from 25 per cent to 75 per cent.

# The upper class

It has been argued that the upper class (the extremely wealthy, property-owning elite who need not work in order to maintain their lifestyle), especially the aristocratic and traditional rich, have declined in wealth, power and influence over the course of the 20th century. In particular, it has been argued by Roberts (2001) that high death duties (now called 'inheritance tax') have resulted in a substantial number of upper-class families losing their family seats (the country houses where their family lived for generations) and experiencing downward social mobility. Some have even been forced to take up salaried employment in the service sector. In other words, it is argued that the upper class is in danger of being assimilated into the upper-middle class. But how true are these assertions? A number of observations can be made on the basis of the evidence available.

## Inherited wealth

The upper class is still very wealthy. We saw earlier how the top 1 per cent have got 'poorer', but only because they have made real efforts to avoid inheritance tax by transferring their wealth via trust funds to the top 10 per cent. Moreover, the top 10 per cent still own about one-half of the country's wealth.

The evidence also suggests that we should talk about wealthy families rather than wealthy individuals. In this context, inheritance is very important. In general, individuals or families are wealthy because their fathers were also rich. Inheritance is responsible for most of the inequality in the distribution of wealth.

## Positions of economic leadership

Scott (1982) argues that there now exists a unified propertied class which has actively used its wealth to maintain its privileged position at the top of the socio-economic structure. He argues that the core of the upper class – the richest 0.1 per cent (between 25 000 and 50 000 people) – occupy positions of leadership in manufacturing, banking and finance. He suggests that this core is made up of three groups:

- entrepreneurial capitalists, who own (or mainly own) businesses founded by their family
- internal capitalists, the senior executives who head the bureaucracies that run the big companies
- finance capitalists, who usually own or run financial institutions such as merchant banks and firms of stockbrokers.

It can be argued that the traditional landed gentry, mainly aristocratic in character, has managed since the turn of the 20th century, through investment and marriage to business and financial leaders, to become an integral part of the three groups that make up the core of the modern upper class.

## Networks and social closure

The upper class is also supported by networks that permeate throughout that class. These may be based on marriage or kinship. For example, there is a tendency for members of the upper class to marry other upper-class individuals. This obviously gives the class a unity based on marriage and kinship, and is instrumental in strengthening business and financial ties between families.

Membership of the upper class is strengthened by **social closure** – the ability to control mobility into upper-class circles. This is partly achieved by networking and being part of an 'in crowd'. Another major means of ensuring social closure is the emphasis on public-school education. Generation after generation of upper-class children have been educated at fee-paying schools, such as Eton, Harrow, Winchester, Westminster, Charterhouse and Rugby. The large movement of such pupils into the elite universities of Oxford and Cambridge reinforces such students' belief in their 'difference' from the rest of society. The 'old-boy network', based very much on common schooling, is a type of networking that financially benefits members of the upper class and reinforces self-recruitment to the upper class. This means that current members of the upper class are likely to be the offspring of wealthy individuals who attended the same schools and universities. Their sons and daughters are very likely to follow the same route.

A good example of the power of social closure can be seen if we examine the current political establishment. Despite the fact that only 7.3 per cent of the UK population attend private fee-paying schools, ex-private-school pupils were disproportionately represented among top politicians in 2008 and included:

- nearly a third of Labour government ministers
- 59 per cent of Conservative MPs
- 17 out of 27 members of David Cameron's shadow cabinet.

In addition:

- 14 members of the Conservative opposition frontbench attended Eton College, including the Conservative leader, David Cameron
- the Conservative mayor of London, Boris Johnson, was educated at Eton
- the two leading Liberal Democrats in 2008, Nick Clegg and Chris Huhne, both attended Westminster School.

## The 'Establishment'

Scott argues that the upper class's influence is not confined to business. There is overwhelming evidence that those in top positions in politics, the civil service, the church, the armed services and the professions come disproportionately from upper-class families. Scott refers to this group as the 'establishment' – a coherent and self-recruiting body of men with a similarity of outlook who are able to wield immense power. However, exactly how this group interacts and whether they do so for their own benefit is extremely difficult to prove.

Although the basis of the wealth of the upper class is no longer primarily land, this class still retains many of the characteristics it possessed 50 years ago, especially the emphasis on public-school education, thus helping to ensure that social closure continues unchallenged.

# The middle classes

## The expansion of the middle classes

In 1911, some 80 per cent of workers were in manual occupations. This number fell to 32.7 per cent in 1991 and is approximately 25 per cent today. Non-manual workers (traditionally seen as middle-class) have now become the majority occupational group in the workforce. As Savage (1995) points out, there are now more university lecturers than coal miners in the UK.

## Reasons for the expansion

The number of manual jobs in both **primary** and **secondary industries** has gone into decline since the 1970s as a result of a range of factors, including new technologies, the oil crisis and globalization (i.e. the same raw materials and goods can be produced more cheaply in developing countries). The tertiary or service sector of the economy that is organized around education, welfare, retail and finance has expanded hugely in the past 20 years. Mass secondary education and the expansion of both further and higher education have ensured the existence of a well-educated and qualified workforce. The service sector is made up of a mainly male professional workforce at its top end but, as a result of changes in women's social position, the bulk of workers in this sector are female.

## The boundary problem

Studying the middle classes can be problematic because not all sociologists agree who should be included in this category. This is the so-called '**boundary problem**'. Traditionally, differentiating between the middle class and working class was thought to be a simple task involving distinguishing between white-collar, or non-manual, workers on the one hand and blue-collar, or manual, workers on the other. Generally, the former enjoyed better working conditions in terms of pay, holidays and promotion possibilities. Today, however, this distinction is not so clear cut. Some sociologists, notably Braverman, argue that some **routine white-collar workers** no longer fit neatly into a middle-class category.

## A fragmented middle class

The term 'middle class' covers a wide range of occupations, incomes, lifestyles and attitudes. Roberts *et al.* (1977) argued that the middle class was becoming fragmented into a number of different groups, each with a distinctive view of its place in the stratification system. They suggest that we should no longer talk of the middle class, but of the 'middle classes'. Savage *et al.* (1992) agree that it is important to see that the middle class is now divided into strata, or '**class fractions**', such as higher and lower professionals, higher and middle managers, the petit bourgeoisie and routine white-collar workers.

### *Professionals*

Savage and colleagues argue that higher and lower professionals mainly recruit internally – in other words, the sons and daughters of professionals are likely to end up as professionals themselves. The position of professional workers is based on the possession of educational qualifications. Professionals usually have to go through a long period of training – university plus professional examinations before they qualify. Savage argues that professionals possess both **economic capital** (a very good standard of living, savings, financial security) and cultural capital (seeing the worth of education and other cultural assets such as taste in high culture), which they pass on to their children. Moreover, they increasingly have social capital (belonging to networks that can influence decision-making by other professionals such as head teachers). Professionals also have strong occupational associations, such as the Law Society and the British Medical Association, that protect and actively pursue their interests (although the lower down the professional ladder, the weaker these associations/unions become). The result of such groups actively pursuing the interests of professionals, especially those in the state sector in areas such as the NHS, is high rewards, status and job security.

Savage concludes that professionals are aware of their common interests and quite willing to take industrial action to protect those interests. In this sense, then, professionals have a greater sense of class identity than other middle-class groups. However, there is a slight danger that as the state sector becomes increasingly privatized, many professionals will face an increased threat of redundancy and reduced promotional opportunities as a result of de-layering (a reduction in the number of 'tiers' of management in an organization).

### *Managers*

Savage and colleagues suggest that managers have assets based upon a particular skill within specific organizations. Such skills (unlike those of professionals) are not easily transferable to other companies or industries. They note that many managers have been upwardly mobile from the routine white-collar sector or the skilled working class. Many have worked their way up through an organization which they joined at an early age. They consequently often lack university degrees. Their social position, therefore, is likely to be the result of experience and reputation rather than qualifications. Savage notes too that most managers do not belong to professional associations or trade unions. Consequently, they tend to be more individualistic in character and are less likely to identify a common collective interest with their fellow managers – whom they are much more likely to see as competitors. Savage argues that managers actively encourage their children to pursue higher education because they can see the benefits of a professional career. However, managers, despite being well paid, are less likely to have the cultural or social capital possessed by professionals.

Savage argues that job security differentiates professionals from managers – managers, particularly middle managers such as bank managers, are constantly under threat of losing their jobs because of recession, mergers and **downsizing**. They are consequently more likely to be potentially downwardly mobile.

However, some sociologists have noted that, in the past 20 years, a super-class of higher executives has appeared who run companies on a day-to-day basis and who are on spectacular salaries and often have share options worth millions. The Income Data Services showed that nearly half of all senior executives of Britain's 350 largest public companies made more than £1 million a year, with eight directors on packages of £5+ million (Cohen 2005). Adonis and Pollard (1998) claim that this 'super-class' or salariat now makes up approximately 15 per cent of middle-class occupations. According to Adonis and Pollard, the lifestyle of this super-class revolves around nannies and servants, second homes, private education for their children, private health schemes, exotic foreign holidays and investment in modern art. The super-class tends to live on private urban estates patrolled by private security companies. Some sociologists have suggested that this super-class is no longer middle-class because it has more in common with the unified property elite that now makes up most of the upper class.

### *The self-employed*

Between 1981 and 1991, the number of people **self-employed**, referred to by Marx as the '**petit-bourgeois**', rose from 6.7 per cent of the workforce to over 10 per cent. Research by Fielding (1995) examined what the self-employed in 1981 were doing in 1991. He showed that two-thirds of his sample constituted a relatively stable and secure part of the workforce in that they remained self-employed over this ten-year period. However, he noted that the character of the self-employed has undergone some change. The number of managers who prefer to work for themselves (for example, as consultants) rose considerably in the 1980s, especially in the finance and computer industries. Some writers argue that many firms now prefer to contract services to outside consultants rather than employ people themselves because it is cheaper and they have fewer legal obligations to such workers.

### *Routine white-collar workers*

Marxists such as Harry Braverman (1974) argue that routine white-collar workers are no longer middle class. Braverman argues that they have been subjected to a process of **proletarianization**. This means that they have lost the social and economic advantages that they enjoyed over manual workers, such as superior pay and working conditions. Braverman argues that, in the past 20 years, employers have used technology, especially computers, to break down complex white-collar skills, such as book-keeping, into simplistic routine tasks. This process is known as '**de-skilling**' and is an attempt to increase output, maximize efficiency and reduce costs. Control over the work process has, therefore, been removed from many non-manual workers.

These developments have been accompanied by the parallel development of the feminization of the routine white-collar workforce (especially in the financial sector and call centres), because female workers are generally cheap to employ and are seen by employers as more adaptable and amenable to this type of work. Braverman concludes that de-skilling means that occupations that once were middle class are today in all respects indistinguishable from those of manual workers.

However, Marshall *et al.* (1988) have challenged the idea of proletarianization. In a national random sample of female workers, they found that it was mainly manual workers who claimed that their work had been de-skilled. Over 90 per cent of non-manual workers felt that little had changed, and most identified with the middle class rather than the working class. Finally, they were also more likely to vote Conservative than Labour. Marshall and colleagues therefore concluded that proletarianization among routine white-collar workers was not taking place.

### *New-technology workers*

In further contrast to Braverman, however, Clark and Hoffman-Martinot (1998) highlight the growth of a technological elite of 'wired workers' – new professionals who are as productive as entire offices of routine non-manual workers because of their use of technology, and who spend most of their days behind computers working in non-hierarchical settings. They enjoy considerable **autonomy**, are paid extremely well, often working flexibly, sometimes from home and are engaged in dynamic problem-solving activities. Such workers can be found in a wide range of new occupations regarded as part of the 'infotech sector' – areas such as web design, systems analysis, e-commerce, software development, graphic design and financial consultancy. At the lower end of this sector, however, are growing numbers of casual workers who spend all day on the telephone in front of a VDU, often working in very poor conditions in call-centres.

In conclusion, then, the middle classes are an important and vibrant part of the class structure. What was once a minority group, perceived as a class apart from the working class in terms of income, lifestyle, status, and culture, has become a much larger, more heterogeneous (diverse) body.

# The working class

## Changes in class solidarity

Fulcher and Scott (1999) point out that, until the late 20th century, the working class had a strong sense of their social-class position. Virtually all aspects of their lives, including gender roles, family life, political affiliation and leisure, were a product of their keen sense of working-

# Focus on research

## Simon Charlesworth

### A phenomenology of working-class experience

Simon Charlesworth's study focuses on working-class people in Rotherham in Yorkshire, the town where he grew up. Charlesworth based his study on 43 unstructured, conversational interviews, although he also clearly spoke to large numbers of people whom he knew socially. Many of the people to whom he spoke were male, but at least a third were female.

Charlesworth finds class seeping into all aspects of life in Rotherham. Generally, he finds that the lives of people are characterized by suffering and depression. The loss of a man's job, for instance, has a physical consequence because it can lead to fear and panic because of loss of earnings. Older people, in particular, are faced with the difficulties of learning to cope with a changing world. One of his main findings is that miserable economic conditions cause people to feel both physically and psychologically unhealthy.

Many of the unemployed workers experienced a lack of identity and a sense of being devalued because of the loss of status which normally accompanies paid work. However, the culture of the working-class lad demands respect and consequently this was pursued by committing crime and antisocial behaviour.

Other working-class lads saw no point in working at education or qualifications because even

if they acquired them, they were not able to obtain decent work. There were further problems for those who did get to university or college, as they felt out of place and excluded from the culture because they were no longer fully part of it.

Charlesworth concludes that changes in the social climate have left people without a sense of belonging to their 'communities' or an understanding of how the world is developing. They have little hope for their future and they worry for their children. He claims that the socially excluded and deprived of Rotherham (which the locals called 'Deadman's Town') feel rage and suffering. The culture that develops out of unemployment and poverty is one of having to make do and buy only what is necessary and cheap. It is therefore marked by social and spiritual decay.

Adapted from Blundell, J. and Griffiths, J. (2002) *Sociology since 1995*, Vol 2, Lewes: Connect Publications

1. **Identify two criticisms that might be made of Charlesworth's methods as described in the passage above.**
2. **What factors have caused working-class culture in Rotherham to be marked by a 'social and spiritual decay'?**



class identity. Lockwood's (1966) research found that many workers, especially in industrial areas, subscribed to a value system he called '**proletarian traditionalist**'. Such workers felt a strong sense of loyalty to each other because of shared community and work experience, and so were mutually supportive of each other. They had a keen sense that capitalist society was characterized by inequality and unfairness. Consequently, they tended to see society in terms of conflict – a case of 'them' (their employers who were seen as exploiting them) versus 'us' (the workers united in a common cause and consciousness).

Later research has claimed that this type of class identity is in decline because the service sector of the economy has grown more important as the traditional industrial and manufacturing sectors have gone into decline. Recession and unemployment linked to globalization have undermined traditional working-class communities and organizations such as trade unions. However, Cannadine (1998) argues that this idea – that once upon a time the working class subscribed to a collective class consciousness and an adversarial view of society – is exaggerated and the evidence lacking. He argues that the history of the working class suggests no clear consistent pattern of class consciousness – collectivism only emerges at particular times and in particular contexts, and even then, is rarely universally shared.

## Middle-class lifestyles?

In the 1960s, Zweig (1961) argued that a section of the working class – skilled manual workers – had adopted the economic and cultural lifestyle of the middle class. This argument became known as the '**embourgeoisement** thesis' because it insisted that skilled workers had become more like the middle class by supporting bourgeois values and the Conservative party, as well as enjoying similar income levels.

This view was investigated in Goldthorpe and Lockwood's famous study of a car factory in Luton (1969). They found little evidence to support Zweig's assertion. Economically, whilst wages were comparable to those of members of the middle classes, they did not enjoy the same working conditions or fringe benefits, such as expense accounts, company car, sick pay or company pensions. They had to work longer hours and had less chance of promotion. They did not readily mix with members of other classes, either inside or outside work, and 77 per cent of their sample voted Labour. Goldthorpe and Lockwood did, however, argue that there were signs of **convergence** between working-class and middle-class lifestyles, but concluded that, rather than an increase in the middle class, what had emerged was a new working class.

### *The privatized new working class*

Goldthorpe and Lockwood identified a new trend, the emergence of the 'privatized instrumentalist' worker who saw work as a means to an end rather than as a source of identity. These affluent workers were more home-centred than traditional working-class groups; they were also less likely to subscribe to the notion of working-class community and 'them-versus-us' attitudes. However, Fiona Devine (1992) undertook a second study of the Vauxhall plant at Luton in the late 1980s, in which she argued that Goldthorpe and Lockwood's study may have exaggerated the degree of working-class privatization. She found that workers retained strong kinship and friendship links, and had a reasonably developed working-class identity in that they were critically aware of class inequalities such as the unequal distribution of wealth and income.

Although the concept of embourgeoisement is now rarely used, it is frequently argued that the working class have fragmented into at least two different layers:

- the traditional working class, in decline and typically situated in the north of England
- a new working class found in the newer manufacturing industries, mainly situated in the south, who enjoy a relatively affluent lifestyle but still see themselves as working-class.

## False consciousness?

However, Marxists reject the view that there is a fragmented working class. They argue that there is still a unified working class made up of manual workers – both Black and White, male and female, and routine white-collar workers. They would argue that the sorts of divisions discussed above are the product of ruling-class ideology, which attempts to divide and rule the working class. The fact that some groups do not see themselves as working class is dismissed by Marxists as false class-consciousness. They would argue that in relation to the means and social relations of production, all so-called 'class fractions' are objectively working class because they are alienated and exploited by the ruling class, whether they realize it or not.

## The underclass

The concept of the **underclass** has entered everyday speech to describe those living at the margins of society, largely reliant on state benefits to make ends meet. However, the concept has been rejected by many sociologists due to its negative and sometimes politically charged connotations. Members of the political right, such as Charles Murray (1994) in the USA, in particular, have focused on the cultural 'deficiencies' of the so-called underclass, blaming them for their situation, and accusing them of being welfare-dependent (i.e. relying on benefits). It is also argued that they supplement their income through petty crime, or compensate for deprivation through excessive drug and alcohol abuse. Murray identifies a Black underclass which, he alleges, is to be found in most American cities. Similar points have been made about members of non-working groups in deprived areas of Britain, particularly single-mothers living in inner-city areas or on deprived council estates (Dennis and Erdos 1993).

## A matter of choice?

Many New Right commentators (such as Saunders 1995) suggest that a large number of the poor see 'poverty' as a choice, as a way of life preferable to work. Young single mothers are often cited as examples of this – for example, by having a second child in order to secure a flat that will be paid for by the state. However, various studies such as those by Morris (1993) and Gallie (1994) have examined the extent to which the poor possess cultural differences that may account for their situation. They found that there is little evidence of an underclass culture and that the most disadvantaged groups actually have a greater commitment to the concept of work than many other groups.

Marxists are also sceptical about the existence of an underclass. They point out that capitalist economies produce large numbers of poorly skilled and insecure workers who are constantly at risk of falling into poverty because capitalism is an unstable and inconsistent economic system. Bottero (2005) notes:

> «*In highly unequal labour markets there is always someone at the bottom, but this does not mean that the lowest brick is any different from the other bricks in the pile. The underclass are simply elements of the working class who have been hit by adverse life-course events or economic recession.*» (p.226)

Rather than blaming the cultural deficiencies of the poor, critics of the underclass thesis prefer to use the concept of social exclusion to explain poverty. Social exclusion can take many forms, the accumulated effects of which can lead to extreme poverty. Consider the current refugee 'crisis' concerning Eastern European immigrants to Britain: these people are excluded from gaining anything but casual low-paid work; they may be ineligible for state benefits; they have language barriers to contend with and may also be socially excluded because of xenophobic attitudes and racism.

Some sociologists have noted that social exclusion may build resentment that can lead to other social ills such as crime or increased suicide rates. Jock Young (1999) suggests that crime rates may be reflecting the fact that a growing number of people do not feel valued or feel that they have little investment in the societies in which they live. Young (2007) suggests that there exists a contradiction between culture that strongly encourages the acquisition of money and material goods and structural exclusion, and this has produced 'social bulimia'. Members of society are strongly encouraged to subscribe to the meritocratic ideal, but society's failure to deliver the material success promised by this has resulted in widespread feelings of **anomie** expressed through a sense of unfairness, relative deprivation and crises of identity that can only be resolved by crime.

## Does class identity still exist?

Postmodernists argue that class identity is no longer relevant as a collective group identity and has now fragmented into numerous separate and individualized identities. Social identity is now more pluralistic, individualistic and diverse. Pakulski and Waters (1996) argue that people now exercise more personal choice about what type of people they want to be, rather than have their identity shaped by their membership of a social class. They argue that gender, ethnicity, age, region and family role interact and impact with consumption and media images to construct postmodern culture and identity.

However, postmodern ideas may be exaggerated as recent surveys indicate that social class is still a significant source of identity for many (e.g. Marshall *et al.* 1988). Members of a range of classes are still aware of class differences and are happy to identify themselves using class categories. On the other hand, according to Savage, class identities have declined in importance because of changes in the organization of the economy (for example, the decline of primary industries and factory work, the expansion of white-collar work as well as the rise of more insecure forms of manual and non-manual work), which he argues have largely dissolved the boundaries between social classes. Consequently, class is rarely viewed as an issue by most people, despite its continuing objective influence on people's social experience and life-chances, as seen clearly in Topic 3.

## Key terms

**Anomie** a breakdown in, absence of or confusion about social norms, rules, etc.

**Autonomy** freedom to choose one's own actions.

**Boundary problem** the constantly shifting nature of work makes it more difficult to draw boundaries between classes of workers.

**Class fractions** the recognition that the main social classes are fragmented into competing and often conflicting internal groups or fractions.

**Convergence** coming together, e.g. of working-class and middle-class lifestyles.

**De-skilling** reducing the skill needed to do a job.

**Downsizing** reducing the size of the permanent workforce.

**Economic capital** money in shares (and so on) which generates more money.

**Embourgeoisement** the idea that the working class is adopting the attitudes, lifestyle and economic situation of the middle classes.

**Primary industries** those involved in extraction of raw materials, e.g. mining, agriculture, fishing.

**Proletarianization** a tendency for lower-middle-class workers to become de-skilled and hence to share the market position of members of the working class.

**Proletarian traditionalist** members of the working class with a strong sense of loyalty to each other because of shared community and work experience.

**Routine white-collar workers** clerical staff involved in low-status, repetitive office work.

**Secondary industries** those involved in producing products from raw materials.

**Self-employed/petit-bourgeois** owners of small businesses.

**Social closure** the process by which high-status groups exclude lower-status groups from joining their ranks.

**Tertiary or service sector** jobs providing services such as transport, retailing, hotel work, cleaning, banking and insurance.

**Underclass** termed used by Charles Murray to describe those living at the margins of society, largely reliant on state benefits to make ends meet.



# Activities

### Research ideas

1. **Ask a sample of adults across a range of occupations how 'flexible' their work is. Ask them about their job security, the sort of tasks they do, their working hours, how much freedom they have, and so on.**
2. **Conduct a survey of your peers in casual part-time employment to find out the conditions of work they experience.**

### Web.task

Try this quiz on the manners and language of the upper class, questions and answers based on the anthropologist Kate Fox's book: Watching the English.

**www.funtrivia.com/playquiz/quiz2786131fe5ce0.html**

## Check your understanding

1. **How has the structure of the upper class changed in the last 50 years?**
2. **What is the 'establishment'?**
3. **Why do some writers suggest that we should no longer talk of the middle class but of the 'middle classes'?**
4. **How do managers differ from professionals?**
5. **Why do Marxists see white-collar workers as experiencing proletarianization?**
6. **What was the 'embourgeoisement thesis' and how was it challenged?**
7. **How do Marxists challenge the view that the working class has fragmented?**
8. **What happened to class identity, according to postmodernists such as Pakulski and Waters?**
9. **What is an 'underclass'?**
10. **How does the New Right view of the underclass differ from the Marxist view?**

## An eye on the exam Changes in the class structure

Describe only – no need for evaluation

Those groups situated on the boundary between the middle-classes and working-classes, e.g. white-collar workers, call-centre workers

**(a) Outline the evidence that some sections of the middle-class are experiencing proletarianization. (20 marks)**

Statistical trends and patterns, research findings and contemporary examples from any module studied and/or your wider sociological knowledge

The trend suggested by Braverman that some middle-class workers have more in common with manual workers because of the impact of technology and de-skilling on their jobs

Describe Britain's class structure in detail using examples and evidence

Britain has a hierarchical class structure composed of an upper class, middle-classes and working-classes

**(b) Outline and assess the view that Britain's class structure is increasingly fragmented. (40 marks)**

Weigh up the evidence that particular social classes are changing, growing or disappearing before reaching a balanced conclusion

Are social classes in the UK unified or are they made up of competing groups?

### Grade booster Getting top marks in question (b)

Begin by constructing a theoretical context in your introduction. Marxists generally focus on the idea of two main opposing classes (i.e. the bourgeoisie and proletariat) with the middle classes cast as the agents of the bourgeoisie, as managers of their factories, for example. Some Marxists, notably Braverman suggest that some middle-class occupational groups are experiencing proletarianization. Other theoretical positions, e.g. Weberians, suggest that the middle-class is fragmented into competing status groups, e.g. professionals, managers, the self-employed. The embourgeoisement theory similarly argues that skilled manual workers have more in common with the middle-classes in terms of lifestyle, voting behaviour etc. than other manual workers. Postmodernists argue that social class has decreased in importance as a source of identity.

Evidence regarding the social groups that make up Britain's class structure should be examined to ascertain the extent of social change. For example – is the upper class in decline? Is the middle-class characterized by competing interest groups? Have some middle-class groups being overtaken in terms of income and lifestyle by some skilled manual workers? Have new social class groupings appeared at the bottom end of society?

# TOPIC 5

# Gender and stratification

## Getting you thinking

**Table 6.7** Occupations 2004

**Employees and self-employed aged 16 and over (Great Britain)**

| Selected occupations | Women (%) | Men (%) |
|---|---|---|
| Receptionists | 95 | 5 |
| Educational assistants | 93 | 7 |
| Nurses | 88 | 12 |
| Care assistants & home carers | 88 | 12 |
| Primary & nursery teachers | 87 | 13 |
| Cleaners and domestics | 80 | 20 |
| Secondary teachers | 54 | 46 |
| Chefs and cooks | 46 | 54 |
| Retail & wholesale managers | 35 | 65 |
| Marketing & sales managers | 26 | 74 |
| IT managers | 18 | 82 |
| Software professionals | 17 | 83 |
| Production, works & maintenance managers | 9 | 91 |

Adapted from ONS (2004) *Labour Force Survey Spring 2004*

**Table 6.8** Full-time earnings by sector 2005

**Mean earnings of employees on adult rates (UK)**

| Industry sectors | Women (£ / hour) | Men (£ / hour) | Gender pay gap* |
|---|---|---|---|
| Banking, insurance & pension provision | 13.98 | 23.86 | 41.4 |
| Health & social work | 11.54 | 17.03 | 32.2 |
| Real estate, renting & business activities | 12.70 | 16.66 | 23.8 |
| Wholesale, retail & motor trade | 9.02 | 11.54 | 21.8 |
| Public admin. & defence | 11.62 | 14.44 | 19.5 |
| Manufacturing | 10.38 | 12.89 | 19.5 |
| Hotels & restaurants | 7.12 | 8.55 | 16.7 |
| Construction | 10.83 | 12.35 | 12.3 |
| Education | 13.87 | 15.68 | 11.5 |
| Transport, storage & communication | 11.02 | 12.09 | 8.9 |
| Public sector | 13.18 | 15.20 | 13.3 |
| Private sector | 10.65 | 13.75 | 22.5 |
| All sectors** | 11.67 | 14.08 | 17.1 |

* 100 – (women's full-time earnings as a percentage of men's full-time earnings)
** Including sectors not shown separately.

Adapted from ONS (2005) *Annual Survey of Hours and Earnings, 2005*

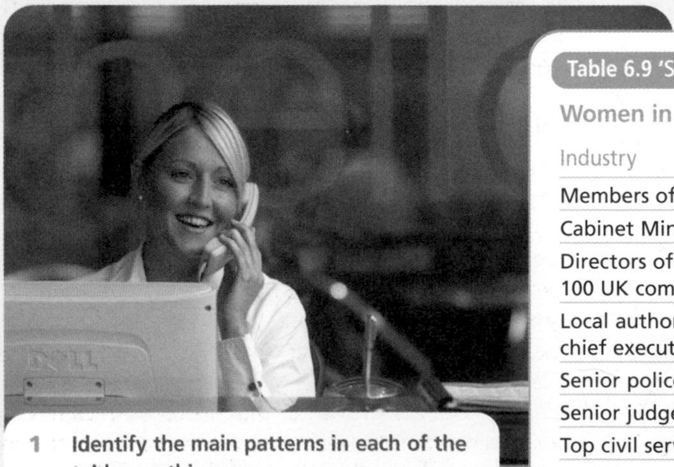

1. **Identify the main patterns in each of the tables on this page.**
2. **Using ideas you have developed from studying your Sociology course, suggest explanations for each of these patterns.**

**Table 6.9** 'Sex and power' 2008 index

**Women in selected 'top jobs' over a five-year period**

| Industry | 2003 | 2004 | 2005 | 2006 | 2007 |
|---|---|---|---|---|---|
| Members of Parliament | 18.1 | 18.1 | 19.7 | 19.5 | 19.3 |
| Cabinet Ministers | 23.8 | 27.3 | 27.3 | 34.8 | 26.1 |
| Directors of the top 100 UK companies | 8.6 | 9.7 | 10.5 | 10.4 | 11.0 |
| Local authority chief executives | 13.1 | 12.4 | 17.5 | 20.6 | 19.5 |
| Senior police officers | 7.5 | 8.3 | 9.8 | 12.2 | 11.9 |
| Senior judges | 6.8 | 8.3 | 8.8 | 9.8 | 9.6 |
| Top civil servants | 22.9 | 24.4 | 25.5 | 26.3 | 26.6 |
| Top health service execs | 28.6 | 27.7 | 28.1 | 37.9 | 36.9 |
| Secondary school heads | 30.1 | 31.8 | 32.6 | 34.1 | 30.0 |

Adapted from Equality and Human Rights Commission (2008) *Sex and Power, 2008* (www.equalityhumanrights.com)

You will probably have noted patterns in each of the tables on the previous page and realized that, despite all the improvements in the social position of women, gender differences in paid work are still very noticeable. You should also have been able to offer some explanations drawn from your past study of the subject. These may well match up with some of those introduced later in this topic, which examines gender inequality in the UK, focusing particularly on paid work. There are many other aspects of gender inequality in British society – you should pay particular attention to gender differences and inequalities in poverty, health, education, and crime and deviance.

## Gender inequality in employment

During the past 30 years, the number of female workers in the UK has risen by 2.45 million, whereas the number of male workers has only risen by 0.5 million. There are a similar number of men and women in work in 2008 – 13.6 million of each sex – compared with 1985, when men filled two million more jobs than women. However, there are still significant differences in the distribution of male and female workers throughout the occupational structure. Catherine Hakim (1979) refers to these differences as 'occupational segregation' because in the UK 'men and women do different kinds of work, so that one can speak of two separate labour forces, one male and one female, which are not in competition with each other for the same jobs'. She suggests that there are two types of occupational segregation:

- **Horizontal segregation** – Men and women are concentrated in different types of jobs in different sectors of the economy.
- **Vertical segregation** – Women occupy the lower levels of pay and status in particular jobs.

### Horizontal segregation

Table 6.7 in the 'Getting you thinking' activity gives us an insight into how occupations are gender segregated. In the public sector, women are mainly employed in health and social work and in education, where they made up 79 per cent and 73 per cent of the workforce respectively in 2006. In the private sector, women are overconcentrated in clerical, administrative, retail and personal services, such as catering, whereas men are mainly found in the skilled manual and upper professional sectors (EOC 2006).

According to the Office of National Statistics (ONS), in 2008 men and women were still likely to follow very different career paths. Men were ten times more likely than women to be employed in skilled trades (19 per cent compared with 2 per cent) and were also more likely to be managers and senior officials. A fifth of women in employment do administrative or secretarial work, compared with 4 per cent of men. Women are also more likely than men to be employed in personal services and in sales and customer services. Men are more likely to be self-employed than women. Nearly three quarters of the 3.8 million self-employed people in 2008 were men, a proportion that has remained the same since early 1997.

There is some evidence that horizontal segregation may be in decline because there has been a decline in men's work, such as that found in the primary (e.g. engineering, coal-mining) and secondary sectors (e.g. car manufacturing) of the economy. Increasing female educational success, especially in higher education, has resulted in more women entering areas of work previously dominated by men, such as the medical, legal and financial sectors of the economy. For example, in 2005, according to the Women and Work Commission, 75 per cent of pharmacists, nearly 40 per cent of accountants and about 50 per cent of solicitors were women.

### Vertical segregation

#### *Skill and status*

The evidence suggests that, within occupational groups, women tend to be concentrated at the lower levels. When women do gain access to the upper professional or management sector, the evidence suggests that they encounter a '**glass ceiling**' – a situation in which promotion appears to be possible, but restrictions or discrimination create barriers that prevent it. For example, 66 per cent of full-time secondary school teachers in 2007 in England were female, but only 30 per cent of secondary school heads were. In 2007, male primary school teachers were three times more likely than female primary teachers to become head teachers.

In 2008, women made up only 11 per cent of directors of the top 100 British companies, a quarter of NHS consultants, 10 per cent of high court judges and just two out of 17 national newspaper editors.

The Equality and Human Rights Commission noted in 2008 that women lack access to the most powerful jobs in society, and that it will take 55 years at the current rate of progress for women to achieve equal status with men at senior levels in the judiciary, and 73 years for equality to be achieved in top management jobs in Britain's top 100 companies.

#### *Pay*

Generally, men are better paid. In 1975, women only earned about 71 per cent of the average full-time male wage. This gap has narrowed over the last 30 years, but the gap between men's pay and women's pay was 17 per cent in 2007. However, the government claims that the gap is lower – 12.6 per cent – if calculated in terms of median pay, i.e. comparing men and women who are in the middle of their respective pay ranges, rather than average pay. The ONS argue that the problem with using average pay to calculate the gender gap is that a few men who are exceptionally well paid (i.e. the top 10 per cent of individuals in the UK, who now receive 40 per cent of all personal income) can artificially inflate the average and therefore distort the true pay gap between men and women. However, whatever method is used, significant differences still exist between men and women.

# Focus on research

## Measuring occupational segregation

**Scott MacEwen (1994) notes that there are two ways of measuring segregation. The first is an objective and scientific measure using survey or census data to calculate the numbers of women and men in an occupation. This is precise but measures broad occupations only, rather than specific jobs. However, it is at the level of specific jobs that segregation is most extreme. For example, the occupation 'cleaner' obscures the fact that it is mainly men who are 'street cleaners' and women who are 'office cleaners'. Similarly, the occupation 'teacher' glosses over the fact that the vast majority of primary teachers are female.**

**The second method is to measure occupational segregation subjectively. Here, interviews or questionnaires are used to ask people whether their type of job is done exclusively or mainly by men or women, or shared equally. This method does have its problems – for example, it relies on the judgement of the respondent – but it does focus more directly on individual jobs**

Adapted from Pilcher, J. and Whelehan, I. (2004) *50 Key Concepts in Gender Studies*, London: Sage

1 **Identify and explain the two methods of measuring occupational segregation identified by MacEwen**

Hourly pay statistics are also only one aspect of the inequality women experience in pay. If specific occupations are examined, the gap is much greater than 12.6 per cent. It rises to 22.3 per cent in the private sector, although it is only 13.4 per cent in the state sector. For example, the difference in earnings in 2006 between men and women in health and social work jobs was 32 per cent, and in banking and insurance it was 41 per cent.

Even women who have managed to reach top positions are not immune from pay inequality. In 2008, the Chartered Management Institute (CMI) showed that the average female executive is earning £32 614 a year, £13 655 less than the average male executive, who earns £46 269 a year. The CMI estimate it will not be until 2195 that women's pay begins to outstrip that of men. Moreover, according to a TUC report in 2008, young women earn 26 per cent less than young men for apprenticeships, and dominate the lowest-paid sectors such as hairdressing and childcare. It is estimated by Trevor Phillips, who chairs the Equality and Human Rights Commission, that women who work full time will earn on average £330 000 less than a man over their working lives and, at the current rate, it will take at least another two decades to close the pay gap.

When annual earnings are examined, the gap between men and women increases quite dramatically. In 2006, the annual earnings gap between men and women was 27.1 per cent. The weekly income gap between males and females increases even further to 44 per cent when all economic activity is considered, i.e. full-time, part-time and self-employment, unemployment and other benefits and pensions. The income gap is widest in retirement, at 47 per cent in 2006. While retired men got nearly half their income from non-state or occupational pensions, retired women got only a quarter of their income from this source.

### *Work situation*

Women are more likely than men to be employed in part-time work. In 2005, 42 per cent of female employees worked part time, compared with only 9 per cent of male employees. Part-time work tends to have worse working conditions, less job security and fewer promotion prospects than full-time work. In 1999, women in part-time work earned, on average, 60 per cent of the average hourly pay of male full-time employees. By 2005, this situation had slightly improved – part-time female employees earned 61.6 per cent of men's average full-time earnings.

## What about men?

Whilst men generally enjoy a greater range of work opportunities, more status and more pay, there is evidence of change in the experience of work for some men, particularly working-class men. This change has been mainly caused by economic recession which has led to unemployment in traditional industries and manufacturing. In parts of the country, women may even have replaced men as the main breadwinner in some families. Some writers suggest that this has led some men to feel frustrated at their inability to fulfil their traditional role as breadwinner and protector. Mac an Ghaill (1996) suggests these men are experiencing a 'crisis in masculinity'. This may threaten marital stability and play some part in causing higher divorce rates in such areas.

Willott and Griffin (1996) have explored this so-called 'crisis'. They researched a group of long-term unemployed men in the West Midlands. Their respondents typified the kinds of men most likely to be marginalized because they had little hope of finding steady employment. However, while their role as provider was undermined, their other masculine characteristics (in particular their sense of authority over their families) remained. Willott and Griffin reject the thesis that men are experiencing a crisis in masculinity. Rather, they suggest that there is merely a weakening of certain elements of traditional masculinity.

# Sociological explanations of gender stratification in employment

## Functionalism and human capital theory

You should be familiar with the functionalist position associated particularly with the work of Talcott Parsons in the mid-20th century. Parsons felt that separate gender roles for men and women were helpful to societies. He claimed that women were more suited to what he called 'expressive roles' – those emphasizing caring and emotions – while men were the ideal candidates for 'instrumental roles' – those that required qualities of competition, aggression and achievement. This view implies that men are more suited to paid employment and women are more suited to domesticity. The implications of Parsons' view are that women will be less motivated and less suited to the labour market than men. Therefore, he suggests that it is not surprising that they will, on average, be paid less.

Some economists have gone on to suggest that the pay gap between men and women is justified because it reflects the fact that men have more '**human capital**' than women because of their greater orientation to paid work. It is suggested that women are less committed to paid work and are more likely to take career breaks or to opt for part-time work in order to continue to care for their families. Men, however, will be able to build up their skills, qualifications and experience because they are in receipt of more education and training and their employment is not interrupted by family commitments.

Human capital theory has been criticized by Olsen and Walby (2004). They used data from the longitudinal British Household Panel Survey to investigate the causes of pay differences between men and women. They accept that pay differentials partly reflect the fact that women tend to experience less full-time employment than men and take more career breaks, but they argue that the main cause of women's low pay is 'systematic disadvantage in acquiring human capital'. For example, pay is lower in occupations where there are high concentrations of women. This could well be because these jobs provide less training and promotion prospects than those jobs in which men are in the majority. Furthermore, human capital theory assumes that experience of employment increases wages, yet experience of part-time work (which is mainly taken up by women) is actually associated with a slight reduction in wages.

## Dual labour-market theory

Many sociologists have looked for explanations for gender stratification within the structure of the labour market as a whole. Barron and Norris (1976) argue that a **dual labour-market** exists, i.e. the labour market is divided into two sectors:

1. a primary sector consisting of secure, well-paid jobs with good prospects
2. a secondary sector characterized by poor pay, insecurity and no ladder of promotion.

It is very difficult to move from the secondary to the primary sector. Barron and Norris argue that women are more likely to be found in the disadvantaged secondary sector for three reasons.

### *1 Women's 'unsuitability'*

There is some evidence that employers may hold stereotypical beliefs about the 'unsuitability' of women for primary-sector roles. Studies by West and Zimmerman (1991) and Hartnett (1990) both noted that employers in the 1990s subscribed to myths and negative stereotypes about women workers such as:

- Male workers do not like working for a female manager – employers are therefore reluctant to promote females to management positions.
- Women are less dependable because they often take time off work to deal with family commitments.
- Women are financially dependent on their husbands and so are either not as committed to work as male breadwinners or they have less need of pay rises/promotion.
- Women will stop work when they marry and have children, so there is little point investing in their long-term training.
- Children are psychologically damaged by their mothers spending long periods of time at work rather than spending quality time with them. In order to protect children, women should not be given management jobs because these involve long and unsociable hours.

### *2 Disrupted career development*

Jobs with good promotion prospects often recruit people at a young age and require several years of continuous service. It is difficult in most jobs to take long periods of time out of work and return to a similar position. However, social pressure to have a family often leads to women taking extensive time out of employment. Consequently, they lack experience compared with men and often miss out on promotion when they do return to the workplace. Abbott and Wallace (1997) argue that women's continuous employment is also undermined by the fact that the husband's career and pay is often regarded as more important. Therefore, if his job requires a move to another part of the country, wives are often forced to interrupt their careers and give up their jobs.

# Focus on research

## Gender, life-chances and stereotyping

### Education

Although girls now outperform boys in terms of numbers of GCSEs and A-level qualifications, there are clear differences in subjects studied. In 2005, 71 per cent of entries for English Literature A-level and 69 per cent of Sociology A-level entries were female, whilst 76 per cent of A-level Physics entries were male. In vocational training in 2005, gender differences were even more marked, with females heavily dominating early-years care and hairdressing (97 per cent and 91 per cent respectively), while plumbing, electrical work and construction were 99 per cent male.

### Power and politics

Although women make up 46 per cent of the workforce, they are underrepresented in many jobs with power and influence. For example, only 19 per cent of MPs, 12 per cent of senior police officers and 9.6 per cent of top judges are women.

### Mass media

Women constituted only 13.6 per cent of editors of national newspapers and 10.5 per cent of the chief executives of large media companies in 2005. The media are a continuing source of conventional gender stereotyping. Toy manufacturers also develop and market toys specifically for girls or boys. Not only are they stereotyped, but many boys' games and toys are noticeably violent and aggressive.

### Family

Even before birth, expectations based on gender may affect how a child is perceived by its parents. Some parents, especially fathers, hope their firstborn will be a son in order to continue the family name and to be a protector to any younger (girl) children that follow. Once a child is born, it is treated in gendered ways, and studies have shown that a mother will react differently to a baby depending on whether they are told that it is a girl or a boy.

More examples of gender stereotyping from the topics you have studied can be found throughout this book and its AS-level companion.

Adapted from *Sex and Power* by the Equality and Human Rights Commission (2008), and various pamphlets and *Facts About Women and Men In Great Britain* by the Equal Opportunities Commission (2006)

### 3 *Weak legal and political framework supporting women*





Both the Equal Pay and Sex Discrimination Acts are ineffective because they fail to protect women's employment rights. Coussins (1976) described the Sex Discrimination Act as 'feeble', because it does not apply to many areas of employment. Further, she doubted the commitment of governments to eliminate gender inequality. She noted that the government has done little to promote free or cheap nursery care and encourage employers to provide crèche facilities for their workers who are mothers. However, recent changes in the legal position of part-time workers have benefited women considerably and some attempt has been made to recognize that men, too, have some responsibility for childrearing, with the introduction of recent legislation to allow unpaid leave for either partner.

### *Evaluation of dual labour-market theory*

Dual labour-market theory has two strengths as an explanation of vertical segregation:

1. It stresses that the social organization of work in Western societies is essentially **patriarchal**, with men in positions of power making gendered discrimination and women's subordinate status at work seem 'normal' and 'natural'.
2. It undermines the popular assumption that better qualifications and increased ambition for women – what Wilkinson calls the 'genderquake' – would automatically dismantle gender divisions in employment. Women with the same qualifications as men will continue to be disadvantaged as long as these two sectors exist and continue to be underpinned with patriarchal stereotypical assumptions about the role of women.

However, Bradley (1996) points out that the theory fails to explain inequalities in the same sector. For example, teaching is not a secondary labour-market occupation yet, as we saw above, women are less likely than men to gain head-teacher posts.

## Feminism

Perhaps the most significant contributions to understanding gender stratification have come from the range of perspectives classified as feminist. Here, we focus on the ways feminists have explained the position of women in employment.

### Liberal feminism

Liberal feminists argue that traditional forms of gender-role socialization found in the family, but also in education and the mass media, are responsible for reproducing a sexual division of labour in which masculinity is largely seen as dominant and femininity as subordinate. For example, parents continue to see a boy's education as more important than a girl's, whilst schools continue to channel boys and girls into stereotypical subject choices which impact in the long term on university and career choices.

Ann Oakley (1974) argues that the main reason for the subordination of women in the labour market is the continuing dominance of the mother–housewife role for women. She argues that patriarchal ideology stresses the view that a woman's major function is to raise children and that family rather than career should be the main focus of their lives. The fact that female professional workers are three times more likely not to be married than their male counterparts also supports this view, as does the fact that being childless increases a woman's chances of becoming a director of a major company.

In the 1990s, some liberal feminists suggested that these processes were coming to an end. Sue Sharpe's work on the attitudes of teenage girls (1994) suggests that education and careers are now a priority for young women. Females have also enjoyed greater educational success than males in recent years. Liberal feminists, therefore, have an optimistic view of the future for women. In the family, they see evidence of both partners accepting equal responsibility for domestic work and childrearing. They also argue that dual-career families in which both partners enjoy equal economic status are becoming the norm. Legislators too are beginning to recognize male responsibility for childcare with the recent increases in paternity rights.

However, liberal feminism has been subject to some criticisms:

- Although there is evidence that masculinity and femininity are socially constructed, it does not explain why this leads to men dominating and women being oppressed.
- It implies that people passively accept their gender identities, underestimating the degree to which women may resist society's expectations of them.
- It fails to acknowledge that women's experiences differ according to social class and race.
- In seeing gender equality as simply a matter of time, real obstacles to progress are being overlooked. During World War II, when women were required to work in munitions factories, for example, free crèche places were made available. Over half a century later, only a small percentage of workplaces provide this facility.

## Marxist feminism

Marxist feminists are heavily influenced by Marxist sociological theory. They argue that the subordination of women to men is directly linked to their position within a capitalist society. According to Margaret Benston (1972), women benefit capitalism in two important ways:

1. Women provide free domestic labour, which functions to make male workers more effective. She notes that women were excluded from paid employment in the early to mid-19th century. Thereafter, the major role of women became the mother-housewife role. Benston argues that if the woman is a full-time housewife, the male wage actually ends up paying for both the labour power of the male and the domestic labour power of the woman. The housewife, by providing a comfortable home, meals, etc., provides emotional and domestic support for her husband so that he can return to work as a healthy and efficient worker. Women have returned to the labour market in large numbers since the 1980s, but it can be argued from a Marxist-feminist perspective that domestic labour is still important because surveys indicate that women in relationships with men still take most of the responsibility for housework and childcare.
2. Women are also responsible for raising the future labour force at no extra cost to the capitalist class. This raising of the next generation of waged workers is referred to as the 'reproduction of labour power'.

According to Ansley (1976), women in relationships with men also function to soak up the male worker's frustration with his paid work (e.g. low pay, low status, little power) in the form of domestic violence.

Other Marxist feminists see women as part of '**reserve army of labour**', which is only hired by prosperous firms in times of rapid economic expansion and fired when recession sets in. Marxists argue that women are more vulnerable to trends such as economic recession, downsizing and mergers, and therefore constitute a more disposable part of the workforce for a number of reasons:

- They change jobs more frequently than men because of pregnancy and childcare, or because their job is secondary to that of their partner, i.e. they may be forced to change jobs if their partner is relocated to another part of the country.
- They are generally less skilled, often part time and less likely to be members of trade unions. As a result, it is easier for employers to sack them.
- Capitalist ideologies are generally patriarchal and so mainly locate women in the home. The idea that married women have less right to a job than men is common among management, unions and even among women themselves. Therefore, when women lose their jobs an ideology of domesticity comes into play which suggests that women are more generally suited to the home and childcare rather than work or a career, 'justifying' discrimination against them in the labour market.

Marxist feminists have been criticized for being tautological, in that the starting point of their argument is also their conclusion. Marxist feminists believed that there had to be a reason why women were excluded from the workforce and why they undertook domestic labour for men. Marxists explained this in terms of its benefits to capitalism. They therefore looked for the benefits to capitalism of women working at home and came to the conclusions that we have seen above. Walby (1986) is critical of this approach because, as she points out, it could quite as easily have been argued that women staying at home harmed capitalism because women competing with men for jobs would probably lower wages and increase profits. Women who earn also have superior spending power, which boosts capitalism.

The reserve army of labour theory has been criticized, too, because it does not explain why male and female labour are put to different uses. In other words, it fails to explain why there are men's jobs and women's jobs.

It also fails to explain why women ended up with responsibility for domestic labour, especially considering that historical evidence suggests that in the pre-industrial period, this was the responsibility of children and older adults of both sexes rather than exclusively female.

Marxist feminism can also be criticized for overlooking the fact that patriarchy can be as influential in its own right, the implication being that once capitalism is abolished, gender inequality will disappear. However, there is no guarantee of this. According to Ellwood (1982), in the communist Soviet Union, women could fly to the moon but they still had to do the ironing once they got home.

## Radical feminism

Radical feminists argue that gender inequality is more important than class inequality. They argue that society is divided into two fundamental gender classes – men and women – whose interests are opposed. Modern societies are patriarchal societies in which women are exploited and oppressed by men in all aspects of social life. Culture, government, tradition, religion, law, education and the media all reflect patriarchal leadership and power.

According to radical feminists, all these types of patriarchal inequality originate not in wider society, but in the intimacy of personal relationships, in sexual partnerships, and in families and households of various kinds. From a radical feminist perspective, all personal relationships are 'political', in that they are based upon different and unequal amounts of power, which are determined by sex and which are reinforced by every aspect of the wider society. Radical feminists particularly focus on the power relationships that are experienced in private – above all, the significance of sexuality and men's use of domestic and sexual violence. Radical feminists note that patriarchal definitions of women's sexuality are used to control women for the benefit of men. Women are told how to look, dress and behave. When patriarchal ideology fails, then women are constantly under the threat of male violence and sexual aggression, which limits their capacity to live as free and independent beings.

However, radical feminism has been criticized for failing to acknowledge historical change, e.g. the fact that women now experience the same rights as men. Radical feminists also fail to take account of divisions between women themselves, caused by class and ethnicity. Black feminists have been particularly critical of the **ethnocentricity** of most feminist approaches, which have assumed that all women experience patriarchy in the same way. Black feminists point out that different forms of inequality actually interact with each other. Bhavani (2000) puts the following question: 'When comparing racism to sexism, which is more fundamental?' In her view, racism and sexism shape each other and both, in turn, are influenced by social class.

Black fem →

Explain the radical feminist argument that 'all personal relationships are political'

## Dual systems approach

Delphy (1977) takes a slightly different approach, emphasizing, like the radical feminists, the key role of the family. Like Marxists, however, she argues that the household is an important and underrated place of work. Indeed, she refers to 'housework' as 'the domestic mode of production' and argues that the work performed by women is highly productive. However, she notes that men dominate households because they have more economic power than women. As a result, the views and wishes of men prevail within families. Some support for this position comes from studies of family poverty (Joseph Rowntree Foundation 1995), which indicate that women rather than men experience the consequences of poverty within families because men are more likely than women to spend money on themselves rather than the family unit.

### *Walby on patriarchy*

Sylvia Walby (1990) suggests that the radical-feminist and Marxist approaches could be combined. She argues that capitalism and patriarchy work alongside each other to exploit women. Walby argues that patriarchy has evolved from 'private patriarchy', in which women were limited to the domestic sphere, to 'public patriarchy', in which women have entered the public arenas of employment, politics and so on, but are still disadvantaged. She notes that 'women are no longer restricted to the domestic hearth, but have the whole society in which to roam and be exploited'.

Walby argues that patriarchy intersects with capitalism and racism to produce a modern form of gender stratification underpinned by six key patriarchal social structures:

1. *The area of paid work* – Women experience discrimination from employers and restricted entry into careers because of the ideology that 'a woman's place

is in the home'; when they enter work they experience low pay, low status, etc.

2 *The household* – Female labour is exploited in the family
3 *The state* – This acts in the interests of men rather than women in terms of taxation, welfare rules, the weakness of laws protecting women at work, etc.
4 *Cultural institutions such as the mass media* – These represent women in a narrow set of social roles, such as sex objects and as mother–housewives or wives and girlfriends, rather than as people in their own right.
5 *Sexuality* – A double standard persists in modern society that values multiple sexual partners for men but condemns the same behaviour in women
6 *Violence against women* – Sexual assault, domestic violence and the threat of violence are used by men to control the behaviour of women.

Walby acknowledges that inequalities between men and women vary over time and in intensity. For example, young women are now achieving better educational qualifications than men and, as a result, the intensity of patriarchy has to some extent lessened. Nevertheless, women continue to be disadvantaged. Walby notes that the most powerful positions in all aspects of society continue to be held by men. She concludes that patriarchy continues to exist but that different **gender regimes** affect groups of women differently. For example, the experience of White single mothers is likely to be different to the experience of Asian women or White female professionals.

## Criticisms of feminist theory

Feminist theory has not gone uncriticized. A huge amount of debate has been generated by the approaches just explored.

- There does not seem to be much agreement between feminists about how patriarchy should be defined, what its causes are and the forms that it takes in modern societies.
- Some feminists have suggested that if patriarchy is universal, i.e. found in all societies, then, its origin may be biological. It has been suggested that whilst women are in the stages of advanced pregnancy, childbirth and childrearing, they are more likely to be dependent on men. Patriarchy may therefore be the product of women's reproductive role rather than culture or capitalism.
- Delamont (2001) has pointed out that feminist writers seem to assume that women share a common position of exploitation. She suggests that there are many divisions between women on grounds of income and social class, ethnicity and religion.
- Feminists often fail to take into account the changing nature of modern societies, which has resulted in women rapidly acquiring social, legal, educational and economic benefits. It is argued that if modern societies were truly patriarchal, women would remain fixed into a subordinate position. This is obviously not the case in the UK today.

## Preference theory

Catherine Hakim (2000) has examined data about gender and work from across the world. She argues that reliable contraception, equal-opportunities legislation, the expansion of white-collar and part-time jobs, and the increase in lifestyle choices give women in modern societies more choices than ever before. However, women do not respond to these choices in the same ways. She identifies three main types of work–lifestyle preferences that women may adopt:

1 *Home-centred* – 20 per cent of women prefer not to be in employment because family life and children are their main priorities.
2 *Adaptive* – The majority of women (about 60 per cent) are those who want to combine family and paid work in some way.
3 *Work-centred* – 20 per cent of women see careers or other involvement in public life as their priority. Childless women are concentrated in this category.

Hakim argues that this choice of preferences creates conflict between different groups of women – the policies and practices that suit one group may not necessarily work in the interests of the others. Men, on the other hand, are much more alike in their preferences – most fit into the 'work-centred' category. This is one reason for the continuation of male dominance or patriarchy.

Hakim's ideas seem to be supported by Scott, who found that support for gender equality appears to be declining across Britain because of concerns that women who play a full role in the workforce do so at the expense of family life (Scott *et al.* 2008). She found that both women and men are becoming more likely to believe that both the mother and the family will suffer if a woman works full time. In 1994, 51 per cent of women in Britain and 52 per cent of men said they believed family life would not suffer if a woman went to work. By 2002, those proportions had fallen to 46 per cent of women and 42 per cent of men. There was also a decline in the number of people thinking the best way for a woman to be independent is to have a job. As Scott notes:

> *«It is conceivable that opinions are shifting as the shine of the 'super-mum' syndrome wears off, and the idea of women juggling high-powered careers while also baking cookies and reading bedtime stories is increasingly seen to be unrealisable by ordinary mortals.»*

However, Scott also found that there was a continuing decline in the proportion of women and men who think 'it is the husband's job to earn income and the wife's to look after the children'. In 1987, 72 per cent of British men and 63 per cent of British women agreed with this proposition, but by 2002, the proportion had fallen to 41 per cent of men and 31 per cent of women.

The Fawcett Society, which campaigns for equal rights for men and women, said the study showed that work and family were still patriarchal institutions. Workplaces –

and, in particular, the culture of long working hours and the lack of flexible working – are still made by men for the benefit of men. Moreover, women still shoulder the bulk of caring and housework at home. Women are therefore often presented with impossible choices – they are forced to choose between caring for a family at home or either maximizing their career opportunities or bringing much needed income into the home.

Hakim's work has provoked much opposition from feminists. For example, Ginn *et al.* (1996) point out that all too often it is employer attitudes rather than women's work orientation that confine women to the secondary labour market or the home.

## Postmodern or 'difference' feminism

**Postfeminism** has two strands. The first asserts that feminism is no longer necessary because women have largely won equality. Faludi (1992) suggests that feminism went too far in criticizing men, the family and femininity, and this has created a male backlash which has undermined the power of the feminist message. Consequently, few girls see themselves as 'feminists' today. She notes how politicians, business leaders and advertisers among others have, on the one hand, recognized women's equality, whilst on the other hand, they have highlighted its cost to women. Magazines in the USA, for example, claim that professional women are more prone to alcoholism, hair loss and infertility, whilst women without children suffer more hysteria and depression.

The second strand abandons the feminist grand theories to adopt a more postmodern position. Brooks (1997) argues that there needs to be a shift from the old debates about equality to debates about difference. Postmodern feminists suggest that terms like 'patriarchy' and 'women' overgeneralize because male ideology does not affect all women in the same way and so all women do not experience oppression in the same way. Postmodern feminists believe that there exist a range of masculinities and femininities; consequently, they reject the idea that some characteristics should be preferred over others. They particularly concentrate on differences between women and how these might affect choices and lifestyles, especially with regard to inequalities in consumption and how women construct their identity.

# Conclusion: which is more important, gender or class?

Feminists, particularly radical feminists, have pointed to the importance of gender inequalities in society. For many of these writers, despite cosmetic improvements to the position of women, gender is still the most significant social division in modern societies.

For many years, when sociologists talked about social inequality, they meant social class. However, Pilcher and Whelehan (2004) identify three key developments since the 1970s that have threatened the predominance of class analysis:

1 *Social and economic changes* – There has been a major shift from heavy industry and manufacturing to an economy dominated by service jobs in retail, finance and the public sector. Some sociologists have seen this feminization of the economy and workplace as a sign that gender may now be more important than social class in shaping our experience of work, inequality, etc.
2 *Feminists,* such as Walby (1990), have pointed out that much conventional sociology has either ignored gender or failed to recognize the importance of gender in structuring other forms of inequality.
3 *Postmodern perspectives* have directed attention towards diversity, difference and choice, which has undermined the traditional focus on large social and economic groupings such as classes.

Today, most sociologists would argue that social class, gender and ethnicity combine to shape our experience of society and social consequences, such as inequality. For example, Skeggs' (1997) research on a group of White, working-class women leads her to conclude that class cannot be understood without gender and vice versa. Similarly, Anthias (2001) argues that class, gender and ethnicity each involve distinctive features, but together create the conditions we live in and the opportunities we have.

## Check your understanding

1 **Using your own words, explain the difference between horizontal and vertical segregation.**
2 **What is the relationship between vertical segregation and the glass ceiling?**
3 **How can dual labour-market theory be used to explain vertical segregation?**
4 **Why have some sociologists argued that a 'crisis of masculinity' exists?**
5 **How does human capital theory justify the gender pay gap? How can it be criticized?**
6 **How does Walby use the concept of patriarchy to explain gender stratification?**
7 **According to Hakim, why are women now able to have different 'preferences' for their work/lifestyle balance?**
8 **What does Faludi mean by the 'male backlash'?**
9 **How does postmodern feminism differ from other forms?**
10 **Why is class analysis less popular with sociologists than 50 years ago?**

# Key terms

**Dual labour-market theory** see Key Terms in Topic 7.

**Ethnocentricity** the view that your own culture is 'normal' and all others 'abnormal'.

**Gender regimes** term used by Walby to illustrate how patriarchy continues to exist but affects different groups of women in different ways.

**Glass ceiling** invisible barrier preventing women from gaining high-status positions in employment.

**Horizontal segregation** gender division in the workplace whereby men and women work in different jobs in different occupational sectors.

**Human capital** education, training and employment experience believed to give some employees pay advantages.

**Patriarchy** system of male domination.

**Postfeminism** recent views on gender influenced by postmodernism.

**Reserve army of labour** Marxist concept used to describe an easily exploitable pool of workers drawn from vulnerable groups, who can be moved in and out of the labour market as it suits capitalists.

**Vertical segregation** gender division in the workplace whereby women occupy the lower levels of pay and status in particular jobs.

# Activities

## Research ideas

1. Try to get hold of a staff list from your school or college. Find out which of the staff are in which positions. To what extent does the institution you are studying in reflect vertical segregation?
2. Interview a sample of younger and older women about feminism. What meaning do they give to feminism? To what extent do their views reflect different types of feminism?

## Web.tasks

Find the latest statistics on the position of men and women in British society the website of the Government Equalities Office at **www.equalities.gov.uk**.

## An eye on the exam Gender and stratification

Describe only – no need for evaluation

Male-dominated

**(a) Outline the evidence that the UK is a patriarchal society.** **(20 marks)**

Statistical trends and patterns, research findings and contemporary examples from any module studied and/or your wider sociological knowledge

Describe the main explanations of gender inequalities in the workplace using appropriate theories, writers and concepts

Weigh up the explanations before reaching a balanced conclusion

**(a) Outline and assess sociological explanations for the existence of gender inequality in the workplace.** **(40 marks)**

The focus should be on horizontal and vertical segregation in jobs as well as pay inequalities

### Grade booster Getting top marks in question (b)

Outline some of the gender inequalities that exist in the modern UK today including those in the workplace (e.g. pay, examples of horizontal and vertical segregation, part-time work) and in the home (e.g. childcare, housework, dual-burden, decision-making). You need to consider a range of different sociological explanations in your answer such as the different varieties of feminism (liberal, Marxist, dual systems and radical), human capital theory, dual labour market, preference theory and postmodernism. In discussing explanations, make use of relevant concepts, such as patriarchy, reserve army of labour, primary and secondary labour markets, and horizontal and vertical segregation. You can develop evaluation by considering evidence for and against different views as well as by using one view to argue against another.

# TOPIC 6

# Ethnicity and stratification

## Getting you thinking

JANE ELLIOTT, a junior school teacher in the USA, began her crusade against racism and discrimination one day after the assassination of Dr Martin Luther King, Jr in 1968. She wanted her students to experience actual racism, so she told the blue-eyed students they were smarter, nicer, cleaner and deserved more privileges than the students with brown eyes. The day became a life-changing experience for the children and for Elliott. On the second day of the experiment, Elliott reversed the situation. What she discovered was amazing. Whoever was on top was not only better-behaved, but also more likely to learn. One dyslexic boy even learned how to read for the first time.

Elliott believed that all people are racists, whether they choose to believe it or not. She was frequently interviewed on TV chat shows as her experiment quickly caught the media's attention. 'I am a racist,' she said. 'If you want to see another racist, turn to the person on your right. Now look at the person on your left.'

Elliott stressed that the world didn't need a colour-blind society, but rather a society that recognizes colour. She said people are conditioned to the myth of White superiority. 'Differences are very valuable', she said. 'Start recognizing them and appreciating them. They are what make up our world.'

The experiment is commonly used today to raise awareness of discrimination issues with students around the world. The following comments were made by an older group of Dutch students in 1998:

'Today, I have learned what it is to be seen by others as a minority. I did not expect that it would be so humiliating! In the end, I really had the feeling that I was a bit inferior. I was against racism and discrimination already, but now I understand what it really is.'

'I was one of the blue-eyes today, and I did not find that funny. I felt greatly discriminated against because we (the blue-eyeds) had to shut our mouth and stand still. The brown eyes were treated well. I really understand that people who are discriminated against must feel very angered, like I felt today. It was very much worth it.'

'When you feel day by day what I today as a blue-eye felt (especially in the beginning of the day) then your life is rotten... Racism is so very easy to do. Before you realize it happens. As a person, you are powerless, it makes more sense to revolt together.'

Source: Magenta Foundation (a web-based antiracist educational organization based in the Netherlands) © 1999 Amsterdam. www.magenta.nl

1. **Why does Jane Elliott believe that all people are racists?**
2. **Is it racist to treat people differently on the basis of characteristics over which they have no control?**
3. **Should people have to control their social or cultural characteristics to conform to the requirements of the dominant culture?**
4. **To what extent can it be argued that it is racist to treat all people in the same way?**

Your discussion may have concluded that racism has several dimensions, and that it is racist both to treat people negatively on the basis of their perceived physical or cultural differences and, ironically, to ignore such difference. Both aspects can also be seen to operate when examining racism sociologically.

It is important to understand that the terms '**race**' and '**ethnicity**' are potentially problematic for a number of reasons. First, the concept of 'race' was once used to suggest biological differences between groups, but has since been discredited in that sense and abandoned in favour of the term 'ethnicity' or 'ethnic minority'. However, Kenyatta and Tai (1999) argue that the concept of 'race' is a superior concept because it focuses attention on power differences, economic exploitation, inequality and conflict. They argue that sociological discussions of 'ethnicity' tend to be focused on culture, religion and identity rather than inequality. However, with regard to

GARE = + inequality + AM Ethnicity:

inequalities in employment, education and health, most sociological literature focuses on differences between the ethnic majority, i.e. Whites, and ethnic minorities. This chapter will generally do the same.

The term 'ethnic minority' is also problematic. There are literally hundreds of different ethnic groups living in the modern UK. However, the sociological literature tends to focus on those who make up about 7 per cent of the UK population, i.e. people from Asian backgrounds who make up about 5 per cent of British society and people from African-Caribbean backgrounds who make up about 2 per cent. However, the terms 'Asian' and 'African-Caribbean' are also problematic. The term 'Asian' does not refer to people from the wider Asian continent – rather it refers only to those people who are from or related to people from the Indian subcontinent, particularly India, Pakistan and Bangladesh, although a large number of Asians came to the UK in the 1970s from East Africa, particularly Uganda and Kenya. Chinese people, therefore, are treated as a separate category. However, the term 'Asian' disguises national, regional and, particularly, religious differences and conflicts between Asian groups. Many sociologists believe that insufficient attention is paid to the specific origins and experience of people of Asian origin in the UK. As Bhopal *et al.* (1991) point out:

> «*The term 'Asian' is applied to people who have come to Britain from many different parts of the world, most notably India, Pakistan, Bangladesh, Uganda, Kenya and Tanzania, and from peasant or urban middle class backgrounds; they are also differentiated in their religion, language, caste, kinship obligations, diet, clothing, health beliefs, and birth and burial practices, and yet there is an inbuilt assumption through the use of the term that they all share a common background and experience.*»

The term 'African-Caribbean' is also fraught with problems. People from African-Caribbean backgrounds originally came from a dozen or so islands that were ex-colonies of the UK and scattered across thousands of miles of ocean. These islands have their own very distinctive and cultural identities and consequently people from them have very little in common apart from the colour of their skin and perhaps support for the West Indies cricket team.

Another problem with using terms like 'ethnic minorities', 'Asians', 'Blacks', etc., is that they imply that people from these backgrounds are recent immigrants and that they have very little in common with British culture. However, it is important to understand that we are now on the third generation of people in the UK from Asian or African-Caribbean origin. Most people from these backgrounds are young British citizens rather than recent migrants.

Finally, the term 'Muslim' has recently taken on an emotional meaning for White people because of the appearance of Islamic terrorism in the UK. This emotional response may have reinforced divisions between the White population and the Muslim minority. However, Samad (2006) notes that such divisions disguise the fact that most Muslims share a great deal in common with White people – especially working-class Whites – in terms of educational attainment, uncertain labour market futures, social exclusion and marginalization.

## Racism

Miles (1989) has argued that a key factor in the fact that ethnic-minority groups are more likely than Whites to be found at the bottom of the stratification system is **racism**. This is a system of beliefs and practices that exclude people from aspects of social life on the grounds of racial or ethnic background.

Racism can be seen to have three key elements: **prejudice**, **racial discrimination** and institutional discrimination.

## Prejudice

Racial prejudice is a type of racism that is expressed through opinion, attitude or fear rather than action, i.e. many prejudiced people do not act upon their beliefs (although some do). Prejudice is a way of thinking that relies heavily on stereotypes or prejudices that are usually factually incorrect, irrational, exaggerated and distorted. These are used to legitimate hostility and mistrust towards members of ethnic groups who are perceived to have negative characteristics.

According to Heath and Rothon (2003), the authors of the 2003 British Social Attitudes survey, in 1983, 35 per cent of adults described themselves as prejudiced against people of other races. This rose to a peak of 39 per cent in 1987 before falling steadily to 25 per cent in 2000 and 2001. However, in 2002, the proportion claiming to be racially prejudiced jumped to 31 per cent, the highest figure since 1994.

Connolly and Keenan (2000) in a survey of Northern Ireland found that a quarter of all their respondents were unwilling to accept either an African-Caribbean, Chinese or South Asian person as a resident in their local area. Similarly, over two out of every five people also stated that they were unwilling to accept a member of any of these three groups as a close friend. Fifty-four per cent of respondents stated that they were unwilling to accept a person of South Asian origin as a relative by way of marriage.

In 2006, a Channel 4 survey, 'How racist is Britain?', into the attitudes of 1000 White Britons towards people from different cultures found that the vast majority (84 per cent) said they were not prejudiced at all and only 1 per cent admitted to being 'very prejudiced'. However, the survey found that people subscribe to very contradictory views on race. Many of the sample were very prejudiced on some issues and very suspicious of unfamiliar cultures. On the other hand, they were also extremely tolerant, e.g. many of them were antiracist and welcomed diversity. The oldest and youngest parts of the sample were the most open-minded about mixing with ethnic-minority people. The most racist were members of the 45 to 65 age group.

Prejudice is part of a society's culture and passed from generation to generation through agencies of socialization such as the family and mass media. Rothon and Heath note that increasing levels of education are responsible for Britain being less racially prejudiced compared with 30 years ago. Their evidence suggests that educated people are the least likely to be racially prejudiced. Less than one

## Focus on research

### Adam Rutland (2005)

### The development and regulation of prejudice in children

**Rutland (2005) tested 155 White children aged between 6 and 16, assessing their responses to stories to discover the extent of their conscious and unconscious racial prejudice. The children were then split into groups according to how acceptable they thought it was to discriminate against Black children. Some children were told that they were being videotaped and that the material would be kept as a record of their answers, whilst others were shown that the cameras in their rooms were not working. In subsequent tests, children who believed they were being recorded and would be judged on the views they expressed toned down their racist opinions and presented more positive reactions to Black people than they had before. In Rutland's words, 'this suggests that they were controlling their explicit ethnic bias in line with what is generally regarded as acceptable. Racially prejudiced White teenagers are simply very skilful at repressing their attitudes'**

**Previous research has suggested that children show signs of racial prejudice as early as 3 years of age, that these attitudes peak around the ages of 7 and 8 and decrease in adolescence. However, Rutland's study indicates that rather than becoming more enlightened and tolerant in their racial attitudes, racially prejudiced White teenagers are simply very skilful at hiding their racial prejudice when they feel it is in their interests to do so.**

**Dr Rutland points to the impact his research should have on the work schools need to do to manage relationships between White and ethnic-minority students if they are to be more successful in eliminating racial discrimination among them.**

Source: Rutland, A. (2005) *The Development and Regulation of Prejudice in Children*, London: ESRC research

1. **What methods were used by Rutland and how might their reliability be questioned?**
2. **What implications do Rutland's findngs have for race relations in the UK?**

in five graduates (18 per cent) admit to being prejudiced compared with more than a third (35 per cent) of those with no qualifications. Rothon and Heath note that younger people are more tolerant and therefore less racially prejudiced than older people. However, research by Rutland (2005) questions this assumption. His data found that rather than becoming more enlightened and tolerant in their racial attitudes, racially prejudiced White teenagers are aware that racial prejudice is not acceptable and consequently they very skilfully hide their prejudicial attitudes because they feel that it is in their interests to do so (see 'Focus on research', left).

Rothon and Heath argue that the rise in prejudice since 2001 has been fuelled by hostile newspaper coverage of immigration and asylum seekers. Barker (1982) agrees and argues that mass media representations of ethnic minorities are symbolic of a new type of prejudice which is the product of New Right politicians and journalists. This type of prejudice highlights 'cultural difference' and suggests that traditional White British/English culture is under threat from ethnic-minority culture because ethnic minorities are allegedly not committed to integration with their White neighbours. The mass media, especially tabloid newspapers, such as the *Sun* and *Daily Mail*, reinforce these prejudices by portraying Black people, Muslims, refugees and migrants from Eastern Europe as a 'problem'. They are often represented as scrounging off welfare benefits, as criminals and as a threat to the British way of life. Barker notes that these media representations play down the problem of White prejudice towards ethnic minorities. Instead, they strongly imply that the fault lies with the 'reluctance' of ethnic minorities to adopt a British way of life.

Rothon and Heath note that although many UK newspapers urged readers not to link Islam and terrorism, numerous articles have made such a connection. They suggest that this may have resulted in a rise in 'Islamophobia' – unfounded hostility and prejudice towards Islam, and therefore fear or dislike of Muslims.

The Runnymede Trust (1997) identified a number of components that they believe make up Islamophobia and make anti-Muslim hostility seem natural and normal:

- Islam is seen as a monolithic bloc, static and unresponsive to change.
- Islam is seen as inferior to the West. Specifically, it is seen as barbaric, irrational, primitive and sexist.
- Islam is seen as violent, aggressive, threatening, supportive of terrorism and engaged in a 'clash of civilizations'.

## Racial discrimination

Racial discrimination is racial prejudice put into practice. It can take many forms.

### *Racist name-calling and bullying*

On an everyday level, racial discrimination may take the form of racist name-calling. Connolly and Keenan's survey found that 21 per cent of respondents stated that their friends had called someone a name to their face because of their colour or ethnicity. They also note that because of the sensitivity of the issue, this figure is likely to be an underestimation of the true incidence of racist name-calling.

Research sponsored by the Department for Education and Skills (2002) found that 25 per cent of pupils from minority-ethnic backgrounds in mainly White schools had experienced racist name-calling within the previous seven days. A third of the pupils of minority-ethnic backgrounds reported experiences of hurtful name-calling and verbal abuse either at school or during the school journey, and for about a half of these (one in six overall) the harassment was continuing or had continued over an extended period of time.

A survey conducted by Mirza (2007) found that nearly 100 000 racist incidents in schools have been recorded by education authorities between 2002 and 2006. Cities such as Leeds, Manchester and Birmingham have seen great increases in reported racism in the classroom. Education authorities suggest such increases are the product of more efficient and robust reporting methods, but Mirza suggests that the problem suffers from under-reporting because of embarrassment and fear of further racist bullying.

### *Racial attacks*

Discrimination may take the form of racial attacks and street violence. According to the Institute of Race Relations, between 1991 and 1997 there have been over 65 murders in Britain with a suspected or known racial motive. Although some of these victims have been White, the overwhelming majority of victims have been Asian, African-Caribbean, African or asylum seekers.

The Crime and Disorder Act created a number of new 'racially aggravated offences' in 1998. It stated that, for crimes such as assault, harassment and wounding, if there was an additional racial element to the offence, punishments should be increased. Racist chanting at football grounds was also made a criminal offence. More than 61 000 complaints of racially motivated crime were made in 2006/07, a rise of 28 per cent in just five years, with increases reported by most police forces in England and Wales. Officers classified 42 551 of the complaints as racially or religiously aggravated offences. Nearly two thirds were offences of harassment, 13 per cent wounding, 12 per cent criminal damage and 10 per cent assault.

However, the number of racial attacks reported to the police may still only be a fraction of the actual attacks that take place. According to the British Crime Survey, those at greatest risk of racially motivated attacks are Pakistani and Bangladeshis at 4.2 per cent, followed by Indians at 3.6 per cent and Black people at 2.2 per cent. This compared with only 0.3 per cent for White people.

A study of racial harassment conducted by Chahal and Julienne (1999) found that the experience of racism had become part of the everyday experience of Black and minority-ethnic people. Being made to feel different in a variety of social situations and locations was largely seen as routine and in some instances expected. Racist abuse was the most common form of everyday racism. The study found that there was limited support for victims of racist harassment and they generally felt ignored, unheard and unprotected.

### *Employer racism*

In 2004, a BBC survey showed ethnic-minority applicants still face major discrimination in the job market. CVs from six fictitious candidates – who were given traditionally White, Black African or Muslim names – were sent to 50 well-known firms covering a representative sample of jobs by Radio Five Live. All the applicants were given the same standard of qualifications and experience, but their CVs were presented differently. White 'candidates' were far more likely to be offered an interview than similarly qualified Black or Asian 'names'. Almost a quarter of applications by two candidates given traditionally 'White' names – Jenny Hughes and John Andrews – resulted in interview offers. But only 9 per cent of the 'Muslim' applications, by the fictitious Fatima Khan and Nasser Hanif, prompted a similar response. Letters from the 'Black' candidates, Abu Olasemi and Yinka Olatunde, had a 13 per cent success rate.

In 2007, the Commission for Racial Equality reported that they had received 5000 complaints from ethnic-minority workers during the first half of 2007 and that 43 per cent of these were related to employment. The most common complaints focused on workplace bullying, lack of career progression and being unable to secure interviews. Employer racism may be partly responsible for the fact that in 2007 the unemployment rate for ethnic minorities was over 11 per cent – twice the national average. The Office for National Statistics have estimated that a Black person is three times more likely to be out of work than a White person. Research from the Joseph Rowntree Foundation suggests that, even when they are in work, people from ethnic-minority groups do not receive the same rewards as people from White backgrounds with similar qualifications. In 2004, White men were paid an average of £1.80 per hour more than ethnic-minority men.

## Institutional racism

Some sociologists argue that racism is a basic feature of the rules and routines of Britain's social institutions, such as the police and courts, the immigration service, central and local government, the mass media, the education system, and the employment and housing markets. Racism is taken for granted and is so common that it is not even recognized as racism. This is known as '**institutional racism**'.

### *Policing*

Lord Macpherson's 1998 report into the murder of the Black teenager Stephen Lawrence by White youths in 1993 concluded that the London Metropolitan Police were guilty of 'institutional racism', which was defined as 'unwitting prejudice, ignorance, thoughtlessness and racial stereotyping which disadvantaged minority-ethnic groups'. For example, when the police arrived at the scene, they initially failed to understand that Stephen had been murdered because he was Black and they also assumed that all Black people near the site of the killing (including Stephen's best friend, who had witnessed the attack) were suspects rather than witnesses. The Macpherson report denounced the Metropolitan Police as fundamentally racist for its handling of the investigation into Stephen's death. No one has been convicted of the crime.

Despite Macpherson's criticisms, chief constables have recently been accused of being complacent about the amount of racial prejudice among police officers. Studies by Holdaway (2005) and by Bowling and Phillips (2007) suggest that there exists an occupational police culture in which some officers take for granted that Black people are 'naturally' more criminal than White people. Such officers as a matter of routine use derogatory language and jokes when discussing ethnic minorities with their fellow officers. A *Panorama* investigation into cadets training to be police officers in Manchester in 2005 suggested that little was being done to prevent recruits with racist tendencies from joining the police. Holdaway's most recent research suggests that ethnic-minority officers experience racist bullying and banter from their fellow White officers. The London Metropolitan's Black Police Officer's Association actually advised Black and Asian people not to join the police in 2008 because of these experiences.

Home Office statistics on police stop and search of Black people support the view that the police may be guilty of racial stereotyping. They reveal that, in 2007, Black people were seven times more likely to be searched than White people, and Asians twice as likely.

### *Immigration*

Britain's immigration laws are often cited as an example of institutional racism. The laws restrict the entry of Black people, while allowing White migrants easier entry. There is also evidence that immigration rules have been implemented in a racist manner. For example, Black visitors are more likely than foreign White visitors to be stopped for questioning by immigration control. The Home Office conceded in 1999 that such practices are institutionally racist.

It is important to understand that institutional racism is not conscious nor intentional. Not all members of key institutions are necessarily racist – they may or may not be. However, it is the manner in which some institutions operate that has racist outcomes. Teachers, for example, may be committed to antiracist education but schools still expel four times as many Black pupils as White.

Another aspect of institutional racism is the failure to recognize that ethnic-minority cultures may differ in key respects from White culture, such as failing to recognize special dietary or religious needs if a Muslim or Hindu is admitted to hospital, or not providing female medical professionals to deal with female members of religious groups.

One way of tackling institutional racism is to increase the numbers of ethnic-minority employees working in key institutions, especially in higher-status positions. The monitoring of the number of ethnic-minority people in key institutions can highlight imbalances that can then be addressed through equal-opportunities strategies. However, these strategies, particularly positive discrimination, may create the potential for resentment among sections of the White population.

## Focus on research

### Health

- Infant mortality is 100 per cent higher among the children of African-Caribbean or Pakistani mothers than among children of White mothers.
- Pakistani and Bangladeshi people are five times more likely to be diagnosed with diabetes and 50 per cent more likely to have coronary heart disease than White people.
- People from African-Caribbean backgrounds experience high levels of strokes compared with other social groups.

### Education

- Pakistani and Black pupils achieve less than other pupils at all stages of compulsory education. In 2006, only 51 per cent of Pakistani pupils and 48 per cent of Black pupils achieved 5 or more GCSEs at grades A* to C, compared with 58 per cent of White pupils and 72 per cent of Indian pupils.
- Male ethnic-minority pupils perform particularly badly. 52 per cent of White boys achieved five or more GCSE grades A* to C in 2006 compared with 38 per cent of African-Caribbean boys and 45 per cent of Pakistani boys.
- 46 per cent of 18-year-old Whites achieved one or more AS-levels compared with 40 per cent of Blacks and 37 per cent of Pakistanis/Bangladeshis.
- Modood (2006) notes that ethnic minorities make up 16 per cent of undergraduates at UK universities, which is nearly double their share of the population. However, he also points out that they are more likely to enter the less prestigious new universities, they are more likely to drop out and they are less likely to finish their degree.
- African-Caribbean pupils are over four to six times more likely to be excluded than White pupils, and three times more likely to be excluded permanently. Many of those excluded are of higher or average ability, although the schools see them as underachieving.
- Ethnic-minority children from poor families measured by receipt of free school meals do better than poor White children, e.g. only 20 per cent of White children with FSM status achieved five or more GCSE grades A* to C compared with 34 per cent of African-Caribbean children, 43 per cent of Bangladeshi children and 35 per cent of Pakistani children.

### Housing

- 70 per cent of all people from ethnic minorities live in the 88 most deprived local authority districts, compared with 40 per cent of the general population.
- Some ethnic-minority groups are more likely to live in poor housing. 30 per cent of Bangladeshi and 22 per cent of Pakistani households live in overcrowded housing compared with 2 per cent of Whites.

## Ethnic minorities and life-chances: empirical evidence

Ethnic minorities are disadvantaged in many areas of social life. Like the White poor, they experience multiple deprivations. However, it is very important to be aware of the significant differences between various minorities, and of the way inequalities also link with gender and class differences. For example, the majority of Muslim immigrants entered Britain at the bottom of the socio-economic ladder. Many (mostly Pakistanis and Bangladeshis) are still concentrated in semi-skilled and unskilled sectors of industry. These communities suffer from unemployment, poor working conditions, poverty, overcrowded housing, poor health, and low educational qualifications. In many ways, they share the experiences of the White urban poor. On the other hand, people from Indian and Chinese backgrounds tend to do reasonably well both in the education system and the labour market.

The 2001 disturbances in Oldham, Burnley and Bradford highlighted how multiple social deprivation can lead to deep disaffection, alienation and frustration. The areas most affected suffered from relatively high levels of youth unemployment, inadequate youth facilities, and a lack of a strong civic identity and shared social values that could have united these diverse local communities. Instead, these communities were strongly polarized along ethnic, cultural, religious and economic lines. A feeling of 'us' and 'them' developed between White and Muslim communities, enabling divisive racist organizations such as the British National Party (BNP) to exploit anti-Muslim feelings among many White people.

## Focus on research

### Jobs, pay and poverty

- In 2004, Whites had the lowest unemployment rates at 5 per cent. The highest unemployment rates were among Black Caribbean men (14 per cent) and men from Black African, Mixed and Bangladeshi groups (each 13 per cent). Unemployment rates were slightly lower for Pakistani and Chinese men (11 per cent and 10 per cent respectively). Indian men had the lowest unemployment rates among the ethnic-minority groups at 7 per cent. In 2004, 37 per cent of Bangladeshis aged 16 to 24 and 35 per cent of Pakistanis were unemployed compared with 11 per cent of White young people.
- Differences can also be seen when unemployment rates are compared by religion. In 2004, the unemployment rate among economically active Muslim men (13 per cent) was twice the rate of Sikh (7 per cent) or Hindu (5 per cent) men. Christian men had the lowest unemployment rates (4 per cent)
- Research by The Joseph Rowntree Foundation (Clark and Drinkwater 2007) found that men from ethnic minorities in managerial and professional jobs earn up to 25 per cent less than their White colleagues. Black African and Bangladeshi men were most likely to face the greatest pay discrimination. Indian men were the least likely to be discriminated against, but they were still earning less than White men doing the same job.

- Research by the Joseph Rowntree Foundation in 2007 showed that 40 per cent of ethnic-minority communities live in poverty – double the poverty rate of the White British communities – and are most likely to live in London, parts of the north and the Midlands than elsewhere in the UK. Half of all ethnic-minority children in the UK live in poverty.
- Ethnic-minority men were less likely than White men in 2004 to be employed in skilled trades (12 per cent compared with 20 per cent) and more likely than White men to be employed in unskilled 'elementary occupations' (16 per cent compared with 12 per cent).
- An African-Caribbean graduate is more than twice as likely to be unemployed as a White graduate, while an African is seven times as likely.
- Ethnic-minority men are overrepresented in the service sector. The distribution industry (including restaurants and retail businesses) is the largest single source of service-sector jobs for men from ethnic-minority groups, employing 70 per cent of Bangladeshi and 58 per cent of Chinese men. In contrast, only 17 per cent of White and 19 per cent of Black men work in this industry (Labour Market Trends 2000).
- However, it is important to acknowledge that a degree of upward social mobility exists within British Asian communities. For example, 47 per cent of Indian men were professional, managerial and technical workers in 2000, compared with 41 per cent of Whites.

### Power and politics: the legal system

- In 2006, 86 per cent of male prisoners were White, 11 per cent were Black and 5 per cent were Asian.
- 14 per 1000 of the White population are subject to police stop and searches compared with 93 per 1000 of the Black population and 29 per 1000 of the Asian population. Black people are therefore nearly seven times and Asian people over twice as likely to be stopped and searched as White people.

Sources: ONS *Labour Market Surveys* (2002–05), *The Guardian*, *Social Trends* 38 (2007) and *Ethnic Minorities Factfile* (CRE 2002).

# Explanations of racism and racial inequality

## Cultural explanations

Racist stereotyping probably originates in a number of diverse cultural sources:

- *Britain's colonial past* – Britain's imperial power exercised during the 19th and 20th centuries clearly saw Black and Asian people as subordinate to and heavily dependent upon White people. The teaching of Britain's imperial history in schools may reinforce stereotypes of ethnic minorities picked up during family socialization and in the media.
- *Language* – Language often contains implicit cultural messages. For example, some socio-linguists have noted that words associated with Black people – e.g. 'things are looking black', accident blackspot, black sheep of the family – are negative. Black is also symbolic of evil and wrong-doing. Whiteness, on the other hand, is associated with innocence, purity, goodness, etc. The use of this type of language may, therefore, reinforce racist stereotypes passed down through socialization.
- *The mass media* – A number of degrading unsympathetic or negative stereotypes of ethnic minorities are common across the media. Van Dijk (1991) conducted a content analysis study of tens of thousands of news items across the world over several decades. He found that Black crime and violence is one of the most frequent issues in ethnic coverage. Ethnic minorities are often portrayed as a threat to the White monopoly of jobs and housing. Moreover, ethnic-minority cultures are often represented as abnormal in terms of their values and norms, and thus as undermining the British way of life. The *Big Brother* racism scandal in 2007, in which the Indian actress, Shilpa Shetty, was racially abused by White housemates, originated in the fact that they regarded her culture and accent as strange and alien.
- *Family* – People may pick up these stereotypes in the course of normal socialization from their parents and other family members.




## The host–immigrant model or assimilation theory

A sociological approach that also stressed the importance of culture was Patterson's (1965) theory – the host–immigrant model – which shares many of the assumptions of functionalist sociology. Patterson depicted Britain as a basically stable, homogeneous and orderly society with a high degree of consensus over values and norms. However, she claims that this equilibrium was disturbed by the arrival of immigrant 'strangers' in the 1950s who subscribed to different cultural values. Patterson argues that this resulted in a culture clash between West Indians (who were regarded as boisterous and noisy) and their English hosts (who valued privacy, quiet and 'keeping oneself to oneself'). Patterson argued that these clashes reflected understandable fears and anxieties on the part of the host community. She claimed that the English were not actually racist – rather they were unsure about how to act towards the newcomers.

She therefore suggested that there were three causes of racial prejudice, discrimination and racial inequality:

1. the host culture's (White people's) fear of strangers, cultural difference and social change
2. the host culture's, particularly the working class's resentment at having to compete with ethnic minorities for scarce resources such as jobs and housing
3. the failure of ethnic minorities to assimilate, i.e. to become totally British and integrate – they tended to live in segregated communities rather than socially mixing.

Patterson's theory is implicitly critical of the insistence of ethnic minorities that they should retain their own cultural values and practices because these allegedly make White people anxious. However, she was reasonably optimistic about the future of race relations in the UK and argued that ethnic minorities would eventually move toward full cultural assimilation by shedding their 'old' ethnic values and taking on English or British values.

There are signs that the Labour government elected in 1997 was very influenced by this assimilationist model. Government ministers implied that racial tensions and inequality are the result of a supposed Asian desire and choice for residential self-segregation – to live in 'comfort zones' with 'their own kind'. Labour has suggested that this self-segregation of areas has led to school segregation; in some primary and secondary schools, Asian pupils have become the majority, and the affluent White middle-class have consequently responded by moving elsewhere – this has become known as 'White flight'. However, the White poor get left behind and have to compete for the same jobs and housing, which has led to racial tensions in areas like Lancashire as some areas allegedly have become no-go areas for White people.

Labour responded by introducing 45-minute multiple-choice nationality or citizenship tests. In order to get British citizenship, immigrants to the UK must successfully answer questions on aspects of British culture and swear an oath of allegiance to the Queen. Some commentators have suggested that this Britishness test should have a language component to ensure all potential citizens can speak and write English. Critics have suggested that Labour believes that racism, racial inequality, racial tensions and the alienation of Muslim youth can only be tackled by ethnic minorities doing more to assimilate – the ideological message quite simply is: embrace British culture and become 'more like us'.

## Criticisms

The evidence from areas in which racial tensions spilled over into riots in 2002, such as Oldham and Burnley, collected by the Commission for Racial Equality (CRE) suggests segregation was a product of discrimination rather than choice. Estate agents in Oldham promoted residential segregation by steering White and ethnic-minority populations into different areas. The CRE also noted evidence that suggests council officers allocated Asians to the most deprived council estates compared with Whites.

How was the New Labour introduction of citizenship tests influenced by the assimilationist model?

Despite Whites and Asians suffering similar levels of economic and social deprivation, this policy did not promote social mixing. This segregation also made it easier for the British National Party (BNP) to stir up rumours and resentment among the White population. The BNP claimed that Asians were being allocated superior council housing despite the fact that 25 per cent of the White population lived in council housing compared with only 9 per cent of Pakistanis. The CRE also point out that Whites are responsible for White flight rather than Asians, because the White middle classes do not want to mix socially with Asians. Being able to afford to move out of an area because ethnic minorities are moving in is a type of racism.

Critics of this assimilationalist host–immigrant approach point out that African-Caribbeans are the most assimilated of all ethnic-minority groups – they speak English as a first language at home, they intermarry into the White population, their children mix freely and easily with White children and they are usually Christian. There are no cultural barriers preventing them from assimilating into British cultural life. However, the economic, social and educational position of African-Caribbean people is no better than it was 50 years ago. They are still more likely to be unemployed and in poverty than Whites and their children are still most likely to fail academically or be excluded from school.

Patterson can be criticized because she failed to acknowledge that the UK is a multicultural society and that the concept of assimilation is ethnocentric – it fails to recognize that no one culture is superior and that all cultures, British and ethnic minority, have similar value. The host–immigrant model also focuses so much on culture that it tends to end up 'blaming the victim' or scapegoating them, by attributing racism and racial inequality to their 'strange' cultures.

Finally, racial hostility has not declined as predicted by Patterson. The basic structure of British society remains unchanged, and the struggle over scarce jobs, housing and money between groups of urban poor, Whites, Asians and African-Caribbeans continues to fuel racial tensions.

## Weberian explanations

The work of Max Weber (1864–1920) has had a significant influence on explanations for racial discrimination and inequality. He noted that modern societies are characterized by a class struggle for income and wealth. In this sense, he would agree with Marxists. However, he also notes that modern societies are also characterized by status inequality. Status and power are in the hands of the majority-ethnic group, thereby making it difficult for ethnic-minority groups to compete equally for jobs, housing, etc. Ethnic minorities who do manual jobs are technically part of the working class, but they do not share the same status as the White working class. This is because they are likely to face prejudice and discrimination from the White working class who see them as in competition for the same scarce resources, e.g. jobs. Ethnic minorities therefore suffer from status inequality as well as class inequality. Even middle-class Asians doing professional jobs may experience status inequality in the form of prejudicial attitudes held by members of both the White middle and working classes.

## Organisation of the job market

Such prejudice and discrimination can be seen in the distribution of ethnic minorities in the labour force. The '**dual labour-market theory**' of Barron and Norris focuses on ethnic inequalities as well as gender inequalities in employment. They suggest that there are two labour markets:

1. *the primary labour sector* – characterized by secure, well-paid jobs, with long-term promotion prospects and dominated by White men
2. *the secondary labour sector* – consisting of low-paid, unskilled and insecure jobs.

Barron and Norris (1976) point out that women and Black people are more likely to be found in this secondary sector. They argue that Black people are less likely to gain primary-sector employment because employers may subscribe to racist beliefs about their unsuitability and even practise discrimination against them, either by not employing them or by denying them responsibility and promotion.

Furthermore, Barron and Norris point out that the legal and political framework supporting Black people is weak. Trade unions are generally White dominated and have been accused of favouring White workers and being less interested in protecting the rights of Black workers. The Race Relations Act 1976 (which was introduced to protect Black people from discriminatory practices) was generally thought to be weak and was rarely used in practice.

However, the recent amendment to the Race Relations Act, which came into force in 2001, increases the need for greater clarity concerning the meaning and status of race. It 'places a general duty on public authorities to work towards the elimination of unlawful discrimination and promote equality of opportunity and good relations between persons of different racial groups'. The modern Race Relations Act, therefore, aims to have a much greater and wider impact – it seeks to ensure that racial discrimination is outlawed throughout the public sector and places a duty on all public bodies and authorities to promote good race relations. However, it is too early to say whether this amendment is having any real impact.

## Underclass

Another Weberian approach is that of Rex and Tomlinson (1979), who argue that ethnic-minority experience of both class and status inequality can lead to poverty, which is made more severe by racism. They believe that a Black underclass has been created of people who feel marginalized, alienated and frustrated. Another aspect of status inequality is that some young Blacks may feel both socially excluded from the standard of living most other members of society take for granted and experience policing as harassment. These feelings may occasionally erupt in the form of inner-city riots.

However, there is considerable overlap between the White and Black population in terms of poverty and unemployment, although the constant threat of racism does suggest that some members of the White working class do not recognize the common economic situation they share with Black and Asian workers. The concept of status inequality may therefore help to explain the apparent divisions between the White and ethnic-minority working class and the outbreaks of racial conflict between White and Asian people in some northern towns in 2001.

## Marxist explanations

Marxists such as Castles and Kosack (1973) argue that ethnic minorities are generally part of the exploited working class and it is this that determines their fate in capitalist society. Marxists see racial conflict, discrimination and inequality as symptoms of some deeper underlying class problem. They see these symptoms as deliberately encouraged by the capitalist class for three ideological reasons:

1. *Legitimization* – Racism helps to justify low pay and poor working conditions because ethnic-minority workers are generally seen as second-class citizens undeserving of the same rights as White workers. Capitalist employers benefit from the cheap labour of ethnic minorities in terms of profits made. Some Marxists note that ethnic minorities, like women, are a **reserve army of labour** that is only taken on in large numbers during periods of economic boom but whose jobs are often the first to be lost in times of recession. However, the existence of racism means that the plight of ethnic minorities in the job market is rarely highlighted.
2. *Divide and rule* – If ethnic minority and White workers unite in a common economic interest, they are in a stronger position to campaign for better wages and conditions. Castles and Kosack argue that racism benefits employers because it divides the workforce. The White workforce will fear losing their jobs to the cheaper labour of ethnic-minority workers. Employers play on these fears during pay negotiations to prevent White workers from demanding higher wages or going on strike.
3. *Scapegoating* – When a society is troubled by severe social and economic problems, then widespread frustration, aggression and demands for radical change can result. However, instead of directing this anger at the capitalist class or economic system, White people are encouraged by racist ideology and agents such as the mass media to blame relatively vulnerable groups such as ethnic minorities for unemployment, housing shortages and inner city decline, e.g. 'they have come over here and stolen our jobs, taken over all our corner shops'. Ethnic minorities become the scapegoats for the social and economic mismanagement of capitalism. This process works in the interest of the wealthy and powerful capitalist class because it protects them from direct criticism and reduces pressure for radical change.

However, some Marxists such as Miles (1989) have been influenced by the Weberian argument that the concept of 'status' should be used alongside the concept of 'class' to explain racism and racial inequality. Miles argues that the class position of ethnic minorities is complicated by the fact that they are treated by White society as socially and culturally different, and consequently they have become the victims of racist ideologies that prevent their full inclusion into UK society. At the same time, ethnic minorities too set themselves apart from the White majority by stressing and celebrating their unique cultural identity. Miles suggests that, as a result of these two processes, ethnic minorities are members of '**racialized class fractions**'. He argues that the White working class stress the importance of their ethnicity and nationality through prejudice and discrimination, whilst ethnic minorities react to such racism by stressing their ethnicity in terms of their observance of particular religious and cultural traditions.

Miles acknowledges that some ethnic minorities may be economically successful and become part of the middle classes. These professionals and owners of businesses may see their interests lying with capitalism. For example, recent statistics suggest there are currently over 5000 Muslim millionaires in Britain. Furthermore, their ethnicity may be a crucial influence in their business practices and financial success. However, the fact of their ethnicity probably makes it difficult for them to be fully accepted by the White middle class. They are, therefore, a racialized class fraction within the middle class.

# Recent approaches

It would be a mistake to think that all ethnic minorities are disadvantaged in UK society. Owen and Green (1992) note that Indians and Chinese are two ethnic groups that have made significant economic progress in the British labour market since the 1980s. Recent figures indicate that their average earnings are very similar to those of White workers. More generally, evidence suggests that increasing numbers from these ethnic minorities are entering the ranks of the professional middle class. Sociologists are also starting to notice the growth of ethnic-minority businesses and the spread of self-employment among ethnic-minority groups, particularly Asians. However, it is important to note that although groups such as Indians are moving into white-collar and professional work, they may experience a 'glass ceiling' as White professionals and managers fill the higher-status positions within this sector.

Some sociologists have also questioned whether self-employment is really such a privileged sector of the economy. The high rate of self-employment among ethnic minorities may be a reaction to the racial discrimination that prevents them from getting employment. In other words, self-employment may be forced upon them. Sometimes, these businesses are precarious ventures in extremely competitive markets (e.g. taxi-driving) and offer small rewards for long hours. Often, the owners of such businesses only manage to survive because they are able to use cheap family labour.

## Postmodernist approaches

Postmodernists, such as Modood (1992), reject Weberian and Marxist explanations that seek to generalize and offer blanket explanations for ethnic groups as a whole. Postmodernists argue that ethnic-minority groups in the UK are characterized by difference and diversity. They point out that the experience of racism is not the same: different groups may have different experiences. For example, police stop-and-search tactics focus on African-Caribbeans rather than other ethnic-minority groups. Postmodernists point out that there are also different ethnic-minority cultural responses to racism.

However, postmodernists tend to focus on 'culture and identity' issues rather than racial inequality. They suggest that both White and ethnic-minority identities are being eroded by globalization and consumption, and so members of such groups are less likely to have their identity shaped by membership of their ethnic group. Postmodernists suggest that in the 21st century, the young, in particular, have begun to 'pick and mix' their identity from a new globalized culture that interacts with both White British culture and the ethnic-minority subcultures that exist in the UK. This process has produced new **hybrid identities**. As a result, racial or ethnic differences are not fixed and imposed by membership of an ethnic group. Instead, identity has become a matter of choice. The implication of these trends is that as ethnicity and race are reduced in importance and influence, so racism and racial disadvantage will decline.

Postmodernists argue that the extent and impact of racism differ from one person to another as identities are chosen and interact. They argue that once identity is better understood, ethnic disadvantage can be targeted and addressed. For example, if we know that Jamaican boys not born in Britain living in a particular area are more likely to drop out of school, then something meaningful can be done to address this problem.

In criticism of postmodernism, evidence from studies of ethnic identity suggest that ethnic and religious identity often overlap, and that through agencies such as the family, community, places of worship and faith schools, ethnic identity is imposed rather than chosen. Such processes are often reinforced by the experience of unemployment, poverty, poor housing, inner-city deprivation and the constant fear of racial harassment. In conclusion, we can argue that postmodern ideas have greatly exaggerated the capacity of both White and ethnic-minority people to resist cultural influences and that they unrealistically play down the social and economic factors, such as everyday racism, that impact on the life-chances of ethnic-minority groups compared with Whites.

## Check your understanding

1. How can it be argued that the term 'race' has more explanatory value than the term 'ethnicity'?
2. Where does racial prejudice come from? Give examples to back up your arguments.
3. Explain why members of organizations deemed 'institutionally racist' may not necessarily be racist individuals.
4. How can institutional racism be tackled?
5. What is wrong with early functionalist explanations of ethnic inequality?
6. How was the Labour government's policy towards race relations influenced by assimilation theory?
7. Briefly summarize three Weberian accounts of ethnic inequality in the workplace.
8. How do Marxists argue that racism benefits capitalism?
9. Why do postmodernists reject Weberian and Marxist explanations of ethnic inequality?

# Activities

## Research ideas

1. Carry out a piece of research to explore local people's knowledge of ethnic differences. Do they understand the distinctions between the various Asian groups? Do they understand the significance of particular festivals? Do they know of prophets or holy books? Can they point on a world map outline to the countries of origin of the various groups?
2. Assess the extent to which an organization such as your school or college might be deemed to be institutionally racist. Look at the distribution of ethnic groups on the various courses. Try to acquire statistics on exclusions, achievement rates and progression. What problems might you encounter in your research and how might you overcome them?

## Web.tasks

Go to the guardianunlimited website at **www.guardianunlimited.co.uk**. Search the archive by typing in 'race equality'. Read the articles highlighting a range of issues from institutional racism, social policy reform to rural racism and racial harassment.

# Key terms

**Dual labour-market theory** the view that two labour markets exist: the first has secure, well-paid jobs with good promotion prospects, while the second has jobs with little security and low pay; vulnerable groups such as women, the young, elderly and ethnic minorities are concentrated in this second sector.

**Ethnicity** cultural heritage shared by members of a particular group.

**Hybrid identities** new identities created by ethnic mixing.

**Institutional racism** where the sum total of an organization's way of operating has racist outcomes.

**Prejudice/Cultural attitudes** a style of thinking that relies heavily on stereotypes that are factually incorrect, exaggerated or distorted.

**Race** variation of physical appearance, skin colour and so on between populations that confers differences in power and status.

**Racial discrimination** racial prejudice put into practice, for example by denying someone a job on the basis of their skin colour or membership of a different ethnic group.

**Racialized class fractions** term used by Miles to describe splits in the working class along racial lines.

**Racism** systematic exclusion of races or ethnic groups from full participation in society.

**Reserve army of labour** Marxist concept used to describe an easily exploitable pool of workers drawn from vulnerable groups such as women, ethnic minorities, the old and the young.

## An eye on the exam Ethnicity and stratification

Describe only – no need for evaluation

Prejudice and discrimination expressed through media representations, policing, housing allocation, employer attitudes, employment, unemployment and pay, racial name-calling and attacks etc.

**(a) Outline the evidence that racism exists in modern British society. (20 marks)**

Statistical trends and patterns, research findings and contemporary examples from any module studied and/or your wider sociological knowledge

Describe the main explanations for ethnic inequality using appropriate theories, concepts and writers

These should focus particularly on employment, unemployment and pay although references to education, housing etc. would be relevant too

**(b) Outline and assess sociological explanations for ethnic inequalities in modern Britain. (40 marks)**

Compare the strengths and weaknesses of different explanations before reaching a balanced conclusion

Focus on comparing the main ethnic minority groups in the UK - Asians such as Pakistanis, Indians and Bangladeshis, and African-Caribbeans - with the White majority

### Grade booster Getting top marks in question (b)

Outline some of the ethnic inequalities that exist in the modern UK today including access to skilled jobs, pay, unemployment as well as poverty, housing and education. You need to consider a range of different sociological explanations in your answer including functionalism, Weberianism, Marxism and postmodernism. In discussing explanations, make use of relevant concepts, such as assimilation, reserve army of labour, primary and secondary labour markets, underclass, and racialized class fractions. You can develop evaluation by considering evidence for and against different views, using one theory to argue against another and by considering how different ethnic minority groups compare against one another in the labour market.

# TOPIC 7

# Age and stratification

## Getting you thinking

- Young people are not allowed to watch films with too much sex or violence in them until the age of 18.
- The legal minimum age to stand for Parliament is 18 years.
- To become a judge, a person needs to have practised law for a minimum of 7 years.
- A person must be 13 years old to register on Facebook, Bebo and MySpace.
- Magistrates must retire at the age of 70.
- A third of job-seekers between the age of 50 and 65 are unable to find work.
- An analysis of fictional representations of the elderly in television drama and sit-coms found that 46 per cent of elderly characters were portrayed as grumpy, interfering, lonely, stubborn and sexless.
- Only 16 per cent of pensioners have a car compared with 77 per cent of all households.

Source: Ray and Sharp (2006) *Ageism: A Benchmark of Public Attitudes in Britain,* Policy Unit, Age Concern England

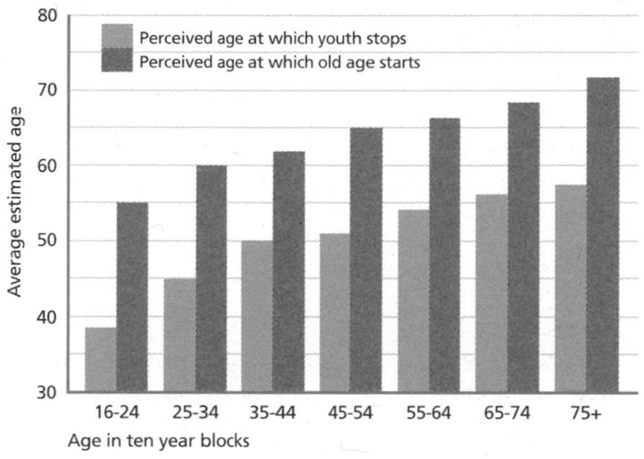


**Study the figure above and the points on the left, and then answer the following questions:**

1. **What does the bar chart tell you about attitudes towards youth and old age?**
2. **What do the listed facts about age tell you about the treatment of the young and the elderly in UK society?**
3. **In your opinion, why are the elderly in particular subjected to such negative treatment in the UK?**

## Age cultures: a natural or social creation?

Ageing is a physical process that all human beings experience. However, in most societies, age is divided up into significant periods – childhood, youth or adolescence (i.e. being a teenager), young adulthood, middle age and old age. These periods have different social meanings attached to them with regard to social expectations about behaviour and lifestyle, responsibilities to others, independence and dependence, and so on. These social meanings are relative to culture and time.

In many pre-industrial and tribal societies, for example, the period of youth is notably absent, because at puberty children go through 'rites of passage' – often involving physical ordeal – that transform them into adults with much the same responsibilities as other adult members of the society. The term 'elder' in these societies symbolizes great wisdom, dignity and authority. The elderly are treated with great respect and consequently have a great deal of status. Vincent (2001) notes that what constitutes 'old age' varies cross-culturally, although how age is defined and treated differs within our own society too. It can be argued that young people and the elderly have a great deal in common in that they both experience low status. The transition to adulthood, however, is celebrated at 18 with a social event whilst those reaching their 100th birthday are regarded as so special they get a message of congratulation from the Queen.

These age categories, or **age strata**, are not 'natural' but created by society. That is, they are **social constructions**. You may have noticed from the exercise above that different age groups have different subjective interpretations of what counts as 'young' and as 'old' – what you see as 'old' may be quite different from how the 'objectively old' (official definitions see 65 years – the age of retirement – as the beginning of old age) view themselves. However, the consequences of these constructions are that members of different age groups will experience differing degrees of social status, self-esteem and prejudice. These, in turn, will produce different experiences of inclusion and exclusion, and often marginalization and inequality.

# The elderly – the demographic picture

The decline in the death rate, the increase in life expectancy and a decline in the birth rate over the last 50 years have led to an ageing of the UK population. There are increasing numbers of people aged 65 and over and declining numbers of children under 16. Between 1971 and 2004, the number of people aged under the age of 16 declined by 18 per cent while the number of people aged over 65 increased by 29 per cent. Consequently, in 2008, about 18 per cent of the population, i.e. approximately 11 million people, were over retirement age. Davidson (2006) points out that, in 2002, in the UK population over the age of 60, for every 100 men there are 127 women; over the age of 80, this ratio increases to 100 : 187. Altogether, over 65 per cent of the elderly are women.

## Age and inequality

Bradley (1996) refers to old age as the most neglected and hidden dimension of social stratification and hence inequality – for example, pensioners are one of the most significant groups that make up the poor. The annual Spotlight report by Help the Aged (2008) suggests that in 2005/6, 11 per cent of UK pensioners, i.e. 1.2 million people, were living in severe poverty on less than half of average earnings. Nearly double that number – 21 per cent, or 2.2 million people – were classified as living in poverty, with incomes less than 60 per cent of average earnings. These figures suggest that nearly a third of the elderly are in poverty. The Spotlight report claims that such poverty is having a negative effect on the health of the elderly – one in four of the elderly poor suffered illness as a direct result of poverty.

There is some evidence that, in 2007, an additional 200 000 pensioners were experiencing 'fuel poverty', meaning that they were spending at least 10 per cent of their income on electricity, gas and coal just to stay warm. The numbers of pensioners likely to be experiencing fuel poverty by 2010 is estimated at 1.2 million.

## Age, gender, ethnicity and social class

Age interacts with social class and gender to bring about inequality. People who are poor in old age are most likely to be those who have earned least in their working lives, i.e. women and those employed in manual jobs. This can be seen especially with regard to pension rights. Many of those working in professions such as teaching and finance can supplement their state pension with a company or private pension. However, many manual occupations fail to provide this extra.

Davidson notes that the majority of those people who are not eligible for – or who cannot afford the contributions required for – participation in private occupational pension schemes are female. This is because they are more likely to have their careers interrupted by pregnancy and childcare, and are more likely to be employed in low-paid, part-time work for a significant period of their lives. Oppenheim and Harker (1996) found that 73 per cent of male employees receive company pensions, compared with only 68 per cent of female full-time employees and only 31 per cent of female part-time workers. Consequently, women are more likely in later life to be dependent on a husband's occupational pension or on a state pension supplemented by benefits. Mordaunt *et al.* (2003) report that as a result twice as many elderly women compared with men rely on benefits and one in four single (never married, widowed or divorced) women pensioners in the UK live in poverty.

Davidson notes that the proportion of ethnic-minority elders reaching retirement is higher now than ever before. She argues that interrupted work patterns, low pay and racial discrimination mean that ethnic-minority workers also have less opportunity to pay into private occupational pension schemes. They also have less economic potential to save and invest for old age. Ethnic-minority women are further disadvantaged. Davidson suggests their old age may be underpinned by race, gender and age discrimination.

Scase and Scales (2000) argue that the elderly are likely to be split between affluent early retirees and those who are on or close to the breadline. This latter group may have to continue working beyond retirement age in order to avoid severe poverty, especially as the value of state pensions relative to earnings has been declining since the early 1990s. Ray *et al.* (2006) also note that the retirement age often differs according to social class and status. For example, senior business executives and political leaders have the power to resist the official legal retirement requirement, and consequently they may avoid the potential poverty and negative connotations associated with being elderly or retired.

## The effects of ageism

Robert Butler (1969) defined ageism as a process of negative stereotyping and discrimination against people purely on the grounds of their chronological age. The elderly have mainly been the victims of this discrimination. For example, Butler argued that ageism is about assuming all older people are the same, despite their different life histories, needs and expectations, but Best (2005) also notes that the young, especially youth, can be victims of ageism too. Moral panics which negatively focus on the activities and cultural habits of young people are cited as evidence of such ageism. However, it can argued that ageism practised against the elderly has greater negative consequences than that practised against the young, in terms of self-esteem and social well-being.

Butler suggested that ageism was composed of three connected elements:

1. prejudicial attitudes towards older persons, old age and the ageing process
2. discriminatory practices against older people
3. institutional practices and policies that perpetuate stereotypes about older people.

He argued that ageism leads to the elderly experiencing fundamental inequalities in the UK in terms of their access to jobs and services, their income and how they are viewed by younger members of society.

# Focus on research

## Milne *et al.* (1999)

### Grey power

A study of elderly people in Britain (Milne *et al.* 1999) found evidence of two distinct 'worlds'. In one world, composed of people in the early years of retirement who live in a shared household with an occupational pension, there is a reasonably comfortable lifestyle. In the second world, made up of those over 80 who live alone with few savings, people can suffer acute poverty.

The former grouping, comprising relatively affluent older people, is much sought after by manufacturers all over the industrialized world, where the term 'grey power' is sometimes used to refer to the consumption habits and patterns of those over 65. Of course, the term cannot be applied to all older people. First, social-class differences continue into retirement. Lifestyle and taste differences, and the impact of different occupations as well as different forms of housing tenure, persist. Second, ill health is also gendered, with men more likely to experience it at an earlier age. The jobs people did also affect their income in old age; ex-professional and managerial workers have more income than ex-manual workers. Finally, older men have generally higher incomes than older women.

Adapted from Abercrombie, N. and Warde, A. (2000) *Contemporary British Society* (3rd edn), Cambridge: Polity Press

1. **Why is it that the term grey power 'cannot be applied to all older people'?**
2. **What might be the circumstances which lead to an older person belonging to either of the 'worlds' described above?**

## Institutional ageism

Greengross (2004) agrees with Butler and argues that ageism is deeply embedded and very widespread in UK society. Moreover, it is often unconscious, which makes it difficult to tackle. She notes that arbitrary age barriers set by the state mean older citizens cannot participate in many voluntary and civic activities – for example, the age limit for being a juror is 65 years whilst all judges and magistrates have to retire at 70 years. In 2006, the government implemented the UK's first age discrimination legislation. This covered all higher and further education, but excluded unpaid voluntary and civic work. Despite this legislation, employers are still able to force workers to retire at the age of 65. In 2008, Age Concern unsuccessfully challenged the compulsory retirement age in the European courts. However, the government have stated that it will eventually move away from insisting on a compulsory legal retirement age.

Greengross argues that the National Health Service (NHS) is guilty of institutional ageism because older patients in the NHS are treated differently from the young. Older people are subjected to discrimination in that they are often omitted from clinical trials or are denied particular treatment or operations on the basis of their chronological age. Greengross notes that these decisions are usually based on prejudiced views of what a 'good innings' is or is based on the view that the interventions are not worth pursuing because a person is 'too old'. There is some evidence that trainee medical professionals may be avoiding specializing in geriatric medicine because it is regarded as a low-status sector of the NHS.

Ray *et al.* (2006) argue that there is a subtle difference between age-discriminatory state practices, e.g. the ageist policies practiced by the NHS as outlined above, and age-differentiated state practices, e.g. protective legislation, positive stereotyping and special treatment. The latter policies and practices are designed to benefit rather than harm the elderly. For example, having an age at which a person becomes eligible for a state pension helps to ensure an adequate income in retirement, whilst concessions on a range of services, such as free or reduced public transport, free NHS prescriptions and free television licences for those over 75, help to reduce the financial burden on the old.

However, Ray and colleagues argue that some of these practices can prove just as harmful for older people as more overtly negative forms of discrimination. For example, the types of concessions mentioned above can reinforce ageist stereotypes of older people as needy and dependent and, by doing so, exclude them from choices and opportunities.

Greengross also notes that the elderly experience ageism with regard to services other members of society take for granted. For example, ageism practised by financial services may mean older people may have difficulty in hiring a car, getting insurance, getting a credit card or negotiating a loan.

## Ageism and the mass media

Another type of institutional ageism is found in the mass media. Featherstone and Wernick (1995) point out that birthday cards in particular indicate the distaste widely held about the ageing process. Representations of men and women in the UK media tend to focus on the 'body beautiful', and television and advertising encourage women in particular to see their bodies as 'projects' in needs of constant care and improvement. Ageing – and its outward signs, such as wrinkles and grey hair often presented as the greatest threat to our well-being, one that needs to be resisted at all costs. Carrigan and Szmigin (2000) argue that the advertising industry either ignores older people or presents them as negative stereotypes – physically unattractive, mentally deficient, senile, cranky, grumpy, cantankerous or difficult. They conclude that advertisers fail to reflect the elderly in any authentic way.

Older people portrayed on television are often marginalized, comical or based on inaccurate stereotypes. Genuine older people are generally underrepresented on television. These stereotypes are often the only experience younger people have of old age. These negative images may, therefore, create perceptions of a future old age as a time of dependency, poor health, poverty and vulnerability, even though this may bear little relationship to the lived experience of many older people.

## The 'demographic timebomb'?

Another aspect of ageism is the debate about the so-called '**demographic timebomb**'. It is predicted that in 2014, people aged over 65 years will outnumber people aged under 16 for the first time, and that the gap will widen thereafter. The number of people over retirement age in 2021 is projected to be 12.2 million. New Right thinkers have assumed, almost without question, that these elderly people are going to be dependent on younger people, that they are going to put intolerable strain on services such as health care, and that they will be a drain on the economy because of the disproportionate costs of the health care, social services and housing assistance they will supposedly need. Generally, then, this demographic timebomb is seen as likely to lead to a potential crisis for the welfare state, family and economy.

However, the concept of a demographic timebomb is based on a number of ageist assumptions that do not stand up to scrutiny:

- One such assumption is that elderly people are likely to be dependent because of poor physical and mental health. Whilst ageing is associated with some biological decline in physical and mental abilities, there is little evidence that this has a significant effect on the lifestyle of the elderly. For example, only one in 20 people over 65 and one in five people over 80 experience dementia. Ray and colleagues argue that overall, research has failed to prove a link between declining health and capability, and ageing.
- In terms of physical health, some authors suggest that there is a 'medical myth' that unfairly suggests ageing is synonymous with disease. However, decline in terms of illness may be due to prolonged and life-long exposure to an unhealthy environment and lifestyle, rather than to the ageing process itself.
- There is also an assumption that the elderly are incapable of doing paid work because the ageing process makes them incompetent. However, Ray and colleagues note that research findings indicate that younger workers are no better at their jobs than older workers, despite the widespread perception that this is the case. In experiments, it has been shown that there is no significant difference between the abilities of younger and older workers, with each group performing particularly well or poorly in different areas. Increasingly, because of the prospect of poverty and inadequate state pensions, the elderly are already returning to work post-retirement in fairly large numbers despite discrimination in the workplace. Over 1 million people are already voluntarily working beyond the state pension age, and research by the Prudential insurance company in 2005 estimated that figure could rise to 2.5 million by the end of the decade because many people won't be able to afford to retire.
- Taylor-Gooby (1996) points out that the number of pensioners increased from 6.5 million in 1951 to 10 million in 1991 without causing any major economic or social problems.

## Ageist attitudes

It can be argued that all these ageist practices result in negative stereotypes underpinning social attitudes about the elderly in the modern UK, so dehumanizing members of this group. The elderly have already lost a major source of status, respect, identity and economic security – work – when they have been forced to retire. However, the sorts of ageist practices and stereotypes outlined above result in their association, particularly by the young, with dependence, vulnerability and disability. The elderly are generally seen as making little or no contribution to society and/or as a burden on society. The ascribed characteristics of age therefore serve to exclude many elderly people from full involvement in society.

The research of Ray and colleagues found that ageism is common in the UK but, despite its negative consequences, it does not have a malicious character. They note that it exists in the form of what they call 'benevolent prejudice', in that the elderly are generally viewed as moral and admirable. Most people in their survey agreed that they should be valued and cherished. However, the sample also generally saw the elderly as 'incompetent, less intelligent but dear dodderers'. Ray and colleagues suggest that disadvantages can arise from both these positive and negative attitudes which can result in the

**Figure 6.2** Population pyramids, 1950 to 2050

Europe, Population Pyramids, UN Ageing Report 2003

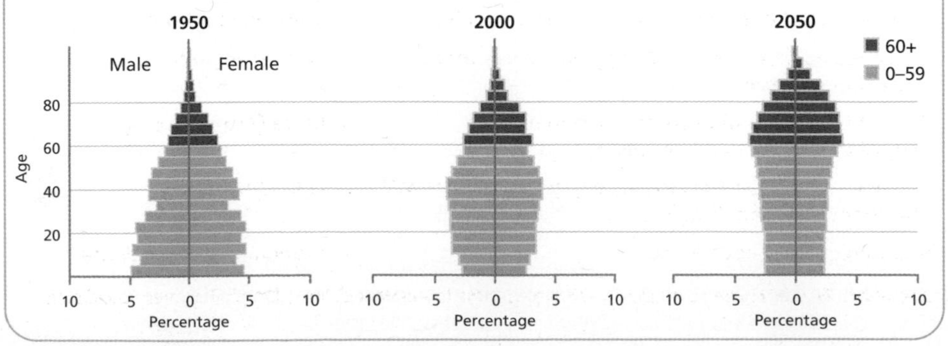

continued socio-economic exclusion of the elderly. At an individual level, they claim that the elderly are infantilized, ignored and treated in a patronizing and disrespectful fashion. It can also lead to conflict if the elderly person fails to live up to these social expectations – for example, they may be treated preferentially when being given a seat on a bus, but may be criticized as selfish for spending their savings on a holiday when they should be looking to provide an inheritance for their families.

At an institutional level, Ray and colleagues claim that ageism can mean exclusion from the workplace and positions of power or decision-making because employers assume lower competence. It might also lead to a failure to offer the elderly choices in health and social care, and to the assumption that older people might not want the sorts of life-chances that younger people do. Finally, it might be assumed that it is natural for older people to have lower expectations and reduced choice and control. Consequently, less account is taken of their views. Ray and colleagues conclude that ageism, and therefore age inequality, can only be tackled if older people are regarded by the state and society as active participants in decisions about their future, rather than as passive victims.

## The young

Like the elderly, the young also make up a large subgroup of the poor. A quarter of children live in households receiving less than 60 per cent of the average median income. In addition, many young people of working age face social deprivation caused by low pay, student loans and, in some cases, ineligibility for benefits and unemployment. In 2005, the unemployment rate for those under 25 was over 18 per cent. However, the increase in those on training schemes masks the true figure. Again, this is affected by other factors, such as ethnicity – for example, twice as many African-Caribbean males are unemployed compared with Whites.

Furthermore, the extended transitions into adulthood that characterize the experience of young people in advanced industrial societies often bring with them extended periods of relative deprivation and reduced social standing. There are now more likely to be intermediate stages between leaving school and entry into the labour market, between living in the parental home and having a home of one's own, and (perhaps) between being a child in a family and being a parent or partner in one, as Table 6.10 demonstrates. Each of these stages is, however, potentially problematic.

Declining opportunities for those in vulnerable groups has led to increases in homelessness and financial hardship amongst the young, especially in run-down urban areas. Beatrice Campbell in *Wigan Pier Re-visited* (1985) and *Goliath* (1993) referred to adaptations some young people make in the absence of access to the mainstream routes to adult status. She suggests that some young women use having a baby as a means of acquiring adult status in a society which has increasingly closed down other options for them. Young men, on the other hand, with little prospect of work, turn to daring crimes such as car theft and joyriding as alternatives which offer the opportunity to show off their skills. Both motherhood and car theft become public ways of achieving status.

### Young people at work

Most young workers earn relatively little, and are given less responsibility and status in almost every occupational sector. Currently, some 227 000 18- to 20-year-old workers earn the minimum wage (Bulman 2003). Young workers are central to many industries, but are generally subjected to the worst pay and conditions and required to be the most 'flexible'. This is particularly evident in retail and catering. More than two-thirds of McDonalds' staff are aged under 20, while the Restauranters' Association says that in the commercial sector of the hospitality industry, 31 per cent of staff are aged 16 to 24. Of the nearly two million young people aged between 16 and 24 in full-time education, 40 per cent are also in paid employment. Two thirds of Pizza Hut's 'crew' staff are in full-time education, as are one-fifth of Sainsbury's store staff (Sachdev and Wilkinson 1998).

There is some evidence that ageism that can affect the young too. Vincent notes that young job applicants may be passed over in favour of older and more mature workers. He notes that reverse discrimination – in which older workers are offered dead-end jobs because it is assumed that younger workers are more ambitious – also takes place.

**Table 6.10** Extended transitions to adulthood

| Childhood | Youth | Adulthood |
|---|---|---|
| School | College or training scheme | Labour market |
| Parental home | Intermediate household, living with peers or alone | Independent home |
| Child in family | Intermediate statuses, including single parenthood, cohabiting partner | Partner–parent |
| More secure housing | Transitional housing in youth housing market, e.g. furnished flats and bedsits | More secure housing |
| 'Pocket money' income | 'Component' or partial income, e.g. transitional NMW (National Minimum Wage) | Full adult income |
| Economic 'dependence' | Economic semi-dependence | Economic 'independence' |

Source: Jones, G. (2002) *The Youth Divide – Diverging Paths to Adulthood*, York: Joseph Rowntree Foundation

Age

# Theoretical explanations of age inequality

## Functionalism

Functionalists such as Parsons (1977) considered age to be of increasing importance in modern societies. In pre-industrial society, Parsons argued, age did not really matter because family determined one's place in society. However, since industrialization, people have been more socially and geographically mobile, and age groups have become more important. Parsons argued that they provide **role sets** that create a link between the kinship group and the wider society. For example, Pilcher (1995) suggests youth is a stage of transition that connects childhood (which is mainly experienced as dependency upon adults in families and schools) to adulthood (which is mainly experienced as independence at work and in relationships that might lead to the setting-up of our own families). In this sense, age is important as a mechanism of social integration – it allows people to move from one social institution to another without too much social disturbance or conflict. However, critics note that there is a strong possibility that such social order might be undermined by unemployment, low pay, the expensive housing market, the lengthening of education and higher education costs. All these trends are likely to lead to more dependence on the family. The difficulties in this transition to economic independence are having a knock-on effect in other areas of social life, e.g. young mothers are marrying later.

Functionalists, such as Cummings and Henry (1961), suggest that the way society treats the old has positive benefits for society. The ageing process and the social reaction to it is part of a mutual process in which the elderly, either by voluntary choice or legal compulsion, are encouraged to abandon their occupational roles within the specialized division of labour. The implication here is that the ageing process inevitably leads to social incompetence. This process of 'social disengagement' functions to allow younger members of society to take the place of the old in the specialized division of labour with minimum disruption to both social order and economic efficiency. However, critics of **disengagement theory** point out that retirement from work and society is often not voluntary. Moreover, this disengagement also has negative consequences for the self-esteem of the elderly in terms of ageism. Critics of functionalism point out that disengagement often leads to the neglect of the experience, skills and talents of older members of society which could still be of great benefit to society. Furthermore, disengagement theory ignores the fact that many old people continue to be active participants in society.

## Marxism

According to Marxists, the young provide a cheap pool of flexible labour that can be hired and fired as necessary. They tend not to have dependants and so are willing to work for low wages. In terms of full-time employment, their lack of experience legitimates low pay, and competition for jobs keeps wages low.

Marxists, such as Phillipson (1982), suggest that the logic of capitalism, which is about exploiting workers and

# Focus on research

## Bynner *et al.* (2002)

### Young people's changing routes to independence

Several studies funded by the Joseph Rowntree Foundation have explored the different patterns of transition from school to work. Some have found that new divisions are appearing among young people entering adulthood and, according to the research, there are winners and losers in the system. The ways in which young people make their domestic transitions to adulthood are polarizing into the majority, whose transitions are extended over many years, and a minority, whose transitions are rapid, stigmatized and potentially problematic. According to Bynner *et al*. (2002), this polarization is increasing. They identify a 'widening gap between those on the fast and the slow lanes to adulthood'. What was previously a middle-class pattern of slow transition is becoming more widespread among the more affluent working class, and is now a majority pattern. This trend may be due to people choosing to marry and have children later in their lives, or because lack of resources and the demands of mortgages and expensive lifestyles cause them to postpone family building. At the other end of the scale, there is a continuation of the working-class pattern of early childbirth, which has become more problematic as the support structures of marriage, extended kinship networks, job security and formal welfare systems have become eroded. In the fast lane, early partnership formation and parenthood is usually followed by partnership breakdown and lone parenthood.

> « *Teenage motherhood … epitomizes the problem: early school leaving, no qualifications, poor job or youth training, pregnancy and childbirth, poor prospects of ever getting a decent job leading to family poverty.* » (Bynner *et al.* 2002)

These slow-track and fast-track patterns are closely linked to socio-economic background and educational level. Working-class and female transitions tend to be more condensed and earlier, while middle-class and male transitions tend to be more protracted and later.

Bynner, J., Elias, P., McKnight, A., Pan, H. and Pierre, G. (2002) *Young People's Changing Routes to Independence*, York: Joseph Rowntree Foundation

1. **What has caused the affluent working class to merge with the 'majority pattern of slow transition'?**
2. **Why is the fast track to adulthood increasingly problematic for the less affluent?**

Age

consumers for profit, is incompatible with the needs of the elderly. The elderly, despite their greater needs, are neglected by the capitalist system because they no longer have the disposable income or spending power which is so attractive to capitalists. Moreover, as Kidd (2001) notes, because their labour-power is no longer of any use to capitalism, the elderly are seen as a drain on its resources through their use of welfare and health provision. Consequently, then, in capitalist societies such as the UK, early retirement and increasing life expectancy mean that the elderly have little or no status because they are likely to possess little economic power. Cultural and ideological stereotypes of the elderly help justify this state of affairs. As a result, the elderly are more likely to be in poverty and to experience ill-health as an aspect of that poverty.

However, some old people, particularly those from an upper-middle-class background have more power and status because their earning power during their working lives was greater and they were able to accumulate savings and wealth. The relationship this group has with capitalism is beneficial. This privileged sector of the elderly has the economic power to consume services, such as private health schemes, and they therefore enjoy greater life expectancy and better health.

## Labelling theory

Ray *et al.* (2006) generally take a social action or interactionist approach to the treatment of the elderly. They note that there is evidence that the mental capability and wellbeing of the elderly can be negatively affected by exposure to stereotypical labels and experiences of ageism. Their labelling theory suggests that a self-fulfilling prophecy may be the result of exposure to ageism, which can cause a person to behave in a way which confirms these beliefs. They note that research has shown that the use of 'baby talk' or infantilized language causes older people to accept the inference that they are no longer independent adults, thus causing them to behave in a passive and dependent manner. In addition, research has shown that the linguistic expression of pity, particularly from medical professionals, conveys the idea that older people are helpless. Some older people may internalize this message and, as a result, increase their dependence on others.

Ray and colleagues argue that negative stereotypes can also impact on older people in other ways. For example, it can affect the way a person reacts to ageing themselves. Negative labels about ageing and the discrimination that follows can cause negative age-related changes to worsen, as the older person sees their life as a downward spiral and therefore takes no counter action. Evidence from the Age Concern and Mental Health Foundation Inquiry into Mental Health and Wellbeing in Later Life found that older people themselves said that the most effective way to improve mental health and wellbeing would be to improve public attitudes to older people.

## Postmodernist theory

Postmodernists such as Blaikie (1999) argue that chronological age, ageism and age-determined inequality are less likely to shape people's life experience in the 21st century. He suggests that UK society has undergone a social transformation from social experiences based on collective identities originating in social class and generation to an increasingly individualized and **consumerist** culture in which old age can be avoided by investing in a diverse choice of youth-preserving techniques and lifestyles.

Featherstone and Hepworth (1991) argue that age is no longer associated with some events and not with others. For example, as Kidd notes, the elderly who were regarded

## Key terms

**Age stratum (pl. strata)** an age layer in society experiencing differential status and market situation relative to other age groups or layers.

**Consumerism** emphasis on lifestyle and purchasing patterns.

**Demographic timebomb** a population trend so potentially grave in its consequences that it could literally damage society in an explosive way.

**Disengagement theory** the proposition that society enhances its orderly operation by disengaging people from positions of responsibility once they reach old age.

**Role set** a group sharing similar characteristics of whom a particular set of roles are expected.

**Social constructions** social categories arising from shared meanings held by members of social groups.

## Check your understanding

1. **'Age is an ascribed characteristic but is also socially constructed.' Explain this statement and give an example of another characteristic that can be understood in this way.**
2. **Give examples which show how some members of both the young and elderly may suffer disadvantages relative to the majority of the population.**
3. **(a) Why do some commentators suggest that the increasing numbers of elderly people constitute a 'demographic timebomb'?**
   **(b) How can this view be criticized?**
4. **What sort of pressures may be put on families as a result of the 'demographic timebomb'?**
5. **What evidence is there that young people experience inequality?**
6. **Why might extended transitions into adulthood become problematic?**
7. **(a) What is an age stratum?**
   **(b) Which age strata would you say enjoy the highest status and market position in the contemporary UK? Why?**
8. **Why, according to Marxists, are both the young and old marginalized in capitalist society?**
9. **What evidence is there of increasing opportunities for consumerism among the elderly?**

as non-sexual only ten years ago are now seen to be able to experience sex and to have an active sexuality.

However, Vincent (2001) suggests that global capitalism is still the major determinant of age-related inequality. He argues that decreasing labour-market stability and rapidly changing employment patterns have increased uncertainty. As a result, the UK is experiencing the growth of a 'fragmented society in which some have been able to use market-position (earnings-related pensions and property-related windfalls) to secure good (i.e. not much reduced) material conditions in old age, while others have missed out. Those who miss out are those with poor market opportunities' (p.5).

## Conclusions

To conclude, it is difficult to generalize about people's experiences of age. This is because these experiences will vary according to other aspects of stratification, such as class, gender and ethnicity. Social class, for example, probably plays a great part in determining people's level of income in old age. Consequently, theories of age which fail to take this into account can never be wholly convincing.

# Activities

## Research idea

Ask a sample of your peers to come up with phrases commonly used to describe the elderly (e.g. 'dirty old man', 'little old lady'). Analyse your results and try to formulate a range of ageist terms highlighting the social exclusion of the elderly in society.

## Web.tasks

Visit the 'Age concern' website at **ageuk.org.uk**

- Use the search facility and type 'statistics'. Download the most recent statistics on inequalities currently faced by the elderly.
- Type 'How ageist is Britain?' to locate their comprehensive study of ageism in 2004.

## An eye on the exam Age and stratification

Describe only – no need for evaluation

Clearly define what you mean by these age-groups

**(a) Outline the evidence that childhood and youth are marginalized statuses in modern Britain. (20 marks)**

Statistical trends and patterns, research findings and contemporary examples from any module studied and/or your wider sociological knowledge

Be careful to operationalize this term carefully

Describe the view using appropriate theories, concepts and writers

Compare the strengths and weaknesses of the view before reaching a balanced conclusion

**(b) Outline and assess the view that age is an important type of stratification in modern Britain. (40 marks)**

Be careful to define this term accurately

No need to compare with the treatment of age in non-industrial or developing societies

### Grade booster Getting top marks in question (b)

Outline the evidence that age is an important type of stratification by focusing on age differences with regard to income and poverty, media representations and ageism in access to work and health care. You need to consider a range of different sociological explanations in your answer including functionalism, Marxism, labelling theory and postmodernism. In discussing explanations, make use of relevant concepts, such as disengagement, institutional ageism, moral panics, prejudice and discrimination. You can develop evaluation by considering how age groups, genders, social classes and ethnic groups compare against each other with regard to the experience of ageism, by considering which theory or theories the evidence supports and challenges and by using one theory to argue against another.

# Exam Practice

**(a) Outline the evidence that males are disadvantaged in the contemporary UK** ***(20 marks)***

The disadvantage of males in the UK is an issue which is much less likely to be looked into, compared with the disadvantage of women. However there are many ways in which men experience disadvantage within society. One of these ways is through work. Development of technology combined with economic recession has lead to many jobs in traditional industries, which were mainly male dominated, being ended and therefore many working class men face unemployment. This, combined with the fact that in some areas of the country women have taken on the role of the breadwinner, has lead to a 'crisis in masculinity' according to Mac an Ghaill. This is where men can no longer fit into their traditional roles and so experience a crisis into what their role is in society.

The candidate is quite correct to note that unemployment has been a disadvantage mainly experienced by men in recent years. However, it is a shame that no evidence is cited in support of this relevant point either in the form of statistical data or sociological studies. The same is true of the relevant point that many women have become family breadwinners. The point about the 'crisis of masculinity' is reasonably well made and rightly links to Mac En Ghaill's study although it would have benefitted from some discussion of the effects of such a crisis.

Another area where men are disadvantaged is the family. Divorce from 1971 to 1996 more than doubled, and the UK has one of the highest divorce rates in the EU. Men who have children and get divorced are much less likely to get fair access to their children. Statistics suggest that more than 90% of single parent households are headed by women, meaning fathers do not have the qualitative relationships with children that women enjoy. Sewell's studies of black teenagers who get involved in street gangs suggests that boys are consequently less likely to have a positive male role model in the form of a father.

The reference to divorce statistics is satisfactory and the point made about fathers' access to children is a reasonably good one. Sewell's study is intelligently used to make a perceptive comment about male children, fatherhood and the potential for deviance.

Boys experience disadvantage from an early age, particularly through education. In the contemporary UK boys are achieving less than girls at every single stage of education. In 2006 48% of females continued to higher education compared with 38% of males. Mac and Ghaill's theory of a crisis in masculinity can also be applied to education, as boys are lacking the motivation to work as hard as they see girls outperforming them throughout school. There is also evidence according to Mitsos and Browne that teachers see boys as being more likely to work less hard and be disruptive and therefore will expect less out of them. Therefore they are not being given the same chance to achieve as girls.

Excellent evidence is cited in this paragraph with regard to higher education and Mac En Ghaill's study is used appropriately again with regard to male motivation. Good reference to teacher labelling of boys.

In terms of crime, according to Heidensohn, women are more likely to be looked upon more sympathetically by the police and women's crime is less likely to be reported by victims, further disadvantaging men. This could begin to explain the difference in crime statistics between men and women. This shows that across all aspects of society, men experience disadvantage by gender.

13/20

This is the weakest paragraph. It is not clear what points the candidate is making with regard to police sympathy or the crimes of women.

## An examiner comments

This candidate demonstrates a reasonably good rather than very good knowledge of evidence relating to male disadvantage. The knowledge cited is appropriate although it is vaguely presented in the final paragraph. It is of a reasonable range and fairly detailed but it lacks enough depth to qualify for a higher band. The quality of written communication is satisfactory. The candidate scores 10 out of 15 marks for knowledge and understanding. With regard to interpretation and application, the candidate scores 3 out of 5 marks because he or she demonstrated a good ability to interpret sociological knowledge and apply it to male disadvantage. Overall, this candidate was awarded 13 marks out of a possible 20.

**(b) Assess functionalist explanations of social inequality** ***(40 marks)***

Functionalism is a structural theory based on the idea that everything in society has a place and is functional for society. Therefore their view on social inequality, which is the difference between the wealthiest and poorest members of society, is that it is functional and necessary for a well operating society.

This is a reasonable introduction albeit a little simplistic. Functionalism is a structural theory but the candidate really needs to explain what this means. The definition of social inequality is a little basic but the point about functionality is satisfactory. However, the essay would have benefitted from an introductory paragraph which set out the theoretical context of the debate, i.e. how the functionalist theory of stratification compares with the Marxist theory of stratification.

Durkheim, who was an influential sociologist of his time, argued that class stratification helps maintain social order. He said that the reasoning behind stratification is that different members of society have different skills which enable them to carry out different jobs. Some jobs are classed as more beneficial to society than others, and therefore these jobs get higher rewards in terms of higher income and status. According to Durkheim, this is the cause of class divisions. Durkheim believed that members of society accept these class divisions and inequality because we accept the fairness of some occupations being more greatly rewarded because they are of greater value to society. Therefore class inequality and stratification reflects value consensus.

This paragraph is quite a good summary of Durkheim's ideas. Try to avoid superfluous statements like 'who was an influential sociologist of his time' – you don't get any marks for saying that a sociologist is famous. However, this paragraph does succinctly express the idea of 'functionality' of some jobs and uses the concept of 'value consensus' reasonably well.

# Exam Practice

Davis and Moore were functionalists who extended Durkheim's views. They believe that in society stratification is permanent as people are placed where they belong. They refer to this as role allocation. They believe people who undertake the most important jobs to society should be rewarded with higher income and status. Another way of allocating what the most important jobs are is by looking into the type of job. They believe the highest paid jobs should be unique, and can only be done by people with either an innate ability or who have been through long periods of training, such as doctors, who they believe should be rewarded at the end of their training with high pay. Davis and Moore also believe jobs which have other positions dependent on them should be well paid as failure to correctly carry out this job could have a wider impact on other jobs.

The knowledge and understanding demonstrated in this paragraph is satisfactory rather than very good. Although the candidate uses the term 'role allocation' the concept needed to be linked to the concept of meritocracy and competition. There also needed to be something on how Davis and Moore see inequality as the key to motivating both the highly and lowly paid.

However there have been a number of criticisms of this theory. One crucial criticism is that functionalists fail to explain why there is widespread resentment about differences in income and wealth, for example the current distrust of well-paid bankers. If all members of society believed in the meritocratic system, this should mean all members of society are happy with the system, which evidently is not true. Some sociologists argue that by only focusing on the positive use of power they are failing to see the way that power is used as a weapon by some to further their own material interests. They also do not explain people who live off, for example, inherited wealth in their meritocratic theory. Moreover they suggest that the only reason for working is economic gain and they ignore other reasons such as a sense of service or a joy in their work. However Davis and Moore believed that these other reasons were overshadowed by the need for economic gain. By stating that stratification is functional for everyone, they ignore the negatives and how some benefit from this system and some suffer.

This is an excellent evaluative paragraph which makes a series of insightful critical comments using contemporary events. However note that it makes reference to concepts such as meritocracy which should have been referenced earlier in the essay.

Marxist theory focuses on the negative repercussions of social inequality. They stress the importance of wealth and the impact this has on social class relationships. They see capitalism as oppressing and exploiting the working-class majority of the population. They criticise functionalist ideas about meritocracy and believe instead that the capitalist system leads workers to create the wealth while the rewards are taken by the employers and property owners. They also dismiss the functionalist view of shared values and instead see a conflict of interests between bosses and workers as it is in bosses' best interests to keep their workers' wages low to increase profits. Finally they dismiss the idea of meritocracy and shared beliefs as instead a system of false class consciousness whereby the bosses use the idea of meritocracy to make them believe they are stuck in the position they are in and to blame the workers for their positions in society.

This evaluative paragraph on Marxism is quite good in that it demonstrates a satisfactory knowledge and understanding of Marxist theory and concepts such as class conflict and false class consciousness. However, some of these ideas are under-developed and would have benefitted from some explanation of how capitalism is organised and concepts such as infrastructure, superstructure and ideology.

Functionalist theory can offer some explanation of social inequality through its theories about the most important jobs reaping the best rewards in society. However it fails to fully explain reasoning behind its faults and therefore cannot be used to offer a full explanation of social inequality.

This is a poor conclusion that adds nothing to the overall debate. The candidate had the opportunity to pick up extra marks by presenting the examiner with an evaluative balanced conclusion that demonstrated a good grasp of the debate. However, the paragraph above adds nothing to our understanding of the debate.

26/40

## An examiner comments

This candidate demonstrates a satisfactory knowledge and understanding of the functionalist theory of stratification. Most of the material was appropriate although there needed to be more reference to concepts such as meritocracy. When concepts such as role allocation were mentioned these required a little more depth and detail both in terms of explanation and illustration. The candidate was therefore awarded 9 marks out of a possible 15 for the skill of knowledge and understanding. With regard to interpretation and application, the candidate showed a good ability overall to interpret sociological ideas about stratification and was awarded 3 out of a possible 5 marks. Finally, this candidate's ability to analyse and evaluate functionalism was very good. Generally the sections which identified and explained specific weaknesses in functionalist theory and outlined Marxism as an alternative were both detailed and precise. However, the response would have benefitted from some discussion of strengths. The candidate was awarded 14 out of a possible 20 marks for evaluation and analysis. Altogether the candidate was awarded 26 out of a possible 40 marks.

# Exploring sociological research into social inequality and difference

| OCR specification | | Coverage |
|---|---|---|
| **All concepts from the AS coverage of methods and the following additional concepts** | | |
| Longitudinal studies | | Topic 1 |
| Case studies | | Topic 1 |
| Pilot studies | | Topic 1 |
| Value freedom | | Topic 6 |
| Objectivity | | Topic 6 |
| Subjectivity | | Topic 6 |
| Respondent validation | | Topic 2 |
| Researcher imposition | | Topic 4 |
| Reflexivity | | Topic 6 |
| Sampling techniques: | • Random | Topic 1 |
| | • Stratified | Topic 1 |
| | • Quota | Topic 1 |
| | • Snowball | Topic 2 |
| | • Purposeful | Topic 2 |
| Target population | | Topic 1 |
| Access | | Topic 2 |
| Gatekeeper | | Topic 2 |
| **Methodological issues and concerns** | | |
| Positivist | | Topic 1 |
| Interpretivist | | Topic 2 |
| Realist | | Topic 3 |
| Feminist | | Topic 3 |

exam 1

# TOPIC 1

# Positivism and quantitative methods

## Getting you thinking

The extract on the right is from a series that appeared in the *Guardian* Saturday Magazine. Each person is asked the simple question 'Are you happy?'

1 What do you mean by happiness? How could you research it?

Design a survey aimed at finding how happy young people are in Britain today.

2 Write down a detailed, step-by-step plan of what you are going to do.

3 How are you going to define and measure happiness?

4 To what extent do you think the results of your survey will give you an accurate picture of the distribution of happiness?

5 What problems are involved in trying to represent concepts such as 'happiness' in figures?

6 Do you think it is possible to measure feelings, beliefs or ideas?

### Are you happy?

BY MAUREEN HILLS-JONES, FORMER NURSE

I STARTED suffering from manic depression after my mother died. It comes and goes. Sometimes I have so much energy, it's ridiculous. I'm extremely happy right now. I undergo periods of extreme excitement followed by a low so deep it feels like grief. It can be a hard thing to explain to my children. The last thing you want to do is inflict it on them.

There are periods of great activity. I buy presents for people and write postcards and letters, even though people don't write letters any more. My kids laugh when they receive them. I talk on the phone. I stay up through the early hours. You can do an enormous amount in the night. I wrote an entire book last year, but then ripped it up. I make the most of these times because I know they're not going to last. It's unpredictable and those around, including my husband, have been very understanding.

I won't take medication. When you do, you're neither happy nor sad – I don't want my life to be like that. I'm open to other solutions to help me, whether that's reflexology or aromatherapy. Manic depression enhances the way you look at the world. When you're in the depression, you plan your funeral, but afterwards it feels as if you've got a new lease of life, a new view of the world – until next time. There will be a next time, but it's best not to dwell on the future. I have learned to live with it.

Source: Craig Taylor, *The Guardian*, Saturday 3 May 2008

You may have concluded from the activity above that it is perfectly possible to investigate happiness by adopting a careful plan, defining terms very clearly and using the precise instrument of a survey. On the other hand, you may have decided that happiness is such a personal and subjective aspect of life that the best way to approach it is through finding out what it means to people by letting them discuss it in their own words. The first scientific approach is likely to be favoured by positivist sociologists and the latter by those who favour an interpretive approach. But rather than splitting them into two completely irreconcilable camps, it is perhaps better to think of sociologists as being either more sympathetic to the use of traditional scientific methods (**positivists**) or more sceptical about whether this is the most useful way to proceed (**interpretive sociologists**).

# The hypothetico-deductive method

Positivists believe that the scientific tradition is the approach that sociology must follow. Accordingly, they seek to follow the **hypothetico-deductive** research method: a series of steps providing what is regarded as the most scientific method of finding information. By following these steps, the sociologist has the highest chance of generating accurate 'scientific' knowledge. These steps consist of the following:

1. *Background reading and personal experience* – Through study and everyday observation the sociologist uncovers an area of interest.
2. *Formation of a hypothesis* – The sociologist formulates a causal link between two events.
3. *Devising the appropriate form of study to isolate the key variables* – This is usually some form of questionnaire, interview or, less often, observation.
4. *Collecting the data* – There are strict rules governing the way questionnaires and interviews are carried out to ensure **validity** and **reliability**.
5. *Analysing the data* – Statistical models are often used here, such as 'tests of confidence', which allow the sociologist to demonstrate to others how likely their research sampling was to produce accurate results.
6. *Confirming, modifying or rejecting the hypothesis* – this is done by searching for weaknesses.
7. *Theory formation or confirmation* – However, no positivists claim their results are proved by their research, merely that they produce the best explanation until others can improve on it or possibly disprove it.

Most real research programmes are rather more complex and overlapping than the classic hypothetico-deductive approach – using some **inductive** features, for example. Nevertheless, it provides the model that positivistic sociologists seek to follow.

**Definition 'Hypothetico-deductive'**

**Hypothetico**

**Refers to a hypothesis, which Punch (1998) defines as 'a predicted answer to a research question'. An example is the fact that people routinely think that there is more violent crime than there really is. A research question might be 'Why is this?' And the predicted answer (or hypothesis) might be that it is 'because the media focus on violent crime and exaggerate its extent'.**

**Deductive**

**Refers to the fact that the hypothesis is drawn from a broader framework of observation, possibly from an existing theory. Deductive refers to the process of working something out from the general to the particular.**





We shall look at an example of the hypothetico-deductive model later, but for the moment, in the next section we will examine some of the key **theoretical** issues it raises.

## Theoretical approaches linked to positivism and quantitative research methods

The key question here is the nature of society. There are two extreme positions. At one extreme is the claim that society really exists 'out there' and largely determines how we think and act. In this model people can arguably be portrayed as puppets of society. At the other pole is the argument that society only exists through the beliefs and activities of individuals interacting. This model of society sees people as creative actors making society.

Positivists generally support a theoretical model of society that is based on the idea that there is some form of structure that exists independently of individual views, perceptions or desires – sometimes known as the structural model of society. As outlined in Chapter 1, there are two main theoretical approaches that are most closely linked to positivism and both base their approaches on the idea of structure: structural functionalism and Marxism.

### *Structural functionalism*

This derives from the work of Parsons (1951) and was heavily influenced by Durkheim and, to a lesser extent by Weber. Functionalism, you will recall, argues that institutions exist in society in the form they do because they contribute to the continuing functioning of society. Underpinning this theoretical model is the acceptance of a social structure that actively guides our actions and beliefs. Durkheim used the term **social facts** to describe the objective 'facts' he claimed existed in society. In his classic study *Suicide: A Study in Sociology* (1897/1952), Durkheim believed that he had demonstrated through using statistics on suicide that clear patterns could be uncovered. The 'social facts' were the numbers and types of suicide.

### *Marxism*

Marxist theory or 'dialectical materialism' was based on the belief that economic and social laws exist that govern human behaviour. Marx hoped that by uncovering these laws he would demonstrate that a communist society was the inevitable future. Although people's consciousness and actions play an important part, ultimately the laws are dominant. It is important to remember that although the original model of society devised by Marx was largely based on positivist ideas, most modern Marxist-inspired research is based on a mixture of quantitative and qualitative ideas.

### *Criticism*

We mentioned earlier that there were two conceptions of the nature of society. We have just looked at the way positivism is largely linked to the structural model.

However, this model of society has been strongly attacked by a range of other sociological perspectives, most notably those coming from a social constructionist perspective, such as symbolic interactionism. Symbolic interactionism derives from the work of Blumer (1962), and is closely linked to labelling theory. Symbolic interactionism, labelling theory and ethnomethodology all stress the way that individuals work at making sense of the society around them. According to these approaches, society is created by the activities of people and not the other way around. Positivistic methods are, therefore, inappropriate, with their assumption of some objective reality. Instead (as we shall see in Topic 2), these social constructionist theories try to grasp the rules (if any) that guide people in their daily tasks of creating reality. This usually involves watching people and analysing their conversations and their activities. This takes us back to our earlier point regarding deductive and inductive reasoning. Whereas positivism generally uses a deductive framework, social constructionists start with an inductive one – building up from observations.

We will explore this approach in more detail in Topic 2, where we look at the methods most closely associated with the social constructionist approaches.

## Quantitative research: the favoured method of positivists

Positivists believe that there is a social world 'out there', relatively independent of individuals, that can be uncovered by testing hypotheses through using rigorous research-collection techniques. They seek out valid **indicators** to represent the variables under study in order to study them in a reliable way.

This approach strongly favours using quantitative methods such as **surveys** and questionnaires.

## Surveys

A social survey involves obtaining information in a standardized manner from a large number of people. This is done in order to maximize reliability and generalizability (see Topic 4).

Before a full social survey is carried out, it is usual for a researcher to carry out a **pilot survey**. This is a small-scale version of the full survey, which is intended to:

- help evaluate the usefulness of the larger survey
- test the quality and the accuracy of the questions
- test the accuracy of the sample
- identify any unforeseen problems.

There are two main types of survey – longitudinal and cross-sectional.

### Cross-sectional surveys

**Cross-sectional surveys** are often called 'snapshot' studies as they gather information at one particular time. These are the most common surveys which we are used to reading in newspapers and textbook and are often called 'opinion polls'. This method is very useful for finding out information on a particular topic at one specific moment. If organized properly, these are quick to do, the results can be collated and analysed very quickly and findings are likely to be highly generalizable. However, there are two real difficulties with cross-sectional surveys:

1 The indicators or questions chosen to measure a particular form of attitude must be accurate. If they are not, then the research will not be valid.
2 The surveys provide information for one particular, static moment – they do not provide information over a period of time, so changes in views cannot be measured.

### Longitudinal surveys

**Longitudinal studies** are surveys that take place over a period of time – sometimes years. The cross-sectional survey already mentioned is a very important method and is widely used by sociologists, in particular because of the very high reliability and generalizability of its findings. However, its weakness is that it provides information for one particular moment only. Changes in attitudes or behaviour over time are simply not measured by it, nor are longer-term factors that might influence behaviour. So, when quantitative sociologists are particularly interested in change, they often switch to using a longitudinal survey. By following groups of people over a period of time, sociologists are able to plot the changes that they are looking for. However, longitudinal surveys suffer from some quite serious drawbacks. The biggest of these is the drop-out rate. Answering questions over time and being the object of study can lead to people getting bored or

**Surveys** Aims and weaknesses

**Aims**

- To uncover straightforward factual information about a particular group of people – for example, their voting intentions or their views on punishment of convicted offenders. This is because a survey allows information to be gathered from a large range and number of people.
- To uncover differences in beliefs, values and behaviour between people, but *only* when these are easily and clearly measurable. If the beliefs and attitudes are complex or it is difficult to find unambiguous indicators for them, then qualitative research may be more appropriate.
- To test a hypothesis, where it is necessary to gain more information to confirm or deny it.

**Weakness**

The *major weakness of all surveys* is that they cannot easily uncover complex views. This means that there is always an issue regarding the *validity* of quantitative research. Issues of indicators and the **operationalization** of concepts in general are crucial in the research design.

# Focus on research

## Parker *et al.* (1998)
## A longitudinal survey

The North-West Longitudinal Study involved following several hundred young people for five years between the ages of 14 and 18. The overall aim of this study was to assess how 'ordinary' young people, growing up in England in the 1990s, developed attitudes and behaviour in relation to the availability of illegal drugs, alongside other options such as alcohol and tobacco.

The main technique was a self-report questionnaire initially administered personally by the researchers (and then by post) to several hundred young people within eight state secondary schools in two, non-inner-city boroughs of metropolitan north-west England.

At the start of the research the sample was **representative** of those areas in terms of gender, class and ethnicity. However, attrition (losing participants) partly reduced this over time with the disproportionate loss of some 'working-class' participants and some from Asian and Muslim backgrounds.

A longitudinal study is able to address issues of validity and reliability far more extensively than one-off snapshot surveys, but in turn must also explain inconsistent reporting that occurs over the years.

In general, the research provides a detailed account of how young people develop attitudes and behaviours through time.

Adapted from Parker, H., Aldrige, J. and Measham, F. (1998) *Illegal Leisure*, London: Routledge, pp. 48–9

**How does this extract illustrate some of the advantages and disadvantages of longitudinal surveys?**

resentful. Also, people move addresses, colleges and friendship groups, so tracking them becomes a complex and expensive task. For both these reasons, longitudinal surveys suffer from low retention.

This is also a problem because the survey will start to lack reliability and generalizability. Quite simply, if the retention rate becomes too low, then the views and behaviour of those who remain may well differ from the views of those who have left the survey.

Such surveys provide us with a clear, ongoing image of changes in attitudes and actions over time. The *British Household Panel Survey* is a longitudinal study that has studied over 10 000 British people of all ages, living in 5500 households. The interviewing started in 1991 and has continued every year since then. The information obtained covers a vast area, including family change, household finances and patterns of health and caring. It is used by the government to help inform social policies.

## Surveys and response rates

The validity and generalizability of all surveys are dependent on having high response rates. Response rates refer to the proportion of people approached in the survey who actually respond to the questionnaire or interview. The greater the proportion of people who return the questionnaires or agree to be interviewed, the greater the chance the survey has of being valid.

# Sampling in quantitative research

One of the main strengths of survey research is that it uses processes that ensure the people in the survey are representative of the whole population. When the people selected are representative, then the results of the survey are likely to be true for the population as a whole and therefore generalizable.

It is very difficult for sociologists to study large numbers of people, as the costs of devising and carrying out the research is just too high. Instead, as we have seen throughout this book, sociologists tend to study a small but representative cross section of the group they are studying. If this small sample truly mirrors the **target population**, then the results from studying this chosen group can be said to be true of the larger population too.

Quantitative surveys have two different methods of ensuring that their sample is representative and, therefore, the results are generalizable to the whole population. These two different methods are **probability** (or **random**) **sampling** and **quota sampling**. There are also other forms of sampling – snowball and purposeful – which are more commonly used in qualitative research. (These are discussed in Topic 2.)

## Probability or (random) sampling

Probability or random sampling is based on the same idea as any lottery or ticket draw. If names are chosen randomly, then each person has an equal chance of being selected. This means that those chosen are likely to be a cross section of the population. As we saw earlier, if the sample is representative, the results are likely to generalizable to the population as a whole.

### *The sampling frame*

In order to make a random sample, sociologists usually prefer to have a **sampling frame**, which is some form of list from which the sample can be drawn. British sociologists typically use Electoral Registers, (which are lists of people entitled to vote) or the Postcode Address File (which is the way that The Post Office links names and addresses to postcodes). However, for smaller studies, sociologists could ask for permission to use the lists of students attending a school, or members of a club that keeps lists of names.

As Bryman (2004) points out, any piece of random sampling can only be as good as the sampling frame, so if this is inaccurate or incomplete then the sampling itself will not be accurate.

### *The different forms of random sampling*

If the names are picked out entirely randomly, then this is known as 'simple random sampling'. However, when given a list of names, it is apparently quite difficult to pick in a truly random way, so very often a method is used whereby every 'nth' name (for example, every fifth or tenth name) on a list is chosen. This is known as **systematic (random) sampling.**

**Stratified sampling** is a further refinement of random sampling. Here, the population under study is divided according to known criteria (for example, it could be divided into 52 per cent women and 48 per cent men, to reflect the sex composition of the UK). Within these broad strata, people are then chosen at random. In reality, these strata can become quite detailed, with further divisions into age, social class, geographical location, ethnic group, religious affiliation, etc.

The final form of random sampling is known as **cluster sampling** and is used when the people the researcher wishes to interview are in a number of different locations (instead of using postal or email questionnaires). In order to cut costs and save time travelling to many different places, the sociologist simply chooses a number of locations at random and then individuals within these locations. This means that it is possible to generalize for the whole population of Britain by interviewing in a relatively few places. This approach has also been developed into **multistage cluster sampling**, in which smaller clusters are randomly chosen within the larger cluster.

Random sampling is generally very easy to use and, even if there is no sampling frame, it is possible to stop every 'nth' person in the street or college and question them. It also has the enormous advantage that if certain statistical tests are used, then it is possible to say with a degree of statistical certainty how accurate the results are.

### *Problems with random sampling*

There are a number of problems that can occur with random sampling. First, it is often difficult to obtain a sampling frame, particularly in the last few years since laws restricting access to information held on computers have been introduced.

Where systematic sampling is undertaken, often by asking every 'nth' person in the street or wherever the appropriate location is, it can be extremely difficult for the researcher to maintain the necessary discipline to ask the correct person. If the person looks unpleasant or threatening, then researchers often skip that person and choose the next one! Also, factors such as the time of day or the weather can have an important influence on how representative the people in the street (or college) are. For example, stopping every tenth person in the high street of a town between 9 am and midday, usually results in a high proportion of retired and unemployed

## Focus on research

### Rees and Lee (2005)
### A scientific survey of young runaways

In 2005, Rees and Lee carried out a survey of 11 000 young people aged 14 to 16 to find out what proportion had run away from home for at least one night, what happened to them and why they had run away.

First, the authors did a full search of previous research in the area of young runaways; their literature search identified a previous study first published in 1999. Rees and Lee therefore decided to use similar methodology, as this would allow them to compare how the situation had changed in the previous seven years.

This study consisted of a representative sample of young people aged 14 to 16, drawn from four or five secondary schools in 16 different areas of the country. Rees and Lee used a questionnaire for the study, which students were asked to complete on their own. In order to ensure that the questionnaire was valid and reliable, they undertook a pilot study with year 10 and 11 groups in three schools and one pupil referral unit. As a result of this, a large number of changes were made.

The questionnaire had six sections and used a 'tick-box' format with space for additional comments. There were a limited number of open-ended questions. The questionnaires were translated into a number of languages reflecting the ethnic background of the students, and there was also large print for partially sighted students.

Rees and Lee took ethical issues very seriously and so provided each school and student with clear statements to explain what the research was about and how it would be used, also explaining that whatever information was obtained would be completely confidential.

Rees, G. and Lee, J. (2005) *Safe and Sound: Still Running II. Findings from the Second National Survey of Young Runaways*, London: The Children's Society

**Why might Rees and Lee's research be viewed as positivistic?**

people. The sample is not representative and the results are therefore not generalizable.

## Non-random (or non-probability) sampling

The main alternative to random sampling in quantitative sociological research is quota sampling.

### *Quota sampling*

For research based on interviews, the main alternative to random sampling, which is commonly used by market research companies, is quota sampling. This can be used in any situation where the key social characteristics of the population under study are already known. For example, census information can give us a detailed picture of the UK population in terms of the proportion of people in each age group, income band, occupational group, geographical location, religious affiliation and ethnicity. There is, therefore, no reason to try to seek a representative sample by random methods. All that has to be done is to select what the key characteristics are and then get the same proportion in the sample as in the main population. Each interviewer is then allocated a quota of people exhibiting the key characteristics. This guarantees that there is a representative coverage of the population.

The main reason for the popularity of quota sampling over random sampling is the very small number of people needed to build up an accurate picture of the whole population (as long as you know what key characteristics to look for). For example, the typical surveys of voting preferences in journals and newspapers use a quota sample of approximately 1200 to represent the entire British electorate.

However, quota sampling has a number of significant drawbacks. The first is that unless the researcher has the correct information on the proportion of people in each key category, then the method is useless. In this situation it is always better to use random sampling. The second drawback is that the statistical tests that can be used with random sampling to ensure that the results of the survey are accurate, cannot be used with quota sampling.

The most important drawback, though, is that quota sampling usually relies upon a researcher choosing people who fall into the quotas they have been given. Relying upon the interviewer's perception of who to interview can lead to all sorts of problems, including the researcher making mistakes in deciding whether people fit into the appropriate categories (for example, thinking people are younger than they are).

# Experiments

An **experiment** is a form of research in which all the variables are closely controlled, so that the effect of changing one or more of the variables can be understood. Experiments are often used in the physical sciences, but are much less common in sociology. The reasons for their lack of use in sociology are, first, that it is almost impossible to isolate a social event from the real world around it. This means that researchers cannot control all the variables, which is the essence of an experiment.

Furthermore, experiments usually involve manipulating people in ways that many people regard as immoral.

> « *When natural scientists carry out their research in laboratories, controlling variables is of crucial importance … Experimentation usually involves manipulating one **independent variable** and creating change in the **dependent variable** … What is important is that all other factors are held constant (or controlled) and are not allowed to contribute to any change which might occur.* » (Moores 1998)

Finally, even if these two problems can be overcome, then what has been found to happen is the problem of the **experimenter effect**, where the awareness of being in an experiment affects the normal behaviour of the participants. Think of your own behaviour when you know you are being photographed, even if you are asked to 'look natural'!

Howell and Frost (1989) conducted a sociological experiment to see which of the three forms of authority identified by Weber (charismatic, traditional and legal-rational) were most effective in getting tasks done. They found 144 student volunteers and divided them into groups. Each group was given tasks to perform, led by actresses who used different authority methods to undertake the tasks. They concluded that charismatic leadership was the most effective form of authority.

One form of experimental method that has been used more often by sociologists is the **field experiment**. This type of experiment takes place in the real world and involves the social scientist manipulating a real situation and observing the outcomes. Garfinkel (1967) asked his students to behave in unconventional ways in order to uncover the assumptions that lie behind everyday behaviour. For example, when asked 'how are you?', they would enquire what was actually meant by the question and then answer in great detail. As you can imagine, people became quite annoyed by this, thus revealing that everyday social life is governed by many complex rules.

# Case studies

A **case study** is a detailed study of one particular group or organization. Instead of searching out a wide range of people via sampling, the researcher focuses on one group. The resulting studies are usually extremely detailed and provide a depth of information not normally available. However, there is always the problem that this intense scrutiny may miss wider issues by its very concentration. Case studies are used widely by both quantitative and qualitative researchers. McKee and Bell (1985), for example, studied a small community to explore the impact of high rates of unemployment on family relationships.

The main problem with case studies is that there is never any proof that the particular group chosen to be studied is typical of the population as a whole, therefore it may not be possible to generalize from the findings to other groups.

# Key terms

**Case study** a highly detailed study of one or two social situations or groups.

**Cross-sectional survey** a survey conducted at one time with no attempt to follow up the people surveyed over a longer time.

**Dependent variable** a social phenomenon that changes in response to changes in another phenomenon.

**Experiment** a highly controlled situation where the researchers try to isolate the influence of each variable. Rarely used in sociology.

**Experimenter effect** unreliability of data arising as a result of people responding to what they perceive to be the expectations of the researchers.

**Field experiment** an experiment undertaken in the community or in real life, rather than in a controlled environment.

**Hypothetico-deductive model** the research process associated with the physical sciences and used by positivists in sociology.

**Independent variable** the phenomenon that causes the dependent variable to change.

**Indicator** a measurable social phenomenon that stands for an unmeasurable concept, e.g using church attendance to measure religious belief.

**Inductive** way of reasoning that starts from the particular and works towards the general. In social research, this might mean identifying patterns and trends, and then developing hypotheses and theories based on them.

**Interpretive sociologists** those whose approach to sociology and research emphasizes understanding society by exploring the way people see society, rather than following traditional scientific analysis.

**Longitudinal survey** a survey that is carried out over a considerable number of years on the same group of people.

**Operationalize** to put into practice.

**Pilot survey** Small-scale trial carried out before the main study in order to identify potential problems and errors.

**Positivists** those sympathetic to the use of traditional scientific methods in sociology.

**Probability sampling** see Random sampling.

**Quantitative research** a positivist approach to research, favouring methods that produce statistical data.

**Quota sampling** where a representative sample of the population is chosen using known characteristics of the population.

**Random sampling** where a representative sample of the population is chosen by entirely random methods.

**Reliability** the need for research to be strictly comparable.

**Representative** a sample is representative if it is an accurate cross-section of the whole population being studied. This allows the researcher to generalize the results for the whole population.

**Sampling frame** a list used as the source for a random sample.

**Social fact** a term used by Durkheim to claim that certain objective 'facts' exist in society that are not influenced by individuals. Examples include the existence of marriage, divorce, work, etc.

**Stratified sampling** where the population under study is divided according to known criteria, such as sex and age, in order to make the sample more representative.

**Survey** a large-scale piece of quantitative research aiming to make general statements about a particular population.

**Systematic sampling** where every nth name (for example, every tenth name) on a list is chosen.

**Target population** The group the sociologist is studying and from whom the sample is drawn. It might be secondary school pupils in London, cannabis smokers, women at home etc.

**Validity** the need to show that what research sets out to measure really is that which it measures.

# Activities

## Research ideas

1 Using the positivist criteria, conduct a small study using what you have learnt to find out what changes students would like to see in your school/college.

2 Carry out a small piece of research into the notion of 'happiness' or another abstract quality.
- Separately, ask a small selection of students in your school or college to define what they mean by 'happy' or 'sexy' or 'attractive' (or any other abstract term you wish).
- Choose three different definitions and then conduct three parallel surveys, asking people on a scale of 1 to 5 how happy/sexy/attractive they think they are.
- Compare and reflect on the result. What problems might your research throw up for positivist research?

## Web.tasks

1 Go to **www.ipsos-mori.com** (the website of MORI, a polling organization). Look through a selection of survey results and and assess the methods of data collection used.

2 The UK government uses positivistic approaches to uncover information about the population. To find out how much information can be obtained, go to: **www.ons.gov.uk**
Click on the 'neighbourhood' heading on the top of the page. Fill in your postcode and explore. The site provides you with detailed information about your area.

# Check your understanding

1 **Explain briefly in your own words the seven stages of the hypothetico-deductive model.**

2 **What is the difference between 'deductive' and 'inductive' reasoning?**

3 **What model of society is positivism based upon?**

4 **Identify two types of random sampling – give one example of when each would be useful.**

5 **What is 'quota' sampling? What is the main advantage of this method?**

6 **Give one reason why sociologists tend not to use experiments.**

7 **What is a case study?**

# An eye on the exam Positivism and quantitative methods

## Raising the 'Meritocracy': Parenting and the Individualization of Social Class

**Val Gillies (2005)**

The aim of Gillies' study was to see how class structure can be part of the process of raising children. A large-scale survey of parents of children aged between eight and twelve was conducted in addition to detailed interviews with 25 mothers and 11 fathers.

The survey adopted a 'mixed methods' strategy: a large scale survey and small but intensive interviewing. The quantitative study aimed to identify social attitudes and socially accepted norms for behaviour. The qualitative study focused on what people actually do in order to reveal a more complex world where people negotiate their relationships.

A total of 1112 parents from different households were contacted. More than half the sample were female and working class with 10% from minority ethnic groups. Questions focused on the assistance that parents might turn to from both formal (financial, educational, behavioural and health organizations) and informal sources (family and friends) and were framed as multiple-choice questions. In addition, some mock case studies were presented to parents who were asked what they should do in these circumstances.

68% of the quantitative sample agreed that they would be willing to participate in the detailed qualitative phase of the study. Researchers eventually sampled 25 mothers and 11 fathers from 27 households across the UK.

The study found that parenting was gendered across all social classes. Mothers took responsibility for the daily care of children despite government initiatives to encourage father-friendly policies encouraging men to form closer relationships with their children.

Parents with high status jobs or access to friends and families with professional work used their contacts and knowledge to give their children advantages. Middle-class parents used a range of resources to support their children, focusing on social skills and education. This was in direct contrast to working-class parents who provided their children with strategies to cope with poverty, low social status and vulnerability to emotional and physical abuse and violence. The parents of working-class children focused on providing emotional strength and strategies to cope with injustice and hardship.

Adapted from Blundell, J. and Griffiths, J. (2008) Sociology since 2000, Lewes: Connect Publications

1 **Outline and explain why longitudinal studies may be used in sociological research.** **(15 marks)**

2 **Outline and assess the view that combining methods is the best strategy when studying social class differences in parenting.** **(25 marks)**

## Grade booster Getting top marks in question 2

In this question you need to start by explaining the idea of a mixed methods strategy and then go on to explain why it might be helpful in this particular research context. Finally, you need to discuss the disadvantages of this approach before reaching a balanced conclusion.

There are a variety of ways of using a mixed methods strategy, including triangulation (see Topic 2). In this research context you can expand on the points raised in the second paragraph: that the survey helped identify attitudes and norms and the interviews were used to identify and explore the actual behaviour of the mothers in relation to their children. The terms reliability, validity and representativeness are likely to appear but they will need to be applied to the study of social class and parenting. Disadvantages might focus on the possible lack of depth when resources are spread over several methods and on criticisms that might be raised by both positivists and interpretive sociologists.

# TOPIC 2

# Interpretive sociology and qualitative methods

## Getting you thinking

<<Last year I had a brief fling with a friend's boyfriend. I had met him two years previously when he asked me out but rejected him, partly because I was put off by the fact that he was older than me. I became friends with the woman shortly before they became a couple. After they had been together for several months, I spent time alone with him by chance and we got on very well. I became increasingly attracted to him but tried to ignore these feelings. We ended up kissing after several drinks and, although I felt guilty, when he suggested meeting next day I agreed. We met up several times over the following weeks, only sleeping together one night after being close many times. I thought I was in love with him and he with me, but this allowed me to disregard the guilt I felt about my friend. I realise now that I was being naive. Eventually, I realised he was not going to choose between us and any sort of pleasure I had got from the relationship was overshadowed by anxiety about the pain we could cause my friend, so I ended it. I have never told her. We live in different towns but are still in touch. I feel very guilty and don't know whether I should tell her or not. She is still with this man.>>

***What should we do?***

Source: *The Guardian*, 8 November 2007

<<I am a student and have been sharing a house for six months with four other people. We all get on well, but one issue is causing disharmony. It may sound trivial, but one of my housemates keeps piles of dirty plates and cutlery – ours as well as his own – in his room for weeks on end. At times, we have been left with only two clean plates between the five of us. We are reluctant to retrieve things from his room, which is squalid and smells terrible. My housemates have threatened to keep their kitchen stuff locked in their rooms, which he says is ridiculous. He makes us feel as if we are the unreasonable ones.>>

***What should we do?***

Source: 'Private Lives', *The Guardian*, 28 February 2008

**1 What are your views about these dilemmas?**

**2 Write down a couple of lines on what you think and then have a group discussion.**

**3 Do you all agree?**

It is likely that the group had quite different views on how best to resolve the dilemmas above. The clear facts have been presented to you and yet different people have interpreted them in different ways and come to different conclusions. Probably this is because you approach the 'facts of the case' from different moral or cultural viewpoints. This is not too dissimilar from sociology, for the theoretical approaches and views on the nature of society that different sociologists favour tend to influence the methods of sociological research they choose.

Essentially, there are two ways to start analysing society. One is to begin by looking at society and how it influences people. To take this starting point reflects the belief that there really is a society 'out there' that is influencing our behaviour and directs us into routine patterns of action.

A second way of starting an analysis is to begin by looking at the individual, and then working up to the social level. In starting here, the researcher sees individual perceptions and ideas as the building blocks of any larger social analysis.

It would be nice if the ideas of those who start at the bottom and work up and those who start at the top and work down met 'in the middle', but, sadly, this is not so. Indeed, the different starting points lead to quite different explanations of what society is like and how it operates.

In the last topic, we looked at the methods used by those who start at the top. These positivistic methods are all based (explicitly in the case of functionalism and Marxism, and implicitly in the case of most quantitative research) on the idea that a society exists in such a way that it can be counted and gauged. In this topic, we are going to look at the methodology of those who believe that analyses ought to start at the bottom – that is, with theories that stress how people perceive the world and interact with one another. These theories include interactionism (and labelling theory, which is a version of it) and there is also an overlap with postmodernism. These various approaches are typically referred to as interpretive approaches.

Recently, there has been a move to try to integrate the two levels of theory, most notably in the work of Giddens (1991), but as we said earlier, so far sociologists have found it very difficult to find methods to combine the levels.

# Theory and interpretive research

Bryman (2004) has argued that if there is one distinction to be made regarding the different aims of positivist and interpretive research, it is that while positivist research sets out to explain human behaviour through *analysing* the forces that act upon it, interpretive sociology sets out to understand varieties of human behaviour by being able to *empathize* with it.

## Weber and *verstehen*

The division between analysis and empathy can be traced back at least as far as Durkheim and Weber. As we have seen in earlier topics, Durkheim's attitude was that society could be treated as a 'thing' that existed beyond the individual and could be explored in a similar way to the physical sciences. For Weber, however, society was very different from an inanimate object. It consisted of thinking, purposeful people who acted as a result of a variety of influences, which could not be understood except by looking through the eyes of the individual actors. Weber used the term '***verstehen***' (similar to the English word 'empathy') to describe the sociological process that looking through the eyes of the individuals involved. In fact, Weber (1947) actually defined sociology as a 'science which attempts the interpretive understanding of social action in order to arrive at causal explanations'.

## Symbolic interactionism and labelling theory

As mentioned in earlier topics, symbolic interactionism derives from the writings of Mead, Cooley and Thomas, who were all at the University of Chicago in the 1950s. This theoretical approach informed and developed alongside labelling theory. In the 1960s, Blumer further developed these ideas and gave the name symbolic interactionism to the approach. According to Blumer (1962), societies do not have an existence independent of people's understanding of it. Social objects, events and situations are all interpreted by people in various socially learned ways and then people respond to them in terms of these learned **meanings**. Labelling theory, which is associated with Lemert (1967) and Becker (1963), shares this belief in the importance of symbols (which they call labels), but largely focuses on situations where one group or individual is able to impose its definition of the situation on others – usually with negative consequences for the people being labelled (see Chapter 2 Topic 4).

Symbolic interactionism and labelling theory tend to use qualitative methods, rejecting the positivist approaches.

## Structuration theory

More recently, Giddens has argued in his structuration theory (1984) that there is a form of structure that exists beyond the control of individuals and which does constrain human action. However, Giddens argues that these structures only exist in so far as people make them exist. So, families exist only as long as people choose to stay within the particular set of relationships that define a family. Research, according to Giddens, must therefore understand the motivations and actions of individuals, before it can see how structures can 'exist'.

A good example of the difference between objective facts and perception of facts is Foster's (1995) **ethnographic** study of a housing estate (consisting mainly of blocks of flats) in East London. Objectively, the estate had a high crime rate – at least according to official statistics. However, residents did not perceive the estate to be particularly threatening. Of particular significance was the existence of 'informal social control'. People expected a certain level of crime, but felt moderately secure because the levels were contained by informal controls and by a supportive network. Neighbours looked after each other and they believed that if any trouble should occur, they could rely upon each other for support. Furthermore, because of the degree of intimacy and social interaction on the estate, most people knew who the offenders were, and felt that this knowledge allowed them some degree of protection, because they could keep an eye on the troublemakers.

Official statistics portrayed this estate as having major problems – yet ethnographic research showed that the estate actually provided a secure environment in which most people were happy.

# Interpretive approaches and method

Interpretive researchers largely reject the use of quantitative methods (that is, statistical surveys and other positivist approaches) and prefer instead **qualitative research**. Qualitative research methods refer to any approach in sociology that sets out to uncover the meaning of social action rather than measure it through statistics. Interpretive researchers prefer qualitative methods for the following reasons.

### *Meaning*

As we have just noted, qualitative research allows sociologists to search for the meaning for participants of events, situations and actions in which they are involved. This reflects the belief of interpretive approaches that only by understanding how individuals build up their patterns of interaction can a full understanding of society be presented.

### *Context*

Interpretive research usually studies small-scale groups and specific situations. This allows the researcher to preserve the individuality of each of these in their analyses (in contrast with positivistic research which is based on large samples). Interpretive-based research provides the

## The differences between **qualitative** and **quantitative** methods

Bryman (2004) suggests that the differences between qualitative and quantitative methods include:

- *Numbers versus words* – Qualitative methods tend to describe social life in words, whilst quantitative research uses far more numbers to paint the sociological picture.
- *Point of view of researcher versus point of view of participants* – In quantitative research the researcher is the one who decides what questions to ask and how to classify the responses. However, in qualitative research, the researcher starts from the point of view of the participants – and writes up what they say, no matter how confusing or contradictory.
- *Researcher is distant versus researcher is close* – In quantitative research, the sociologist usually stays 'outside' and is uninvolved with the participants. The sociologist distributes, collects and analyses the questionnaires or interview results. In qualitative research, sociologists attempting to understand what is going on become heavily involved with the people being researched.
- *Theories tested versus theories emerge* – In quantitative research, sociologists usually have a hypothesis that they wish to test and this forms the basis for the research. In qualitative research, however, the theory may well emerge from the actual process of research. This is known as **'grounded theory'**.
- *Structured versus unstructured* – Quantitative research is usually very well structured as the information needs to be gained in a way that is reliable. Qualitative research, on the other hand, is usually far less structured and is more flexible and open. Incidentally, this does not mean that it is less well organized.
- *Hard reliable data versus rich, deep data* – Quantitative research almost always aims at being **generalizable** and thus is designed to be statistically correct. So, a survey should provide information about the population as a whole. Qualitative research places much greater emphasis on a detailed understanding of the particular group being studied.

researcher with an understanding of the events, actions and meanings as they are influenced by specific circumstances. It is only within the contexts that action makes sense.

### *Unanticipated phenomena and influences*

Positivistic research tends to fall into a format whereby researchers look for evidence to back up a hypothesis and then amend or reject it. In other words, positivistic researchers tend to anticipate certain outcomes – research does not start in a vacuum, but is based on a fairly clear idea of what should happen if variables react as expected. In qualitative research, the researcher does not necessarily have to have a clear idea of what they are looking for (see 'grounded theory', in the panel on the right) – researchers often start with an interest in a particular area and absolutely no idea of where it might lead. Without the 'blinkers' of the hypothetico-deductive model, researchers are much more open to the unexpected, and to fresh ideas.

### *Process*

Positivistic forms of research are generally interested in outcomes (what happens if), however qualitative research is more interested in the process (what is happening). This reflects a belief by positivists that they are looking for patterns that can be generalized across society – they are not interested necessarily in the details of the actual processes that lead to the outcome. Interpretive sociologists, on the other hand, will be interested in the actual dynamics of the situation – the process.

## Types of qualitative research methods

Qualitative research covers a wide range of methods, but the most common are: observational research (ethnography); focus groups; qualitative interviewing; and secondary sources. In this topic, we will concentrate on just observational research and focus groups, leaving the interviewing and secondary sources to be discussed in the next two topics.

**A note on ethnography:** We will be using the term *ethnography* quite often in this topic and it can be quite confusing. Ethnography is a general term commonly used by sociologists for participant observation or observation plus in-depth interviewing. So it is best to think of ethnography as a useful term for sociologists immersing themselves in the lives of the people under study, generally joining in as much social activity as possible, so that they can gain an in-depth understanding of the lives of a particular group.

## Ethnographic research

Any sociologist undertaking this form of research has quite a number of decisions to make about what is the best form of observational research for their purposes. The key decisions facing the researcher are:

- the extent of involvement with the group under study

- the amount of information that the sociologist gives the group about their research.

The following two examples illustrate the differences between the methods.

### *Extent of involvement with the group under study*

Sociologists can choose the extent of their participation in a group from one extreme of simply being an external observer with no contact with the group whatsoever – this is known as **non-participant observation**, through to the other extreme of complete immersion in the group – in fact, actually becoming a full group member – known as **participant observation**. Of course, in reality, observational research usually falls somewhere in between.

In deciding the extent of their involvement in the group, researchers have to decide what they wish to obtain from their research and weigh up the advantages and disadvantages of the role they adopt. Usually, qualitative researchers ask themselves three questions:

1. *What is possible?* – Is it actually possible to become a member of the group and be accepted? Differences in age, social-class background, gender, lifestyle and education can all have an impact on this.
2. *What is ethically correct?* – Is it acceptable to join a group that is possibly engaging in harmful activities. What harm will come to them by the sociologist's actions? There is also an ethical dimension to the decision. It is one thing to observe a group engaging in immoral or illegitimate activity; it is quite another actually to be involved.
3. *What method will produce the most valid results? Will becoming a full member of the group actually improve the quality of the research?* – The more the researcher becomes involved with the group, the greater their chances of really getting in-depth information. The sociologist is able to see the situation through the eyes of the group being studied and so will be able to empathize with the group.

On the other hand, by not getting too involved with the group being studied, the sociologist can avoid getting personal feelings mixed up with research perceptions and is much less likely to influence the group in any way (which would ruin the research).

### *Amount of information the sociologist gives*

Sociologists have the choice to be completely honest about the role they are playing – this is known as **overt observation** – or they can tell the participants nothing and pretend to be full members of the group – this is known as **covert observation**.

Once again, the sociologist will make the choice by balancing the three elements:

1. *What is possible?* – Is it actually possible to get away with being a member of the group? Will they find out and the cover be blown. For example, even if the sociologist is young looking and can get accepted by a youth group, how is it possible to hide their job and background?
2. *What is ethically correct?* – Is it acceptable to pretend to be a member of a group without letting them know what is really happening? The ethical guidelines that most sociologists follow insist that informed consent is always obtained. What harm will come to them by the sociologists actions?
3. *What method will produce the most valid results?* – If, by pretending to be a member of a group, the researcher is able to enter groups normally closed to researchers and is able to obtain information that results in greater sociological knowledge, then there is a strong argument for using this form of observation.

By balancing these three issues, in terms of the overt/covert and participant/non-participant decisions, the researcher can then decide exactly what form of observational research role to use.

Gold (1958) has suggested that the result of making these decisions can lead to the researcher taking one of four roles:

- *Complete participant* – A fully functioning member of the group, acting in a covert (hidden) role.
- *Participant as observer* – The researcher joins in as a participant, but is overt (open) about their role.
- *Observer as participant* – The researcher is mainly there to interview and observe.
- *Complete observer* – The researcher simply observes what is going on around them, making no attempt to interview or discuss.

## The process of participant observation

### *Making contact and gaining entry to the group*

Participant observational research by its very nature is interested in groups about whom it is difficult to gain information by survey methods. In the majority of cases, it involves studying groups who are marginal to society in some way, very often engaging in deviant behaviour. Most sociologists are not already members of such groups!

The first problem is to gain **access**, that is to make contact and then find some way to gain entry to the group. Most researchers use a contact or **gatekeeper** who opens the door for them. In Bourgois' (2003) study of East Harlem in the 1990s, it was a local part-time crack dealer, Primo, who befriended him. However, not all groups studied are deviant, and many researchers simply ask their colleagues if they can study them (see 'Convenience sampling'), or get a job, or perhaps join a society where they can observe people.

### *Acceptance by the group*

Gaining access and being introduced to a group does not necessarily mean that the group will accept the researcher as a member or observer. The next stage is to work out how one is going to be accepted. This has two elements: role and relationships:

1. *Role* refers to the decision to be covert or overt. Most sociologists take a fairly pragmatic view of what role to take, in the sense that they will adopt the role that gives them the greatest chance of getting the research material they want. The factors limiting that

will be relationship issues and ethical issues about how much harm the researcher may cause by acting covertly.

2 *Relationships* refer to the similarities and differences between the researcher and the group being studied. Age, ethnicity, gender, religion and social class are amongst the wide range of factors that influence the possibility of the researcher getting close to the people being studied and being able to empathize with them.

### *Recording the activities of the group*

Once settled into a group, one of the biggest problems faced by the researcher in participant observation is how to record information. This is particularly problematic for researchers engaged in covert observation. There are a number of answers to the problem of how to keep a **field diary**.

The first is simply to remember as much as possible and then to write this up as soon after the events as possible. This has the enormous advantage of allowing the researcher to pay full attention to what is going on at the time, rather than being distracted by writing notes. Indeed, in covert observation, this is probably the only possible method. But the big problem is that the researcher is bound to forget things, and of course, it may be the things that are forgotten that are the most important.

The second method is to make notes wherever possible as the action is unfolding. This leads to great accuracy, but is almost guaranteed to disrupt normal social interaction, as one person in a group making copious notes of what is going on rather stands out! In Ditton's (1977) study of workplace 'fiddles', he used to go to the toilets to write up his research, using the toilet paper for his notes!

### *Getting at the truth: influencing the group / being influenced by the group*

In observational research, it is hard to remain objective. Close contact with the group under study means that the sociologist's feelings almost always slip into their field diaries and research notes at some time. The closer to the group the researcher gets, the more likely it is that bias of some sort will creep in. For example, Bourgois became close friends with some of the crack dealers in his study: 'I interviewed and in many cases befriended, the spouses, lovers, siblings, mothers, grandmothers … of the crack dealers featured in these pages.'

Not only can the activities of the group influence the researcher, positively or negatively, but the researcher can also influence the group. If the group is small and perhaps less educated than the sociologist, then the researcher's ideas might influence the group – thereby ruining the research. In his classic study of youths in Liverpool, Howard Parker actually gave them legal advice when they were caught by the police for stealing from cars (Parker *et al.* 1998).

### *Leaving the group*

Everyone engaging in participant observation or ethnographic research must, at some time, leave the group. There are two issues here. The first is, when to leave. Glaser and Strauss (1967) argue that the correct time to get

## Spotlight on …

### Participant observation

Ethnographers usually live in the communities they study and they establish long-term, close relationships with the people they write about. In other words, in order to collect 'accurate data', ethnographers become intimately involved with the people we study …

I spent hundreds of nights on the street and in crackhouses observing dealers and addicts. I regularly tape-recorded their conversations and life histories. Perhaps more important, I also visited their families, attended parties and intimate reunions. I interviewed and in many cases befriended, the spouses, lovers, siblings, mothers, grandmothers of the crack dealers featured in these pages.

Adapted from Bourgois, P. (2003) *In Search of Respect* (2nd edn), Cambridge: Cambridge University Press

### Non-participant observation

Stephen Moore studied the attitudes of a local community to street drinkers who spent most of their time gathering in the high street of an inner-city area. Members of the community became increasingly punitive in their views and formed action groups to force the local authority and the police to harass the street drinkers. The police and local authority, however, took a much more liberal stance and argued that if the street drinkers were not committing a crime they had the same rights as anyone else to gather.

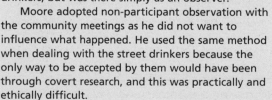

Moore attended all the meetings called by the action groups and the city council, noting the events as they happened, but did not speak or make his presence too obvious. After the meetings, he talked to various speakers about their attitudes, but only to gain permission to quote what they had said. Similarly, he spent some time with professionals who worked with the street drinkers, but was there simply as an observer.

Moore adopted non-participant observation with the community meetings as he did not want to influence what happened. He used the same method when dealing with the street drinkers because the only way to be accepted by them would have been through covert research, and this was practically and ethically difficult.

Moore, S. (2008) 'Street life, neighbourhood policing and the community', in P. Squires *ASBO Nation*, Bristol: Policy Press

**Identify differences in the roles taken by the observer in the two pieces of research described above.**

## **Participant observation** Advantages and disadvantages

### Advantages

- *Experience* – Participant observation allows the researcher to fully join the group and see things through the eyes (and actions) of the people in the group.
- *Generating new ideas* – Often this can lead to completely new insights and generate new theoretical ideas. Also good for validity.
- *Getting the truth* – One of the problems with questionnaires, and to a lesser extent with interviews, is that the respondent can lie. Participant observation prevents this because the researcher can see the person's actual behaviour. This leads to high levels of validity.
- *Digging deep* – Participant observation can create a close bond between the researcher and the group under study, and individuals in the group may be prepared to confide in the researcher. Excellent for validity.
- *Dynamic* – Participant observation takes place over a period of time and allows an understanding of how changes in attitudes and behaviour take place. Again can raise level of validity.
- *Reaching into difficult areas* – Participant observation is normally used to obtain research information on hard-to-reach groups, such as drug users and young offenders.
- Scores very high for validity.

### Disadvantages

- *Bias* – The main problem lies with bias, as the (participant) observer can be drawn into the group and start to see things through their eyes. Loses objectivity and therefore validity.
- *Influence of the researcher* – The presence of the researcher may make the group act less naturally as they are aware of being studied, unless the researcher is operating covertly.
- *Ethics* – How far should researchers allow themselves to be drawn into the activities of the group – particularly if these activities are immoral or illegal?
- *Proof* – There is no way of knowing whether the findings of participant observation are actually true or not, since there is no possibility of replicating the research. In other words the results may lack reliability.
- *Too specific* – Participant observation is usually used to study small groups of people who are not typical of the wider population. It is therefore difficult to claim that the findings can be generalized across the population as a whole.
- *Studying the powerless* – Most (participant) observational studies are concerned with the least powerful groups in society. What about the powerful and their activities?
- Scores very low for reliability and generalizability.



out of an ethnographic study is when new information does no more than confirm what the sociologist has already found out. They use the term 'theoretical saturation' to describe this situation.

The second issue is actually how to leave. This can be a very difficult thing. If the researcher likes the group and gets on well with the group being studied, then it might be very emotional to leave and may upset both group members and the researcher. On the other hand, if the researcher is engaged in deviant behaviour, it may actually be very dangerous to leave and so a strategy must be developed. In one classic study of a violent Glasgow youth gang, 'James Patrick' the researcher used a false name to infiltrate the gang, knowing that if they found him after he left, they would get their revenge. Indeed, to this day his real name is not widely known.

Of course, some people never quite leave. Philippe Bourgois (2003) admits to going back regularly to East Harlem in New York and has kept in touch with his principal gatekeeper, Primo. Interestingly, Primo was heavily influenced by Bourgois and turned from a crack user and part-time dealer into a small-time businessman who gave up alcohol and drugs.

## Causing harm: The ethical dimension of ethnographic studies

Of all forms of research, apart from experiments, participant observation possibly carries the most difficult ethical dilemmas. At virtually any stage in the proceedings, participant observation (particularly covert) can lead to harm to the researcher, to the participants, or to the public.

Even if no harm comes to others, there is still the controversial issue that covert participant observation takes place without the consent of the people being studied. This contradicts one of the bases of all modern research, that those being studied give their informed consent. Holdaway (1983), for example, was a police officer studying his colleagues without their knowledge. He knew that he was leaving the police force to work at a university once his research was completed. When the research, which was critical of his colleagues, was published, some were angry as they felt that he had taken advantage of them.

Sociologists therefore have to be very careful about what they do, and this can lead to many moral dilemmas. This is the last part of the introduction to Bourgois' (2003) study of East Harlem (New York) where he studied crack dealers and users.

<< *Finally, I want to thank my family. I will always be grateful to Charo Chacon-Mendez for coming with me to El Barrio, where we married at the very beginning of the research project. Her help was invaluable. I apologize for imposing so much anxiety on her when I regularly stayed out all night on the street and in crackhouses for so many years. I hope that it is not one of the reasons why we are no longer together. If it is, I regret it profoundly.* >>

## Focus groups

A second very common form of qualitative research method is the focus group. A focus group consists of a relatively small number of people, usually less than 12, who are requested to discuss a specific topic. Focus groups ideally are representative of a particular **population** and are obtained through the most appropriate sampling techniques. (These can include both traditional qualitative or quantitative sampling methods.)

Focus groups give researchers an opportunity to hear an issue being discussed, with people being able to discuss and challenge each other's views. Compared with the rather static interview method, focus groups are much more dynamic, with people demonstrating the thought process involved in how they came to their views. In the actual discussions, issues emerge that researchers may never have thought of and so these groups are often innovative. Finally, the focus group members have the power to concentrate more on issues they consider important than on the researcher's priorities. See the panel above for a summary of advantages and limitations of focus groups and Topic 3 for a feminist perspective on focus groups.

### Focus groups Advantages and limitations

**Advantages**

- Allows researchers to understand *why* people hold certain opinions.
- People can modify and change views, so demonstrating how strongly held their views are.
- Because it is a discussion, the focus group will prioritize issues it thinks are more important. This may be different from the researcher's ideas.
- Focus groups are dynamic, with people probing each other's views and defending their own views.
- Focus groups study group views and interactions.

**Limitations**

- Researchers have limited control over what happens. The group discussion can veer off into irrelevant (for the researcher) areas.
- Membership of focus groups needs to be carefully run to ensure real discussion, and 'louder' people who dominate discussion need to be controlled.
- Focus groups generate a huge amount of material which is not clearly structured, this means that analysing the material is very difficult.

## Sampling in qualitative research

There are three main types of sampling associated with qualitative research: convenience, snowball and purposeful.

### Convenience sampling

This refers to any group used for research that is easily available to the researcher. Convenience sampling is very commonly used in ethnography because problems of entry and acceptance by the group being studied are kept to a minimum. Typically, convenience sampling is used for research into occupational groups such as nurses, teachers and students.

Though this is widely used, it can have serious drawbacks. Engaging in covert research can make a person feel like a spy. As seen earlier, where colleagues know and accept the researcher, any results that are critical of them may lead to problems between the researcher and colleagues after the research is over.

### Snowball sampling

This is used in all forms of qualitative research, but is most common in studying deviant groups. This method involves finding one person initially who agrees to act as gatekeeper and through them building up an ever bigger network of contacts. The main problem with this form of sampling is that the sample tends to be restricted to one group who have contacts. This may result in a very partial picture of social interaction.

> << *A snowball sample of men and women was built up by making contacts through various institutions such as luncheon clubs, local history groups and other social networks. Many were recommended to us by someone who had already participated, and we were able to interview some members of the same family.* >> (Hood and Joyce 1999)

### Purposeful sampling

Sometimes a researcher will decide that information from certain individuals would be very useful to the research and will therefore select these individuals as research participants. In these cases, moving the research forward is seen as more important than a representative sample.

For example, a sociologist studying gender inequality in a large call centre might want to talk to individuals who had applied for promotion, union representatives and anyone who had worked there for more than two years.

# Criticisms of research methods used in interpretive sociology

Positivist sociologists have not been shy in criticizing the methods used by qualitative researchers in the following ways.

## Values

Positivists argue that although a value-free sociology may not be possible, there are reasonable limits to observe. Qualitative research is shot through with issues related to value bias, and it is almost impossible to untangle the personal biases of the researcher from the research 'insights' generated. The approach taken by feminists such as Mies, which commits itself to a particular value approach, is seen as going beyond the acceptable limit. However, the very opposite can occur too. In Lee-Treweek's (2000) study of carers in homes for the elderly, she found that she increasingly disliked the 'carers' she was studying. Their attitudes to the old people so angered her that it was difficult to continue her study in the value-neutral way she wanted.

## Transferability/generalizability

Qualitative research is often small scale and specific to a particular group. Positivists claim that it is difficult to transfer the results of research in one specific situation to others – that is, there are problems with results being **transferable**.

Generalizability follows from transferability. To what extent can general statements be made from highly localized and specific studies that aim to uncover the meaning of the interaction of a group in a specific situation?

Interpretive approaches to sociology have generated a range of sophisticated methods that can justifiably claim to provide extremely useful insights into the nature of social action. Interpretive approaches seek, above all else, to understand how people perceive the world about them and how this influences their actions – and the consequences of these actions for both themselves and others. The nature of the questions asked by these approaches therefore leads interpretive sociologists to use qualitative methods, rather than qualitative ones. Whether qualitative approaches are 'better' or 'worse' than qualitative approaches is like asking whether in theory, structural approaches are 'better' or 'worse' than interpretive approaches. There is no simple answer, except to say that each approach asks different questions that need to be studied in different ways.

## Lack of transparency

According to Bryman and Burgess (1994), in the qualitative methods associated with interpretive sociology, it is often unclear how conclusions are reached, resting heavily upon the intuition and understanding of the researcher. The reader of the research has to take it on trust that the perception of the situation as described by the interpretive researcher is accurate.

Sometimes a researcher will discuss their findings with research participants, either during the data collection or at the end of the research. This process is known as **respondent validation**. It allows findings to be checked against the understandings of the research participants.

Respondent validation creates two main problems.

1. What will actually be shown to the participants? They cannot be expected to read thousands of words and may not understand sociological language.
2. Participants may disagree with the researcher's point of view and the process of respondent validation may end up in conflict.

Despite these problems, Lincoln and Guba (1985) point out that respondent validation has the advantages of adding to the credibility of a study and reassuring the researcher that their understandings match the perceptions and experiences of participants.

# Triangulation (multistrategy research)

In order to be clear about the different research strategies used by sociologists, we have made very clear distinctions between quantitative and qualitative research. In real life research, however, things are rather more complicated. While one group of sociologists is largely in favour of using quantitative methods wherever possible, and other sociologists are largely in favour of using qualitative methods, both groups will dip into the 'other side's' methods if they think it will be useful.

So, quantitative researchers may well back up their work by including some observation or some in-depth, unstructured interviewing, whilst qualitative researchers may well engage in some structured interviewing or draw upon secondary sources in order to strengthen their research. This use of multiple methods is generally known as **triangulation** (though, strictly speaking it is really multistrategy research).

The term 'triangulation' originally referred to the use of different methods so that the data gathered from each could be checked. However, over time the term has come to mean the use of multiple methods in a particular piece of research, with the aim of improving its validity, reliability and generalizability.

## Check your understanding

1. What two ways are there for starting an analysis of society? What terms do sociologists use for these approaches?
2. Explain the meaning of *verstehen* in your own words. Why is it different from Durkheim's approach to sociology?
3. Identify and explain three reasons why interpretive sociologists prefer the use of qualitative methods in research.
4. What advantages does observational research have over quantitative methods?
5. Suggest two examples of research where it would be possible to justify covert observation.
6. Identify two advantages and two disadvantages of focus groups in research.
7. Why do interpretivist-based approaches have a difficulty with generalizability, according to positivist critics?
8. What are the advantages of triangulation?

## Activities

### Research idea

Design a research strategy using positivist ideas to discover why some young people are attracted to 'clubbing'. Now, design an alternative piece of research using interpretive ideas. How is the research different? How could each piece of research be criticized?

### Web.task

Increasingly, sociologists are conducting ethnographic research on the internet. Go to the chat room, The Student Room at **www.thestudentroom.co.uk/** and explore the informal rules of conduct that govern the interaction.

## Key terms

**Access** gaining entry to a group or research situation

**Covert observation** where the sociologist does not admit to being a researcher.

**Ethnography** term used to describe the work of anthropologists who study simple, small-scale societies by living with the people and observing their daily lives. The term has been used by sociologists to describe modern-day observational studies.

**Field diary** a detailed record of events, conversations and thoughts kept by participant observers, written up as often as possible.

**Gatekeeper** individual who can give the researcher access to a group or social situation.

**Generalizability** the ability to apply the findings of research into one group accurately to other groups.

**Grounded theory** an approach to theory construction in which theory is generated during research.

**Meaning** the word used by Blumer to describe the sense people make of a particular situation.

**Non-participant observation** where the sociologist simply observes the group but does not seek to join in their activities.

**Overt observation** where the sociologist is open about the research role.

**Participant observation** where the sociologist joins a group of people and studies their behaviour.

**Population** the entire group the sociologist is focusing on.

**Qualitative research** a general term for approaches to research that are less interested in collecting statistical data, and more interested in observing and interpreting the ways in which people behave.

**Respondent validation** Checking the findings of research by sharing them with research participants.

**Transferability** the ability to transfer the results of research in one specific situation to others.

**Triangulation (multistrategy research)** a term often used to describe the use of multiple methods (qualitative and quantitative) in research.

**Verstehen** term first used by Weber in sociology to suggest that the role of sociology is to understand partly by seeing through the eyes of those who are being studied. Similar to 'empathy' in English.

## An eye on the exam — Interpretive sociology and qualitative methods

# 'We Can't All Be White': Racist Victimization in the UK

**Kusminder Chahal and Louis Julienne (1999)**

There is very little qualitative information on the consequences of racist victimization for the everyday lives of minority ethnic individuals and their families. This study attempted to address that gap by listening to the voices and experiences of the victims of racist victimization.

The study involved 74 victims of racist victimization from four cities – Belfast, Cardiff, Glasgow and London. The researchers made contact with as many voluntary, community and government agencies as they could, meeting police, local authority housing department staff, Racial Equality Council members and so on. These agencies helped them identify potential respondents.

Two main methods of data collection were used: focus groups and in-depth interviews. There were eight focus groups, involving a total of 32 people. The discussions covered experiences of racist victimization among people who had not necessarily reported incidents and not all of whom identified themselves as victims. The purpose was to find out how people made sense of racist experiences, how they understood them to be racist, and the consequences of these experiences. The sessions were recorded and transcribed.

The 34 in-depth interviews involved 42 respondents who had been victims of incidents in or near their homes that they had reported. Sometimes partners were present at the interviews. The researchers experienced difficulty in getting some potential respondents to agree to be interviewed, and in getting agencies to put forward names of potential respondents.

In order to analyse the interviews, themes in the data were identified and coded. This provided a framework in which the data could be analysed.

The study found that the fear and experience of victimization had considerable effects on people's lives. Most had not been physically attacked, but experience of victimization had changed their lives for the worse. Many suffered stress, depression and sleeplessness, and some women had miscarriages which they attributed to the harassment. A few had actually given up their homes. Victims used all the resources at their disposal to attempt to continue to lead a normal life such as contacting agencies for help such as the police and housing departments. But it was often felt that their complaints were not taken seriously. Agencies failed to see how harassment appeared to the victims and could not appreciate the pain of everyday racism.

Adapted from Blundell, J. and Griffiths, J. (2003) Sociology since 1995 Volume 2, Lewes: Connect Publications

1 **Outline and explain why focus groups may be used in sociological research.** **(15 marks)**

2 **Outline and assess the view that sociologists should use interpretive approaches to study racist victimization.** **(25 marks)**

## Grade booster — Getting top marks in question 2

In this question you need to start by explaining interpretive approaches and then go on to explain why they might be helpful in this particular research context. Finally, you need to discuss the disadvantages of these approaches before reaching a balanced conclusion.

Try to use sociological concepts (e.g. verstehen) and theories (interactionism) when explaining the idea of interpretive approaches and make sure they are linked to the use of ethnographic methods. Use the aims of the research to justify the choice of methods – read the first paragraph carefully. The sensitivity of the issue of racist victimization and the difficulty of obtaining valid data are also likely to feature among the reasons for using interpretive methods. Disadvantages may include problems of reliability, representativeness and generalizability associated with interpretive approaches, meaning that the impact of the research on this important issue may be seen as less credible and the social policy implications less clear.

# TOPIC 3

# Postmodern, feminist and realist methodologies

## Getting you thinking

1. **Compare the photos of people and buildings in London in 1950 and today. What differences can you see?**
2. **What other major social changes affecting contemporary life can you identify?**
3. **Suggest some explanations for these changes?**
4. **Briefly think about the major theories of Marxism and functionalism – do you think they are relevant for an understanding of recent social changes?**

« Mass production, the mass consumer, the big city, big-brother state, the sprawling housing estate, and the nation-state are in decline: flexibility, diversity, differentiation, mobility, communication, decentralization and internationalization are in the ascendant. In the process our own identities, our sense of self, our own subjectivities are being transformed. We are in transition to a new era. »

Source: cited in Callinicos, A. (1989) *Against post-modernism: a Marxist critique*, Cambridge: Polity Press

One of the most exciting developments in sociology over the past 20 years has been the emergence of postmodernism. In many ways this is rather strange, as apparently one of the key messages of postmodernism is that it rejects the very project of understanding society – the aim of sociology itself!

However, some sociologists have enthusiastically taken on board some of its messages and have incorporated them into what they see as a consequently revitalized and radical sociology.

In this topic, we look at the impact of postmodernism on research methods and explore how, by influencing methods, postmodernism has also led sociology into studying new areas previously considered outside its domain.

## Postmodernism and the rejection of positivism

Postmodernists, such as Bauman (1990), Lyotard (1984) and Baudrillard (1998), argue that the coherent 'picture' of the social and physical worlds drawn by modernists, is no more 'true' or 'real' than the picture previously painted by the religions that dominated thought processes before **modernity**. Postmodernists see a fragmented, discontinuous world in which the desire for order has led people to impose a framework which ignores those things that do not fit neatly into the classifications and theories that have been constructed.

This idea of artificial structures imposed on a fragmented world has also been applied to sociology itself. Postmodernists argue that the nature of sociological theorizing is rooted in this false idea of structure and order. Not only this, but the methods used by sociologists are also a reflection of the mistaken belief in an organized, structured social world out there.

The postmodern critique of sociological methods has three strands: **relativity,** knowledge as control, and **narrative** and **discourse**.

### Relativity

As you know, the assumption underlying positivism is that there is an objective world 'out there' waiting to be uncovered by research. Postmodernists dispute this. They see, instead, many different, competing 'worlds' that exist only in particular contexts and at particular times. There is, quite simply, no objective reality waiting to be discovered. The objective, scientific analysis based upon a scrupulous following of the rules does not produce knowledge about the world – it simply produces another relative version of society . According to Sarap (1993), Lyotard argues that knowledge is only deemed to be true if it is accepted by those who are regarded as the appropriate people to decide upon its worth.

### Knowledge as control

Scientists and other professionals and academics are not objective intellectuals engaged in a struggle to find the truth. According to Foucault (1963/1975), they, like any other group in society, are engaged in a struggle to have their concept of knowledge (as opposed to other, competing ones) accepted as reality. The reason for engaging in this struggle is that whoever has control over what is regarded as knowledge, and how to obtain it, gains considerable power in society. Scientists and professionals are therefore not disinterested and objective, but key players in a power struggle. A particularly good example of this can be found in medical knowledge. Despite the fact that about 20% of people in hospital actually contract another illness or are medically harmed in some way by the very 'healing process', doctors have gained control over the task of healing and of defining what is or is not a healthy body. Other ways of dealing with health have been labelled as 'complementary medicine' or 'alternative therapies', and denied equal status on the grounds that they are not scientifically rigorous.

### Narrative and discourse

We have seen that, according to postmodernists, sociologists are yet another group seeking to impose their form of knowledge on society, which they do by claiming expert knowledge based on sociology as a form of science.

The outcome of sociological research is the production of explanations or theories that explain social phenomena. Postmodernists call these explanations 'narratives'. The implication is that they are no more than stories, giving a partial account.

Where sociologists have provided large-scale 'grand-theories', which claim to provide a full and complete explanation for human behaviour (e.g. functionalism), the term used by postmodernists is 'meta-narrative'. The reason for the dismissal of these theories is simply that there is no world out there waiting to be explained. All explanation is partial and grounded in the context of people's lives and experiences.

Linked to narrative is the concept of discourse. Discourse can be seen as the framework of language within which discussions about issues occur. Discourse therefore limits and locates discussion.

## Postmodernist research

Postmodernism has also been a positive force in three main ways relevant to research:

1. It has introduced new methods and approaches to research.
2. It has introduced different topics to study.
3. It has encouraged people to speak for themselves, thereby allowing their narratives to stand without necessarily interpreting them.

### Deconstruction: a new method

Postmodernism argues that all knowledge is relative and that some knowledge is more powerful than others. Postmodernist writers such as Baudrillard (1998) argue that these 'narratives' about what we consider to be knowledge crucially affect how we act. However, they do not influence us in the way that Marxists or functionalists would argue, rather they interact with people to create new and fragmentary patterns of thought and behaviour that alter according to place, time and an unknowable range of other factors. The task of postmodernists is to try to uncover the linkages and possible patterns that underlie these narratives.

Foucault suggests this process of **deconstruction** is like the activities of an archaeologist, in that the sociologist carefully digs down layer after layer to explore the construction of narratives. The postmodern researcher is, however, not concerned to give the 'truth' but to look instead at how particular narratives emerge at different times and in different contexts. Furthermore, they are not seeking to make claims for anything beyond the particular area studied.

One particular area to which deconstruction is applied is the subject of sociology itself, so traditional concepts are taken apart and looked at in new ways.

### Transgression: new areas of study

The second innovation that postmodernism brought to research was that of topic areas. Traditionally, sociologists have divided the subject matter of society into various categories and classifications – so we study religion, work, social divisions, crime, and so on. If there is no world out there, and if sociology is just one narrative amongst many others (with no claim of superiority), then we also need to look critically at the sociological enterprise itself. Why do we have these divisions? They don't actually exist and we don't divide ourselves into separate chapters as we live our lives!

Postmodernists suggest that we should **transgress** classification boundaries and think in new ways. Take criminology, for example. Traditionally this studies people who commit crime. But the category 'crime' covers a massive range of actions, which sociologically have little in common. Crimes are just what some people have managed to have declared illegal, no more, no less. A different way of looking at the area is to study why people do harm to others – irrespective of what form that takes. Immediately, torture by the state, low wages, child labour and a million other forms of harmful activity enter the area of study – thus transgressing traditional boundaries.

Furthermore, if all areas of knowledge are equally relative, then how do we know what is more important or relevant than anything else? This has liberated sociologists to study issues such as the body, sexuality, eating and time – all areas which traditionally have been seen as marginal to sociology.

# Feminism and methods

Feminist theory and methods are linked to the postmodern movement in this topic, mainly because they have contributed importantly to the current fragmentation of sociology. Feminism and postmodernism have provided the most powerful intellectual critiques of traditional sociology and opened up massive new areas for study, as well as new methods to use.

Traditional theoretical and methodological approaches (Marxism, functionalism and even interpretive approaches) assumed that sexual identities, including the role of women, were of no sociological interest. This resulted in females and the female perspective simply being ignored. However, by the 1960s and increasingly in the 1970s, some writers, such as Firestone (1970) and Millett (1970), suggested that knowledge (and methods) are linked to gender. Men and women have different experiences and different starting points from which they construct their knowledge. So, all knowledge is related to gender. Incidentally, this argument has also been extended to different forms of knowledge based on 'ethnicity', religion, disability and sexual identity. Studies of society are then actually studies of male society.

This resulted in a rapid growth of feminist theory, which sought to understand gender relations. We discuss feminist theory in Chapter 6, but for now the important point is that this emergence of feminist theory was paralleled with the development of different feminist methods of research.

Harding (1987) has suggested that there are three key elements of this feminist methodology, as follows.

### *1 Women's experiences: a new resource*

Harding argues that most research has been devised and conducted by male sociologists and that this has resulted in a concentration on issues of interest to males. Women have different interests and perspectives, which open up new areas for sociological investigation. For example she asks 'Why do men find childcare and housework so distasteful?'

### *2 New purposes of social science: for women*

Harding suggests the purpose of feminist sociological research ought to be to improve the position of women. Traditional social science has been concerned to 'pacify, control and exploit' women, but feminist research is committed and open about its own commitment – unlike the value-free model that has been used as a cover to control women. This commitment is known as a 'feminist **standpoint**'.

### *3 Locating the researcher in the same critical plane as the subjects*

This third element of feminist research aims to bridge the gap between female researchers and female subjects of research. Harding argues that the feminist researcher must examine all her 'assumptions, beliefs and behaviours' and make these clear to both the subjects of research and to the people who read the research. Not only this, but the 'class, race and gender' of the researcher must also be clearly stated. In doing so, the feminist researcher does not appear 'as an invisible, anonymous voice of authority, but as a real, historical individual with concrete, specific desires and interests'. Maynard has added that feminist research should include the perspective of the women being studied, so that research is seen as a joint activity, rather than one in which the sociologist is an expert who studies powerless subjects (Maynard and Purvis 1994).

These ideas have led to in-depth interviewing/discussion and participant observation being particularly favoured in feminist research.

Harding also addresses two other key points which concern feminists – the relative truth of male and female sociologists' accounts of the world, and the question of whether men can ever undertake feminist research. The first question revolves around the problem faced by feminist sociologists that they can sometimes arrive at completely different accounts of society from those of male sociologists. So, who is right? Both? Or only one? Or neither? Harding's reply is quite simple – women are more able to understand society than men and therefore their accounts are to be preferred. The second question concerning men conducting feminist research is one where Harding gives a possibly surprising answer. She believes men can do feminist research – particularly because there are areas, to do with male sexuality and male friendships, where they have greater potential for insight compared with females. However, they would have to follow the three key elements of feminist research mentioned above.

## Focus groups

Feminist sociologists routinely use focus groups for their research. Wilkinson (1999) argues that this method fits the ethos of feminism in three ways. First, focus group research is less artificial than other methods because it emphasizes group interaction which is a normal part of social life. As women are able to discuss issues in the company of other women, they are more likely to divulge their true 'lived experiences' than in more artificial interviewing situations. Second, feminist research is concerned to minimize differences in power and status that can occur in research situations, where the more powerful sociological researcher may dominate the interaction. Focus groups tend to even out the power, by giving a group of women the chance to take control over the discussion. Finally, Madriz (2000) has further suggested that where focus groups consist of 'marginalized' women such as 'lower-socioeconomic-class women of colour' then the focus group gives them the sense of solidarity to make sense of their 'experience of vulnerability and subjugation'.

## Feminist ethnography

Reinharz (1992) suggests that the most effective way to study women is to use ethnographic methods. She argues that these allow the full documentation of women's lives, especially those aspects that are regarded by males as unimportant (such as domestic tasks). Further, she suggests that ethnography allows researchers to see activities from the viewpoint of women, rather than from the traditional male sociological angle. Finally, Reinharz argues that feminist ethnographic research is less exploitative of the women being studied than traditional male ethnography. For example, Skeggs (2001) points out that in her ethnographic research (see 'Focus on research' below), she was seeking to 'emphasize the words, voices and lives of the women', which fits well with the argument of feminist researchers for a feminist standpoint.

## Qualitative interviewing

Feminist sociologists have adopted the in-depth interview as their most used tool of research, according to Bryman (2004). Oakley (1981) argues that traditional structured interviewing is exploitative, offering the interviewee nothing in exchange for their information and reflects a power imbalance between researcher and interviewee, with the researcher deciding what is worth talking about. Therefore feminist unstructured/in-depth interviewing emphasizes that the two women involved are engaged in a discussion based on equality, in which the interviewee is equal in power with the interviewer and has equal right to decide on the direction of the discussion. In her own research interviews on the transition into motherhood, Oakley was asked questions on a range of issues by the respondents and felt that by replying and even advising the women, she was fulfilling the criteria of feminist research methods.

However, feminist writers have had some problems, in that their interpretation of women's responses to their questions do not necessarily square with the respondents'. For example, Millen (1997) interviewed 32 British female scientists about their work. However, her approach, based on feminist ideas, was largely rejected by the respondents. Millen comments:

> *«From my external, academically privileged position vantage point, it is clear that sexism pervades these professions. However, the women did not generally see their careers and interactions with male scientists in terms of gendered social relations. There is therefore a tension between their characterization of their experience and my interpretation of it.»*

## Evaluation of feminist methods

This strong approach to the uniqueness and superiority of feminist research has not gone unchallenged.
Mary Maynard, herself a feminist sociologist, disagrees with Harding's arguments. She suggests that the strong position taken by Harding belongs to an early era of feminism when there was a need to stake out its territory and stamp its mark upon sociology (Maynard and Purvis 1994). She also argues that no matter what central themes there are to feminist research, in the end if it is not rigorous and compelling in its accuracy, then it cannot claim to be sociological research.

She argues that the continuing stress on listening to women's experiences, particularly through in-depth interviews, has become political correctness and other forms of research are being prevented. Oakley (1998), although strongly associated with the use of qualitative interviewing methods, argues that the use of qualitative research methods in feminist studies reflected a desire by feminists to distance their work from the traditional scientific/positivist approaches much favoured by the male sociology 'establishment'. According to Oakley, it is important for feminist researchers to use quantitative as well as qualitative methods in their research. This will allow them access to the prestige, funding and influence on government policy currently enjoyed by those following more positivistic methods. Interestingly, Oakley was one of the first feminist writers to argue for the use of in-depth, qualitative interviews, but clearly she feels that the wheel has turned too far and the total rejection of quantitative methods is harming feminist research.

# Realism

Another angle on the relationship between qualitative and quantitative methods is provided by realism. To understand this approach we need to look at the methodology of the physical sciences.

Sayer (1992) has pointed out that the model of the physical sciences presented to the public may be misleading. He argues that we need to distinguish between open and closed systems. Sciences such as chemistry or physiology operate in **closed systems**, in which all variables can be controlled. This allows experiments to be carried out.

However, other physical sciences such as meteorology and seismology, operate in **open systems**, in which the variables cannot be controlled. These sciences recognize unpredictability. Seismology cannot predict when earthquakes will occur, though it does understand the conditions leading to earthquakes. Meteorologists can explain the forces producing weather, but the actual weather itself is difficult to predict. Certain sciences, therefore, do not necessarily follow the process which it is claimed is a hallmark of science.

From Sayer's viewpoint the social sciences are no different from the physical sciences operating within unpredictable open systems where variables cannot be controlled. So, just as seismology investigates the relationship between the conditions that cause earthquakes to the actual earthquakes themselves, the aim of sociology should be to uncover the relationship between wider social structures and the way we relate to other people in everyday life. For example, we can only understand the relationship between a student and teacher by referring to the education system, inequalities of power, the aims of education, and so on.

In terms of methods, realism suggests that there is a need for both qualitative research, which can explore people's meanings and motives, and quantitative research which can reveal the patterns and trends in the structure of society that provide the context for those meanings and motives. For example, using semi-structured interviews may be an effective method of investigating changing attitudes to gender, but these attitudes can only be understood within the context of the changing structure of the labour market and the family – aspects of social structure which may be best examined using quantitative methods and official statistics.

# Focus on research

## Bev Skeggs (1997)

### Formations of class and gender

Beverley Skeggs studied 83 White, working-class young women over a period of 12 years using ethnographic measures, involving participant observation and in-depth interviews. The research began with the women enrolling on a health and social care course at a college in the North-West of England and Skeggs followed them through the rest of their education, their employment and their family lives. According to Skeggs, her work was feminist in that she was politically committed to providing a means for 'marginalized' women to express themselves. Furthermore, she wished to show how the young women's perceptions of the society they encountered influenced their actual behaviour.

Skeggs argues that she did not exploit the women for her own career benefits, but that her research gave her 'subjects' a sense of self-worth and that she 'provided a mouthpiece against injustice, particularly with regard to disclosures of violence, child abuse and sexual harassment'.

Skeggs, B. (1997) *Formations of Class and Gender*, London: Sage Publications

**In what ways can Skeggs' research be described as feminist?**

# Activities

## Research idea

Design a piece of research influenced by the feminist approach. Decide what you want to investigate, what methods you will use and how the research will be carried out.

## Web.task

Search YouTube for the two-part interview with Sharlene Nagy Hesse-Biber about feminist research. Watch the interview and note the key points she makes.

# Key terms

**Closed system** environment in which all variables can be controlled.

**Deconstruction** the breaking down of a taken-for-granted subject to uncover the assumptions within it.

**Discourse** the linguistic framework within which discussion takes place.

**Modernity** a period in history with specific ways of thinking largely based on rational, scientific thought applied to both the physical and social worlds.

**Narrative** an accepted explanation or theory for some occurrence.

**Open system** environment where the variables cannot be controlled.

**Realism** the view that sociology should aim to uncover the relationship between the wider structures that determine the way we relate to other people in everyday life.

**Relativity** the idea that there is no fixed truth 'out there' waiting to be found. All knowledge is relative to a particular situation.

**Standpoint feminism** the researcher rejects the traditional notion of being neutral and value free, taking the side of the women being researched.

**Transgress** to cross accepted academic boundaries.

# Check your understanding

1. **Give two examples of meta-narratives in sociology.**
2. **Why does the postmodernist stress on the relativity of knowledge imply criticism of positivism?**
3. **Explain in your own words what is meant by 'discourse'. Give an example.**
4. **How do postmodernists view experts and professionals?**
5. **What do postmodernists do when they deconstruct a concept or theory?**
6. **Give one example of:**
   - **(a) a traditional subject looked at in a new way by postmodernists**
   - **(b) a new subject brought into the domain of sociology by postmodernists.**
7. **What are the three key elements of feminist methodology, according to Harding?**
8. **Give one criticism of Harding's approach.**
9. **What approach to methodology is likely to be taken by those adopting a realist position?**

## An eye on the exam **Postmodern, feminist and realist methodologies**

# The Company She Keeps: An Ethnography of Girls' Friendships

**Val Hey, 1997**

Hey's study was written within the context of feminist sociology and is an ethnographic study of girls and their friendships in two London comprehensive schools.

Many studies of youth culture have ignored young females, seeing them as conformists and therefore as uninteresting compared to the exciting lives of dangerous and rebellious males. Hey's work is an attempt to redress the balance.

Hey adopted a reflexive approach and adapted her research to situations as they emerged. She reveals elements of her own personal history and emotional states in her discussion of female friendships. She also refers to some of the issues which arose as a result of her role as a female researcher conducting a study in a school in which the issue of gender equality was sensitive and challenging to many of the school staff.

The aims of the study were to:

- investigate how girls create their identities through talking and writing
- gain an understanding of the processes that take place in girls' social networks
- recognise how females negotiate their relationships with a male-dominated outside world
- investigate the way that girls create intensely pleasurable emotional 'lived' personal lives in the face of gendered repression.

Hey spent her time with girls doing what they were doing: attending lessons, going on cross-country runs and even truanting. She is open about the fact that a trading situation was occurring. She would exchange small gifts of time, sometimes money, excuses to miss lessons, attention and advice in return for access to information about the girls' social lives and emotions.

Hey made friends with girls. Sometimes these relationships were fairly close so that the girls were able to explain the meanings of their slang and the social context in which exchanges were occurring. One particular study group of working-class girls were frequent truants and so Hey necessarily spent time with them outside school.

One of her main sources of data was the notes which girls wrote to each other in class. She collected a wide variety of these and was also given examples by sympathetic staff. Girls gave her examples of notes that had been saved for long periods of time, years in some cases.

Hey found that cliques tend to form among girls of the same social class. They involve a core of best friends and some others who move in and out of favour with the core groups. There is much jostling and negotiating within these groups, with some girls acting in competition with each other for the company of a favoured partner. Middle-class girls have more freedom and autonomy in terms of sexual behaviours but are often seen as 'boffins' and unattractive sexually by the working-class girls. Conversely, working-class girls are dangerous and excluding to middle-class girls who reject the over-feminised and over-sexualised behaviour of the working-class girls.

Adapted from Blundell, J. and Griffiths, J. (2002) Sociology since 1995 Volume 1, Lewes: Connect Publications

**1** **Outline and explain why ethnographic methods may be used in sociological research.** **(15 marks)**

**2** **Outline and assess the view that sociologists should use feminist approaches when studying young female peer groups.** **(25 marks)**

## Grade booster **Getting top marks in question 2**

In this question you need to start by explaining feminist approaches and then go on to explain why they might be helpful in this particular research context. Finally, you need to discuss the disadvantages of feminist approaches before reaching a balanced conclusion.

The ideas and implications of feminist methodologies will need to be explained carefully so try to introduce ideas of male domination of sociology, standpoint feminism and the commitment to equal relationships between researcher and researched. In terms of the study of female peer groups, note the point in the first paragraph about previous studies of youth culture, Hey's use of the ethnographic methods favoured by feminists and her relationship with the girls. The insightful points in her analysis of the findings indicate that her approach led to high levels of validity. However, there are important critical issues to raise – about ethics and objectivity, lack of reliability and the small size and particular location of her sample. Feminist approaches have come under serious attack from those who favour more scientific, positivist research.

# TOPIC 4

# Questionnaires and interviews in research

## Getting you thinking

### Which Austen heroine are you?

**1 You identify most with:**

a Sleeping Beauty
b Cinderella
c Beauty and the Beast
d The wicked queen (in Snow White)
e Tinkerbell
f The Little Mermaid

**2 Your favourite movie star is:**

a Dark, French and sexily brooding
b George Clooney
c Colin Farrell
d Matthew McConaughey
e Viggo Mortensen
f Harrison Ford

...

**10 What do you drink?**

a What have you got?
b Champagne
c White wine/spritzers
d The latest trendy cocktail
e Red wine, vodka, and/or brandy
f You don't really drink much.

**11 You flirt:**

a With anyone who'll flirt back – gender immaterial
b With any good-looking man who crosses your path
c With men you like, but it's more mutual teasing and quick-witted banter than sexual innuendo
d Discreetly. It may feel to you like flirting, but your friends would never call you a flirt
e Yes, but you're uncomfortable if the conversation gets too sexually provocative
f Not really. It's rare that you meet someone you really connect with.

**12 You dress:**

a Down – jeans, sweaters, trainers
b Classy but sexy – you like to be noticed
c Attractive, but not flashy
d In the latest trends, and you like to show skin – low-rise jeans and a belly-button piercing
e Feminine – skirts, pretty tops, kitten heels
f To express your personality.

**Scoring**

| | | | | | | |
|---|---|---|---|---|---|---|
| Q1 | a 2 | b 1 | c 3 | d 4 | e 5 | f 6 |
| Q2 | a 4 | b 3 | c 5 | d 2 | e 6 | f 1 |
| Q10 | a 5 | b 4 | c 2 | d 3 | e 6 | f 1 |
| Q11 | a 4 | b 5 | c 3 | d 1 | e 2 | f 6 |
| Q12 | a 1 | b 4 | c 3 | d 5 | e 2 | f 6 |

**41–51 You are Elizabeth** (*Pride and Prejudice*) – outgoing, funny and direct. You want a serious relationship, but it's essential for you to find someone you can have fun with or teach to have fun. Your best matches are: Mr Darcy, Henry Tilney, Captain Wentworth ...

**64–71 You are Lydia** (*Pride and Prejudice*) – flirty, wild and thoughtless. You're not ready for a serious relationship – what you need is a series of fun flings, and any of these wild boys will do nicely – Henry Crawford, Willoughby, Mr Wickham ...

Source: *The Times*, 29 August 2005

**This is part of a 15-question quiz about personality types published in *The Times*. The questionnaire and answers are good fun – but if we were serious in asking questions about personality types, what sorts of questions might you ask?**

The most common form of research in social science is based on simply asking questions and noting down the answers. Questions, either in questionnaires or interviews, are used equally in both qualitative and quantitative research. In this topic, we will explore the issues linked to the use of questionnaires and interviews and their relationship to particular methodological and theoretical approaches in sociology.

However, not all sociologists agree that just asking questions is enough:

> <<*Interviews and questionnaires allow access to what people say, but not to what they do. The only way to find out what 'actually happens' in a given situation is through observation.*>> (Darlington and Scott 2002)

## Questionnaires and interviews in qualitative and quantitative research

### Quantitative approaches

Quantitative approaches commonly use one of the following:

- *Questionnaires* – written questions that respondents are requested to complete by themselves. To emphasize this and distinguish them from **structured interviews** (see opposite), quantitative-style questionnaires are often referred to as 'self-completion questionnaires'.

## Designing questionnaires Key issues

- **Validity** – Do the questions actually get to the truth of the matter? Crucially, this depends upon whether the sociologist has operationalized (put them in a form that can be measured) concepts through the use of indicators (things that are real, measurable).
- **Reliability** – The sociologist has ensured that, as far as possible, every interview or questionnaire is the same as the other. This means that they can be counted as the same.
- **Replicability** – The research is organized in such a clear way that if the study were conducted by someone else, they would get exactly the same results.
- **Generalizability** – The result of reaching high levels of reliability and validity is the confidence that the research outcomes are true for a much wider population than those studied.
- **Ethics** – The questions must never embarrass or humiliate the person responding and they must be certain that their answers will not be used in a way that could lead to this.

This style of questionnaire is likely to contain a majority of **closed questions**, i.e. questions with a very specific answer or with a given set of answers from which the respondent must choose.

- *Structured interviews* – a series of questions read out directly by the researcher to the respondent. No variation or explanation is allowed. There is the possibility of using scripted **prompts**. These are best viewed as oral questionnaires.

### Qualitative approaches

Qualitative researchers usually use **semi-structured** or **unstructured** interviews. These use a series of questions as a starting point for the in-depth exploration of an issue. Qualitative researchers also use similar discussion techniques in group interviews (more than one person interviewed at the same time) or in focus groups (where a topic is introduced by the researcher and then the group take the discussion where they wish).

## Self-completion questionnaires: a quantitative method

Questionnaires are used by sociologists when they are looking for specific information on a topic (often to support a hypothesis). They are extremely useful in surveys as they can reach a large number of people, since the printed questions can be handed out, mailed out, or put on the internet. Even though they are distributed to a large number or a widely dispersed group of people, they are still very easy to administer and can be very quickly organized and distributed. They provide clear information, which can be converted into statistical data through the use of coding.

In terms of the sorts of questions asked, most questionnaires generally use closed, rather than **open**, questions, as without a researcher present, people may become confused if the questions are complex. Questionnaires are also particularly useful when it comes to asking embarrassing questions, where having an interviewer present may make the respondent feel uncomfortable.

### Reliability

Questionnaires are highly standardized, so clearly everyone receives the same questions in the same format. This should make them highly reliable. However, it is never possible to know if everyone interprets the questions in the same way.

### Generalizability and representativeness

Questionnaires are widely used in survey work. If the sampling has been correct, then the questionnaire should produce questions that are generalizable to the whole population. However, postal or internet questionnaires are not necessarily answered by the person they were sent to. Anyone in the household or with access to a computer could complete the questionnaire. This throws some doubt on representativeness and generalizability.

The second main problem with all self-completion questionnaires is the low **response rate**. Unfortunately, many people cannot be bothered to reply to questionnaires – unless there is some benefit to them, such as the chance to win a prize. This is a serious drawback of questionnaires in research. A low response rate (that is when only a small proportion of people asked actually replies) makes a survey useless, as you do not know if the small number of replies is representative of all who were sent the questionnaire. Those who reply might have strong opinions on an issue, whereas the majority of people may have much less firm convictions – without an adequate number of replies, you will never know. This often occurs when questions are asked about moral issues such as experiments on animals, or abortion/termination. This is a crucial issue, which impacts on the generalizability of any research using self-completion questionnaires.

### Validity

Questionnaires can have high **validity** if they are well designed and seek out answers to relatively simple issues. However, there are a number of problems that they have to overcome to ensure these high levels of validity. People who reply to the questionnaire may interpret the questions in a different way from that which the researcher originally intended. So their replies might actually mean something different from what the researcher believes they mean. Even more problematic than this is the danger of people deliberately lying or evading the truth. There is little that the researcher can do, apart from putting in 'check questions' – which are questions that ask for the same information, but are phrased differently. However, without an interviewer present, the researcher can never really know if the answers are true. Parker *et al.* (1998) used questionnaires to find out what sorts of drugs young people were using over a period of time. Later, in follow-up interviews, one respondent said:

> «*The first time we had this questionnaire, I thought it was a bit of a laugh. That's my memory of it. I can't remember if I answered it truthfully or not. … It had a list of drugs and some of them I'd never heard of, and just the names just cracked me up.*»

### Designing a good questionnaire

When constructing a questionnaire, the sociologist has to ensure:

- *that the indicators are correct* – so that it asks the right questions, which unearth exactly the information wanted – in sociological terms, 'the concepts have been well operationalized'
- *that there is clarity* – the questions are asked in a short, clear and simple manner that can be understood by the people completing the questionnaire
- *that it is concise* – that it is as short as possible, since people usually cannot be bothered to spend a long time completing questionnaires
- *that it is unbiased* – the respondent is not led to a particular viewpoint or answer.

### Collating and analysing self-completion questionnaires

As these are usually closed questionnaires, sociologists use a system known as 'coding'. This consists of allocating each answer a particular number and then putting all the answers into a type of spreadsheet. This spreadsheet can then be interrogated for information. All the different answers to the questions can be summarized and compared against each other. Sociologists have numerous statistical software packages for this.

## Structured interviews: a quantitative approach

Quantitative researchers use highly structured interviews, with the interviewer simply reading out questions from a prepared questionnaire. Effectively, they are oral questionnaires in which the researcher writes down the answers. (Hence the use of the term 'self-completion questionnaire' to distinguish it from the highly structured interview.)

Structured interviews are often used in conjunction with quota sampling (see Topic 1), as researchers often have to go out in the streets to seek people who fall into the categories allocated to them. Once the person is identified, then the researcher will proceed with the structured interview.

The aim of the structured interview is to increase the reliability of questionnaires; the interviewer's role is deliberately restricted to reading out the questions and recording the answers. In limiting the role of the interviewer to the minimum, the possibility of **interviewer bias** is minimized and the possibility of reliability is maximized.

The advantages and disadvantages of structured versus unstructured interviewing are fully discussed in the next section.

## Interviews: a mainly qualitative approach

Sociologists generally use interviews if the subject of enquiry is complex, and a self-completion questionnaire would not allow the researcher to explore the issues adequately.

### Types of interviews

As we have seen, interviews fall between two extremes: structured and unstructured:

- At their most structured, they can be very tightly organized, with the interviewer simply reading out questions from a prepared questionnaire.
- At the other extreme, interviews can be highly unstructured – more like a conversation, where the interviewer simply has a basic area for discussion and asks any questions that seem relevant.
- In between is the semi-structured interview, where the interviewer has a series of set questions, but may also explore various avenues that emerge by **probing** the respondent for more information.

There are a three further types of specialist unstructured interviews sometimes used by sociologists:

1. *Oral history interviews* – Respondents are asked about specific events that have happened in their lifetimes, but not necessarily to them. These interviews are almost always used to link up with other secondary sources.
2. *Life history interviews* – These are a second form of unstructured interview in which people are asked to recount their lives. Like oral history interviews, this method is almost always linked to secondary sources.
3. *Group interviews* – Interviews are usually conducted on a one-to-one basis, but there are occasions when group interviews are useful and these have similar issues in terms of reliability and validity to focus groups (see Topic 2). Group interviews are commonly used where the researcher wants to explore a 'group dynamic', believing that a 'truer' picture emerges when the group is all together. An example of this is Mairtin Mac an Ghaill's *The Making of Men: Masculinities, Sexualities and Schooling* (1994), in which a group of gay students discuss their experiences of school.

### Reliability

Interviews always involve some degree of interaction between researcher and respondent. As in every interaction, there is a range of interpersonal dynamics at work. Differences in age, ethnicity, social class, education and gender, amongst many other things, will impact on the interview. The less structured the interview, the greater the impact of these factors. Reliability levels are, therefore, much lower than for questionnaires and are directly related to the degree of structure of the interview. According to May (2001), the greater the structure, the higher the reliability – as the greater the chance of these variables being excluded and of the different interviews being comparable. However, Brenner *et al*. (1985) argue that 'any misunderstandings on the part of the interviewer and interviewee can be checked immediately in a way that is just not possible when questionnaires are being completed'. So, they believe that reliability is actually greater.

## Representativeness and generalizability

Interviews are much more likely to be used in qualitative research, mainly because they allow for greater depth and exploration of ideas and emotions. Qualitative research tends to be more interested in achieving validity than representativeness. There is no reason why interviews should be any less generalizable than questionnaires, but as they are more likely to be used in non-representative studies, interviews have a reputation for being less generalizable. However, there is a much higher response rate with interviews than with questionnaires, as the process is more personal and it is often more difficult to refuse a researcher who approaches politely.

## Validity

Interviews, particularly unstructured ones, have high levels of validity. The point of an unstructured interview is to uncover meaning and untangle complex views. Interviewing also has a significant advantage over self-completion questionnaires in that the interviewer is present and can often see if the respondent is lying or not. However, there are some problems ensuring that validity is high in interviewing.

Many of these centre around what is sometimes referred to as **researcher imposition** – the ways in which the sociologist can unknowingly influence the data they collect. Let's look at this idea in more detail.



## Focus on research

### Zoe James (2007)
### Policing gypsies and travellers

Zoe James wanted to study groups who have a difficult relationship with the police and who are regarded both by themselves and the majority of people as 'marginal' to the wider society around them.

One part of James' study was on 'New Travellers', sometimes known as 'New Age Travellers'. The study was particularly difficult to do, as New Travellers are suspicious of outsiders and particularly researchers. Her study consisted of 17 in-depth interviews and one focus group with New Travellers living on unauthorized sites throughout the south-west region of England in 2005. Interviews were gained through use of 'snowball' sampling via initial contacts made by a 'gatekeeper'.

The research interviews were carried out in the form of 'guided conversations' (semi-structured interviews) that were not tape recorded, as the New Travellers were very wary of having their views directly recorded. James made notes of the conversations, but also took detailed notes of what she observed on the sites. These notes were 'taken contemporaneously, either in the field (often quite literally), or as soon as possible on leaving the research setting'.

James negotiated with the New Travellers over the form of research methodology and it was only after their full agreement – both as to the methods and the limits of James's research – that they agreed to take part in her work.

James found that despite new laws that provide the police and other enforcement agencies with a range of powers to control and evict travellers from sites, the travellers were determined to continue living their style of nomadic life – even if this meant breaking the law.

James, Z. (2007) 'Policing marginal spaces: Controlling Gypsies and Travellers', *Criminology and Criminal Justice*, 7(4), pp. 367–89

**How does the extract above illustrate some of the problems involved in using questioning as a method of data collection?**

We saw earlier that every interview is a social interaction with issues of class, gender, ethnicity and so on impacting on the relationship between the two people. Not only does this make each interview slightly different, it also means that validity can be affected. In particular, this can lead to the specific issue of interviewer bias – the extent to which the relationship between interviewer and respondent can change the respondents' answers to questions. There is a whole range of possibilities, from respondents wishing to please the interviewer at one extreme, to seeking to mislead at the other.

In fact, there is no reason why people should tell the truth to researchers, and this is particularly true when a sensitive issue is being researched. When questioned about sexual activities or numbers of friends, for example, people may well exaggerate in order to impress the interviewer. This can influence the validity of the research project. So it is rare now for interviews to be used for personal or embarrassing issues, with sociologists preferring self-report questionnaires.

It is easy for researchers, unknowingly, to slip their values into the research. Usually this happens in questionnaires as a result of the language used. In interviews there is a much wider possible range of influences to bias the research – as well as the language, there is the body language or facial expression of the researcher, or even their class, gender or ethnic background. In particular, interviewers should avoid leading questions.

Loaded words and phrases can also generate bias, i.e. the researchers use particular forms of language that either indicate a viewpoint or may generate a particular positive or negative response. For example, 'termination of pregnancy' (a positive view) or 'abortion' (a negative view); 'gay' or 'homosexual'.

## The advantages of interviewing

- Interviewers can pick up non-verbal cues from interviewees.
- The interviewer can see whether the respondent might be lying, by seeing the situation through their own eyes.
- There is a higher response rate than with questionnaires.
- Interviews take place where interviewees feel comfortable.
- The more structured the interview, the higher the chance of replicating it and therefore of high reliability.
- The less structured the interview, the higher the validity as meaning can be explored.

## Ethical issues in interviews

There can be significant ethical issues when using interviews in research, as the interviewer can gain considerable information about the interviewee – some of which is potentially embarrassing for the interviewee. Trust needs to be established very early on and the person being interviewed has to have a reassurance that the information will be confidential. Any information that is published will be done in such a way that the interviewee remains anonymous.

Dorothy Scott studied child abuse in a children's home (Darlington and Scott 2002).

> «*Confidentiality also proved to be difficult as I became increasingly aware of the difficulty of presenting findings of research based on an intensive analysis of cases without using illustrations which might be recognizable to the staff or the clients.*» (p.38)

## Collating and analysing interview data

Interviews are usually recorded and this recording is then **transcribed** (written up) into notes. This is an extremely time-consuming activity. For example. Tizard and Hughes (1991) recorded interviews with students to find out how they went about learning – and every one hour of interview took 17 hours to transcribe and check. However, researchers still prefer to do this, as taking notes at the time of the interview usually interrupts the flow, disrupting the atmosphere. The transcription is then studied for key themes. Increasingly, sociologists use special software that can be set up to look for key words or phrases and will then collate these into categories. By recording and transcribing interviews, sociologists have independent evidence to support their claims, which they can also provide to other researchers should they wish to replicate the research. This is very important for qualitative sociologists, who are often criticized by quantitative researchers for their failure to provide independent evidence.

# Key terms

**Closed questions** questions that require a very specific reply, such as 'yes' or 'no'.

**Interviewer bias** the influence of the interviewer (e.g. their age, 'race', gender) on the way the respondent replies.

**Open questions** questions that allow the respondent to express themselves fully.

**Probing** encouraging the interviewee to expand on an answer, e.g. by asking them directly to expand or simply remaining silent as if expecting more detail from the respondent.

**Prompts** possible answers to a question.

**Researcher imposition** the ways in which the sociologist can unknowingly influence the data they collect

**Response rate** the proportion of questionnaires that is returned (could also refer to the number of people who agree to be interviewed).

**Semi-structured interview** where the interviewer has a series of set questions, but may also explore avenues that emerge by probing the respondent for more information.

**Structured interview** where the questions are delivered in a particular order and no explanation or elaboration of the questions is allowed by the interviewer.

**Transcribing** the process of writing up interviews that have been recorded.

**Unstructured interview** where the interviewer is allowed to explain and elaborate on questions.

**Validity** refers to the problem of ensuring that the questions actually measure what the researcher intends them to.

# Check your understanding

1 **Identify and explain three of the key issues in asking questions.**

2 **What do we mean when we talk about loaded questions and leading questions? Illustrate your answer with an example of each and show how the problem could be overcome by writing a 'correct' example of the same questions.**

3 **Why are 'response rates' so important?**

4 **When is it better to use questionnaires rather than interviews?**

5 **When would it be more appropriate to use unstructured interviews?**

6 **Give any two advantages of structured interviews compared with unstructured ones.**

7 **How can researcher imposition affect the validity of data collected from interviews?**

8 **What is meant by 'transcribing'?**

# Activities

## Research idea

Find out about a sample of young people's experience of schooling. Draft a closed questionnaire to collect this data. Collect and analyse the data quantitatively. Then draft guide questions for an unstructured interview to find out about the same issue. Conduct two or three of these interviews, either taping or making notes of the responses.

Compare the two sorts of data. What differences are there? Why do those differences occur?
Which method do you think was most effective for that particular purpose? Why?

## Web.task

Go to the website of the polling organization Ipsos-Mori at **www.ipsos-mori.com**. Browse the section on 'Research Techniques'. List the different ways the organization asks questions. How is the internet used to gather data about attitudes and opinions?

## An eye on the exam **Questionnaires and interviews in research**

# Social Exclusion of Pakistani and Bangladeshi Women

**Angela Dale (2002)**

This research is based in Oldham near Manchester. The Pakistani and Bangladeshi communities in the north of England often live in relative poverty, with many of the boroughs of Oldham among the most deprived in the country. This research seeks to discover whether family factors and education are a significant influence on young women and their participation in work, or whether there are structural factors created by the opportunities for work available.

The study combines quantitative data collected at a national level and qualitative data drawn from interviews and focus groups involving the Pakistani and Bangladeshi communities in Oldham. Statistics were gathered from UCAS (the organization that manages university applications) about the rate of applications to higher education from Pakistani and Bangladeshi young people and their preferred subject choices compared to other ethnic groups.

The qualitative data was gathered through interviewing young people in focus groups. Students aged between 14 and 16 were drawn from two contrasting secondary schools, one with a high proportion of Bangladeshi students and one with a more mixed intake. Focus groups also took place with white girls from the mixed school. In addition young people aged 16–21 were recruited from a further education and sixth form college and informal contacts were made with young people who had chosen to leave education. In total, 82 Pakistani and Bangladeshi young people were part of this process.

Detailed individual interviews were conducted with Pakistani and Bangladeshi women selected to represent different stages of life, different levels of education and different work statuses. Economically inactive women were recruited by calling at houses in areas with large Pakistani or Bangladeshi populations. Women in work were contacted through a variety of processes of convenience and snowball sampling. This group consisted of younger women born and educated in Britain and also older women. All interviews were transcribed. There is no claim that the samples were representative, so survey data from other sources was used as a control.

The study finds that social exclusion originates in 'early patterns of residential segregation, an absence of well paid jobs and a lack of understanding between white and Pakistani and Bangladeshi communities'.

However, there is very clear evidence of change across generations:

'By contrast with their mothers' generation, younger women who had been educated in the UK saw paid work as a means to independence and self-esteem. Women with higher level qualifications often showed considerable determination in managing to combine paid work and child-care. Whilst most women subscribed strongly to the centrality of the family, it is clear that the majority will follow very different routes through the life-course from their mothers. However, even with higher level qualifications, women are facing considerable barriers to employment - not just in Oldham but nationally. '

Adapted from Blundell, J. and Griffiths, J. (2003) Sociology since 1995 Volume 2, Lewes: Connect Publications

1 **Outline and explain why snowball samples may be used in sociological research.** **(15 marks)**

2 **Outline and assess the view that interviews provide the most useful method for sociological research into the social exclusion of Pakistani and Bangladeshi women.** **(25 marks)**

## Grade booster **Getting top marks in question 2**

In this question you need to start by explaining the different types of interview and then go on to explain why they might be helpful in this particular research context. Finally, you need to discuss the disadvantages of interviewing before reaching a balanced conclusion.

This study uses both individual interviews and focus groups – describe the differences. Explain how interviews can have different levels of structure, depending on the needs of the research. Move on to look at the advantages of both focus groups and individual interviews for studying this topic. Focus groups are used with young people – will this method encourage them to speak more freely about this sensitive issue? What extra insights might be gained from group interviews? Raise points about interviews allowing for prompting and the establishment of rapport, which should add to validity, especially if the interviewers share the cultural background of the participants. Disadvantages might relate to the issue of researcher imposition and interviewer bias; cultural similarities between interviewers and participants might lead to over-rapport and cultural differences to lack of understanding and, therefore, validity. You might also wish to raise issues of reliability and representativeness in qualitative interviews.

# TOPIC 5

# Secondary data

## Getting you thinking

It is beautiful day in September 1944 near the end of the Second World War in a little mountain village in Tuscany, Italy. The United States and British forces are about fifty miles away and slowly advancing and pushing the occupying German forces back.

At the village of Cerpiano, Cornelia Paselli and the rest of the family had been woken early by her father.

"Wake up! Wake up! The Germans are burning houses, it's not safe here. Go and take refuge in the church."

At about 9 o'clock there was a banging on the (church) doors and the German troops shouted at them to come out. The soldiers ushered them down a track ... towards the cemetery and ... told them to get inside.

"A number of the women began to shout and cry and everyone was pushing, she says, forwards, backwards – like a waving mass" says Cornelia.

A German came in with a machine gun and set it up in the left hand corner in front of them and began loading cylinders of ammunition onto and beside the gun.

Suddenly, one woman began to panic. 'I want to go to my daughter!' she shouted, running forward. She was shot dead immediately.

"Then there was a kind of jolt," says Cornelia, "an explosion so intense that I was thrown into the air and landed in the middle of the crowd'. People were shouting and crying, calling out names, others screaming for help and then the machine gun started firing. Bodies started falling on top of her and around her. The she fainted. When she came to again, more bodies were piled around her. She could hear voices and then her mother calling out "Cornelia, Cornelia are you still alive?"

"Mama please be quiet", she whispered back. "Don't talk otherwise they will kill you". But her mother called out for her other daughter. Then a shot rang out.

"Dead bodies are really heavy", she says, "but eventually I managed to free myself". There was no one about except the dead and wounded. She thought to go back to Cerpiano, but she could still see troops and heard shouting from the village and so, instead ran down the valley barefoot through the brambles and scrub.

191 people were killed in the cemetery.

Adapted from: Holland, J. (2008) *Italy's Sorrow: A Year of War 1944–45*, London: Harper Press (pp. 379–81)

1. **What are your immediate reactions to the extract above?**
2. **How do you think the author obtained the information?**
3. **Do you believe it?**
4. **Do you think there could be another side to the story (i.e. that of the Germans)?**
5. **How could we find out?**
6. **If you wanted to study something that happened in 1945, what would you do?**
7. **Can you think of any problems that might result from using information about an occurrence where you were not present?**

In this topic, we explore the way that sociologists can make use of material collected by other people for whatever reason. Because these resources are 'second-hand', when the sociologist comes to examine the data, they are called **secondary data**. However, it is important to remember that they have equal status amongst sociologists with **primary data**, and can be just as difficult to collect and interpret as primary sources. Both qualitative and quantitative researchers make use of secondary sources for a variety of reasons, which we will explore in this topic.

A huge range of material can be considered as secondary data. Bryman (2004) suggests the following categories:

- *Life (personal) documents* – These include diaries, letters, emails, photographs and video recordings. They may be written down, or in visual or aural (i.e. can be heard) form.
- *Official documents* – These derive from the state and include official statistics, government and local authority reports, minutes of government meetings and of Parliament, and the whole range of officially sanctioned publications available.
- *Other documents that derive from organizational sources* – By this, Bryman means the publications of profit-making companies, charities and any other organization that produces some form of formal output.
- *The contents of the mass media* – This is a whole area of study by itself. The mass media refers to all organizations producing information and entertainment for a public audience. This includes radio, television, the internet, newspapers and magazines, and novels.
- *Previous sociological research* – This covers all previously published sociological research and datasets.

Webb *et al.* (1981) also argue for the use of **trace measures** – these are the physical changes produced by human action, such as the number of lager cans left around a building after a group of young people go home after hanging around for the evening.

# Approaches to secondary data

Sociologists take different approaches towards analysing and using secondary data. There are three main approaches, outlined below.

## Extraction

**Extraction** simply involves taking statistics or research examples from the original texts. It is commonly used when sociologists examine previous sociological sources and databases.

## Content analysis

In **content analysis**, documents and other sources are examined in great detail to see what themes run through them. There are two ways of doing this:

- Qualitative content analysis stresses exploring the meaning and looking for examples to illustrate the themes. This method is particularly commonly used in studies of the mass media.
- On the other hand, quantitative analysis will almost certainly use computer programs, which will count the number of times certain words (which are regarded as indicators of themes) or themes are used.

## Semiotics

**Semiotics** is the study of signs. A sign is something that stands for something other than itself. For example, a Mohican haircut may indicate a rebellious attitude, or a St George's Cross painted on a face signifies support for an England sports team. Semiotics is often used in the study of youth culture, and is apparent in the work of both Marxist cultural studies writers and of postmodernist writers. Both these groups seek to analyse the meaning of the particular clothes, music and 'argot' used by young people. Similarly, sociologists interested in semiotics try to uncover the hidden meaning within the secondary data. It is particularly used in the study of **life documents**, especially photos and in music.

# Advantages and disadvantages of using secondary sources

## Advantages of using secondary sources

All sociological research begins with a **literature search**, or review, of all relevant previous sociological research on the particular topic under investigation. If the information required already exists, even if in a different form, the researcher does not have to repeat the original research. Alternatively, the researcher may use the original data to re-examine previously published data or studies in order to interpret them in a new theoretical light.

Often, sociologists want to look back in history for information but there is no one able to provide a life or oral history. In these cases, the sociologist must use secondary sources, such as **official documents** and letters.

Sometimes, it is impossible for the researcher actually to visit or talk to the group directly. This could be for financial reasons, or because the group may be geographically too distant or scattered. More commonly, the sociologist thinks that studying the group directly would be too obtrusive. This is where trace measures are often used.

For instance, sociologists studying crime and deviance are often faced with situations where direct studies of the group might be considered unethical – a good example is research on children where it may not be possible to get informed consent. Although some sociologists are prepared to engage in participant observational methods, for example, that can involve them in illegal or immoral activities, other sociologists prefer to study these activities with the use of secondary data.

Finally, and overlapping with the previous point, there are groups engaged in activities that they do not want sociologists to study, because they may be illegal, deviant or immoral. For sociologists studying these groups, one of the few ways to gain information is to access any secondary data available.

## Disadvantages of using secondary sources

All secondary sources (except trace sources) are created for a reason; this could well create bias and distortion. Government statistics are often neutral, but they are also often constructed in such a way as to throw a positive light on events or statistics. At worst, they can be simple propaganda. Private organizations, such as companies, are concerned to produce a positive image of themselves. They will, therefore, only produce information that promotes this image. This applies equally to charities and any other form of organization.

Life documents, such as a diary, give a very one-sided view of what happened and are almost always bound to be sympathetic to the writer.

Historical sources contain the possibility of bias, which we have already noted for other secondary sources, but there is the even greater problem, according to May (2001), of their being influenced by particular historical events or cultural ways of thinking that the sociologist may not be aware of.

Finally, as we have seen throughout the book, the work of sociologists may contain errors and biases.

# Assessing the quality of secondary data

Scott (1990) suggests that there are four criteria to use when judging the usefulness of secondary data to the researcher. These are:

1. *Authenticity* – Is the origin of the data known and does the evidence contained there seem genuine?
2. *Credibility* – Are the data free from error and distortion?
3. *Representativeness* – Is the evidence shown by the data typical of its kind?
4. *Meaning* – Is the evidence clear and comprehensive?

We will use these to guide us through the usefulness of each type of secondary source.

# Types of secondary data

## Life documents

Life documents include virtually all written, aural and visual material that derives from people's personal lives, including diaries, letters, emails, photographs and video recordings.

Traditionally, the material used by sociologists was written, but, increasingly, there has been a growth in visual material such as photographs and home videos.

Life documents can give sociologists a detailed and very personal look into people's lives; as a way of seeing events through their eyes, it is an unrivalled method. They are also particularly useful when there is no other way to get hold of information, for example if the events happened a long time ago and there is no one to interview. However, the writers may have distorted views of what happened, or they may well be justifying or glorifying themselves in their accounts.

Plummer (2000) suggested that the main forms of life documents include diaries, letters, photographs, film and what he calls '**miscellanea**', which consist of anything else reflecting one's life. We will examine each of these in turn.

### *Diaries*

The key thing about diaries is that they chronicle events as they happen, rather than being filtered by memory or later events, as is the case with autobiographies. Diaries are also very detailed as they cover events day by day. This daily writing is also useful as if gives the sociologist a real idea of the exact timing of when things happened.

However, diaries cannot be relied upon for 'the truth', as people are not objective about their own lives. Instead they filter what happens around them according to their own **biases** and perceptions. It is also important to remember why the diaries were being written, as many politicians and journalists have published diaries that were specifically written for later publication. This would suggest that the contents will be biased to ensure that they come to be perceived by the reader in a positive fashion.

### *Letters*

The most famous example of the use of letters in sociology is Thomas and Znaniecki's *The Polish Peasant* (1918). This is a study of the correspondence of recent immigrants to the United States with their families back in Poland. Thomas and Znaniecki placed an advert in the Chicago newspaper offering to pay for each letter handed to them, and received hundreds of letters. The letters gave them insights into the ordinary lives of immigrants and the issues that concerned them in their new lives in the USA. It also told them about the changes that occurred in family life and relationships as a result of the movement. The letters were divided into various categories by Thomas and Znaniecki, so there were:

- ceremonial letters, which marked formal occasions such as marriages, deaths and birthdays
- informal letters about everyday life
- sentimental letters about love and how family members were missed
- letters asking for and sending money and financial advice.

However, letters are always written with some purpose in mind and to convey a particular image of a person. For example, in Thomas and Znaniecki's work, the immigrant letter writers wanted to demonstrate to the people left in Poland what a success they had made of their lives, and so this 'filter' had to be taken into account when reading the letters.

### *Visual images*

Millions of photographs and images are produced every year by families as the most common form of documenting their lives. Photographs have a very long history in sociology, and in the early days of sociology in America, almost all research was illustrated with photographs. More recently, some sociologists have used photographs to 'capture' images of people's lives as a form of ethnographic study. Jackson (1978) used mainly photographs to explore the lives of prisoners, and Harper (1978) photographed the lives of homeless people. These two sociologists argued that using image rather than text provides a powerful insight into people's lives.

Sutton (1992), however, is very critical of the use of photographs in sociological research. He points out that photographs are almost always taken when groups or families are engaged in holiday or festive occasions and that the photographs are also constructed to reflect a happy image ('Say cheese!'). He conducted a study of visits to Disneyland and concluded that these happy images reinforced the pleasant memories that families had of their visits, helping to forget the more negative experiences. Sutton therefore suggests that to use photographs (and videos) in research has serious drawbacks. However, as Plummer (2000) points out, photographs of events are not restricted to family holidays and occasions, and there is a wide variety of photographic images available which are not necessarily biased.

### *Miscellanea*

Plummer uses this category to include the huge variety of other personal 'documents' that sociologists have used. For example, Schwartz and Jacobs (1979) studied people's suicide notes to try to understand the thoughts and emotion of people in their last hours before death.

However, the same point has to be made regarding miscellanea as for all other life documents. The documents were produced for an effect; they do not necessarily represent the truth or even what people really thought. Taking the example of suicide notes, Schwartz and Jacobs point out that they were often intended to make other people feel guilty and to punish them. They were, therefore, written for an audience and may not necessarily tell their true feelings.

## Official publications

Statistics compiled by governments and reputable research organizations are routinely used by sociologists. Governments have entire departments devoted to the production of statistics. In the UK, the Office for National Statistics produces statistics and collates them from other departments. These statistics provide far greater scale and detail than sociologists can generally achieve and offer a source of information that is readily available, comprehensive and cheap to access.

Usually, the government will produce these statistics over a number of years – for example, the government statistical publication *Social Trends* has been published for over 35 years. It is therefore possible to make comparisons at various points in time.

Although these official statistics have many advantages, there are also some problems facing researchers using them. The statistics are collected for administrative reasons and the classifications used may omit crucial information or might classify groupings or activities in a way that is inappropriate for the researcher. A researcher might be interested in the link between religion and income, but the official statistics may be collated on the grounds of ethnic origin or gender and average income.

Official statistics may also be affected by political considerations, as government will always seek to present the statistics in the most positive light. They may also reflect a complex process of interaction and negotiation – as is the case with crime statistics – and may well need to be the focus of investigation themselves!

### *Reports and government inquiries*

The Civil Service and other linked organizations will often produce official reports that investigate important problems or social issues. However, although they draw together much information on these issues, they are constrained by their 'remit', which states the limits of their investigations. The government and other powerful bodies are therefore able to exclude discussion of issues that they do not want to become the centre of public attention. For example, McKie *et al.* (2004) examined official government policy documents on health improvements for families in Britain. They used a particular perspective in their analysis, in that they explored exactly what benefits there would be for women as opposed to other family members. They conclude that there were significant gender inequalities in the official documents, with assumptions about the role of women being to care for other family members.

### *Documents from other sources*

An enormous range of documents is produced by non-governmental organizations (NGOs) – that is, private companies, charities and other social groups. These include annual reports, press releases, advertisements and a range of statistical information about the company's aims and achievements. Increasingly, these are brought into the public domain via the internet.

However, sociologists are even more wary of taking NGOs' materials than they are of taking government ones. Most companies – and even non-profit-making organizations – have a vested interest in ensuring that their public image is positive. It is, therefore, extremely unlikely that negative information will be published by a company about itself. The complexity of using formal information produced by NGOs is illustrated by Forster's (1994) study of career-development opportunities in a large, multinational corporation. The more detail that Forster went into, the more contradictory the information he received:

> «*One of the clearest themes to emerge was the apparently incompatible interpretations of the same events and processes amongst the three subgroups within the company – senior executives, HQ personnel and regional personnel managers. These documents were not produced deliberately to distort or obscure events or processes being described, but their effect was precisely to do this.*» (p. 160)

## The mass media

The mass media produce an overwhelming amount of information each day, which not only reflects the concerns and values of society but also helps to shape these values. The mass media thus provide fertile ground for sociological researchers.

Content analysis is used by sociologists in order to discover how particular issues are presented. They can do this in two ways:

1 Using quantitative techniques, researchers simply count the number of times a particular activity or term appears in the media being analysed. This helps to prove a particular hypothesis, e.g. regarding the numbers of people from minority-ethnic backgrounds appearing on television. A slightly more sophisticated version of this might be to construct a content analysis grid, where two or more themes can be linked, e.g. the number of times that newspapers run stories that link people from minority-ethnic backgrounds with negative events.
2 In a similar way to the second form of quantitative analysis, researchers may use a qualitative form of content analysis to draw out general themes from the newspapers, film or television. They will, for example, seek to establish not just whether there is a negative association between ethnicity and social problems, but what forms any such association might take.

Quantitative approaches are useful for several reasons:

- They provide clear, unambiguous statistics on the number of times topics appear in the press or are broadcast.
- They can clearly state the criteria they use for the selection of themes.
- They are replicable – other sociologists can return to the original sources and check their accuracy.

However, qualitative approaches have the strength of being able to explore the meaning of the theme or item being researched. Just having the number of times that an item is mentioned in the media does not give a true image of what is being discussed or the importance of the discussion. So, qualitative analyses tend to be more valid but less reliable.

Content analysis is very widely used in sociology because accessing mass-media material and analysing it is simple and relatively cheap. Furthermore, there are no problems in finding a representative sample, as it is possible to obtain a wide variety of newspapers or television programmes. Importantly, it is an unobtrusive method of research – recording a television programme and then analysing it for its content themes does not impact in any way on the making of the programme.

However, Macdonald and Tipton (1993) suggest there is considerable risk of bias and distortion, for two main reasons:

- There are errors of various kinds, most importantly, errors of fact, as the standards of journalists are not as high as those of academics.
- There is distortion of the facts – Newspapers and television programmes have various preferences as to what can be considered news and what 'angle' to approach the news from. The influences include journalistic values, proprietor's values and, perhaps most important in a competitive market, the audience at which the journalists perceive themselves to be aiming the news.

Furthermore, as Cohen (2002) points out, there is no single correct way to 'read' a newspaper's or television programme's hidden meanings. Each sociologist will approach the interpretation of the contents from their own perspective. Therefore, both reliability and validity are low in content-analysis studies.

One final further difficulty sociologists have in content analysis is actually knowing how the viewers or readers interpret the media output. We know from Morley's research (1980) that people approach and understand television programmes from very different perspectives. Sociologists cannot assume that the interpretation they have – even as a group of researchers agreeing on the content's meaning – will be the same as that of the viewer.

## Sociological research and data archives

There are a number of **data archives** in Britain where the results of large research studies are stored. These can be accessed and the information reused by other researchers. Many of these can be found at The Data Archive (www.data-archive.ac.uk), based at the University of Essex. This holds over 4000 datasets from government, academic researchers and opinion poll organizations.

The huge advantage of these datasets is that they provide ready-made material. However, the information that the original researchers were seeking may not be the same as what is needed by the researcher using them as secondary data. If the researcher is not careful, it is possible to be led astray by the focus of the original research.

Although we have categorized data sets as purely sociological research, it is worth knowing that some are wholly or part-funded by the government. However, as they tend to collect information that is sociological in character rather than politically sensitive, most sociologists classify government-sponsored datasets as sociological research.

Perhaps the best-known data set is the Census, a survey of all people and households in the country, which takes place every ten years (the last Census was 2001, the next is 2011). All households in Britain are required to complete this by law. It is intended to be the most complete picture of Britain available. In recent years, there has been some concern that not everyone completes the Census – in particular, certain minority-ethnic groups, refugees and asylum seekers, and transient populations such as the homeless and travellers. It may, therefore, underrepresent certain categories of the population.

Other well-known data sets include the longitudinal British Household Panel Survey and the General Household Survey which collects information on:

- housing patterns
- income
- education
- demographic changes
- ownership of consumer items
- household and family information.
- health services usage
- employment
- smoking and drinking

## Previous sociological research studies

### *Previous studies as a starting point*

Whenever sociologists undertake a study, the first thing they do is to carry out a literature search – that is, go to

# Focus on research

## Blanden and Machin (2007)
### Intergenerational social mobility

In 2005, Jo Blanden and Stephen Machin investigated what changes have taken place in intergenerational mobility in the UK. In order to do this, they had to rely upon secondary data, which involved comparing the mobility of people born in 1958 compared to 1970.

Blanden and Machin used data that was already available in other surveys, but combined the results and used a slightly different method of categorizing mobility. Specifically, they used information from two very large national surveys: the British Household Panel Survey and the Millennium Cohort Study.

By doing this, they avoided duplicating work already done; they saved time and money and they were able to access historical information (about those born in 1958) which it would have been impossible to obtain – unless they could engage in time-travel!

The study indicated that levels of social mobility have declined recently. Their evidence for this conclusion came from analyses of income similarities between parents and children and also in educational attainment across generations – both pieces of information were obtained from surveys which were originally carried out for very different purposes.

Blanden, J. and Machin, S. (2007) *Recent Changes in Intergenerational Mobility in Britain*, London: The Sutton Trust

**Explain why Blanden and Machin used secondary data in their research.**

the library or the internet and look up every available piece of sociological research on the topic of interest. They can then see the ways in which the topic has been researched before, the conclusions reached and the theoretical issues thrown up. Armed with this information, the researcher can then construct the new research study to explore a different 'angle' on the problem or simply avoid the mistakes made earlier.

### *Reinterpreting previous studies*

Often, sociologists do not want to carry out a new research project, but prefer instead to examine previous research in great detail in order to find a new interpretation of the original research results; the secondary data (that is, the original piece of sociological research) provide all the information that is needed. Sometimes, sociologists might conduct a **meta-analysis**. This is a formal term for the process of looking at the whole range of research on a topic and seeking to identify and draw together common findings.

A good example of how previous sociological work was used as secondary data is provided by Goodwin and O'Connor's (2005) re-examination of a little-known sociological study undertaken in the early 1960s on the lives of young people as they left school and entered work. They compared this with the transition from school to work today. The early work provided them with a detailed and rich database from which they could form hypotheses and make comparisons with contemporary research.

Sometimes, however, there are methodological errors in published research, as well as possible bias in the research findings. There have been many examples of research that has formed the basis for succeeding work and that only many years later has been found to be faulty. A famous piece of anthropological research which was used for 40 years before it was found to be centrally flawed was Mead's *Coming of Age in Samoa* (1928). Mead made a number of mistakes in her interpretation of the behaviour of the people she was studying, but as no one knew this, many later studies used her (incorrect) findings in their work.

## Trace measures

One of the problems faced by all sociological researchers is the degree to which their presence and activities actually changes the natural behaviour of the participants. This problem is well recognized in participant observation and experimentation, but also exists to a lesser degree in survey work.

Webb has argued that sociology should use 'unobtrusive measures' in research wherever this is possible, so that this problem is eliminated (Webb *et al.* 1966). He points out that when people interact, they will often leave behind them some physical sign of their activities, the trace measures referred to earlier. According to Webb, there are two types of trace measures:

1 *Erosion measures, which refer to things missing* – The most famous example of erosion measures (and the origin of the term) was the fact that the tiles around a particular exhibit in the Chicago Museum of Science and Industry, which showed real chicks hatching out from their eggs, had to be replaced every six weeks because they became worn out by the sheer

numbers of people visiting this exhibit. However, the rest of the museum only needed its tiles replacing after some years.

**2** *Accretion measures, which refer to things being added* – They were used by Rathje and Murphy (2002) in their study of rubbish thrown out by households, but they have also been used in studying graffiti in Belfast (to indicate 'ownership' of particular areas) and litter patterns (to demonstrate public use of space).

## Check your understanding

1. What are secondary data?
2. Why do sociologists use secondary sources?
3. What are the disadvantages of using secondary sources?
4. What are the advantages and disadvantages of using official statistics and other government documents?
5. What are the advantages and disadvantages of using qualitative secondary data, such as diaries?
6. Give two examples of data archives. How can these be used by sociologists?
7. How can sociologists use trace measures in research?

## Key terms

**Bias** where the material reflects a particular viewpoint to the exclusion of others; this may give a false impression of what happened and is a particular problem for secondary sources.

**Content analysis** exploring the contents of the various media in order to find out how a particular issue is presented.

**Data archives** where statistical information is stored.

**Extraction** taking statistics or research examples from the original texts.

**Life (personal) documents** personal data in written, visual or aural form, including diaries, letters, emails, photographs and video recordings.

**Literature search/review** the process whereby a researcher finds as much published material as possible on the subject of interest, usually through library catalogues or the internet.

**Meta-analysis** studying a range of research on a particular topic in order to identify common findings.

**Miscellanea** a term used by Plummer (2000) to refer to a range of life documents other than letters and diaries.

**Official documents** publications produced by the government.

**Primary data** Data collected by the sociologist themselves.

**Secondary data** data already collected by someone else for their own purposes.

**Semiotics** the study of the meaning of signs; data are examined for symbolic meaning and reinterpreted in this light.

**Trace measures** physical changes as a result of human actions.

## Activities

### Research idea

You can conduct a simple trace measure experiment. Go around your house/garden and look at the objects lying around (anything from a photograph or a scratch in some wood to a CD) and think about the memories that these bring up. Think about the changes in you and your family since these first appeared, and what your feelings are.

### Web.task

You are probably a member of a social networking site, such as Facebook. Log on and look through the photos, descriptions, etc., of any friends or other contacts you have on it. What kinds of images do people want to present of themselves? Are there some common themes?

## An eye on the exam Secondary data

# The Educational Backgrounds of Members of The House of Commons and House Of Lords

**The Sutton Trust (2005)**

The researchers obtained information about the education of all members of the House of Commons and the House of Lords. There were a few individuals for whom information could not be obtained and also a number who had been educated in other countries. In all, information was collected about the schools of 587 of the 641 MPs (91%) and the university data for 625 (97%). For the House of Lords, school data was found for 631 of the 723 peers (87%) and university data for 656 (91%). Sources of information included 'Who's Who', government and party websites and online reference libraries such as 'KnowUK'.

The researchers also wanted to look at changes in the educational backgrounds of politicians over the last 50 years and so used data from the British General Election Studies which are produced after each election. For both aspects of the research therefore, the main method used was analysis of secondary data. The absence of some of the relevant data, in this case the educational backgrounds of some MPs and peers, is a common problem with secondary data. However, it can be assumed that the data were valid and reliable as they were based on information that can be checked.

About one third of current MPs attended a private school, although private schools educate only 7% of the population. 72% of MPs attended university, with 43% attending one of the leading 13 universities and 27% attending Oxford or Cambridge. Less than half of MPs had attended a comprehensive school (42%) and 25% had attended grammar schools. There were fewer younger MPs who had been to grammar schools because of the phasing out of these schools as the comprehensive system expanded. Only 20% of Conservative MPs attended a comprehensive school, although such schools now educate 88% of secondary schoolchildren. 13 of 15 Old Etonians (past students of Eton) are Conservatives, with one each in the Labour and Liberal Democrat parties, and eight of these 13 held offices within the Conservative Party.

Conservative MPs were more likely to have attended private schools (59%) while Labour MPs were the least likely to have done so (18%). Conservatives were also more likely to have been to a leading university. 164 MPs from the three main parties had been to Oxbridge and 100 (61% of these) to Oxford.

MPs who held office in their parties were more likely than non-office holders to have attended private school or to have attended Oxbridge. The figures were most noticeable for the Labour Party (25% of members of the government in 2005 had been to private school but only 16% of backbenchers).

Members of the House of Lords were twice as likely as MPs to have been educated at private schools (62% had attended a private school). Of the remaining hereditary lords, 98% had been to private schools; for appointed peers the figure was 56%. 79% of Conservative peers and 34% of Labour peers had attended private school. Of those educated in the state sector, more than half had been to a grammar school. Lords were as likely as MPs to have been to university but rather more had been to one of the leading universities.

Over the past fifty years, the study found that the proportion of MPs who had been privately educated had fallen, although not dramatically.

Adapted from Blundell, J. and Griffiths, J. (2008) Sociology since 2000, Lewes: Connect Publications

1 **Outline and explain why official statistics may be used in sociological research.** **(15 marks)**

2 **Outline and assess the view that secondary data are the most effective source of information when studying the educational background of MPs.** **(25 marks)**

## Grade booster Getting top marks in question 2

In this question you need to start by explaining the various types of qualitative and quantitative secondary data and then go on to explain why they might be helpful in this particular research context. Finally, you need to discuss the disadvantages of secondary data in studying this topic before reaching a balanced conclusion.

The advantages of using secondary data include the wide range of sources (both official and non-official) available about MPs, which will allow for some cross-checking of data to eliminate errors. Some advantages are practical, for example the difficulties of obtaining primary data from MPs. Also, MPs might be reluctant to admit to privileged backgrounds so there may be question marks over validity.

Disadvantages include the fact that sociologists will not usually be able to check the accuracy of individual sources and the data may not be presented in the ways that the sociologist requires, for example, the information about education may not specify whether a particular educational institution was a state or an independent school. There may also be question marks over bias in some of the sources.

# TOPIC 6

# Values and ethics

## Getting you thinking

**1 Do you agree that we should continue to experiment on animals?**

**2 Do you think that it is acceptable to engage in**

**(a) picketing and protests**

**(b) illegal, possibly violent activities,**

**in order to stop animal testing?**

**3 Imagine you have been given an opportunity to study scientists working in a lab who actually perform the 'experiments' on the animals.**

**(a) What would you like to find out?**

**(b) What would the first three questions of your questionnaire be?**

**(c) Do you think that you could conduct a series of interviews with the scientists without letting your views come across?**



One of the most bitterly contested concepts in sociology has been over the question of the place of personal and political values in theory and research. Three distinct positions can be identified on this issue.

1. At one end of the debate are those sociologists who argue that if sociology wants to make any claim to scientific status then it has to be free of **subjective**, personal and political biases. This is known as **value freedom** or **objectivity**.
2. A second position is that, ideally, our personal values should not intrude into our sociological studies, but that in practice it is simply impossible to keep them out – sociology as **value laden**.
3. At the other extreme from value freedom are those who argue that anyone doing sociology must surely use their studies to improve the condition of those most oppressed in society. Sociology is, therefore, more a tool that helps bring about social change – **committed** sociology – than just an academic subject studying society.

## Value-free sociology

As we saw in Topics 1 and 2, there is a significant current of opinion in sociology (deriving from Emile Durkheim) that argues that we should seek to copy the methodology of the physical sciences such as biology or chemistry. One of the key ideas that these sociologists, or **positivists**, have taken from the physical sciences is that of the importance of objectivity in research.

As discussed earlier, positivists argue that the nature of sociological research is no different from that of the physical sciences – both branches of science (the physical and the social) study a series of phenomena that exist totally independently of the scientists, and which can be measured and classified. On the basis of this, theories can be constructed and tested.

The 'social facts' positivists refer to are the statistics obtained by surveys and, possibly, from official publications. Properly constructed, they claim, these should be a perfect reflection of the subject under study. The evidence to show that surveys are objective and accurate exists in the accuracy of opinion polls on a range of subjects including voting and general elections; market research; extent of drug use and even sexual behaviour.

According to O'Connell Davidson and Layder (1994), personal biases and political opinions of researchers are irrelevant as long as the research is well designed and there is no attempt to distort or alter the findings. Finally, to ensure that no biases have inadvertently intruded, there is the check coming from publication of the research findings, which will include a discussion of methods used. The publication will be read and possibly criticized by other researchers.

# Value-laden sociology

Other sociologists believe that whether it is desirable or not, sociology cannot be value free and it is a mistake to see it as such. They further claim that sociologists arguing that sociology is value free are actually doing a disservice to the subject, and they identify a number of issues as evidence in support of their position.

## Historical context

Gouldner (1968) has pointed out that the argument for a value-free sociology is partially based in a particular historical context. Weber has traditionally been associated with the idea that personal and political values should be excluded from research. Yet Gouldner claims that Weber was writing at a time when the Prussian (now German) government was making a strong attack on intellectual freedom. According to Gouldner, Weber was merely trying to prevent the government from interfering in sociology by claiming it was value free.

## Paying for research

Sociological research has to be financed, and those who pay for the research usually have a reason why they want it done. Sociologists working for British government departments, for instance, usually have to sign an agreement that if the department does not like the ideas or findings, then it has the right to prevent publication.

In *Market Killing*, Philo and Miller (2000) have argued that, increasingly, all sciences are having their critical researchers silenced through a combination of targeted funding by those who only want research undertaken into the topics of benefit to them and by the intrusion of commercial consultancies into research. This means that scientists benefit financially from certain outcomes and lose out if other outcomes are uncovered. They also point out that scientists allow their findings to be manipulated by public-relations companies, operating for the benefit of the funders – even when the findings do not necessarily support the funder's claims.

## Career trajectories

As Gouldner (1968) pointed out, all sociologists have personal ambitions and career goals. They want to publish, get promoted, become renowned in their field. These desires can intrude either knowingly or subconsciously into their research activities. According to Kuhn (1962/1970), this involves accepting the dominant 'paradigms' at any particular time within sociology.

## Personal beliefs and interests

Sociologists are no different from other people, in that they hold a set of values and moral beliefs. They might set out to eliminate these as best they can, but, ultimately, all our thoughts and actions are based on a particular set of values and it is impossible to escape from these. The best that can be done is to attempt to make these values clear to both ourselves and to the readers of the research.

Similarly, sociologists find certain areas of study 'interesting'. Why are they drawn to these areas in the first place? Often they reflect personal issues and a desire to explore something important to them. This makes it more difficult to extricate personal values from the research process itself. An example of this is the work of Ken Plummer (2000), who has published widely on sexual issues and is a sociologist associated with 'queer theory'. He makes it plain that his own sexual preference encouraged him to become interested in gay issues:

> «*So, in a sense, I was actually exploring my own life side by side with exploring sociological theory. And I suppose that has shaped the way I think about these things today.*»

Similarly, feminist writers are drawn to subjects of particular interest to women. Indeed, Harding (1986) accuses male sociologists of being biased in their choice of subject matter, and in their selection of 'facts'.

## The domain of sociology

Today, sociology does have academic status and has been accepted as a 'social science'. As a subject, it has developed a range of accepted ways of exploring the world, of sensible questions to be asked and reasonable research methods. It has joined other subjects in rejecting other non-orthodox approaches that claim to provide knowledge. For example, Collins and Pinch (1998) studied parapsychology and found that other social scientists believed that parapsychology was simply fantasy, therefore any research conducted by parapsychologists was dismissed out of hand. Any positive outcomes were simply regarded as the result of poor experimental methods or quite simply fraudulent.

The reasons why social scientists have rejected non-orthodox approaches become clear when we consider the work of postmodernists and of Foucault below. A good contemporary example is discussed by Mark J. Smith (2008), who points to the great difficulty that environmental or 'green' sociology has had in getting its concerns about the environment accepted by the sociological 'establishment' – as green concerns are seen as peripheral to the subject.

## The postmodern critique

Postmodernists such as Lyotard (1984) and Baudrillard (1998) argue that the whole process of sociological and scientific thinking is itself based on a series of values about the nature of society. Postmodernists dispute the assertion that rational thinking based upon verifiable evidence is superior to any other approach to understanding the world. They argue that, in fact, scientific thinking is just one of many possible ways of approaching an understanding of the world and that it is not inherently better – nor does it provide any superior 'truths'. Quite simply, the process of science is based upon a set of values, and all that a sociologist does is derived from a set of values, which are no 'truer' than any other set of values. In writing about their research, postmodernists have adopted two tactics:

1. **Reflexivity** – This involves sociologists including information about themselves and their roles when actually constructing the research, and constantly reflecting on their own biases and the ways in which they may have influenced the research.
2. **Narratives** – This is the name given to the different viewpoints and voices that the researcher allows to be heard in the research. Here, the postmodern sociologist is not trying to dominate the account of the research but to put forward different views of the various subjects of the research. Plummer (2000) has used this in his accounts of gay men's life histories.

### Foucault

A similar argument is put forward by Foucault (1977) in his analysis of knowledge. He argues that what is considered to be knowledge reflects the ability of more powerful groups to impose their ideas on the rest of society. By gaining control over the production of knowledge (methodology), one also gains control over what is considered knowledge. In an argument similar to that of postmodernists, Foucault therefore argues that the 'value-free' process itself is actually based on a set of values.

## Committed sociology

The third approach comes from those who argue that sociology should not be value free but should have some explicit values guiding its approach to study (i.e. it should be committed). The most ardent advocates of this approach are feminist writers and critical (or Marxist) sociologists. It has also been used by writers who are challenging racism and discrimination against people with disabilities. However, it was two sociologists from rather different traditions who started this approach.



### Whose side are we on?

In the 1970s, a famous debate took place between Howard Becker and Alvin Gouldner. Both sociologists agreed that sociology should not be value free, but the debate that followed went on to ask: 'Well, if we are going to be committed, then what side shall we be on?'

Becker (1970) started the debate by arguing that sociology (or at least the study of deviance, his speciality) had traditionally been on the side of the more powerful, and so had looked at issues from the viewpoint of the police officer, the social worker or the doctor, rather than from those of the criminal, the client or the 'mental patient'. Becker called for sociology to look instead from the viewpoint of the 'underdog'. By examining issues from their perspective, new questions and 'facts' could emerge. This sort of approach is the one that was taken by labelling theorists such as Becker (see Chapter 2 Topic 4).

Gouldner (1968) attacked Becker for this argument, claiming that it did not go far enough – and, indeed, merely strengthened the status quo. Gouldner argued that Becker's work still focused on the less powerful. After all, what real power do police officers, social workers and doctors actually have? According to Gouldner, sociology needs to study the really powerful, those who create the structures of oppression of which police officers are merely unimportant agents.

### Marxist view

Exactly this sort of argument was taken up by **critical sociologists** or Marxists. Althusser (1969), a writer in the Marxist tradition, has argued that the role of sociology (which he viewed as a science) is to uncover the ways in which the ruling class control the mass of the population. In doing so, sociologists hope to achieve the breakdown of capitalism by exposing the truth of how it operates for the benefit of a few.

A good example of this form of argument comes from the critical (Marxist) criminologists Taylor, Walton and Young who argued in *The New Criminology* (1973) that 'radical criminological strategy ... is to show up the law, in its true colours, as the instrument of the ruling class ... and that the rule-makers are also the greatest rule-breakers'. Interestingly, however, Young was later to co-found a very different school of sociology, **left realism**, which we explore below.

### Feminist view

Feminist writers, such as Spender (1985), would agree with the idea of exposing the workings of an oppressive society, but also argue that the key is to explore how males dominate and control society. Again, the aim is exposing the truth, but the result is to free women from patriarchy.

There are four elements to feminist research, according to Hammersley (1992) – all of which demonstrate a rejection of searching for objectivity:

1. Feminist research starts with the belief that the subordination of women runs through all areas of social life.
2. Rather than seeking to exclude women's feelings and personal experience, these should form the basis of all analysis.
3. The **hierarchical** division between the researcher and the researched should be broken down so that the subjects of research should be drawn in to help interpret the data obtained. This would help the research belong to the women under study.
4. As the overall aim of feminist research is the emancipation of women, the success of research should only be measured in this, not solely in terms of academic credibility.

Feminist writers accuse sociology of traditionally being '**malestream**', that is, interested in male views and concerns, rather than trying to include views of both males and females.

Feminist writers such as Cain (1986) and Smart (1990) also argue that the categorization by sociologists into areas of study (criminology, social class, politics, and so on) has failed to show the pattern of oppression that women face in all these areas – only by transgressing these categories can feminists gain a real view of their situation and of patriarchy.

## Left realism

Marxist or critical sociologists saw the role of sociology as uncovering the means by which capitalism oppressed the majority of the population. This call to arms was responded to enthusiastically by criminologists such as Taylor, Walton and Young. However, one of these writers, Jock Young, later rejected this approach and helped co-found a very different, and currently influential new school of thought in sociology, now known as 'left realism' (Lea and Young 1984). Left realists argue that rather than wait for a Marxist revolution, it is better to apply sociological research and analysis to social problems as less powerful groups in society experience them, and then to seek ways to resolve these problems. The crucial difference is that this resolution of problems is within capitalism. These left realists are therefore committed, but to improvements within the currently existing political and economic arrangements. See Chapter 2 Topic 5 for more detail on left realism

# Research ethics

By **ethics**, we refer to the moral dilemmas that sociologists face when undertaking and writing up their research. Research ethics are closely interwoven with the debates over value freedom and objectivity, although there are other distinctive concerns that go beyond the value-freedom debate.

Whatever the view of the researcher regarding the importance of values in research, no sociologist would wish the actual procedure of research to harm those being studied or to produce a piece of research that was not as 'true' to the facts uncovered as possible. Ethical procedure is so important to sociologists that the British Sociological Association – the official body of sociology in Britain – has actually issued a guide to ethics that all researchers are expected to follow. Punch (1994) has summarized the main ethical concerns of sociology as follows:

- *Harm* – Any research undertaken must not cause any harm either directly or indirectly to those being studied (although a further question arises: what should a researcher do if the people under study are going to harm someone else?).
- *Consent* – Any person or group being studied, wherever possible, should give their consent to being the subject of research. This usually involves an honest explanation of the research being undertaken and the future use of the material obtained.
- *Deception* – The researcher should, wherever possible, be clear about their role to those being studied.
- *Privacy and confidentiality of data* – The information obtained should not breach the privacy of the person being studied, and nothing should be published that the person regards as confidential. Research should not, therefore, provide the real name or address of a person being studied.

## Dealing with ethical issues

These ethical concerns may seem necessary, but following them can pose great difficulties for sociologists engaged in certain research methods, such as **covert participant observation**. Difficulties also arise in certain areas of research – for example amongst young people, those engaged in criminal or deviant activities, and those with learning difficulties or suffering from mental illness.

An example of both of these fine lines between acting ethically and crossing the boundary can be found in Hobbs' ethnographic study of East End criminals and local CID officers (1988). During his study he found out about many illegal activities committed by both villains and police officers, including acts of violence. Hobbs decided not to pass any information from one group to the other, and despite knowing about criminal activities, he decided that the most 'ethical' thing to do was not to interfere in any way.

Hobbs also mixed overt and covert styles of research with the police. Overtly, he was conducting research through interviews, but covertly he befriended a number of police officers and carefully studied them in their social lives without telling them what he was doing. Hobbs' work can be questioned for its rather dubious ethics in terms of condoning law-breaking behaviour (which was sometimes serious) and in researching the detectives informally without their consent. However, in doing both these activities, he produced a more vibrant and possibly more accurate piece of research than if he had adhered to the 'correct procedures'.

# Key terms

**Committed** where an approach is open in its support of particular values, usually used with reference to Marxist sociologists, feminist sociologists and those wishing to confront racism and discrimination against people with disabilities.

**Covert participant observation** when the researcher joins a group as a full member, and studies them, but does not tell them that he or she is a researcher.

**Critical sociology** a term used for sociology influenced by Marxism.

**Ethics** refers to issues of moral choices.

**Hierarchical** some people are regarded as more important than others.

**Left realism** an approach to social problems that argues it is better to cooperate with the authorities to solve social problems, even if fundamental social change is not brought about.

**Malestream** a feminist term implying criticism of traditional sociology for excluding women from the subject both as sociologists and as the subjects of research.

**Narratives** the name given to the different viewpoints and voices that the researcher allows to be heard in the research.

**Objectivity** the exclusion of values from research.

**Positivism** an approach to sociological research which aims to use the rigour and methods of the physical sciences.

**Reflexivity** constant awareness of, and reflection on, personal biases and values while conducting research

**Subjective** based on personal attitudes, values, meanings and feelings.

**Value freedom** the exclusion of values from research.

**Value laden** the belief that sociology cannot be value free and that it is a mistake to see it as such.

# Focus on research

## Hobbs (1988)

### Studying criminals and policing

Hobbs conducted a famous study of minor criminals and policing in East London. In this study Hobbs needed to spend a large amount of time with police officers in both working and social environments. Indeed, Hobbs became so close to the detectives that he states: 'I often had to remind myself that I was not in a pub to enjoy myself, but to conduct an academic inquiry and repeatedly woke up the following morning with an incredible hangover, facing the dilemma of whether to bring it up or write it up.'

Although Hobbs enjoyed the company of the police officers, he also disapproved of many of the activities which they engaged in – some potentially illegal. He sometimes faced a moral dilemma in that he allowed things to happen that normally he might consider objecting to.

Hobbs, D. (1988) *Doing the Business: Entrepreneurship, the Working Class and Detectives in the East End of London*, Oxford: Oxford University Press

**1** **When faced with a moral choice which could lead to either the end of the research project or a getting a book published, with the consequent academic prestige, what do you think most sociologists choose?**

**2** **How can sociologists ensure that research is ethical?**

# Check your understanding

1. What is meant by 'positivism'?
2. How do positivistic sociologists think the problem of values can be overcome?
3. How can the funding for research influence its content, according to Philo and Miller?
4. Compare the views of Becker and Gouldner on values in sociology.
5. Why do postmodernists see it as impossible to even try to overcome the issue of values?
6. What do we mean by 'committed sociology'? Give two examples.
7. Identify and explain three ethical issues faced by sociologists.

# Activities

## Research idea

Design two questionnaires aiming to discover young women's views on feminism. The first must discover that feminism is still important and relevant to young women, the second that it has gone too far and young women do not support it.

What different questions could you use to get these different results? Could you interpret answers in different ways?

## Web.task

1. Go to the MORI website at **www.ipsos-mori.com**. This contains a wide range of opinion surveys. Take a few examples of their surveys. Check who is sponsoring the research and see if you can identify any evidence of the intrusion of values, for example in the motives for the research and in the sorts of questions asked.

2. The British Sociological Association website lists all ethical issues that sociologists should consider when they undertake research. There is a summary by Punch in the main text, but it is worth exploring the original.

   Go to **www.britsoc.co.uk** and then click on 'Equality and Ethics'. On this page choose 'Statement of Ethical Practice'; finally go through each of the headings on this page.

   Based on what you find there, what would you have to do if you wished to interview 14-year-old students in a local comprehensive to find out their views on drug use?

## An eye on the exam Values and ethics

# Below the Breadline: Life on the Minimum Wage

**Fran Abrams (2002)**

Fran Abrams was a journalist for the Guardian newspaper who was asked to study what life is like relying on the minimum wage. Abrams took on three different jobs in three different parts of the country for a period of four weeks in each location and attempted to live on the minimum wages paid by her employers. The jobs were a cleaner in London, working in a food and preserve factory in Doncaster and in an old people's home in an unidentified town in Scotland.

Abrams did not tell people that she was an investigative journalist and attempted to live fully among the people she met during the course of her research. This was possible because she was the appropriate age and sex to have taken on casual labour and so was able to blend into her assumed roles. It was not necessary for her to change her name although she is careful to hide the identities of those whose lives she describes. The book is dedicated to them.

Abrams found it easy to find low-paid work but very difficult to live on the minimum wage. Often companies stopped part of her wages for essential items such as uniforms and safety equipment, thus bringing down pay even more. Work was generally boring and demeaning with most satisfaction coming from her relationships with other workers.

Adapted from Blundell, J. and Griffiths, J. (2003) Sociology since 1995 Volume 2, Lewes: Connect Publications

**1** **Outline and explain why ethical issues are important in sociological research.** **(15 marks)**

**2** **Outline and assess the view that sociologists should always be value free when researching the experience of low-paid work.** **(25 marks)**

### Grade booster Getting top marks in question 2

In this question you need to start by explaining the idea of value freedom and then go on to discuss why value freedom might be desirable in sociological research on this subject. Finally, you need to discuss the problems and disadvantages of attempting to be value free when studying this topic before reaching a balanced conclusion.

The idea of value freedom is associated with a positivist approach to research which holds that sociologists should be objective and focus on 'social facts' – Abrams approach clearly does not match these criteria – explain why.

However, there are a range of problems with the idea of value freedom, for example is it possible or practical to be value free when immersing yourself in the situation you are studying? Critical sociologists such as feminists and Marxists believe that value freedom is not even desirable – Abrams should be committed to taking the side of the low-paid women. The concept of reflexivity might be useful in a balanced conclusion.

# Exam Practice

## The Family and Community Life of Older People

**Chris Phillipson et al. (2001)**

The aim of the study was to research the family and community life of older people in three locations and, by comparing the findings with those of earlier studies, to discover what changes and developments had occurred.

The research involved two phases. The first phase consisted of questionnaires returned by 627 older people from three areas selected for the research: Bethnal Green in East London, Woodford in Essex and Wolverhampton in the West Midlands. These areas were chosen as they had been the location for previous studies of old age and thus could provide baseline data to map changes over time. The researchers used a random sample drawn from the registers of General Practitioners in these areas. The response rates in the three areas were 63%, 65% and 78% respectively.

The samples were stratified by age and gender, and also by ethnicity in the case of Bethnal Green. 62% of respondents were women and 38% men, reflecting the proportions of older men and women in the population. The sample's marital status closely reflected that predicted by other research: 55% married, 31% widowed, 9% single, 5% divorced or separated.

The second phase involved in-depth interviews producing qualitative data. 62 people over 75 who had indicated in the first phase that they were willing to take part were interviewed. There were also 18 interviews with younger people who were named by these respondents as part of their social network. Finally, there were 23 interviews with Bangladeshi and Punjabi families in Bethnal Green and Wolverhampton, and two group interviews with people working with older members of these ethnic groups.

The questions in the questionnaire and interview were designed to investigate seven main issues:

- Changes in household composition
- Changes in the geographical proximity of kin and relatives
- Extent and type of help provided by family
- Contact and relationship with neighbours
- Relationships with friends
- Involvement in social and leisure activities
- Experiences of minority ethnic groups

The main finding of the research is that over the last fifty years there has been a shift from old age being experienced within the family group to old age being shaped within personal communities in which friends may be as important as immediate family.

Adapted from Blundell, J. and Griffiths, J. (2002) Sociology since 1995 Volume 1, Lewes: Connect Publications

**1 Outline and explain why sociologists often use representative samples when doing research.** ***(15 marks)***

Representative refers to whether a sample represents the target population of the study. If a sociologist does not use a representative sample, the research cannot be generalized to the target population and the research lacks validity. Therefore using a representative sample is a very important factor in carrying out research. In order to carry out research which is representative, sociologists use large samples, which are often stratified as shown in Phillipson's questionnaires. If a large sample is used, it is more likely to represent the views of most/all participants of the target population. This is further achieved by stratifying the sample by the most important factors as chosen by the researcher, for example in the questionnaires in 'The family and community life of older people' the sample was stratified by age and gender, as well as ethnicity in one case. Quantitative data is more likely to use a representative sample as it is usually a quicker method and therefore possible to contact a larger sample, however qualitative methods can still be representative. A sample which is not representative of the target population will not provide the researcher with the information they set out to find.

10/15

Good idea to start with a definition of representative but try to avoid repeating parts of the word you are defining – the word 'cross-section' would have displayed more understanding. The concept of 'generalized' is crucial to this answer so it is important to use in the first few lines. However, it could have been further explained and illustrated by using the Phillipson study as an example. The crucial factor in determining the representativeness of a sample is not so much the size of the sample as the way the sample is stratified to match the characteristics of the target population. This answer does not really make clear how stratifying a sample helps its representativeness.

In general, there is evidence of good understanding but the answer would have benefited from more examples drawn from both the study provided and from the candidate's wider sociological knowledge.

# Exam Practice

**2 Outline and assess the view that questionnaires provide the most useful method for sociological research into the lives of older people. *(33 marks)***

Questionnaires are a frequently used method by sociologists. They have a number of advantages over other methods. One example of this is the high levels of reliability. As if all questionnaires given to participants are the same and are a highly standardised method, the research can be easily replicated by using the same questionnaires. Questionnaires are particularly good for finding specific information, especially for supporting a hypothesis. Therefore questionnaires are a method which could easily be used by sociologists to find out about the lives of older people and gain an overall picture, before continuing with more research. If the participant is likely to be embarrassed by the questions being asked, the fact there is no interviewer with them should reduce this and this may be especially useful in the case of the lives of older people, as they can be more reluctant to voice personal information than younger people.

The start of the answer would have been helped by a quick definition of a questionnaire and an explanation of the different types e.g. closed questions, self-completion etc. The idea of reliability is applied accurately but the idea of 'specific information' needs to unpacked. What exactly does this mean? The paragraph goes on to link to the topic in the question but could have been much more specific, for example by using the list of issues provided in the extract. Which of these would have been suitable to investigate using a questionnaire? Why?

Another area addressed by using questionnaires to research into the lives of older people is the access to a sample. Questionnaires provide easy access to a large sample of older participants which means the data gathered is more likely to be able to be broadly generalized. Questionnaires also provide an easy way to contact older people. If they are unable to go out to take part in the research, the researcher can contact these people through email or mail, and older people without access to the internet will be able to receive the questionnaire via mail, or have them given to them by hand. Questionnaires are also easy to analyze as they provide clear information to the researcher, particularly if they are coded. Well-designed questionnaires can provide highly valid data to researchers.

The first couple of sentences are a little confused. It's not the questionnaire itself that provides access to a large sample or an easy way to contact older people. In the extract, it appears that doctors' surgeries were used to provide access to the sample. It is true, however, that questionnaires offer a quick and convenient method of collecting data from a large number of people.

However there are some issues with using questionnaires to carry out research. One of these is that unless all the key concepts are very clearly operationalised, each older person will interpret the question in their own way or may not understand the question. This reduces the validity, which is a key flaw of the questionnaire. Another way in which the validity is reduced is that without a researcher present while the participant fills out the questionnaire, the researcher cannot know for certain that it was filled out by the older person it was designed for, as it could be filled out by any member of the household. This would therefore reduce how representative the research was. Another key issue in carrying out questionnaires is the low response rate. Without an incentive, many participants do not bother taking part in questionnaires and those who do take part often have particularly strong feelings on the subject and therefore people who do not have strong feelings on the matter will not have their views represented, again affecting the validity of the study.

This is the part of the answer devoted to critical assessment. There are some good points but the opportunity is missed to link each one to the issue of older people. For example, many older people may respond better to an interviewer who can establish rapport than to a faceless self-completion questionnaire. Links to interpretive criticisms of positivistic methods could also be introduced at this point as interpretivists would argue that questionnaires will be much less effective at exploring older people's subjective meanings and experiences than the more qualitative method also used in the research above.

Questionnaires can be a very useful and efficient way of carrying out research. However without careful planning and caution taken when undertaking the research, they can provide results which do not give a clear picture of what is being studied, therefore reducing the validity. In order to check, questionnaires should be piloted before being fully carried out and questionnaires should be very carefully organised.

16/25

This conclusion is a bit vague and does not really add much to the answer. It could really apply to any method.

### An examiner comments

Two key improvements would really benefit this answer. First, more references to the extract provided – make sure you spend enough time reading through the summary and annotating key points after reading the question – and to other examples of sociological research. Second, a consideration of the link between the questionnaire method and positivism would have created more opportunities to provide criticisms from an interpretive point of view.

**Table 8.1** Units of study and assessment

| Unit | Title | Topics | Length of exam | Form of assessment |
|---|---|---|---|---|
| G673 | Power and control | • Crime and deviance<br>• Education<br>• Mass media<br>• Power and politics | 1.5 hours | There are three essay questions on each topic. You must answer two, on the same topic or on different topics. |
| G674 | Exploring social inequality and difference | • Social inequality and difference<br>• Exploring sociological research | 2 hours | The exam is based on a summary of one piece of research. The first two questions on methods are compulsory, then there is a choice of two 'options', each consisting of two further questions on social inequality and difference. |

The 'Social inequality and difference' unit also covers sociological research methods in relation to the study of social inequality and difference.

# How will I be assessed?

## Skills

The skills you will acquire and develop in your A2 course are tested in the examinations by two 'assessment objectives'.

### *Assessment objective one (AO1): Knowledge and understanding*

This requires you to demonstrate your knowledge and understanding of the topic area that forms the basis of the assessment. It covers knowledge and understanding of relevant sociological theories, methods, concepts, studies and other forms of evidence. You should also be able to refer to relevant social policies, issues and events. Also included in AO1 is the skill of communication. While this is not assessed separately, and therefore does not carry a particular mark weighting, it is an important skill, as poor communication will prevent you from showing the examiner what you mean.

### *Assessment objective two (AO2): Analysis, evaluation and application*

Good analysis is shown by presenting an informed, detailed and accurate discussion of a particular theory, perspective, study or event, and also by the ability to present your arguments and evidence in a clear and logical manner. Evaluation refers to your ability to recognise and discuss the strengths and weaknesses of theories, perspectives, studies, sociological methods and data presented in a variety of forms. Application involves the ability to apply what you know to the set question in an appropriate way.

### *Units of assessment/exams*

The basic structure of the units of assessment is shown in Table 8.1, and the question structure is discussed in more detail in the next section. The weighting given to each of the two A2 Units is given in Table 8.2, which shows the percentage of the marks allocated to each unit and to each set of skills in terms of the full A level.

Remember that the first 50% of A-level marks are allocated for the AS course.

# How can I do well in the written examinations?

## Question style and structure

### *Power and control (G673)*

Three essay questions are provided for each of the four topics available (Crime and deviance, Education, Mass media, Power and politics). The essay questions will ask you to 'Outline and assess ....'. The subject of the question may be a particular view, theoretical position or sociological explanation for example. You can choose two essays on the same topic or answer on two different topics. Each essay is worth 50 marks and you should give yourself about 40 minutes for each of

**Table 8.2** Weighting given to A2 units at A-level

| Unit | Title | % of total A level | Skills tested |
|---|---|---|---|
| G673 | Power and control | 25% | AO1: 12%<br>AO2: 13% |
| G674 | Exploring social inequality and difference | 25% | AO1: 11%<br>AO2: 14% |

the two you are required to answer. This will leave you a little time for planning and reading through your answers.

### *Exploring social inequality and difference (G674)*

In this exam you are provided with a summary of a piece of sociological research that investigates an aspect of social inequality and difference. Unlike the first AS exam, this is not provided in advance. The first two questions are compulsory and will focus on sociological methods and on your ability to interpret and apply material from the study to your answers. The first is worth 15 marks and will ask you to 'Outline and explain' why a particular method or approach is used by sociologists. It is likely that the subject of the question will be linked in some way to the stimulus material. The second question is worth 25 marks and will ask you to 'Outline and assess ...'. The subject of this question will be a particular aspect of the research strategy used in the stimulus material and you will be asked to assess this in relation to the subject matter of the study.

These two questions require you to interpret and apply material from the study provided and to use your wider sociological knowledge of research methods from both the AS and A2 parts of the course. Examples of these types of question are provided in the 'Eye on the Exam' features throughout Chapter 7.

You will then be given a choice for the last two questions – two sets of questions are provided and you select one set. They cover issues of social inequality and difference. The first will ask you to 'Outline the evidence that ...'. The subject of the question will be an aspect of social inequality and difference. You need to display a range of knowledge (for example, studies, statistical patterns and trends and contemporary events) about this aspect of your study. There is no need to evaluate material or look at any alternative views – doing this will simply be wasting your time. The evidence may be drawn from any AS or A2 topic you have studied, and from your wider sociological knowledge. The best answers will cover a wide range of evidence in some detail. This question is worth 20 marks and you should spend about the same number of minutes answering it.

The second question is an essay-style task, written in the same style as the 'Power and control' paper. You will be asked to 'Outline and assess ...' a view, theory, sociological explanation etc. This question is worth 40 marks and you should spend at least the same number of minutes on it.

Don't feel you have to draw material only from this unit - you are encouraged to introduce ideas and evidence from other topics you have studied, at both AS and A2 as well as from your broader sociological knowledge.

Giving yourself roughly one minute for each of the 100 marks available in this exam will allow you 20 minutes to read and annotate the study provided and to plan and read through your answers.

### *Command words in the A2 exams*

Questions in the A2 exams will include the following command words:

- *Outline:* provide an overview and summary of the key points.
- *Explain:* pick out distinguishing features and say why they are important. Often you will need to give reasons or causes for social changes, trends, relationships or research decisions.
- *Assess:* look at all the theories and evidence that relate to the question and reach a balanced conclusion.

## How can I find out more?

The specification, examiners' reports, past papers, mark schemes and other guidance material are available from the OCR website at www.ocr.org.uk.

## Exam tips

- **Read the whole question carefully before you begin your answer. If you find you are trying to use the same material twice, make sure you have fully understood the questions as the examiner strives to prevent duplication of material.**
- **Keep an eye on the time - it is very important that you allow sufficient time for each question. Before the exams, work out roughly the time when you should be starting each question.**
- **In all your answers, refer to appropriate theories, perspectives, studies and evidence to support and inform your response. Where possible, bring in examples of recent or current events or social policies to illustrate the points you are making.**
- **Finally, make sure that you answer the question that the examiner has set, rather than the one that you wished for. This is a serious point as many candidates fail to achieve marks because they have not kept to the focus of the question. No question is likely to ask you simply to 'Write everything you know about ...', and yet this is what some students do. However, it is better to write something than to sit there doing nothing. Leaving a blank means you cannot score any marks, but if you write something, it could be correct enough or relevant enough to pick up some marks.**

# BIBLIOGRAPHY


Abbott, P. (1990) 'A re-examination of "Three theses re-examined"', in G. Payne (ed.) *The Social Mobility of Women,* London: Routledge

Abercrombie, N. and Warde, A. (2000) *Contemporary British Society* (3rd edn), Cambridge: Polity Press

Abercrombie, N., Hill, S. and Turner, B.S. (1980) *The Dominant Ideology Thesis*, London: Allen and Unwin

Abraham, J. (1996) *Are Girls Necessary? Lesbian writing and modern histories,* London: Routledge

Adler, I. (1975) *Sisters in Crime*, New York: McGraw-Hill

Adonis, A. and Pollard, S. (1998) *A Class Act: the Myth of Britain's Classless Society,* Harmondsworth: Penguin

Adorno, T.W. (1991) *The Culture Industry: Selected Essays on Mass Culture*, London: Routledge

Agbetu, T. (2006) *Institutional Racism and the British Media*, www.ligali.org

Age Concern (2000) *How Ageist is Britain?* www.ageconcern.org.uk

Akers, R.L. (1967) 'Problems in the sociology of deviance: social definitions and behaviour', *Social Forces* 46 (4)

Akinti, P. (2003) 'Captivate us', *The Guardian,* 21 February

Albert, B., McBride, R. and Seddon, D. (2002) *Perspectives on Disability, Poverty and Technology*, Norwich: University of East Anglia

Alexander, J. (1985) *Neo-Functionalism*, London: Sage

Allen, J. (2000) 'Power: its institutional guises (and disguises)', in G. Hughes and R. Fergusson (eds) *Ordering Lives: Family, Work and Welfare*, London: The Open University/Routledge

Almy, M. *et al.* (eds) (1984) *Difference: On Representation and Sexuality*, New York: The New Museum of Contemporary Art

Althusser, L. (1969) *For Marx*, Harmondsworth: Penguin

Althusser, L. (1971) 'Ideology and ideological state apparatuses', in *Lenin and Philosophy and Other Essays*, London: New Left Books

Althusser, L. (1971) *Lenin and Philosophy and Other Essays*, London: New Left Books

Ameli, S., Marandi, S., Ahmed, S., Kara, S. and Merali, A. (2007) *The British Media and Muslim Representations: The Ideology of Demonisation*, London: Islamic Human Rights Commission

Anderson, S., Kinsey, R., Loader, I. and Smith, C. (1994) *Young People, Crime and Policing in Edinburgh,* Aldershot: Avebury

Ansley (1976) quoted in J. Bernard, *The Future of Marriage*, Harmondsworth: Penguin, p.233

Anthias, F. (2001) 'The concept of social division and theorising social stratification: looking at ethnicity and class', *Sociology,* 35(4), pp.835–54

Arber, A., Dale, S. and Gilbert, N. (1986) 'The limitations of existing social class classification of women', in A. Jacoby (ed.) *The Measurement of Social Class*, Guildford: Social Research Association

Aron, R. (1967) 'Social class, political class, ruling class' in R. Bendix and S.M. Lipset (eds) *Main Currents in Sociological Thought,* Vols 1 and 2, Harmondsworth: Penguin

Aubert, V. (1952) 'White collar crime and social structure', *American Journal of Sociology*, 58

Aust, R. and Simmons, J. (2002) *Rural Crime in England and Wales 2001/02*, London: Home Office

Babb, P., Haezewindt, P. and Martin, J. (eds) (2004) *Focus on Social Inequalities,* London: Office for National Statistics

Bachrach, P. and Baratz, M.S. (1970) *Power and Poverty: Theory and Practice*, Oxford: Oxford University Press

Bagdikian, B. (2004) *The New Media Monopoly*, Boston: Beacon Press

Baldwin, J. and Bottoms, A.E. (1976) *The Urban Criminal,* London: Tavistock

Ball, S. (2002) *Class Strategies and the Education Market: The Middle Classes and Social Advantage,* London: RoutledgeFalmer

Ball, S.J. (1981) *Beachside Comprehensive: A Case-Study of Secondary Schooling*, Cambridge: Cambridge University Press

Ball, S.J., Bowe, R. and Gerwitz, S. (1994) 'Market forces and parental choice', in S. Tomlinson (ed.) *Education Reform and Its Consequences*, London: IPPR/Rivers Oram Press

Bandura, A., Ross, D. and Ross, S.A. (1963) 'The imitation of film mediated aggressive models', *Journal of Abnormal and Social Psychology*, 66(1), pp. 3–11

Barak, G. (ed.) (1991) *Crimes by the Capitalist State: An introduction to state criminality*, Albany: State University of New York Press

Barclay, G. and Tavares, C. (1999) *Information on the Criminal Justice System in England and Wales Digest 4*, London: Home Office

Barker, P. (1982) *The Other Britain: A New Society Collection*, London: Routledge & Kegan Paul

Barnett, S. and Weymour , E. (1999) *A Shrinking Iceberg Slowly Travelling South: Changing Trends in British Television*, London: Campaign for Quality Television

Barron, R.G. and Norris, G.M. (1976) 'Sexual divisions and the dual labour market', in D.J. Barker and S. Allen (eds) *Dependence and Exploration in Work and Marriage*, London: Longman

Bartkey, S.C. (1992) 'Reevaluating French feminism', in N. Fraser and S.C. Bartkey (eds) *Critical Essays in Difference, Agency and Culture*, Bloomington: Indiana University Press

Bartley, M., Carpenter, L., Dunnell, K. and Fitzpatrick, R. (1996) 'Measuring inequalities in health: an analysis of mortality patterns using two social classifications', *Sociology of Health and Illness,* 18(4) pp.455–74

Batchelor, S.A., Kitzinger, J. and Burtney, E. (2004) 'Representing young people's sexuality in the 'youth' media', *Health Education Research*, 19(6), pp. 669–76

Bates, I. (ed.) *Youth and Inequality*, Milton Keynes: Open University Press

Baudrillard, J. (1980) *For a Critique of the Political Economy of the Sign*, New York: Telos Press

Baudrillard, J. (1994) *The Illusion of the End*, Cambridge: Polity Press

Baudrillard, J. (1998) *Selected Writings* (M. Poster ed.), Cambridge: Polity Press

Bauman, Z. (1978) *Hermeneutics and Social Sciences: Approaches to Understanding*, London: Hutchinson

Bauman, Z. (1983) 'Industrialism, consumerism and power', *Theory, Culture and Society*, 1(3)

Bauman, Z. (1990) *Thinking Sociologically*, Oxford: Blackwell

Bauman, Z. (2000) 'Sociological enlightenment – For whom, about what?', *Theory, Culture and Society*, 17(2), pp.71–82

BBC (2002) *BBC Race Survey*

BBC (2005) *News Online Survey*

Beck, U. (1992) *Risk Society: Towards a New Modernity*, London: Sage

Becker, A. et al. (2003) 'Binge eating and binge eating disorder in a small-scale, indigenous society: the view from Fiji', published online in Wiley InterScience (www.interscience.wiley.com)

Becker, H. (1963) *The Outsiders: Studies in the Sociology of Deviance,* New York: Free Press

Becker, H. (1970) 'Whose side are we on?', in H. Becker, *Sociological Work*, New Brunswick: Transaction Books

Becker, H. (1971) 'Social class variations in the teacher–pupil relationship', in B. Cosin (ed.) *School and Society,* London: Routledge & Kegan Paul

Benston, M. (1972) 'The political economy of women's liberation', in N. Glazer-Mahlbin and H.Y. Wahrer (eds) *Women in a Man-made World*, Chicago: Rand MacNally

Bernstein, B. (1971) *Class, Codes and Control* (Vol. 1), London: Routledge & Kegan Paul

Berry, C. (1986) 'Message misunderstood', *The Listener* 27 Nov

Best, L. (1993) '"Dragons, dinner ladies and ferrets": Sex roles in children's books', *Sociology Review*, 2(3), Oxford: Philip Allan

Best, S. (2005) *Understanding Social Divisions*, London: Sage

Best, S. and Kellner, D. (1999) 'Rap, Black rage, and racial difference', *Enculturation* 2(2), Spring

Bhaskar, R. (1986) *Scientific Realism and Human Emancipation*, London: Verso

Bhaskar, R. (1998) *The Possibility of Naturalism: A Philosophical Critique of the Contemporary Human Sciences* (3rd edn), New York and London: Routledge

Bhavani, K. (2000) *Feminism and Race*, Oxford: Oxford University Press

Bhopal, R., Phillimore, P. and Kohli, H.S. (1991) 'Inappropriate use of the term "Asian": an obstacle to ethnicity and health research', *Journal of Public Health Medicine*, 13, pp.244–6

Billig, M., Condor, S., Edwards, D., Gane, M., Middleton, D. and Radley, A.R. (1988) *Ideological Dilemmas*, London: Sage Publications

Blackman, S. (1995) *Youth: Positions and Oppositions, Style, Sexuality and Schooling*, Aldershot: Avebury

Blackstone, T. and Mortimore, J. (1994) 'Cultural factors in child-rearing and attitudes to education' in B. Moon and A.S. Mayers (eds) *Teaching and Learning in the Secondary School*, London: Routledge

Blanden, J., Gregg, P. and Machin, S. (2005) *Intergenerational Mobility in Europe and North America*, London: London School of Economics, Centre for Economic Performance

Blumer, H. (1962) 'Society as symbolic interaction', in N. Rose (ed.) *Symbolic Interactionism*, Englewood Hills, NJ: Prentice-Hall

Blumler, J.G. and McQuail, D. (1968) *Television in Politics: Its Uses and Influence*, London: Faber & Faber

Blundell, J. and Griffiths J. (2002) *Sociology since 1995 vol. 1*, Lewes: Connect Publications

Blundell, J. and Griffiths J. (2002) *Sociology since 1995 vol. 2*, Lewes: Connect Publications

Blundell, J. and Griffiths, J. (2008) *Sociology since 2000,* Lewes: Connect Publications

Bocock, B.J. (1986) *Hegemony*, London: Tavistock

Bonger, W. (1916) *Criminality and Economic Conditions,* Chicago: Little Brown

Book Marketing Limited (2000) *Reading the Situation: Book Reading, Buying and Borrowing Habits in Britain*, Library and Information Commission Research Report 34, Book Marketing Limited

Borsay P. (2007) 'Binge drinking and moral panics: historical parallels?' History & Policy website, www.historyandpolicy.org/papers/policy-paper-62.html

Bottero, W. (2005) *Stratification: Social Division and Inequality*, London: Routledge

Bourdieu, P. (1977) 'Cultural reproduction and social reproduction', in J. Karabel and A.H. Halsey (eds) *Power and Ideology in Education*, New York: Oxford University Press, pp.487–511

Bourdieu, P. and Passeron, J. (1977) *Reproduction in Education, Society and Culture*, London: Sage

Bourgois, P. (2003) *In Search of Respect* (2nd edn), Cambridge: Cambridge University Press

Bowles, S. and Gintis, H. (1976) *Schooling in Capitalist America: Educational Reform and the Contradictions of Economic Life*, New York: Basic Books

Bowling, B. (1999) *Violent Racism: Victimisation, Policing and Social Context* (revised edn), Oxford: Oxford University Press

Bowling, B. and Phillips, C. (2002) *Racism, Crime and Justice*, Harlow: Pearson

Box, S. (1981) *Deviance, Reality and Society* (2nd edn), Eastbourne: Holt Rheinhart Wilson

Box, S. (1983) *Crime, Power and Mystification*, London: Tavistock

Boyle, R. (2005) 'Press the red button now: television and technology', *Sociology Review*, Nov

Boyle, R. (2007) 'The "now" media generation, *Sociology Review*, Sep

Bradley, H. (1996) *Fractured Identities: Changing Patterns of Inequality*, Cambridge: Polity Press

Bradley, H. (1999) *Gender and Power in the Workplace*, Basingstoke, Macmillan

Braithwaite, J. (1984) *Corporate Crime in the Pharmaceutical Industry*, London: Routledge

Braithwaite, J. (2000) *Regulation, Crime and Freedom*, Aldershot: Ashgate

Brake, M. (1980) *The Sociology of Youth and Youth Subcultures*, London: Routledge

Brantingham, P.J. and Brantingham, P.L. (1984) *Patterns of Crime*, New York: Macmillan

Brantingham, P.J. and Brantingham, P.L. (1991) *Environmental Criminology* (revised edn), Prospect Heights: Waveland Press

Braverman, H. (1974) *Labour and Monopoly Capitalism*, New York: Monthly Press

Brenner, M., Brown, J. and Canter, M. (1985) *The Research Interview: Uses and Approaches*, London: Academic Press

Bristol Fawcett Society (2008) *Representation, Misrepresentation, No Representation: Women in the Media*, Bristol Fawcett Society/Bristol Feminist Network

British Attitude Survey, www.statistics.gov.uk/STATBASE/Source.asp?ComboState=Show+Links&More=Y&vlnk=619&LinkBtn.x=26&LinkBtn.y=14

*British Youth Lifestyles Survey* (2000) Home Office Research Study 209

Brooks, A. (1997) *Postfeminisms: Feminisms, Cultural Theory and Cultural Forms*, London: Routledge

Brown, Gordon (2006) Donald Dewar memorial lecture, Glasgow, 12 October 2006

Brown, S. (1997) 'High and low quality performance in manufacturing firms', *TQM Journal,* 9(4), pp.292–9

Bryman, A. (2004) *Social Research Methods* (2nd edn), Oxford: Oxford University Press

Bryman, A. and Burgess, A. (1994) *Analysing Qualitative Data,* London: Routledge

Buckingham, D. (1996) *Moving Images: Understanding Children's Emotional Responses to Television*, Manchester: Manchester University Press

Buckingham, D. (ed.) (1993) *Reading Audiences: Young People and the Media*, Manchester: Manchester University Press

Bulman, J. (2003) 'Patterns of pay: results of the 2002 New Earnings Survey', *Labour Market Trends*, London: HMSO

Burns, J. and Bracey, P. (2001) 'Boys' underachievement: Issues, challenges and possible ways forward', *Westminster Studies in Education*, 24, pp.155–66

Buswell, C. (1987) *Training for Low Pay*, Basingstoke: Macmillan

Butler, D. and Stokes, D. (1971) *Political Change in Britain*, London: Macmillan

Butler, R. (1969) 'Ageism: another form of bigotry', *The Gerontologist*, 9, p.243

Butler, T. and Hamnetta, C. (2007) 'The Geography of Education: Introduction', *Urban Studies,* 44(7), June 2007, pp. 1161–74

Butsch, R. (1992) 'Class and gender in four decades of television situation comedy', *Critical Studies in Mass Communication*, 9, pp.387–99

Button, J. (1995) *The Radicalism Handbook*, London: Cassell

Cain, M. (1986) 'Realism, feminism, methodology and law', *International Journal of the Sociology of Law,* 14

Callendar, C. and Jackson, J. (2004) *Fear of Debt and Higher Education Participation,* London: South Bank University

Campbell, B. (1985) *Wigan Pier Revisited,* London: Virago Press Ltd

Campbell, B. (1993) *Goliath: Britain's Dangerous Places*, London: Methuen

Cannadine, D. (1998) *Class in Britain*, London: Yale University Press

Cantril, H. (1940) *The Invasion from Mars: A study in the psychology of panic*, Princeton, NJ: Princeton University Press

Caplow, T. (1954) *The Sociology of Work*, New York: McGraw-Hill

Carlen, P. (1988) *Women, Crime and Poverty*, Milton Keynes: Open University Press

Carlen, P. (1992) 'Criminal women and criminal justice: the limits to and potential of feminist and left realist perspectives', in R. Matthews and J. Young (eds) *Issues in Realist Criminology,* London: Sage

Carrabine, E., Iganski, P., Lee, M., Plummer, K. and South, N. (2004) *Criminology: A Sociological Introduction*, London: Routledge

Carrigan, M. and Szmigin, I. (2000) 'The ethical advertising covenant: regulating ageism in UK advertising', *International Journal of Advertising,* 19(4), pp.509–28

Carrington, B., Francis, B., Skelton, C., Hutchings, M., Read, B. and Hall, I. (2007 in press) 'A Perfect Match? Pupils' and teachers' views of the impact of matching educators and learners by gender', Research Papers in Education

Cashmore, W. E. (1989) *United Kingdom? Class, Race and Gender since the War*, London: Unwin Hyman

Castles, S. and Kosack, G.C. (1973) *Immigrant Workers and Class Structure in Western Europe*, Oxford: OUP

Chahal, K. and Julienne, L. (1999) *We Can't All Be White*, York: Joseph Rowntree Foundation

Chambliss, W.J. (1975) 'Towards a political economy of crime', *Theory and Society,* Vol. 2 pp.149–70

Chambliss, W.J. and Mankoff, M. (1976) *Whose Law? What Order?*, New York: John Wiley & Sons

Chandler, D. (1994) *Notes on the Construction of Reality in TV News Programmes*, www.aber.ac.uk/media/Modules

Chapman, S. and Langley P. (2010) *Key Studies in Crime and Deviance*, Lewes: Connect Publications

Chapman, S. and Langley P. (2010) *Key Studies in Education*, Lewes: Connect Publications

Charlton, T., Gunter, B. and Hannan, A. (2000) *Broadcast Television Effects in a Remote Community*, Hillsdale, NJ: Lawrence Erlbaum

Childs, S. and Campbell, R. (2008) 'Is politics gendered?', *Sociology Review*, November

Clark, T.N. and Hoffman-Martinot, V. (eds) (1998) *The New Political Culture*, Boulder CO: Westview

Clarke, M. (1990) *Business Crime: Its Nature and Control*, Bristol: Policy Press

Clarke, R.V.G. (1995) 'Situational crime prevention', in M. Tonry and D. Farrington (eds) *Building a Safer Society*, Chicago: University of Chicago

Clarke, R.V.G. (ed.) (1992) *Situational Crime Prevention,* New York: Harrow & Heston

Clegg, S.R. (1989) *Frameworks of Power*, London: Sage

Clinard, M.B. (1974) *Sociology of Deviant Behavior*, New York: Holt, Rhinehart & Winston

Cloward, R. and Ohlin, L. (1960) *Delinquency and Opportunity*, London: Collier Macmillan

Coard, B. (1971) *How the West-Indian Child is Made Educationally Subnormal in the British School System*, London: New Beacon Books

Cohen, A. (1955) *Delinquent Boys*, New York: The Free Press

Cohen, L.E. and Felson, M. (1979) 'Social change and crime rate trends: a routine activities approach', *American Sociological Review*, 44

Cohen, N. (2005) 'Capital punishment', *The Observer*, 6 November

Cohen, N. (2009) *Waiting for the Etonians: Reports from the Sickbed of Liberal England*, London: Fourth Estate

Cohen, P. (1984) 'Against the new vocationalism', in L. Bates, J. Clarke, R. Moore and P. Willis *Schooling for the Dole*, Basingstoke: Macmillan

Cohen, R. and Kennedy, P. (2000) *Global Sociology*, London: Palgrave Macmillan

Cohen, R. and Rai, S. (eds) (2000) *Global Social Movements*, Athlone: Continuum International Publishing Group

Cohen, S. (1972, 1980 [2nd edn]) *Folk Devils and Moral Panics*, London: Paladin

Cohen, S. (1985) *Visions of Social Control*, Cambridge: Polity

Cohen, S. (2002) 'Moral panics as cultural politics', (New introduction), in *Folk Devils and Moral Panics: The Creation of the Mods and Rockers* (3rd edn), London: Routledge

Cohen, S. and Young, J. (1981) *The Manufacture of News,* London: Constable

Collins, H. and Pinch, T. (1998) *The Golem: What You Should Know About Science* (2nd edn) Cambridge: Cambridge University Press

Collison, M. (1995) *Police, Drugs and Community*, London: Free Association Books

Collison, M. (1996) 'In search of the high life', *British Journal of Criminology,* 36(3), pp.428–44

Colman, A. and Gorman, L. (1982) 'Conservatism, dogmatism and authoritarianism amongst British police officers', *Sociology*, 16(1)

Conklin, J.E. (1977) *Illegal but not Criminal: Business Crime in America*, Englewood Cliffs, NJ: Prentice Hall

Connell, R.W. (1995) *Masculinities*, Cambridge: Polity Press

Connolly, P. (1998) *Racism, Gender Identities and Young* Children, London: Routledge & Kegan Paul

Connolly, P. and Keenan, M. (2000) *Racial Attitudes and Prejudice in Northern Ireland* (Report 1), Belfast: Northern Ireland Statistics and Research Agency

Cornford, J. and Robins, K. (1999) 'New media', in J. Stokes and A. Reading (eds) *The Media in Britain: Current debates and developments*, London: MacMillan

Couldry, N., Curran J. et al. (2007a) *Media Ownership and the News*, Submission to House of Lords Select Committee on Communications, Goldsmiths Media Research Group

Couldry, N., Livingstone, S. and Markham, T. (2007b) *Media Consumption and Public Engagement: Beyond the Presumption of Attention,* London: Palgrave Macmillan

Coussins, J. (1976) *The Equality Report*, NCCL Rights for Women Unit: London

Coxall, W.N. (1981) *Parties and Pressure Groups*, London: Longman

Craib, I. (1992) *Anthony Giddens*, London: Routledge

Craig, S. (ed.) (1992) *Men, Masculinity and the Media*, Newbury Park, CA: Sage

Crewe, I. (1984) 'The electorate: partisan de-alignment ten years on', in H. Berrington (ed.) *Change in British Politics*, London: Frank Cass

Crick, B. (2000) *Essays on Citizenship*, London: Continuum

Croall, H. (2001) *Understanding White-collar Crime*, Milton Keynes: Open University Press

Crook, S., Pakulski, J. and Waters, M. (1992) *Postmodernisation: Change in Advanced Society*, London: Sage

Cuff, E.C., Sharrock W.W. and Francis, D.W. (1990) *Perspectives in Sociology*, London: Routledge

Cumberbatch, G. (2004) *Video Violence: Villain or Victim?* Report for the Video Standards Council available at www.videostandards.org.uk/video_violence.htm

Cummings, E. and Henry, W. (1961) *Growing Old: The Process of Disengagement*, New York: Basic Books

Curran, J. (2003) 'Press History' in J. Curran and J. Seaton (2003) – *see next entry*

Curran, J. and Seaton, J. (2003) *Power without Responsibility: the press, broadcasting, and new media in Britain* (6th edn), London: Routledge

Dahl, R. (1961) *Who Governs: Democracy and Power in an American City*, New Haven: Yale University Press

Dalton, K. (1964) *The Pre-menstrual Syndrome and Progesterone Therapy,* London: Heinemann Medical

Darlington, Y. and Scott, D. (2002) *Qualitative Research in Practice: Stories from the Field*, Milton Keynes: Open University Press

Davidson, K. (2006) 'Gender and an ageing population', *Sociology Review*, 15(4), Apr

Davies, N. (2008) *Flat Earth News,* London: Chatto & Windus

Davies, T. (1994) 'Disabled by society', *Sociology Review*, 3(4), April

Davis, K. and Moore, W.E. (1955) 'Some principles of stratification', in Bendix, R. and Lipset, S.M. (eds) *Class, Status and Power* (2nd edn 1967), London: Routledge & Kegan Paul

Davis, M. (1990) *City of Quartz*, London: Vintage

Deacon, D.N., Golding, P. and Billig, M. (2001) 'Press and broadcasting: "real issues" and real coverage', in P. Norris, P. (ed) *Britain Votes 2001*, Oxford: Oxford University Press

Delamont, S. (2001) *Changing Women: Unchanged Men: Sociological Perspectives on Gender in a Post-Industrial Society*, Buckingham: Open University Press

Delphy, C. (1977) *The Main Enemy*, London: Women's Research & Resources Centre

Dennis, N. and Erdos, G. (1993) *Families without Fatherhood*, London: IEA

Denscombe, M. (1999) *Sociology Update*, Leicester: Olympus Books

Denscombe, M. (2001) 'Uncertain identities and health-risking behaviour: the case of young people and smoking in late modernity', *British Journal of Sociology*, 52, March

Department for Education and Skills (DfES) (2004) *Every Child Matters. Change for Children in Schools,* London: DfES/HMSO

Department for Education and Skills (DfES) (2006) *Social Mobility: Narrowing Social Class Educational Attainment Gaps,* London: Office for National Statistics

Department for Education and Skills (DfES) (2007) *Green Paper: Raising Expectations: Staying in education and training post-16*, London: DfES

Devine, F. (1992) *Affluent Workers Revisited*, Edinburgh University Press: Edinburgh

Diani, M. (1992) 'The concept of social movement', *Sociological Review*, 40, pp.1–25

Dietz, T. (1998) 'An examination of violence and gender role portrayals in video games: Implications for gender socialization and aggressive behavior', *Sex Roles*, 38, pp. 425–42

Ditton, J. (1977) *Part-time Crime: An Ethnography of Fiddling and Pilferage*, Basingstoke: Macmillan

Doherty, B. (1998) 'Opposition to road building', *Parliamentary Affairs*, 51(3), pp.370-83

Downes, D. (1966) *The Delinquent Solution,* London: Routledge

Doyle (2002) *Media Ownership*, London: Sage

Drew, D. (1995) *Race, Education and Work: The Statistics of Inequality*, Aldershot: Avebury

Duncan, M.C. and Messner, M.A. (2005) *Gender in Televised Sports: News and Highlights Shows, 1998-2004*, Los Angeles: Amateur Athletic Foundation of Los Angeles

Dunn, M. and Gazeley, L. (2008) 'Teachers, social class and underachievement', *British Journal of the Sociology of Education* 29(5) pp. 451-463

Durkheim, E. (1893/1960 reissue) *The Division of Labour in Society*, Glencoe: Free Press

Durkheim, E. (1895/1982 reissue) *The Rules of Sociological Method* (ed. S. Lukes), London: Macmillan

Durkheim, E. (1897/1952) *Suicide: A Study in Sociology*, London: Routledge Kegan Paul

Duverger, M. (1972) *Party Politics and Pressure Groups*, London: Nelson

Dworkin, A. (1988) *Pornography: Men Possessing Women*, New York: E.P. Dutton

Dyer, R. (2002) *The Matter of Images: Essays on Representation*, London: Routledge

Easthope, A. (1990) *What a Man's Gotta Do: The Masculine Myth in Popular Culture*, Boston, MA: Unwin Hyman

Economic and Social Research Council (1997) *Twenty-Something in the 90s: Getting on, Getting by, Getting Nowhere*, Research Briefing, Swindon: ESRC

Edwards, D. and Cromwell, E. (2008) *Guardians of Power: The Myth of the Liberal Media*, London: Pluto Press

Edwards, T. (1997), *Men in the Mirror: Fashion, Masculinity and Consumer Society*, London: Cassell

Elias, N. (1978) *The Civilizing Process: The History of Manners*, Oxford: Blackwell Publishing

Elliot, A. (2002) 'Beck's sociology of risk: a critical assessment', *Sociology*, 36(2), pp.293–315

Ellwood, W. (2001) *The No-Nonsense Guide to Globalisation*, London: Verso

Epstein, D. (1998) 'Real boys don't work: "underachievement", masculinity and the harassment of "sissies"', in D. Epstein, J. Ellwood, V. Hey and J. Maw (eds) *Failing Boys? Issues in Gender and Achievement,* Buckingham: Open University Press

Equal Opportunities Commission (2006) *Facts about Women and Men in Great Britain*, EOC

Ethnic Focus (2004) quoted in I. Burrell, 'Terrestrial TV either ignores Asians or casts them in stereotypical roles', *Independent*, 17 Aug

Etzioni, A. (1993) *The Spirit of Community*, New York: Crown Publishers

Evans, G. (1992) 'Is Britain a class-divided society? A re-analysis and extension of Marshall *et al.*'s study of class consciousness', *Sociology*, 26(2), pp.233–58

Evans, J. and Chandler, J. (2006) 'To buy or not to buy: family dynamics and children's consumption', *Sociological Research Online*, 11(2)

Fahmy, E. (2004) *Encouraging Young People's Political Participation in the UK*, London: Routledge,

Faludi, S. (1992) *The Undeclared War against Women*, London: Chatto & Windus

Farrington, D.P. (1995) 'The development of offending and anti-social behaviour from childhood: key findings from the Cambridge Study in Delinquent Development', *Journal of Child Psychology and Psychiatry*, 36, pp.929–64

Farrington, D.P. and Morris, A.M. (1983) 'Sex, sentencing and reconviction' in *British Journal of Criminology* 23(3)

Farrington, D.P. and Painter, K.A. (2004) *Gender Differences in Offending: Implications for risk focussed prevention,* Home Office Online Report 09/04 www.homeoffice.gov.uk/rds/onlinepubs1.html

Farrington, D.P. and West, D.J. (1990) 'The Cambridge Study in Delinquent Development: a long-term follow-up of 411 London males', in H.J. Kerner and G. Kaiser (eds) *Criminality; Personality, Behaviour and Life History*, Berlin: Springer-Verlag

Faulks, K. (1999) *Political Sociology: A Critical Introduction*, New York University Press

Fawbert, J. (2008) 'Hoodies: moral panic or justifiable concern?', www.beds.ac.uk/news/2008/feb/080214-hoodies

Featherstone, M. and Hepworth, M. (1991) The mask of ageing and the postmodern life course', in M. Featherstone, M. Hepworth and B.S. Turner (eds) *The Body: Social Process and Cultural Theory*, London: Sage

Featherstone, M. and Wernick, A. (1995), *Images of Ageing: Cultural Representations of Later Life*, London & New York: Routledge

Feeley, M. and Simon. J. (1992) 'The new penology: notes on the emerging strategy of corrections and its implications', *Criminology*, 30(4), pp.449–74

Feinstein, L *et al* (2007) *Reducing Inequalities*, London: National Children's Bureau

Ferguson, M. (1983) *Forever Feminine: Women's Magazines and the Cult of Femininity*, London: Heinemann

Ferrell, J. (1999) 'Cultural criminology', *Annual Review of Sociology*, 25(1)

Fesbach, S. and Sanger, J.L. (1971) *Television and Aggression*, San Francisco: Jessey-Bass

Festenstein, M. 'Contemporary Liberalism', in A. Lent (ed) *New Political Thought, London: Lawrence and Wishart*

Feyerabend, P. (1975) *Against Method*, London: New Left Review Editions

Fielding, A. (1995) 'Migration and middle-class formation in England and Wales', in T. Butler and M. Savage (eds) *Social Change and the Middle Class*, London: UCL

Finch, M. 1990 'Sex and address in *Dynasty*', in J.O. Thomson (eds) *The Media Reader*, London: BFI

Finn, D. (1987) *Training without Jobs*, Basingstoke: MacMillan

Firestone, S. (1970) *The Dialectic of Sex*, New York: Bantam Books

Fiske, J. (1987) *Television Culture*. London: Methuen

Fiske, J. and Hartley, J. (2003) *Reading Television*, London: Methuen

Fitzgerald, M., Stockdale, J. and Hale, C. (2003) *Young People's Involvement in Street Crime*, London: Youth Justice Board

Flood-Page, C., Campbell, S., Harrington, V. and Miller, J. (2000) *Youth crime: findings from the 1998/99 Youth Lifestyles Survey*, London: Home Office

Forster, N. (1994) 'The analysis of company documentation', in C. Cassell and G. Symon (eds) *Qualitative Methods in Organizational Research*, London: Sage

Foster, J. (1995) 'Informal social control and community crime prevention', *British Journal of Criminology*, 35

Foucault, M. (1963/1975) *The Birth of the Clinic*, New York: Vintage Books

Foucault, M. (1977) *Discipline and Punish: The Birth of the Prison,* London: Allen Lane

Foucault, M. (1980) *Power/Knowledge: Selected Interviews and Other Writings 1972–77* (ed. C. Gordon), Brighton: Harvester Press

Fouts, G. (1999) quoted on www.mediaawareness.ca/english/issues/stereotyping/women_and-girls/women_beauty.cfm

Francis, B. (1998) *Power Plays: Primary School Children's Constructions of Gender, Power and Adult Work*, Stoke-on-Trent: Trentham Books

Francis, B. (2000) *Boys, Girls and Achievement: Addressing the Classroom Issues,* London: Routledge Falmer

Francis, B. (2005) *The Impact of Gender Constructions on Pupils' Learning and Educational Choices: Final project report*, London: ESRC

Francis, B. and Skelton, C. (2005) *Reassessing Gender and Achievement*, London: Routledge/Falmer

Francis, B., Archer, L., Osgood, J. and Dalgety, J. (2005) *Gender Equality in Work Experience Placements for Young People*. Equal Opportunities Commission

Friedman, L. M. (1999) *The Horizontal Society*, New Haven: Yale University Press

Fulcher, J. and Scott, J. (1999) *Sociology*, Oxford: Oxford University Press

Fuller, M. (1984) 'Black girls in a London comprehensive', in R. Deem (ed.) *Schooling for Women's Work*, London: Routledge

Furlong, A. and Cartmel, F. (1997) *Young People and Social Change*, Buckingham: Open University Press

Furlong, A. and Cartmel, F. (2005) *Vulnerable Young Men in Fragile Labour Markets: Employment, unemployment and the search for long-term security*, York: Joseph Rowntree Foundation

Furlong, A., Cartmel, F., Biggart, A., Sweeting, H. and West, P. (2006) 'Social class in an 'individualised' society', *Sociology Review*, 15(4), pp.28–32

Gallagher (1980) quoted in L. Van Zoonen (1996) *Feminist Media Studies*, London: Sage

Gallie, D. (1994) 'Are the unemployed an underclass: some evidence from the Social Change and Economic Life Initiative', *Sociology*, 28

Galtung, J. and M. H. Ruge (1970) 'The structure of foreign news', in J. Tunstall (ed.),*Media Sociology: A Reader*, London: Constable

Garfinkel, H. (1967) *Studies in Ethnomethodology*, Englewood Hills, NJ: Prentice-Hall

Garland, D. (2001) *The Culture of Control: Crime and Social Order in Contemporary Society*, Chicago: University of Chicago Press

Gauntlett, D. (2008) *Media, Gender and Identity: An Introduction* (2nd edn), London, Routledge

Geis, G. (1967) 'The heavy electrical equipment anti-trust cases of 1961', in M.B. Clinard and R. Quinney (eds) *Criminal Behaviour Systems*, New York: Holt, Rhinehart & Winston

*General Household Survey* (2001) London: ONS, HMSO

Gerbner (2002) p188

Gewirtz, S. (2002) *The Managerial School: Post-welfarism and Social Justice in Education*, London, Routledge

Ghaill, M. Mac an (1988) *Young, Gifted and Black*, Milton Keynes: Open University Press

Ghaill, M. Mac an (1992) 'Coming of age in 80s England: reconceptualising black students' educational experience', in D. Gill, B. Mayor and M. Blair (eds) *Racism and Education: Structures and Strategies*, London: Sage

Giddens, A. (1964) *Structuration and Related Theories of Social Life and Communication*, London: Routledge

Giddens, A. (1973) *The Class Structure of the Advanced Societies,* London: Hutchinson

Giddens, A. (1976) *The New Rules of Sociological Methods*, London: Hutchinson

Giddens, A. (1984) *The Constitution of Society: Outline of the Theory of Structuration*, Cambridge: Polity Press

Giddens, A. (1991) *Modernity and Self-Identity*, Cambridge: Polity Press

Giddens, A. (1993) *New Rules of Sociological Method : A positive critique of interpretative sociologies* (2nd edn), Cambridge: Polity Press.

Giddens, A. (1994*) Beyond Left or Right*, Cambridge: Polity Press

Giddens, A. (2001) *Sociology* (4th edn), Cambridge: Polity Press

Giddens, A. (2006) *Sociology* (5th edn), Oxford: Polity Press

Giddens, A. and Diamond, P. (2005) *The New Egalitarianism*, Cambridge: Polity

Giddens, A. and Pierson, C. (1998) *Conversations with Anthony Giddens: Making Sense of Modernity*, Cambridge: Polity Press

Gill, R. (2007) *Gender and the Media*, Cambridge: Polity Press

Gill, R. (2008) 'Empowerment/sexism: figuring female sexual agency in contemporary advertising', *Feminism and Psychology*, 18(1), pp. 35-60

Gillborn, D. (1990) *'Race', Ethnicity and Education: Teaching and Learning in Multi-ethnic Schools*, London: Unwin Hyman

Gillborn, D. (2002) *Education and Institutional Racism*, London: Institute of Education

Gillborn, D. and Gipps, B. (1996) *Recent Research in the Achievement of Ethnic Minority Pupils*, London: HMSO

Gillborn, D. and Mirza, H.S. (2000) *Educational Inequality: Mapping Race and Class*, London: OFSTED

Gillborn, D. and Youdell, D. (1999) *Rationing Education: Policy, Practice, Reform and Equity*, Milton Keynes: Open University Press

Gilroy, P. (1982a) 'Steppin' out of Babylon: race, class and autonomy', in *The Empire Strikes Back: Race and Racism in Britain*, London: CCCS/Hutchinson

Ginn, J., Arber, S., Brannen, J., Dale, A., Dex, S., Elias, P., Moss, P., Pahl, J., Roberts, C. and Rubery, J. (1996) 'Feminist fallacies: a reply to Hakim on women's employment', *British Journal of Sociology*, 47

Glaser, B.G. and Strauss, A.L. (1965) *Awareness of Dying*, Chicago: Aldine

Glasgow University Media Group (1985) *War and Peace News*, Milton Keynes: Open University Press

Glasgow University Media Group (GUMG) (2000) *Viewing the World: News Content and Audience Studies*, London: Department for International Development

Glass, D.V. (1954) *Social Mobility in Britain*, London: RKP

Goffman, E. (1968) *Asylums*, Harmondsworth: Penguin

Gold, K. (2003) 'Poverty is an excuse', *Times Educational Supplement*, 7 March

Gold, R. (1958) 'Roles in sociological field investigation', *Social Forces*, 36, pp.217–23.

Goldthorpe, J. (1980) *Social Mobility and the Class Structure in Modern Britain*, Oxford: Clarendon Press

Goldthorpe, J. (1983) 'Women and class analysis: in defence of the conventional view', *Sociology*, 17(4)

Goldthorpe, J. (1996) 'Class analysis and the reorientation of class theory', *British Journal of Sociology*, 47(3), pp.481–505

Goldthorpe, J. and Jackson, M. (2007) 'Intergenerational class mobility in contemporary Britain: political concerns and empirical findings', *The British Journal of Sociology*, 58(4) Dec

Goldthorpe, J. and Lockwood, D. (1969) *The Affluent Worker in the Class Structure* (3 vols), Cambridge: Cambridge University Press

Goode, E. and Ben-Yehuda, N. (1994) *Moral Panics: The Social Construction of Deviance*, Oxford: Blackwell

Goodwin, J. and O'Connor, H. (2005) 'Exploring complex transitions: looking back at the golden age of from school to work', *Sociology*, 39(2), pp.201–20

Gordon, P. (1988) 'Black people and the criminal law: rhetoric and reality', *International Journal of the Sociology of Law*, 16

Gouldner, A.W. (1968) 'The sociologist as partisan: sociology and the welfare state', *The American Sociologist*, May

Graef, R. (1989) *Talking Blues: The Police in Their Own Words,* London: Collins Harvill

Graham, J. and Bowling, B. (1995) *Young People and Crime*, Home Office Research Study 145, London: Home Office

Gramsci, A. (1971) *Selections from the Prison Notebooks*, London: Lawrence and Wishart

Grant, W. (1999) *Pressure Groups and British Politics*, Basingstoke: Palgrave

Green, P. and Ward, A. (2004) *State Crime: Governments, Violence and Corruption*, London: Pluto Press

Greengross, S. (2004) 'Why ageism must be eradicated', *BBC News* 7 Dec

Greenslade, R. (2005) *Seeking Scapegoats: The Coverage of Asylum in the UK Press*, London: Institute of Public Policy Research

Griffin, C. (1985) *Typical Girls: Young Women from School to the Job Market*, London: Routledge & Kegan Paul

Gunter, B. (2008) 'Why study media content?', *Sociology Review*, Nov

Habermas, J. (1979) *Communication and the Evolution of Society*, London: Heinemann

Hagan, J. (1987) *Modern Criminology: Crime, Criminal Behaviour and its Control*, New York: McGraw-Hill

Hakim, C. (1979) *Occupational Segregation*, Department of Employment Research Paper no.9, London: HMSO

Hakim, C. (2000) *Work–Lifestyle Choices in the 21st Century*, Oxford: Oxford University Press

Hall, S. and Jacques, M. (1983) *The Politics of Thatcherism*, London: Lawrence & Wishart

Hall, S. and Jefferson, T. (1976) *Resistance through Rituals*, London: Hutchinson

Hall, S., Critcher, C., Jefferson, A., Clarke, J. and Robert, B. (1978) *Policing the Crisis: Mugging, the State and Law and Order,* London: Palgrave Macmillan

Hallam, S., Ireson, J. and Davies, J. (2004) 'Primary pupils' experiences of different types of grouping in school', *British Journal of Educational Research*, 30, pp. 515–33

Halloran, J., Elliott, P. and Murdock, G. (1970) *Demonstrations and Communications: A Case Study*, Harmondsworth: Penguin

Hallsworth, S. (1994) 'Understanding New Social Movements', *Sociology Review*, 4(1), Oxford: Philip Allen

Hamilton, K.and Waller, G. (1993), 'Media influences on body size estimation in anorexia and bulimia: an experimental study', *British Journal of Psychiatry*, Vol. 162 pp.837-40

Hammersley, M. (1992) 'By what criteria should ethnographic research be judged?', in M. Hammersley, *What's Wrong with Ethnography?*, London: Routledge

Hannan, J. (2000) *Improving Boys' Performance*, Dunstable: Folens

Hansard (2008) www.publications.parliament.uk/pa/cm200708/cmhansrd/cm080610/text/80610w0027.htm

Haque, Z. and Bell, J.F. (2001) 'Evaluating the performances of minority ethnic pupils in secondary schools', *Oxford Review of Education*, 27(3), pp.359–68

Haralambos, M. and Holborn, M. (2008) *Sociology: Themes and Perspectives (7th edn),* London: Collins Educational

Harding, S. (1986) *The Science Question in Feminism*, Milton Keynes: Open University Press

Harding, S. (1987) *Feminism and Methodology*, Bloomington, IN & Buckingham: Indiana University Press & Open University Press

Hargreaves, D.H. (1967) *Social Relations in a Secondary School*, London: Routledge & Kegan Paul

Harper, D. (1978) 'At home on the rails: ethics in a photographic research project', *Qualitative Sociology*, 1, pp.66–77

Harper, P., Pollak, M., Mooney, J., Whelan, E. and Young, J. (1986) *The Islington Crime Survey,* London Borough of Islington

Hart, A. (1989) 'Gender and class in England' , *New Left Review,* 1/175

Hartnett, O. (1990) 'The sex role system', in P. Mayes (ed.) *Gender*, Longman: London

Harvey, D. (1990) *The Condition of Modernity*, Blackwell: Oxford

Haste, H. (2005) 'Joined-up texting: mobile phones and young people', *Young Consumers*, Quarter 2, 6(3), pp.56–67

Hastings, M. (2005) 'They've never had it so good', *The Guardian* , 6 Aug

Hatcher, R. (1996) 'The Limitations of the New Social-Democratic Agendas: Class, equality and agency', in R. Hatcher and K. Jones (eds) *Education after the Conservatives*, Stoke-on-Trent: Trentham Books

Hay, C. (1997) 'Divided by a common language: political theory and the concept of power, *Politics* 17(1) pp. 45-52

Hayek, F.A. (1944/1986) *The Road to Serfdom*, London: Routledge

Hayward, K.J. and Yar, M. (2006) 'The "Chav" phenomenon: consumption, media and the construction of a new underclass', *Crime, Media, Culture*, 2(1), pp.9–28

Heath, A. (1991) *Understanding Political Change: The British Voter, 1964–87*, Oxford: Butterworth Heinemann

Heath, A. and C. Payne (1999) *Twentieth Century Trend in Social Mobility in Britain,* University of Oxford Centre for Research into Elections and Social Trends, Working Paper No. 70

Hedderman, C. and Hough, M. (1994) *Does the Criminal Justice System Treat Men and Women Differently?* Research Findings 10, London: HMSO

Heidensohn, F. (1989, 1996 [2nd edn]) *Women and Crime*, London: Macmillan

Heidensohn, F. (2002) 'Gender and crime', in M. Maguire, R. Morgan and R.

Held, D. (ed.) (2000) *A Globalising World: Culture, Economics*, Politics, London: Routledge

Held, D. and McGrew, A. (2002) *Globalization and Anti-Globalization*, Cambridge: Polity Press

Henry, S. and Milovanovich, D. (1996) *Constitutive Criminology: Beyond Postmodernism*, London: Sage

Herman, E. and Chomsky, N. (1988) *Manufacturing Consent*, New York: Pantheon Books

Hetherington, K. (1998) *Expressions of Identity: Space, Performance, Politics*, London: Sage

Higher Education Statistics Agency (2007) *Higher Education Students Early Statistics Survey 2007–08*, HESES07, London. Higher Education Funding Council for England

Hill, K.A. and Hughes, J.E. (1997) 'Computer-mediated political communication: The Usenet and political communities', *Political Communication* 14 pp. 3-14

Hirsch, D. (2006) Experiences of Poverty and Educational Disadvantage, York: Joseph Rowntree Foundation

Hirschi, T. (1969) *Causes of Delinquency*, Berkeley, CA: University of California Press

Hirst, P.Q. (1975) 'Radical deviancy theory and Marxism: a reply to Taylor, Walton and Young', in E. Taylor, P. Walton and J. Young (eds) *Critical Criminology*, London: Routledge

Hobbs, D. (1988) *Doing the Business, Entrepreneurship, the Working Class and Detectives in the East End of London*, Oxford: Oxford University Press

Hobbs, D. (1998) *Bad Business: Professional Crime in Britain*, Oxford: Oxford University Press

Hobbs, D. (2003) *The Night-time Economy*, London: Alcohol Research Forum Papers

Hobbs, D., Lister, S., Hadfield, P. and Winlow, S. (2000) 'Receiving shadows: governance and liminality in the night-time economy', *British Journal of Sociology*, 51(4) pp.682–700

Holdaway, S. (1983) *Inside the British Police*, Oxford: Blackwell

Hollows, J. (2000) *Feminism, Femininity and Popular Culture*, Manchester: Manchester University Press

Home Office (1998) *British Crime Survey*, Research and Statistics Directorate of the Home Office

Hood, R. and Joyce, K. (1999) 'Three generations: oral testimony of crime and social change in London's East End', *British Journal of Criminology*, 39(1), pp.136–60

Hooks, B. (2003) *Rock My Soul: Black People and Self-Esteem*, New York: Pocket Books

Hopkins, M. (2002) 'Crimes against businesses', *British Journal of Sociology*, (42)4, pp.782–97

Horkheimer, M. (1974) *Eclipse of Reason*, New York: Oxford University Press

Howell, J.M. and Frost P.J. (1989) 'A Laboratory Study of Charismatic Leadership', *Organizational Behavior and Human Decision Processes*, 43, pp.243–69

Hutton, W. (1996) *The State We're In*, London: Vantage

Hyde, M. (2001) 'Disabled people in Britain today: discrimination, social disadvantage and empowerment', *Sociology Review*, 10(4), April

Inland Revenue (2004) Distribution of Personal Wealth – www.hmrc.gov.uk/stats/personal_wealth/menu.htm

Institute of Practitioners in Advertising (2006) quoted in *Guardian*, 25 Jan

Ireson, J., Hallam, S. and Hurley, C. (2002) *Ability grouping in the Secondary School: Effects on GCSE attainment in English, mathematics and science*, Paper presented at the British Educational Research Association Annual Conference, Exeter University, Exeter, 10–14 September, 2002.

Jackson, B. (1978) 'Killing time: life in the Arkansas penitentiary', *Qualitative Sociology*, 1 pp.21 –32

Jackson, C. (2006) *Lads and Ladettes in School: Gender and the fear of failure*, Milton Keynes: Open University Press

Jasper, L. (2002) 'School system failing black children', Guardian, 16 March

Jencks, C., Smith, M., Acland, H., Bane, M.J., Cohen, D., Gintis, H. *et al.* (1972) *Inequality: A reassessment of the effect of family and schooling in America*, New York: Basic Books

Jenkins, H. (2008) *Convergence Culture: Where Old and New Media Collide*, New York: New York University Press

Jessop, B. (2002) *The Future of the Capitalist State*, Cambridge: Polity Press

Jewkes, Y. (2006) 'Creating a stir? Prisons, popular media and the power to reform' in P. Mason (ed.) *Captured by the Media: Prison Discourse in Media Culture*, Cullompton: Willan

Jones, A. and Singer, L. (2008) *Statistics on Race and the Criminal Justice System 2006/7*, London: Ministry of Justice

Jones, B., Kavanagh, D., Moran, M. and Norton, D. (2004), *Politics UK* (5th edn), London: Pearson Longman

Jones, T., Maclean, B. and Young, J. (1995) *The Second Islington Crime Survey*, London Borough of Islington

Joseph Rowntree Foundation (1995) *Income and Wealth: Report of the JRF Inquiry Group*, York: JRF

Karpf, A. (1988) 'Give us a break, not a begging bowl', *New Statesman*, 27 May

Katz, E. and P. Lazarsfeld (1965). *Personal Influence*, New York, Free Press

Katz, J. (1988) *Seductions of Crime: Moral and Sensual Attractions in Doing Evil*, New York: Basic Books

Kay, T. (1996) 'Women's work and women's work': implications of women's changing employment patterns', *Leisure Studies*, 15, pp.49–64

Kellner, D. (1999) in B. Smart (ed) *Resisting McDonaldisation*, London: Sage

Kenyatta, M.L. and Tai, R.H. (1999) *Critical Ethnicity: Countering the Waves of Identity Politics*, Oxford: Rowman and Littlefield

Kershaw, C., Nicholas, S. and Walker, A (eds.). (2008) *Crime in England and Wales 2007/8*, London: Home Office

Kidd, W. (2001) 'Time to think about age', *Sociology Review*, 10(3) Feb

Kirby, R. (2000) *Underachievement in Boys*, Winchester: www.practicalparent.org.uk

Kitsuse, J. (1962) 'Societal reaction to deviant behaviour', *Social Problems*, (9) Winter

Klapper, J.T. (1960) *The Effects of Mass Communication*, New York: The Free Press

Klein, N. (2001) *No Logo*, London: Flamingo

Kramer, R. (2006) 'The Space Shuttle *Challenger* explosion', in R. Michalowski and R. Kramer (2006) *State-Corporate Crime: Wrongdoing at the intersection of business and government*, New Brunswick, NJ: Rutgers University Press

Kuhn, T.S. (1962/1970) *The Structure of Scientific Revolutions* (2nd edn), Chicago: University of Chicago Press

Kynaston, D. (2008) 'The road to meritocracy is blocked by private schools', *The Guardian*, 22 Feb

Lakatos, I. (1970) 'Falsification and the methodology of scientific research programmes', in I. Lakatos and A. Musgrave (eds) *Criticism and the Growth of Knowledge*, Cambridge: Cambridge University Press

Landis (2002) quoted on www.tc.umn.edu/~rbeach/teaching media/module5/9.htm

Lawler, S. (2005) 'Introduction : class, culture, identity', *Sociology* 39(5)

Lea, J. and Young, J. (1984, 1993 revised edn) *What is to be Done about Law and Order?*, Harmondsworth: Penguin

Lee, M.M., Carpenter, B. and Meyers, L.S. (2007) 'Representation of older adults in television adverts', *Journal of Ageing Studies*, 21 pp. 23-30

Lees, S. (1986) *Losing Out: Sexuality and Adolescent Girls*, London: Hutchinson

Lee-Treweek, G. (2000) 'The insight of emotional danger: research experiences in a home for the elderly', in G. Lee-Treweek and S. Lingogle (eds) *Danger in the Field: Risk and Ethics in Social Research*, London: Routledge

Lemert, E. (1972) *Human Deviance, Social Problems and Social Control*, Englewood Cliffs, NJ: Prentice-Hall

Levi, M. (1987) *Regulating Fraud*, London: Tavistock

Levi, M., Burrows, J., Fleming, J. and Hopkins, M. (2007) *The Nature, Extent and Economic Impact of Fraud in the UK*, London: ACPO

Li, N. and Kirkup, G. (2007) 'Gender and cultural differences in internet use': a study of China and the UK, *Computers and Education*, 48(2), Feb

Liazos, A. (1972) 'The poverty of the sociology of deviance: nuts, sluts and perverts', *Social Problems*, 20

Ligali (2006) www.ligali.org/

Lobban, G. (1974) 'Data report on British reading schemes', *Times Educational Supplement*, 1 March 1974

Lockwood, D. (1966) 'Sources of variation in working-class images of society', *Sociological Review*, 14

Lukes, S. (1974) *Power: A Radical View*, London: Macmillan

Lukes, S. (1986) 'Domination by economic power and authority', in S. Lukes (ed.) *Power*, Oxford: Blackwell

Lull, J. (1995) *Media, Communication, Culture: A global approach*, New York: Columbia University Press.

Lyng, S. (1990) 'Edgework: a social psychological analysis of voluntary risk-taking', *American Journal of Sociology*, 95(4), pp.851–6

Lyotard, J.-F. (1984) *The Post-Modern Condition: A Report on Knowledge*, Manchester: University of Manchester Press

Mac an Ghaill, M. (1994) *The Making of Men: Masculinities, Sexualities and Schooling*, Milton Keynes: Open University Press

Mac an Ghaill, M. (ed.) (1996) *Understanding Masculinities: Social Relations and Cultural Arenas*, Buckingham: Open University Press

Macdonald, K. and Tipton, C. (1993) 'Using documents', in N. Gilbert (ed.) *Researching Social Life*, London: Sage

Mack, J. and Lansley, S. (1985) *Poor Britain*, London: Allen & Unwin

Madriz, M. (2000) 'Focus groups in feminist research', in N.K. Denzin and Y.S. Lincoln (eds) *Handbook of Qualitative Research* (2nd edn), Thousand Oaks, CA: Sage

Maffesoli, M. (1996) *The Time of the Tribes*, London: Sage

Maguire, M. (2002) 'Crime statistics: the data explosion and its implications', in M. Maguire, R. Morgan and R. Reiner (eds) *The Oxford Handbook of Criminology* (3rd edn), Oxford: Oxford University Press

Maguire, M., Morgan, R. and Reiner, R. (eds) (1997) *The Oxford Handbook of Criminology* (2nd edn), Oxford: Oxford University Press

Malinowski, B. (1982) *Magic, Science and Religion and Other Essays*, London: Souvenir Press

Mann, M. (1986) *The Sources of Social Power*, Vol. 1, Cambridge: Cambridge University Press

Mannheim, K. (1960) *Ideology and Utopia*, London: Routledge

Marcuse, H. (1964/1991) *One Dimensional Man: Studies in the Ideology of Advanced Industrial Societies*, London: Routledge

Marmot, M.G., Smith, G.D., Stansfeld, S., Patel, C., North, F., Head, J., White, I., Brunner, E. and Feeney, A. (1991) 'Health inequalities among British civil servants: the Whitehall II study', *The Lancet*, 337, pp.1387–93.

Mars, G. (1982) *Cheats at Work: An Anthropology of Workplace Crime*, London: George Allen & Unwin

Marshall, B., Webb, B. and Tilley, N. (2005) *Rationalisation of Current Research on Guns, Gangs and Other Weapons: Phase 1*, London: Jill Dando Institute of Crime Science, University College London

Marshall, G. (1987) 'What is happening to the working class?', *Social Studies Review*, January

Marshall, G. (1998) *A Dictionary of Sociology*, Oxford: OUP

Marshall, G. (2005) *A Dictionary of Sociology*, 3rd edition, Oxford: OUP

Marshall, G., Newby. H., Rose, D. and Vogler, C. (1988) *Social Class In Modern Britain*, London, Hutchinson

Marsland, D. (1996) *Welfare or Welfare State?*, Basingstoke: Macmillan

Marx, K. (1867/1973) *Capital: A Critique of Political Economy*, Harmondsworth: Penguin

Marx, K. and Engels, F. (1848, reissued 2002) *Manifesto of the Communist Party*, North Charleston, SC: BookSurge

Matthews, R. and Young, J. (eds) (1992) *Issues in Realist Criminology*, London: Sage

Matza, D. (1964) *Delinquency and Drift*, New York: Wiley

May, T. (2001) *Social Research: Issues, Methods and Process*, Buckingham: Open University Press

Mayhew, H. (1851) *London Labour and the London Poor* (republished 1985), Harmondsworth: Penguin

Mayhew, P., Aye Maung, N. and Mirrlees-Black, C. (1993) *The 1992 British Crime Survey*, Home Office Research Study 111, London: Home Office

Maynard, M. and Purvis, J. (eds) (1994) *Researching Women's Lives from a Feminist Perspective*, London: Taylor & Francis

McCabe, K. A. and Martin, G.M. (2005) *School Violence, the Media, and Criminal Justice Response*, York: Peter Lang Publishing

McChesney, R. (2002) in K. Borjesson (ed) *Into the Buzzsaw: Leading Journalists Expose the Myth of a Free Press*, Amherst, NY: Prometheus

McKee, L. and Bell, C. (1985) 'Marital and family relations in times of male unemployment', in B. Roberts, R. Finnegan and D. Gallie (eds) *New Approaches to Economic Life*, Manchester: Manchester University Press

McKendrick, J.H., Sinclair, S., Irwin. A., O'Donnell H., Scott, G. and Dobbie, L. (2008) *The Media, Poverty and Public Opinion in the UK*, York: Joseph Rowntree Foundation

McKenzie, R.T. and Silver, A. (1968) 'The working class Tory in England', in P. Worsley *Angels in Marble*, London: Heinemann

McKie, L., Bowlby, S. and Gregory, S. (2004) 'Starting well: gender, care and health in the family context', *Sociology*, 38(3), pp.593–611

McQuail, D. (1992) *Mass Communication* (5th edn), London : Sage

McRobbie, A and Thornton, S. (1995) 'Rethinking "moral panic" for multi-mediated social worlds', *British Journal of Sociology*, 46(4), pp.559–74

McRobbie, A. (1994) *Feminism and Youth Culture*, London: Macmillan

McRobbie, A. (1999) *In the Culture Society : Art, Fashion and Popular Music,* London: Routledge

Mead, G.H. (1934) *Mind, Self and Society* (ed. C. Morris) Chicago: University of Chicago

Mead, M. (1928) *Coming of Age in Samoa*, New York: Morrow

Melucci, A. (1989) *Nomads of the Present*, London: Hutchinson

Merton, R.K. (1938) 'Social structure and anomie', *American Sociological Review*, 3

Merton, R.K. (1949; revised and expanded, 1957 and 1968) *Social Theory and Social Structure*, New York: The Free Press

Messerschmidt, J. (1993) *Masculinities and Crime*, Lanham, MD: Rowman & Littlefield

Michalowski, R. and Kramer, R. (1987) 'The space between laws: the problem of corporate crime in a transnational context', *Social Problems*, 34

Miles, R. (1989) *Racism*, London: Routledge

Miliband, R. (1970/1973) *The State in Capitalist Society*, London: Quartet

Millen, D. (1997) 'Some methodological and epistemological issues raised by doing feminist research on non-feminist women', *Sociological Research* Online www.socresonline.org.uk/socresonline/2/3/3.html

Miller, W.B. (1962) 'Lower class culture as a generating milieu of gang delinquency', in M.E. Wolfgang, L. Savitz and N. Johnston (eds) *The Sociology of Crime and Delinquency*, New York: Wiley

Millett, K. (1970) *Sexual Politics*, New York: Doubleday

Mills, C.W. (1959) *The Sociological Imagination*, Oxford: Oxford University Press

Millwood Hargrave, A. (2003) *How Children Interpret Screen Violence*, London: BBC/BBFC/BSC/ITC

Milne, A., Hatzidimitradou, E. and Harding, T. (1999) *Later Lifestyles: A Survey by Help the Aged and* Yours *Magazine*, London: Help the Aged

Ministry of Justice (2008) *Statistics on Race and the Criminal Justice System – 2006/7*, www.justice.gov.uk/docs/stats-race-criminal-justice.pdf

Mirza, H. (1992) *Young, Female and Black*, London: Routledge

Mirza, H. (2007) quoted in 'Revealed: Racism in Schools', *Channel 4 News*, 24 May

Mitchell, D. (2007) 'You are what you own', *Guardian*, 29 Aug

Mitsos E. and Browne, K. (1998) 'Gender differences in education: the underachievement of boys', *Sociology Review*, 8(1)

Modood, T. (1992) *Not Easy Being British: Colour, Culture and Citizenship*, Runnymede Trust and Trentham Books

Modood, T. (2003), 'Ethnic differentials in educational performance', in D. Mason (ed.) *Explaining Ethnic Differences: Changing Patterns of Disadvantage in Britain*, Bristol: The Policy Press.

Modood, T. (2004) 'Capitals, ethnic identity and education qualifications', *Cultural Trends*, 13(2), pp. 87–105.

Modood, T. (2006) 'Ethnicity, Muslims and higher education entry in Britain', *Teaching in Higher Education*, 11(2) pp. 247-50

Mokhiber, R. (1988) *Corporate Crime and Violence*, San Francisco: Sierra Club

Monaghan, L. (1999) 'Creating "the perfect body": a variable project', *Body and Society,* 5(2–3), pp.267–90

Monaghan, L. (2005) 'Get ready to duck: bouncers and the realities of ethnographic research on violent groups', *British Journal of Criminology*, 41, pp.536–48

Monbiot, G. (2004) 'Our lies led us into war', *Guardian,* 20 June

Moore, M. (2001) *Stupid White Men*, London: Penguin

Moore, M. (2003) *Dude, Where's My Country?,* London: Penguin

Moores, M. (1998) 'Sociologists in white coats', *Sociology Review*, 7(3)

Mordaunt, S., Rake, K., Wanless, H. and Mitchell, R. (2003) *One in Four*, Age Concern

Morgan, I. (1999) *Power and Politics*, London: Hodder & Stoughton

Morgan, R. (1980) 'Theory and practice: pornography and rape', in L. Lederer (ed) *Take Back the Night: Women on Pornography*, New York: William Morrow

Morgan, R. and Russell, N. (2000) *The Judiciary in the Magistrates' Courts*, Home Office and LCD Occasional Paper 66, London: Home Office/LCD

Morley, D. (1980) *The Nationwide Audience*, London: BFI

Morris, L. (1993) *Dangerous Classes: The Underclass and Social Citizenship*, London: Routledge

Morris, T.P. (1957) *The Criminal Area: A study in Social Ecology*, London: Routledge

Morrison, D.E. (1999) *Defining Violence: The Search for Understanding*, Luton: University of Luton Press

Mort, F. (1988), 'Boy's own? Masculinity, style and popular culture', in R. Chapman and J. Rutherford, *Male Order: Unwrapping Masculinity*, London: Lawrence & Wishart

Mosca, G. (1939) *The Ruling Class*, New York: McGraw Hill

Mouzelis, N. (1995) *Sociological Theory: What Went Wrong?,* London: Routledge

Mulvey, L. (1975) 'Visual pleasures and narrative cinema', *Screen*, 16(3)

Murray, C. (1990) *The Emerging British Underclass*, London: Institute of Economic Affairs, Health and Welfare Unit

Murray, C. (1994) *Underclass: The Crisis Deepens*, London: IEA

Myhill, D. (1999) 'Bad boys and good girls: patterns of interaction and response in whole class teaching', Exeter University School of Education paper

Nahdi, F. (2003) 'Doublespeak: Islam and the media', Open Democracy, 3 Apr

Nairn, T. (1988) *The Enchanted Glass: Britain and its Monarchy*, London: Radius

Nelken, D. (2002) 'White collar crime', in M. Maguire, R. Morgan and R. Reiner, *The Oxford Handbook of Criminology* (3rd edn), Oxford: Oxford University Press

Newman, D. (2006) *The Architecture of Social Stratification: Social Class and Inequality*, London: Sage

Newman, O. (1972) *Defensible Space: Crime prevention through urban design*, New York: Collier

Newton, K. (1969) 'A Critique of the Pluralist Model', *Acta Sociologica*, 12

Nightingale, C. (1993) *On the Edge*, New York: Basic Books

Norris, P. (1999) *On Message: Communicating the Campaign*, London: Sage

O'Connell Davidson, J. and Layder, D. (1994) *Methods, Sex and Madness*, London: Routledge

O'Donnell, M. (1991) *Race and Ethnicity*, Harlow: Longman

O'Donnell, M. and Sharpe, S. (2000) *Uncertain Masculinities: Youth, Ethnicity and Class in Contemporary Britain*, London: Routledge

Oakley, A. (1974) *Housewife*, London: Allen Lane

Oakley, A. (1981) 'Interviewing women: a contradiction in terms', in H. Roberts (ed.) *Doing Feminist Research*, London: Routledge

Oakley, A. (1998) 'Gender, methodology and people's ways of knowing: some problems with feminism and the paradigm debate in social science', *Sociology*, 32, pp.707–31

Olsen, W. and Walby, S. (2004) *Modelling Gender Pay Gaps*, Manchester: Equal Opportunities Commission

Orbach, S. (1991) *Fat is a Feminist Issue*, London: Hamlyn

Orton, M. and Rowlingson, K. (2007) *Public Attitudes to Economic Inequality*, York: Joseph Rowntree Foundation

Osler, A. (2006) *Response to the Equalities Review Interim Report of the Cabinet Office (2006)* sponsored by the Joseph Rowntree Foundation, Centre for Citizenship and Human Rights Education, University of Leeds

Owen, D.W. and Green, A.E. (1992) 'Labour market experience and occupational change amongst ethnic groups in Great Britain', *New Community*, 19, pp.7–29

Pakulski, J. and Waters, M. (1996) *The Death of Class*, London: Sage

Pareto, V. (1935) *The Mind and Society*, New York: Dover

Park, A. (1999) 'Young people and political apathy', in R. Jowell, J. Curtice, A. Park, K. Thomson and L. Jarvis (eds) *British Social Attitudes: the 15th Report*, Ashgate: Aldershot

Parker, H. (1974, 1992 [2nd edn]) *View from the Boys*, Aldershot: Ashgate

Parker, H., Aldridge, J. and Measham, F. (1998) *Illegal Leisure: the Normalization of Adolescent Recreational Drug Use*, London: Routledge

Parkin, F. (1972) *Class Inequality and Political Order*, St. Albans: Paladin

Parsons, C., Godfrey, R., Annan, G., Cornwall, J., Dussart, M., Hepburn, S., Howlett, K. and Wennerstrom, V. (2005) *Minority Ethnic Exclusions and the RR (A)A 2000*, Report 616/2004, London: DfESResearch

Parsons, T. (1937) *The Structure of Social Action*, New York: McGraw-Hill

Parsons, T. (1951) *The Social System*, New York: Free Press

Parsons, T. (1963) 'On the concept of political power', *Proceedings of the American Philosophical Society*, 107

Parsons, T. (1964) *Essays in Social Theory*, New York: The Free Press

Parsons, T. (1977) *The Evolution of Societies*, J. Toby (ed.), Englewood Cliffs, NJ: Prentice-Hall

Patel, S. (1999) 'The media and its representation of Islam and Muslim women', in J. Waghorn (ed) *Young Women Speak: A Message to the Media*, London: The Women's Press

Patterson, S. (1965) *Dark Strangers*, Harmondsworth: Penguin

Pawson, R. (1989) *A Measure For Measures*, London: Routledge

Payne, G. (1987) *Economy and Opportunity*, Basingstoke: Macmillan

Payne, G. (1992) 'Competing views of contemporary social mobility and social divisions', in R. Burrows and C. Marsh (eds) *Consumption and Class*, Basingstoke: Macmillan

Peace, M. (1998) quoted on www.sociologystuff.com

Pearce, F. (1976) *Crimes of the Powerful: Marxism, Crime and Deviance*, London: Pluto

Pearce, F. and Tombs, S. (1998) *Toxic Capitalism: Corporate Crime and the Chemical Industry*, Aldershot: Ashgate

Phillips, C. and Brown, D. (1998) *Entry into the Criminal Justice System: A Survey of Police Arrests and their Outcomes*, Home Office Research Study 185, London: Home Office

Phillips, K. (2004) *American Dynasty; Aristocracy, Fortune and the Politics of Deceit in the House of Bush*, London: Penguin

Phillips, M. and Murray. C. (2001) *Charles Murray and the Underclass (Civil Society) Ten Years On*, London: Civitas

Phillips, M. (1997) *All Must Have Prizes*, London: Little Brown

Phillipson, C. (1982) *Capitalism and the Construction of Old Age*, Basingstoke: Macmillan

Philo, G. (2001) 'Media effects and the active audience', *Sociology Review,* 10(3), Feb

Philo, G. and Beattie, L. (1999) 'Race, migration and media', in G. Philo (ed) *Message Received: Glasgow Media Group Research 1993-1998*, Harlow: Longman

Philo, G. and Miller, D. (2000) *Market Killing: What the Free Market Does and What Social Scientists Can Do About It,* Harlow: Longman

Piacentini, L. and Walters, R. (2006) 'The politicization of youth crime in Scotland and the rise of the "Burberry Court"', *Youth Justice*, 6, pp.43-59

Pilcher, J. (1995) *Age and Generation in Modern Britain*, Oxford: OUP

Pilcher, J. and Whelehan, I. (2004) *50 Key Concepts in Gender Studies*, London: Sage

Pirie, M. (2001) 'How exams are fixed in favour of girls', The Spectator, 20 January

Platt, L. (2005) 'The intergenerational social mobility of minority ethnic groups', *BSA Publications*, Volume 39(3), pp.445–61

Platt, T. and Takagi, P. (1977) 'Intellectuals for Law and Order: a Critique of the New Realists', *Crime and Social Justice* 8 pp 1-

Plummer, K. (2000) *Documents of Life*, Thousand Oaks, CA: Sage

Poole, E. (2000) 'Media representation and British Muslims', *Dialogue Magazine*, Apr

Popper, K. (1959) *The Logic of Scientific Discovery*, London: Hutchinson

Portnoy, F. (2003) *Infectious Greed: How Deceit and Risk Corrupted the Financial Markets*, New York: Times Books

Postman, N. (1986) *Amusing Ourselves to Death*, London: Methuen

Poulantzas, N. (1973) *Political Power and Social Classes*, London: New Left Books

Power, S., Edwards, T., Whitty, G. and Wigfall, V. (2003) *Education and the Middle Class*, Milton Keynes: Open University Press

Punch, K.F. (1998) *Introduction to Social Research*, London: Sage

Punch, M. (1994) 'Politics and ethics in qualitative research', in N.K. Denzin and Y.S. Lincoln (eds) *Handbook of Qualitative Research*, Thousand Oaks, CA: Sage

Punch, M. (1996) *Dirty Business: Exploring Corporate Misconduct*, London: Sage

Putnam, R. (1995) Bowling alone: America's declining social capital', *Journal of Democracy*, 6(1), Jan, pp. 65-78

Ramazanoglu, C. (1992) 'On feminist methodology: male reason versus feminist empowerment', *Sociology*, 26(2), pp.213–18

Ranson, S. (2005) 'The participation of volunteer citizens in school governance', *Education Review*, 57

Rathje, W.L. and Murphy, C. (2002, originally 1992) *Rubbish! The Archaeology of Garbage,* Phoenix: University of Arizona Press

Ray, S., Sharp, E. and Abrams, D. (2006) Ageism: A benchmark of public attitudes in Britain, London: Age Concern/University of Kent

Raymond, G. J. (2002) *A Comparative Study of Women Trafficked in the Migration Process: Patterns, Profiles and Health: Consequences of Sexual Exploitation in Five Countries*, New York: UN

Reay, D. (1998) 'Rethinking social class: qualitative perspectives on gender and social class', *Sociology*, 32(2), pp.259–75

Reay, D., David, M. *et al.* (2005) *Degrees of Choice: Social class, race and gender in higher education,* New York: Oxford University Press

Redhead, S. (ed.) (1993) *Rave off: Politics and Deviance in Contemporary Youth Culture*, Aldershot: Avebury

Reiman, J. (2003 [7th edn], 2006 [8th edn]) *The Rich Get Richer and the Poor Get Poorer: Ideology, Class and Criminal Justice*, Harlow: Allyn & Bacon / Pearson Longman

Reiner, R. (1992) *The Politics of the Police,* Hemel Hempstead: Wheatsheaf

Reiner, R. (2007) 'Policy on police', in M. Maguire, R. Morgan, R. Reiner (eds) *The Oxford Handbook of Criminology* (2nd edn) Oxford: OUP

Reinharz, S. (1992) *Feminist Methods in Sociological Research*, New York: Oxford University Press

Reiss, A.J. (1961) 'The social integration of queers and peers', *Social Problems*, 9(2), p.102–20

Rex, J. and Tomlinson, S. (1979) *Colonial Immigrants in a British City*, London: Routledge & Kegan Paul

Reynolds, D. (1984) *Constructive Living,* Hawaii: Kolowalu Books, University of Hawaii Press

Richardson, J. (2001) 'British Muslims in the broadsheet press: a challenge to cultural hegemony ?', *Journalism Studies*, 2(2)

Riseborough, G. (1993) 'The gobbo barmy army: one day in the life of YTS boys', in

Roberts, K. (2001) *Class in Modern Britain,* Basingstoke: Palgrave

Roberts, K. and Chadwick, C. (1991) *Transitions into the Labour Market: The New Routes of the 1980s*, Youth Cohort Series 16, Research and Development Series 65, Sheffield: Employment Department

Roberts, K., Cook, F.G., Clark, S.C. and Semeonoff, E. (1977) *The Fragmentary Class Structure*, London: Heinemann

Robinson, T., Gustafson, B. and Popovich, M. (2008) 'Perceptions of negative stereotypes of older people in magazine adverts: comparing the perceptions of other adults and college students', *Ageing and Society*, 28, pp. 233-251

Rock, P. (1988) 'The present state of British criminology' in *The British Journal of Criminology*, 28(2)

Rodgers, J. (2008) *Criminalising Social Policy: Its Nature and Consequences,* London: Sage

Room, G. (1995) *Beyond the Threshold: The measurement and analysis of social exclusion*, Bristol: The Policy Press

Rorty, R. (1980) *Philosophy and the Mirror of Nature,* Oxford: Blackwell

Rosenthal, R. and Jacobson, L. (1968) *Pygmalion in the Classroom*, New York: Holt, Rinehart & Winston

Ross, J.I. (ed.) (2000) *Varieties of State Crime and Its Control*, Monsey, NJ: Criminal Justice Press

Rowbotham, S. (1982) 'The trouble with patriarchy', in M. Evans (ed) *The Woman Question*, London: Fontana

Rowntree, B.S. (1901) *Poverty: A Study of Town Life*, London: Macmillan

Rubin, H. (1998) The Princessa: Machiavelli for Women, London: Bloomsbury

Ruggiero, V. (1996) *Organized and Corporate Crime in Europe: Offers That Can't Be Refused*, Aldershot: Dartmouth

Runciman, W. (1966) *Relative Deprivation and Social Justice*, London: Routledge

Runnymede Trust (1997) *Islamophobia: A challenge for us all*, London: Runnymede Trust

Rusche, G. and Kircheimer, O. (1939) *Punishment and Social Structure,* New York: Columbia University Press

Rutherford, J. (1988) 'Who's that man?', in R. Chapman and J. Rutherford (eds) *Male Order: Unwrapping Masculinity*, London: Laurence & Wishart

Rutland, A. (2005) *The Development and Regulation of Prejudice in Children*, London: ESRC research

Sachdev, S. and Wilkinson, F. (1998) *Low Pay and the Minimum Wage*, Institute of Employment Rights

Samad, Y. (2006) 'Muslims in Britain today', *Sociology Review*, 15(4)

Sampson, R.J., Raudenbusch, S.W. and Earls, F. (1997) 'Neighbourhoods and violent crime: a multi-level study of collective efficacy', *Science*, 277, pp.918–24

Sarap, M. (1993) *An Introductory Guide to Post-structuralism and Postmodernism*, Hemel Hempstead: Harvester Wheatsheaf

Saunders, P. (1979) *Urban Politics*, Harmondsworth: Penguin

Saunders, P. (1990) *Social Class and Stratification*, London: Routledge

Saunders, P. (1995) *Capitalism – A Social Audit*, Buckingham: Open University Press

Saunders, P. (1996) *Unequal but Fair? A Study of Class Barriers in Britain*, London: Institute of Economic Affairs

Savage, M. (1995) 'The middle classes in modern Britain', *Sociology Review*, 5(2), Oxford: Philip Allan

Savage, M. (2000) *Class Analysis and Social Transformation*, Buckingham: Open University Press

Savage, M. and Egerton, M. (1997) 'Social mobility, individual ability and the inheritance of class inequality', *Sociology*, 31(4)

Savage, M., Bagnall, G. and Longhurst, B. (2001) 'Ordinary, ambivalent and defensive class identities in the North West of England', *Sociology*, 35(4), pp.875–92

Savage, M., Barlow, J., Dickens, P. and Fielding, I. (1992) *Prosperity, Bureaucracy and Culture: Middle-class Formation in Contemporary Britain*, London: Routledge

Sayer, A. (1992) *Method in Social Science: A Realist Approach* (2nd edn), London: Routledge

Scarman, Lord (1981) *The Scarman Report*, Harmondsworth: Penguin

Scase, R. and Scales, J. (2000) *Fit and Fifty*, Swindon: Economic and Social Research Council

Schlesinger, P. (1990) 'Rethinking the sociology of journalism: source strategies and the limits of media-centrism', in M. Ferguson (ed) *Public Communication: The New Imperative*, London: Sage

Schutz, A. (1972) *The Phenomenology of the Social World*, London: Heinemann

Schwartz, H. and Jacobs, J. (1979) *Qualitative Sociology: A Method to the Madness*, London: Collier-Macmillan

Scott MacEwen, A. (1994) 'Gender segregation and the SCELI research', in A. Scott MacEwen (ed.) *Gender Segregation and Social Change*, Oxford: Oxford University Press

Scott, A. (1990) *Ideology and The New Social Movements*, London: Unwin Hyman

Scott, J. (1982) *The Upper Classes: Poverty and Privilege in Britain*, London: Macmillan

Scott, J. (1991) *Who Rules Britain?*, Cambridge: Polity Press

Scott, J. (2005) 'Social mobility: occupational snakes and ladders', *Sociology Review* 15(2) Nov

Scott, J. Dex, S. and Joshi, H. (2008) *Women and Employment: Changing Lives and New Challenges*, Cheltenham: Edward Elgar Publishing

Scraton, P. (1985) *The State of the Police*, London: Pluto

Scraton, P. (1987) *Law, Order and the Authoritarian State: Readings in Critical Criminology*, Milton Keynes: Open University Press

Scraton, P. (1997) 'Whose "childhood"? What "crisis"?', in P. Scraton (ed.) *Childhood' in 'Crisis?*, London: UCL Press

Scraton, P. (2002) 'Defining "power" and challenging "knowledge": critical analysis and resistance in the UK', in K. Carrington and R. Hogg (eds) *Critical Criminology: Issues, debates, challenges*, Cullompton: Willan Publishing

Scraton, P. and Chadwick, K. (1982) 'The theoretical and political priorities of critical criminology', in G. Mars, *Cheats at Work, an Anthropology of Workplace Crime*, London: Allen & Unwin

Sewell, A. (2004) 'Where white liberals fear to tread', *Guardian*, 30 March

Sewell, T. (1996) *Black Masculinities and Schooling*, Stoke on Trent: Trentham Books

Shah, S. (2008) 'Too many black and Asian faces on TV', *Guardian*, 26 June

Shapin, S. (1995) 'Here and everywhere: sociology of scientific knowledge', *Annual Review of Sociology*, 21

Sharp, C. and Budd, T. (2005) Minority Ethnic Groups and Crime: Findings from the Offending, Crime and Justice Survey 2003 (2nd edn), London: Home Office

Sharp, R. and Green, A. (1975) *Education and Social Control*, London: Routledge and Keegan Paul

Sharpe, S. (1976) *Just Like a Girl*, Harmondsworth: Penguin (2nd edn 1994)

Sharpe, S. (1994) *Just Like a Girl: How Girls Learn to be Women – From the Seventies to the Nineties*, Harmondsworth: Penguin

Sharrock, W., Hughes, J. and Martin, P. (2003) *Understanding Modern Sociology*, London: Sage

Shaw, C.R. and McKay, H.D. (1931) *Social Factors in Juvenile Delinquency*, Washington, DC: Government Printing Office

Shaw, C.R. and McKay, H.D. (1942) *Juvenile Delinquency and Urban Areas,* Chicago: University of Chicago Press

Shearing, C. and Stenning, P. (1983) 'Private security: implications for social control', *Social Problems,* 30(5), pp.493–506

Skeggs, B. (1997) *Formations of Class and Gender*, London: Sage

Skeggs, B. (2001) 'Feminist ethnography', in P. Atkinson, A. Coffey, S. Delamont, J. Lofland and L. Lofland (eds) *Handbook of Ethnography*, London: Sage

Skelton, C. (2001) *Schooling the Boys: Masculinities and Primary Education*, Buckingham: Open University Press

Sklair, L. (2004) *Globalization: Capitalism and its Alternatives*, Oxford: Oxford University Press

Skogan, W.G. (1990) *Disorder and Decline: Crime and the Spiral of Decay in American Neighbourhoods*, New York: Free Press

Skolnick, J. (1966) *Justice without Trial*, New York: Wiley

Slapper, G. and Tombs, S. (1999) *Corporate Crime*, Harlow: Longman

Smart, C. (1990) 'Feminist approaches to criminology; or postmodern woman meets atavistic man', in L. Gelsthorpe and A. Morris (eds) *Feminist Perspectives in Criminology,* Milton Keynes: Open University Press

Smart, C. (1990) 'Feminist approaches to criminology; or postmodern woman meets atavistic man', in L. Gelsthorpe and A. Morris (eds) *Feminist Perspectives in Criminology,* Milton Keynes: Open University Press

Smelser, N. (1962) *Theory of Collective Behaviour*, London: Routledge & Kegan Paul

Smith, D. (1973) 'Women's perspective as a radical critique of sociology', *Sociological Inquiry*, 44

Smith, D.J. and Gray, J. (1985) *People and Police in London*, London: Gower

Smith, M.J. (2008) *Environment and Citizenship: Integrating Justice, Responsibility and Civic Engagement*, London: Zed Publications

Smith, T. and Noble, M. (1995) *Poverty and Schooling in the 1990s*, London: Child Poverty Action Group

South, N. (2004) in Carrabine, E., Iganski, P., Lee, M., Plummer, K. and South, N. (2004) *Criminology: A Sociological Introduction*, London: Routledge

Spencer-Thomas, O. (2008) 'What is Newsworthy?' www.btinternet.com/~owenst/index.html

Spender, D. (1985) *Man Made Language*, London: Routledge

*Statistics on Race and the Criminal Justice System 2007/8*, London: Ministry of Justice

Stinchcombe, A. (1963) 'Institutions of privacy in the determination of police administration', *American Journal of Sociology,* 69

Stone, M. (1981) The Education of the Black Child in Britain, Glasgow: Fontana

Storr, M. (2002) 'Sociology and social movements: theories, analyses and ethical dilemmas', in P. Hamilton and K. Thompson (eds) *The Uses of Sociology*, Oxford: The Open University/Blackwell

Strand, S. (2007) *Minority Ethnic Pupils in the Longitudinal Study of Young People in England (LSYPE)*, Centre for Educational Development Appraisal and Research, University of Warwick/Department for Children, Schools and Families

Sullivan, A. (2001) 'Cultural capital and educational attainment', *Sociology*, 35(4), pp.893–912

Sutherland, E.H. (1940) 'White-collar criminality', *American Sociological Review*, 5, pp.1–12

Sutherland, E.H. and Cressey, D. (1966) *Principles of Criminology* (revised edn), Chicago: University of Chicago Press

Sutton Trust (2005) *The Educational Backgrounds of Members of the House of Commons and the House of Lords*, London: The Sutton Trust

Sutton Trust (2007) *The Educational Backgrounds of the UK's Leading 500 People*, London: Sutton Trust

Sutton, R.I. (1992) 'Feelings about a Disneyland visit: photography and the reconstruction of bygone emotions', *Journal of Management Enquiry*, 1, pp.278–87

Swale (2006) 'Meet the "NEETS": media accounts of the underclass debate', *Sociology Review*, 14(1) Sep

Swann Report (1985) *Education for All*, London: HMSO

Swartz, J. (1975) 'Silent killers at work', *Crime and Social Justice*, 3, pp.15–20

Tarling, R. (1988) *Police Work and Manpower Allocation,* Paper 47, London: Home Office

Taylor, I. (1999) *Crime in Context: A Critical Criminology of Market Societies,* Cambridge: Polity Press

Taylor, J., Walton, P. and Young, J. (1973) *The New Criminology*, London: Routledge

Taylor-Gooby, P. (with Vic George) (1996) *Welfare Policy: Squaring the Welfare Circle*, Basingstoke: Macmillan

Tebbel, C. (2000) *The Body Snatchers: How the Media Shapes Women*, New South Wales: Finch Publishing

Thomas, W.I. and Znaniecki, F. (1918) *The Polish Peasant in Europe and America,* Chicago: University of Chicago Press

Thompson, N. (1993) *Antidiscriminatory Practice*, Basingstoke: MacMillan

Thornton, J. and Beckwith, S. (2004) *Environmental Law* (2nd edn), London: Sweet & Maxwell

Thornton, S. (1995) *Club Cultures: Music, media and subcultural capital*, Cambridge: Polity Press

Thrasher, F. (1927) *The Gang,* Chicago: University of Chicago Press

Tikly, L., Haynes, J., Caballero, C., Hill, J. and Gillborn, D. (2006) *Evaluation of Aiming High Report*, University of London Research Report RR801, London: DFES/HMSO

Tizard, B. and Hughes, M. (1991) 'Reflections on young people learning', in G. Walford (ed.) *Doing Educational Research*, London: Routledge

Tombs, S. (2002) 'Understanding regulation: a review essay', *Social and Legal Studies*, 11(1), p.111–31

Tombs, S. (2007) 'A political economy of corporate killing ', *Criminal Justice Matters*, 70(1), Winter, pp.29–30

Tombs, S. and Whyte, D. (2003) *Unmasking the Crimes of the Powerful: Scrutinizing States and Corporations,* New York: Peter Lang

Tombs, S. and Whyte, D. (2007) *Safety Crimes*, Cullompton: Willan

Tomlinson, S. (2005) *Education in a post-Welfare Society*, 2nd edition, Buckingham: Open University Press

Touraine, A. (1982) *The Voice and The Eye*, Cambridge: Cambridge University Press

Townsend, P. (1979) *Poverty in the United Kingdom*, Harmondsworth: Penguin

Trowler, P. (2003) *Education Policy*, London: Routledge

Tuchman, G., Kaplan Daniels, A. and Benit, J. (eds) (1978) *Hearth and Home: Images of Women in the Mass Media*, New York: Oxford University Press

Tunstall, J. (2000) *The Media in Britain*, London: Constable

Tunstall, J. and Palmer, M. (1991) *Media Moguls*, London: Routledge

Turner, B.S. (1994) 'From regulation to risk', in B.S. Turner (ed.) *Orientalism, Postmodernism and Globalism*, London: Routledge

United Nations Development Programme (UNDP) (1999) *Human Development Report 1999*, New York/Oxford: Oxford University Press. http://hdr.undp.org/en/reports/global/hdr1999/

United Nations Office on Drugs and Crime (UNODC ) (2005) World Drugs Report *www.unodc.org/pdf/WDR_2005/volume_1_web.pdf*

Universities UK (2005) *Survey of Higher Education Students' Attitudes to Debt and Term-time Working and their Impact on Attainment*, London South Bank University, London

Urry, J. (1990) *The Tourist Gaze*, London: Sage

Valier, C. (2001) *Theories of Crime and Delinquency,* Harlow: Longman

Van Dijk, T. (1991) *Racism and the Press*, London: Routledge

Vincent, J. (2001) 'The life course and old age', Sociology Review, 11(2) Nov

Vulliamy, G. (1978) 'Culture clash and school music: a sociological analysis', in L. Barton and R. Meighan (eds) *Sociological Interpretations of Schooling and Classrooms: a Re-appraisal*, Driffied: Nafferton Books

Walby, S. (1986) *Patriarchy at Work*, Cambridge: Polity Press

Walby, S. (1990) *Theorizing Patriarchy*, Oxford: Blackwell

Walker A., Flateley J., Kershaw, C., Moon, D. (2009) (eds.) *Crime in England and Wales 2008/9 Volume 1*, London: Home Office

Walters, R. (2007) 'Crime, regulation and radioactive waste', in P. Beirne and N. South (eds) *Issues in Green Criminology: Confronting harms against humanity, animals and nature*, Cullompton: Willan

Walters, R. (2008) *Eco Crime and Genetically Modified Food*, London: Cavendish Routledge

Wanless Report (2007) *Getting It, Getting It Right*, London: Department for Education and Skills (HMSO)

Waters, M. (1995) *The Death of Class*, London: Sage

Watson, J. (2008) *Media Communication: An Introduction to the Theory and Process* (3rd ed), Basingstoke: Palgrave

Wayne, M. (2007) 'The media and young people – hyping up the new folk devils', *Socialist Worker*, 2069, 22 Sep

Webb, E., Campbell, D., Schwartz, R. and Sechrest, L. (1981) *Nonreactive Measures in the Social Sciences* (2nd edn), Boston: Houghton Mifflin

Weber, M. (1947) *The Theory of Social and Economic Organisation,* New York: Free Press

Webster, C. (2007) *Understanding Race and Crime*, Buckingham : Open University Press

Weiner, G. (1995) 'Feminisms and education', in *Feminism and Education*, Buckingham: OUP

Weiner, G., Arnot, M. and David, M. (1997) 'Is the future female? Female success, male disadvantage, and changing gender patterns in education', in A.H. Halsey *et al.* (2002) *Education: Culture, Economy, Society*, Oxford: OUP

West, A. and Hind, A. (2003) Secondary School Admissions in England: Exploring the extent of overt and covert selection, Centre for Educational Research, Department of Social Policy, London School of Economics and Political Science.

West, C. and Zimmerman, D.H. (1991) 'Doing gender', in J. Larber and S.A. Farrell (eds) *The Social Construction of Gender*, London: Sage, pp.13–37

West, D.J. and Farrington, D.P. (1973) *Who Becomes Delinquent?*, London: Heineman

Westergaard, J. (1996) 'Class in Britain since 1979; facts, theories and ideologies', in D. Lee and B. Turner (eds) *Conflicts about Class: Debating Inequality in Later Industrialisation*, Harlow: Longman

Westwood, S. (1999) 'Representing gender', *Sociology Review*, September

Westwood, S. (2002) *Power and the Social*, London: Routledge

Whannel, G. (2002) 'David Beckham, identity and masculinity', *Sociology Review*, 11. pp.2–4

Whitaker, B. (2002) 'Islam and the British press after September 11', www.albab.com/media/articles/bw020620.htm

White, C. (2004) *The Middle Mind: Why Consumer Culture is Turning Us Into The Living Dead*, London: Penguin

Whyte , D. (2007) 'The crimes of neo-liberal rule in occupied Iraq', *British Journal of Criminology*, 47, pp.177–95

Whyte, W.F. (1943) *Street Corner Society: The Social Structure of an Italian Slum*, Chicago: University of Chicago Press

Wilkins, L. (1964) *Social Deviance: Social Policy, Action and Research,* London: Tavistock

Wilkinson, H. (1994) *No Turning Back: Generations and the Genderquake*, London: Demos

Wilkinson, H. and Mulgan, G. (1997) 'Freedom's children and the rise of generational politics', in G. Mulgan (ed.) *Life After Politics: New Thinking for the Twenty-first Century*, London: Fontana

Wilkinson, R. (1996) *Unhealthy Societies: The Afflictions of Inequality*, Routledge: London

Wilkinson, S. (1999) 'Focus groups: a feminist method', *Psychology of Women Quarterly*, 23, pp.221–44

Wilks-Heeg, S. (2008) *Purity of Elections in the UK: Causes for Concern*, York: The Joseph Rowntree ReformTrust Ltd

Wilkstrom, P.H. (1991) *Urban Crime, Criminals and Victims: the Swedish Experience in an Anglo-American Comparative Perspective*, New York: Springer-Verlag

Williams, H. (2006) *Britain's Power Elites*, London: Constable

Willis, P. (1977) *Learning to Labour: How Working-class Kids get Working-class Jobs*, Farnborough: Saxon House

Willott, S.A. and Griffin, C.E. (1996) 'Men, masculinity and the challenge of long-term unemployment', in M. Mac An Ghaill (ed.) *Understanding Masculinities: Social Relations and Cultural Arenas*, Buckingham: Open University Press

Wilson, J.Q. and Kelling, G. (1982) 'Broken windows: the police and neighbourhood safety', *Atlantic Monthly*, March, pp.29–38

Wilson, W.J. (1996) *When Work Disappears: The World of the New Urban Poor*, New York: Albert Knopf

Winlow, S. (2004) 'Masculinities and crime', *Criminal Justice Matters*, 55(18)

Winship, J. (1987) *Inside Women's Magazines*, London: Pandora Press

Wolf, N. (1990) *The Beauty Myth*, London: Vintage

Wood, J. (1993) 'Repeatable pleasures: notes on young people's use of video', in D. Buckingham (ed.) *Reading Audiences: Young People and the Media*, Manchester: Manchester University Press

Woods, P. (1983) *Sociology and the School: An Interactionist Viewpoint*, London: Routledge & Kegan Paul

Woolf, A. (2002) *Does Education Matter? Myths about Education and Economic Growth*, Harmondsworth: Penguin

Wright Mills, C. (1956) *The Power Elite*, Oxford: Oxford University Press

Wright, C. (1992) 'Early education: multi-racial primary classrooms', in D. Gill, B. Mayor and M. Blair (eds) *Racism and Education: Structures and Strategies*, London: Sage

Yougov (2008) *The Culture of Youth Communities,* London: The Princes Trust

Young, J. (1971) *The Drug Takers,* London: Paladin

Young, J. (1986) 'The Failure of Criminology: The Need for a Radical Realism' in J. Young and R. Matthews (eds.) *Confronting Crime*, London: Sage

Young, J. (1999) *The Exclusive Society: Social Exclusion, Crime and Difference in Late Modernity*, London: Sage

Young, J. (2007) *The Vertigo of Late Modernity*, London: Sage

Zweig, E. (1961) *The Worker in an Affluent Society*, London: Heinemann

Zylinska, J. (2003) 'Guns n' rappers: moral panics and the ethics of cultural studies', *Culture Machine*,

# INDEX

# NOTES

**Acknowledgements**

William Collins' dream of knowledge for all began with the publication of his first book in 1819. A self-educated mill worker, he not only enriched millions of lives but also founded a flourishing publishing house. Today, staying true to this spirit, Collins books are packed with inspiration, innovation and practical expertise. They place you at the centre of the world of possibility and give you exactly what you need to explore it.

**Collins. Do More.**

Published by Collins
An imprint of HarperCollins*Publishers* Limited
77-85 Fulham Palace Rd
Hammersmith
London
W68JB

Browse the complete Collins catalogue
at www.collinseducation.com



ISBN 978-0-00-735374-3



British Cataloguing in Publication Data.
A cataloguing record for this publication is available from the British Library.

Commissioned by: Charlie Evans
Consultant editor: Peter Langley
Proofread by Val Shore
Student answers: Rachel Hewitt
Internal layout: Ken Vail Graphic Design
Cover Design: Oculus
Index: Robert Spicer
Production: Simon Moore
Printed and bound by L.E.G.O. S.p.A. Italy

**Credits**

Photographs

Getty images (1, 2); Alamy, Robert Llewellyn (4); courtesy Apple Corp (10); David Gauntlett (15); Rex Features (18, 20, 28, 32, 33); On Asia Images, Gerhard Joren (35T); Rex Features (35B); Corbis (41); Rex Features (42); Still Pictures (44); Corbis/Bassouls Sophie/Sygma (45); Rex Features/Dennis Stone (49); Getty Images (51T); Alamy/Janine Wiedel (51B); Getty Images, Jon Gray (56); Rex Features/Image Source (61); Photofusion/Paula Solloway (66); Impact Photos/Steve Parry (72); PA Photos (75); educationphotos.co.uk/Walmsley (87, 89BL); Sally Greenhill (89 TR, BR); Richard Greenhill (89TL); Photofusion/Stan Gamester (96T); Network Photographers/Mike Abrahams (96C); Sally Greenhill (96B); Photos.com (99); Photofusion/Crispin Hughes (106); education.co.uk/Walmsley (107); Richard Greenhill (112, 113BR); Bubbles Photo Library (113TR/TL); Rex Features (113BL); Getty Images (114); Istockphoto (117 both); Istockphoto/Marjan Paliuskevic (133); Istockphoto/George Peters (132L); Istockphoto (132R); Istockphoto/Tammy Bryngelson (134); Istockphoto (137); Istockphoto/Robert Billstone (146); Flickr/Janis Krums (151); Rex Features (153); Associated Press (161); Advertising Archives (162TL); Rex Features (162B); PA Photos (162TC); Kobal (162TR); Rex Features (165, 167, 169); Advertising Archives (192); Rex Features (194, 195); Getty Images (201); Rex Features (203); Ronald Grant Archive (186); Kobal (170 both); Corbis/Joe Mahoney (207); Rex Features (204 Barrack Obama. Osama bin Laden); Getty (204 Policewoman); Rex Features/Richard Young (204 Madonna); Rex Features (204 Simon Cowell); Corbis/Robert Bisson (218); Alamy (222); PA Photos (225); Rex Features (220); Punchstock (237); www.johnbirdsall.co.uk (238T); Alamy (238C); Alamy/Robert Judges (238B); Alamy/John Philips (243); Alamy/geogphotos (245); Getty Images (249); Alamy (253L); Rex Features (SIPA Press) (253R); Alamy (258); Getty Images (262TL); Rex Features (262TR); Punchstock/Flying Colours Ltd (262BL); Alamy/David Levenson (262BR); Alamy/Profimedia (266); Alamy (270); Photofusion/Jacky Chapman (272); Alamy (276, 282); Punchstock/Imagestate (285); Getty Images (287); Photofusion/David Montford (293); Punchstock/David de Lossy (303); Rex Features (306); Alamy (307, 315, 321L, 321R); Corbis (321BL); Alamy (325); PA Photos (330); Alamy (339); PA Photos (342).

Text permissions

The publishers gratefully acknowledge all those organizations that have given us permission to reproduce material from their publications. Sources are given in the text where the material is quoted.

Whilst every effort has been made to contact the copyright holders, this has not proved possible in every case.